1 2 APR 2024

WITHDRAWN

College of Ripon & York St. John

3 8025 00319431 6

The British Cinema Source Book

University College of
Ripon & York St. John
YORK CAMPUS
REFERENCE ONLY
NOT TO BE TAKEN OUT
OF THE LIBRARY

THE
BRITISH CINEMA
SOURCE BOOK

BFI Archive Viewing Copies
and Library Materials

Edited by Elaine Burrows
with Janet Moat, David Sharp
and Linda Wood

COLLEGE OF RIPON
AND YORK ST. JOHN
YORK CAMPUS
LIBRARY

BRITISH FILM INSTITUTE

bfi

BFI PUBLISHING

First published in 1995 by the
British Film Institute
21 Stephen Street
London W1P 2LN

The British Film Institute exists to promote appreciation,
enjoyment, protection and development of moving
image culture in and throughout the whole of the United
Kingdom. Its activities include the National
Film and Television Archive; the National Film
Theatre; the Museum of the Moving Image; the
London Film Festival; the production and
distribution of film and video; funding and support
for regional activities; Library and Information
Services; Stills, Posters and Designs; Research;
Publishing and Education; and the monthly *Sight
and Sound* magazine.

Copyright © British Film Institute 1995

This book has been published as a contribution to
the celebrations of the centenary of the cinema in
the United Kingdom, which are being organised
by Cinema 100 on behalf of all sectors of the
industry.

Cinema 100 aims to ensure that everyone is aware
of the Centenary; that filmgoing audiences
increase; that knowledge of the cinema industry's
history and culture is enhanced; and that the
cinema's second century is heralded.

British Library Cataloguing-in-Publication Data.
A catalogue record for this book is available from
the British Library.

ISBN: 0–85170–474–3

Cover design by John Gibbs

Typesetting by
Fakenham Photosetting Limited, Fakenham,
Norfolk
Printed in Great Britain by
Page Bros Limited, Norwich

Cover photo:
Celia Johnson and Trevor Howard
in *Brief Encounter*

Contents

Introduction

It is self-evident that archival materials – even those as physically vulnerable and hard-won as the film and paper collections preserved in the British Film Institute – can, like protected cave paintings, have only a twilight life if they are not made progressively and permanently available for research, study and public use. It is equally truistic to say that, if the BFI has one priority commitment above all others, it is to British cinema – its continuous encouragement, protection, scholarship and enjoyment.

These two basic factors are importantly combined in *The British Cinema Source Book*, which, in its exposure of the range and scale of accessible holdings of a hundred years of national cinema collected and created by the BFI, is unprecedented in the generally beleaguered world of film preservation, where the cataloguing cards are often held close to the chest. It is testimony also to the fact that the patient, thorough and determined acquisition and conservation policies which are an envied characteristic of the Institute's archive and library will eventually reap their own reward, as more and more of the materials in the collections, once secured, can be made visible and available once again.

This volume lists more than 8,300 British films, fiction and non-fiction, for which the NFTVA has a viewing copy or the Library a script or press book, as well as giving details of the BFI's comprehensive collection of books and pamphlets on British cinema: a vast and timely resource to place on record and put on show in the cinema's centenary year. We hope the user – whether student, researcher, programmer or serious browser – will delve deeply into the possibilities it offers, not only for plain information, but also for a discovery of British cinema and the pleasure and knowledge it can give.

CLYDE JEAVONS
Curator, National Film and Television Archive

GILLIAN HARTNOLL
Head of Library and Information Services
British Film Institute, 1995

Acknowledgments

The BFI's National Film and Television Archive and Library and Information Services are grateful to the many people who assisted with the preparation of this catalogue. Thanks must, first of all, be extended to Wilf Stevenson, Director of the British Film Institute, for his support for the project and for the provision of the financial resources which made publication possible.

The efficient downloading of data from the BFI's database to machine-readable files for typesetting was the work of the Computer Unit, in particular Frank Carberry and Mark Richardson, to whose enthusiasm and skills we are indebted. For expert advice on typesetting and design layout, we thank Ed Buscombe and John Smoker (BFI Publishing) and John Gibbs; thanks go also to the Stills, Posters & Designs collection of the NFTVA.

Sincere thanks for sharing their opinions on what constitutes 'a film' (rather than a television programme) as well as other help and advice go to colleagues in the NFTVA's three Acquisitions sections, Fiction, Non-Fiction and Television. Thanks, too, are due to colleagues in the Cataloguing Section, particularly Simon Baker, Olwen Terris and Luke McKernan whose experience on previous publications has proved invaluable.

Special thanks must go to Tise Vahimagi, who was always ready to research queries and to offer advice. Thanks, too, to Markku Salmi, who provided information and corrections with his usual enthusiasm, and to Chris Duyt, whose proof-reading skills were an enormous asset.

For the LIS section of the catalogue, thanks should go to Stephen Pearson for writing the software (and transferring it to a lap-top) to enable us to manipulate the data and build the index, to Jackie Madden and Cherry-Ann Chandler (who also helped proof-read) for data entry, assistance with subject headings and arrangement, and to Lisa Wood for preparatory work.

Finally, particular thanks go to Clyde Jeavons and Anne Fleming, Curator and Deputy Curator of the NFTVA, and to Gillian Hartnoll, Head of Library and Information Services, for all their support. Without that support this book would not have appeared.

ELAINE BURROWS
National Film and Television Archive

JANET MOAT, DAVID SHARP
Library and Information Services

LINDA WOOD
formerly Library and Information Services

About this Volume

The British Cinema Source Book is divided into two parts. The first of these is a listing of British films for which the National Film and Television Archive (NFTVA) and the BFI's Library and Information Services (LIS) between them hold viewing copies, scripts or press-books. The second part gives details of LIS's collection of books and pamphlets on all aspects of British cinema.

Part One of the book lists all British films – more than 8,300 – for which the National Film and Television Archive holds a viewing copy or for which the BFI's Library and Information Services holds a script or a press-book. It has sometimes been difficult to decide what to include or what to leave out as, in recent years, the distinction between what is a film and what is a television programme has become increasingly blurred. In general, entries are for productions which have been released – whether theatrically or non-theatrically – before television transmission. Also included, however, are productions which seem to have been intended to be seen cinematically even though they may first have appeared on television. Some fairly arbitrary decisions have been made on occasion.

By listing all viewing copies of British fiction and non-fiction films held in the NFTVA, this volume fulfils the function of a new edition of the Archive's *Catalogue of Viewing Copies*, last published ten years ago. The 1985 edition listed approximately 8,000 titles of films and television programmes, both fiction and non-fiction (but excluding newsfilm), from all countries. Ten years later, the Archive has available about the same number of *just* British fiction and non-fiction films (excluding, this time, both newsfilm and television), for study and research on the Archive's premises, for screening at the National Film Theatre and Museum of the Moving Image, and for loan to BFI-supported cinemas and educational venues and to archives and festivals outside the UK. Most of these screenings and loans are arranged by the Archive's Viewing Service, whose staff can give details of availability and cost.

The first part of the *Source Book* also notes British titles (again, excluding newsfilm and television) for which the British Film Institute's Library and Information Services holds unpublished scripts and press-books. (Published scripts are listed in the second part of the book.)

LIS has a large collection of film scripts. The unpublished ones are a mixture of production scripts (screenplays and shooting scripts) and post-production scripts, which document the finished film. Press-books are produced by distributors for exhibitors, providing information about ways of publicising the film. In the heyday of the cinema they were often quite lavish and might include full credits, synopsis, footage and running time, production stories and photographs, biographies, interviews, illustrated catalogues of available publicity materials, competitions, displays, and product tie-ins.

The information on all these elements has been drawn from the BFI's database, SIFT (Summary of Information on Film & Television), which contains data input by LIS, by the NFTVA's Cataloguing Section, and by other BFI departments.

Part Two of the Source Book, which is based mainly on the areas of the collection not yet accessible by computer, consists of information on Library and Information Services holdings – as of the end of 1993 – on all aspects of British cinema and those who worked in it. Some 1,800 entries give details of virtually every book – and many pamphlets – published on British cinema, as well as brief details of relevant Special Collections. Topics covered by the books and pamphlets include genre films, non-fiction films, the role of the British Government in the film industry, censorship, cinemas (there is a growing number of publications dedicated to the cinemas in particular localities), biographies, published scripts and 'books of the film'.

Special Collections is the term used to refer to the papers donated by individuals and companies, a rich and growing research tool, including materials from practitioners such as Sir Carol Reed, Derek Jarman, Sir Michael Balcon, Joseph Losey, Ivor Montague, Anna Neagle and David Puttnam. The materials in these collections incorporate such items as scrapbooks of cuttings, correspondence, scripts (often annotated), contracts and other business papers, production material and cinema ephemera.

For logistical reasons, some Library materials have been consciously omitted. These include news cuttings, publicity and press releases, film periodicals, all works purely about television, and most works on popular culture except where they concentrate on British cinema.

All non-film materials listed in this volume – including the scripts and press-books documented in the first section – are held in the BFI's Library and Information Services. Enquiries about Special Collections materials should be directed to the Special Materials Unit in LIS.

Arrangement

Part One

The listing is divided into five broad date-bands, up to and including 1914, 1915–1928, 1929–1945, 1946–1964, and 1965 onward. These date-bands are then divided alphabetically by title, on a letter-by-letter basis, thus:

ALL FOR THE SAKE OF MARY
ALLOTMENT HOLDER'S ENEMIES
AL STARITA AND HIS SAXOPHONE

Numerals have been filed as though written out: 1492 appears as though it were FOURTEEN NINETY TWO. Decisions on filing – for example, £100 REWARD as 'a hundred' or 'one hundred' – have been based on day to day Archive usage.

The same pragmatic approach has been used for abbreviations: BBC – THE VOICE OF BRITAIN and OHMS have been filed by the letters of the abbreviations rather than under BRITISH BROADCASTING CORPORATION . . . or ON HIS MAJESTY'S SERVICE, as that is how they are commonly referred to. On the other hand DR . . . and MR . . . , to take two examples, have been filed conventionally as DOCTOR and MISTER.

Because of the semi-chronological approach, series entries may be split over two or more date-bands.

The information on each title is basic filmographic data – title, date, director. This is followed by a note of what material the Institute holds: VC = an NFTVA viewing copy; SC = LIS script; PB = LIS press-book. For example:

BLACK NARCISSUS (1948)
d Michael Powell, Emeric Pressburger
VC SC PB

An index by directors' names, which lists titles and dates, is to be found on p. 167. From this the correct date-band for the entry can be found.

SIFT does not yet carry details of the base or format on which viewing copies are held, nor does it include running times for particular copies. For this reason, the *Source Book* does not include that information. As a rough guide, virtually all the silent material will be on 35mm film, the 30s to the 70s will be mainly 35mm with an admixture of 16mm, while the 80s and 90s will consist of a high percentage of VHS with some 16mm and 35mm copies. This reflects not only the formats on which the films were originally made, but also the fact that the NFTVA now acquires, by direct off-air recording, about 25% of Independent and Channel 4 Television transmissions, many of which are of 'films'. Details about the format and length of particular copies can be obtained from the Archive's Viewing Service.

Part Two

The Library and Information Service entries, each of which is identified by a unique *Source Book* number, are arranged in three sub-sections by film title, personality and subject. These sub-sections are followed by an index by book author. Special Collections covering several film titles or personalities are listed at the end of the appropriate section. Where there are several entries under one heading in any of these sub-sections, the secondary filing order will be by book title. As in the first part of the book, the alphabetical arrangement is letter-by-letter, and film or book titles which consist of or start with numbers are filed as though the number were written out.

Sample entry:
1420. British Films for Liberated Europe by the Ministry of Information.
N.p., 1944. 6p.
Lists British features and shorts shown in France and Italy.

The first two sections, title and personality, are self-defining and also relatively straightforward to consult. The subject section is more complex. Within it, the arrangement initially echoes the date-band system of the first part of the *Source Book* with books on the general history of British cinema being listed first, at the start of the subject sequence. The sub-section then continues with sequences on companies and studios, the industry, Government and Cinema, the British Film Institute, film production, social aspects of the cinema including censorship and propaganda, and cinemas (in specific locations) and the audience. The final sections of this part of the book cover criticism and theory, genres, animation, the non-fiction film, and reference books and catalogues.

An index by names of the authors of books listed is to be found on p. 209.

Abbreviations

bibliog.	bibliography
col.	colour
d	director
et al.	and others
filmog.	filmography
illus.	illustrated
n.d.	no date
n.p.	publisher not known or no publisher
p.	pages (as in 216p.)
PB	press-book
SC	script
VC	viewing copy
photos.	photographs
teleog.	teleography (television programmes)
theatrog.	theatrography

Part One
NFTVA Viewing Copies and
BFI Library and Information Services
Scripts and Press-books

ABENTEUER ZWEIER KINDER (1910)
VC

ACCIDENTS WILL HAPPEN (1907)
VC

AERIAL SUBMARINE, the (1910)
d W R Booth
VC

AIRSHIP DESTROYER, the (1909)
d W R Booth
VC

ALGY'S YACHTING PARTY (1908)
d Percy Stow
VC

ALICE IN WONDERLAND (1903)
d Percy Stow, Cecil M Hepworth
VC

ALL'S FAIR (1913)
d Hay Plumb
VC

ALL'S FAIR IN LOVE (1912)
d Percy Stow
VC

AMANN, THE GREAT IMPERSONATOR
(1898)
VC

AMBULANCE CROSSING THE MODDER
(1900)
VC

ANARCHIST AND HIS DOG, the (1907)
VC

ANARCHIST'S DOOM, the (1913)
d Alexander Butler
VC

AND THEN HE WOKE UP (1909)
d Dave Aylott
VC

ANIMATED COTTON (1909)
d W R Booth
VC

ANSWERING A CALL (1901)
VC

ANTIQUE VASE, the (1913)
d H O Martinek
VC

ANTWERP UNDER SHOT AND SHELL (The
Whirlpool of War series) (1914)
VC

ANXIOUS DAY FOR MOTHER, an (1907)
d Percy Stow
VC

APPLE PICKING (1910)
VC

ARE WE DOWN HEARTED? (1909)
VC

ARE YOU THERE? (1901)
d James Williamson
VC

ARLBERG RAILWAY, the (1906)
VC

ARMS DRILL (1914)
VC

**ARRIVAL OF TRAIN-LOAD OF VISITORS
AT HENLEY STATION** (1899)
VC

ARTISTIC CREATION (1901)
d W R Booth
VC

ARTIST'S MODEL, the (1898)
VC

**ASCENT OF MONT BLANC, 15,781 FEET
HIGH, the** (1902)
d Frank Ormiston-Smith
VC

AS SEEN THROUGH A TELESCOPE (1900)
d G A Smith
VC

ATLANTIC WHALING (1909)
VC

AT MESSRS PILKINGTONS GLASSWORKS
(1913)
VC

**ATTACK ON A CHINESE MISSION –
BLUEJACKETS TO THE RESCUE** (1900)
d James Williamson
VC

ATTACK ON A MISSION STATION (1900)
VC

ATTEMPT TO SMASH A BANK, an (1909)
d Theo Bouwmeester
VC

AT THE FOOT OF THE SCAFFOLD (1913)
d Warwick Buckland
VC

AT THE MERCY OF THE TIDE (1910)
VC

AUSTRALIAN SPORTS AND PASTIMES
(1908)
VC

AUTOMATIC MOTORIST, the (1911)
d W R Booth
VC

BABY'S TOILET (1905)
VC

BAD DAY FOR LEVINSKY, a (1909)
d T J Gobbett
VC

BARNARD CASTLE AND DISTRICT (1913)
VC

BATHERS, the (1900)
d Cecil M Hepworth
VC

**BATTLE OF SPION KOP: AMBULANCE
CORPS CROSSING THE TUGELA RIVER**
(1900)
VC

BATTLE OF THE SNOW, the (1903)
VC

**BATTLESHIP ODIN WITH ALL HER GUNS
IN ACTION, the** (1900)
VC

**BAU EINER EISENBAHNSTRECKE IN
AMERIKA** (1910)
VC

BEE HUNTER, the (1910)
d J C Bee-Mason
VC

BEES AND THEIR ENEMIES (1910)
d J C Bee-Mason
VC

BEE'S EVICTION, the (1909)
d J C Bee-Mason
VC

BEGGAR'S DECEIT, the (1900)
d Cecil M Hepworth
VC

BELFAST STREET SCENES 1890s (1899)
VC

BELINDA'S ELOPEMENT (1913)
d Dave Aylott
VC

BERCHTESGADEN AND LAKE KÖNIGSEE
(1913)
VC

BERTIE BUYS A BULLDOG (1909)
d A E Coleby
VC

BESUCH IM AQUARIUM, ein (1910)
VC

BIG SWALLOW, the (1901)
d James Williamson
VC

BILL POSTER, the (1899)
d Charles Goodwin Norton
VC

BILLY'S BIBLE (1911)
d Dave Aylott
VC

BIRDS, BEASTS AND REPTILES (1912)
VC

BIRD'S EYE VIEW OF PARIS, a (1910)
VC

BIRTH OF A BIG GUN, the (1908)
VC

BIRTH OF A FLOWER, the (Urban Science
series) (1910)
VC

BITER BIT, the (1900)
VC

BITER BIT, the (1909)
d A E Coleby
VC

BLACK AND WHITE WASHING (1900)
VC

BLACK BEAUTY (1906)
d Lewin Fitzhamon
VC

BLACKPOOL HIGH TIDE (1913)
VC

BLACKSMITH'S DAUGHTER, the (1904)
VC

**BLAINA ANNUAL SUNDAY SCHOOL
DEMONSTRATION MONDAY JULY 1912**
(1912)
VC

BLIND MAN'S DOG, a (1912)
d Lewin Fitzhamon
VC

BLOEMFONTEIN: UNFURLING THE FLAG
(1900)
VC

BLOOD & BOSH (1913)
d Hay Plumb
VC

BLUEJACKETS' DRILL AND EXERCISES – VOLLEY FIRING (1898)
VC

BOAT RACE (1900)
VC

BOBBY THE BOY SCOUT; or, The boy detective (1909)
d Percy Stow
VC

BOER ATTACK ON A RED CROSS OUTPOST (1900)
VC

BOLD VENTURE, a (1912)
VC

BO'NESS PUBLIC SCHOOL: QUEEN ANNIE PEACE (1912)
VC

BÖSEN BUBEN UND DER SCHULMEISTER, die (1908)
VC

BOURNEMOUTH (1911)
VC

BOXING MATCH FOR CHAMPIONSHIP OF THE WORLD (1907)
VC

BOY AND THE CONVICT, the (1909)
d Dave Aylott
VC

BOYS BATHING – VENICE (1898)
VC

BOY SCOUTS TO THE RESCUE (1909)
VC

BOYS OF HMS TERRIBLE GETTING THEIR GUNS INTO POSITION (1899)
VC

BOYS SLIDING (1900)
VC

BRAVE CHILDREN; or, The young thief catchers (1908)
d A E Coleby
VC

BREACH OF PROMISE CASE, a (1908)
VC

BREWSTER TROUPE OF HIGH KICKERS AND DANCERS, the (1902)
VC

BRIDE'S FIRST NIGHT, the (1898)
VC

BRITISH COLUMBIA: LOGGING IN WINTER (1908)
VC

BROWN'S HALF HOLIDAY (1905)
d James Williamson
VC

BUILDING A BRITISH RAILWAY – CONSTRUCTING THE LOCOMOTIVE (1905)
VC

BUILDING A MOTOR CAR (1913)
VC

BULLY BOY (Bully Boy series) (1914)
d Lancelot Speed
VC

BULLY BOY series
see
BULLY BOY (1914)
GENERAL FRENCH'S CONTEMPTIBLE LITTLE ARMY (1914)
SEA DREAMS (1914)
SLEEPLESS (1914)

BURGLAR FOR ONE NIGHT, a (1911)
d Bert Haldane
VC

BURGLARS IN THE HOUSE (1911)
VC

BURNHAM BEECHES (1909)
VC

BURNING HOME, the (1909)
VC

BUSINESS IS BUSINESS (1912)
d Wilfred Noy
VC

BUSY LONDON – TRAFFIC PASSING IN FRONT OF BANK OF ENGLAND AND MANSION HOUSE (1905)
VC

BUSY MAN, the (1907)
d Lewin Fitzhamon
VC

BUY YOUR OWN CHERRIES (1904)
VC

BY THE SIDE OF THE ZUYDER ZEE (Cinematophone Singing Pictures series) (1907)
VC

CABBY'S DREAM, the (1906)

CANADIAN CAR RIDE (1900)
VC

CANDLE-MAKING (1910)
VC

CATCHING A BURGLAR (1908)
d Lewin Fitzhamon
VC

CATCHING THE MILK THIEF (1899)
VC

CATHOLIC GUILD PROCESSION (1910)
VC

CHARLEY SMILER JOINS THE BOY SCOUTS (1911)
d Dave Aylott
VC

CHEAP REMOVAL, a (1909)
d Lewin Fitzhamon
VC

CHEEKIEST MAN ON EARTH, the (1908)
d J B McDowell
VC

CHEESE MITES (The Unseen World series) (1903)
VC

CHEESE MITES; or, Lilliputians in a London restaurant, the (1901)
d W R Booth
VC

CHESS DISPUTE, a (1903)
d R W Paul
VC

CHILD, DOG AND PRAM, the (1900)
VC

CHILDREN IN THE NURSERY (1898)
d R W Paul
VC

CHILDREN'S DENTAL LEAGUE, the (1912)
VC

CHILD STEALERS, the (1904)
d Alf Collins
VC

CHRISTMAS CAROL, a (1914)
d Harold Shaw
VC

CHRISTMAS DAY IN THE WORKHOUSE (1914)
d George Pearson
VC

CHURCH AND STAGE (1912)
d Warwick Buckland
VC

CHURNED WATERS (1899)
VC

CINEMATOPHONE SINGING PICTURES series
see
BY THE SIDE OF THE ZUYDER ZEE (1907)
CINEMATOPHONE SINGING PICTURES SERIES NO.106 (1907)
FLY ANN (1907)
I WOULD LIKE TO MARRY YOU (1907)
WHERE OH WHERE HAS MY LITTLE DOG GONE? (1907)

CINEMATOPHONE SINGING PICTURES SERIES NO.106 (1907)
VC

CITY OF WESTMINSTER (1909)
VC

CLIFF CLIMBING; THE EGG HARVEST OF FLAMBOROUGH HEAD (1908)
VC

CLOWN AND HIS DONKEY, the (1910)
d Charles Armstrong
VC

CLOWN AND POLICE (1900)
d Cecil M Hepworth
VC

COLLAPSING BRIDGE, the (1902)
VC

COLOGNE – CORPUS CHRISTI PROCESSION (1903)
VC

COLOGNE – THE CORPUS CHRISTI PROCESSION (1904)
VC

COME ALONG, DO! (1898)
d R W Paul
VC

COMIC COSTUME RACE (1896)
d R W Paul
VC

COMIC FACES – OLD MAN DRINKING A GLASS OF BEER (1898)
VC

CONSTABLE SMITH AND THE MAGIC BATON (1912)
d Edwin J Collins
VC

CONSTABLE SMITH'S DREAM OF PROMOTION (1911)
d A E Coleby
VC

CONVICT AND THE CURATE, the (1904)
d Percy Stow
VC

COOLIE BOYS DIVING FOR COINS (1900)
VC

CORONATION OF THEIR MAJESTIES KING EDWARD VII AND QUEEN ALEXANDRA, the (1902)
VC

CORONATION OF THEIR MOST GRACIOUS MAJESTIES KING GEORGE AND QUEEN MARY (1911)
VC

CORONATION PROCESSION AT ST BOSWELLS (1901)
VC

CORPORAL'S KIDDIES, the (1914)
d Warwick Buckland
VC

CORPORATION ROAD SCHOOLS 4.3.11 (1911)
VC

COSTER'S WEDDING, the (1913)
d Percy Stow
VC

COUNTRY CATTLE SHOW, a (1897)
d Charles Goodwin Norton
VC

COUNTRYMAN AND THE CINEMATOGRAPH, the (1901)
d R W Paul
VC

CROWD OF PEOPLE IN A BACK STREET (1905)
VC

CUP TIE FINAL: LIVERPOOL V BURNLEY 1914 (1914)
VC

CURFEW MUST NOT RING TONIGHT; A ROMANCE OF THE DAYS OF CROMWELL, the (1906)
d Alf Collins
VC

CUTTING THE FIRST SOD, ROYAL EDWARD DOCK, 1902 (1902)
VC

DADDY'S DID'UMS ON A HOLIDAY (1912)
d Wilfred Noy
VC

DADDY'S LITTLE DID'UMS DID IT? (1910)
d Wilfred Noy
VC

DAISY DOODAD'S DIAL (1914)
d Florence Turner
VC

DANCER'S DREAM, the (1905)
d J H Martin
VC

DARING DAYLIGHT BURGLARY, a (1903)
d Frank Mottershaw
VC

DASH TO THE NORTH POLE, a (1909)
VC

DAUGHTER OF ROMANY, a (1914)
d Charles J Brabin
VC

DAVID COPPERFIELD (1913)
d Thomas Bentley
VC

DAVID GARRICK (1912)
VC

DAY IN THE HAYFIELDS, a (1904)
VC

DAY IN THE LIFE OF A COAL MINER, a (1910)
VC

DAY IN THE LIFE OF A RICKSHA BOY, a (1912)
VC

DAY WITH POACHERS, a (1912)
VC

DEAR BOYS HOME FOR THE HOLIDAYS, the (1904)
d James Williamson
VC

DEATH OF NELSON, the (1905)
d Lewin Fitzhamon
VC

DECEPTION, the (1912)
VC

DEER HUNTING IN CANADA (1908)
VC

DEONZO BROTHERS, the (1901)
d R W Paul
VC

DERBY, the (1910)
VC

DESPATCH BEARER, the (1900)
VC

DESPERATE POACHING AFFRAY (1903)
d William Haggar
VC

DIABOLO NIGHTMARE, a (1907)
d W R Booth
VC

DICKE KOPF IM KLEINEN TOPF, der (1909)
VC

DIVING AT PORT SKILLION, ISLE OF MAN (1897)
VC

DR BRIAN PELLIE AND THE SECRET DESPATCH (1912)
d Wilfred Noy
VC

DOG OUTWITS THE KIDNAPPERS, the (1908)
d Lewin Fitzhamon
VC

DONKEY DERBY, the (1900)
VC

DRAT THAT BOY (1904)
VC

DREAMLAND ADVENTURES (1907)
d W R Booth
VC

DREAMS OF TOYLAND (1908)
d Arthur Melbourne-Cooper
VC

DRINK AND REPENTANCE; A CONVICT STORY (1905)
VC

DRINK CURE, a (1907)
d A E Coleby
VC

DUMB SAGACITY (1907)
d Lewin Fitzhamon
VC

DUSTY DICK'S AWAKENING (1911)
VC

EASTER ON SHIPLEY GLEN (1912)
VC

EAST LYNNE (1913)
d Bert Haldane
VC

EDWARD VII LAYS FOUNDATION STONE (1903)
VC

EGYPT AND HER DEFENDERS (1914)
VC

ELECTRIC SHOCK, the (1904)
d Alf Collins
VC

ELECTRIC TRANSFORMATION (1909)
d Percy Stow
VC

ELECTRO-CARDIOGRAPH, the (1912)
VC

ELEPHANTS WORKING AT MacGREGOR'S TIMBER YARDS AND MILLS AT RANGOON (1903)
VC

EMPIRE'S MONEY MAKER, an (1910)
VC

ENGINE STARTING WITH SCOTCH EXPRESS FROM EUSTON (1913)
VC

ENGLISCHE UHRENFABRIKATION (1910)
VC

ENTRY OF THE SCOTS GUARDS INTO BLOEMFONTEIN (1900)
VC

EUGENE ARAM (1914)
d Edwin J Collins
VC

EUROPE'S WINTER PLAYGROUND (1913)
VC

EVEN A WORM WILL TURN (1907)
d A E Coleby
VC

EXCHANGE OF HEADS, an (1914)
VC

EXCURSION THROUGH ABRUZZI (1910)
VC

EXPLOITS OF THREE-FINGERED KATE series, the
see
KATE PURLOINS THE WEDDING PRESENTS (1912)

EXPLOSION OF A MOTOR CAR (1900)
d Cecil M Hepworth
VC

EXPRESS DELIVERY (1913)
d Edwin J Collins
VC

EXTRAORDINARY CAB ACCIDENT (1903)
VC

FALSELY ACCUSED (1905)
d Lewin Fitzhamon
VC

FAMILIAR REPTILES (Urban Science series) (1914)
VC

FANCY SKATING ON THE BEAR ICE RINK AT GRINDELWALD (1902)
VC

FARMER GILES IN LONDON (1909)
VC

FARMER JENKINS' VISIT TO THE WHITE CITY (1910)
VC

FARMERLEBEN IN AMERIKA (1910)
VC

FASTEST MOTOR BOAT IN THE WORLD, URSULA, the (1909)
VC

FATHER BUYS AN ARMCHAIR (1909)
d Joseph Rosenthal
VC

FATHER BUYS A PICTURE (1908)
d A E Coleby
VC

FATHER, MOTHER WANTS YOU! (1906)
VC

FATHER'S LESSON (1908)
d Lewin Fitzhamon
VC

FATHER'S PICNIC ON THE SANDS (1905)
VC

FATHER'S SATURDAY AFTERNOON (1911)
VC

FAVOURITE FOR THE JAMAICA CUP, the (1913)
d Charles Raymond
VC

FEEDING THE PIGEONS IN SAINT MARK'S SQUARE, VENICE (1898)
VC

FEEDING THE SEAGULLS (1899)
VC

FEEDING THE TIGERS (1899)
VC

FESTIVAL DAY AT REEDHAM ORPHANAGE, 1910 (1910)
VC

FETE IN VENICE, a (1910)
VC

FIGHT FOR THE COAST, the (The Whirlpool of War series) (1914)
VC

FINDING HIS COUNTERPART (1913)
VC

FIRE! (1901)
d James Williamson
VC

FIRE BRIGADE TURN-OUT IN THE COUNTRY (1899)
d Charles Goodwin Norton
VC

FIREMEN TO THE RESCUE (1903)
d Cecil M Hepworth
VC

1ST ANNIVERSARY OF THE CLITHEROE CORONATION PROCESSION IN HONOUR OF THE CROWNING OF KING GEORGE & QUEEN MARY 1911 (1912)
VC

1ST SW LONDON (PUTNEY) BOY SCOUTS IN CAMP AT POLZEATH, CORNWALL (1910)
VC

FIRST X-RAY CINEMATOGRAPH FILM EVER TAKEN, SHOWN BY DR MacINTYRE AT THE LONDON ROYAL SOCIETY 1897 (1897)
VC

FISHING WITH CORMORANTS, ISLE OF YESO, JAPAN (1911)
VC

FLAPPER AND THE FAN, the (1914)
VC

FLY ANN (Cinematophone Singing Pictures series) (1907)
VC

FLY DANGER, the (Urban Science series) (1911)
VC

FLYING DESPATCH, the (1912)
d Stuart Kinder
VC

FLYING THE FOAM AND SOME FANCY DIVING (1906)
d James Williamson
VC

FOILED BY A GIRL (1912)
d Wilfred Noy
VC

FRED'S POLICE FORCE (1912)
VC

FREE RIDE, a (1904)
d Percy Stow
VC

FROM ANTWERP TO OSTEND (1914)
VC

FROM BEHIND THE FLAG (1912)
VC

FROM GIPSY HANDS (1910)
d Dave Aylott
VC

FROM LAUSANNE TO MONTREUX (1914)
VC

FROM MONTREUX TO ROCHERS DE NAYE VIA TERRITET (1913)
VC

FROM TRAU TO SPALATO ON THE DALMATIAN COAST (1910)
VC

FRUSTRATED ELOPEMENT, the (1902)
d Percy Stow
VC

FUNERAL OF PROVOST YOUNG (1914)
VC

FUNERAL OF THE LATE GENERAL BOOTH, AUG 29 1912 (1912)
VC

FURNISHING EXTRAORDINARY (1913)
d Dave Aylott
VC

GAIETY DUET, a (1909)
VC

GAME OF HOCKEY, a (1902)
VC

GAME OF SNOWBALLING, a (1900)
VC

GAMIN'S GRATITUDE, a (1909)
d Lewin Fitzhamon
VC

GENERAL FRENCH'S CONTEMPTIBLE LITTLE ARMY (Bully Boy series) (1914)
d Lancelot Speed
VC

GENTLEMAN RANKER, the (1912)
VC

GERMAN OCCUPATION OF HISTORIC LOUVAIN, the (1914)
VC

GERMAN SPY PERIL, the (1914)
d Bert Haldane
VC

GETTING CLOSE TO THE SPIDER (Urban Science series) (1909)
VC

GIANTS AND PYGMIES OF THE DEEP (1909)
VC

GIBRALTAR (1911)
VC

GLASS OF GOAT'S MILK, a (1909)
d Percy Stow
VC

GOODBYE SWEETHEART GOODBYE (1907)
VC

GORDON BENNETT MOTOR CAR RACE 1903 (1903)
VC

GORDON HIGHLANDERS IN LADYSMITH (1900)
VC

GRAND CANAL, VENICE, the (1898)
VC

GRANDFATHER'S BIRTHDAY; or, The last roll-call (1908)
d A E Coleby
VC

GRANDMA THREADING HER NEEDLE (1900)
d G A Smith
VC

GRANDMA'S READING GLASS (1900)
d G A Smith
VC

GRAND NATIONAL, the (1911)
VC

GRAND NATIONAL, the (1914)
VC

GREAT TEMPTATION, a (1906)
d Harold Hough
VC

GREAT WESTERN ROAD 1914 (1914)
VC

GUARDIAN OF THE BANK, the (1908)
d A E Coleby
VC

GUILLEMOTS (1907)
VC

HALIFAX DAY BY DAY (1910)
VC

HAMLET (1913)
d Hay Plumb
VC

HANGING OUT THE CLOTHES; or, Master, mistress and maid (1897)
d G A Smith
VC

HAPPY EVENT IN THE POORLUCK FAMILY, a (1911)
d Lewin Fitzhamon
VC

HARRY THE FOOTBALLER (1911)
VC

HAUNTED CURIOSITY SHOP, the (1901)
VC

HAWKEYE, SHOWMAN (1913)
d Hay Plumb
VC

HEART OF A FISHERGIRL, the (1910)
d Lewin Fitzhamon
VC

HECHT, EIN SÜSSWASSERRÄUBER, der
(1910)
VC

HENLEY REGATTA, the (1901)
VC

HENLEY REGATTA 1911 (1911)
VC

HERE WE ARE AGAIN (1913)
d Edwin J Collins
VC

HER FATHER'S PHOTOGRAPH (1911)
d H O Martinek
VC

HIGHLAND REEL (1899)
VC

HILDA'S LOVERS (1911)
d Bert Haldane
VC

HIS BRAVE DEFENDER (1901)
d R W Paul
VC

**HIS MAJESTY KING EDWARD ON THE
DECK OF HIS YACHT** (1897)
VC

HIS ONLY PAIR (1902)
VC

HIS ONLY PAIR OF TROUSERS (1907)
d A E Coleby
VC

HISTORIC MUTINY SITES (1914)
VC

**HISTORY OF A BUTTERFLY; A ROMANCE
OF INSECT LIFE, the** (1910)
VC

HIS WEDDING MORN (1908)
d A E Coleby
VC

**HOLIDAY TRIP TO THE CLYDE COAST OF
SCOTLAND VIA L & NW RAILWAY, a**
(1909)
VC

HORNET AND HER NEST, the (1911)
d J C Bee-Mason
VC

**HORSE STEALER; or, A casual
acquaintance, the** (1905)
d Tom Green
VC

**HORSHAM CRICKET WEEK AND GRAND
CARNIVAL, THURSDAY JULY 24TH** (1913)
VC

HOUSE THAT JACK BUILT, the (1900)
VC

**HOW A BRITISH BULLDOG SAVED THE
UNION JACK** (1906)
VC

**HOW BROWN BROUGHT HOME THE
GOOSE** (1905)
d Alf Collins
VC

HOW IT FEELS TO BE RUN OVER (1900)
d Cecil M Hepworth
VC

**HOW PERCY WON THE BEAUTY
COMPETITION** (1909)
VC

HOW TO STOP A MOTOR CAR (1902)
d Percy Stow
VC

**HURRIED DEPARTURE – EXEUNT
OMNES, a** (1910)
VC

I DO LIKE TO BE WHERE THE GIRLS ARE
(1912)
VC

IM URWALD AUF JAVA (1910)
VC

IN A SOUTH AMERICAN PORT (1911)
d Dave Aylott
VC

**INCIDENTS IN THE LIFE OF THOMAS
ATKINS** (1911)
VC

INCOMING TIDE, the (1898)
VC

**INDIAN CHIEF AND THE SEIDLITZ
POWDER, the** (1901)
d Cecil M Hepworth
VC

INDIAN WASHING THE BABY, an (1906)
VC

**INDUSTRIAS ARGENTINAS – SALINAS
CHICAS** (1910)
VC

IN EINER ENGLISCHEN FARM (1910)
VC

INHABITANTS OF JUNGLE TOWN, the
(1912)
VC

INTERESTING STORY, an (1905)
d James Williamson
VC

INTERNATIONAL EXCHANGE, the (1905)
VC

INTERRUPTED HONEYMOON, an (1905)
d Lewin Fitzhamon
VC

IN THE SCOTTISH HIGHLANDS (PART 2)
(1908)
VC

INVADERS, the (1909)
d Percy Stow
VC

**INVESTITURE OF HRH PRINCE EDWARD
AS PRINCE OF WALES AT CAERNARVON**
(1911)
VC

INVISIBILITY (1909)
d Cecil M Hepworth, Lewin Fitzhamon
VC

**ITALIAN MARBLE QUARRIES AT
CARRARA, the** (1913)
VC

**IT'S LOVE THAT MAKES THE WORLD GO
ROUND** (1913)
d Percy Stow
VC

IT'S NOT MY PARCEL (1906)
VC

IVANHOE (1913)
d Leedham Bantock
VC

I WOULD LIKE TO MARRY YOU
(Cinematophone Singing Pictures series) (1907)

**JACK'S GAME OF CRICKET ON BOARD
HMS GIBRALTAR** (1900)
VC

**JAIL-BIRD; or, The bishop and the
convict, the** (1905)
d Charles Raymond
VC

JAPANESE ACROBATS (1914)
VC

JAPANESE FUNERAL, a (1904)
VC

JAPANESE SCHOOL CHILDREN (1904)
VC

**JEALOUS DOLL; or, The frustrated
elopement, the** (1910)
d Percy Stow
VC

JERBOA OR JUMPING MOUSE, the (1914)
VC

JESSIE (1914)
VC

JETHART'S HERE (1900)
VC

JEWEL THIEVES OUTWITTED, the (1912)
d Frank Wilson
VC

JIM OF THE MOUNTED POLICE (1911)
d Lewin Fitzhamon
VC

JOHN BULL'S HEARTH (1903)
VC

JOHN GILPIN'S RIDE (1908)
d Lewin Fitzhamon
VC

**JONAH MAN; or, The traveller bewitched,
the** (1904)
d Cecil M Hepworth, Lewin Fitzhamon
VC

JUGGINS' MOTOR SKATES (1909)
d Percy Stow
VC

JUST IN TIME (1906)
d Lewin Fitzhamon
VC

JUVENILE SCIENTIST, a (1907)
VC

**KATE PURLOINS THE WEDDING
PRESENTS** (The Exploits of Three-Fingered
Kate series) (1912)
VC

KETTEN LOKOMOBIL, das (1910)
VC

KIDDIES AND RABBITS (1901)
VC

**KING EDWARD VII OPENS SHEFFIELD
UNIVERSITY** (1905)
VC

KING JOHN (1899)
d William Kennedy-Laurie Dickson
VC

KING OF COINS (1903)
d Alf Collins
VC

KING'S VISIT TO THE ROYAL AGRICULTURAL SHOW, SHREWSBURY 3RD JULY 1914, the (1914)
VC

KISSING COUPLE, the (1900)
VC

KISS IN THE TUNNEL (1899)
VC

KISS IN THE TUNNEL (1900)
VC

KOIARI DANCE (1904)
VC

KOITA BAMBOO DANCE, MAGINOGO (1904)
VC

KOITA DANCE (1904)
VC

KOITA DANCE, EHOLASI (1904)
VC

KOITA DANCES (1904)
VC

LADIES SWIMMING RACE THROUGH PARIS, the (1910)
VC

LAKWAHARU DANCE, TUPUSELEI VILLAGE (1904)
VC

LANDING OF SAVAGE SOUTH AFRICA AT SOUTHAMPTON, the (1899)
VC

LANDWIRTSCHAFT UND VIEHZUCHT IN AUSTRALIEN (1909)
VC

LASSIE AND HER DOG, the (1901)
VC

LAUNCH OF HMS ALBION AT BLACKWALL (1898)
VC

LAUNCH OF THE WORTHING LIFEBOAT: COMING ASHORE (1898)
VC

LAUNCH OF THE WORTHING LIFEBOAT: EMERGING FROM THE BOATHOUSE (1898)
VC

LAW IN THEIR OWN HANDS, the (1913)
VC

LCC FIRE BRIGADE COMPETITION (1910)
VC

LEAP FROG (1900)
VC

LESSON ON ELECTRICITY, a (1909)
d Percy Stow
VC

LET ME DREAM AGAIN (1900)
d G A Smith
VC

LIE, the (1914)
d Frank Wilson
VC

LIEUTENANT DARING AND THE PLANS OF THE MINE FIELDS (1912)
d Dave Aylott
VC

LIEUTENANT DARING QUELLS A REBELLION (1912)
d Charles Raymond
VC

LIEUTENANT LILLY AND THE SPLODGE OF OPIUM (1913)
d Hay Plumb
VC

LIEUT PIMPLE AND THE STOLEN SUBMARINE (1914)
d Fred Evans, Joe Evans
VC

LIEUTENANT PIMPLE'S DASH FOR THE POLE (1914)
VC

LIEUTENANT ROSE AND THE CHINESE PIRATES (1910)
d Percy Stow
VC

LIEUTENANT ROSE AND THE GUNRUNNERS (1910)
d Percy Stow
VC

LIEUTENANT ROSE AND THE HIDDEN TREASURE (1912)
d Percy Stow
VC

LIEUTENANT ROSE AND THE ROBBERS OF FINGALL'S CREEK (1910)
d Percy Stow
VC

LIEUTENANT ROSE AND THE ROYAL VISIT (1911)
d Percy Stow
VC

LIEUTENANT ROSE AND THE SEALED ORDERS (1914)
d Percy Stow
VC

LIEUTENANT ROSE AND THE STOLEN CODE (1911)
d Percy Stow
VC

LIEUTENANT ROSE RN AND HIS PATENT AEROPLANE (1912)
d Percy Stow
VC

LIEUTENANT ROSE RN AND THE STOLEN BATTLESHIP (1912)
d Percy Stow
VC

LIFE IN JAFFA (1905)
VC

LIFE OF A RACING PIGEON, the (1912)
VC

LIFE OF CHARLES PEACE, the (1905)
d William Haggar
VC

LIGHTS AND SHADES ON THE BOSTOCK CIRCUS FARM (1911)
VC

LIGHTWEIGHT CHAMPIONSHIP OF THE WORLD AND £1,900 AT THE NATIONAL SPORTING CLUB, the (1910)

LIVELY QUARTER-DAY, a (1906)
VC

LONG NIGHT DANCE (1900)
VC

LORD AND LADY OVERTOUN'S VISIT TO McINDOE'S SHOW (1906)
VC

LORD KITCHENER'S ARRIVAL AT SOUTHAMPTON – JULY 12TH (1902)
VC

LORD ROBERTS' VISIT TO HAWICK (1913)
VC

LOST IN THE SNOW (1906)
d Frank Mottershaw
VC

LOVE AND THE VARSITY (1913)
d Percy Stow
VC

LOVE STORY OF ANN THOMAS, THE MAID OF CEFN YDFA, the (1914)
d William Haggar Jr
VC

LOVE'S STRATEGY (1908)
VC

LOVE'S VICTORY OVER CRIME (1912)
d Fred Rains
VC

LURE OF LONDON, the (1914)
d Bert Haldane
VC

MacNAB'S VISIT TO LONDON (1905)
d Arthur Melbourne-Cooper
VC

MAGIC EXTINGUISHER, the (1901)
d James Williamson
VC

MAGIC GLASS, the (1914)
d Hay Plumb
VC

MAGIC SWORD, the (1901)
d W R Booth
VC

MAKING CHRISTMAS CRACKERS (1910)
VC

MAKING FIREWORKS (1911)
VC

MAKING OF A MODERN RAILWAY CARRIAGE, the (1912)
VC

MALTA – SAILORS ON SHORE LEAVE (1901)
VC

MAN'S SHADOW, a (1912)
d Edwin J Collins
VC

MAN TO BEAT JACK JOHNSON, the (1910)
VC

MANUFACTURE OF WALKING STICKS, the (1912)
VC

MAN WHO NEVER MADE GOOD, the (1914)
VC

MANX MOTOR RACE, the (1910)
VC

MARY JANE'S MISHAP; or, Don't fool with the paraffin (1903)
d G A Smith
VC

MASQUES AND GRIMACES (1901)
VC

MATCHES (MADE IN ENGLAND) (1910)
VC

MAUDIE'S ADVENTURE (1913)
d Percy Stow
VC

MAY MOORE DUPREZ: WHILST YOU WAIT (1912)
VC

MAYOR KINGSTON'S CALL TO ARMS DEMONSTRATION, DEC 5TH 1914 (1914)
VC

MAYOR'S SUNDAY (1913)
VC

MEDIUM EXPOSED: or, A modern spiritualistic seance, the (1906)
VC

MENAI BRIDGE – THE IRISH DAY MAIL FROM EUSTON ENTERING THE TUBULAR BRIDGE OVER THE MENAI STRAITS (1898)
VC

MESSAGE FROM THE SEA, a (1905)
d William Haggar
VC

METROPOLITAN FIRE BRIGADE TURN OUT (1899)
VC

MIGHTY ATOM, the (1911)
d A E Coleby
VC

MIGHTY ATOM, the (1914)
VC

MIKE MURPHY AS PICTURE ACTOR (1914)
d Dave Aylott
VC

MILITARY FUNERAL OF THE LATE SURGEON CAPTAIN ALFRED A BEEKS, RAMC (1913)
VC

MILITARY SUNDAY IN YORK (1910)
VC

MILLER AND THE SWEEP, the (1897)
d G A Smith
VC

MILLING THE MILITANTS; A COMICAL ABSURDITY (1913)
d Percy Stow
VC

MIND YOUR OWN BUSINESS (1907)
d Jack Smith
VC

MISER'S LESSON, the (1910)
VC

MISSING LEGACY; or, The story of a brown hat, the (1906)
d Alf Collins
VC

MISS SIMPKINS' BOARDERS; THE INCIDENT OF THE CURATE AND THE GHOST (1910)
d Percy Stow
VC

MISTER MOON (1901)
VC

MR POORLUCK BUYS SOME CHINA (1911)
d Lewin Fitzhamon
VC

MR POORLUCK'S LUCKY HORSESHOE (1910)
d Lewin Fitzhamon
VC

MISTLETOE BOUGH, the (1904)
d Percy Stow
VC

MIXED BABIES (1905)
d Frank Mottershaw
VC

MODERN CHINA (1910)
VC

MONKEY AND THE ICE CREAM, the (1904)
d Jasper Redfern
VC

M LEFEBVRE MAKING ASCENT ON A WRIGHT BIPLANE (1909)
VC

MOONLIGHT TRIP ON THE NILE (1909)
VC

MOTHER GOOSE NURSERY RHYMES (1902)
VC

MOTHER'S GRATITUDE, a (1910)
d Frank Wilson
VC

? MOTORIST, the (1906)
d W R Booth
VC

MOTOR PIRATES (1906)
d Arthur Melbourne-Cooper
VC

MOTU DANCES IN HANUABADA VILLAGE (1904)
VC

MOUNTAINEER'S ROMANCE, the (1912)
d Charles Raymond
VC

MOUNT PILATUS RAILWAY, the (1900)
VC

MUGGINS, VC (1909)
d Dave Aylott
VC

MYSTERY OF MR MARKS, the (1914)
d Warwick Buckland
VC

MYSTIC GLOVE, the (1914)
VC

MYSTIC MAT, the (1913)
d Dave Aylott
VC

MYSTIC RING, the (1912)
d Dave Aylott
VC

NANKIN ROAD, SHANGHAI (1901)
d Joseph Rosenthal
VC

NAPOLEON AND THE ENGLISH SAILOR (1908)
d Alf Collins
VC

NATIVE LIFE IN NORTH BORNEO (1908)
VC

NATIVE STREET IN INDIA, a (1906)
VC

NATURAL HISTORY STUDIES AT THE ZOO (1911)
VC

NATURE'S CHILDREN IN THEIR NATIVE HAUNTS (1910)
VC

NAVAL GUNS FIRING AT COLENSO (1899)
VC

NEVER LATE; or, The conscientious clerk (1909)
d Percy Stow
VC

NEW BABY, the (1910)
VC

NEW HAT FOR NOTHING, a (1910)
d Lewin Fitzhamon
VC

NEW UNIQUE COLLECTION OF THE KING AND ROYAL VISITORS TO HELSINGOR, SHOWING 32 SOVEREIGNS, PRINCES AND PRINCESSES OF THE IMPERIAL AND ROYAL HOUSES OF EUROPE, the (1901)
VC

NIGHT DUTY (1904)
d Alf Collins
VC

NIGHT I FOUGHT JACK JOHNSON, the (1912)
VC

1912 GRAND NATIONAL (1912)
VC

NOBBY THE NEW WAITER (1913)
d W P Kellino
VC

NORTH WALES, ENGLAND: THE LAND OF CASTLES AND WATERFALLS (1907)
VC

NORWAY – HARDANGER AND GEIRANGER FJORDS (1904)
VC

NORWICH – TRAMWAY RIDE THROUGH PRINCIPAL STREETS (1902)
VC

NURSE SHOWS TOOTHBRUSHES (1912)
VC

OHMS (1913)
d Alexander Butler
VC

OLD CHORISTER, the (1904)
d James Williamson
VC

OLD KING COLE AND BLACKBIRD PIE (1903)
d G A Smith
VC

OLD LONDON (1914)
VC

OLD MAID'S VALENTINE, the (1900)
d G A Smith
VC

OLD SERGEANT, the (1910)
VC

OLD SOLDIER, an (1910)
VC

ON A GOOSE FARM (1909)
VC

£100 REWARD (1908)
d James Williamson
VC

ON THE BANKS OF THE ZUYDERSEE
(HOLLAND) (1912)
VC

OTHER SIDE OF THE HEDGE, the (1905)
d Lewin Fitzhamon
VC

OUR BANANA SUPPLY (1908)
VC

OUR CAVALRY'S MAGNIFICENT
HORSEMANSHIP (1914)
VC

OUR NEW ERRAND BOY (1905)
d James Williamson
VC

OUR NEW POLICEMAN (1907)
VC

OUTWITTED (1911)
VC

OVERCHARGED (1912)
d Frank Wilson
VC

OVER-INCUBATED BABY, an (1901)
d W R Booth
VC

OXFORD AND CAMBRIDGE BOAT RACE
1911 (1911)
VC

PADDLING PARTY, a (1902)
VC

PAGEBOY'S JOKE, the (1908)
VC

PANORAMA OF GRAND HARBOUR,
MALTA, SHEWING BATTLESHIPS, ETC.
(1901)
VC

PANORAMA OF THE PARIS EXHIBITION
NO.3 (1900)
VC

PANORAMIC VIEW OF THE VEGETABLE
MARKET AT VENICE (1898)
VC

PANTHER HUNTING IN THE ISLE OF
JAVA (1909)
VC

PASSIONS OF MEN, the (1914)
d Wilfred Noy
VC

PA TAKES UP PHYSICAL CULTURE (1907)
VC

PATIENT US ARMY MULE AND NEGRO
CAVALRY, the (1911)
VC

PATRICK STREET, CORK (1900)
VC

PEACE AND WAR; PENCILLINGS BY
HARRY FURNISS (1914)
VC

PEEPS INTO NATURE'S REALM (1909)
VC

PELICANS AT THE ZOO (1898)
VC

PEPPERY AFFAIR, a (1912)
d Percy Stow
VC

PERCY'S PERSISTENT PURSUIT (1912)
d Percy Stow
VC

PERIL OF THE FLEET, the (1909)
d S Wormald
VC

PETTICOAT LANE ON SUNDAY (1904)
VC

PHANTOM RIDE – CHAMONIX (1900)
VC

PHOTOGRAPH TAKEN FROM OUR AREA
WINDOW, a (1901)
d G A Smith
VC

PICTURESQUE NIAGARA, ONTARIO,
CANADA – GRAND TRUNK RAILWAY
SYSTEM (1910)
VC

PICTURESQUE NORTH WALES series
  see
    NORTH WALES, ENGLAND: THE LAND
      OF CASTLES AND WATERFALLS
      (1907)

PILFERED PORKER, the (1905)
VC

PIMPLE'S BATTLE OF WATERLOO (1913)
d Fred Evans, Joe Evans
VC

PIMPLE'S COMPLAINT (1913)
d Fred Evans, Joe Evans
VC

PIMPLE'S MOTOR BIKE (1913)
d Fred Evans, Joe Evans
VC

PIMPLE'S NEW JOB (1913)
d Fred Evans, Joe Evans
VC

PIMPLE'S WONDERFUL GRAMOPHONE
(1913)
d Fred Evans, Joe Evans
VC

PING-PONG (1902)
VC

PLAYING TRUANT (1910)
VC

PLUCKY LAD, a (1910)
d H O Martinek
VC

PLUMBER AND THE LUNATICS, the (1908)
VC

PLUM PUDDING STAKES, the (1911)
d H O Martinek
VC

POET AND HIS BABIES, a (1906)
d Lewin Fitzhamon
VC

POISON OR WHISKEY (1904)
d Lewin Fitzhamon
VC

POLICEMAN (1900)
d G A Smith
VC

POORLUCKS' FIRST TIFF, the (1910)
d Lewin Fitzhamon
VC

PORT MORESBY: DANCE OF MEN OF
THE ARMED NATIVE CONSTABULARY
FROM THE MAMARE DISTRICT (1904)
VC

POSTMAN AND THE NURSEMAID, the
(1899)
d Charles Goodwin Norton
VC

PREHISTORIC PEEPS (1905)
d Lewin Fitzhamon
VC

PRESIDENT DAY. FULWOOD BOWLING
CLUB, SATURDAY JULY 25 1914 (1914)
VC

PRESS – ILLUSTRATED, the (1904)
VC

PRESTIDIGITATEUR, le (1906)
VC

PRESTON GOLF CLUB; FOURSOME
MATCH BETWEEN VARDON &
M'CINTOSH V TAYLOR AND BROWN
(1913)
VC

PRESTON'S EMPIRE DAY, 22 MAY 1909
(1909)
VC

PRIZE FIGHT OR GLOVE FIGHT
BETWEEN JOHN BULL AND PRESIDENT
KRUGER, a (1900)
d John Sloane Barnes
VC

PROFESSOR WHO DRANK INK, the (1900)
VC

PUT A... (1909)
d Percy Stow
VC

PUZZLED BATHER AND HIS ANIMATED
CLOTHES, the (1901)
d James Williamson
VC

QUARRYING FRENCH STONES FOR OUR
ROADS (1910)
VC

QUEENSBURY TUNNEL (1898)
VC

QUEEN VICTORIA (1910)
VC

QUEER PETS (1912)
VC

QUICK SHAVE AND BRUSH-UP, a (1900)
d G A Smith
VC

RACE FOR A KISS, a (1904)
d Lewin Fitzhamon
VC

RAILWAY COLLISION, a (1900)
d W R Booth
VC

RAILWAY RIDE OVER THE TAY BRIDGE
(1897)
VC

RAILWAY TRAFFIC (1898)
VC

REEDHAM ORPHANAGE BOYS FANCY
DRILL (1907)
VC

REITER EVOLUTIONEN ENGLISCHER
HUSAREN (1910)
VC

REPAIRING THE BROKEN BRIDGE AT
FRERE (1899)
VC

RESCUED BY ROVER (1905)
d Lewin Fitzhamon
VC

RESCUED IN MID-AIR (1906)
d Percy Stow
VC

RESERVIST, BEFORE THE WAR, AND AFTER THE WAR, a (1902)
d James Williamson
VC

RETURN OF TRH THE PRINCE AND PRINCESS OF WALES (1903)
d R W Paul
VC

REVOLVING TABLE, the (1903)
d Percy Stow
VC

RICE PLANTATIONS OF BALI, the (1913)
VC

RIGOLLO, THE MAN OF MANY FACES (1910)
VC

RING AND THE RAJAH, the (1914)
d Harold Shaw
VC

RIVAL BARBERS, the (1906)
d James Williamson
VC

RIVAL CYCLISTS, the (1908)
d James Williamson
VC

ROAD TO RUIN, the (1913)
d Bert Haldane, George Gray
VC

ROBBERS AND THE JEW, the (1908)
d Jack Smith
VC

ROBBERY (1897)
d R W Paul
VC

ROBINSON CRUSOE (1902)
d G A Smith
VC

ROLLICKING RAJAH, the (1914)
VC

ROTHWELL INFIRMARY PROCESSION (1913)
VC

ROTHWELL PARISH CHURCH SCHOOL FEAST, 1913 (1913)
VC

ROUGH SEA (1900)
VC

ROUGH SEA AT DOVER (1895)
d Birt Acres
VC

ROYAL PROGRESS TO THE GUILDHALL, JUNE 29, 1911, the (1911)
VC

ROYAL VISIT TO BOLTON. STREET SCENES AND DECORATIONS (1913)
VC

ROYAL VISIT TO IRELAND 1903 (1903)
VC

RUDGE-WHITWORTH – BRITAIN'S BEST BICYCLE (1900)
VC

RUGBY AT RICHMOND (1900)
VC

RUNAWAY LORRY, the (1911)
VC

SAILMAKING: REPAIRING CLEAN RENT IN FABRIC (1914)
VC

SAILORS DRILLING WITH CLUBS (1900)
VC

ST KILDA, ITS PEOPLE AND BIRDS (1908)
d Oliver Pike
VC

SALLY IN OUR ALLEY (1913)
VC

SALVATION ARMY CONGRESS LONDON (1914)
VC

SANTA CLAUS (1898)
d G A Smith
VC

SARAH BERNHARDT (1914)
VC

SATURDAY SHOPPING (1903)
d Cecil M Hepworth
VC

SAVAGE SOUTH AFRICA – ATTACK AND REPULSE (1899)
VC

SAVED BY A BURGLAR (1909)
VC

SAVED BY CARLO (1909)
d A E Coleby
VC

SAWNEY SAM'S DILEMMA (1914)
VC

SCANDALOUS BOYS AND THE FIRE-CHUTE, the (1908)
d Percy Stow
VC

SCANDAL OVER THE TEACUPS (1900)
d G A Smith
VC

SCAPEGRACE, the (1913)
d Edwin J Collins
VC

SCENE ON MR N SMIT'S OSTRICH FARM, IMPANZI, NATAL, SOUTH AFRICA (1900)
VC

SCENES AND INCIDENTS AT ORPINGTON ATHLETIC SPORTS. THURSDAY JULY 17TH (1913)
VC

SCENES IN JERSEY (1910)
VC

SCENES IN MOSCOW AND TIFLIS (1914)
VC

SCENES IN TARANAKI, NEW ZEALAND (1913)
VC

SCENES IN THE SCILLY ISLES (1912)
VC

SCENES ON THE CORNISH RIVIERA (1904)
VC

SCENES ON THE RIVER JHELUM, THE CHIEF WATERWAY OF SRINAGAR, THE CAPITAL OF CASHMERE (1903)
VC

SCHLITTENPARTIE (1910)
VC

SCROOGE (1913)
d Leedham Bantock
VC

SCROOGE; or, Marley's ghost (1901)
d W R Booth
VC

SCULPTOR'S DREAM, the (1910)
VC

SEA DREAMS (Bully Boy series) (1914)
d Lancelot Speed
VC

SEASIDE GIRL, a (1907)
d Lewin Fitzhamon
VC

SEASIDE INTRODUCTION, a (1911)
d Lewin Fitzhamon
VC

SELKIRK COMMON RIDING 1899 [sic] (1909)
VC

SHAKESPEARE LAND (1910)
VC

SICK KITTEN, the (1903)
d G A Smith
VC

SIGHTS IN NEW YORK (1910)
VC

SINGAPORE (1910)
VC

SISTER MARY JANE'S TOP NOTE (1907)
d Lewin Fitzhamon
VC

SLEEP BREAKERS, the (1910)
d Alf Collins
VC

SLEEPING BEAUTY, the (1912)
d Elwin Neame
VC

SLEEPLESS (Bully Boy series) (1914)
d Lancelot Speed
VC

SMALLEST CAR IN THE LARGEST CITY IN THE WORLD, the (1913)
d F S Bennett
VC

SOLD AGAIN (1907)
d Frank Mottershaw
VC

SOLDIER'S RETURN, the (1902)
d James Williamson
VC

SOMNAMBULIST'S CRIME, the (1908)
d A E Coleby
VC

SORCERER'S SCISSORS, the (1907)
d W R Booth
VC

SPITHEAD REVIEW, JUNE 24 1911, the (1911)
VC

SPORTS ON BOARD SHIP (1898)
VC

SQUADRONE GUARDIE DEL RE (1906)
VC

SQUATTER'S DAUGHTER, the (1906)
d Lewin Fitzhamon
VC

SS ST PAUL WHICH RAN-DOWN THE CRUISER (1910)
VC

STAGE-STRUCK CARPENTER, the (1911)
d Percy Stow
VC

STAG HUNTING IN FRANCE (1907)
VC

STAPELLAUF EINES KRIEGSSCHIFFES (1907)
VC

STILTON CHEESE (1904)
VC

STOLEN CLOTHES (1909)
d Lewin Fitzhamon
VC

STOLEN GUY, the (1905)
d Lewin Fitzhamon
VC

STOLEN PICTURE, the (1912)
d Frank Wilson
VC

STOLEN PIG, the (1904)
d Percy Stow
VC

STOP THIEF! (1901)
d James Williamson
VC

STOP THIEF (1910)

STRENGTH AND AGILITY OF INSECTS, the (1911)
VC

STUDENT, THE SOOT AND THE SMOKE, the (1904)
VC

STUDIES OF REPTILE LIFE (Urban Science series) (1913)
VC

SUFFRAGETTE'S DOWNFALL; or, Who said 'Rats'?, the (1911)
d Fred Rains
VC

SWITCHBACK RAILWAY, a (1898)
VC

SWORD DANCE PERFORMED BEFORE THE KING AND QUEEN IN INDIA (1911)
VC

SZENEN AUS DEM FERNEN OSTEN (1909)
VC

TABLES TURNED, the (1910)
d H O Martinek
VC

TALE OF A COAT, the (1905)
d Alf Collins
VC

TALE OF THE ARK, the (1909)
d Arthur Melbourne-Cooper
VC

TAME ANIMALS AT WORK (1909)
VC

TEMPEST, the (1908)
d Percy Stow
VC

TEMPTER, the (1913)
d F Martin Thornton, R H Callum
VC

TERROR AND THE TERRIER, the (1910)
d A E Coleby
VC

TETHERBALL, OR DO-DO (1898)
d R W Paul
VC

THAT FATAL SNEEZE (1907)
d Lewin Fitzhamon
VC

THEIR FIRST SNOWBALLS (1907)
VC

THERE'S GOOD IN THE WORST OF US (1913)
d Ethyle Batley
VC

THOMAS V SULLIVAN AT NATIONAL SPORTING CLUB NOV 14TH 1910 (1910)
VC

THRILLING STORY, a (1910)
d Dave Aylott
VC

THROUGH PARIS ON THE SEINE (1911)
VC

TILLY'S PARTY (1911)
d Lewin Fitzhamon
VC

TILLY THE TOMBOY VISITS THE POOR (1910)
d Lewin Fitzhamon
VC

TIMOTHY TODDLES AT THE LADIES TRAINING CENTRE (1914)
VC

TINY HONEY GATHERERS (Urban Science series) (1911)
VC

TOADS – LEAPING BATRACHIANS (1908)
VC

TOBOGANNING (1903)
VC

TO DEMONSTRATE HOW SPIDERS FLY (Urban Science series) (1909)
VC

TOMKINS BUYS A DONKEY (1908)
d Lewin Fitzhamon
VC

TOM MERRY, LIGHTNING CARTOONIST, SKETCHING KAISER WILHELM II (1895)
d Birt Acres
VC

TOMMY ATKINS IN THE PARK (1898)
d R W Paul
VC

TOPPER TRIUMPHANT (1914)
d Hay Plumb
VC

TOPSY'S DREAM OF TOYLAND (1911)
d A E Coleby
VC

TOPSY TURVEY DANCE BY THREE QUAKER MAIDENS (1900)
d G A Smith
VC

TOREADOR SONG, the (1909)
VC

TORPEDO ATTACK ON HMS DREADNOUGHT (1907)
VC

TOUCH OF NATURE, a (1911)
VC

TRAGEDY ON THE CORNISH COAST (1912)
d Sidney Northcote
VC

TRAIN ENTERING HOVE STATION (1900)
VC

TRAMP AND THE BABY'S BOTTLE, the (1899)
VC

TRAMPS IN CLOVER (1905)
VC

TRICKY STICK, the (1914)
d Dave Aylott
VC

TRIP ON THE METROPOLITAN RAILWAY FROM BAKER ST TO UXBRIDGE AND AYLESBURY, a (1910)
VC

TRIP THROUGH BRITISH NORTH BORNEO, a (1907)
VC

TRIP TO THE WHITE SEA FISHERIES, a (1909)
d Joseph Rosenthal
VC

TROUPE OF RUSSIAN DANCERS, a (1903)
VC

TRUANT'S CAPTURE, the (1906)
d Percy Stow
VC

TUNIS AND SURROUNDINGS (1912)
VC

TWINS' TEA PARTY, the (1896)
d R W Paul
VC

'TWIXT LOVE AND DUTY; or, A woman's heroism (1908)
d A E Coleby
VC

TWO COLUMBINES, the (1914)
d Harold Shaw
VC

TWO LITTLE WAIFS (1905)
d James Williamson
VC

TWO OLD SPORTS (1900)
d G A Smith
VC

UNCLEAN WORLD, the (1903)
d Percy Stow
VC

UNDANK IS DER WELT LOHN (1909)
VC

UNDRESSING EXTRAORDINARY; or, The troubles of a tired traveller (1901)
d W R Booth
VC

UNIQUE STUDIES OF NATURE; SERIES 2 (1913)
VC

UNSEEN WORLD series, the
see
CHEESE MITES (1903)
WATER FLEA AND ROTIFERS (1903)

UNVEILING OF THE MEMORIAL STATUE OF THE LATE SIR GEORGE LIVESEY BY EARL GREY (1909)
VC

UPSIDE DOWN; or, The human flies (1899)
VC

URBAN SCIENCE series
see
BIRTH OF A FLOWER, the (1910)
FAMILIAR REPTILES (1914)
FLY DANGER, the (1911)
GETTING CLOSE TO THE SPIDER (1909)
STUDIES OF REPTILE LIFE (1913)
TINY HONEY GATHERERS (1911)
TO DEMONSTRATE HOW SPIDERS FLY
   (1909)

VALE; DANCED BY THE VILLAGERS OF THE HOOD PENINSULA (1904)
VC

VENETIAN SHORES, the (1914)
VC

VERARMTER ADLIGER DER SEINE NOT VERBERGEN WILL, ein (1910)
VC

VICE VERSA (1910)
d Dave Aylott
VC

VICTIM OF MISFORTUNE, a (1905)
VC

VICTORIA FALLS – ZAMBESI RIVER (1907)
VC

VICTORIAN LADY IN HER BOUDOIR, a (1896)
d Esmé Collings
VC

VIEW FROM AN ENGINE FRONT – BARNSTAPLE (1898)
VC

VIEW FROM AN ENGINE FRONT – ILFRACOMBE (1898)
VC

VIEW FROM AN ENGINE FRONT – SHILLA MILL TUNNEL (1899)
VC

VILLAGE BLACKSMITH, the (1907)
VC

VISIT OF THE BRITISH FLEET TO BARCELONA (SPAIN) (1914)
VC

VISIT TO EARL'S COURT, a (1911)
VC

VISIT TO LOCOMOTIVE WORKS, CREWE, a (1913)
VC

VISIT TO PEEK FREAN AND CO'S BISCUIT WORKS, a (1906)
VC

VISIT TO WHITBY, YORKS, a (1913)
VC

VIVAPHONE FILM (1909)
VC

VOLCANOS OF JAVA, the (1914)
VC

WAIF AND THE WIZARD; or, The home made happy, the (1901)
d W R Booth
VC

WAIMA DANCE, KOVEA, a (1904)
VC

WARM RECEPTION, a (1914)
d Toby Cooper
VC

WASHING THE SWEEP (1898)
d James Williamson
VC

WASP, the (1912)
VC

WATER BABIES; or, The little chimney sweep, the (1907)
d Percy Stow
VC

WATERFALLS OF WALES, the (1904)
VC

WATER FINDERS, the (1914)
VC

WATER FLEA AND ROTIFERS (The Unseen World series) (1903)
VC

WATER POLO – WORTHING SWIMMING CLUB (1898)
VC

WAYS OF THE WOOD ANT, the (1911)
VC

WEARY WILLIE (1898)
VC

WELLMAN POLAR EXPEDITION, the (1906)
VC

WEYBRIDGE AVIATION (1913)
VC

WHALING AFLOAT AND ASHORE (1908)
VC

WHAT THE CURATE REALLY DID (1905)
d Lewin Fitzhamon
VC

WHEN DADDY COMES HOME (1902)
d Percy Stow
VC

WHEN EXTREMES MEET (1905)
d Alf Collins
VC

WHEN FATHER GOT A HOLIDAY (1906)
d Percy Stow
VC

WHEN THE DEVIL DRIVES (1907)
d W R Booth
VC

WHERE OH WHERE HAS MY LITTLE DOG GONE? (Cinematophone Singing Pictures series) (1907)
VC

WHERE THERE'S A WILL THERE'S A WAY (1906)
d James Williamson
VC

WHIRLPOOL OF WAR series, the
see
ANTWERP UNDER SHOT AND SHELL
   (1914)
FIGHT FOR THE COAST, the (1914)
WITH THE BRITISH & FRENCH IN
   FLANDERS (1914)
WITH THE WARRIORS AT YPRES (1914)

WHISPER AND I SHALL HEAR (1913)
VC

WHO'S WHO IN ZOOLAND (1914)
VC

WIFE'S REVENGE; or, The gambler's end, a (1904)
VC

WILD ANIMALS (1908)
VC

WILD GOOSE CHASE, a (1908)
d Percy Stow
VC

WILL EVANS, THE MUSICAL ECCENTRIC (1899)
VC

WILLIAM AND BRAMWELL BOOTH AT SA CONGRESS – ?1904 (1904)
VC

WILLIE'S MAGIC WAND (1907)
d W R Booth
VC

WINKY AND THE 'DWARF?' (1914)
d Cecil Birch
VC

WINKY'S RUSE (1914)
d Cecil Birch
VC

WINKY'S WEEKEND (1914)
d Cecil Birch
VC

WINTER SPORTS AT TIVERTON (1906)
VC

WISHAW CO-OPERATIVE SOCIETY GALA DAY 26TH JUNE 1909 (1909)
VC

WITH THE BRITISH & FRENCH IN FLANDERS (The Whirlpool of War series) (1914)
VC

WITH THE WARRIORS AT YPRES (The Whirlpool of War series) (1914)
VC

WOMAN AGAINST WOMAN (1910)
VC

WOMAN'S TREACHERY, a (1910)
d Theo Bouwmeester
VC

WOMAN'S WIT, a (1913)
d Warwick Buckland
VC

WOMEN'S RIGHTS (1899)
VC

WOMEN'S WORK IN WARTIME (1914)
VC

WON'T YOU COME HOME (1903)
VC

WOODEN ATHLETES, the (1912)
d Arthur Melbourne-Cooper
VC

WORKMEN LEAVING THE FACTORY (1900)
VC

WORKS AND WORKERS OF DENTON HOLME (1910)
VC

WORLD FAMOUS MUSICAL COMEDY ARTISTS SEYMOUR HICKS AND ELLALINE TERRIS IN A SELECTION OF THEIR DANCES, the (1912)
VC

WOULD-BE CONJURER, the (1900)
VC

WRECK IN A GALE, a (1900)
VC

WRESTLING BURLESQUE (1903)
VC

X-RAY CINEMATOGRAPHY OF FROG'S LEGS (1897)
VC

YOUTHFUL HERO, a (1909)
VC

1915–1928

ABBEY GRANGE, the (The Further Adventures of Sherlock Holmes series) (1922)
d George Ridgwell
VC

ABOVE THE CLOUDS (1917)
VC

ACROSS THE FOOTLIGHTS series
see
POT POURRI (1925)

ACROSS UGANDA TO THE MOUNTAINS OF THE MOON (1924)
VC

ADAGIO, the (On with the Dance series) (1927)
d Harry B Parkinson
VC

ADAM'S APPLE (1928)
d Tim Whelan
VC

ADVENTURES OF SHERLOCK HOLMES series, the
see
BERYL CORONET, the (1921)
CASE OF IDENTITY, a (1921)
DEVIL'S FOOT, the (1921)
DYING DETECTIVE, the (1921)
HOUND OF THE BASKERVILLES, the (1921)
MAN WITH THE TWISTED LIP, the (1921)

ADVENTURES OF WEE ROB ROY NO.1, the (1916)
VC

AERIAL SURVEY OF AFRICA (1927)
VC

AEROPLANE ON WHEELS, an (1928)
VC

AEROPLANES (1919)
VC

AFRICAN WAR COMFORTS SERVICE (1918)
VC

AFTER-DINNER MAGIC (1920)
VC

AGAINST THE GRAIN (1918)
d Henry Edwards
VC

AGITATED ADVERTS (1918)
d Anson Dyer
VC

AIR AND SUN (1924)
VC

ALBERT SANDLER AND HIS VIOLIN... CZARDAS – MONTI (British Phototone series) (1928)
d J B Sloan
VC

ALBERT SANDLER AND HIS VIOLIN... SERENADE – SCHUBERT (British Phototone series) (1928)
d J B Sloan
VC

ALDERMAN MATTHEWS MAYOR'S PROCESSION, NOVEMBER 9TH 1924 (1924)
VC

ALF'S BUTTON (1920)
d Cecil M Hepworth
VC

ALL ABOUT WITNEY BLANKETS (1924)
VC

ALL FOR THE SAKE OF MARY (1920)
VC

ALLOTMENT HOLDER'S ENEMIES (Smallholder series) (1918)
VC

AL STARITA AND HIS SAXOPHONE ...'AT DAWNING' (British Phototone series) (1928)
d J B Sloan
VC

AL STARITA AND HIS SAXOPHONE ... 'LANETTE' (British Phototone series) (1928)
d J B Sloan
VC

ALWAYS TELL YOUR WIFE (1923)
d Hugh Croise, Alfred Hitchcock, Seymour Hicks
VC

AMATEUR CYCLING CHAMPIONSHIPS (1924)
VC

AMBULANCE SUNDAY AT HERNE BAY JULY 1 1928 (1928)
VC

ANGEL ESQUIRE (1919)
d W P Kellino
PB

ANIMAL WORLD SERIES NO.1, the (1915)
VC

ANNUAL INSPECTION OF THE BODYGUARD BY HIS EXCELLENCY LORD LYTTON (1925)
VC

ANTARCTICA: ON THE GREAT WHITE TRAIL SOUTH (1920)
VC

ANTIDOTE, the (1927)
d Thomas Bentley
VC

ANT-LION, the (Secrets of Nature series) (1927)
VC

APPEAL FROM HEART TO POCKET, an (1925)
VC

APPLICATION OF PLASTER OF PARIS ON PATIENT SUFFERING FROM CERVICAL CARIES (1920)
VC

AQUARIUM IN A WINE GLASS, an (Secrets of Nature series) (1926)
VC

ARMISTICE DAY IN PORT SUNLIGHT (1927)
VC

ARMISTICE DAY MEMORIAL SERVICE AND PARADE AT FLINT, 1928 (1928)
VC

ARMISTICE SERVICE IN VICTORIA PARK, WHITEINCH (1928)
VC

ARMISTICE SUNDAY IN FLINT 1926 (1926)
VC

ARMY SPORTS DAY – WORLD WAR I (1920)
VC

AROUND THE TOWN series
see
AROUND THE TOWN NO.110 (1922)
AROUND THE TOWN NO.114 (1922)
AROUND THE TOWN NO.115 (1922)
AROUND THE TOWN NO.116 (1922)
CREATOR OF 'LIGHTNING' SKETCHES ALICK P F RITCHIE, the (1921)
CUPID ON A WEDDING CAKE (1923)
ITALIAN ROSE IN AN ENGLISH GARDEN – PINA MENICHELLI, an (1922)
JOLLY DUTCH GIRL, the (1920)
LONG AND SHORT OF IT, the (1922)
LOVE'S AWAKENING (1922)
SOME CLASSICAL DANCING BY THE PUPILS OF MARGARET MORRIS (1922)
TERPSICHOREAN TECHNICALITIES BY HELEN MAY (1922)
TRIP DOWN THE CLYDE – DUMBARTON ROCK, a (1921)

AROUND THE TOWN NO.110 (1922)
VC

AROUND THE TOWN NO.114 (1922)
VC

AROUND THE TOWN NO.115 (1922)
VC

AROUND THE TOWN NO.116 (1922)
VC

ARRIVAL OF THE EARL OF LYTTON AT CALCUTTA (1922)
VC

ARRIVAL OF THE MAIL STEAMERS LERWICK (1920)
VC

ASCENT OF THE JUNGFRAU, the (1924)
VC

AT THE VILLA ROSE (Eminent British Authors series) (1920)
d Maurice Elvey
VC

BALACLAVA (1928)
d Maurice Elvey, Milton Rosmer
PB

BARBARA'S SECRET (1923)
VC

BARGAIN, the (1921)
d Henry Edwards
VC

BARGING THROUGH LONDON (Wonderful London second series) (1924)
d Harry B Parkinson, Frank Miller
VC

BASUTOLAND AND ITS PEOPLE (1927)
VC

BATTLE OF THE PLANTS, the (Secrets of Nature series) (1926)
VC

BATTLE OF THE SOMME, the (1916)
VC

BATTLES OF CORONEL AND FALKLAND ISLANDS, the (1927)
d Walter Summers
VC

BEAU BROCADE (1916)
d Thomas Bentley
PB

BEAUTY SPOTS OF ITALY NO.1 (1922)
VC

BECKET (1923)
d George Ridgwell
VC

BEDFORD HOSPITAL FETE (1926)
VC

BEDTIME STORIES OF ARCHIE THE ANT series
see
BERTIE'S CAVE (1925)
PIT AND THE PLUM, the (1925)
TALE OF A TENDRIL, the (1925)

BELOVED VAGABOND, the (1923)
d Fred Leroy Granville
VC

BENGUELA RAILWAY; A MILESTONE IN AFRICAN CIVILISATION, the (1928)
VC

BERNE AND THE BERNESE OBERLAND (1926)
VC

BERTIE'S CAVE (Bedtime Stories of Archie the Ant series) (1925)
d Percy Smith
VC

BERYL CORONET, the (The Adventures of Sherlock Holmes series) (1921)
d Maurice Elvey
VC

BHUTAN (1928)
VC

BID FOR FORTUNE, a (1917)
d Sidney Morgan
VC

BIG PUSH, the (1927)
VC

BINDLE series
see
BINDLE'S COCKTAIL (1926)

BINDLE'S COCKTAIL (Bindle series) (1926)
d Harry B Parkinson
VC

BIOCOLOR PICTURE THEATRES DEFY THE 'CLERK OF THE WEATHER', WEDY JULY 21ST 20 (1920)
VC

BIRMINGHAM'S WATER SUPPLY (1923)
VC

BIRTHPLACE OF GOETHE, the (1925)
VC

BLACK COTTON (The Empire series) (1927)
VC

BLACKGUARD, the (1925)
d Graham Cutts
PB

BLEAK HOUSE (1920)
d Maurice Elvey
VC

BLIGHTY (1927)
d Adrian Brunel
VC

BLUEBOTTLES (1928)
d Ivor Montagu
VC

BLUE PETER, the (1928)
d Arthur Rooke
VC PB

BLUNDERS OF MR BUTTERBUN series, the
see
TRIPPS AND TRIBUNALS (1918)

BOADICEA (1926)
d Sinclair Hill
PB

BOEING AIRPLANE NB1 IN A FLAT SPIN FROM AN ALTITUDE OF 4,000 FT (1925)
VC

BOHEMIAN GIRL, the (1922)
d Harley Knoles
VC

BONNIE BANKS OF LOCH LOMOND, the (Master Film Song Album series) (1922)
d George Wynn
VC

BONZO series
see
BONZO (1924)
BONZO (1925)
BONZO NO.4 (1925)
BONZOBY (1925)
BONZOLINO; or, Bonzo broadcasted (1925)
BOOSTER BONZO (1925)
CHEEKEE – THE VAMP (1925)
DETECTIVE BONZO AND THE BLACK HAND (1925)
OUT ON THE TILES AFTER A CAT BURGLAR (1925)
PLAYING THE 'DICKENS' IN AN OLD CURIOSITY SHOP (1925)
POLAR BONZO (1925)
SCOUT'S GOOD TURN, the (1925)
TOPICAL BONZETTE (1925)

BONZO (Bonzo series) (1924)
VC

BONZO (Bonzo series) (1925)
VC

BONZO NO.4 (Bonzo series) (1925)
VC

BONZOBY (Bonzo series) (1925)
VC

BONZOLINO; or, Bonzo broadcasted (Bonzo series) (1925)
VC

BOOKWORMS (1920)
d Adrian Brunel
VC

BOOSTER BONZO (Bonzo series) (1925)
VC

BOTTLE-MAKING UP TO DATE (Pathé Pictorial series) (1921)
VC

BOY SCOUT'S INTERNATIONAL JAMBOREE, OLYMPIA, LONDON 1920 (1920)
VC

BOY WHO WANTED TO MAKE PICTURES, the (1924)
VC

BRIGADIER GERARD (1915)
d Bert Haldane
PB

BRIGHTON CELEBRATION WEEK FESTIVITIES, the (1928)
VC

BRITAIN KEEPS HER WORD (1923)
VC

BRITAIN'S LONELIEST ISLE (1923)
VC

BRITISH AIRSHIPS IN THE EAST (1917)
VC

BRITISH LEGION CLUB (1926)
VC

BRITISH PHOTOTONE series
see
ALBERT SANDLER AND HIS VIOLIN ... CZARDAS – MONTI (1928)
ALBERT SANDLER AND HIS VIOLIN ... SERENADE – SCHUBERT (1928)
AL STARITA AND HIS SAXOPHONE ... 'AT DAWNING' (1928)
AL STARITA AND HIS SAXOPHONE ... 'LANETTE' (1928)
TEDDY BROWN AND HIS XYLOPHONE (1928)

BRITISH SCREEN TATLER series
see
EASTERN IDYLL, an (1920)

BRITISH SPORTS AND PASTIMES SERIES NO.5 (1916)
VC

BRITISH SUBMARINES IN THE MEDITERRANEAN (1916)
VC

BROADCASTING (John Henry Calling series) (1926)
d Challis N Sanderson, Widgey R Newman
PB

BROKEN IN THE WARS (1918)
d Cecil M Hepworth
VC

BROKEN ROAD, the (Eminent British Authors series) (1921)
d René Plaisetty
VC

BRUCE PARTINGTON PLANS, the (The Further Adventures of Sherlock Holmes series) (1922)
d George Ridgwell
VC

BUCKLEY JUBILEE 1925 (1925)
VC

BUCKLEY JUBILEE 1928 (1928)
VC

BUILDING AND LAUNCH OF THE 'CREPATH' AT BARNSTAPLE, the (1918)
VC

BUILDING AND OPERATION OF INDUSTRIAL MUSEUMS, the (1928)
VC

BUILDING OF A LOCOMOTIVE AT CREWE, the (1920)
VC

BULLDOG BREED, the (1926)
VC

BULLDOG GRIT (1915)
d Ethyle Batley
VC

BUMP, the (1920)
d Adrian Brunel
VC

CAB, the (Little Dramas of Everyday Life series) (1926)
d William J Elliott
VC

CABBAGES AND THINGS (Secrets of Nature series) (1923)
VC

CALCUTTA TOPICAL (1926)
VC

CALCUTTA TOPICAL NO.1 FOR 1925 (1925)
VC

CALCUTTA TOPICAL NO.2 FOR 1925
(1925)
VC

CALL OF THE HEATHER, the (1924)
VC

CALL OF THE ROAD, the (1920)
   d A E Coleby
VC

CALL OF THE SEA, the (1919)
VC

CALVARY (1919)
   d Edwin J Collins
SC

CAMEO OPERAS series
   see
   TRAVIATA, la (1927)

CANDY CUSHIONS (1920)
VC

CAN YOU BEAT IT? (1925)
VC

CAPE TO CAIRO (1926)
   d C Court Treatt, Stella Court Treatt
VC

CARDBOARD BOX, the (The Last
Adventures of Sherlock Holmes series) (1923)
   d George Ridgwell
VC

CARNIVAL (1921)
   d Harley Knoles
VC PB

CARNIVAL WEEK AT MORECAMBE (1923)
VC

CASE OF IDENTITY, a (The Adventures of
Sherlock Holmes series) (1921)
   d Maurice Elvey
VC

**CÉLÈBRE SPA SUISSE, LOÈCHE-LES-
BAINS, le** (1915)
VC

CENTRE OF THE WORLD (Wonderful
London first series) (1924)
   d Harry B Parkinson, Frank Miller
VC

CHAMPAGNE (1928)
   d Alfred Hitchcock
VC

CHANGING HUES (1922)
VC

CHANNINGS, the (1920)
   d Edwin J Collins
PB

**CHARACTERS IN THE ALL STARS
CIRCUS BY THE 3RD SALISBURY TROOP**
(1921)
VC

CHEEKEE – THE VAMP (Bonzo series) (1925)
VC

CHESTER FORGETS HIMSELF (Cuthbert
series) (1924)
   d Andrew P Wilson
VC

CHINESE BUNGALOW, the (1926)
   d Sinclair Hill
VC

CHRISTMAS EVE (1915)
   d Alfonse Frenguelli
VC

**CHURCH PARADE OF GLASGOW
LOWLAND SIGNAL UNITS, SUNDAY 20TH
JUNE 1926** (1926)
VC

CIRCUS JIM (1921)
   d B E Doxat-Pratt
VC

CITY IN DANGER, a (1928)
VC

**CLASSIC RACES OF THE YEAR: TOURIST
TROPHY RACES, ISLE OF MAN 1923**
(1923)
VC

CLICKING OF CUTHBERT, the (Cuthbert
series) (1924)
   d Andrew P Wilson
VC

CLIMBING MOUNT EVEREST (1922)
   d J B L Noel
VC

CLIMBING THE JUNGFRAU (1915)
VC

COALS AND COURTSHIP (1919)
VC

COBWEB, the (1916)
   d Cecil M Hepworth
PB

COCAINE (1922)
   d Graham Cutts
VC

COCK O' THE WALK (1915)
   d Hay Plumb
VC

COD – A MELLOW DRAMA (1928)
   d Lloyd T Richards, Desmond Dickinson,
     Gerald Gibbs, Harcourt Templeman
VC

**COMIC FOOTBALL MATCH. MOTHERS
ATHLETIC V FATHERS RHEUMATIC,
WALTON-ON-THAMES** (1927)
VC

COMIN' THRO' THE RYE (1923)
   d Cecil M Hepworth
VC PB

COMMUNITY SONG series
   see
   KENTUCKY LULLABY (1927)
   PERHAPS YOU'LL THINK OF ME (1927)

COMRADESHIP (1919)
   d Maurice Elvey
VC

CONSCRIPTION (1915)
   d Dave Aylott
VC

CORNER MAN, the (1921)
   d Einar J Bruun
VC

CORNISH RIVIERA, the (1916)
VC

COSMOPOLITAN LONDON (Wonderful
London first series) (1924)
   d Frank Miller, Harry B Parkinson
VC

**CREATOR OF 'LIGHTNING' SKETCHES
ALICK P F RITCHIE, the** (Around the Town
series) (1921)
VC

CROOKED MAN, the (The Last Adventures of
Sherlock Holmes series) (1923)
   d George Ridgwell
VC

CROSSING THE GREAT SAGRADA (1924)
   d Adrian Brunel
VC

CROSSING THE GREAT SAHARA (1924)

CROXLEY MASTER, the (1921)
   d Percy Nash
VC

CRY OF THE CRIPPLED CHILDREN (1921)
VC

CUCKOO'S SECRET, the (Secrets of Nature
series) (1922)
VC

CUPID ON A WEDDING CAKE (Around the
Town series) (1923)
VC

CUTHBERT series
   see
   CHESTER FORGETS HIMSELF (1924)
   CLICKING OF CUTHBERT, the (1924)
   ORDEAL BY GOLF (1924)
   RODNEY FAILS TO QUALIFY (1924)

**CUT IT OUT; A DAY IN THE LIFE OF A
CENSOR** (1925)
   d Adrian Brunel
VC

DADDY'S BIRTHDAY (1919)

**DAILY DISPATCH AND MANCHESTER
EVENING CHRONICLE APPEAL FOR
FLEETWOOD** (1927)
VC

DAILY JESTERS series
   see
   JOHN CITIZEN (1927)

DAMAGED GOODS (1919)
   d Alexander Butler
VC

**DANCING GRACE – STUDIES OF
MADAME LOPOKOVA** (Eve's Film Review
series) (1922)
VC

DANCING MAD (On with the Dance series)
(1927)
   d Harry B Parkinson
VC

DANIEL DERONDA (1921)
   d Walter Courtenay Rowden
PB

**DARK GROUND ILLUMINATION OF
EXPLANTS** (1928)
VC

DAUGHTER OF LOVE, a (1925)
   d Walter West
VC

DAVID GARRICK (Tense Moments with Great
Authors series) (1922)
VC

DAWN (1928)
   d Herbert Wilcox
VC

DAY IN A SANATORIUM, a (1926)
VC

**DAY IN THE LIFE OF A MUNITION
WORKER, a** (1917)
VC

DAY OF REMEMBRANCE (1927)
VC

DAY OF REST, a (1915)
VC

DAYS OF CHIVALRY (1928)
d Hazel ffennell
VC

DECAMERON NIGHTS (1924)
d Herbert Wilcox
VC

DERBY DAY (Wonderful London second series) (1924)
d Harry B Parkinson, Frank Miller
VC

DESTRUCTION OF A GERMAN BLOCKHOUSE BY 9.2 HOWITZER (1916)
VC

DETECTIVE BONZO AND THE BLACK HAND (Bonzo series) (1925)
VC

DEVIL'S FOOT, the (The Adventures of Sherlock Holmes series) (1921)
d Maurice Elvey
VC

DIANA OF THE CROSSWAYS (1922)
d Denison Clift
VC

DICKENS' LONDON (Wonderful London first series) (1924)
d Harry B Parkinson, Frank Miller
VC

DICKY DEE CARTOONS NO.3 (1915)
d Anson Dyer
VC

DIRECT CINEMATOGRAPHY (1924)
VC

DISAPPEARANCE OF LADY FRANCES CARFAX, the (The Last Adventures of Sherlock Holmes series) (1923)
d George Ridgwell
VC

DR SIN FANG ADVENTURE series
see
TORTURE CAGE, the (1928)

DR WISE ON INFLUENZA (1919)
VC

DON QUIXOTE (1923)
d Maurice Elvey
VC

DOWN BY THE SEA (1925)
VC

DOWN ON THE FARM (1920)
VC

DOWNHILL (1927)
d Alfred Hitchcock
VC

DRUM, the (Thrilling Stories from the Strand Magazine series) (1924)
d Sinclair Hill
VC

DUKE OF YORK'S VISIT TO HORROCK'S MILL, the (1922)
VC

DUKE'S SON (1920)
d Franklin Dyall
VC

DUMMY, the (1916)
d W P Kellino
VC

DYING DETECTIVE, the (The Adventures of Sherlock Holmes series) (1921)
d Maurice Elvey
VC

EASTERN IDYLL, an (British Screen Tatler series) (1920)
VC

EAST IS EAST (1916)
d Henry Edwards
VC

EASY VIRTUE (1927)
d Alfred Hitchcock
VC

ECONOMIST, the (1921)
d Walter Forde
VC

EDGE OF YOUTH, the (1920)
d C C Calvert
PB

EDUCATION AUTHORITY OF GLASGOW SPECIAL SERVICES (1925)
VC

EDUCATION WEEK (1925)
VC

EENA, DEENA, DINAH, DOH! (Till Our Ship Comes In series) (1919)
d Frank Miller
VC

EIGHTH ANNUAL SPORTS AT KINGSTON, AUGUST 2ND, 1926, the (1926)
VC

ELECTRIC WOMEN (Eve's Film Review series) (1927)
VC

ELGA COLLINS – THE VERSATILE ENTERTAINER (1927)
VC

ELSIE AND THE BROWN BUNNY (1921)
VC

EMERALD OF THE EAST (1928)
d Jean de Kuharski
VC

EMINENT BRITISH AUTHORS series
see
AT THE VILLA ROSE (1920)
BROKEN ROAD, the (1921)
FOX FARM (1922)
HUNDREDTH CHANCE, the (1920)
MELODY OF DEATH (1922)
OPEN COUNTRY (1922)
RIVER OF STARS, the (1921)
TIDAL WAVE, the (1920)

EMPIRE series, the
see
BLACK COTTON (1927)
NIGERIA (1928)

ENGLAND: CHANGING GUARD AT HORSE GUARDS AND ST JAMES'S PALACE (1916)
VC

ENGLISH CONGREGATIONAL CHURCH FOUNDATION STONE LAYING, FLINT 28.9.27 (1927)
VC

ENO'S 'FRUIT SALT' (1923)
VC

EPIC OF EVEREST (1924)
d J B L Noel
VC

ERUPTION OF MOUNT ETNA, the (1928)
VC

ETERNAL TRIANGLE, the (1925)
d Alexander Butler
VC

E13 AVENGED, the (1915)
VC

EVER BEEN HAD (1917)
d Dudley Buxton
VC

EVE'S FILM REVIEW series
see
DANCING GRACE – STUDIES OF MADAME LOPOKOVA (1922)
ELECTRIC WOMEN (1927)
FASHIONS OF FIFTY YEARS AGO (1928)
MERELY MINNIE; A SINCERE PARROT WHO WANTED TO GET INTO THE MOVIES (1925)
SOMETHING NEW IN CABARETS (1927)
STARS AT HOME – MISS MAY MOORE-DUPREZ, the (1921)
TIED-DYEING – A NEW ART FOR THE HOME (1927)

EXPLOITS OF TUBBY series, the
see
TUBBY'S REST CURE (1916)

EYES OF THE ARMY; WITH THE RFC AT THE FRONT, the (1916)
VC

FABRIC FINE (1925)
VC

FAILURE, the (1917)
d Henry Edwards
VC

FAKE, the (1927)
d Georg Jacoby
PB

FAMINE – THE RUSSIAN FAMINE OF 1921 (1922)
VC

FARMER'S WIFE, the (1928)
d Alfred Hitchcock
VC

FASHIONS OF FIFTY YEARS AGO (Eve's Film Review series) (1928)
VC

FIERY HAND, the (The Mystery of Dr Fu-Manchu series) (1923)
d A E Coleby
VC

15.6 DURANT MOTOR CAR, the (1923)
VC

FIGHTING GLADIATOR, the (Romances of the Prize Ring series) (1926)
d Harry B Parkinson
VC

FILM PIE series
see
VERY UNSUCCESSFUL COMPETITOR IN THE TOFFEE APPLE COMPETITION, a (1920)

FINAL PROBLEM, the (The Last Adventures of Sherlock Holmes series) (1923)
d George Ridgwell
VC

FIND THE WOMAN (Romances of the Prize Ring series) (1926)
d Harry B Parkinson
VC

FIRST BORN, the (1928)
d Miles Mander
VC

FIRST SECTION 4TH LOYAL NORTH LANCASHIRE'S ROLL OF HONOUR FILM (1915)
VC

FISH'S TALE, a (1920)
VC

FLAG LIEUTENANT, the (1926)
d Maurice Elvey
VC PB

FLIGHT COMMANDER, the (1927)
d Maurice Elvey
SC

FLOWERS OF LONDON (Wonderful London second series) (1924)
d Harry B Parkinson, Frank Miller
VC

FLYING SQUADRONS OF BEMPTON CLIFFS, the (1921)
VC

FOOD SUPPLY (1921)
VC

FORGIVE US OUR TRESPASSES (1919)
d L C MacBean
VC

FOR 'MY LADY'S' HAPPINESS (Romances of the Prize Ring series) (1926)
d Harry B Parkinson
VC

FORWARD COVENTRY! HOW A FAMOUS BRITISH MOTOR CYCLE IS MADE (1927)
VC

FOUR JUST MEN, the (1921)
d George Ridgwell
VC

FOX FARM (Eminent British Authors series) (1922)
d Guy Newall
VC

FRENCH BATTLEFIELD SCENES (1918)
VC

FRIVOLITIES OF 1924 (1924)
VC

FUGITIVE FUTURIST; A Q-RIOSITY BY 'Q', the (1924)
d Gaston Quiribet
VC

FURTHER ADVENTURES OF SHERLOCK HOLMES series, the
see
ABBEY GRANGE, the (1922)
BRUCE PARTINGTON PLANS, the (1922)
MUSGRAVE RITUAL, the (1922)
RED CIRCLE, the (1922)
STOCKBROKER'S CLERK, the (1922)

GAME CHICKEN, the (Romances of the Prize Ring series) (1926)
d Harry B Parkinson
VC

GAME FOR TWO, a (Grand Guignol series) (1921)
d Fred Paul, Jack Raymond
VC

GARDEN OF RESURRECTION, the (1919)
d Arthur Rooke
VC

GARSTANG FANCY DRESS PARADE, 1921 (1921)
VC

GEM OF THE BRITISH ISLES, a (1920)
VC

GEMS OF LITERATURE series
see
TAMING OF THE SHREW, the (1923)

GENERAL BOOTH IN THE CITY OF NAGOYA, AICHI PREFECTURE (1926)
VC

GENERAL BOOTH IN THE CITY OF OSAKA (1926)
VC

GENERAL BOOTH RECEIVED IN AUDIENCE BY PRINCE REGENT AT AKASAKA IMPERIAL PALACE (1926)
VC

GENERAL POST (1920)
d Thomas Bentley
VC

GENI AND A GENIUS (SERIES 1), a (1919)
d Victor Hicks
VC

GENI AND A GENIUS (SERIES 2), a (1919)
d Victor Hicks
VC

GEORGE BENNIE RAILPLANE SYSTEM OF TRANSPORT, the (1928)
VC

GEORGES CARPENTIER V DICK SMITH (1919)
VC

GERMAN TRENCHES AFTER THREE DAYS' BOMBARDMENT, the (1915)
VC

GHOSTS OF YESTERDAY series
see
LADY GODIVA (1928)

GIANT LEAVES HOME; A LOCOMOTIVE SIDELIGHT, the (Pathé Pictorial series) (1925)
VC

GIBBS DENTIFRICE (1923)
VC

GIRL OF LONDON, a (1925)
d Henry Edwards
VC

GIRLS LEAVING 'THE AMBER' AND THE CASTLE SILK MILLS, FLINT (1925)
VC

GLASGOW AND THE CLYDE COAST (1927)
VC

GLASS MAKERS OF MURANO, VENICE (Pathé Pictorial series) (1928)
VC

GLIMPSE OF THE PAST, a (1925)
VC

GLORIA SCOTT, the (The Last Adventures of Sherlock Holmes series) (1923)
d George Ridgwell
VC

GLORIOUS ADVENTURE, the (1922)
d J Stuart Blackton
VC

GOLDEN EAGLE, the (Secrets of Nature series) (1926)
VC

GOLD MINING IN CENTRAL COLORADO (Pathé Weekly Pictorial series) (1918)
VC

GOVERNMENT HOUSE GARDEN PARTY 1923 (1923)
VC

G P AS BASIL THE BRAINLESS (1915)
d G P Huntley
VC

GRAND GUIGNOL series
see
GAME FOR TWO, a (1921)
JEST, the (1921)
LAST APPEAL, the (1921)
OATH, the (1921)

GRANGER'S MARVELS OF THE UNIVERSE series
see
BEAUTY SPOTS OF ITALY NO.1 (1922)
HARVEST OF THE SEA, the (1922)
PORT-OF-SPAIN, TRINIDAD (1920)

GREAT FIGHT, the (1920)
VC

GREAT INTERNATIONAL CONTEST: JIM DRISCOLL V CHARLES LEDOUX (1919)
VC

GREAT MOMENTS IN BIG FIGHTS (1924)
VC

GREAT WHITE SILENCE, the (1924)
VC

GREAT WORK, a (1925)
VC

GUNS OF LOOS, the (1928)
d Sinclair Hill
VC

HAMPTON COURT (Haunted Houses and Castles of Great Britain series) (1926)
d Bert Cann
VC

HAPPY CAPTIVES, the (1925)
VC

HARLEQUINADE (1923)
VC

HARVEST OF THE SEA, the (Granger's Marvels of the Universe series) (1922)
VC

HAUNTED HOTEL, the (Kinekature Comedies series) (1918)
VC

HAUNTED HOUSES AND CASTLES OF GREAT BRITAIN series
see
HAMPTON COURT (1926)
WARWICK CASTLE IN FEUDAL DAYS (1926)

HAWICK COMMON RIDING – JUNE 18TH 1923 (1923)
VC

HAWICK COMMON RIDING 1926 (1926)
VC

HAWICK COMMON RIDING 1928 (1928)
VC

HAWICK WAR MEMORIAL UNVEILING CEREMONY (1919)
VC

HEALTH AND CLOTHING (1928)
d H W Bush
VC

HEART OF A COSTER, the (1915)
VC

HEART OF ASIA series, the
see
IN A PERSIAN TOWN (1928)
PERSIAN CARAVAN, a (1928)

HEIGHTS OF LOMBARDY, the (1919)
VC

HELLO FOOTBALL 1926–1927! (1926)
VC

HENNESSY'S BRANDY (1923)
VC

HER EXCELLENCY LADY LYTTON AT THE VICTORIA MEMORIAL (1922)
VC

HER GREATEST PERFORMANCE (1916)
d Fred Paul
VC

HEROES OF THE NORTH SEA (1925)
VC

HIGH TIMES AT THE CHILDREN'S TEA PARTY, HENRIETTA STREET, SOUTH TOTTENHAM, ON SATURDAY, AUGUST 16, 1919 (1919)
VC

HINDLE WAKES (1927)
d Maurice Elvey
VC

HINT OR TWO ON THE ART OF SELF-DEFENCE BY JACK BLOOMFIELD CRUISER-WEIGHT, a (1926)
VC

HINTS AND HOBBIES NO.1 (1926)
VC

HINTS AND HOBBIES NO.7 (1926)
VC

HINTS AND HOBBIES NO.11 (1926)
VC

HINTS TO MOTORISTS IN SAFETY FIRST BY S F EDGE (1926)
VC

HIS LAST BOW (The Last Adventures of Sherlock Holmes series) (1923)
d George Ridgwell
VC

HRH – SCENES FROM THE LIFE OF OUR PRINCE (1928)
VC

HRH THE PRINCE OF WALES KG VISITS HALIFAX (1926)
VC

HRH THE PRINCE OF WALES' VISIT TO BURY (1921)
VC

HRH THE PRINCE OF WALES' VISIT TO FLEETWOOD (1921)
VC

HRH THE PRINCE OF WALES' VISIT TO MANCHESTER (1921)
VC

HIS ROYAL HIGHNESS THE PRINCE OF WALES' VISIT TO ROTHERHAM (1923)
VC

HRH THE PRINCE OF WALES' VISIT TO SCOTLAND (1919)
VC

HIS WINNING WAYS (Studdy's War Studies series) (1915)
d G E Studdy
VC

HOLY YEAR JUBILEE PROCESSION BELFAST (1926)
VC

HOMECOMING CELEBRATIONS (1926)
VC

HOME COMING OF THE BEDFORDS (1918)
VC

HOME-COMING WELCOME TO HAWICK TROOPS (1919)
VC

HOME CONSTRUCTION (John Henry Calling series) (1926)
d Challis N Sanderson, Widgey R Newman
PB

HOSPITAL SUNDAY (1915)
VC

HOT WATER AND VEGETABUEL (1928)
d Widgey R Newman
VC

HOUND OF THE BASKERVILLES, the (The Adventures of Sherlock Holmes series) (1921)
d Maurice Elvey
VC

HOUSE OF PERIL, the (1922)
d Kenelm Foss
VC

HOWARD'S DAIRIES (1927)
VC

HOW I BEGAN (John Henry Calling series) (1926)
d Challis N Sanderson, Widgey R Newman
PB

HOW KITCHENER WAS BETRAYED (1921)
d Percy Nash
VC

HOXTON, SATURDAY JULY 3RD, BRITANNIA THEATRE (1920)
VC

HUMAN LAW (1926)
d Maurice Elvey
VC

HUNDREDTH CHANCE, the (Eminent British Authors series) (1920)
d Maurice Elvey
VC

HUSBAND HUNTER, the (1920)
d Fred W Durrant
VC

IF THOU WERT BLIND (1917)
d F Martin Thornton
VC

IF WINTER COMES (Jerry the Troublesome Tyke series) (1926)
d Sidney G Griffiths
VC

IF YOUTH BUT KNEW (1926)
d George A Cooper
VC

IMPERIAL AIRWAY; THE WORK OF THE BRITISH AIRWAYS, the (1924)
VC

IN A PERSIAN TOWN (The Heart of Asia series) (1928)
VC

INCIDENTS DURING THE LIFE OF THE HEIR TO THE THRONE (1923)
VC

IN OLD ST ALBANS (1920)
VC

INSCRUTABLE DREW, INVESTIGATOR series
see
MOON DIAMOND, the (1926)

INTERNATIONAL PAGEANT (1922)
VC

IN THE LAND OF WILLIAM TELL (1919)
VC

INTRODUCING THE JUGGLING DEMONS (1920)
VC

IRRADIATION OF LIVING TISSUE IN VITRO BY BETA AND GAMMA RAYS (1927)
d R G Canti
VC

ITALIAN ROSE IN AN ENGLISH GARDEN – PINA MENICHELLI, an (Around the Town series) (1922)
VC

IT IS FOR ENGLAND! (1916)
d Lawrence Cowen
VC

JACK SPRATT'S PARROT GETS HIS OWN BACK (1916)
d Toby Cooper
VC

JAFFA ORANGES (The Sunshine series) (1928)
VC

JANE SHORE (1915)
d F Martin Thornton, Bert Haldane
VC

JAPAN (1927)
VC

JERRY THE TROUBLESOME TYKE series
see
IF WINTER COMES (1926)

JERUSALEM (1926)
VC

JESSICA'S FIRST PRAYER (1921)
d Bert Wynne
VC

JEST, the (Grand Guignol series) (1921)
d Fred Paul
VC

JIMMY WILDE (TYLORSTOWN) V YOUNG SYMONDS (PLYMOUTH) (1916)
VC

JIMMY WILDE V TANCY LEE (1915) (1915)
VC

JOE BECKETT V BOY McCORMICK (1921)
VC

JOHN BULL'S ANIMATED SKETCH BOOK (1915)
d Dudley Buxton
VC

JOHN BULL'S ANIMATED SKETCH BOOK NO.4 (1915)
d Dudley Buxton
VC

JOHN CITIZEN (1927)
d Widgey R Newman
VC

JOHN HENRY CALLING series
see
BROADCASTING (1926)
HOME CONSTRUCTION (1926)
HOW I BEGAN (1926)
LISTENING IN (1926)
LOUD SPEAKER, the (1926)
OSCILLATION (1926)

The Magic Lantern
Hand-coloured
engraving (1822). LIS
pre-cinema collection

*A Victorian Lady in her
Boudoir* (Esmé
Collings, 1896)

ST. AIDAN'S CHURCH EXPENSE FUND.
HAND-IN-HAND CLUB,
FOLEY STREET. KIRKDALE.
MONDAY, FEB. 25th. 1884.
MR. W. HINTON
WILL GIVE HIS
Farcical, Extravaganzical, Mechanical, Epidemical,
Whimsical, Vocal, Side-Splittical,
PANORAMICAL
AND
BIOGLYPTICAL
ENTERTAINMENT
ENTITLED
ARTEMUS WARD
AMONG THE MORMONS.

The following Ladies and Gentlemen will render assistance at intervals during the Evening:
**Mrs. Moore, Miss Maude Smith, Miss Pearce, Miss E. Firth,
Mr. Parkinson, Mr. Hunter and Master McVeigh.**
Pianiste
Miss FIRTH

Tickets, One Shilling, may be obtained from the Churchwardens (Messrs. Bargory & Cleverly),
and Messrs. Croxton, Bainbridge and Swinnerton.
Doors Open at 7-30. to Commence at 8. Carriages may be Ordered for 10.
C. F. SMITH & CO., General Printers, &c., St. John's Lane, Liverpool.

Above: *Artemus Ward
Among the Mormons*
Poster (1884) LIS
ephemera

Birt Acres filming the
1895 Derby [381]

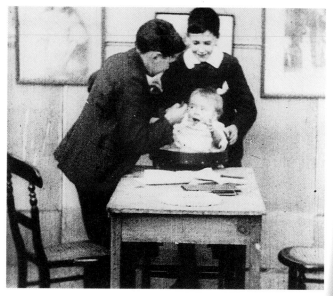

The Dear Boys Home for the Holidays (James Williamson, 1903)

Rescued in Mid-Air (Percy Stow, 1906)

Paul's Theatrograph Brochure (1896). LIS ephemera

The Life of Charles Peace (William Haggar, 1905)

Reflecting on Photography Catalogue of the Cotter Collection, 1839–1902. LIS pre-cinema collection

Dreams of Toyland
(Arthur Melbourne-
Cooper, 1908)

*A Day in the Life of a
Coal Miner* (1910)

Scenes in Moscow and Tiflis (1914)

David Copperfield
(Thomas Bentley,
1913)

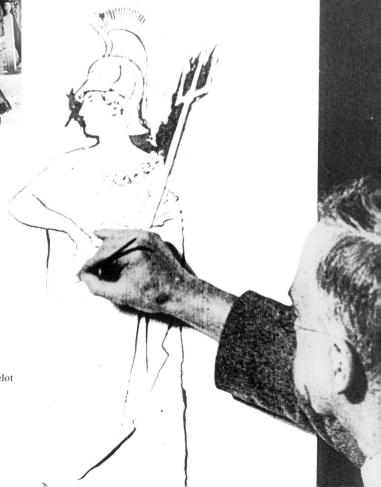

Bully Boy (Lancelot
Speed, 1914)

JOLLY DUTCH GIRL, the (Around the Town series) (1920)
VC

JONES' SCARE (1923)
VC

JUBILEE OF THE INCORPORATION OF THE BOROUGH OF LUTON (1926)
VC

JUNGLE WOMAN, the (1926)
d Frank Hurley
VC

JUNKING WAR METAL FOR USES OF PEACE (1920)
VC

KENSINGTON MYSTERY, the (The Old Man in the Corner series) (1924)
d Hugh Croise
VC

KENTUCKY LULLABY (Community Song series) (1927)
VC

KIDDIEGRAPH series
see
LITTLE RED RIDING HOOD (1922)

KINEKATURE COMEDIES series
see
HAUNTED HOTEL, the (1918)

KINGDOM OF THE BEES. PART 2: BATTLES OF LIFE AND DEATH, the (1921)
VC

KING GEORGE V PAGEANT AT ALCESTER, a (1920)
VC

KING OF THE CASTLE (1925)
d Henry Edwards
VC PB

KINGS, the (Pathé Pictorial series) (1921)
VC

KING'S HIGHWAY, the (1927)
d Sinclair Hill
VC PB

KING'S TOUR ROUND THE NAPIER MOTOR WORKS, the (1917)
VC

KINGTON SPORTS AUG 1ST, 1927 (1927)
VC

KINO THE GIRL OF COLOUR (1920)
d William Friese-Greene, Claude Friese-Greene
VC

KITE BALLOONS (1915)
VC

KNIGHT OF THE PIGSKIN, a (1926)
d Walter West
VC

KNOCKNAGOW (1918)
d Fred O'Donovan
VC

KNOWN LONDON (Wonderful London first series) (1924)
d Harry B Parkinson, Frank Miller
VC

LADS OF THE VILLAGE, the (1919)
d Harry Lorraine
VC

LADY AUDLEY'S SECRET (1920)
d Jack Denton
VC

LADY GODIVA (Ghosts of Yesterday series) (1928)
d George J Banfield, Leslie Eveleigh
VC

LADY JANE GREY (1923)
d Edwin Greenwood
VC

LADY OF THE LAKE, the (1928)
d James A Fitzpatrick
VC

LADY OWNER, the (1923)
d Walter West
VC

LADY WINDERMERE'S FAN (1916)
d Fred Paul
VC

LAMBS OF DOVE COURT, the (1920)
d Maurice Sandground
VC

LAMPS OLD AND NEW (1924)
VC

LAST ADVENTURES OF SHERLOCK HOLMES series, the
see
CARDBOARD BOX, the (1923)
CROOKED MAN, the (1923)
DISAPPEARANCE OF LADY FRANCES CARFAX, the (1923)
FINAL PROBLEM, the (1923)
GLORIA SCOTT, the (1923)
HIS LAST BOW (1923)
MISSING THREE QUARTER, the (1923)
MYSTERY OF THOR BRIDGE, the (1923)
STONE OF MAZARIN, the (1923)

LAST APPEAL, the (Grand Guignol series) (1921)
d Fred Paul
VC

LAST ROSE OF SUMMER, the (1920)
d Albert Ward
VC

LAUGHTER AND TEARS (1921)
d B E Doxat-Pratt
VC

LEOPARD'S SPOTS, the (1918)
d Cecil M Hepworth
VC

LGOC SCENES OF LONDON (1924)
VC

LIBRARY AT WORK, the (1922)
VC

LIFE IN THE SUDAN (1925)
VC

LIFE OF JACK HOBBS, the (1925)
VC

LIGHT WOMAN, a (1928)
d Adrian Brunel
PB

LIQUID SUNSHINE (1921)
d Victor Saville
VC

LISTENING IN (John Henry Calling series) (1926)
d Challis N Sanderson, Widgey R Newman
PB

LITTLE BIT OF FLUFF, a (1928)
d Jess Robbins, Wheeler Dryden
VC PB

LITTLE DRAMAS OF EVERYDAY LIFE series
see
CAB, the (1926)

LITTLE PEOPLE, the (1926)
d George Pearson
VC PB

LITTLE RED RIDING HOOD (Kiddiegraph series) (1922)
d Anson Dyer
VC

LIVERPOOL CATHEDRAL (Pathé Pictorial series) (1927)
VC

LIVINGSTONE (1925)
d M A Wetherell
PB

LODGER; A STORY OF THE LONDON FOG, the (1926)
d Alfred Hitchcock
VC

LONDON BY NIGHT (Wonderful London first series) (1924)
d Harry B Parkinson, Frank Miller
VC

LONDON, MIDLAND AND SCOTTISH RAILWAY (1923)
VC

LONDON OFF THE TRACK (Wonderful London first series) (1924)
d Harry B Parkinson, Frank Miller
VC

LONDON OLD AND NEW (Wonderful London first series) (1924)
d Harry B Parkinson, Frank Miller
VC

LONDON'S CONTRASTS (Wonderful London first series) (1924)
d Harry B Parkinson, Frank Miller
VC

LONDON'S FAMOUS CABARET series (second edition)
see
METROPOLE MIDNIGHT FOLLIES (1925)

LONDON'S OUTER RING (Wonderful London first series) (1924)
d Harry B Parkinson, Frank Miller
VC

LONDON'S SUNDAY (Wonderful London first series) (1924)
d Harry B Parkinson, Frank Miller
VC

LONG AND SHORT OF IT, the (Around the Town series) (1922)
VC

LOUD SPEAKER, the (John Henry Calling series) (1926)
d Challis N Sanderson, Widgey R Newman
PB

LOVE IN THE WILDERNESS (1920)
d Alexander Butler
VC

LOVE'S AWAKENING (Around the Town series) (1922)
VC

LOWLAND CINDERELLA, a (1921)
d Sidney Morgan
VC

LUCK OF THE NAVY, the (1927)
d Fred Paul
VC

LURE OF CROONING WATER, the (1920)
d Arthur Rooke
VC

LURE OF DRINK, the (1915)
d A E Coleby
VC

MACHINES THAT THINK (1922)
VC

MADAME POMPADOUR (1927)
d Herbert Wilcox
VC PB

MADEMOISELLE FROM ARMENTIERES (1926)
d Maurice Elvey
PB

MAID OF THE SILVER SEA, a (1922)
d Guy Newall
VC

MAISIE'S MARRIAGE (1923)
d Alexander Butler
VC

MAKING OF HIGH CLASS SOAPS, SOAP-POWDERS ETC, the (1927)
VC

MAKING SCHOOL SLATES (1920)
VC

MALAYA (1928)
VC

MALAYA NO.12: ITS RELATION TO THE EMPIRE (1927)
VC

MALVERN HILLS, the (1920)
VC

MANCHESTER – WHERE ENGLISH DOG RACING ORIGINATED (1923)
VC

MANIFESTATIONS, DIAGNOSIS AND TREATMENT OF SYPHILIS, the (1925)
d L W Harrison
VC

MANUFACTURE OF ART PAPER, the (1921)
VC

MAN WHO CHANGED HIS NAME, the (1928)
d A V Bramble
PB

MAN WHO FORGOT, the (1919)
d F Martin Thornton
VC

MAN WITHOUT DESIRE, the (1922)
d Adrian Brunel
VC

MAN WITH THE TWISTED LIP, the (The Adventures of Sherlock Holmes series) (1921)
d Maurice Elvey
VC

MARINE PARADE, the (Secrets of Nature series) (1922)
VC

MARKETS AND FOOD SUPPLIES OF MANCHESTER, the (1925)
VC

MASKS AND FACES (1917)
d Fred Paul
VC

MASTER FILMS SONG ALBUM series
see
BONNIE BANKS OF LOCH LOMOND, the (1922)

MAYOR'S SUNDAY AT PRESTON (NOVEMBER 8TH 1925) (1925)
VC

MECHANICAL AGE, the (1927)
VC

MEDICAL MYSTERY, a (1925)
d Harcourt Templeman
VC

MELODY OF DEATH (Eminent British Authors series) (1922)
d F Martin Thornton
VC

MEMOIRS OF MIFFY series
see
RUNNING A CINEMA (1921)

MERELY MINNIE; A SINCERE PARROT WHO WANTED TO GET INTO THE MOVIES (Eve's Film Review series) (1925)
VC

MESSRS BARLOW AND JONES LTD, MANCHESTER AND BOLTON (1919)
VC

METROPOLE MIDNIGHT FOLLIES (London's Famous Cabaret series, second edition) (1925)
d Harry B Parkinson
VC

MIDNIGHT MAIL, the (1915)
d Warwick Buckland
VC

MILWARD'S FAMOUS NEEDLES (1923)
VC

MIRACLE, the (The Mystery of Dr Fu-Manchu series) (1923)
d A E Coleby
VC

MIRAGE, the (1920)
d Arthur Rooke
VC

MISSING THREE QUARTER, the (The Last Adventures of Sherlock Holmes series) (1923)
d George Ridgwell
VC

MR ... GOES MOTORING (1928)
VC

MIST IN THE VALLEY (1923)
d Cecil M Hepworth
VC

MRS ERRICKER'S REPUTATION (1920)
d Cecil M Hepworth
PB

MODERN BOOT MANUFACTURING (1920)
VC

MODERN CARRIERS AT WORK (1928)
VC

MONS (1926)
d Walter Summers
VC PB

MOODY'S CLUB FOLLIES (1923)
VC

MOON DIAMOND, the (1926)
d A E Coleby
VC

MOTHERHOOD; A LIVING PICTURE OF LIFE TODAY (1917)
d Percy Nash
VC

MOULIN ROUGE (1928)
d E A Dupont
VC

MOUNTAIN OBSERVATORY, a (1920)
VC

MOVEMENT OF THE BRITISH NAVY AFTER GREAT ENGLISH VICTORY OF JUTLAND (1916)
VC

MUSEUMS OF THE NEW AGE (1927)
VC

MUSGRAVE RITUAL, the (The Further Adventures of Sherlock Holmes series) (1922)
d George Ridgwell
VC

MUSTARD CLUB TOPICAL BUDGET, the (1926)
VC

MYSTERIES OF LONDON, the (1915)
d A E Coleby
VC

MYSTERY OF A LONDON FLAT, the (1915)
d Walter West
VC

MYSTERY OF DR FU-MANCHU series, the
see
FIERY HAND, the (1923)
MIRACLE, the (1923)
QUEEN OF HEARTS, the (1923)
SHRINE OF SEVEN LAMPS, the (1923)

MYSTERY OF THOR BRIDGE, the (The Last Adventures of Sherlock Holmes series) (1923)
d George Ridgwell
VC

NAVAL MANOEUVRES (1924)
VC

NELSON; THE STORY OF ENGLAND'S IMMORTAL NAVAL HERO (1918)
d Maurice Elvey
VC

NEW BELLS FOR OLD (1918)
VC

NEW TYNE BRIDGE, the (1927)
VC

NEW WORLDS FOR OLD; QUAKER RELIEF IN STRICKEN EUROPE (1923)
VC

NIGERIA (The Empire series) (1928)
VC

NIGHT AT THE REGENT DANCE HALL, BRIGHTON, a (1924)
VC

NIONGA (1925)
VC

NOBODY'S CHILD (1919)
d George Edwardes Hall
VC

NORTHWARD HO: TO KAMBOVE AND THE CONGO (1918)
VC

NOT FOR SALE (1924)
d W P Kellino
VC

NOTHING ELSE MATTERS (1920)
d George Pearson
VC

NOT QUITE A LADY (1928)
d Thomas Bentley
PB

NURSERY OF THE CORMORANT, the (Secrets of Nature series) (1927)
VC

OATH, the (Grand Guignol series) (1921)
d Fred Paul
VC

OFFICIAL RECORD OF THE TOUR OF HRH THE PRINCE OF WALES (1925)
VC

OFFICIAL VISIT TO PARISH CHURCH OF THE NEW MAYOR, COUNCILLOR R DURHAM (1927)
VC

OH! WHAT A LITTLE QUEEN (1926)
VC

OLD BILL 'THROUGH THE AGES' (1924)
d Thomas Bentley
VC

OLD LINEN CHEST, the (1923)
VC

OLD MAN IN THE CORNER, the
see
KENSINGTON MYSTERY, the (1924)

OLD SHOE FOR LUCK, an (1923)
VC

ONE ARABIAN NIGHT (1923)
d Sinclair Hill
VC

ONE COLOMBO NIGHT (1926)
d Henry Edwards
VC PB

ONE GOOD TURN... (1928)
VC

ONLY WAY, the (1926)
d Herbert Wilcox
VC PB

ON THE EQUATOR (1923)
d Cherry Kearton
VC

ON WITH THE DANCE series
see
ADAGIO, the (1927)
DANCING MAD (1927)
ON WITH THE DANCE (1927)
WHIRL OF CHARLESTON, the (1927)

ON WITH THE DANCE (On with the Dance series) (1927)
d Harry B Parkinson
VC

OPEN COUNTRY (Eminent British Authors series) (1922)
d Sinclair Hill
VC

OPENING OF TAKORADI HARBOUR, the (1928)
VC

OPENING OF THE CELTIC CARNIVAL (1925)
VC

OPENING OF THE DUMFRIES AND MAXWELLTOWN WORKING GIRLS' CLUB, 1924 (1924)
VC

OPENING OF THE NEW BOWLING GREEN AT ACREGATE CLUB BY HIS WORSHIP THE MAYOR, ALD T PARKINSON JP (1920)
VC

OPENING OF WEMBLEY HOSPITAL BY TRH THE DUKE AND DUCHESS OF YORK, 2ND JUNE 1928 (1928)
VC

OPEN ROAD, the (1925)
VC

ORDEAL BY GOLF (Cuthbert series) (1924)
d Andrew P Wilson
VC

ORDER OF ST JOHN, the (1927)
VC

ORDER OF THE BATH, the (1926)
VC

ORGY OF DESTRUCTION (1924)
VC

OSCILLATION (John Henry Calling series) (1926)
d Challis N Sanderson, Widgey R Newman
PB

OTHELLO (1920)
d Anson Dyer
VC

OUR BOYS IN GERMANY; THE WATCH ON THE RHINE (OFFICIAL PHOTOGRAPHS) PART TWO (1919)
VC

OUR GREATEST AMBASSADOR (1922)
VC

OUR LOCAL TERRIERS (1924)
VC

OUR NAVAL SQUADRON IN THE MEDITERRANEAN (1918)
VC

OUT ON THE TILES AFTER A CAT BURGLAR (Bonzo series) (1925)
VC

OWD BOB (1924)
d Henry Edwards
VC

OXFORD (1928)
d C C Calvert
VC

OXFORD UNIVERSITY PRESS AND THE MAKING OF A BOOK, the (1925)
d Percy Nash
VC

PADDY – THE VERY BEST THING IN BURMA (1925)
VC

PALACE OF DREAMS, the (Wonderful London second series) (1924)
d Harry B Parkinson
VC

PALAIS DE DANSE (1928)
d Maurice Elvey
VC

PALAVER; A ROMANCE OF NORTHERN NIGERIA (1926)
d Geoffrey Barkas
VC

PALESTINE (1925)
VC

PALM OIL, LUMBER AND RUBBER IN SOUTHERN NIGERIA (1924)
VC

PAPWORTH HALL, CAMBRIDGE (1924)
VC

PARADISE (1928)
d Denison Clift
VC

PARIS (1922)
VC

PARKS DEPARTMENT (1922)
VC

PASSIONATE FRIENDS, the (1922)
d Maurice Elvey
VC

PATHÉ PICTORIAL series
see
BOTTLE MAKING UP TO DATE (1921)
GIANT LEAVES HOME; A LOCO-MOTIVE SIDELIGHT, the (1925)
GLASS MAKERS OF MURANO, VENICE (1928)
KINGS, the (1921)
LIVERPOOL CATHEDRAL (1927)
PATHÉ PICTORIAL NO.531 (1928)
UNCLE SAM'S CENSUS (1920)
WHAT'S LEFT OF THE BISON HERDS (1921)

PATHÉ PICTORIAL NO.531 (1928)
VC

PATHÉ WEEKLY PICTORIAL series
see
GOLD MINING IN CENTRAL COLORADO (1918)

PEACE CELEBRATIONS AT HASLINGDEN JULY 19TH 1919 (1919)
VC

PEARL OF THE SOUTH SEAS (1927)
d Frank Hurley
VC PB

PEEP AT MELBOURNE'S PICTURESQUE TREASURY GARDENS, a (1922)
VC

PENCIL AND ALICK P F RITCHIE, a (1915)
VC

PERHAPS YOU'LL THINK OF ME (Community Song series) (1927)
VC

PERSIAN CARAVAN, a (The Heart of Asia series) (1928)
VC

PERSIAN OIL INDUSTRY; THE STORY OF A GREAT NATIONAL ENTERPRISE, the (1925)
VC

PETER'S PICTURE POEMS (1918)
d Anson Dyer
VC

PHANTOM FOE, the (Romances of the Prize Ring series) (1926)
d Harry B Parkinson
VC

PIMPLE'S PART (1916)
d Fred Evans, Joe Evans
VC

PIMPLE'S THE WHIP (1917)
d Fred Evans, Joe Evans
VC

PIMPLE'S THREE MUSKETEERS (1922)
d Fred Evans, Joe Evans
PB

PIMPLE'S UNCLE (1915)
d Fred Evans, Joe Evans
VC

PIT AND THE PLUM, the (Bedtime Stories of Archie the Ant series) (1925)
d Percy Smith
VC

'PLANE TALE, a (1918)
d Anson Dyer
VC

PLANT MOVEMENTS (1920)
VC

PLAYING THE 'DICKENS' IN AN OLD CURIOSITY SHOP (Bonzo series) (1925)
VC

PLEASURE GARDEN, the (1925)
d Alfred Hitchcock
VC

POLAR BONZO (Bonzo series) (1925)
VC

POPPIES OF FLANDERS (1927)
d Arthur Maude
VC

PORT SUNLIGHT (1919)
VC

POSSESSION (1919)
d Henry Edwards
PB

POTATO AND WHEAT CULTURE IN ENGLAND (1917)
VC

POT POURRI (Across the Footlights series) (1925)
d Harry B Parkinson
VC

PREHISTORIC MAN, the (1924)
d A E Coleby
VC

PRESTON AND DISTRICT ROLL OF HONOUR (1915)
VC

PRESTON CONSERVATIVE FETE AND GALA JULY 18TH 1925 (1925)
VC

PRESTON INFANT WELFARE BABY DAY JULY 28 1927 (1927)
VC

PRESTON LABOUR GALA (1925)
VC

PRESTON: MAYORAL PROCESSION AND CHURCH PARADE OF ALDERMAN T PARKINSON (1921)
VC

PRESTON'S NEW CHIEF CONSTABLE (1926)
VC

PRINCE OF WALES' VISIT TO BILSTON, the (1923)
VC

PRINCESS MARY PRESENTS NEW COLOURS TO THE ROYAL SCOTS AT MARYHILL BARRACKS (1926)
VC

PROCESSION AND CROWNING OF THE ROSE QUEEN OF FLINT, 7 JULY 1928 (1928)
VC

PROCESSION OF CHURCH OF ENGLAND SUNDAY SCHOOL SCHOLARS (1920)
VC

PROCESSION OF NONCONFORMIST SUNDAY SCHOOL SCHOLARS (1922)
VC

PROCESSION OF THE AMALGAMATED FRIENDLY SOCIETIES (1922)
VC

PRODIGAL SON, the (1923)
d A E Coleby
VC

PRODUCTION OF 'THE TIMES', the (1927)
VC

PRUDE'S FALL, the (1924)
d Graham Cutts
VC

Q-SHIPS (1928)
d Geoffrey Barkas, Michael Barringer
VC

QUEEN MARY VISITS FAZAKERLEY HOSPITAL (1916)
VC

QUEEN OF HEARTS, the (The Mystery of Dr Fu-Manchu series) (1923)
d A E Coleby
VC

QUEEN OF THE BALLET, the (1922)
VC

QUEEN WAS IN THE PARLOUR, the (1927)
d Graham Cutts
VC

RACING OUTLOOK NO.1– STEEPLECHASING (Sporting Life; a Racing Outlook series) (1924)
d John Betts
VC

RACING OUTLOOK NO.2 – STEEPLECHASING (Sporting Life; a Racing Outlook series) (1924)
d John Betts
VC

RACING OUTLOOK NO.4 – STEEPLECHASING (Sporting Life; a Racing Outlook series) (1924)
d John Betts
VC

RACING OUTLOOK NO.5 – STEEPLECHASING (Sporting Life; a Racing Outlook series) (1924)
d John Betts
VC

RACING OUTLOOK NO.7 (Sporting Life; a Racing Outlook series) (1924)
d John Betts
VC

RACING OUTLOOK NO.8 (Sporting Life; a Racing Outlook series) (1924)
d John Betts
VC

RACING OUTLOOK NO.9 (Sporting Life; a Racing Outlook series) (1924)
d John Betts
VC

RACING OUTLOOK NO.10 (Sporting Life; a Racing Outlook series) (1924)
d John Betts
VC

RACING OUTLOOK NO.11 (Sporting Life; a Racing Outlook series) (1924)
d John Betts
VC

RACING OUTLOOK NO.12 (Sporting Life; a Racing Outlook series) (1924)
d John Betts
VC

RADIO AND RADIANCE; FEATURING 2LO, SAVOY HILL, LONDON (1925)
VC

RAT, the (1925)
d Graham Cutts
VC

RAT MENACE, the (1925)
VC

READY FOR THE ENEMY (1916)
VC

RECRUITING FOR THE 5TH ESSEX (1915)
VC

RED CIRCLE, the (The Further Adventures of Sherlock Holmes series) (1922)
d George Ridgwell
VC

RED CROSS FAIR (1917)
VC

RED TAPE FARM (1927)
VC

REPENTANCE (1922)
d Edward R Gordon
PB

REVEILLE (1924)
d George Pearson
SC

RIDING THE BOUNDARIES, MORPETH, APRIL 24TH, 1924 (1924)
VC

RT HON LORD LAMBOURNE LAYS FOUNDATION STONE OF PUBLIC OFFICES, CHINGFORD (1928)
VC

RING, the (1927)
d Alfred Hitchcock
VC

RINGER, the (1928)
d Arthur Maude
VC

RING OUT THE OLD! (1925)
VC

RIVER OF STARS, the (Eminent British Authors series) (1921)
d F Martin Thornton
VC

ROB ROY (1922)
d W P Kellino
VC

ROCK GARDEN, the (1928)
VC

ROCKS OF VALPRÉ, the (1919)
d Maurice Elvey
VC

RODEO, the (1924)
VC

RODNEY FAILS TO QUALIFY (Cuthbert series) (1924)
d Andrew P Wilson
VC

ROGUES OF LONDON (1915)
VC

ROMANCE OF MAYFAIR, a (1925)
d Thomas Bentley
VC

ROMANCE OF OLD BAGDAD, a (1922)
d Kenelm Foss
VC

ROMANCES OF THE PRIZE RING series
see
FIGHTING GLADIATOR, the (1926)
FIND THE WOMAN (1926)
FOR 'MY LADY'S' HAPPINESS (1926)
GAME CHICKEN, the (1926)
PHANTOM FOE, the (1926)

ROMANY LASS, a (1918)
d F Martin Thornton
VC

ROYAL CITY OF CANTERBURY, the (1915)
VC

ROYAL GARDEN PARTY (1915)
VC

ROYAL VISIT TO BRISTOL (1928)
VC

RULE, BRITANNIA (1918)
VC

RUNNING A CINEMA (Memoirs of Miffy series) (1921)
VC

RUNNING; A SPORT THAT CREATES BOTH BODILY AND MENTAL HEALTH PLUS ENDURANCE AND COURAGE ('Sporting Life' and what not to do but how to do it series) (1924)
d John Betts
VC

RUSSIA'S GREAT HAUL (1915)
VC

ST HELENS HEALTH WEEK, 1923 (1923)
VC

ST JOHN AMBULANCE (1928)
VC

SALISBURY AND DISTRICT BAND OF HOPE DEMONSTRATION, JUNE 22ND 1921 (1921)
VC

SALTCOATS PILGRIMAGE TO LOURDES (1921)
VC

SALVAGE IN AUSTRIA (1922)
VC

SANDEMAN'S PORT(1923)
VC

SANDRINGHAM, THE COUNTRY SEAT OF OUR KING (1920)
VC

SAY IT WITH FLOWERS (1927)
VC

SCALLYWAG, the (1921)
d Challis N Sanderson
PB

SCARLET WOMAN, the (1924)
d Terence Greenidge
VC

SCENES AT HIS EXCELLENCY THE VICEROY'S GARDEN PARTY AT BELVEDERE (1926)
VC

SCENES AT THE PROCESSION IN AID OF THE WALTON MATERNITY HOME, JULY 10TH (1928)
VC

SCENES OF THE FIRST WORLD WAR (1918)
VC

SCOTTIE AND THE FROGS (1915)
d Cecil Birch
VC

SCOTTISH WOMEN'S HOSPITAL (NUWSS) (1917)
VC

SEA URCHIN, the (1926)
d Graham Cutts
VC

SECRET KINGDOM, the (1925)
d Sinclair Hill
VC

SECRETS OF NATURE series
see
ANT-LION, the (1927)
AQUARIUM IN A WINEGLASS, an (1926)
BATTLE OF THE PLANTS, the (1926)
CABBAGES AND THINGS (1923)
CUCKOO'S SECRET, the (1922)
GOLDEN EAGLE, the (1926)
MARINE PARADE, the (1922)
NURSERY OF THE CORMORANT, the (1927)
STORY OF WESTMINSTER HALL, the (1923)
SWALLOW-TAIL BUTTERFLY, the (1924)
TIGER-BEETLE, the (1923)
TRAGEDY OF THE SEA, a (1922)
VAPOURER MOTH, the (1924)
WASP, the (1923)
WINTER (1923)

SEWAGE DEPARTMENT (1922)
VC

SHADOW OF EGYPT, the (1924)
d Sidney Morgan
PB

SHAKESPEARE'S COUNTRY (Wonderful Britain series) (1926)
VC

SHARPS AND FLATS (1915)
d Cecil Birch
VC

SHE (1925)
d Leander de Cordova
VC

SHIMMY SHEIK, the (1923)
d Adrian Brunel
VC

SHINE, SIR? (1916)
VC

SHIPS OF THE SNOW (1920)
VC

SHOOTING STARS (1927)
d A V Bramble, Anthony Asquith
VC

SHORTAGE OF MUNITIONS (1916)
VC

SHRINE OF SEVEN LAMPS, the (The Mystery of Dr Fu-Manchu series) (1923)
d A E Coleby
VC

SIDELIGHTS OF LONDON (Wonderful London second series) (1924)
d Harry B Parkinson
VC

SIGNALLING ON THE EALING AND SHEPHERDS BUSH RAILWAY (1922)
VC

SILVER LINING, the (1927)
d Thomas Bentley
VC

SIMONE EVRARD; or, Deathless devotion (Wonder Women of the World series) (1923)
d Edwin Greenwood
VC

SIR ERNEST SHACKLETON (1921)
VC

SIR OR MADAM (1928)
d Carl Boese
PB

SIR RUPERT'S WIFE (1922)
d Challis N Sanderson
VC

SMALLHOLDER series
see
ALLOTMENT HOLDER'S ENEMIES (1918)

SMOKE FROM GRAND-PA'S PIPE, the (1920)
d J S Anderson
VC

SNAPSHOTS OF LONDON (Wonderful London second series) (1924)
d Harry B Parkinson, Frank Miller
VC

SO THIS IS LONDON (1928)
VC

SO THIS WAS PARIS! (1928)
VC

SOLVING THE HOUSING PROBLEM AT BOURNVILLE (1919)
VC

SOME CLASSICAL DANCING BY THE PUPILS OF MARGARET MORRIS (Around the Town series) (1922)
VC

SOMETHING NEW IN CABARETS (Eve's Film Review series) (1927)

SOME WAR-TIME TYPES: THE WLA GIRL (1918)
VC

SOMME, the (1927)
d M A Wetherell
VC

SONG OF THE SEA, a (1922)
VC

SONS OF THE SEA (1925)
d H Bruce Woolfe
VC

SOUTH; SIR ERNEST SHACKLETON'S GLORIOUS EPIC OF THE ANTARCTIC (1919)
VC

SOUTHWARD ON THE 'QUEST' (1922)
VC PB

SPITZBERGEN; OXFORD UNIVERSITY ARCTIC EXPEDITION 1924 (1924)
VC

SPORT AND INTEREST IN A FRESH LIGHT (1926)
d John Betts
VC

SPORTING HOLIDAYS IN DEVON (1926)
VC

SPORTING LIFE; A RACING OUTLOOK series
see
RACING OUTLOOK NO.1– STEEPLECHASING (1924)
RACING OUTLOOK NO.2 – STEEPLECHASING (1924)
RACING OUTLOOK NO.4 – STEEPLECHASING (1924)
RACING OUTLOOK NO.5 – STEEPLECHASING(1924)
RACING OUTLOOK NO.7 (1924)
RACING OUTLOOK NO.8 (1924)
RACING OUTLOOK NO.9 (1924)
RACING OUTLOOK NO.10 (1924)
RACING OUTLOOK NO.11 (1924)
RACING OUTLOOK NO.12 (1924)

'SPORTING LIFE' AND WHAT NOT TO DO BUT HOW TO DO IT series
see
RUNNING; A SPORT THAT CREATES BOTH BODILY AND MENTAL HEALTH PLUS ENDURANCE AND COURAGE (1924)
SWIMMING (1924)
TENNIS; THE MOST DEMOCRATIC OF GAMES FOR BOTH SEXES (1924)

SPORT OF KINGS, the (1922)
d Arthur Rooke
VC

SQUIBS (1921)
d George Pearson
VC

SQUIBS MP (1923)
d George Pearson
PB

SQUIBS WINS THE CALCUTTA SWEEP (1922)
d George Pearson
VC

SQUIRE OF LONG HADLEY, the (1925)
d Sinclair Hill
PB

STARLINGS OF THE SCREEN; TESTING BRITISH FILM ASPIRANTS AT CRICKLEWOOD (1925)
VC

STARLIT GARDEN, the (1923)
d Guy Newall
VC

STARS AT HOME – MISS MAY MOORE DUPREZ, the (Eve's Film Review series) (1921)
VC

STICKLEBACK, the (The World About Us series) (1923)
d W P Pycraft
VC

STOCKBROKER'S CLERK, the (The Further Adventures of Sherlock Holmes series) (1922)
d George Ridgwell
VC

STONE OF MAZARIN, the (The Last Adventures of Sherlock Holmes series) (1923)
d George Ridgwell
VC

STOPPING THE ROT (1926)
VC

STORMFLOWER (1922)
d Bert Wynne
VC

STORY OF OIL, the (1921)
d Victor Saville
VC

STORY OF OUR FOOD SUPPLY, the (1928)
d H W Bush
VC

STORY OF THE CUCKOO, the (1922)
VC

STORY OF WESTMINSTER HALL, the (Secrets of Nature series) (1923)
VC

STRATFORD-ON-AVON (1925)
VC

STRAWBERRY FETE (1917)
VC

STRIKE SCENE AT CHISWICK WORKS (1926)
VC

STUDDY'S WAR STUDIES series
see
HIS WINNING WAYS (1915)

SUEZ CANAL, the (1926)
VC

SUEZ CANAL AND THE RED SEA, the (1926)
VC

SUNSHINE series, the
see
JAFFA ORANGES (1928)

SURRENDER OF THE U-BOATS, the (1919)
VC

SURREY WOMEN WAR WORKERS; DEMONSTRATION AT CROSS FARM, SHACKLEFORD (1916)
VC

SWALLOW-TAIL BUTTERFLY, the (Secrets of Nature series) (1924)
VC

SWAMPS OF THE SEMLIKI, the (1923)
VC

SWEENEY TODD (1928)
d Walter West
VC

SWIMMING ('Sporting Life' and what not to do but how to do it series) (1924)
d John Betts
VC

TABLE TENNIS TODAY (1928)
d Ivor Montagu
VC

TALE OF A TENDRIL, the (Bedtime Stories of Archie the Ant series) (1925)
d Percy Smith
VC

TAMING OF THE SHREW, the (Gems of Literature series) (1923)
d Edwin J Collins
VC

TANCY LEE V JIMMY WILDE (1915)
VC

TANGLED HEARTS (1920)
d William Humphrey
PB

TEDDY BROWN AND HIS XYLOPHONE (British Phototone series) (1928)
d J B Sloan
VC

TENNIS AND HOW TO PLAY IT (1922)
VC

TENNIS; THE MOST DEMOCRATIC OF GAMES FOR BOTH SEXES ('Sporting Life' and what not to do but how to do it series) (1924)
d John Betts
VC

TENSE MOMENTS WITH GREAT AUTHORS series
see
DAVID GARRICK (1922)
VANITY FAIR (1922)

TERPSICHOREAN TECHNICALITIES BY HELEN MAY (Around the Town series) (1922)
VC

TESTIMONY (1920)
d Guy Newall
VC

TESTS FROM AEROPLANES (1916)
VC

THEY FORGOT TO READ THE DIRECTIONS (1924)
d J W Smith, William Maxwell Aitken
VC

THIRD ROUND, the (1925)
d Sidney Morgan
VC

THREE LITTLE PIGS, the (1918)
d Anson Dyer
VC

THRILLING STORIES FROM THE STRAND MAGAZINE series
see
DRUM, the (1924)

THROUGH THREE REIGNS (1922)
VC

TIDAL WAVE, the (Eminent British Authors series) (1920)
d Sinclair Hill
VC

TIED-DYEING – A NEW ART FOR THE HOME (Eve's Film Review series) J(1927)
VC

TIGER-BEETLE, the (Secrets of Nature series) (1923)
VC

TILL OUR SHIP COMES IN series
see
EENA, DEENA, DINAH, DOH! (1919)

TIN-CAN FUSILIERS, the (1926)
VC

TINKER, TAILOR, SOLDIER, SAILOR (1918)
d Rex Wilson
VC

TIPTOES (1927)
d Herbert Wilcox
SC

TO ALL OUR PATRONS – A MERRY CHRISTMAS (1922)
VC

TOILERS, the (1919)
d Tom Watts
VC

TOM BROWN'S SCHOOLDAYS (1916)
d Rex Wilson
VC

TONI (1928)
d Arthur Maude
VC

TONIC, the (1928)
d Ivor Montagu
PB

TONS OF MONEY (1924)
d Frank Hall Crane
VC

TOPICAL BONZETTE (Bonzo series) (1925)
VC

TOPSEY TURVEY (1926)
d Bertram Phillips
VC

TORTURE CAGE, the (Dr Sin Fang Adventure series) (1928)
d Fred Paul
VC

TOTTENHAM STILL GOING STRONG IN TEA FIGHTS AUGUST 30, 1919 (1919)
VC

TOURIST TROPHY RACES 1922, the (1922)
VC

TOUR OF A BRITISH COALMINE (1928)
d Charles Hanmer
VC

TOWN CRIER STILL KEPT UP IN MANY TOWNS, the (1916)
VC

TOYLAND TOPICS (1928)
VC

TRAFALGAR SQUARE CELEBRATION (1915)
VC

TRAGEDY OF THE NEAR EAST, the (1923)
VC

TRAGEDY OF THE SEA, a (Secrets of Nature series) (1922)
VC

TRAINING GROUP B'S MILITARY SPORTS, BELTON PARK, JULY 5, 1917 (1917)
VC

TRAINING LONDON'S FIRE BRIGADE – DISPLAY AT HEADQUARTERS (1928)
VC

TRAPPED BY LONDON SHARKS (1916)
d L C MacBean
VC

TRAPPED BY THE MORMONS (1922)
d Harry B Parkinson
VC

TRAVEL CUNARD LINE – CANADIAN ROUTE (1923)
VC

TRAVEL THE CHEAP WAY – BY TRAM WAY (1925)
VC

TRAVIATA, la (Cameo Operas series) (1927)
d Harry B Parkinson
VC

TRIP ALONG THE MANCHESTER SHIP CANAL, a (1921)
VC

TRIP DOWN THE CLYDE, a (1922)
VC

TRIP DOWN THE CLYDE – DUMBARTON ROCK, a (Around the Town series) (1921)
VC

TRIPPS AND TRIBUNALS (The Blunders of Mr Butterbun series) (1918)
d Fred Rains
VC

TRIP TO ULLSWATER AND PATTERDALE, a (1925)
VC

TRISTAN DA CUNHA (1927)
VC

TRIUMPH OF THE RAT, the (1926)
d Graham Cutts
VC

TRIUMPH OF THE SCARLET PIMPERNEL, the (1928)
d T Hayes Hunter
PB

TROJAN CAR ADVERT (1926)
VC

TROUBLESOME WIVES (1928)
d Harry Hughes
VC

TUBBY'S REST CURE (The Exploits of Tubby series) (1916)
d Frank Wilson
VC

TWELVE POUND LOOK, the (1920)
d Jack Denton
VC

TWENTY YEARS AGO (1928)
VC

TWISTED TALES series
see
ETERNAL TRIANGLE, the (1925)

TWO OF NATURE'S WONDERS (1916)
VC

TYPICAL BUDGET; THE ONLY UNRELIABLE FILM REVIEW (1925)
d Adrian Brunel
VC

ULTUS AND THE THREE-BUTTON MYSTERY (1917)
d George Pearson
SC

UNCLE SAM'S CENSUS (Pathé Pictorial series) (1920)
VC

UNDERGROUND (1928)
d Anthony Asquith
VC

UNDER SAIL IN THE FROZEN NORTH (1926)
VC

UNDERWEAR AND HOSIERY (1924)
VC

UNION OF POST OFFICE WORKERS, the (1927)
VC

UNKNOWN LONDON (Wonderful London first series) (1924)
d Harry B Parkinson
VC

UNVEILING CEREMONY OF THE CAMERONIANS' 'SCOTTISH RIFLES' REGIMENTAL MEMORIAL BY FIELD MARSHAL EARL HAIG (1920)
VC

UNVEILING OF KIRKCALDY WAR MEMORIAL (1920)
VC

UNVEILING OF THE KIRKHAM WAR MEMORIAL ON SUNDAY NOVEMBER 7TH 1926 (1926)
VC

UNVEILING OF THE WAR MEMORIAL ON TUNSTALL VILLAGE GREEN ON SATURDAY NOVEMBER 25TH 1922, the (1922)
VC

UNVEILING OF WAR MEMORIAL BY ADMIRAL OF THE FLEET EARL JELLICOE OF SCAPA GCB, OM, GCVO, ON SUNDAY JUNE 13 (1926)
VC

UP THE RIVER WITH MOLLY; A STEREOSCOPIC SCENIC GEM (1921)

VANITY FAIR (Tense Moments with Great Authors series) (1922)
d Walter Courtenay Rowden
VC

VAPOURER MOTH, the (Secrets of Nature series) (1924)
VC

VENGEANCE OF NANA, the (1915)
d Charles Weston
VC

VENICE: CANAL AND RIALTO BRIDGE (1918)
VC

VERY UNSUCCESSFUL COMPETITOR IN THE TOFFEE APPLE COMPETITION, a (Film Pie series) (1920)
d Geoffrey H Malins, Neville Bruce
VC

VICKERS AIRCRAFT (1926)

VICTORY AND PEACE (1918)
d Herbert Brenon
VC

VICTORY NAVAL REVIEW (1919)
VC

VISIT OF HRH THE PRINCE OF WALES KG, MC, TO NOTTINGHAM, AUG 1ST 1923 (1923)
VC

VISIT OF HRH THE PRINCE OF WALES TO MESSRS WIGGINS TEAPE CO (1919) LTD (1921)
VC

VISIT OF HRH PRINCESS MARY AND VISCOUNT LASCELLES TO HALIFAX 13.3.25 (1925)

VISIT OF THEIR MAJESTIES THE KING AND QUEEN TO THE NORTH-EAST COAST SHIP-BUILDING ENGINEERING WORKS ON THE WEAR (1917)
VC

VORTEX, the (1927)
d Adrian Brunel
VC

VOTE FOR HARRY KEMP (1920)
VC

WAIT AND SEE (1928)
d Walter Forde
VC

WALTER MAKES A MOVIE (1922)
d Tom Seymour, Walter Forde
VC

WALTER THE PRODIGAL (1926)
d Tom Seymour, Walter Forde
VC

WANDERING JEW, the (1923)
d Maurice Elvey
VC

WAR NEUROSES: NETLEY 1917, SEALE HAYNE MILITARY HOSPITAL 1918 (1918)
VC

WARNING, the (1928)
d Reginald Fogwell
PB

WARRIOR STRAIN, the (1919)
d F Martin Thornton
VC

WARWICK CASTLE IN FEUDAL DAYS (Haunted Houses and Castles of Great Britain series) (1926)
d Fred Paul
VC

WASP, the (Secrets of Nature series) (1923)
VC

WATFORD BECOMES A BOROUGH (1922)
VC

WAY TO A CHILD'S HEART, the (1925)
VC

WEST AFRICA CALLING (1928)
VC

WHAT NEXT? (1928)
d Archibald Nettlefold
PB

WHAT'S LEFT OF THE BISON HERDS
(Pathé Pictorial series) (1921)
VC

WHATSOEVER A MAN SOWETH (1917)
d Joseph Best
VC

WHAT'S THE USE OF GRUMBLIN'? (1918)
d Henry Edwards
VC

WHAT'S WRONG WITH THE CINEMA?
(1925)
VC

WHEN GEORGE WAS KING (1922)
d George F Whybrow
VC

WHEN GREEK MEETS GREEK (1922)
d Walter West
PB

WHERE DREAMS COME TRUE (1926)
VC

WHERE THEIR CARAVAN WAS WRESTED
(1915)
VC

WHERE THE RAINBOW ENDS (1921)
d H Lisle Lucoque
PB

WHERE THERE'S LIFE THERE'S 'OPE
(1927)
d D M Connan
VC

WHIRL OF CHARLESTON, the (On with the
Dance series) (1927)
d Harry B Parkinson
VC

WHITE SHEIK, the (1928)
d Harley Knoles
VC

WIFE THE WEAKER VESSEL (1915)
d Frank Wilson
VC

WILDLIFE ACROSS THE WORLD series
see
SWAMPS OF THE SEMLIKI, the (1923)

**WILD LIFE IN THE TREE TOPS – THE
STORY OF THE HERON** (1921)
VC

**WINNERS OF 'THE CAPITOL'
CHALLENGE CUP** (1928)
VC

WINTER (Secrets of Nature series) (1923)
VC

WITCH'S FIDDLE, the (1924)
d Peter Le Neve Foster
VC

**WITH A SKIRMISHING PARTY IN
FLANDERS** (1915)
VC

**WITH BRITAIN'S MONSTER GUNS IN
ACTION** (1916)
VC

WITH COBHAM TO THE CAPE (1926)
VC

WITH THE BRITISH FORCES IN FRANCE
(1915)
VC

**WITH THE CRUSADERS IN THE HOLY
LAND: ALLENBY – THE CONQUEROR**
(1917)
VC

WOMAN HE SCORNED, the (1928)
d Paul Czinner
VC

WOMAN REDEEMED, a (1927)
d Sinclair Hill
PB

**WOMEN'S WORK ON MUNITIONS OF
WAR** (1918)
VC

WONDERFUL ADVENTURE, a (1927)
VC

**WONDERFUL ADVENTURES OF PIP,
SQUEAK AND WILFRED, THE FAMOUS
'DAILY MIRROR' PETS, the** (1921)
d Lancelot Speed
VC

WONDERFUL BRITAIN series
see
SHAKESPEARE'S COUNTRY (1926)

WONDERFUL LONDON first series
see
CENTRE OF THE WORLD (1924)
COSMOPOLITAN LONDON (1924)
DICKENS' LONDON (1924)
KNOWN LONDON (1924)
LONDON BY NIGHT (1924)
LONDON OFF THE TRACK (1924)
LONDON OLD AND NEW (1924)
LONDON'S CONTRASTS (1924)
LONDON'S OUTER RING (1924)
LONDON'S SUNDAY (1924)
UNKNOWN LONDON (1924)

WONDERFUL LONDON second series
see
BARGING THROUGH LONDON (1924)
DERBY DAY (1924)
FLOWERS OF LONDON (1924)
PALACE OF DREAMS, the (1924)
SIDELIGHTS OF LONDON (1924)
SNAPSHOTS OF LONDON (1924)
WONDERS OF WESTMINSTER (1924)

WONDERFUL STORY, the (1922)
d Graham Cutts
VC PB

WONDERS OF WESTMINSTER (Wonderful
London second series) (1924)
d Harry B Parkinson
VC

WONDER WOMEN OF THE WORLD series
see
LADY JANE GREY (1923)
SIMONE EVRARD; or, Deathless devotion
(1923)

WOOING OF EVE, the (1927)
d Max Mack
VC

**WORK OF AN INFANT WELFARE
CENTRE, the** (1924)
VC

WORLD ABOUT US series, the
see
STICKLEBACK, the (1923)

WRECKER, the (1928)
d Geza von Bolvary
SC

YELLOW WEEK AT STANWAY, the (1923)
d J M Barrie
VC

YORK (1920)
VC

YOU (1916)
d Harold Shaw
VC

YOUNG LOCHINVAR (1923)
d W P Kellino
VC

YPRES (1925)
d Walter Summers
VC

ZANZIBAR AND THE CLOVE INDUSTRY
(1926)
VC

ZEEBRUGGE (1924)
d H Bruce Woolfe, A V Bramble
VC PB

ZERO HOUR (1928)
VC

1929–1945

ABCD OF HEALTH (1942)
d Jack Ellitt
VC

ABDUL THE DAMNED (1935)
d Karl Grune
VC PB

ABERDEEN CELEBRATES THE CORONATION (1937)
VC

ABU AND THE POISONED WELL (1943)
d John Halas, Joy Batchelor
VC

ACCIDENT SERVICE (1944)
d A Reginald Dobson
VC

ACCUSED (1936)
d Thornton Freeland
VC PB

ACE OF SPADES, the (1935)
d George Pearson
VC PB

ACHIMOTA (1945)
d John Page
VC

ACROSS BOLIVIA (1930)
d Mamerto Urriolagoita
SC

ACROSS LAPLAND; THE STORY OF A WOMAN'S ADVENTUROUS JOURNEY IN THE ARCTIC (1933)
VC

ACROSS THE SAHARA; THE RECORD OF A JOURNEY TO TIMBUKTU (1933)
d Walter Summers
VC

ACROSS THE WORLD (1932)
VC

ACTION AGAINST THE MEANS TEST (1935)
VC

ACTION FOR SLANDER (1937)
d Tim Whelan
VC PB

ADESTE FIDELES (1941)
d Ralph Keene, Ralph Bond
VC

ADMIRALS ALL (1935)
d Victor Hanbury
VC PB

ADMIRAL'S SECRET, the (1934)
d Guy Newall
PB

ADOLF'S BUSY DAY (1940)
d Lance White
VC

ADVANCE DEMOCRACY (1938)
d Ralph Bond, Basil Wright
VC

ADVENTURE LIMITED (1934)
d George King
PB

AERIAL CIRCUS (1930)
VC

AERIAL MILESTONES (1939)
VC

AEROBATICS (1931)
VC

AERO ENGINE (1933)
d Arthur Elton
VC

AFRICAN PEASANT FARMS – THE KINGOLWIRA EXPERIMENT (1937)
d L A Notcutt
VC

AFRICAN SKYWAY (1939)
d Donald Taylor
VC

AFTER OFFICE HOURS (1932)
d Thomas Bentley
VC PB

AFTER THE BALL (1932)
d Milton Rosmer
SC

AGAINST IMPERIALIST WAR – MAY DAY 1932 (1932)
VC

AGAINST THE TIDE (1937)
d Alex Bryce
PB

AGRICULTURE (Britain under National Government series) (1935)
VC

AID TO CHINA (1939)
VC

AIRCRAFT DESIGN (1935)
VC

AIRMAN'S LETTER TO HIS MOTHER, an (1941)
d Michael Powell
VC

AIR OUTPOST (1937)
d John Taylor, Ralph Keene

AIRPORT (1934)
d Roy Lockwood
VC

AIR POST (1934)
d Geoffrey Clark
VC

AIR RAID PRECAUTIONS NO.5 (1939)
VC

AIRSCREW (1940)
d Grahame Tharp
VC

ALBERT'S SAVINGS (1940)
d Harold Purcell
VC

ALF'S BUTTON AFLOAT (1938)
d Marcel Varnel
VC SC

ALF'S CARPET (1929)
d W P Kellino
VC

ALIBI (1942)
d Brian Desmond Hurst
VC

ALICE IN SWITZERLAND (1940)
d Alberto Cavalcanti
VC

ALL ABOARD (1937)
VC

ALL ABOUT CARROTS (1941)
d Ronald Haines
VC

ALL AT SEA (1939)
d Herbert Smith
PB

ALLEY CAT, the (1929)
d Hans Steinhoff
VC

ALL HANDS (1940)
d John Paddy Carstairs
VC

ALL IN (1936)
d Marcel Varnel
SC

ALL THE FUN OF THE 'AIR (1937)
d Anson Dyer
VC

ALL THOSE IN FAVOUR (1941)
d Donald Alexander
VC

ALMOST A HONEYMOON (1930)
d Monty Banks
VC

ALMOST A HONEYMOON (1938)
d Norman Lee
VC

ALMOST ARCADY (1930)
VC

ALONG THE CAMBRIAN COAST (1930)
VC

ALWAYS 62° (1930)
VC

AMATEUR GENTLEMAN, the (1936)
d Thornton Freeland
PB

AMAZING QUEST OF ERNEST BLISS, the (1936)
d Alfred Zeisler
VC PB

AMERICAN PRISONER, the (1929)
d Thomas Bentley
VC

ANCIENT WINDSOR (1930)
VC

AND NOW THEY REST (1939)
d Brian Salt, J V Durden, Robert Fairthorne
VC

ANDRÉE HOWARD – 'POMPETTE' (1931)
VC

ANGLING AT KEGWORTH (1933)
VC

ANGLO-IRANIAN OIL COMPANY'S OPERATIONS IN IRAN, 1921 (1939)
VC

ANIMAL KINGDOM series
see
ZETLAND BIRDS (1939)

ANIMAL LIFE IN THE HEDGEROWS (Secrets of Life series) (1936)
VC

ANIMAL MOVEMENT (1939)
d Mary Field
VC

ANNE ONE HUNDRED (1933)
d Henry Edwards
PB

ANNIE, LEAVE THE ROOM! (1935)
d Leslie Hiscott
VC

**ANNUAL FIRE BRIGADE COMPETITION –
JUNE 30TH, 1934** (1934)
VC

ANOTHER LITTLE DROP... (1942)
VC

ANSWER, the (1940)
d Alex Bryce
VC

ANYBODY'S BUGBEAR (1940)
d Alex Bryce
VC

ANY OLD IRON (1940)
VC

ANY RECORDS CHUMS? (1942)
VC

ANYTHING TO DECLARE? (1938)
d Redd Davis
PB

ANYTOWN (1936)
VC

A1 AT LLOYD'S (1941)
VC

APHIS, the (Secrets of Nature series) (1930)
d Mary Field
VC

APPEARANCES ARE DECEPTIVE (1942)
VC

ARACHNIDA (1940)
d J V Durden
VC

ARCHITECTS OF ENGLAND (1941)
VC

AREN'T MEN BEASTS! (1937)
d Graham Cutts
VC PB

AREN'T WE ALL? (1932)
d Harry Lachman
PB

ARE YOU A MASON? (1934)
d Henry Edwards
PB

ARMS AND THE MAN (1932)
d Cecil Lewis
VC

AROMA OF THE SOUTH SEAS (1931)
d W P Kellino
SC

AROUND SNOWDONIA (1937)
d Duncan Robbins
VC

AROUND THE VILLAGE GREEN (1937)
d Evelyn Spice, Marion Grierson
VC

**ARP BIRMINGHAM. GLOUCESTER
STREET EXPERIMENT** (1939)
VC

ARP FILM (1940)
VC

**ARP NORTHAMPTON. SHELTER TEST
20.3.39** (1939)
VC

ARSENAL STADIUM MYSTERY, the (1939)
d Thorold Dickinson
VC PB

**ARSENAL V NEWCASTLE FA CUP FINAL,
WEMBLEY 1932** (1932)
VC

**ARTHUR LUCAN (OLD MOTHER RILEY) –
BRIDGET'S NIGHT OUT** (1936)
VC

**ARTHUR PRINCE AND JIM IN A
VENTRILOQUIAL SKETCH** (1935)
VC

AS GOOD AS NEW (1933)
d Graham Cutts
PB

ASHANTI (1939)
VC

ASHLEY GREEN GOES TO SCHOOL (1940)
d John Eldridge
VC

ASK A POLICEMAN (1939)
d Marcel Varnel
VC PB

ASK BECCLES (1933)
d Redd Davis
PB

ASKING FOR TROUBLE (1942)
d Oswald Mitchell
PB

ASPHALT LAKE (1938)
VC

ASTACUS (1940)
d J V Durden
VC

AS YOU LIKE IT (Eve's Film Review series)
(1929)
VC

AS YOU LIKE IT (1936)
d Paul Czinner
PB

ATLANTIC (1929)
d E A Dupont
VC PB

ATLANTIC (1940)
d Mary Field
VC SC

ATLANTIC CHARTER (1942)
VC

ATLANTIC FERRY (1941)
d Walter Forde
VC

AT SCHOOL IN TANGANYIKA (1936)
d Ralph Cutler
VC

AT THE THIRD STROKE (1939)
d Richard Massingham
VC

AT THE VILLA ROSE (1939)
d Walter Summers
VC SC PB

AULD AYRSHIRE (Pathé Pictorial series)
(1930)
VC

AUNT SALLY (1933)
d Tim Whelan
VC

AURORA (1932)
VC

**AUSTRALIAN MEMORIAL AT VILLIERS-
BRETONNEAU, FRANCE, the** (1938)
VC

AUSTRALIAN WINES (1931)
VC

AUTUMN CROCUS (1934)
d Basil Dean
VC SC

AVENTURE MALGACHE (1944)
d Alfred Hitchcock
VC

BABES IN THE WOOD (1940)
d Mary Field
VC

BABY ON THE ROCKS (Secrets of Life
series) (1934)
d Mary Field
VC

BACHELOR'S BABY (1932)
d Harry Hughes
SC

BACK CHAT (1935)
d John Cobham
VC

BACK-ROOM BOY (1942)
d Herbert Mason
VC

BACKYARD FRONT, the (1940)
d Andrew Buchanan
VC

BADGER'S GREEN (1934)
d Adrian Brunel
PB

BAGGED (1934)
d John Harlow
SC

BAILEY BRIDGE (1944)
d Arthur W Barnes
VC

BAILIFFS (1932)
d Frank Cadman
VC

BAIRD TELEVISION (1930)
VC

BALL AT SAVOY (1936)
d Victor Hanbury
PB

BALLOON SITE 568 (1942)
d Ivan Moffat
VC

BANANA RIDGE (1941)
d Walter C Mycroft
SC

BAND WAGGON (1940)
d Marcel Varnel
VC PB

BANK HOLIDAY (1938)
d Carol Reed
VC SC PB

BARNACLE BILL (1934)
d Harry Hughes
PB

BAROUD (1932)
d Rex Ingram
VC

BARTON MYSTERY, the (1932)
d Henry Edwards
PB

BASSETSBURY MANOR (1936)
VC

BATTLE, the (1934)
d Nikolas Farkas
VC

BATTLE FOR FREEDOM (1942)
d Alan Osbiston
VC

BATTLE FOR MUSIC (1943)
d Donald Taylor
VC

BATTLE OF SUPPLIES (1942)
VC

BATTLE OF THE BOOKS, the (1941)
d J D Chambers
VC

BATTLE OF THE FORESTS (1944)
VC

BBC BRAINS TRUST NO.1, the (1943)
d Howard Thomas, Donald Taylor
VC

BBC – DROITWICH (1935)
d Harry Watt
VC

BBC THE VOICE OF BRITAIN (1935)
d Stuart Legg
VC

BEAD BUTTERFLIES (Eve's Film Review series) (1929)
VC

BEAUTY AND THE BARGE (1937)
d Henry Edwards
PB

BED AND BREAKFAST (1930)
d Walter Forde
PB

BED AND BREAKFAST (1938)
d Walter West
PB

BEDROCK (1930)
d Carlyle Blackwell
PB

BEES IN PARADISE (1944)
d Val Guest
VC SC

BEFORE THE RAID (1943)
d Jiří Weiss
VC

BEGINNERS PLEASE! (Fitness Wins series) (1940)
d Donald Carter
VC

BEHIND THE MASK (1945)
VC

BEHIND THE SCENES (1938)
d Evelyn Spice
VC

BEHIND THE SPANISH LINES (1938)
d Thorold Dickinson, Sidney Cole
VC

BEHIND YOUR BACK (1937)
d Donovan Pedelty
PB

BELFAST TELEGRAPH, the (1934)
VC

BELLA DONNA (1934)
d Robert Milton
PB

BELL-BOTTOM GEORGE (1944)
d Marcel Varnel
VC

BELLES OF ST CLEMENT'S, the (1936)
d Ivar Campbell
PB

BELLS GO DOWN, the (1943)
d Basil Dearden
VC

BESIDE THE SEASIDE (1935)
d Marion Grierson
VC

BEST OF THEIR KIND, the (1938)
VC

BETHLEHEM (Pathé Pictorial series) (1929)
VC

BEVERLEY CELEBRATES ITS 800TH BIRTHDAY AS A CHARTER BOROUGH BY A SPECIAL SERVICE IN THE MINSTER (1929)
VC

BEVERLEY COMMEMORATES THE ANNIVERSARY OF THE BATTLE OF BRITAIN (1943)
VC

BEYOND OUR HORIZON (1939)
d Norman Walker
VC

BEYOND THE CITIES (1931)
d Carlyle Blackwell
PB

BEYOND THE DEVIL'S PUNCHBOWL! (Eve's Film Review series) (1930)
VC

BIG BLOCKADE (1942)
d Charles Frend
SC PB

BIG BUSINESS (1930)
d Oscar M Sheridan
PB

BIG CITY, the (1940)
d Ralph Bond
VC

BIG FELLA, the (1937)
d J Elder Wills
PB

BIG GAME OF LIFE, the (1935)
d Cherry Kearton
VC PB

BIG MONEY (1938)
d Harry Watt
VC

BIG NOISE, the (1936)
d Alex Bryce
PB

BIG TOP, the (1940)
VC

BIKANER (Secrets of India series) (1934)
d Geoffrey Barkas
PB

BILL AND COO (1931)
d John Orton
VC

BINGO series
see
BINGO THE BATTLING BRUISER (1930)

BINGO THE BATTLING BRUISER (Bingo series) (1930)
d Norman Cobb
VC

BIRDS OF PREY (1930)
d Basil Dean
VC SC

BIRMINGHAM (Cities of Britain series) (1931)
VC

BIRMINGHAM AIR RAID PRECAUTIONS (1938)
see
THIS IS A MATTER WHICH VITALLY CONCERNS YOU (1938)

BIRMINGHAM CENTENARY PAGEANT 1938, the (1938)
VC

BIRTH-DAY (1945)
d Budge Cooper
VC

BIRTH OF AN EMPIRE, the (1937)
VC

BIRTH OF THE ROBOT, the (1935)
d Len Lye
VC SC

BIRTH OF THE YEAR (1938)
d Evelyn Spice
VC

BITER BIT, the (1943)
VC

BITTER SWEET (1933)
d Herbert Wilcox
PB

BLACK AND WHITE (1929)
VC

BLACK DIAMONDS (1932)
d Charles Hanmer
VC

BLACK EYES (1939)
d Herbert Brenon
VC

BLACK HAND GANG, the (1930)
d Monty Banks
VC SC

BLACK LIMELIGHT (1938)
d Paul L Stein
SC

BLACKMAIL (1929)
d Alfred Hitchcock
VC SC

BLACKOUT (1941)
VC

BLACK SHEEP OF WHITEHALL, the (1941)
d Will Hay, Basil Dearden
VC

BLARNEY STONE, the (1933)
d Tom Walls
VC

BLITHE SPIRIT (1945)
d David Lean
VC SC PB

BLITZED CITIES OF BRISTOL AND BATH, the (1942)
VC

BLONDES FOR DANGER (1938)
d Jack Raymond
PB

BLOOD (Hygiene series) (1935)
d Donald Carter
VC

BLOOD TRANSFUSION (1942)
d Hans M Nieter
VC

BLOSSOM TIME (1934)
d Paul L Stein
VC PB

BLOW BUGLES BLOW (1936)
d Rudolph Messel
VC SC

BLOW-FLY, the (1935)
VC

BLUE SMOKE (1935)
d Ralph Ince
PB

BLUE SQUADRON, the (1934)
d George King
PB

BOB IN THE POUND (1943)
VC

BOB'S YOUR UNCLE (1941)
d Oswald Mitchell
VC PB

BOILER HOUSE PRACTICE (1943)
d George Wynn
VC

BOLTON ROYAL INFIRMARY JUBILEE YEAR 1933, the (1933)
VC

BOMB FEVER (1930)
VC

BONNIE SCOTLAND CALLS YOU (1938)
d Howard Gaye
VC

BON VOYAGE (1944)
d Alfred Hitchcock
VC

BOOK BARGAIN (1937)
d Norman McLaren
VC

BOOTS! BOOTS! (1934)
d Bert Tracy
VC

BORDER COLLIE (1939)
d Germain Burger
VC

BOTTLE PARTY (1936)
d R A Hopwood
PB

BOUQUET OF THE MONTH – NICE GIRL (1939)
VC

BOXING FOR VICTORY (1943)
VC

BOYS' BRIGADE JUBILEE CELEBRATIONS AT GLASGOW, 8–11TH SEPTEMBER 1933 (1933)
VC

BOYS OF THE OLD BRIGADE (1945)
d A Stanley Williamson
PB

BOYS WILL BE BOXERS (Pathétone Weekly series) (1931)
VC

BOYS WILL BE BOYS (1935)
d William Beaudine
VC SC

BRACELETS (1931)
d Sewell Collins
PB

BREAD (1934)
VC

BREAK THE NEWS (1938)
d René Clair
VC PB

BREATH OF DANGER, a (1941)
d Stanley Irving
VC

BREWSTER'S MAGIC (Secrets of Nature series) (1933)
d Mary Field
VC

BREWSTER'S MILLIONS (1935)
d Thornton Freeland
VC PB

BRICKS (1936)
VC

BRIDES TO BE (1934)
d Reginald Denham
PB

BRIEF ECSTASY (1937)
d Edmond T Gréville
VC

BRIEF ENCOUNTER (1945)
d David Lean
VC SC

BRIGGS FAMILY, the (1940)
d Herbert Mason
VC

BRIGHTER COUNTRYSIDE, a (Britain under National Government series) (1935)
VC

BRINGING HOME THE CUP (1930)
VC

BRINGING IT HOME (1940)
d John E Lewis
VC

BRITAIN AT BAY (1940)
d Harry Watt
VC

BRITAIN BEATS THE CLOCK (1943)
VC

BRITAIN CAN TAKE IT (1940)
d Harry Watt, Humphrey Jennings
VC

BRITAIN FIRST (1929)
VC

BRITAIN'S COUNTRYSIDE (1937)
d Marion Grierson
VC

BRITAIN'S YOUTH (1940)
d Jack Ellitt
VC

BRITAIN TODAY (1936)
VC

BRITAIN UNDER NATIONAL GOVERNMENT (1935)
VC

BRITAIN UNDER NATIONAL GOVERNMENT series
see
AGRICULTURE (1935)
BRIGHTER COUNTRYSIDE, a (1935)
EMPIRE TRADE (1934)
GREAT RECOVERY, the (1934)
PRICE OF FREE TRADE, the (1932)
RT HON RAMSAY MACDONALD, the (1935)
SAM SMALL AT WESTMINSTER (1935)
SPEECH BY THE RT HON JOHN SIMON (1935)
SPEECH BY THE RT HON STANLEY BALDWIN (1935)
TWO LANCASHIRE COTTON WORKERS DISCUSS SAFEGUARDING (1935)
YORKSHIRE WOOLLEN WORKERS DISCUSS SAFEGUARDING (1931)

BRITANNIA OF BILLINGSGATE (1933)
d Sinclair Hill
SC

BRITISH GRAHAMLAND EXPEDITION (1937)
VC

BRITISH MADE (1939)
d George Pearson
VC

BRITISH NAVY, the (1939)
VC

BRITISH PROPAGANDA FILM (1942)
VC

BRITISH SCREEN TATLER NO.68 (1929)
VC

BRITISH STEEL (1939)
VC

BRITISH UNION OF FASCISTS MARCH OCTOBER 3RD 1937 (1937)
VC

BROADWAY CINEMA, WALHAM GREEN; OLD AGE PENSIONERS' SEASIDE HOLIDAY TO SOUTHEND-ON-SEA, WEDNESDAY 20TH JULY 1938 (1938)
VC

BROKEN BLOSSOMS (1936)
d John Brahm
VC

BROKEN DYKES (1945)
VC

BROKEN MELODY, the (1929)
d Fred Paul
PB

BROKEN MELODY, the (1934)
d Bernard Vorhaus
VC

BROTHER ALFRED (1932)
d Henry Edwards
VC

BUILDERS (1942)
d Pat Jackson
VC

BUILDING OF ODEON LEICESTER SQUARE (1933)
VC

BULLDOG DRUMMOND AT BAY (1937)
d Norman Lee
VC SC

BULLDOG JACK (1935)
d Walter Forde
VC PB

BULLDOG SEES IT THROUGH (1940)
d Harold Huth
PB

BULL RUSHES (1931)
d W P Kellino
SC

BULWARK OF THE LEGIONS – CHESTER, a (1934)
VC

BURIED TREASURE (1939)
d Donald Carter
VC

BUSMAN'S HOLIDAY (1937)
VC

BUZZARD, the (1934)
VC

CABLE SHIP (1933)
d Alexander Shaw, Stuart Legg
VC

CAESAR AND CLEOPATRA (1945)
d Gabriel Pascal
VC PB

CAFE COLETTE (1937)
d Paul L Stein
SC PB

CAFE MASCOT (1936)
d Lawrence Huntington
PB

CALENDAR, the (1931)
d T Hayes Hunter
SC

CALENDAR OF THE YEAR (1936)
d Evelyn Spice
VC

CALLED BACK (1932)
d Reginald Denham, Jack Harris
PB

CALL FOR ARMS, the (1940)
d Brian Desmond Hurst
VC

CALLING ALL STARS (1937)
d Herbert Smith
VC

CALLING MR SMITH (1940)
d Stefan Themerson, Franciszka Themerson
VC

CALLING THE TUNE (1936)
d Reginald Denham
VC PB

CALL ME SPEEDY (1930)
VC

CAMBRIDGE (1931)
d G F Noxon, Stuart Legg
VC

CAMBRIDGE (1944)
d Richard Massingham
VC

CAMELS ARE COMING, the (1934)
d Tim Whelan
VC

CAMERA MAKES WHOOPEE (1935)
d Norman McLaren
VC

CAMERAMEN AT WAR (1944)
d Len Lye
VC

CAMERA REFLECTIONS (1945)
VC

CAMPANIONS (1938)
d A Frank Bundy
VC

CAMP CONCERT (1943)
VC

CANDLELIGHT IN ALGERIA (1943)
d George King
VC PB

CANDLES AT NINE (1944)
d John Harlow
VC PB

CANON STUART MORRIS OF BIRMINGHAM (1937)
VC

CANTERBURY TALE, a (1944)
d Michael Powell, Emeric Pressburger
VC SC

CAPE FORLORN (1930)
d E A Dupont
VC

CAPITOL CORONATION GAZETTE – MAY 12TH, 1937, the (1937)
VC

CAPITOL'S JUBILEE GAZETTE (1935)
VC

CAPITOL THEATRE PRESENTS SCENES AND EVENTS, the (1930)
VC

CAPTAIN BILL (1935)
d Ralph Ceder
SC

CAPTAIN'S ORDERS (1937)
d Ivar Campbell
VC

CAPTAIN'S TABLE, the (1936)
d Percy Marmont
VC

CARBON DIOXIDE ABSORPTION TECHNIQUE, the (The Technique of Anaesthesia series) (1944)
d Yvonne Fletcher
VC

CARCINOMA OF THE BREAST TREATED WITH RADIUM (1929)
d Geoffrey Keynes
VC

CARGOES (1940)
d Humphrey Jennings
VC

CARGO FOR ARDROSSAN (1939)
d Ruby Grierson
VC

CARGO FROM JAMAICA (1933)
d Basil Wright
VC

CARMEN (Colourtune series) (1936)
d Anson Dyer
VC

CAR OF DREAMS (1935)
d Graham Cutts, Austin Melford
VC SC

CARRYING THE LOAD; BRITISH RAILWAYS AT WAR (1945)
VC

CARRY ON CHILDREN (1940)
d Michael Hankinson
VC

CARRY ON SAVING ETC (1941)
VC

CASE FOR THE CROWN, the (1934)
d George A Cooper
PB

CASE OF GABRIEL PERRY, the (1935)
d Albert de Courville
PB

CASE OF THE FRIGHTENED LADY, the (1940)
d George King
VC SC

CASH (1933)
d Zoltan Korda
PB

CASTLES AND FISHERFOLK (1933)
d Walter Creighton
VC

CATHEDRALS OF ENGLAND (1937)
d Marion Grierson
VC

CATHERINE THE GREAT (1934)
d Paul Czinner
VC SC PB

CATTLE AUCTION IN THE HEBRIDES, a (1932)
VC

CAUSE COMMUNE, la (1940)
d Alberto Cavalcanti
VC

CAUTIONARY TALE, a (1944)
d Lister Laurance
SC

CAVALCADE OF VARIETY (1941)
d Thomas Bentley
VC

CAVES OF PÉRIGORD, the (1939)
d Caroline Byng Lucas
VC

CENTRAL INDIAN TOWN: UDAIPUR, a (1937)
VC

CEREAL SEED DISINFECTION (1943)
d Andrew Buchanan
VC

CHALLENGE, the (1938)
d Milton Rosmer, Luis Trenker
VC SC

CHALLENGE TO FASCISM; GLASGOW'S MAY DAY (1938)
d Helen Biggar
VC

CHAMPAGNE CHARLIE (1944)
d Alberto Cavalcanti
VC

CHANNEL CROSSING (1933)
d Milton Rosmer
VC

CHANNEL INCIDENT (1940)
d Anthony Asquith
VC

CHANNEL ISLANDS 1940–45, the (1945)
d Gerard Bryant
VC

CHAPLIN'S FIRST FILMS (1942)
VC

CHAPTER AND VERSE (1936)
d Stanley Hawes
VC

CHARLEY'S (BIG-HEARTED) AUNT (1940)
d Walter Forde
VC

CHARM OF VENICE; A TRAVEL TALK, the (1932)
VC

CHECKMATE (1935)
d George Pearson
PB

CHEER, BOYS, CHEER (1939)
d Walter Forde
VC PB

CHEER UP! (1936)
d Leo Mittler
VC SC

CHELSEA LIFE (1933)
d Sidney Morgan
PB

CHICK (1936)
d Michael Hankinson
VC

CHILDREN AT SCHOOL (1937)
d Basil Wright
VC

CHILDREN MUST LAUGH (1944)
d Aleksander Ford
VC

CHILDREN OF THE CITY (1944)
d Budge Cooper
VC PB

CHILDREN'S CHARTER (1945)
d Gerard Bryant
VC

CHILDREN SEE IT THRU, the (1941)
d Yvonne Fletcher
VC

CHILDREN'S EXERCISES (1931)
d H W Bush
VC

CHILDREN'S STORY, the (1938)
d Alexander Shaw
VC

CHILTERN COUNTRY, the (1939)
VC

CHINA (1942)
VC

CHINESE BUNGALOW, the (1940)
d George King
PB

CHORAL CAMEOS (1930)
d R E Jeffrey
VC

CHRISTMAS MESSAGE FROM MR OSCAR DEUTSCH, a (1939)
VC

CHRISTMAS UNDER FIRE (1941)
d Harry Watt
VC

CHU-CHIN-CHOW (1934)
d Walter Forde
VC PB

CHURCH BELLS OF ENGLAND, the (1941)
VC

CHURCH MOUSE, the (1934)
d Monty Banks
PB

CIRCULATION (Hygiene series) (1935)
d Donald Carter
VC

CITADEL, the (1938)
d King Vidor
VC PB

CITIES OF BRITAIN series
see
BIRMINGHAM (1931)

CITIZEN'S ADVICE BUREAU (1941)
d Francis Searle
VC

CITY, the (1939)
d Ralph Elton
VC

CITY AND COUNTY OF KINGSTON UPON HULL 'VICTORY IN EUROPE' CELEBRATIONS MAY 1945 (1945)
VC

CITY AND WESTMINSTER, the (1931)
VC

CITY BOUND (1941)
d Robin Carruthers
VC

CITY OF BEAUTIFUL NONSENSE (1935)
d Adrian Brunel
PB

CITY OF BIRMINGHAM: CORONATION OF THEIR MAJESTIES KING GEORGE VI AND QUEEN ELIZABETH, 10TH MAY 1937 (1937)
VC

CITY OF PARIS, the (1932)
d I Isaacs, Christopher A Radley
VC

CITY OF PLAY, the (1929)
d Denison Clift
PB

CITY OF PROGRESS (1941)
VC

CITY OF SHIPS (1939)
VC

CITY OF SONG (1930)
d Carmine Gallone
VC PB

'CITY OF ST ALBAN' AND THE FORGOTTEN CITY OF VERULAMIUM, the (1933)
d Christopher A Radley
VC

CITY REBORN, a (1945)
d John Eldridge
VC

CIVILIAN FRONT (1940)
d Mary Field
VC

CLAIRVOYANT, the (1935)
d Maurice Elvey
VC SC

CLAUDE DEPUTISES (1930)
d R E Jeffrey
VC

CLEANER MILK (1935)
VC

CLEANING UP (1933)
d Leslie Hiscott
PB

CLIMBING HIGH (1938)
d Carol Reed
VC SC

CLIMBING PLANTS (1938)
d J V Durden
VC

CLOCKS AND WATCHES (1940)
VC

CLOSE-UPS OF THE STARS – PATRICIA ROC (1939)
VC

CLOSE-UPS OF THE STARS – VALERIE HOBSON (1938)
VC

CLOTHES AND THE WOMAN (1937)
d Albert de Courville
PB

CLUE OF THE GLEAMING HAIR, the (1937)
VC

CLYDE FOOTBALL CLUB SPORTS (1932)
VC

COAL FACE (1935)
d Alberto Cavalcanti
VC

COASTAL COMMAND (1942)
d J B Holmes
VC

COASTAL VILLAGE (1943)
d Stanley Irving
VC

COCK O' THE NORTH (1935)
d Oswald Mitchell, Challis N Sanderson
PB

COELENTERATA (1937)
d J V Durden
VC

COLD BLOODED FRIENDS (1931)
VC

COLLAPSIBLE METAL TUBES (1942)
d Len Lye
VC

COLLOIDS IN MEDICINE (1940)
d Marcus Cooper
VC

COLONEL BLOOD (1933)
d W P Lipscomb
PB

COLOUR BOX, a (1935)
d Len Lye
VC

COLOURTUNE series
see
CARMEN (1936)

COME AGAIN (1943)
d Ralph Elton
VC

COME BACK TO ERIN (1933)
VC

COME FOR A STROLL (1938)
d Richard Massingham
VC

COME ON, GEORGE! (1939)
d Anthony Kimmins
VC

COME OUT OF THE PANTRY (1935)
d Jack Raymond
VC PB

COMING OF AUREA (1932)
VC

COMING OF THE DIAL, the (1933)
d Stuart Legg
VC

COMMAND PERFORMANCE (1937)
d Sinclair Hill
PB

COMMON BUTTERFLY, the (1929)
VC

COMMON CAUSE (1942)
d Henry Cass
VC

COMMON ROUND, the (1935)
d Stephen Harrison
VC

COMMON TOUCH, the (1941)
d John Baxter
VC PB

COMPOSER'S DREAM, the (1936)
VC

COMPROMISING DAPHNE (1930)
d Thomas Bentley
PB

COMPULSORY HUSBAND, the (1930)
d Harry Lachman
PB

CONDEMNED TO DEATH (1932)
d Walter Forde
PB

CONQUERING SPACE – THE STORY OF MODERN COMMUNICATIONS (1934)
VC

CONQUEST (1930)
VC

CONQUEST OF A GERM (1944)
d John Eldridge
VC

CONQUEST OF NATURAL BARRIERS (1932)
VC

CONQUEST OF THE AIR, the (1934)
VC

CONQUEST OF THE AIR, the (1940)
VC

CONSTANT NYMPH, the (1933)
d Basil Dean
VC PB

CONSTRUCTION (1935)
VC

CONSUMPTION (TUBERCULOSIS OF THE LUNGS) (1932)
d H W Bush
VC

CONTACT (1933)
d Paul Rotha
VC

CONTAGIOUS ABORTION (The Health of Dairy Cattle series) (1944)
VC

CONTRABAND (1940)
d Michael Powell
VC PB

CONTRABAND LOVE (1931)
d Sidney Morgan
PB

CONTRARIES (1943)
d Roger McDougall, Alexander Mackendrick
VC

CONTROL OF EDENTULOUS POSTERIOR FRAGMENT BY SURGICAL WIRING, the (Maxillo-Facial Surgery series) (1942)
VC

CONTROL ROOM (1942)
d Geoffrey Bell
VC

CONVICT 99 (1938)
d Marcel Varnel
VC SC

CONVOY (1940)
d Pen Tennyson
VC PB

COOKERY HINTS series
see
HERRINGS (1940)
STEAMING (1940)

CO-OPTIMISTS, the (1929)
d Edwin Greenwood
VC

COPENHAGEN CAMEOS (1930)
VC

CORNWALL, THE WESTERN LAND (1938)
VC

CORONATION OF THEIR MAJESTIES KING GEORGE VI AND QUEEN ELIZABETH, the (1937)
VC

COTSWOLD CLUB (1944)
d Charles de Lautour
VC

COTTAGE ON DARTMOOR (1929)
d Anthony Asquith
VC SC

COTTAGE TO LET (1941)
d Anthony Asquith
VC

COTTON GROWING IN THE SUDAN C.1925–1930 (1930)
VC

COTTON QUEEN (1937)
d Bernard Vorhaus
VC PB

COTTON SPINNING (1930)
VC

COUGHS AND SNEEZES (1945)
d Richard Massingham
VC

COUNTRY COMES TO TOWN (1932)
d Basil Wright
VC

COUNTRY FARE; A FILM OF THE FARM (1937)
VC

COUNTRY TOWN (1945)
d Julian Wintle
VC

COUNTRYWOMEN, the (1942)
d John Page
VC

COUNTY OF THE WHITE ROSE (1934)
d Robin Carruthers
VC

CP CONGRESS – BIRMINGHAM 1938 (1938)
VC

CRACKERJACK (1938)
d Albert de Courville
VC

CRAFTSMAN series, the
see
WHEELWRIGHT, the (1935)

CREEPING SHADOWS (1931)
d John Orton
SC

CRICKET (1929)
VC

CRIME AT BLOSSOMS, the (1933)
d Maclean Rogers
PB

CRIME ON THE HILL (1933)
d Bernard Vorhaus
VC PB

CRIMES AT THE DARK HOUSE (1940)
d George King
PB

CRIMES OF STEPHEN HAWKE, the (1936)
d George King
VC

CRIME UNLIMITED (1935)
d Ralph Ince
VC

CRIMSON CIRCLE, the (1936)
d Reginald Denham
VC

CROOK'S TOUR (1940)
d John Baxter
VC PB

CROSS BEAMS (1940)
d Aveling Ginever
PB

CROSS CURRENTS (1935)
d Adrian Brunel
PB

CROSS MY HEART (1937)
d Bernard Mainwaring
PB

CROWN AND GLORY (1937)
VC

CROWNING CEREMONY; FLINT ROSE QUEEN 1930 (1930)
VC

CROWNING GLORY (1936)
VC

CROWN OF THE YEAR, the (1943)
d Ralph Keene
VC

CROWN V STEVENS (1936)
d Michael Powell
VC

CROYDON TO HAVE SUNDAY CINEMAS (1931)
VC

CRUSH FRACTURE OF THE MIDDLE THIRD OF THE FACE (Maxillo-Facial Surgery series) (1942)
VC

CTO; THE STORY OF THE CENTRAL TELEGRAPH OFFICE (1935)
VC

CUCKOO, the (Featherland series) (1931)
VC

CUCKOO IN THE NEST, a (1933)
d Tom Walls
VC PB

CULTIVATION OF LIVING TISSUE, the (1933)
d R G Canti
VC

CULTIVATION OF SKELETAL TISSUES: THE DEVELOPMENT IN VITRO OF THE LOWER LIMB BUD OF THE EMBRYONIC FOWL, the (1929)
VC

CUPBOARD LOVE (1931)
d Bernard Mainwaring
VC

CUP OF KINDNESS, a (1934)
d Tom Walls
VC SC

CURLEW AND THE OWL, the (Featherland series) (1931)
VC

CURSE OF THE SWASTIKA, the (1940)
VC

DAILY BREAD (1940)
d Montgomery Tully
VC

DAILY ROUND (1937)
d Richard Massingham, Karl Urbahn
VC

DAIMLER ARMOURED CAR series, the
see
DAY IN THE FIELD, a (1942)
GENERAL DESCRIPTION (1942)

DAISY BELL COMES TO TOWN (1937)
d J B Holmes
VC

DANCE BAND (1935)
d Marcel Varnel
VC PB

DANCE MOMENTS FROM 'RIO RITA' – THE NEW MUSICAL PLAY AT THE PRINCE EDWARD THEATRE, LONDON (Eve's Film Review series) (1930)
VC

DANCE OF THE HARVEST (1934)
VC

DANCE PRETTY LADY (1932)
d Anthony Asquith
VC

DANDY DICK (1935)
d William Beaudine
VC

DANGER AREA (1943)
d Henry Cass
VC

DANGEROUS COMPANIONS (1934)
d A N C Macklin
VC

DANGEROUS FINGERS (1938)
d Norman Lee
PB

DANGEROUS GROUND (1934)
d Norman Walker
PB

DANGEROUS MOONLIGHT (1941)
d Brian Desmond Hurst
VC PB

DANGERS IN THE DARK (1941)
d Richard Massingham, Lewis Grant Wallace
VC

DARJEELING (Secrets of India series) (1934)
d Geoffrey Barkas
PB

DARK EYES OF LONDON (1939)
d Walter Summers
PB

DARK GROUND ILLUMINATION, SHOWING THE INTERNAL STRUCTURES OF THE CELL (1930)
d R G Canti
VC

DARK JOURNEY (1937)
d Victor Saville
PB

DARK RED ROSES (1929)
d Sinclair Hill
VC

DARK TOWER, the (1943)
d John Harlow
VC

DARK WORLD (1935)
d Bernard Vorhaus
PB

DARTMOUTH; THE ROYAL NAVAL COLLEGE (1942)
d Michael Hankinson
VC

DASSAN; AN ADVENTURE IN SEARCH OF LAUGHTER, FEATURING NATURE'S GREATEST LITTLE COMEDIANS (1930)
d Cherry Kearton, Ada Kearton
VC

DAWN GUARD, the (1941)
d Roy Boulting
VC

DAWN OF IRAN (1938)
d John Taylor
VC

DAY AND NIGHT. LATITUDE AND LONGITUDE (The Earth in Space series) (1936)
VC

DAY AT DENHAM, a (1939)
VC

DAY AT OUNDLE SCHOOL, a (1931)
VC

DAY AT SEA, a (1937)
VC

DAY-DREAMS (1929)
d Ivor Montagu
VC

DAY IN LIVERPOOL, a (1929)
d Anson Dyer
VC

DAY IN THE FIELD, a (The Daimler Armoured Car) (1942)
VC

DAY IN THE LIFE OF A MSUKUMA CALLED KINGA MKONO BARA, a (1937)
d Ralph Cutler
VC

DAY ON THE SANDHILLS, a (Featherland series) (1931)
VC

DAY WILL DAWN, the (1942)
d Harold French
VC

DEAD MAN'S SHOES (1939)
d Thomas Bentley
VC PB

DEAD MEN ARE DANGEROUS (1939)
d Harold French
PB

DEAD MEN TELL NO TALES (1938)
d David Macdonald
VC PB

DEAD OF NIGHT (1945)
d Alberto Cavalcanti, Robert Hamer, Charles Crichton, Basil Dearden
VC PB

DEAR OCTOPUS (1943)
d Harold French
VC SC

DEATH AT BROADCASTING HOUSE (1934)
d Reginald Denham
VC PB

DEATH DRIVES THROUGH (1935)
d Edward L Cahn
VC PB

DEBRIS TUNNELLING (1943)
d Kay Mander
VC

DEBT OF HONOUR (1936)
d Norman Walker
VC PB

DECLARATION OF THE POLL AT CHERTSEY TOWN HALL, the (1931)
VC

DECONTAMINATION OF STREETS (1942)
d Louise Birt
VC

DEEP PAN BOTTLING TOMATOES (1945)
d Henry Cooper
VC

DEFEAT DIPHTHERIA (1941)
d Bladon Peake
VC

DEFENCE OF MADRID, the (1936)
d Ivor Montagu
VC

DEFERRED PAYMENT (1929)
d Mary Field
VC

DEMI-PARADISE, the (1943)
d Anthony Asquith
VC PB

DEMOBBED (1944)
d John E Blakeley
PB

DESERT VICTORY (1943)
d Roy Boulting
VC PB

DEVELOPMENT OF THE CHICK, the (1937)
VC

DEVELOPMENT OF THE ENGLISH RAILWAYS, the (1936)
d Andrew Miller Jones
VC

DEVELOPMENT OF THE ENGLISH TOWN (1942)
d Mary Field
VC

DEVELOPMENT OF THE RABBIT (1942)
VC

DEVELOPMENT OF THE TROUT, the (1938)
d J V Durden
VC

DEVIL DANCERS OF SIKKIM (Secrets of India series) (1934)
d Geoffrey Barkas
VC PB

DEVIL'S ROCK (1938)
d Germain Burger, Richard Hayward
VC

DIAL 999 (1938)
d Lawrence Huntington
PB

DIAMOND CUT DIAMOND (1932)
d Fred Niblo, Maurice Elvey
PB

DIANA GOULD – LAMENT, 'GOOD HUMOURED LADIES' (1931)
VC

DIARY OF A POLISH AIRMAN (1942)
d Eugene Cekalski
VC

DICK SHEPPARD, FOUNDER OF THE PEACE PLEDGE UNION (1937)
VC

DICK TURPIN series
see
NEMESIS (1929)

DICTATOR, the (1935)
d Victor Saville
VC PB

DIESEL TRAIN DRIVER PART 2, DRIVING THE TRAIN (1945)
VC

DIG FOR VICTORY (1941)
d Michael Hankinson
VC

DIGGING FOR GOLD (1936)
d R A Hopwood
PB

DINNER AT THE RITZ (1937)
d Harold Schuster
VC

DINNER HOUR (1935)
d Edgar Anstey
VC

DIRTY WORK (1934)
d Tom Walls
VC

DISCORD (1932)
d Henry Edwards
PB

DISCOVERIES (1939)
d Redd Davis
VC

DISCOVERY OF A NEW PIGMENT; THE STORY OF MONASTRAL BLUE, the (1935)
VC

DISHONOUR BRIGHT (1936)
d Tom Walls
VC

DISTILLATION (1940)
d Peter Baylis
VC

DISTRICT NURSE, the (1942)
d John Page
VC

DITCHING (1942)
d Margaret Thomson
VC

DIVORCE OF LADY X, the (1938)
d Tim Whelan
VC PB

DIZZY LIMIT, the (1930)
d Edward Dryhurst
PB

DOCK WORKERS (1938)
d H A Green
VC

DR JOSSER KC (1931)
d Norman Lee
SC

DOCTOR'S ORDERS (1934)
d Norman Lee
SC

DR SYN (1937)
d Roy William Neill
VC PB

DO IT NOW (1939)
VC

DOMINANT SEX, the (1937)
d Herbert Brenon
PB

DON CHICAGO (1945)
d Maclean Rogers
PB

DON'T GET ME WRONG (1937)
d Reginald Purdell, Arthur Woods
VC PB

DON'T TAKE IT TO HEART (1944)
d Jeffrey Dell
VC

DOOR IN THE WALL, the (1934)
d Raymond ffennell
SC

DOOR WITH SEVEN LOCKS, the (1940)
d Norman Lee
VC PB

DORA (1933)
d St John Legh Clowes
VC

DOSS HOUSE (1933)
d John Baxter
VC

DOUBLE DROP, the (Pathétone Weekly series) (1931)
VC

DOUBLE EVENT (1934)
d Leslie Howard Gordon
PB

DOUBLE EXPOSURES (1937)
d John Paddy Carstairs
PB

DOUBLE THREAD (1943)
d Mary Field
VC

DOWN AT THE LOCAL (1945)
d Richard Massingham
VC

DOWN MELODY LANE (1943)
VC

DOWN ON THE FARM (1942)
d Charles Ridley
VC

DOWN OUR STREET (1932)
d Harry Lachman
PB

DOWN RIVER (1931)
d Peter Godfrey
SC

DOWN SOMERSET WAY (1942)
VC

DOWN THE RHEIDOL VALLEY (1929)
VC

DRAKE OF ENGLAND (1935)
d Arthur Woods
VC

DREAMERS, the (1933)
d Frank Cadman
SC

DREAMING (1944)
d John Baxter
VC PB

DREAMING LIPS (1937)
d Lee Garmes, Paul Czinner
VC

DREAMS COME TRUE (1936)
d Reginald Denham
VC

DREYFUS (1931)
d Milton Rosmer, F W Kraemer
VC PB

DRIFTERS (1929)
d John Grierson
VC PB

DRY DOCK (1936)
d Stanley Hawes
VC

DUAL CONTROL (1932)
d Walter Summers
VC

DUCHESS OF YORK AT STUDLEY COLLEGE, the (1929)
VC

DUCHY OF CORNWALL, the (1938)
d William Pollard
VC

DUKE IN THE NORTH, the (1936)
VC

DUMMY TALKS, the (1943)
d Oswald Mitchell
PB

DUSTBIN PARADE (1942)
d John Halas, Joy Batchelor
VC

DUSTY ERMINE (1936)
d Bernard Vorhaus
VC PB

EARLY ACTUALITIES (1936)
VC

EARLY BIRD, the (1936)
d Donovan Pedelty
PB

EARLY TO BED (1933)
d Ludwig Berger
VC

EARTH IN SPACE series, the
see
DAY AND NIGHT. LATITUDE AND LONGITUDE (1936)

EASTERN VALLEY (1937)
d Donald Alexander, Paul Rotha
VC

EAST LYNNE ON THE WESTERN FRONT (1931)
d George Pearson
PB

EAST MEETS WEST (1936)
d Herbert Mason
VC PB

EAST OF PICCADILLY (1941)
d Harold Huth
VC PB

EASY MONEY (1934)
d Redd Davis
PB

EASY RICHES (1938)
d Maclean Rogers
PB

EATING AT WORK (1942)
d Ralph Bond
VC

EATING OUT WITH TOMMY TRINDER (1941)
d Desmond Dickinson
VC

EBB TIDE (1932)
d Arthur Rosson
PB

ECHO MURDERS, the (1945)
d John Harlow
PB

EDGE OF THE WORLD, the (1937)
d Michael Powell
VC PB

EDINBURGH (1934)
VC

EFENDULA: MARRIAGE CEREMONIES, KUANYAMA TRIBE (1937)
d P H G Powell-Cotton
VC

18 MINUTES (1935)
d Monty Banks
VC

EIGHTH PLAGUE, the (1945)
VC

8TH WONDER, the (1938)
VC

EIGHTY DAYS, the (1944)
d Humphrey Jennings
VC

ELDER BROTHER, the (1937)
d Frederick Hayward
PB

ELEMENTARY – MY DEAR WATSON (1945)
VC

ELEPHANT BOY (1937)
d Zoltan Korda, Robert Flaherty
VC

ELIZA COMES TO STAY (1936)
d Henry Edwards
VC

ELLA SHIELDS (1936)
d John Baxter
VC

ELOPEMENT IN FRANCE (1944)
d Richard Massingham
VC

ELSTREE CALLING (1930)
d Adrian Brunel
VC

ELSTREE 'ERBS, the (1930)
d Joe Noble
VC

EMBEX (1942)
VC

EMIL AND THE DETECTIVES (1935)
d Milton Rosmer
PB

EMINENT SCIENTISTS series
see
MR WILLIAM MORRIS MORDEY (1934)

EMPIRE series, the
see
NORTHERN TERRITORIES – THE GOLD COAST, the (1929)

EMPIRE TRADE (Britain under National Government series) (1934)
VC

ENDOTRACHEAL ANAESTHESIA (The Technique of Anaesthesia series) (1944)
d Margaret Thomson
VC

ENDURANCE; THE STORY OF A GLORIOUS FAILURE (1933)
VC

ENGINE SHED (1938)
VC

ENGLAND AWAKE (1932)
d John Buchan, H Bruce Woolfe
VC

ENGLAND'S PLAYGROUND (1934)
d Vernon J Clancey
VC

ENGLAND'S SHAKESPEARE (1939)
VC

ENGLISH ELECTRIC COMPANY AND THE GRID, the (1933)
VC

ENGLISH HARVEST (1938)
d Humphrey Jennings
VC

ENGLISH POTTER, the (1932)
VC

ENGLISH WITHOUT TEARS (1944)
d Harold French
VC

ENOUGH TO EAT (1936)
d Edgar Anstey
VC

ENTHRONEMENT OF ARCHBISHOP CYRIL FORSTER GARBETT IN YORK MINSTER ON 11TH JUNE 1942 (1942)
VC

ERECTING AEROPLANE ENGINES (1932)
VC

ESCAPE (1930)
d Basil Dean
VC

ESCAPE ME NEVER (1935)
d Paul Czinner
VC PB

ESCAPE TO DANGER (1943)
d Lance Comfort, Max Greene
PB

ETERNAL FEMININE, the (1930)
d Arthur Varney
PB

ETERNAL PRAGUE (1942)
d Jiří Weiss
VC

EUROPE TODAY (1934)
VC

EUSTON HOUSE (1934)
VC

EVENSONG (1934)
d Victor Saville
VC PB

EVERGREEN (1934)
d Victor Saville
VC PB

EVERYBODY DANCE (1936)
d Charles F Riesner
VC SC

EVERYTHING IN LIFE (1936)
d J Elder Wills
SC

EVERYTHING IS RHYTHM (1936)
d Alfred Goulding
VC PB

EVERYTHING IS THUNDER (1936)
d Milton Rosmer
VC PB

EVE'S FILM REVIEW series
see
AS YOU LIKE IT (1929)
BEAD BUTTERFLIES (1929)
BEYOND THE DEVIL'S PUNCHBOWL! (1930)
DANCE MOMENTS FROM 'RIO RITA' – THE NEW MUSICAL PLAY AT THE PRINCE EDWARD THEATRE, LONDON (1930)

EVE'S FILM REVIEW NO.503 (1931)
EVE'S FILM REVIEW NO.575 (1932)
JUST FEET – HERS AND HIS (1930)
SILKEN SUPPLENESS (1930)
VELVET AND SABLE; A NEW PATHÉCOLOR MODE (1929)
WAS EVE SO SLOW THIRTY YEARS AGO? (1930)

EVE'S FILM REVIEW NO.503 (Eve's Film Review series) (1931)
VC

EVE'S FILM REVIEW NO.575 (Eve's Film Review series) (1932)
VC

EXHIBITS AFTER DARK (1944)
VC

EXPANSION OF GERMANY 1870–1914, the (1936)
d Andrew Miller Jones
VC

EXPERIMENTAL ANIMATION 1933 (1933)
d Len Lye
VC

EYE AND THE EAR, the (1944)
d Stefan Themerson, Franciszka Themerson
VC

FABRICATION OF PLANT IN ACID RESISTING STEELS, the (1930)
VC

FACE AT THE WINDOW, the (1939)
d George King
VC PB

FACE OF BRITAIN series, the
see
FACE OF BRITAIN, the (1935)
SHIPYARD (1935)

FACE OF BRITAIN, the (The Face of Britain series) (1935)
d Paul Rotha
VC PB

FACE OF SCOTLAND, the (1938)
d Basil Wright
VC

FACES (1934)
d Sidney Morgan
PB

FACING THE MUSIC (1933)
d Harry Hughes
VC SC

FACING THE MUSIC (1941)
d Maclean Rogers
PB

FAILURE OF A STRATEGY (1944)
VC

FAILURE OF THE DICTATORS (1945)
VC

FAIR CITY OF UDAIPUR, the (Secrets of India series) (1934)
d Geoffrey Barkas
PB

FAIRY OF THE PHONE, the (1936)
d William Coldstream
VC

FAITHFUL FOR EVER (1941)
d Germain Burger
PB

FAITHFUL HEART, the (1932)
d Victor Saville
VC PB

FAITH TRIUMPHANT (St Paul series) (1938)
  d Norman Walker
  VC

FALCONS OF CZECHOSLOVAKIA, the
(1943)
  VC

FALLING FOR YOU (1933)
  d Robert Stevenson, Jack Hulbert
  VC SC

FALLING IN LOVE (1934)
  d Monty Banks
  PB

FALSE EVIDENCE (1937)
  d Donovan Pedelty
  PB

FAME (1936)
  d Leslie Hiscott
  PB

FAMILY OF GREAT TITS, a (1934)
  d Oliver Pike
  VC

**FAMOUS SCENES FROM SHAKESPEARE
series**
  see
  JULIUS CAESAR (1945)
  MACBETH (1945)

FANNY BY GASLIGHT (1944)
  d Anthony Asquith
  VC SC

FARES FAIR (1936)
  d Francis Searle
  VC

FAREWELL AGAIN (1937)
  d Tim Whelan
  VC PB

FARMER'S BOY, a (1945)
  d Peter Price
  VC

FARMER'S DAY, a (1940)
  d Brian Smith
  VC

FARMER'S WIFE, the (1941)
  d Norman Lee, Leslie Arliss
  VC SC

FARM FACTORY, the (1935)
  d Mary Field
  VC

FARMING FOR BOYS (1930)
  VC

FARMING IN SPRING (Farming in Suffolk
series) (1934)
  d Mary Field
  VC

FARMING IN SUFFOLK series
  see
  FARMING IN SPRING (1934)
  FARMING IN SUMMER (1934)
  FARMING IN WINTER (1934)

FARMING IN SUMMER (Farming in Suffolk
series) (1934)
  d Mary Field
  VC

FARMING IN WINTER (Farming in Suffolk
series) (1934)
  d Mary Field
  VC

FARM IS RECLAIMED, a (1944)
  d Alan J Harper
  VC

FARM WORK (1945)
  d Michael S Gordon
  VC

FAST AND SLOW (1945)
  VC

FATAL HOUR, the (1937)
  d George Pearson
  PB

FATHER AND SON (1945)
  d Leon Schauder
  VC

FATHER STEPS OUT (1937)
  d Maclean Rogers
  VC

FAUN (1931)
  VC

FAUST (1936)
  d Albert Hopkins
  VC

FEAR AND PETER BROWN (1940)
  d Richard Massingham
  VC

FEAR SHIP, the (1933)
  d James Edwards
  PB

FEAST OF HARMONY, a (1930)
  d R E Jeffrey
  VC

FEATHER, the (1929)
  d Leslie Hiscott
  PB

FEATHER BED, the (1933)
  d J Bertram Fryer
  VC SC

FEATHERED GANGSTERS (1932)
  VC

FEATHERLAND series
  see
  CUCKOO, the (1931)
  CURLEW AND THE OWL, the (1931)
  DAY ON THE SANDHILLS, a (1931)
  GOLDEN PLOVER AND REDSHANK, the
    (1931)
  TAWNY OWL, the (1931)

FEATHER YOUR NEST (1937)
  d William Beaudine
  VC PB

FENLANDS (The Pattern of Britain series)
(1945)
  d Ken Annakin
  VC

FEW OUNCES A DAY, a (1941)
  d Paul Rotha
  VC

FIDDLERS THREE (1944)
  d Harry Watt
  VC SC

FIGHTER PILOT (1940)
  VC

FIGHTING FIELDS (1940)
  VC

FIGHTING STOCK (1935)
  d Tom Walls
  VC PB

FILM AND REALITY (1942)
  d Alberto Cavalcanti
  VC

**FILM ON NEUROLOGICAL SEQUELAE OF
STARVATION IN PRISONERS OF WAR
FROM JAPANESE PRISON CAMPS** (1945)
  VC

FILTER, the (1934)
  d Mary Field
  VC

FIND, FIX AND STRIKE (1942)
  d Compton Bennett
  VC

FIND THE LADY (1936)
  d Roland Gillett
  PB

FINE FEATHERS (1937)
  d Leslie Hiscott
  PB

FINE FEATHERS, the (1941)
  d Andrew Buchanan
  VC

FIRE HAS BEEN ARRANGED, a (1935)
  d Leslie Hiscott
  VC

FIRE OVER ENGLAND (1937)
  d William K Howard
  VC PB

FIRE RAISERS, the (1933)
  d Michael Powell
  VC PB

FIRES IN TENEMENT BUILDINGS (1930)
  VC

FIRES WERE STARTED (1943)
  d Humphrey Jennings
  VC

FIRST A GIRL (1935)
  d Victor Saville
  VC SC

FIRST AID IN ACTION (1944)
  d Richard Massingham
  VC

**FIRST BIG OUTING FOR LOCAL
CHILDREN** (1936)
  VC

FIRST DAYS, the (1939)
  d Harry Watt, Pat Jackson, Humphrey
    Jennings
  VC

FIRST MRS FRASER, the (1932)
  d Sinclair Hill
  VC PB

FIRST NIGHT (1937)
  d Donovan Pedelty
  PB

FIRST OFFENCE (1936)
  d Herbert Mason
  VC PB

FIRST OF THE FEW, the (1942)
  d Leslie Howard
  VC PB

FIRST PASSENGER RAILWAY 1804, the
(1930)
  VC

FISHERFOLK OF NORTHUMBRIA (1942)
  VC

FISHY TALE!, a (1931)
  VC

FITNESS WINS series
see
BEGINNERS PLEASE! (1940)
FITNESS WINS THE GAME (1940)
5 FIT FELLOWS (1938)
4 AND 20 FIT GIRLS (1940)
20 MEN AND A LEADER (1940)

FITNESS WINS THE GAME (Fitness Wins series) (1940)
d Donald Carter
VC

FIVE AND UNDER (1941)
d Donald Alexander
VC

FIVE FACES OF MALAYA (1938)
d Alexander Shaw
VC

5 FIT FELLOWS (Fitness Wins series) (1938)
VC

FLAG LIEUTENANT, the (1932)
d Henry Edwards
VC

FLAME IN THE HEATHER (1935)
d Donovan Pedelty
PB

FLAME OF LOVE, the (1930)
d Richard Eichberg, Walter Summers
VC SC PB

FLAX (1944)
VC

FLEMISH FARM, the (1943)
d Jeffrey Dell
VC PB

FLOOD TIDE (1934)
d John Baxter
VC

FLORAL MATCHMAKERS (1931)
VC

FLY CATCHERS, the (1931)
VC

FLYING CINDERS (1939)
VC

FLYING FOOL, the (1931)
d Walter Summers
VC SC

FLYING FORTRESS (1942)
d Walter Forde
VC PB

FLYING SCOTSMAN, the (1930)
d Castleton Knight
VC

FLYING SQUAD, the (1940)
d Herbert Brenon
VC

FLYING START, a (1944)
d Ken Annakin
VC

FLYING TO INDIA BY IMPERIAL AIRWAYS 1932 & 1934 (1934)
VC

FOCUS ON THE EMPIRE series
see
NONQUASSI (1939)
TWELVE OP (1940)

FOLKESTONE SPEEDWAY THRILLS (1929)
VC

FOLKESTONE, THE GEM OF THE KENTISH COAST (1931)
VC

FOLLOW YOUR STAR (1938)
d Sinclair Hill
PB

FOOD FLASHES (1944)
VC

FOOD FLASHES (1945)
VC

FOR ALL ETERNITY (1935)
d Marion Grierson
VC

FORBIDDEN TERRITORY (1934)
d Phil Rosen
VC

FORD AT DAGENHAM, the (1935)
VC

FOREIGN AFFAIRES (1935)
d Tom Walls
VC PB

FOREMAN WENT TO FRANCE, the (1942)
d Charles Frend
VC

FOREVER ENGLAND (1935)
d Walter Forde, Anthony Asquith
VC PB

FOR FREEDOM (1940)
d Maurice Elvey, Castleton Knight
VC SC

FORGET-ME-NOT (1936)
d Zoltan Korda, Stanley Irving
VC PB

FORGOTTEN MEN; THE WAR AS IT WAS (1934)
d Norman Lee
VC

FOR LOVE OF YOU (1933)
d Carmine Gallone
VC

FOR THOSE IN PERIL (1944)
d Charles Crichton
VC SC

49TH PARALLEL (1941)
d Michael Powell
VC SC

FOR VALOUR (1937)
d Tom Walls
VC PB

FOR YOU ALONE (1945)
d Geoffrey Faithfull
SC PB

FOUNDER'S DAY, BEVERLEY GRAMMAR SCHOOL (1942)
VC

4 AND 20 FIT GIRLS (Fitness Wins series) (1940)
d Mary Field
VC

FOUR BARRIERS, the (1937)
d Alberto Cavalcanti
VC

FOUR FEATHERS, the (1939)
d Zoltan Korda
VC PB

FOUR JUST MEN, the (1939)
d Walter Forde
VC PB

FOUR MASKED MEN (1934)
d George Pearson
VC

FOURTH ESTATE; A FILM OF A BRITISH NEWSPAPER, the (1940)
d Paul Rotha
VC

FOURTH EVEREST EXPEDITION, the (1933)
VC

FOX HUNT (1936)
d Hector Hoppin, Anthony Gross
VC

FOYER DE DANSE (1932)
VC

FRAIL WOMEN (1932)
d Maurice Elvey
VC

FREEDOM OF THE HILLS, the (1930)
VC

FREEDOM OF THE SEAS (1934)
d Marcel Varnel
VC

FREEDOM RADIO (1940)
d Anthony Asquith
VC

FREE THAELMANN! (1935)
d Ivor Montagu
VC

FRENCH LEAVE (1937)
d Norman Lee
PB

FRENCH TOWN (1945)
d Alexander Shaw
VC

FRENCH WITHOUT TEARS (1939)
d Anthony Asquith
VC PB

FRIDAY THE THIRTEENTH (1933)
d Victor Saville
VC SC

FRIENDLY FLIES (Secrets of Nature series) (1931)
d Mary Field
VC

FROG, the (1937)
d Jack Raymond
VC

FROM ACORN TO OAK (1938)
d Montgomery Tully
VC

FROM COAL-MINE TO ROAD (1931)
VC

FROM MINUET TO FOXTROT (1940)
VC

FROM SAND TO SIDEBOARD (1933)
VC

FROM THE FOUR CORNERS (1941)
d Anthony Havelock-Allan
VC

FROM THE ORCHARD TO THE HOME (1931)
VC

FRONT LINE, the (1940)
d Harry Watt
VC

FRONT LINE KIDS (1942)
d Maclean Rogers
VC PB

FROTHBLOWER, the (Secrets of Nature series) (1932)
d Mary Field
VC

FROZEN LIMITS, the (1939)
d Marcel Varnel
VC SC

FRUITLANDS OF KENT (Regional Geography series) (1934)
d Mary Field
VC

FUEL FOR BATTLE (1944)
d John Eldridge
VC

FULL SPEED AHEAD (1936)
d Lawrence Huntington
PB

FULL STEAM (1935)
d R A Hopwood
PB

FURRY FOLK (1931)
VC

GABLES MYSTERY, the (1938)
d Harry Hughes
SC

GAINSBOROUGH MINIATURES series
see
SHAKESPEARE'S COUNTRY (1940)

GANG'S ALL HERE, the (1939)
d Thornton Freeland
VC SC

GANG SHOW, the (1937)
d Alfred Goulding
VC

GANGWAY (1937)
d Sonnie Hale
VC SC

GAOL BREAK (1936)
d Ralph Ince
PB

GARDEN FRIENDS AND FOES (1943)
d Darrel Catling
VC

GARDEN TOOLS (1943)
d Margaret Thomson
VC

GASBAGS (1940)
d Marcel Varnel
VC SC

GASLIGHT(1940)
d Thorold Dickinson
VC PB

GAUMONT-BRITISH STARLET series
see
JESSIE MATTHEWS (1937)

GAUNT STRANGER, the (1938)
d Walter Forde
VC SC

GAY OLD DOG, the (1935)
d George King
VC

GEMS OF WALES – CONWAY (1942)
VC

GENERAL DESCRIPTION (The Daimler Armoured Car series) (1942)
VC

GENERAL REPAIR (1938)
VC

GENTLEMAN OF PARIS, a (1931)
d Sinclair Hill
SC

GENTLEMEN'S AGREEMENT (1935)
d George Pearson
PB

GENTLE SEX, the (1943)
d Leslie Howard
VC PB

GERMANY CALLING (1941)
d Charles Ridley
VC

GERMS (1931)
d H W Bush
VC

GERT AND DAISY CLEAN UP (1942)
d Maclean Rogers
PB

GERT AND DAISY'S WEEKEND (1941)
d Maclean Rogers
VC PB

GHOST CAMERA, the (1933)
d Bernard Vorhaus
VC PB

GHOST GOES WEST, the (1935)
d René Clair
VC PB

GHOST OF ST. MICHAEL'S, the (1941)
d Marcel Varnel
VC

GHOST TRAIN, the (1931)
d Walter Forde
VC PB

GHOST TRAIN, the (1941)
d Walter Forde
VC SC

GHOUL, the (1933)
d T Hayes Hunter
SC PB

GIRL FROM MAXiM'S, the (1933)
d Alexander Korda
VC PB

GIRL IN THE FLAT, the (1934)
d Redd Davis
PB

GIRL IN THE NEWS, the (1940)
d Carol Reed
VC SC

GIRL MUST LIVE, a (1939)
d Carol Reed
VC

GIRLS PLEASE! (1934)
d Jack Raymond
VC

GIRLS WILL BE BOYS (1934)
d Marcel Varnel
VC PB

GIRO THE GERM (1934)
VC

GIVE HER A RING (1934)
d Arthur Woods
VC PB

GIVE THE KIDS A BREAK (1936)
d Donald Taylor
VC

GIVE US THE MOON (1944)
d Val Guest
VC

GLAMOROUS NIGHT (1937)
d Brian Desmond Hurst
VC PB

GLAMOUR GIRL (1938)
d Arthur Woods
PB

GLASGOW'S FESTIVAL OF FELLOWSHIP (1937)
VC

GLASS MAKERS OF ENGLAND (1932)
VC

GLIMPSES OF MODERN RUSSIA (1930)
d Ralph Bond
VC

GLORIOUS RIBBLESDALE (1940)
VC

GLORIOUS SIXTH OF JUNE, the (1934)
VC

GOAL, the (1935)
d Pat Wilson
VC

GOD'S CHILLUN (1938)
VC

GOING GAY (1933)
d Carmine Gallone
PB

GOLD COAST, the (1938)
VC

GOLDEN ARROW (1930)
VC

GOLDEN PLOVER AND REDSHANK, the (Featherland series) (1931)
VC

GOODBYE, MR CHIPS (1939)
d Sam Wood
VC

GOOD COMPANIONS, the (1933)
d Victor Saville
VC SC

GOOD KING WENCESLAS (1945)
VC

GOOD MORNING, BOYS! (1937)
d Marcel Varnel
VC PB

GOODNIGHT VIENNA (1932)
d Herbert Wilcox
VC PB

GOOD OLD DAYS, the (1939)
d Roy William Neill
PB

GOOD VALUE (1942)
d Hans M Nieter
VC

GOOSE STEPS OUT, the (1942)
d Will Hay, Basil Dearden
VC PB

GORNO'S ITALIAN MARIONETTES (1930)
d Jack Harrison
VC

GOVERNMENT OF SPAIN, the (Spain Today series) (1936)
VC

GPO FILM DISPLAY (1938)
VC

GRAIN HARVEST (1936)
d John C Elder
VC

GRAND FINALE (1936)
d Ivar Campbell
PB

GRAND HOTEL (1932)
d J G Ratcliffe
VC

GRAND WASHING CONTEST (1930)
VC

GRANTON TRAWLER (1934)
d John Grierson
VC

GRAPES OF CORINTH (1929)
VC

GRASS AND CLOVER SEED PRODUCTION (1944)
VC

GRASSY SHIRES, the (The Pattern of Britain series) (1944)
d Ralph Keene
VC

GREAT BARRIER, the (1937)
d Milton Rosmer, Geoffrey Barkas
VC PB

GREAT CIRCLE (1944)
d J B Napier-Bell
VC

GREAT CRUSADE; THE STORY OF A MILLION HOMES, the (1936)
d Fred Watts
VC

GREAT DAY (1945)
d Lance Comfort
VC PB

GREAT DEFENDER, the (1934)
d Thomas Bentley
VC PB

GREATEST BOXING TOURNAMENT OF CORONATION YEAR (1937)
VC

GREAT GAME, the (1930)
d Jack Raymond
PB

GREAT HARVEST, the (1942)
VC

GREAT MR HANDEL, the (1942)
d Norman Walker
VC PB

GREAT RECOVERY, the (Britain under National Government series) (1934)
VC

GREAT STUFF (1933)
d Leslie Hiscott
PB

GREAT WESTERN PORTS (1929)
VC

GREEK STREET (1930)
d Sinclair Hill
VC PB

GREEK TESTAMENT, the (1943)
d Charles Hasse
VC SC

GREEN COCKATOO, the (1937)
d William Cameron Menzies
VC SC PB

GREEN GIRDLE, the (World Window series) (1941)
d Ralph Keene
VC

GREENLAND: RYMILL 1933 (1933)
d John R Rymill
VC

GREEN PACK, the (1934)
d T Hayes Hunter
PB

GROWTH OF ROAD TRAVEL, the (1929)
VC

GUESS WHAT? NO. 2 (1944)
VC

GUILTY MELODY (1936)
d Richard Pottier
SC PB

GUS ELEN IN 'IT'S A GREAT BIG SHAME' (Pathétone Weekly series) (1932)
VC

GUV'NOR, the (1935)
d Milton Rosmer
VC SC

GUY FAWKES (1930)
d Maurice Elvey
VC

GYPSY (1937)
d Roy William Neill
PB

GYPSY MELODY (1936)
d Edmond T Gréville
SC PB

HAIL AND FAREWELL (1936)
d Ralph Ince
PB

HAIR; A TALE OF IMAGINATION (1933)
d James K Urquhart
VC

HALF A DAY'S TRIP (Seeing London series) (1930)
VC

HALFWAY HOUSE, the (1943)
d Basil Dearden
VC SC

HAMSTER, the (1929)
VC

HANDLE WITH CARE (1935)
d Redd Davis
PB

HANDLING AND CARE OF THE PATIENT (The Technique of Anaesthesia series) (1944)
d Rosanne Hunter
VC

HANG IT (1931)
VC

HAPPIDROME (1943)
d Phil Brandon
PB

HAPPY (1934)
d Fred Zelnik
VC

HAPPY DAYS ARE HERE AGAIN (1936)
d Norman Lee
VC PB

HAPPY ENDING (1931)
d Millard Webb
PB

HAPPY EVER AFTER (1932)
d Paul Martin, Robert Stevenson
PB

HAPPY FAMILIES (1940)
d Paul Barralet
PB

HAPPY FAMILY, the (1936)
d Maclean Rogers
PB

HAPPY IN THE MORNING (1938)
d Alberto Cavalcanti
VC

HARD STEEL (1942)
d Norman Walker
VC PB

HAREM-SCARE-'EM (1933)
VC

HARMONY HEAVEN (1930)
d Thomas Bentley
VC

HARNESSING THE WAVE (Simplified Science series) (1931)
VC

HARPENDEN'S WONDERFUL MILK SUPPLY (1930)
VC

HARRY LAUDER SONGS series
see
I LOVE A LASSIE (1931)
ROAMIN' IN THE GLOAMIN' (1931)
SAFTEST O' THE FAMILY, the (1931)

HARVEST SHALL COME, the (1942)
d Max Anderson
VC

HATTER'S CASTLE (1941)
d Lance Comfort
VC SC

HAVE YOU HAD YOUR CHILD IMMUNIZED AGAINST DIPHTHERIA? (1942)
VC

HAWICK COMMON RIDING JUNE 1932 (1932)
VC

HAWICK COMMON RIDING 1934 (1934)
VC

HAWICK COMMON RIDING 1931 (1931)
VC

HAWICK COMMON RIDING 1933 (1933)
VC

HAWICK COMMON RIDING 1929 (1929)
VC

HEAD OVER HEELS (1937)
d Sonnie Hale
VC PB

HEADS WE GO! (1933)
d Monty Banks
VC PB

HEALTH FOR THE NATION (1939)
d John Monck
VC

HEALTH IN WAR (1940)
d Pat Jackson
VC

HEALTH OF A NATION (1943)
d Lister Laurance
VC

HEALTH OF DAIRY CATTLE series, the
see
CONTAGIOUS ABORTION (1944)
MASTITIS (1945)
TUBERCULOSIS (1944)

HEALTH OF THE NATION, the (1936)
d Charles Barnett
VC

HEALTHY HOLIDAYS (Strength and Beauty series) (1937)
d Donald Carter
VC PB

HEART OF AN EMPIRE, the (1936)
d Alexander Shaw
VC

HEART OF BRITAIN, the (1941)
d Humphrey Jennings
VC

HEART'S DESIRE (1935)
d Paul L Stein
VC PB

HEARTS OF HUMANITY (1936)
d John Baxter
VC SC

HEATHLANDS (1938)
d Margaret Thomson
VC

HEAT WAVE (1935)
d Maurice Elvey
PB

HEAVEN IS ROUND THE CORNER (1944)
d Maclean Rogers
PB

HEDGING (1942)
d Margaret Thomson
VC

HE FOUND A STAR (1941)
d John Paddy Carstairs
VC

HELLO! WEST INDIES (1943)
d John Page
VC

HELL'S CARGO (1939)
d Harold Huth
VC PB

HELL UNLTD (1936)
d Norman McLaren, Helen Biggar
VC

HENRY V (1944)
d Laurence Olivier
VC

HERE AND THERE IN THE BRITISH ISLES (1931)
VC

HERE COMES THE SUN (1945)
d John Baxter
VC

HEREDITY IN MAN (1937)
d J V Durden
VC

HERE IS FASCISM'S WORK (Spain Today series) (1936)
VC

HERE IS THE LAND (1937)
d Stanley Hawes
VC

HERE WE COME GATHERING (1945)
d Barry Delmaine
VC

HER FATHER'S DAUGHTER (1941)
d Desmond Dickinson
VC

HER FIRST AFFAIRE (1932)
d Allan Dwan
VC

HERITAGE OF THE SOIL, the (1937)
d Widgey R Newman
VC

HER LAST AFFAIRE (1935)
d Michael Powell
VC PB

HERON AND THREE BIRDS OF PREY, the (1930)
VC

HER REPUTATION (1931)
d Sidney Morgan
PB

HERRINGS (Cookery Hints series) (1940)
d Jay Lewis
VC

HE SNOOPS TO CONQUER (1944)
d Marcel Varnel
SC

HEY! HEY! USA! (1938)
d Marcel Varnel
VC SC

HI, GANG! (1941)
d Marcel Varnel
VC

HIGH COMMAND, the (1937)
d Thorold Dickinson
VC PB

HIGHLAND DOCTOR (1943)
d Kay Mander
VC

HIGH SEAS (1929)
d Denison Clift
VC SC

HIGH TREASON (1929)
d Maurice Elvey
VC

HIGHWAY (1933)
d Eric Spear
VC

HIGHWAY CODE (1936)
d Charles Barnett
VC

HINDLE WAKES (1931)
d Victor Saville
VC PB

HIS LORDSHIP (1936)
d Herbert Mason
PB

HIS LORDSHIP REGRETS (1938)
d Maclean Rogers
PB

HRH PRINCE GEORGE VISITS HALIFAX INDUSTRIES, MONDAY JULY 13TH 1931 (1931)
VC

HOLD MY HAND (1938)
d Thornton Freeland
VC SC

HOLIDAY HORIZONS (1939)
VC

HOLIDAY'S END (1937)
d John Paddy Carstairs
PB

HOME FROM HOME (1939)
d Herbert Smith
PB

HOME OF THE WASP (1931)
d Christopher A Radley, Charles Head
VC

HOME PRODUCE FOR THE NATION (1939)
VC

HOMES FOR THE PEOPLE (1945)
d Kay Mander
VC

HOMES FOR WORKERS (1939)
VC

HOME SWEET HOME (1933)
d George A Cooper
PB

HOME SWEET HOME (1945)
d John E Blakeley
PB

HONEY BEES (1939)
VC

HONEY FOR THE QUEEN (1932)
VC

HONEYMOON FOR THREE (1935)
d Leo Mittler
PB

HONEYMOON MERRY-GO-ROUND (1940)
d Alfred Goulding
VC

HOOTS MON! (1939)
d Roy William Neill
VC

HOP GARDENS OF KENT (1933)
VC

HORSEY MAIL, the (1938)
d Pat Jackson
VC

HOSPITAL NURSE (1941)
d Francis Searle
VC

HOSPITAL SCHOOL (1944)
d Arthur W Barnes
SC

HOTEL RESERVE (1943)
d Victor Hanbury, Lance Comfort, Max Greene
VC PB

HOTEL SPLENDIDE (1932)
d Michael Powell
VC

HOT EVIDENCE (1939)
d John E Lewis
VC

HOT STUFF (1935)
VC

HOUND OF THE BASKERVILLES, the (1931)
d V Gareth Gundrey
VC

HOURS OF TRIUMPH (1945)
VC

HOUSE BROKEN (1936)
d Michael Hankinson
PB

HOUSEMASTER (1938)
d Herbert Brenon
VC PB

HOUSE OF SILENCE, the (1937)
d R K Neilson Baxter
VC

HOUSE OF THE ARROW, the (1940)
d Harold French
SC PB

HOUSE OF THE SPANIARD, the (1936)
d Reginald Denham
VC

HOUSING IN SCOTLAND (1945)
d Gilbert Gunn
VC

HOUSING PROBLEMS (1935)
d Arthur Elton, Edgar Anstey
VC

HOUSING PROGRESS (1937)
d Matthew Nathan
VC

HOW A BICYCLE IS MADE (1945)
d Norman Lee
VC

HOW HE LIED TO HER HUSBAND (1931)
d Cecil Lewis
VC

HOW TALKIES TALK (1934)
d Donald Carter
VC

HOW THE DAILY MAIL IS PRODUCED (1930)
VC

HOW THE DIAL WORKS (1937)
VC

HOW THE TELEPHONE WORKS (1938)
d J D Chambers, Ralph Elton
VC

HOW TO COOK (1937)
d J B Holmes
VC

HOW TO COOK GREEN VEGETABLES (1944)
d Andrew Buchanan
VC

HOW TO DIG (1941)
d Jack Ellitt
VC

HOW TO FIT A GAS MASK (1939)
VC

HOW TO SAVE SOAP (1942)
VC

HOW TO TELL (1931)
VC

HOW TO THATCH (1941)
d Ralph Bond
VC

HPO, the (1938)
d Lotte Reiniger
VC

HUNTING TIGERS IN INDIA (1930)
PB

HYGIENE
see
BLOOD (1935)
CIRCULATION (1935)

I AM FROM SIAM (1934)
VC

ICELAND; THE LAND OF ICE AND FIRE (1929)
VC

IDEAL SOUND CINEMAGAZINE NO.361 (1933)
VC

I DIDN'T DO IT (1945)
d Marcel Varnel
SC PB

IF I WERE BOSS (1938)
d Maclean Rogers
PB

IF WAR SHOULD COME (1939)
VC

I GIVE MY HEART (1935)
d Marcel Varnel
VC

IGNITION; INSTRUCTIONAL FILM NO.5 (1942)
VC

I KNOW WHERE I'M GOING! (1945)
d Michael Powell, Emeric Pressburger
VC PB

I LIVED WITH YOU (1933)
d Maurice Elvey
VC

I LIVE IN GROSVENOR SQUARE (1945)
d Herbert Wilcox
VC SC

I'LL BE YOUR SWEETHEART (1945)
d Val Guest
VC

I LOVE A LASSIE (Harry Lauder Songs series) (1931)
d George Pearson
VC

ILP SUMMER SCHOOL (1935)
VC

I MET A MURDERER (1939)
d Roy Kellino
VC PB

IMMORTAL GENTLEMAN, the (1935)
d Widgey R Newman
VC

IMMORTAL SWAN, the (1935)
d Edward Nakhimoff
VC

IMPASSIVE FOOTMAN, the (1932)
d Basil Dean
SC PB

IMPRESSIONS OF DISRAELI (1931)
VC

IMPRESSION TECHNIQUE FOR FRACTURED JAWS (Maxillo-Facial Surgery series) (1942)
VC

IMPROPER DUCHESS, the (1936)
d Harry Hughes
PB

IN A LOTUS GARDEN (1930)
d Fred Paul
PB

INCIDENT IN SHANGHAI (1938)
d John Paddy Carstairs
PB

INDIAN CONVOY (1940)
VC

INDIA'S NAVY GROWS (1941)
VC

INDISCRETIONS OF EVE (1932)
d Cecil Lewis
VC

INDUSTRIAL BRITAIN (1931)
d Robert Flaherty
VC

IN ENEMY HANDS (1942)
VC

INFATUATION (1930)
d Sasha Geneen
VC

INFECTED FRACTURE OF THE LEFT ANGLE, an (Maxillo-Facial Surgery series) (1942)
VC

INFORMER, the (1929)
d Arthur Robison
VC

INLAND VOYAGE; OBAN TO INVERNESS, the (1937)
d John C Elder
VC

INNOCENTS OF CHICAGO, the (1932)
d Lupino Lane
VC SC

IN OUR TIME (1933)
d Aveling Ginever
VC

INQUEST (1939)
d Roy Boulting
VC PB

INSIDE GOODS (1938)
VC

INSPECTOR HORNLEIGH (1939)
d Eugene Forde
PB

INSPECTOR HORNLEIGH GOES TO IT (1941)
d Walter Forde
VC PB

INSPECTOR HORNLEIGH ON HOLIDAY (1939)
d Walter Forde
PB

INTERNATIONAL BRIGADE (1938)
VC

INTERRUPTED HONEYMOON, the (1936)
d Leslie Hiscott
PB

IN THE ARENA (Secrets of India series) (1934)
d Geoffrey Barkas
VC PB

IN THE CAUSE OF CHARITY AND GOOD BOXING (1931)
VC

IN THE HEART OF THE COTSWOLDS: CHELTENHAM (1929)
VC

IN THE LAND OF THE TOBAS (1930)
VC

IN THE SOUP (1936)
d Henry Edwards
VC PB

INTIMATE RELATIONS (1937)
d Clayton Hutton
PB

INTO BATTLE series
see
LIFT YOUR HEAD, COMRADE (1942)
THESE ARE THE MEN (1943)

IN TOWN TONIGHT (1936)
VC

INTRAVENOUS ANAESTHESIA (The Technique of Anaesthesia series) (1944)
d Yvonne Fletcher
VC

INTRODUCING LADY CRIPPS (1942)
VC

INTRODUCING – ROGERSON HALL (1938)
VC

INVADER, the (1936)
d Adrian Brunel
PB

INVISIBLE ENEMY, the (1931)
VC

INVITATION TO THE WALTZ (1935)
d Paul Merzbach
VC SC

IN WHICH WE LIVE (1943)
d Richard Massingham
VC

IN WHICH WE SERVE (1942)
d David Lean, Noël Coward
VC SC

IRISH FOR LUCK (1936)
d Arthur Woods
PB

IRON DUKE, the (1935)
d Victor Saville
VC PB

I SEE ICE! (1938)
d Anthony Kimmins
SC

ISLANDERS, the (1939)
d Maurice Harvey
VC

ISLAND PEOPLE (1940)
VC

I SPY (1933)
d Allan Dwan
VC

IT ALL DEPENDS ON YOU (1942)
d T R Thumwood
VC

IT COMES FROM COAL (1940)
d Paul Fletcher
VC

I THANK YOU (1941)
d Marcel Varnel
VC SC

IT HAPPENED IN PARIS (1935)
d Carol Reed, Robert Wyler
VC PB

IT HAPPENED ONE SUNDAY (1944)
d Carl Lamac
PB

IT MIGHT BE YOU...! (1938)
d Major Lloyd
VC

IT'S A BET (1935)
d Alexandre Esway
VC SC

IT'S A BOY! (1933)
d Tim Whelan
VC

IT'S A COP (1934)
d Maclean Rogers
PB

IT'S A GRAND OLD WORLD (1937)
d Herbert Smith
PB

IT'S A KING (1932)
d Jack Raymond
PB

IT'S IN THE AIR (1938)
d Anthony Kimmins
VC PB

IT'S IN THE BAG (1936)
d William Beaudine
VC

IT'S IN THE BLOOD (1938)
d Gene Gerrard
PB

IT'S JUST THE WAY IT IS (1943)
d Leslie Fenton
VC

IT'S LOVE AGAIN (1936)
d Victor Saville
VC PB

IT'S NOT CRICKET (1937)
d Ralph Ince
PB

IT'S THAT MAN AGAIN (1943)
d Walter Forde
VC

I'VE GOT A HORSE (1938)
d Herbert Smith
PB

IVORY GATE (1932)
VC

I WANT TO BE AN ACTRESS (1943)
VC

I WAS A SPY (1933)
d Victor Saville
VC PB

JACK AHOY! (1934)
d Walter Forde
SC PB

JACK COURTNEY AT THE COMPTON ORGAN (1935)
VC

JACK LONDON VS BRUCE WOODCOCK (1945)
VC

JACK OF ALL TRADES (1936)
d Jack Hulbert, Robert Stevenson
VC SC

JACK PETERSEN V LEN HARVEY (1935)
VC

JACK'S THE BOY (1932)
d Walter Forde
VC PB

JACK TAR AFLOAT AND ASHORE (1931)
VC

JAILBIRDS (1939)
d Oswald Mitchell
PB

JAMAICA INN (1939)
d Alfred Hitchcock
VC SC

JAMAICAN HARVEST (1938)
d A Frank Bundy
VC

JANE STEPS OUT (1938)
d Paul L Stein
PB

JAVA HEAD (1934)
d J Walter Ruben
VC PB

JAZZ TIME (1929)
d R E Jeffrey
VC

JCB 1920 (1933)
VC

JEANNIE (1941)
d Harold French
VC

JERICHO (1937)
d Thornton Freeland
VC

JERUSALEM AND BETHLEHEM ARE VISITED FROM JAFFA (1929)
VC

JESSIE MATTHEWS (Gaumont-British Starlet series) (1937)
VC

JEWEL, the (1933)
d Reginald Denham
PB

JEW SÜSS (1934)
d Lothar Mendes
VC SC

JOB IN A MILLION, a (1937)
d Evelyn Spice
VC

JOB TO BE DONE, a (1940)
d Donald Alexander
VC

JOE'S GOT A SAUCE (1942)
VC

JOHN ATKINS SAVES UP (1934)
d Arthur Elton
VC

JOHN HALIFAX, GENTLEMAN (1938)
d George King
VC

JOHNNY FRENCHMAN (1945)
d Charles Frend
VC PB

JOHN SMITH WAKES UP (1940)
d Jiří Weiss
PB

JOHN THE BULL (1930)
VC

JOLLY FARMERS, the (1930)
d R E Jeffrey
VC

JOSSER IN THE ARMY (1932)
d Norman Lee
SC

JOSSER JOINS THE NAVY (1932)
d Norman Lee
VC SC

JOSSER ON THE RIVER (1932)
d Norman Lee
SC

JOURNEY TOGETHER (1945)
d John Boulting
VC PB

JOY LOADER AND SHUTTLE CAR, the (1945)
VC

JOY RIDE (1935)
d Harry Hughes
VC SC

J QUARMBY AND SON (1939)
VC

JUBILEE (1935)
VC

JUBILEE WINDOW (1935)
d George Pearson
PB

JUGGERNAUT (1936)
d Henry Edwards
VC PB

JULIUS CAESAR (Famous Scenes from Shakespeare series) (1945)
d Henry Cass
VC

JUMP FOR GLORY (1937)
d Raoul Walsh
VC

JUNGLE MARINERS (1945)
d Ralph Elton
VC

JUNO AND THE PAYCOCK (1930)
d Alfred Hitchcock
VC PB

JURY'S EVIDENCE (1936)
d Ralph Ince
VC

JUST FEET – HERS AND HIS (Eve's Film Review series) (1930)
VC

JUST LIKE A WOMAN (1938)
d Paul L Stein
PB

JUST SMITH (1933)
d Tom Walls
SC PB

JUST WILLIAM (1939)
d Graham Cutts
VC

KAMALAM (1935)
VC

KAMET CONQUERED; AN EPIC ADVENTURE ON THE ROOF OF THE WORLD (1932)
d F S Smythe
VC

KATE PLUS TEN (1938)
d Reginald Denham
VC PB

KATHLEEN MAVOURNEEN (1937)
d Norman Lee
VC

KATMANDU (Secrets of India series) (1934)
d Geoffrey Barkas
VC PB

KEEPERS OF YOUTH (1931)
d Thomas Bentley
SC

KEEP FIT (1937)
d Anthony Kimmins
PB

KEEP SMILING (1938)
d Monty Banks
VC PB

KEEP YOUR SEATS, PLEASE (1936)
d Monty Banks
VC PB

KENSINGTON CALLING (1935)
VC

KENTUCKY MINSTRELS (1934)
d John Baxter
VC

KEY TO HARMONY (1935)
d Norman Walker
PB

KEY TO SCOTLAND, the (1935)
d Marion Grierson
VC

KILLING FARM RATS (1944)
d Graham Wallace
VC

KILL OR BE KILLED (1943)
d Len Lye
VC

KING ARTHUR WAS A GENTLEMAN (1942)
d Marcel Varnel
VC

KING OF HEARTS (1936)
d Oswald Mitchell, Walter Tennyson
PB

KING OF PARIS, the (1934)
d Jack Raymond
VC

KING OF THE CASTLE (1936)
d Redd Davis
PB

KING OF THE DAMNED (1936)
d Walter Forde
VC PB

KING OF THE KEYBOARD; A GREAT ENGLISH PIANIST, ARTHUR DULAY (1943)
d Phil Oakes
VC

KING'S BREAKFAST, the (1937)
d Lotte Reiniger
PB

KING'S CUP, the (1933)
d Herbert Wilcox
VC PB

KING'S MEN, the (1940)
VC

KING SOLOMON'S MINES (1937)
d Robert Stevenson
VC SC

KING'S STAMP, the (1935)
d William Coldstream
VC

KING WITH A TERRIBLE TEMPER, the (1937)
d Anson Dyer
VC

KING WITH THE TERRIBLE HICCUPS, the (1937)
d Anson Dyer
VC

KIPPS (1941)
d Carol Reed
VC

KISSING CUP'S RACE (1930)
d Castleton Knight
PB

KITTY (1929)
d Victor Saville
VC SC PB

KNIGHT WITHOUT ARMOUR (1937)
d Jacques Feyder
VC PB

KNOWING MEN (1930)
d Elinor Glyn
VC

KOENIGSMARK (1936)
d Maurice Tourneur
PB

KUANYAMA: MEDICINE WOMEN INITIATION (1936)
d P H G Powell-Cotton
VC

KUANYAMA: POTTER'S METHODS IN BUILDING POTS (1936)
d P H G Powell-Cotton
VC

KUANYAMA: SKINNING AND DRESSING SKINS (1936)
d P H G Powell-Cotton
VC

KUKUKUKU (1937)
VC

LABURNUM GROVE (1936)
d Carol Reed
VC PB

LADDIE'S DAY OUT (1939)
d Lance Comfort
PB

LADY BE KIND (1941)
d Rodney Ackland
VC

LADY FROM THE SEA, the (1929)
d Castleton Knight
VC

LADY IN DANGER (1934)
d Tom Walls
VC SC

LADY INTO FOX (1945)
VC

LADY IS WILLING, the (1934)
d Gilbert Miller
PB

LADY VANISHES, the (1938)
d Alfred Hitchcock
VC PB

LAMBETH WALK, the (1939)
d Albert de Courville
PB

LAMP STILL BURNS, the (1943)
d Maurice Elvey
VC PB

LANCASHIRE, HOME OF INDUSTRY (1935)
d Donald Taylor
VC

LANCASHIRE LUCK (1937)
d Henry Cass
PB

LAND GIRL (1942)
d John Page
VC

LAND OF INVENTION (1941)
d Andrew Buchanan
VC

LAND OF RHODES, the (1938)
VC PB

LAND OF THE BOOK, the (1941)
VC

LAND OF THE SPRINGBOK (1945)
VC

LAND OF THE VIKINGS (1933)
d C E Hodges
VC

LANDSLIDE (1937)
d Donovan Pedelty
PB

LAND WITHOUT MUSIC (1936)
d Walter Forde
VC PB

LANGFORD REED'S LIMERICKS (1935)
d A F C Barrington
PB

LASH, the (1934)
d Henry Edwards
PB

LASSIE FROM LANCASHIRE (1938)
d John Paddy Carstairs
SC

LAST ADVENTURERS, the (1937)
d Roy Kellino
VC PB

LAST COUPON, the (1932)
d Thomas Bentley
VC

LAST CURTAIN, the (1937)
d David Macdonald
PB

LAST JOURNEY, the (1935)
d Bernard Vorhaus
VC

LAST SHOT, the (1945)
d John Ferno
VC

LAST WALTZ, the (1936)
d Leo Mittler, Gerald Barry
VC

LATIN QUARTER (1945)
d Vernon Sewell
PB

LAUGH IT OFF (1940)
d John Baxter
VC

LAUNCHING A SHIP (1936)
VC

LAURENCE OLIVIER HOME MOVIES (1932)
VC

LAZYBONES (1934)
d Michael Powell
VC PB

LEADED LIGHTS (1936)
VC

LEARNING A JOB (1944)
d Andrew Buchanan
VC

LEARNING TO LIVE (1943)
d Harold Purcell
VC

LEAVE IT TO ME (1933)
d Monty Banks
VC SC

LEND ME YOUR HUSBAND (1935)
d Frederick Hayward
VC PB

LESSONS FROM THE AIR (1944)
d Harold Purcell, James E Rogers
VC

LEST WE FORGET (1934)
d John Baxter
SC

LET GEORGE DO IT! (1940)
d Marcel Varnel
VC SC

LET ME EXPLAIN DEAR (1932)
d Gene Gerrard
SC

LET'S BE FAMOUS (1939)
d Walter Forde
VC SC

LET'S LOVE AND LAUGH (1931)
d Richard Eichberg
VC SC

LET'S MAKE A NIGHT OF IT (1937)
d Graham Cutts
VC SC

LET'S SEE (1945)
d Robert Le Presle
VC

LETTER FROM HOME (1941)
d Carol Reed
VC

LETTER FROM ULSTER, a (1943)
d Brian Desmond Hurst
VC

LETTER OF WARNING, a (1932)
d John Daumery
PB

LETTERS TO LINERS (1937)
VC

LET THE PEOPLE SING (1942)
d John Baxter
VC PB

LETTING IN THE SUNSHINE (1933)
d Lupino Lane
VC

LIFE (1933)
VC

LIFE AND DEATH OF COLONEL BLIMP, the (1942)
d Michael Powell, Emeric Pressburger
VC PB

LIFE BEGINS AGAIN (1942)
d Donald Alexander
VC

LIFE CYCLE OF THE MAIZE, the (1942)
d Mary Field
VC

LIFE CYCLE OF THE NEWT, the (1942)
d Mary Field
VC

LIFE CYCLE OF THE PIN MOULD, the (1942)
d Mary Field
VC

LIFE HISTORY OF THE ONION, the (1944)
d Mary Field
VC

LIFE IN HUNZA (1938)
VC

LIFE ON LAND AND SEA IN BRITAIN (1939)
VC

LIFTING (1943)
d George Wynn
VC

LIFT THE BLACKOUT (1941)
VC

LIFT YOUR HEAD, COMRADE (Into Battle series) (1942)
d Michael Hankinson
VC

LIGHTNING CONDUCTOR (1938)
d Maurice Elvey
VC PB

LIGHTS O' LONDON (1938)
VC

LILAC DOMINO, the (1937)
d Fred Zelnik
VC

LILY CHRISTINE (1932)
d Paul L Stein
PB

LILY MORRIS – 'WHY AM I ALWAYS THE BRIDESMAID?' (1930)
VC

LILY OF KILLARNEY (1934)
d Maurice Elvey
VC

LIMELIGHT (1936)
d Herbert Wilcox
VC PB

LIMPING MAN, the (1936)
d Walter Summers
PB

LINE ENGAGED (1935)
d Bernard Mainwaring
PB

LINER CRUISING SOUTH (1933)
d Basil Wright
VC

LINE TO THE TSCHIERVA HUT (1937)
d Alberto Cavalcanti
VC

LION HAS WINGS, the (1939)
d Michael Powell, Brian Desmond Hurst, Adrian Brunel
VC SC

LION OF JUDAH, the (1941)
d Eric Boothby
VC

LISTEN TO BRITAIN (1942)
d Humphrey Jennings, Stewart McAllister
VC

LITTLE ANNIE'S RAG BOOK (1942)
d L Bradshaw
VC

LITTLE DAMOZEL, the (1932)
d Herbert Wilcox
PB

LITTLE FELLA (1932)
d William McGann
PB

LITTLE FRIEND (1934)
d Berthold Viertel
VC SC

LITTLE MISS SOMEBODY (1937)
d Walter Tennyson
PB

LITTLE SHIPS OF ENGLAND, the (1943)
VC

LITTLE STRANGER (1934)
d George King
VC

LIVERPOOL – GATEWAY OF EMPIRE (1933)
VC

LIVING DANGEROUSLY (1936)
d Herbert Brenon
VC

LIVING IN THE NETHERLANDS (1937)
d George H Green
VC

LLOYD OF THE CID (1931)
d Henry MacRea
PB

LOBSTERS (1936)
d John Mathias, László Moholy-Nagy
VC SC PB

LOCAL GOVERNMENT (1944)
d Bernard Mainwaring
VC

LOCOMOTIVES (1934)
d Humphrey Jennings
VC

LONDON (1933)
VC

LONDON AUTUMN 1941 (1941)
VC

LONDON CAN TAKE IT (1940)
d Harry Watt, Humphrey Jennings
VC

LONDONDERRY AIR, the (1938)
d Alex Bryce
PB

LONDONERS, the (1939)
d John Taylor
VC

LONDON FIRE RAIDS 29TH–30TH DECEMBER 1940 (1940)
VC

LONDON MAY 7TH 1933. THE WORKERS UNITED FRONT IN ACTION (1933)
VC

LONDON 1942 (1942)
d Ken Annakin
VC

LONDON ON PARADE (1937)
VC

LONDON PIGEON, the (1940)
d Mary Field
VC

LONDON PRIDE (1945)
VC

LONDON RIVER (1939)
d Andrew Buchanan
VC

LONDON SCRAPBOOK (1942)
d Derrick de Marney, Eugene Cekalski
VC

LONDON'S REPLY TO GERMANY'S FALSE CLAIMS (1940)
VC

LONDON'S RIVER (FROM WESTMINSTER TO WOOLWICH) (1936)
VC

LONDON TERMINUS (1943)
d George A Cooper
VC

LONDON TOWN (1933)
d Marion Grierson
VC

LONDON WORKERS OUTING, HIGH BEECH (1935)
VC

LONELY ROAD, the (1936)
d James Flood
VC

LOOKING ON THE BRIGHT SIDE (1932)
d Basil Dean, Graham Cutts
VC

LOOKING THROUGH GLASS (1943)
d Cecil Musk
VC

LOOK UP AND LAUGH (1935)
d Basil Dean
VC

LOOSE ENDS (1930)
d Norman Walker
VC

LORD BURLEIGH (1931)
VC

LORD CAMBER'S LADIES (1932)
d Benn W Levy
VC PB

LORD EDGWARE DIES (1934)
d Henry Edwards
VC

LORD HURST OF WITTON. ELECTRICAL ENGINEERING INDUSTRIAL PIONEER (1936)
VC

LORD OF THE MANOR (1933)
d Henry Edwards
PB

LORNA DOONE (1934)
d Basil Dean
VC SC

LOST CHORD, the (1933)
d Maurice Elvey
VC PB

LOST PRIZE, the (1930)
d H P Tarrant
VC

LOUIS V FARR FIGHT, the (1937)
VC

LOVE AT SEA (1936)
d Adrian Brunel
VC

LOVE AT SECOND SIGHT (1934)
d Paul Merzbach
SC PB

LOVE FROM A STRANGER (1937)
d Rowland V Lee
VC PB

LOVE IN EXILE (1936)
d Alfred Werker
VC PB

LOVE LIES (1931)
d Lupino Lane
VC PB

LOVE, LIFE AND LAUGHTER (1934)
d Maurice Elvey
SC

LOVE ON LEAVE (1940)
d Horace Shepherd
VC

LOVE ON THE DOLE (1941)
d John Baxter
VC PB

LOVE ON THE RANGE (1939)
d George Pál
VC

LOVE ON THE WING (1939)
d Norman McLaren
VC

LOVE ON WHEELS (1932)
d Victor Saville
VC

LOVES OF ROBERT BURNS, the (1930)
d Herbert Wilcox
VC

LOVE STORY (1944)
d Leslie Arliss
VC PB

LOVE TEST, the (1935)
d Michael Powell
VC

LOVE UP THE POLE (1936)
d Clifford Gulliver
PB

LOVE WAGER, the (1933)
d A Cyran
PB

LOWLAND VILLAGE (1942)
d Darrel Catling
VC

LOYALTIES (1933)
d Basil Dean
VC

LUBRICATION OF THE PETROL ENGINE (1937)
d Grahame Tharp
VC

LUCK OF THE IRISH, the (1935)
d Donovan Pedelty
PB

LUCK OF THE TURF, the (1936)
d Randall Faye
PB

LUCKY DAYS (1936)
d Reginald Denham
PB

LUCKY DOGS (1935)
d R W Lotinga
PB

LUCKY JADE (1937)
d Walter Summers
VC PB

LUCKY NUMBER, the (1933)
d Anthony Asquith
VC SC

LUCKY SWEEP, a (1931)
d A V Bramble
PB

LUCKY TO ME (1939)
d Thomas Bentley
VC

LURE, the (1933)
d Arthur Maude
PB

LYONS MAIL, the (1931)
d Arthur Maude
PB

MACBETH (Famous Scenes from Shakespeare series) (1945)
d Henry Cass
VC

MACHYNLLETH (Pathé Pictorial series) (1929)
VC

MAD HATTERS, the (1935)
d Ivar Campbell
PB

MADONNA OF THE SEVEN MOONS (1944)
d Arthur Crabtree
VC PB

MADRID TODAY (1937)
VC

MAGIC MYXIES (Secrets of Nature series) (1931)
  d Mary Field
  VC

MAGNIFICENT BERLIN (1930)
  VC

MAID OF THE MOUNTAINS, the (1932)
  d Lupino Lane
  VC PB

MAJOR BARBARA (1941)
  d Gabriel Pascal
  VC PB

MAJOR GENERAL THE EARL OF SCARBOROUGH (1931)
  VC

MAKE UP (1937)
  d Alfred Zeisler
  PB

MAKING A COMPOST HEAP (1941)
  d Margaret Thomson
  VC

MAKING A MIRROR (1936)
  VC

MAKING FASHION (1938)
  d Humphrey Jennings
  VC

MAKING GRASS SILAGE (1943)
  d Margaret Thomson
  VC

MAKING OF WEDGWOOD, the (1938)
  d Darrel Catling
  VC

MALARIA (1941)
  d Grahame Tharp
  VC

MAN AT SIX, the (1931)
  d Harry Hughes
  PB

MAN AT THE GATE, the (1941)
  d Norman Walker
  VC

MAN BEHIND THE MASK, the (1936)
  d Michael Powell
  PB

MANCHESTER ACHIEVEMENT, a (1934)
  VC

MAN FROM CHICAGO, the (1930)
  d Walter Summers
  PB

MAN FROM MOROCCO, the (1945)
  d Max Greene
  VC PB

MAN FROM TORONTO, the (1933)
  d Sinclair Hill
  VC

MANIFOLD VALLEY LIGHT RAILWAY, the (1932)
  VC

MAN IN GREY, the (1943)
  d Leslie Arliss
  VC

MAN IN THE MIRROR, the (1936)
  d Maurice Elvey
  VC PB

MAN I WANT, the (1934)
  d Leslie Hiscott
  PB

MAN OF ARAN (1934)
  d Robert Flaherty
  VC SC

MAN OF MAYFAIR (1931)
  d Louis Mercanton
  PB

MAN OF THE HOUR; THE RT HON NEVILLE CHAMBERLAIN MP, the (1938)
  VC

MAN OF THE MOMENT (1935)
  d Monty Banks
  VC PB

MAN ON THE BEAT, the (1944)
  d Roger McDougall
  VC

MAN OR MACHINE? (Point of View series) (1941)
  VC

MANUFACTURE OF COPPER RODS AND OTHER ACTIVITIES AT THE ENFIELD ROLLING MILLS AND CABLE WORKS, the (1933)
  VC

MANUFACTURE OF GAS, the (1938)
  d Frank Sainsbury
  VC

MAN WHO CHANGED HIS MIND, the (1936)
  d Robert Stevenson
  VC SC

MAN WHO COULD WORK MIRACLES, the (1936)
  d Lothar Mendes
  VC PB

MAN WHO KNEW TOO MUCH, the (1934)
  d Alfred Hitchcock
  VC PB

MAN WHO MADE DIAMONDS, the (1937)
  d Ralph Ince
  PB

MAN WITH THE NOTEBOOK, the (1944)
  VC

MAN WITHOUT A FACE, the (1935)
  d George King
  VC PB

MANXMAN, the (1929)
  d Alfred Hitchcock
  VC

MANY TANKS MR ATKINS (1938)
  d Roy William Neill
  VC

MARCH AGAINST STARVATION (1936)
  VC

MARCH OF HEALTH (1936)
  VC

MARIGOLD (1938)
  d Thomas Bentley
  VC SC

MARKET TOWN (1942)
  d Mary Field
  VC

MAROONED (1933)
  d Leslie Hiscott
  PB

MARRIAGE BOND, the (1932)
  d Maurice Elvey
  PB

MARRIAGE OF CORBAL, the (1936)
  d Karl Grune
  PB

MARRY ME (1932)
  d Wilhelm Thiele
  VC SC

MARRY THE GIRL (1935)
  d Maclean Rogers
  PB

MARS AND VENUS (1931)
  VC

MASTERY OF THE SEA (1940)
  d Alberto Cavalcanti
  VC

MASTITIS (The Health of Dairy Cattle series) (1945)
  VC

MATERNITY AND CHILD WELFARE (1930)
  d H W Bush
  VC

MATTER OF GOOD TASTE, a (1930)
  d George Dewhurst
  VC

MAUDE LLOYD – 'LA BELLE ECUYERE' (1931)
  VC

MAXILLO-FACIAL SURGERY series
  see
  CONTROL OF EDENTULOUS POSTERIOR FRAGMENT BY SURGICAL WIRING, the (1942)
  CRUSH FRACTURE OF THE MIDDLE THIRD OF THE FACE (1942)
  IMPRESSION TECHNIQUE FOR FRACTURED JAWS (1942)
  INFECTED FRACTURE OF THE LEFT ANGLE, an (1942)
  TECHNIQUE OF ARCH WIRING FOR FRACTURED JAWS, the (1942)
  TECHNIQUE OF EYELET WIRING, the (1942)
  TECHNIQUE OF INTER-MAXILLARY FIXATION BY DIRECT WIRING, the (1942)
  TECHNIQUE USED IN CONSTRUCTION OF CAST METAL CAP SPLINTS, the (1942)
  TREATMENT OF FIBROUS NON-UNION BY BONE CHIPS (1942)
  TREATMENT OF A GUNSHOT WOUND OF THE MANDIBLE (1942)
  TREATMENT OF A GUNSHOT WOUND OF THE MANDIBLE WITH EXTENSIVE LOSS OF BONE (1942)

MAYFAIR GIRL (1933)
  d George King
  PB

MAYFAIR MELODY (1937)
  d Arthur Woods
  PB

MAY THE FIRST, 1937 (1937)
  VC

McGLUSKY THE SEA ROVER (1935)
  d Walter Summers
  PB

MEADOW ANT, the (1943)
  VC

ME AND MARLBOROUGH (1935)
  d Victor Saville
  VC

ME AND MY PAL (1939)
  d Thomas Bentley
  VC

MECO-MOORE CUTTER LOADER (1945)
  VC

MEDAL FOR THE GENERAL (1944)
  d Maurice Elvey
  PB

MEDIAEVAL VILLAGE (1936)
d J B Holmes
VC

MEDICAL TALK ON A SERIOUS PROBLEM, a (1939)
VC

MEDITERRANEAN ISLAND, a (1932)
VC

MEET GEORGE (Pathé Pictorial series) (1931)
VC

MEET ME AT EIGHT (1945)
VC

MEET MR PENNY (1938)
d David Macdonald
VC SC

MEET MR YORK! A SPEAKING LIKENESS (1929)
d Joe Noble, Bertram Phillips
VC

MEET MY SISTER (1933)
d John Daumery
VC

MEET SEXTON BLAKE (1944)
d John Harlow
PB

MEET THE OVALTINEYS (1937)
VC

MELODY AND ROMANCE (1937)
d Maurice Elvey
PB

MEMBER OF THE JURY (1937)
d Bernard Mainwaring
PB

MEMORIES (Secrets of Life series) (1944)
VC

MEN ARE NOT GODS (1936)
d Walter Reisch
VC PB

MEN BEHIND THE METERS (1936)
d Edgar Anstey
VC

MEN IN DANGER (1939)
d Pat Jackson
VC

MEN LIKE THESE (1931)
d Walter Summers
VC

MEN OF AFRICA (1940)
d Alexander Shaw
VC

MEN OF STEEL (1932)
d George King
VC

MEN OF THE ALPS (1937)
d Alberto Cavalcanti
VC

MEN OF THE FOOTPLATE (1939)
VC

MEN OF THE LIGHTSHIP (1940)
d David Macdonald
VC

MEN OF TOMORROW (1932)
d Leontine Sagan
PB

MEN OF YESTERDAY (1936)
d John Baxter
PB

MEN WHO WORK (1935)
VC

MEN WITHOUT HONOUR (1939)
d Widgey R Newman
VC

MERCHANT SEAMEN (1941)
d J B Holmes
VC

MERLIN, the (Secrets of Nature series) (1930)
d Mary Field
VC

MERSEYSIDE (1941)
VC

MESSAGE FROM CANTERBURY (1944)
d George Hoellering
VC

MESSAGE FROM GENEVA (1936)
d Alberto Cavalcanti
VC

MESSAGE OF THE DRUM, the (1930)
d Walter Creighton
VC

MESSENGER BOY (1937)
VC

METHODS OF COMMUNICATION (1934)
VC

MICHAEL AND MARY (1931)
d Victor Saville
VC

MICHAEL FARADAY 1791–1867 (1931)
VC

MIDDLE EAST (1942)
d Grahame Tharp
VC

MIDDLE WATCH, the (1939)
d Thomas Bentley
SC PB

MIDNIGHT AT MADAME TUSSAUD'S (1936)
d George Pearson
PB

MIDNIGHT MENACE (1937)
d Sinclair Hill
VC SC

MIDSHIPMAID, the (1932)
d Albert de Courville
VC SC

MIDSHIPMAN EASY (1935)
d Carol Reed
VC SC

MIDSUMMER DAY'S WORK (1939)
d Alberto Cavalcanti
VC

MIGHTY ATOM (1934)
VC

MIKADO, the (1938)
d Victor Schertzinger
VC PB

MILLIONS LIKE US (1943)
d Frank Launder, Sidney Gilliat
VC PB

MIMI (1935)
d Paul L Stein
VC PB

MIND OF MR REEDER, the (1939)
d Jack Raymond
SC PB

MINING AND SMELTING OF IRON: KUANYAMA (OVAMBO GROUP) (1937)
d P H G Powell-Cotton
VC

MINING REVIEW NO.5 (1945)
VC

MINISTER OF THE INTERIOR (1943)
VC

MINOR MINERS (1934)
VC

MINSTREL BOY, the (1937)
d Sidney Morgan
PB

MIRACLES DO HAPPEN (1938)
d Maclean Rogers
VC

MISS GRANT GOES TO THE DOOR (1940)
d Brian Desmond Hurst
VC

MISSING PEOPLE, the (1939)
d Jack Raymond
PB

MISSING RECORD, the (1936)
VC

MR ATTLEE IN SPAIN (1938)
VC

MR BILL THE CONQUEROR (1932)
d Norman Walker
VC

MR BORLAND THINKS AGAIN (1940)
d Paul Rotha
VC

MR CHAMBERLAIN SPEAKING AT THE ALBERT HALL (1937)
VC

MISTER CINDERS (1934)
d Fred Zelnik
VC

MR EMMANUEL (1944)
d Harold French
PB

MR ENGLISH AT HOME (1940)
d Gordon Hales
VC

MR PROUDFOOT SHOWS A LIGHT (1941)
d Herbert Mason
VC

MR REEDER IN ROOM 13 (1938)
d Norman Lee
VC PB

MR SATAN (1937)
d Arthur Woods
VC PB

MR SMITH WAKES UP! (1929)
d Jack Harrison
VC

MR STRINGFELLOW SAYS NO (1937)
d Randall Faye
PB

MR WHAT'S-HIS-NAME (1935)
d Ralph Ince
PB

MR WILLIAM MORRIS MORDEY (Eminent Scientists series) (1934)
VC

MRS DANE'S DEFENCE (1933)
d A V Bramble
PB

MRS MOPP ASKS WHY (1943)
VC

MRS MOPP'S BIRTHDAY (1942)
VC

MRS PYM OF SCOTLAND YARD (1939)
d Fred Elles
PB

MRS RAWLINS (1931)
VC

MIXED DOUBLES (1933)
d Sidney Morgan
PB

MIXING WITH THE MURGATROYDS (1943)
VC

MOBILE CANTEEN (1941)
d Jay Lewis
VC

MODEL HUSBANDS (1945)
VC

MODEL MASTER, the (Pathé Pictorial series) (1931)
VC

MODERN ASEPTIC SURGERY TECHNIQUE (1938)
d J Barlow
VC

MODERN LAUNDRY, a (1935)
VC

MODERN ORPHANS OF THE STORM (1937)
VC

MODERN STEELCRAFT (1938)
d Darrel Catling
VC

MONEY FOR NOTHING (1931)
d Monty Banks
SC PB

MONEY FOR SPEED (1933)
d Bernard Vorhaus
PB

MONEY MEANS NOTHING (1932)
d Harcourt Templeman, Herbert Wilcox
PB

MONEY TALKS (1932)
d Norman Lee
PB

MONKEY INTO MAN (1938)
d Stanley Hawes
VC

MONSOON ISLAND (1934)
VC

MOONLIGHT SONATA (1937)
d Lothar Mendes
VC PB

MORALS OF MARCUS, the (1935)
d Miles Mander
VC

MORE EGGS FROM YOUR HENS (1942)
d James E Rogers
VC

MORNING PAPER (1942)
d Darrel Catling
VC

MOROCCO POTTER (1936)
d P H G Powell-Cotton
VC

MOSCOW NIGHTS (1935)
d Anthony Asquith
VC PB

MOSQUITOES IN THE MAKING (1945)
VC

MOTHER AND BABY (1943)
VC

MOTHER AND CHILD (1940)
d Frank Sainsbury
VC

MOTORING SKETCH (1930)
VC

MOVEMENT OF RAIN IN A THUNDERSTORM (1933)
d James Fairgrieve
VC

MOVIE MIXTURE (1945)
d E W White
VC

MURDER (1930)
d Alfred Hitchcock
VC

MURDER AT THE CABARET (1936)
d Reginald Fogwell
PB

MURDER IN REVERSE (1945)
d Montgomery Tully
PB

MURDER IN SOHO (1938)
d Norman Lee
PB

MURDER ON THE SECOND FLOOR (1932)
d William McGann
VC

MURDER TOMORROW (1938)
d Donovan Pedelty
PB

MUSEUM MYSTERY (1937)
d Clifford Gulliver
PB

MUSICAL MEDLEY (1930)
VC

MUSICAL MOMENTS; AN INTERLUDE OF SONG AND DANCE (1930)
VC

MUSICAL POSTER NO.1 (1940)
d Len Lye
VC

MUSIC HATH CHARMS (1935)
d Roffe Thompson
VC

MUSIC HATH CHARMS (1935)
d Alexandre Esway, Walter Summers, Arthur Woods, Thomas Bentley
VC PB

MUTINY OF THE ELSINORE, the (1937)
d Roy Lockwood
SC PB

MY FIGHT FOR PROSPERITY (1934)
VC

MY HEART IS CALLING (1934)
d Carmine Gallone
VC SC

MY IRISH MOLLY (1938)
d Alex Bryce
VC SC

MY LEARNED FRIEND (1943)
d Will Hay, Basil Dearden
VC SC

MY LUCKY STAR (1933)
d Louis Blattner, John Harlow
PB

MY OLD CHINA (1931)
d W P Kellino
SC

MY OLD DUCHESS (1933)
d Lupino Lane
SC PB

MY OLD DUTCH (1934)
d Sinclair Hill
VC PB

MYRA HESS (1945)
VC

MY SONG FOR YOU (1934)
d Maurice Elvey
VC PB

MY SONG GOES FORTH (1937)
d Joseph Best
VC

MY SONG GOES ROUND THE WORLD (1934)
d Richard Oswald
VC SC

MYSTERIOUS MR DAVIS, the (1936)
d Claude Autant-Lara
SC

MYSTERY OF MARRIAGE, the (1931)
d Mary Field
VC

MY WIFE'S FAMILY (1931)
d Monty Banks
VC

MY WIFE'S FAMILY (1941)
d Walter C Mycroft
SC

NATIONAL FIRE SERVICE (LONDON REGION) FIGHTS THE FLYING BOMBS, the (1944)
VC

NATION SPRINGS TO ARMS, a (1940)
VC

NATURE'S CHARMS (1933)
VC

NAVAL OPERATIONS (1942)
d Grahame Tharp
VC

NAVY AT WORK, the (1939)
VC

NEED FOR SELF DENIAL, the (1931)
VC

NEGOMBO COAST (1934)
d Basil Wright
VC

NELL GWYN (1934)
d Herbert Wilcox
VC PB

NEMESIS (1929)
d Leslie Eveleigh
VC

NET RESULT (1938)
VC

NETTING SALMON (1938)
VC

NEURO-PSYCHIATRY (1943)
d Michael Hankinson
VC

NEUTRAL PORT (1940)
d Marcel Varnel
PB

NEW ACRES (1941)
d R K Neilson Baxter
VC

NEW BEGINNING, a (1945)
d Stefan Osiecki
VC

NEW BREAD, the (1941)
VC

NEW BRITAIN, the (1940)
d Ralph Keene
VC

NEW BUILDERS (1944)
d Kay Mander
VC

NEW CIVIC CENTRE FOR CONWAY (1937)
VC

NEW CROP, the (1944)
d Ken Annakin
VC

NEW FIELDS FOR INDUSTRY (1939)
d A Frank Bundy
VC

NEW FIRE BOMB, a (1942)
d J B Napier-Bell
VC

NEW GENERATION, the (Secrets of Life series) (1937)
d Mary Field
VC

NEW MILL RADIO, the (1939)
VC

NEW MINE (1945)
d Irene Wilson
VC

NEW OPERATOR, the (1934)
d Stuart Legg
VC

NEW ROAD TRANSPORT TRAIN, a (1932)
VC

NEWS BY WIRE (1939)
VC

NEWSPAPER TRAIN (1942)
d Len Lye
VC

NEW TOWNS FOR OLD (1942)
d John Eldridge
VC

NEW WORLDS FOR OLD (1938)
d Frank Sainsbury
VC

NEXT OF KIN, the (1942)
d Thorold Dickinson
VC SC

NIGHT ALONE (1938)
d Thomas Bentley
VC SC

NIGHT AND DAY (1945)
d Jiří Weiss
VC

NIGHT CLUB QUEEN (1934)
d Bernard Vorhaus
VC

NIGHT HAS EYES, the (1942)
d Leslie Arliss
SC

NIGHTINGALES (1943)
d Derrick de Marney
VC

NIGHT IN MONTMARTRE, a (1931)
d Leslie Hiscott
SC

NIGHT MAIL (1936)
d Harry Watt, Basil Wright
VC

NIGHT OF THE GARTER (1933)
d Jack Raymond
PB

NIGHT OF THE PARTY, the (1934)
d Michael Powell
VC PB

NIGHT PORTER, the (1930)
d Sewell Collins
PB

NIGHT SHIFT (1942)
d J D Chambers
VC

NIGHT TRAIN TO MUNICH (1940)
d Carol Reed
VC PB

NIGHTWATCHMAN'S STORY; A ROMANCE OF INDUSTRY, the (1933)
d Walter Creighton
VC

NIKKO ('SUNSHINE'). ONE OF THE BEAUTY SPOTS OF THE ORIENT (1929)
VC

NINE FOR SIX (1939)
VC

NINE HUNDRED, the (1945)
d Jerrold Krimsky
VC

NINE MEN (1942)
d Harry Watt
VC SC

19 METRE BAND (1941)
d William MacQuitty
VC

1938 HOSPITAL CARNIVAL AND AROUND THE TOWN (1938)
VC

1930 TT (1930)
VC

90° SOUTH (1933)
d Herbert G Ponting
VC

NIPPER, the (1930)
d Louis Mercanton
PB

NITROUS OXIDE-OXYGEN-ETHER ANAESTHESIA (The Technique of Anaesthesia series) (1944)
d Margaret Thomson
VC

NOEL (1944)
d Sidney Gausden
VC

NO ESCAPE (1934)
d Ralph Ince
PB

NO ESCAPE (1936)
d Norman Lee
VC PB

NO FUNNY BUSINESS (1933)
d John Stafford, Victor Hanbury
VC PB

NO LADY (1931)
d Lupino Lane
PB

NO MONKEY BUSINESS (1935)
d Marcel Varnel
VC PB

NONQUASSI (Focus on the Empire series) (1939)
d Leon Schauder
VC

NON-STOP NEW YORK (1937)
d Robert Stevenson
SC PB

NO PARKING (1938)
d Jack Raymond
PB

N OR NW (1937)
d Len Lye
VC

NORTHERN OUTPOST (1941)
d Walter Tennyson
VC

NORTHERN PROVINCES (1930)
VC

NORTHERN SUMMER (1934)
d Alexander Shaw
VC

NORTHERN TERRITORIES – THE GOLD COAST, the (The Empire series) (1929)
VC

NORTH SEA (1938)
d Harry Watt
VC

NOSE HAS IT, the (1942)
d Val Guest
VC

NOTES AND NOTIONS (1929)
d R E Jeffrey
VC

NOTHING LIKE PUBLICITY (1936)
d Maclean Rogers
PB

NOT SO QUIET ON THE WESTERN FRONT (1930)
d Monty Banks
SC

NOW YOU'RE TALKING (1940)
d John Paddy Carstairs
VC

NUMBER, PLEASE (1931)
d George King
PB

NUMBER SEVENTEEN (1932)
d Alfred Hitchcock
VC

NO. 6207; A STUDY IN STEEL (1935)
VC

NURSEMAID WHO DISAPPEARED, the (1939)
d Arthur Woods
VC

OBEDIENT FLAME, the (1939)
d Norman McLaren
VC

OBELIA (1936)
d H R Hewer
VC

The Glorious Adventure (J Stuart Blackton, 1922)
Left: souvenir programme. LIS ephemera
Above: from the NFTVA restoration

The Edge of Youth (C C Calvert, 1920) Press-book. LIS

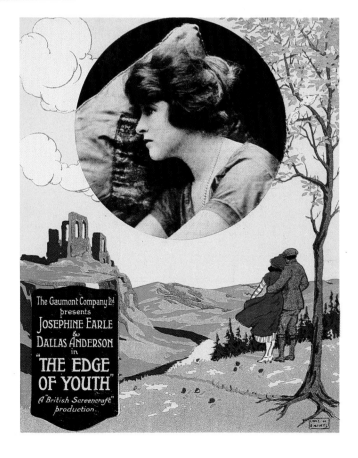

Squibs MP (George Pearson, 1923) Press-book. LIS [932–933]

Mist in the Valley
(Cecil M Hepworth,
1923)

Port Sunlight (1919)

The Prehistoric Man
(A E Coleby, 1924)

Little Red Riding Hood
(Anson Dyer, 1922)

Woman to Woman
(Graham Cutts, 1923)
[453]

The Abbey Grange
(George Ridgewell,
1922)

The Little People
(George Pearson,
1926)

The Tale of a Tendril
(Percy Smith, 1925)

The Epic of Everest
(J B L Noel, 1924)

Boadicea (Sinclair
Hill, 1926)

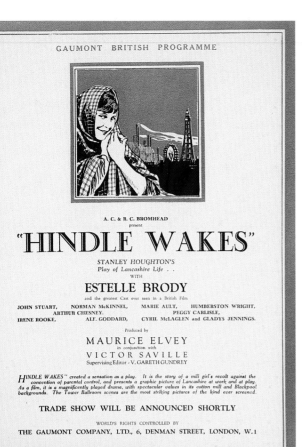

GAUMONT BRITISH PROGRAMME

A. C. & R. C. BROMHEAD
present

"HINDLE WAKES"

STANLEY HOUGHTON'S
Play of Lancashire Life . .
WITH

ESTELLE BRODY

and the greatest Cast ever seen in a British Film

JOHN STUART,   NORMAN McKINNEL,   MARIE AULT,   HUMBERSTON WRIGHT,
ARTHUR CHESNEY.   PEGGY CARLISLE,
IRENE ROOKE,   ALF. GODDARD,   CYRIL McLAGLEN and GLADYS JENNINGS.

Produced by

MAURICE ELVEY

in conjunction with

VICTOR SAVILLE

Supervising Editor - V. GARETH GUNDREY

"HINDLE WAKES" created a sensation as a play. It is the story of a mill girl's revolt against the convention of parental control, and presents a graphic picture of Lancashire at work and at play. As a film, it is a magnificently played drama, with spectacular values in its cotton mill and Blackpool backgrounds. The Tower Ballroom scenes are the most striking pictures of the kind ever screened.

TRADE SHOW WILL BE ANNOUNCED SHORTLY

WORLD'S RIGHTS CONTROLLED BY

THE GAUMONT COMPANY, LTD., 6, DENMAN STREET, LONDON, W.1

Hindle Wakes
(Maurice Elvey, 1927)
Publicity brochure for
Gaumont British
Films. LIS ephemera

Top: *The Vortex*
(Adrian Brunel, 1927)

Champagne (Alfred
Hitchcock, 1928)

Piccadilly (E A
Dupont, 1928)

The King's Highway
(Sinclair Hill, 1927)
Press-book. LIS

BS. 48

NEW ERA
present

MATHESON LANG

in

"The King's Highway"

with
JOAN LOCKTON

STOLL
PRODUCTION

Directed by
SINCLAIR HILL

ODD NUMBERS (1929)
d R E Jeffrey
VC

O'ER HILL AND DALE (1932)
d Basil Wright
VC

OF ALL THE GAY PLACES; AN INTERLUDE IN BATH (1938)
d William Pollard
VC

OFF DUTY (1943)
d Maxwell Munden
VC

OFFICERS' MESS, the (1931)
d Manning Haynes
PB

OFF THE BEATEN TRACK IN GERMANY (1930)
VC

OH, BOY! (1938)
d Albert de Courville
VC SC PB

OH DADDY (1935)
d Graham Cutts, Austin Melford
VC SC

OH, MR PORTER! (1937)
d Marcel Varnel
VC SC

OHMS (1937)
d Raoul Walsh
VC SC

OH NO DOCTOR! (1934)
d George King
VC

OH WHISKERS (1939)
VC

OIL FROM THE EARTH (1938)
d J A D Cartwright
VC

O-KAY FOR SOUND (1937)
d Marcel Varnel
VC SC

OK CHIEF (1931)
d Bernard Mainwaring
VC

OLD BILL AND SON (1940)
d Ian Dalrymple
VC

OLD BONES OF THE RIVER (1938)
d Marcel Varnel
VC SC

OLD CURIOSITY SHOP, the (1935)
d Thomas Bentley
VC PB

OLD IRON (1938)
d Tom Walls
PB

OLD MAN, the (1931)
d Manning Haynes
PB

OLD MOTHER RILEY (1937)
d Oswald Mitchell
PB

OLD MOTHER RILEY AT HOME (1945)
d Oswald Mitchell
VC PB

OLD MOTHER RILEY, DETECTIVE (1943)
d Lance Comfort
VC

OLD MOTHER RILEY IN BUSINESS (1940)
d John Baxter
PB

OLD MOTHER RILEY IN PARIS (1938)
d Oswald Mitchell
VC PB

OLD MOTHER RILEY IN SOCIETY (1940)
d John Baxter
VC PB

OLD MOTHER RILEY JOINS UP (1939)
d Maclean Rogers
VC

OLD MOTHER RILEY MP (1939)
d Oswald Mitchell
VC

OLD MOTHER RILEY OVERSEAS (1943)
d Oswald Mitchell
VC PB

OLD MOTHER RILEY'S CIRCUS (1941)
d Thomas Bentley
PB

OLD MOTHER RILEY'S GHOSTS (1941)
d John Baxter
VC PB

OLD ROSES (1935)
d Bernard Mainwaring
PB

OLD SOLDIERS NEVER DIE (1931)
d Monty Banks
SC PB

OLD SPANISH CUSTOMERS (1932)
d Lupino Lane
VC PB

OLD SUSSEX (1933)
d Stanley Allen
VC

ON APPROVAL (1930)
d Tom Walls
PB

ON APPROVAL (1944)
d Clive Brook
VC

ONCE A CROOK (1941)
d Herbert Mason
SC PB

ONCE A THIEF (1935)
d George Pearson
PB

ONCE IN A NEW MOON (1935)
d Anthony Kimmins
VC

ONE EXCITING NIGHT (1944)
d Walter Forde
PB

ONE FAMILY (1930)
d Walter Creighton
VC

ONE GOOD TURN (1936)
d Alfred Goulding
PB

ONE MINUTE, PLEASE (1940)
VC

ONE MOMENT, PLEASE (1934)
VC

ONE OF OUR AIRCRAFT IS MISSING (1942)
d Michael Powell, Emeric Pressburger
VC PB

ONE PRECIOUS YEAR (1933)
d Henry Edwards
PB

ONLY GIRL, the (1933)
d Friedrich Hollaender
VC PB

ON PARADE (1936)
d George Pál
VC SC

ON SECRET SERVICE (1933)
d Arthur Woods
VC SC

ON THE AIR (1934)
d Herbert Smith
PB

ON THE MOORS (1942)
VC

ON THE NIGHT OF THE FIRE (1939)
d Brian Desmond Hurst
VC PB

ON THE WAY TO WARWICK (1930)
VC

ON THE WAY TO WORK (1936)
d Edgar Anstey
VC

ON THE WINGS OF THE WIND (1935)
VC

OPEN AIR BOXING AT THE COMRADES' CLUB, WALTON-ON-THAMES, JULY 9TH 1934 (1934)
VC

OPEN ALL NIGHT (1934)
d George Pearson
PB

OPEN DROP ETHER (The Technique of Anaesthesia series) (1944)
d Margaret Thomson
VC

OPENING OF MATERNITY HOSPITAL AT CATFORD (1937)
VC

'OPPIN' (1930)
d H W Bush
VC

ORANGE TIP BUTTERFLY, the (1931)
d Charles Head
VC

ORDER OF LENIN (1943)
d Gilbert Gunn
VC

ORDERS IS ORDERS (1933)
d Walter Forde
PB

OTHER PEOPLE'S SINS (1930)
d Sinclair Hill
PB

OUR CAVALCADE (1937)
d Joe Crossman
VC

OUR CLUB MAGAZINE NO.3 (1945)
VC

OUR CLUB MAGAZINE NO.5 (1945)
VC

OUR CLUB MAGAZINE NO.6 (1945)
VC

OUR COUNTRY (1944)
d John Eldridge
VC

OUR FIGHTING NAVY (1933)
d John Betts
PB

OUR FIGHTING NAVY (1937)
d Norman Walker
SC

OUR FILM (1942)
d Harold French
VC

OUR FIRST AMBASSADOR (1929)
VC

OUR ISLAND series
see
WESTERN HIGHLANDS (1934)

OUR ISLAND NATION (1937)
d John Hunt
VC

OUR MR SHAKESPEARE (1944)
d Harold Baim
VC

OUR SCHOOL (1941)
d Donald Alexander
VC

OURSELVES ALONE (1936)
d Walter Summers, Brian Desmond Hurst
VC PB

OUTCAST, the (1934)
d Norman Lee
VC PB

OUTDOOR TOMATO GROWING (1945)
d Andrew Buchanan
VC

OUT OF CHAOS (1944)
d Jill Craigie
VC

OUT OF THE BLUE (1931)
d John Orton, Gene Gerrard
VC PB

OUT OF THE NIGHT (1941)
d Max Anderson
VC

OUT OF THE SHADOW (1938)
d Andrew Buchanan
VC

OUTSIDER, the (1931)
d Harry Lachman
PB

OUTSIDER, the (1939)
d Paul L Stein
PB

OUT TO PLAY (1936)
d Harold Lowenstein
VC

OVER AND OVER (Pathé Pictorial series) (1931)
VC

OVER SHE GOES (1937)
d Graham Cutts
VC PB

OVER THE GARDEN WALL (1934)
d John Daumery
PB

OVER THE MOON (1937)
d Thornton Freeland
VC SC PB

OWD BOB (1938)
d Robert Stevenson
VC PB

OWL, the (1931)
VC

OXFORD (1940)
d Ralph Bond
VC

PAGEANT OF EMPIRE, a (1933)
VC

PAGEANT OF THE SUN-GOD (Secrets of India series) (1934)
d Geoffrey Barkas
PB

PAGLIACCI (1936)
d Karl Grune
VC

PAINTED BOATS (1945)
d Charles Crichton
VC SC

PAPER PEOPLE LAND (1939)
d Cyril Jenkins
VC

PA PUTS HIS FOOT DOWN (1934)
d Zoltan Korda
VC

PAPWORTH VILLAGE SETTLEMENT (1945)
d James Carr
VC

PARADISE FOR TWO (1937)
d Thornton Freeland
PB

PARAFFIN YOUNG, PIONEER OF OIL (1938)
d Ralph Bond
VC

PARAMECIUM (1937)
d J V Durden
VC

PARTNERS IN CRIME (1942)
d Frank Launder, Sidney Gilliat
VC

PASSING OF THE THIRD FLOOR BACK, the (1935)
d Berthold Viertel
VC PB

PASSPORTS AND CUSTOMS (1937)
VC

PASSPORT TO EUROPE (1938)
d Ralph Bond
VC

PASTOR HALL (1940)
d Roy Boulting, John Boulting
VC PB

PATHÉ PICTORIAL series
see
AULD AYRSHIRE (1930)
BETHLEHEM (1929)
MACHYNLLETH (1929)
MEET GEORGE (1931)
MODEL MASTER (1931)
OVER AND OVER (1931)
PATHÉ PICTORIAL NO.201 (1940)
PATHÉ PICTORIAL NO.276 (1941)
PATHÉ PICTORIAL NO.439 (1944)
PATHÉ PICTORIAL NO.592 (1929)
PATHÉ PICTORIAL NO.631 (1930)
PATHÉ PICTORIAL NO.632 (1930)
PATHÉ PICTORIAL NO.683 (1931)
PORTABLE CAR, the (1929)
RULER OF CAMBODGE PASSES BY, the (1933)
SAFETY PETROL (1932)
SUPER GLIDER, the (1930)

PATHÉ PICTORIAL NO.201 (1940)
VC

PATHÉ PICTORIAL NO.276 (1941)
VC

PATHÉ PICTORIAL NO.439 (1944)
VC

PATHÉ PICTORIAL NO.592 (1929)
VC

PATHÉ PICTORIAL NO.631 (1930)
VC

PATHÉ PICTORIAL NO.632 (1930)
VC

PATHÉ PICTORIAL NO.683 (1931)
VC

PATHÉ SOUND MAGAZINE (1930)
VC

PATHÉTONE PARADE OF 1940 (1940)
d Fred Watts
PB

PATHÉTONE WEEKLY series
see
BOYS WILL BE BOXERS (1931)
DOUBLE DROP, the (1931)
GUS ELEN IN 'IT'S A GREAT BIG SHAME' (1932)
PATHÉTONE WEEKLY NO.103 (1932)
PATHÉTONE WEEKLY NO.517 (1940)
ULTRA-MODERN HOUSE, an (1931)
WORKSHOP OF THE WORLD: BIRMINGHAM, the (1930)

PATHÉTONE WEEKLY NO.103 (1932)
VC

PATHÉTONE WEEKLY NO.517 (1940)
VC

PATRICIA GETS HER MAN (1937)
d Reginald Purdell
PB

PATTERN OF BRITAIN series, the
see
FENLANDS (1945)
GRASSY SHIRES, the (1944)

PAWS AND CLAWS (Secrets of Life series) (1944)
d Mary Field
VC

PAYBOX ADVENTURE (1936)
d W P Kellino
PB

PEACE AND PLENTY (1939)
d Ivor Montagu
VC

PEACE OR WAR? (1933)
VC

PEARL ARGYLE – 'SHALOTT' (1931)
VC

PEG OF OLD DRURY (1935)
d Herbert Wilcox
PB

PENICILLIN (1944)
d Alexander Shaw, Kay Mander
VC

PENICILLIN; LABORATORY TECHNIQUES (1944)
VC

PENICILLIN PEREGRINATIONS II; NORTH AFRICA 1943 (1943)
VC

PENNY JOURNEY (1938)
d Humphrey Jennings
VC

PENNY PARADISE (1938)
d Carol Reed
VC

PENNY POOL, the (1937)
d George Black
VC

PEOPLE AND PLACES (1935)
d Alexander Shaw
VC

PEOPLE OF BRITAIN (1936)
d Paul Rotha
VC

PEOPLE WHO COUNT, the (1937)
d Geoffrey Collyer
VC

PERFECT CRIME, the (1937)
d Ralph Ince
VC

PERFECT LADY, the (1931)
d Milton Rosmer, Frederick Jackson
SC

PERFECT STRANGERS (1945)
d Alexander Korda
VC PB

PERFECT UNDERSTANDING (1933)
d Cyril Gardner
PB

PERMANENT WAY, the (1944)
d Sidney Gausden
VC

PEST, the (Secrets of Life series) (1945)
VC

PETERVILLE DIAMOND, the (1942)
d Walter Forde
VC

PETT AND POTT (1934)
d Alberto Cavalcanti
VC

PHANTOM LIGHT, the (1935)
d Michael Powell
VC

PICCADILLY (1929)
d E A Dupont
VC SC

PICTURE PEOPLE (1943)
d John Behr
VC

PILOT IS SAFE, the (1941)
d Jack Lee
VC

PIMPERNEL SMITH (1941)
d Leslie Howard
VC PB

PINE AND SAND (1936)
VC

PINK GUARDS ON PARADE, the (1934)
VC

PINK STRING AND SEALING WAX (1945)
d Robert Hamer
VC PB

PLACE OF ONE'S OWN, a (1944)
d Bernard Knowles
VC PB

PLANE SAILING (1937)
d Philip Wills, Bosworth Goldman
VC

PLAN FOR LIVING (1938)
d Donald Carter
VC

PLANTATION PEOPLE (1936)
d A R Taylor
VC

PLASTIC SURGERY IN WARTIME (1941)
d Frank Sainsbury
VC

PLAYTHING, the (1929)
d Castleton Knight
PB

PLAYTIME (1941)
d Raymond Elton
VC

PLAYTIME FOR WORKERS (1943)
d Harold Baim
VC

PLEASE TEACHER (1937)
d Stafford Dickens
PB

PLEASURE ISLE (1939)
VC

PLENTY OF TIME FOR PLAY (1934)
d Alexandre Esway
VC

PLUMS THAT PLEASE (1934)
VC

PLUNDER (1931)
d Tom Walls
VC PB

POINT OF VIEW series
see
MAN OR MACHINE? (1940)
SHOULD WE GROW MORE FOOD?
(1939)

POISON PEN (1939)
d Paul L Stein
VC SC

POLSKI MAGAZYN FILMOWY NO.1 (1941)
VC

POLYCHROME FANTASY (1935)
d Norman McLaren, T D Allen, W H
  Finlayson
VC

PONTYPOOL HOSPITAL CARNIVAL, the
(1933)
VC

POOR OLD BILL (1931)
d Monty Banks
PB

POPPET VALVE ENGINE (1941)
VC

PORTABLE CAR, the (Pathé Pictorial series)
(1929)
VC

POST HASTE (1933)
d Frank Cadman
SC

POST HASTE (1934)
d Humphrey Jennings
VC

POST 23 (1942)
d Ralph Bond
VC

POTATO BLIGHT (1943)
d Rosanne Hunter
VC

POTIPHAR'S WIFE (1931)
d Maurice Elvey
VC PB

POT LUCK (1936)
d Tom Walls
VC SC

POTS AND PLANS (1937)
d J B Holmes
VC

POWER FOR THE HIGHLANDS (1943)
d J D Chambers
VC

POWER IN STORE (1941)
VC

POWER OVER MEN (1929)
d George J Banfield
VC

POWER TO ORDER (1941)
VC

POWER UNIT (1937)
d J A D Cartwright, Grahame Tharp
VC

PRECISION AND PRACTICE (1937)
VC

PRECISION MAKES PERFECT (1934)
VC

PRELUDE TO FLIGHT (1938)
VC

PREMIERE (1938)
d Walter Summers
VC

PRÉSENCE AU COMBAT (1945)
d Marcel Cravenne
VC

PRICE OF FREE TRADE, the (Britain under
National Government series) (1932)
VC

PRICE OF WISDOM, the (1935)
d Reginald Denham
VC PB

PRIDE OF THE FORCE, the (1933)
d Norman Lee
VC SC

PRIME MINISTER, the (1941)
d Thorold Dickinson
VC

PRIMROSE PATH, the (1934)
d Reginald Denham
PB

**PRINCE GEORGE'S VISIT TO
SCUNTHORPE, OCT 26TH, 1933** (1933)
VC

PRINCE OF WALES, the (1933)
PB

PRINCESS CHARMING (1934)
d Maurice Elvey
VC SC

PRISON WITHOUT BARS (1938)
d Brian Desmond Hurst
PB

PRIVATE LIFE OF DON JUAN, the (1934)
d Alexander Korda
VC

PRIVATE LIFE OF HENRY VIII, the (1933)
d Alexander Korda
VC PB

PRIVATE LIFE OF THE GANNETS, the
(1934)
  d Julian Huxley
  VC

PRIVATE SECRETARY, the (1935)
  d Henry Edwards
  VC PB

**PRODUCTION AND DISTRIBUTION OF
MEDICAL GASES, the** (1939)
  d T R Thumwood
  VC

**PRODUCTION OF GRADE A
(TUBERCULIN TESTED) MILK, the** (1929)
  d D M Connan
  VC

PRODUCTION OF OIL, the (1940)
  VC

PROSPEROUS NEW YEAR 1932, a (1932)
  VC

PROUD VALLEY, the (1940)
  d Pen Tennyson
  VC SC

**PRUDENCE AND STANLEY JUDSON,
'GISELLE' PAS DE DEUX** (1932)
  VC

**PSITTACOSIS VIRUS; A STUDY IN TISSUE
CULTURE** (1935)
  VC

PUBLIC LIFE OF HENRY THE NINTH, the
(1934)
  d Bernard Mainwaring
  SC

PUBLIC NUISANCE NO.1 (1936)
  d Marcel Varnel
  VC

PUPPET PARADE (1939)
  VC

PUPPETS OF FATE (1933)
  d George A Cooper
  VC

PURSE STRINGS (1933)
  d Henry Edwards
  PB

**PWLLHELI MAY DAY CELEBRATIONS
1929** (1929)
  VC

PWLLHELI MAY QUEEN 1931 (1931)
  VC

PYGMALION (1938)
  d Anthony Asquith, Leslie Howard
  VC SC

Q PLANES (1939)
  d Tim Whelan
  VC PB

QUARTERLY FILLING 1941 (1941)
  VC

QUEEN COTTON (1941)
  VC

QUEEN OF HEARTS (1936)
  d Monty Banks
  VC PB

QUEEN'S AFFAIR (1934)
  d Herbert Wilcox
  PB

QUEER CARGO (1938)
  d Harold Schuster
  SC

QUIET WEDDING (1941)
  d Anthony Asquith
  VC

RACING ROMANCE (1937)
  d Maclean Rogers
  PB

RADIO PARADE OF 1935 (1934)
  d Arthur Woods
  VC PB

**RAIDERS PASSED; A SIDELIGHT ON THE
EPIC OF MALTA** (1943)
  VC

**RAID REPORT; HOW THE RAF ASSESS
BOMB DAMAGE** (1943)
  VC

RAINBOW DANCE (1936)
  d Len Lye
  VC

RAISE THE ROOF (1930)
  d Walter Summers
  VC PB

RAISING AIR FIGHTERS (1940)
  VC

RAISING SAILORS (1940)
  VC

RAKE'S PROGRESS, the (1945)
  d Sidney Gilliat
  VC PB

RAMSAY MACDONALD COMPILATION
(1933)
  VC

REAL BLOKE, a (1935)
  d John Baxter
  SC

RED ENSIGN (1934)
  d Michael Powell
  VC

RED PEARLS (1930)
  d Walter Forde
  VC PB

RED RIGHT AND BLOO (1937)
  VC

RED WAGON (1934)
  d Paul L Stein
  VC SC

REGIONAL GEOGRAPHY series
  see
  FRUITLANDS OF KENT (1934)

RELIEF WORK IN BRITAIN (1941)
  VC

RELIGION AND THE PEOPLE (1940)
  d Andrew Buchanan
  VC

REMBRANDT (1936)
  d Alexander Korda
  VC

REMEMBER WHEN (1937)
  d David Macdonald
  PB

REMEMBRANCE DAY PARADE 1929
(1929)
  VC

RESEEDING FOR BETTER GRASS (1943)
  d Margaret Thomson
  VC

RESPIRATORY AND CARDIAC ARREST
(The Technique of Anaesthesia series) (1945)
  d Rosanne Hunter
  VC

RETURN OF BULLDOG DRUMMOND, the
(1934)
  d Walter Summers
  VC SC

RETURN OF CAROL DEANE, the (1938)
  d Arthur Woods
  VC PB

RETURN OF RAFFLES, the (1932)
  d Mansfield Markham
  VC

RETURN OF THE FROG, the (1938)
  d Maurice Elvey
  VC

**RETURN OF THE SCARLET PIMPERNEL,
the** (1937)
  d Hanns Schwarz
  VC

RETURN OF THE VIKINGS (1944)
  d Charles Frend
  SC

RETURN TO YESTERDAY (1940)
  d Robert Stevenson
  SC PB

REVOLT OF THE FISHERMEN (1935)
  VC

REYROLLES AND THE NATIONAL GRID
(1933)
  VC

RHODES OF AFRICA (1936)
  d Berthold Viertel
  VC

RHYTHM OF THE ROAD (1936)
  VC

RHYTHM RACKETEER (1937)
  d James Seymour
  PB

RICH AND STRANGE (1932)
  d Alfred Hitchcock
  VC SC

RIDERS TO THE SEA (1935)
  d Brian Desmond Hurst
  VC

RIDE WITH UNCLE JOE, a (1943)
  d Ken Annakin
  VC

**RT HON GEORGE LANSBURY, PC, MP,
the** (1937)
  VC

RT HON RAMSAY MACDONALD, the (1931)
  VC

RT HON RAMSAY MACDONALD, the
(Britain under National Government series)
(1935)
  VC

RIGHT POLICY, the (1943)
  VC

RIGHT SPIRIT, the (1931)
  VC

RING OF STEEL (1940)
  VC

RINGER, the (1931)
  d Walter Forde
  PB

RIPE EARTH (1938)
d Roy Boulting
VC

RIVER CLYDE (1939)
VC

RIVER WOLVES, the (1933)
d George Pearson
PB

RMS ORFORD AND THE RMS ORONTES, the (1929)
VC

ROAD HOUSE (1934)
d Maurice Elvey
SC PB

ROADS ACROSS BRITAIN (1939)
d Sidney Cole
VC

ROAD TO FORTUNE (1930)
d Arthur Varney
PB

ROAD TO HEALTH, the (1938)
d Brian Salt
VC

ROAD TO HELL, the (1933)
d Rudolph Messel
VC

ROAD TO MOSCOW (1944)
VC

ROAD TO YESTERDAY (1944)
d Widgey R Newman
VC

ROADWARDS (1934)
d Paul Rotha
VC

ROADWAYS (1937)
d William Coldstream, Stuart Legg, Ralph Elton
VC

ROAMIN' IN THE GLOAMIN' (Harry Lauder Songs series) (1931)
d George Pearson
VC

ROBBER SYMPHONY, the (1936)
d Friedrich Féher
PB

ROBBIE FINDS A GUN (1945)
d Anson Dyer
VC

ROCKS OF VALPRÉ, the (1935)
d Henry Edwards
PB

RODNEY STEPS IN (1931)
d Guy Newall
PB

ROGER ANDERSON PIN APPARATUS (1943)
VC

ROGER ANDERSON PIN TECHNIQUE, the (1943)
VC

ROGER THE RAVEN (1936)
d Mary Field
VC

ROMAN CATHOLIC MAY CELEBRATIONS AT FLINT, SUNDAY, 4 MAY 1930 (1930)
VC

ROMANCE À LA CARTE (1938)
d Maclean Rogers
PB

ROMANCE OF A RAILWAY (1935)
d Walter Creighton
VC

ROMANCE OF ODEON, the (1937)
VC

ROMANCE OF SEVILLE, a (1929)
d Norman Walker
VC SC

ROMANTIC INDIA (1935)
VC

ROME EXPRESS (1932)
d Walter Forde
VC

ROOF OVER YOUR HEAD, the (1937)
VC

ROOKERY NOOK (1930)
d Tom Walls
VC

ROOM FOR TWO (1940)
d Maurice Elvey
VC

ROOTS (1934)
VC

ROOTS OF VICTORY, the (1941)
d Jay Lewis
VC

ROPE (1936)
VC

ROSE IN BUD (1942)
d Rex Calvert
VC

ROSE OF TRALEE (1937)
d Oswald Mitchell
PB

ROSE OF TRALEE, the (1942)
d Germain Burger
PB

ROUND FIGURES (1944)
VC

ROUNDING OFF A SQUARE MEAL (1943)
VC

ROUND THE WIRRAL WITH A MOVIE CAMERA (1934)
VC

ROYAL CAVALCADE (1935)
d Norman Lee, Walter Summers, W P Kellino, Herbert Brenon
VC PB

ROYAL DEMAND, a (1933)
d Gustave Minzenty
PB

ROYAL DIVORCE, a (1938)
d Jack Raymond
VC

ROYAL EAGLE (1936)
d George A Cooper, Arnold Ridley
SC

ROYAL MILE, EDINBURGH, the (1943)
d Terry Bishop
VC

ROYAL REMEMBRANCES (1929)
VC

ROYAL TOUR OF KING GEORGE AND QUEEN ELIZABETH (1939)
VC

ROYAL TOUR OF THE NORTH-WEST (1937)
VC

ROYAL VISIT TO CANADA (1939)
VC

RULER OF CAMBODGE PASSES BY, the (Pathé Pictorial series) (1933)
VC

RUMANIAN FOLK DANCES (1939)
VC

RUNAWAY PRINCESS, the (1929)
d Fritz Wendhausen, Anthony Asquith
VC

RUSH HOUR (1941)
d Anthony Asquith
VC

RYNOX (1931)
d Michael Powell
VC

SABOTAGE (1936)
d Alfred Hitchcock
VC SC

SABOTAGE! (1942)
d Peter Pickering
VC

SADNESS AND GLADNESS (1929)
VC

SAFE AFFAIR, a (1931)
d Herbert Wynne
PB

SAFETY FIRST AT SEA (1935)
VC

SAFETY PETROL (Pathé Pictorial series) (1932)
VC

SAFTEST O' THE FAMILY, the (Harry Lauder Songs series) (1931)
d George Pearson
VC

SAID O'REILLY TO McNAB (1937)
d William Beaudine
VC

SAILING ALONG (1938)
d Sonnie Hale
VC PB

SAILORS DON'T CARE (1940)
d Oswald Mitchell
VC

SAILORS THREE (1940)
d Walter Forde
VC

SAILORS WITHOUT UNIFORM (1940)
VC

SAINT IN LONDON, the (1939)
d John Paddy Carstairs
VC PB

ST JAMES'S PARK (1934)
d Marion Grierson
VC

ST MARTIN'S LANE (1937)
d Tim Whelan
VC

ST PAUL series
see
FAITH TRIUMPHANT (1938)

ST PAUL'S CATHEDRAL (1944)
d James E Rogers
VC

SALLY IN OUR ALLEY (1931)
d Maurice Elvey
VC

SALOON BAR (1940)
d Walter Forde
VC PB

SALT OF THE EARTH (1939)
SC

SALUTE THE SOLDIER (1944)
d Michael C Chorlton
VC

SALVAGE WITH A SMILE (1940)
d Adrian Brunel
VC

SAM AND HIS MUSKET (1935)
d Anson Dyer
VC

SAM SMALL AT WESTMINSTER (Britain
under National Government series) (1935)
VC

SAM SMALL LEAVES TOWN (1937)
d Alfred Goulding
VC

SAN DEMETRIO – LONDON (1943)
d Charles Frend
VC PB

SANDERS OF THE RIVER (1935)
d Zoltan Korda
VC

SATURDAY NIGHT REVUE (1937)
d Norman Lee
VC

SAVE A LITTLE SUNSHINE (1938)
d Norman Lee
VC

SAVE FUEL FOR BATTLE (1944)
VC

SAVING OF BILL BLEWITT, the (1936)
d Harry Watt
VC

SAWMILL IN THE FOREST (1935)
VC

SAY IT WITH FLOWERS (1934)
d John Baxter
VC

SCABIES MITE, the (1943)
VC

SCARLET PIMPERNEL, the (1935)
d Harold Young
VC

SCARLET RUNNER & CO (Secrets of Nature
series) (1930)
d Mary Field
VC

**SCENES AT THE GRAND CARNIVAL FETE
AND 'DAILY MAIL' PUSH BALL
COMPETITION** (1934)
VC

**SCENES AT THE WALTON AMATEUR
REGATTA SAT JUNE 9TH 1934** (1934)
VC

SCHOOL FOR HUSBANDS (1937)
d Andrew Marton
VC PB

SCHOOL FOR STARS (1935)
d Donovan Pedelty
PB

SCHWEIK'S NEW ADVENTURES (1943)
d Carl Lamac
VC

SCIENTIFIC RESEARCH (1938)
VC

SCOOP, the (1934)
d Maclean Rogers
PB

SCOTLAND FOR FITNESS (1938)
d Brian Salt
VC

SCOTLAND, THE MAGIC NORTH (1934)
d Albert H Arch
VC

SCRAGS (1930)
d Challis N Sanderson
PB

SCRATCH MEAL (1936)
d Arthur Elton
VC

SCROOGE (1935)
d Henry Edwards
VC

SEA CHANGE (1935)
d Alexander Shaw
VC

SEA FORT (1940)
d Ian Dalrymple
VC

SEA HARVEST (1938)
VC

SEAMAN FRANK GOES BACK TO SEA
(1942)
d Eugene Cekalski
VC

**SECOND ADVENTURE OF 'ORACE THE
'ARMONIOUS 'OUND, the** (1929)
d Joe Noble
VC

**SECONDARY SCHOOL GYMNASTICS;
LEYTON COUNTY HIGH SCHOOL FOR
BOYS** (1936)
VC

SECOND FREEDOM, the (1943)
d Lister Laurance
VC

SECOND MR BUSH, the (1940)
d John Paddy Carstairs
SC

SECRET AGENT (1936)
d Alfred Hitchcock
VC

SECRET ALLIES (1939)
d Jiří Weiss
VC

SECRET JOURNEY (1939)
d John Baxter
VC PB

SECRET LIVES (1937)
d Edmond T Gréville
SC

SECRET MISSION (1942)
d Harold French
VC

SECRET OF STAMBOUL, the (1936)
d Andrew Marton
VC PB

SECRETS OF INDIA series
see
BIKANER (1934)
DARJEELING (1934)
DEVIL DANCERS OF SIKKIM (1934)
FAIR CITY OF UDAIPUR, the (1934)
IN THE ARENA (1934)
KATMANDU (1934)
PAGEANT OF THE SUN-GOD (1934)

SECRETS OF LIFE series
see
ANIMAL LIFE IN THE HEDGEROWS
(1936)
BABY ON THE ROCKS (1934)
MEMORIES (1944)
NEW GENERATION, the (1937)
PAWS AND CLAWS (1944)
PEST, the (1945)
SINGING WHILE THEY WORK (1942)
STRIFE IN THE HEDGEROWS (1945)
SWAN SONG (1938)
WAKE UP AND FEED (1936)

SECRETS OF NATURE series
see
APHIS, the (1930)
BREWSTER'S MAGIC (1933)
FRIENDLY FLIES (1931)
FROTHBLOWER, the (1932)
MAGIC MYXIES (1931)
MERLIN, the (1930)
SCARLET RUNNER & CO (1930)
SUNDEW (1930)
WORLD IN A WINEGLASS, a (1931)

SEEDS AND SCIENCE (1943)
d Alan Osbiston
VC

**SEED TIME TO HARVEST ON A SMALL
ENGLISH WHEAT FARM** (1940)
VC

SEEING ISN'T BELIEVING (1941)
VC

SEEING LONDON series
see
HALF A DAY'S TRIP (1930)

**SELECTION OF EARLY FILMS 1896–1913,
a** (1938)
VC

SELLING TRANSPORT (1937)
VC

SENSATION (1937)
d Brian Desmond Hurst
VC

SENSIBLE BUYING (1942)
d Peter Hennessy
VC

SERVICE FOR LADIES (1932)
d Alexander Korda
PB

SEVEN SINNERS (1936)
d Albert de Courville
VC PB

SEVENTH SURVIVOR, the (1941)
d Leslie Hiscott
VC

SEVENTH VEIL, the (1945)
d Compton Bennett
VC

77 PARK LANE (1932)
d Albert de Courville
PB

SHADOW, the (1933)
d George A Cooper
VC

SHADOWS (1931)
d Alexandre Esway
VC

SHAKESPEARE'S COUNTRY
(Gainsborough Miniatures series) (1940)
VC

SHAMING OF THE TRUE, the (1930)
VC

SHELTERED WATERS (1934)
d Evelyn Spice
VC

SHEPHERD AND HIS DOG, the (1938)
VC

SHEPHERD'S WATCH (1937)
d Basil Wright
VC

SHE SHALL HAVE MUSIC (1935)
d Leslie Hiscott
VC

SHINING HIGHWAY, the (1936)
d J B Sloan
VC

SHIPBUILDERS, the (1943)
d John Baxter
VC

SHIPS WITH WINGS (1941)
d Sergei Nolbandov
VC SC

SHIPYARD (1935)
d Paul Rotha
VC

SHIPYARD SALLY (1939)
d Monty Banks
VC PB

SHIRLEY SCHOOLS, the (1929)
d H W Bush
VC

**SHOCK TREATMENT OF
SCHIZOPHRENIA** (1944)
VC

SHOT IN THE DARK, a (1933)
d George Pearson
VC

SHOULD A DOCTOR TELL? (1930)
d Manning Haynes
PB

SHOULD WE GROW MORE FOOD? (Point
of View series) (1939)
VC

SHOW FLAT (1936)
d Bernard Mainwaring
PB

SHOW GOES ON, the (1937)
d Basil Dean
VC

SHUNTER BLACK'S NIGHT OFF (1941)
d Maxwell Munden
VC

SHUSTAR (1939)
VC

SHUTTERED WINDOWS (1934)
VC

SIGN OF FOUR, the (1932)
d Graham Cutts
VC PB

**SIGNS AND STAGES OF ANAESTHESIA,
the** (The Technique of Anaesthesia series)
(1945)
d Margaret Thomson
VC

SIGNS OF THE TIMES NO.58 (1941)
VC

SILENT BATTLE, the (1939)
d Herbert Mason
PB

SILENT HOUSE, the (1929)
d Walter Forde
VC PB

SILENT PASSENGER, the (1935)
d Reginald Denham
VC SC

SILENT VILLAGE, the (1943)
d Humphrey Jennings
VC

SILKEN SUPPLENESS (Eve's Film Review
series) (1930)
VC

SILVER BLAZE (1937)
d Thomas Bentley
PB

SILVER FLEET, the (1943)
d Gordon Wellesley, Vernon Sewell
VC

SILVER – ITS CRAFT AND TRADITIONS
(1940)
VC

SILVER LINING (1935)
d John Alderson
VC

SILVER TOP (1938)
d George King
PB

SIMPLE SOUPS (1941)
d Ronald Haines
VC

SIMPLIFIED SCIENCE series
see
HARNESSING THE WAVE (1931)

**SINGAPORE; BRITAIN'S FAR EASTERN
OUTPOST** (1936)
VC

SING AS YOU SWING (1937)
d Redd Davis
PB

SINGING WHILE THEY WORK (Secrets of
Life series) (1942)
VC

**SIPHON SPILLWAY ON THE YESHWANT
SAGAR RESERVOIR, INDORE CITY
WATER SUPPLY** (1936)
VC

SIR ARCHIBALD PAGE (1942)
VC

**SIR FRANK GILL KCMG, OBE; A
TELEPHONE PIONEER** (1942)
VC

SIR FRANK SMITH (1943)
VC

SIX-THIRTY COLLECTION (1934)
d Harry Watt, Edgar Anstey
VC

SIXTY GLORIOUS YEARS (1938)
d Herbert Wilcox
VC PB

SKIN GAME, the (1931)
d Alfred Hitchcock
VC SC

**SKY GIANT; THE STORY OF THE AVRO
LANCASTER** (1942)
VC

SKY PIRATES (1937)
d George Pál
VC

SKY'S THE LIMIT, the (1937)
d Lee Garmes, Jack Buchanan
VC

SKY'S THE LIMIT, the (1945)
d Alberto Cavalcanti
VC

SLATE (1936)
VC

SLATE QUARRYING OF NORTH WALES
(1935)
VC

SLEEPING CAR (1933)
d Anatole Litvak
VC SC

SLEEPLESS NIGHTS (1932)
d Thomas Bentley
VC

SLEEVE-VALVE ENGINE (1941)
VC

SMALL MONTANA V PAT PALMER (1935)
VC

SMOKE MENACE, the (1937)
d John Taylor
VC

SNOW PLOUGH, the (1936)
VC

SOCIAL CREDIT PARTY 1920–1938 (1938)
VC

SOCIALIST CAR OF STATE (1930)
VC

SOFT LIGHTS AND SWEET MUSIC (1936)
d Herbert Smith
VC

SOLDIER COMES HOME, a (1945)
d John Eldridge
VC

SOLDIER SAILOR (1945)
d Alexander Shaw
VC

SOLDIERS OF THE KING (1933)
d Maurice Elvey
VC PB

**SOME ACTIVITIES OF THE BERMONDSEY
BOROUGH COUNCIL** (1931)
d H W Bush
VC

SOME LIKE IT ROUGH (1944)
d Richard Massingham
VC

**SOME OF THE GLORIES OF DEVON AND
ITS INDUSTRIES** (1935)
VC

SOMETHING ALWAYS HAPPENS (1934)
d Michael Powell
VC

SOMETIMES GOOD (1934)
d W P Kellino
PB

SOMEWHERE IN CAMP (1942)
d John E Blakeley
PB

SOMEWHERE IN CIVVIES (1943)
d Maclean Rogers
PB

SOMEWHERE ON LEAVE (1942)
d John E Blakeley
PB

SONG AT EVENTIDE (1934)
d Harry Hughes
PB

SONG COPATION (1929)
d R E Jeffrey
VC

SONG OF CEYLON (1934)
d Basil Wright
VC

SONG OF FREEDOM, the (1936)
d J Elder Wills
VC PB

SONG OF HAPPINESS (1934)
VC

SONG OF THE CLYDE (1942)
d James E Rogers
VC

SONG OF THE ROAD (1937)
d John Baxter
VC

SONG YOU GAVE ME, the (1933)
d Paul L Stein
PB

SORRELL AND SON (1933)
d Jack Raymond
VC

SOS (1940)
d John Eldridge
VC

SO THIS IS LANCASHIRE (1933)
d Donald Taylor
VC

SO THIS IS LONDON (1933)
d Marion Grierson
VC

SO THIS IS LONDON! (1936)
VC

SOUND ADVICE (1935)
d William J Dodds
VC

SOUTH AMERICAN GEORGE (1941)
d Marcel Varnel
SC

SOUTHERN MAID, a (1933)
d Harry Hughes
VC PB

SOUTHERN PROVINCES OF NIGERIA, the
(1940)
VC

SOUTHERN ROSES (1936)
d Fred Zelnik
VC

SOUTHERN UPLANDS (1937)
d John C Elder
VC

SOUTH RIDING (1938)
d Victor Saville
VC SC

SOUTH SEA SWEETHEARTS (1938)
d George Pál
VC SC

SOWING AND PLANTING (1941)
d Jack Ellitt
VC

SO YOU WON'T TALK! (1935)
d William Beaudine
VC

SPAIN AND ITS PEOPLE (1931)
VC

SPAIN TODAY series
see
GOVERNMENT OF SPAIN, the (1936)
HERE IS FASCISM'S WORK (1936)

SPANISH ABC (1938)
d Thorold Dickinson, Sidney Cole
VC

SPANISH BASQUE COUNTRY, the (1931)
VC

SPARE TIME (1939)
d Humphrey Jennings
VC

SPEAKING FROM AMERICA (1938)
d Humphrey Jennings
VC

SPECIAL EDITION (1938)
d Redd Davis
PB

SPEECH BY THE RT HON JOHN SIMON
(Britain under National Government series)
(1935)
VC

**SPEECH BY THE RT HON STANLEY
BALDWIN** (Britain under National Government
series) (1935)
VC

SPEED UP ON STIRLINGS (1943)
d Grahame Tharp
VC

SPIDER, the (1939)
d Maurice Elvey
VC

SPIES OF THE AIR (1939)
d David Macdonald
SC

SPINAL ANAESTHESIA (The Technique of
Anaesthesia series) (1944)
d Yvonne Fletcher
VC

SPLINTERS (1929)
d Jack Raymond
VC

SPLINTERS IN THE AIR (1937)
d Alfred Goulding
VC

SPLINTERS IN THE NAVY (1932)
d Walter Forde
VC

SPORT AND COUNTRY (1945)
d Harry Gordon
SC

SPOTLIGHT ON A STAR first series
see
TOMMY HANDLEY (1943)

SPRING HANDICAP (1937)
d Herbert Brenon
VC

SPRING IN THE FIELDS (1936)
VC

SPRING MEETING (1941)
d Walter C Mycroft
VC SC

SPRING OFFENSIVE (1940)
d Humphrey Jennings
VC

SPRING ON THE FARM (1933)
d Evelyn Spice
VC

SPRING ON THE FARM (1943)
d Ralph Keene
VC

SPRINGTIME IN THE HOLY LAND (1939)
d George Wynn
VC

SPY FOR A DAY (1940)
d Mario Zampi
VC

SPY IN BLACK, the (1939)
d Michael Powell
VC PB

SPY OF NAPOLEON (1936)
d Maurice Elvey
VC PB

SQUADRON 992 (1940)
d Harry Watt
VC

SQUEAKER, the (1937)
d William K Howard
VC

SQUIBS (1935)
d Henry Edwards
VC

SS IONIAN (1939)
d Humphrey Jennings
VC

STAMPEDE (1929)
d C Court Treatt, Stella Court Treatt
VC

**STANLEY URBAN DISTRICT 'SALUTE
THE SOLDIER' APPEAL 13TH MAY 1944**
(1944)
VC

STAR AND THE SAND, the (1945)
d Gilbert Gunn
VC

STAR FELL FROM HEAVEN, a (1936)
d Paul Merzbach
VC

STARK NATURE (1930)
d Arthur Woods, C Court Treatt
VC PB

STARLIGHT SERENADE (1943)
d Denis Kavanagh
VC

STAR OF THE CIRCUS (1938)
d Albert de Courville
VC

STARS LOOK DOWN, the (1939)
d Carol Reed
VC SC

STARS ON PARADE (1936)
d Challis N Sanderson, Oswald Mitchell
VC

START A LAND CLUB (1942)
d Andrew Buchanan
VC

START IN LIFE, a (1944)
d Brian Smith
VC

STEAMING (Cookery Hints series) (1940)
d Jay Lewis
VC

STEEL GOES TO SEA (1941)
d John E Lewis
VC

STEVE OF THE RIVER (1937)
d Roland Davies
VC

STEVE STEPS OUT (1937)
d Roland Davies
VC

STOLEN LIFE (1939)
d Paul Czinner
VC PB

STOOKING AND STACKING (1943)
d Rosanne Hunter
VC

STORING VEGETABLES INDOORS (1942)
d Margaret Thomson
VC

STORM IN A TEACUP (1937)
d Victor Saville, Ian Dalrymple
VC

STORMY WEATHER (1935)
d Tom Walls
SC

STORY OF A DISTURBANCE, the (1936)
d Donald Carter
VC

STORY OF AN AIR COMMUNIQUE, the (1940)
VC

STORY OF A TIDE, the (1939)
VC

STORY OF BOURNVILLE, the (1932)
VC

STORY OF COTTON, the (1940)
VC

STORY OF THE ULSTER HOME GUARD, the (1945)
VC

STORY OF THE WHEEL (1935)
d Humphrey Jennings
VC

STRANGE BOARDERS (1938)
d Herbert Mason
VC

STRANGERS (1942)
VC

STRANGERS ON HONEYMOON (1936)
d Albert de Courville
VC

STRANGLEHOLD (1931)
d Henry Edwards
PB

STRANGLER, the (1932)
d Norman Lee
SC

STREET PROCESSION IN AID OF THE WALTON, HERSHAM & OATLANDS COTTAGE HOSPITAL (1932)
VC

STREET SONG (1935)
d Bernard Vorhaus
VC PB

STRENGTH AND BEAUTY series
see
HEALTHY HOLIDAYS (1937)

STRICKEN PENINSULA (1945)
d Paul Fletcher
VC

STRICTLY BUSINESS (1932)
d Jacqueline Logan, Mary Field
VC

STRIFE (1935)
VC

STRIFE IN THE HEDGEROWS (1945)
VC

STRIP! STRIP!! HOORAY!!! (1932)
d Norman Lee
VC

STRONGER SEX, the (1930)
d V Gareth Gundrey
VC PB

STRONG SILENT AXLES (1933)
VC

STUDENT NURSE (1945)
d Francis Searle
VC

STUDENT'S ROMANCE, the (1935)
d Otto Kanturek
VC PB

SUBJECT DISCUSSED (1944)
d Charles de Lautour
VC

SUB-LIEUTENANT BURGOYNE (1945)
VC

SUCH IS THE LAW (1930)
d Sinclair Hill
VC

SUGAR BEET (PART 1) (1945)
d Ralph Cathles
VC

SUMMER ON THE FARM (1943)
d Ralph Keene
VC

SUMMER TRAVELLING (1945)
d W M Larkins
VC

SUNDEW (Secrets of Nature series) (1930)
d Mary Field
VC

SUNSHINE AHEAD (1936)
d Wallace Orton
VC

SUNSHINE, FUN AND LAUGHTER (1932)
d Albert H Arch
VC

SUNSHINE SUSIE (1931)
d Victor Saville
VC PB

SUPER GLIDER, the (Pathé Pictorial series) (1930)
VC

SUPPLIES TO THE SOVIETS (1945)
d Michael Hankinson
VC

SURFACE TENSION (1936)
VC

SUSPENSE (1930)
d Walter Summers
VC SC

SUSSEX 1939 (1939)
VC

SUSSEX PEOPLES' SCRAPBOOK 1938 (1938)
VC

SWALLOWTAIL BUTTERFLY, the (1933)
VC

SWAN SONG (Secrets of Life series) (1938)
d Mary Field
VC

SWEENEY TODD, THE DEMON BARBER OF FLEET STREET (1936)
d George King
VC

SWEET DEVIL (1938)
d René Guissart
PB

SWEET SUCCESS (1936)
d Ralph Smart
VC

SWEET VALE OF AVOCA (1936)
VC

SWINGING THE LAMBETH WALK (1940)
d Len Lye
VC

SWORD OF HONOUR (1939)
d Maurice Elvey
VC

SWORD OF THE SPIRIT, the (1942)
d Henry Cass
VC

SYMPHONY IN TWO FLATS (1930)
d V Gareth Gundrey
VC

TAKE A CHANCE (1937)
d Sinclair Hill
VC

TAKE MY TIP (1937)
d Herbert Mason
VC

TALE OF TWO CITIES (1942)
d John Monck
VC

TALK ABOUT JACQUELINE (1942)
d Paul L Stein
PB

TALKING FEET (1937)
d John Baxter
VC PB

TALKING SHOP (1939)
d John E Lewis
VC

TALK OF THE DEVIL (1936)
d Carol Reed
VC

TAM O'SHANTER (1930)
d R E Jeffrey
VC

TAM TRAUCHLE'S TROUBLES (1934)
VC

TANGLED EVIDENCE (1934)
d George A Cooper
VC

TA-RA-RA BOOM DE-AY (1945)
d Fred Weiss
VC

TARGET FOR TONIGHT (1941)
d Harry Watt
VC PB

TAWNY OWL, the (Featherland series) (1931)
VC

TAWNY PIPIT (1944)
d Charles Saunders, Bernard Miles
VC

TECHNIQUE OF ANAESTHESIA series, the
see
  CARBON DIOXIDE ABSORPTION
    TECHNIQUE, the (1944)
  ENDOTRACHEAL ANAESTHESIA (1944)
  HANDLING AND CARE OF THE
    PATIENT (1944)
  INTRAVENOUS ANAESTHESIA (1944)
  NITROUS OXIDE-OXYGEN-ETHER
    ANAESTHESIA (1944)
  OPEN DROP ETHER (1944)
  RESPIRATORY AND CARDIAC ARREST
    (1945)
  SIGNS AND STAGES OF ANAESTHESIA,
    the (1945)
  SPINAL ANAESTHESIA (1944)

**TECHNIQUE OF ARCH WIRING FOR
FRACTURED JAWS, the** (Maxillo-Facial
Surgery series) (1942)
VC

TECHNIQUE OF EYELET WIRING, the
(Maxillo-Facial Surgery series) (1942)
VC

**TECHNIQUE OF INTER-MAXILLARY
FIXATION BY DIRECT WIRING, the**
(Maxillo-Facial Surgery series) (1942)
VC

**TECHNIQUE USED IN CONSTRUCTION OF
CAST METAL CAP SPLINTS, the** (Maxillo-
Facial Surgery series) (1942)
VC

TELEFOOTLERS (1941)
d John Paddy Carstairs
VC

TELEPHONE (ABSTRACT) (1934)
VC

TELEPHONE WORKERS (1933)
d Stuart Legg
VC

TELEVISION DEMONSTRATION FILM
(1937)
d Dallas Bower
VC

TELL ENGLAND (1931)
d Anthony Asquith, Geoffrey Barkas
VC

TELL-TALE HEART, the (1934)
d Brian Desmond Hurst
VC

TELL-TALES (1930)
VC

TEMBI (1929)
d Cherry Kearton
PB

TEN MINUTE ALIBI (1935)
d Bernard Vorhaus
PB

TENNIS (1930)
VC

TENTH MAN, the (1936)
d Brian Desmond Hurst
VC

TEN YEAR PLAN, the (1945)
d Lewis Gilbert
VC

TERROR, the (1938)
d Richard Bird
VC SC

TERROR ON TIPTOE (1936)
d Louis Renoir
VC

TEST FOR LOVE, a (1937)
d Vernon Sewell
VC

TESTIMONY ON NON-INTERVENTION
(1938)
d Ivor Montagu
VC

THAMES, the (1929)
VC

THANKS! MERCHANT NAVY (1944)
d Stanley Russell
VC

THAT NIGHT IN LONDON (1932)
d Rowland V Lee
PB

THAT'S A GOOD GIRL (1933)
d Jack Buchanan
VC

THAT'S MY UNCLE (1935)
d George Pearson
VC PB

THEATRE ROYAL (1943)
d John Baxter
VC PB

THEIR NIGHT OUT (1933)
d Harry Hughes
VC SC

THERE AIN'T NO JUSTICE (1939)
d Pen Tennyson
VC

THERE GOES SUSIE (1934)
d John Stafford, Victor Hanbury
PB

THERE GOES THE BRIDE (1932)
d Albert de Courville
VC PB

THERE'S A FUTURE IN IT (1943)
d Leslie Fenton
VC

THESE ARE THE MEN (Into Battle series)
(1943)
VC

THESE CHARMING PEOPLE (1931)
d Louis Mercanton
PB

THESE CHILDREN ARE SAFE (1939)
d Alexander Shaw
VC

THEY ALSO SERVE (1940)
d Ruby Grierson
VC

THEY CAME TO A CITY (1944)
d Basil Dearden
VC SC

THEY DRIVE BY NIGHT (1939)
d Arthur Woods
VC PB

THEY FLEW ALONE (1942)
d Herbert Wilcox
VC

THEY KNEW MR KNIGHT (1945)
d Norman Walker
VC

THEY LIVE AGAIN (1944)
d A Reginald Dobson
VC

THEY MADE THE LAND (1938)
d Mary Field
VC

THEY MET IN LONDON (1941)
VC

THEY MET IN THE DARK (1943)
d Carl Lamac
VC

THEY'RE OFF! (1933)
d John Rawlins
SC

THEY WERE SISTERS (1945)
d Arthur Crabtree
VC

THIEF IN THE NIGHT, a (1930)
VC

THIEF OF BAGDAD, the (1940)
d Ludwig Berger, Tim Whelan, Michael
  Powell
VC SC PB

THINGS THAT HAPPEN NO. 1 (1936)
VC

THINGS THAT HAPPEN NO. 3 (1937)
VC

THINGS TO COME (1936)
d William Cameron Menzies
VC SC

39 STEPS, the (1935)
d Alfred Hitchcock
VC

THIS BUTTON BUSINESS (1935)
d Anson Dyer
VC

THIS ENGLAND (1941)
d David Macdonald
VC PB

THIS HAPPY BREED (1944)
d David Lean
VC SC

**THIS IS A MATTER WHICH VITALLY
CONCERNS YOU** (1938)
VC

THIS IS COLOUR (1942)
d Jack Ellitt
VC

THIS IS ENGLAND (1941)
d Humphrey Jennings
VC

THIS IS PARIS! THAT WAS! (1933)
VC

THIS IS POLAND (1941)
VC

THIS'LL MAKE YOU WHISTLE (1936)
d Herbert Wilcox
VC

THIS MAN IN PARIS (1939)
d David Macdonald
PB

THIS MAN IS NEWS (1938)
d David Macdonald
PB

THIS MILK BUSINESS (1939)
VC

THIS PROGRESS (1934)
d Aveling Ginever
VC

THISTLEDOWN (1938)
d Arthur Woods
PB

THIS WAS JAPAN (1945)
d Basil Wright
VC

THIS WEEK OF GRACE (1933)
d Maurice Elvey
PB

THORNCLIFFE (1935)
VC

THOROUGHBRED (1940)
VC

THOSE KIDS FROM TOWN (1942)
d Lance Comfort
PB

THOSE WERE THE DAYS (1934)
d Thomas Bentley
VC SC

THOUSAND HAPPY DAYS, a (1938)
VC

THREE CADETS (1944)
VC

THREE MEN IN A BOAT (1933)
d Graham Cutts
VC

THREE OWLS INN, the (1939)
VC

THREE SILENT MEN (1940)
d Thomas Bentley
VC

THREE WITNESSES (1935)
d Leslie Hiscott
PB

THUNDER IN THE AIR (1935)
d Hans M Nieter
VC

THUNDER ROCK (1942)
d Roy Boulting
VC PB

THURSDAY'S CHILD (1943)
d Rodney Ackland
VC SC

THYROIDECTOMY (1943)
VC

TICKET OF LEAVE (1935)
d Michael Hankinson
PB

TIGER BAY (1933)
d J Elder Wills
VC

TIMBUCTOO (1933)
d Walter Summers, Arthur Woods
VC

TIME AND TIDE (1945)
d John Eldridge
VC

TIN GODS (1932)
d F W Kraemer
VC

TISSUE CULTURE OF GLIOMATA (1935)
VC

TO BE A LADY (1934)
d George King
PB

TOCHER; A FILM BALLET BY LOTTE REINIGER, the (1938)
d Lotte Reiniger
VC

TODAY AND TOMORROW (1936)
d Ruby Grierson, Ralph Bond
VC

TODAY AND TOMORROW; A STORY OF THE MIDDLE EAST (1945)
d Robin Carruthers
VC

TODAY WE LIVE; A FILM OF LIFE IN BRITAIN (1937)
d Ruby Grierson, Ralph Bond
VC

TOM MANN; A HUMBLE TRIBUTE TO A TRULY GREAT COMRADE (1936)
VC

TOMMY HANDLEY (Spotlight on a Star first series) (1943)
d Walter Forde
VC

TOMMY HANDLEY'S VICTORY SONG (1945)
VC

TOMORROW IS THEIRS (1940)
d James Carr
VC

TOMORROW WE LIVE (1936)
d Manning Haynes
VC SC

TOM'S RIDE (1944)
d Darrel Catling
VC

TOO MANY CROOKS (1930)
d George King
PB

TOO MANY HUSBANDS (1938)
d Ivar Campbell
SC

TORQUAY INTEREST FILM (1935)
VC

TOTAL WAR IN BRITAIN (1945)
d Paul Rotha
VC

TOUGH 'UN, the (1938)
d Mary Field
VC

TOWER OF TERROR, the (1941)
d Lawrence Huntington
SC

TO WHAT RED HELL (1929)
d Edwin Greenwood
VC

TRACTOR ENGINE OVERHAUL (1945)
d Andrew Buchanan
VC

TRADE TATTOO (1937)
d Len Lye
VC

TRAINING FOR MECHANISED MINING (1945)
d Andrew Buchanan
VC

TRAITOR SPY (1939)
d Walter Summers
VC PB

TRANSFER OF POWER; THE HISTORY OF THE TOOTHED WHEEL (1939)
d Geoffrey Bell
VC

TRANSFER OF SKILL (1940)
d Geoffrey Bell
VC

TRANSPORT IN ENGLAND (1933)
VC

TRAVELLING DE LUXE TO THE CONTINENT (1930)
VC

TRAVELLING POST OFFICE (1936)
VC

TREATMENT OF A GUNSHOT WOUND OF THE MANDIBLE (Maxillo-Facial Surgery series) (1942)
VC

TREATMENT OF A GUNSHOT WOUND OF THE MANDIBLE WITH EXTENSIVE LOSS OF BONE (Maxillo-Facial Surgery series) (1942)
VC

TREATMENT OF FIBROUS NON-UNION BY BONE CHIPS (Maxillo-Facial Surgery series) (1942)
VC

TREATMENT OF WAR WOUNDS WITH PENICILLIN, NORTH AFRICA, 1943 (1943)
VC

TRIAL FOR MARRIAGE (1936)
VC

TRIUMPH OF SHERLOCK HOLMES, the (1935)
d Leslie Hiscott
VC

TROPICAL BREEZES (1930)
d Sidney G Griffiths, A Goodman, H Brian White
VC

TROPICAL HOOKWORM (1936)
d L A Notcutt
VC

TROPICAL LUMBERING (1938)
VC

TROUBLE AT TOWNSEND (1945)
VC SC

TROUBLE BREWING (1939)
d Anthony Kimmins
VC SC

TRUE STORY OF LILI MARLENE, the (1944)
d Humphrey Jennings
VC

TRUNK CRIME (1939)
d Roy Boulting
VC

TRY WHAT LOVE WILL DO (1939)
d J B Sloan
VC

T S ELIOT 1942 (1944)
d William MacQuitty
VC

TUBERCULOSIS (The Health of Dairy Cattle series) (1944)
VC

TUDOR ROSE (1936)
d Robert Stevenson
VC

TUNISIAN VICTORY (1943)
d Roy Boulting, Frank Capra
VC

TUNNEL, the (1935)
d Maurice Elvey
VC

Film Titles 1929–1945

TURNED OUT NICE AGAIN (1941)
d Marcel Varnel
VC SC

TURNING HER ROUND (1934)
d John Gifford
VC

TURN OF THE FURROW (1941)
d Peter Baylis
VC

TURN OF THE TIDE (1935)
d Norman Walker
VC

TUSALAVA (1929)
d Len Lye
VC

'TWAS ON A MONDAY MORNING (1945)
d Louise Birt
VC

TWELVE OP (Focus on the Empire series)
(1940)
d Leon Schauder
VC

20 MEN AND A LEADER (Fitness Wins series)
(1940)
d Donald Carter
VC

21 DAYS (1937)
d Basil Dean
VC

21 MILES (1942)
d Harry Watt
VC

TWICE BRANDED (1936)
d Maclean Rogers
PB

TWIN FACES (1937)
d Lawrence Huntington
PB

TWITCHING FEET (1931)
d C C Ungley
VC

TWO FATHERS (1944)
d Anthony Asquith
VC

TWO GOOD FAIRIES (1944)
d Germain Burger
VC

TWO HEARTS IN WALTZ TIME (1934)
d Carmine Gallone, Joe May
PB

**TWO LANCASHIRE COTTON WORKERS
DISCUSS SAFEGUARDING** (Britain under
National Government series) (1935)
VC

TWO MORE (1929)
VC

TWO ON A DOORSTEP (1936)
d Lawrence Huntington
PB

TWO-SPEED SUPERCHARGER (1942)
VC

TWO THOUSAND WOMEN (1944)
d Frank Launder
VC

TWO WAY STREET (1931)
d George King
VC

TWO WHITE ARMS (1932)
d Fred Niblo
PB

TWO WORLDS (1930)
d E A Dupont
VC

TYNESIDE (1941)
VC

**TYPICAL DAY IN THE LIFE OF A
KUANYAMA FAMILY, a** (1937)
d P H G Powell-Cotton
VC

UAB (1935)
VC

ULSTER (1940)
d Ralph Keene
VC

ULTRA-MODERN HOUSE, an (Pathétone
Weekly series) (1931)
VC

UMBRELLA, the (1933)
d Redd Davis
VC PB

UNCENSORED (1942)
d Anthony Asquith
VC

UNCLE TIMOTHY'S TEA PARTY (1944)
d Hans M Nieter
VC

UNDER A CLOUD (1937)
d George King
VC PB

UNDERCOVER (1943)
d Sergei Nolbandov
SC

UNDER THE GREENWOOD TREE (1929)
d Harry Lachman
VC

UNDER THE RED ROBE (1937)
d Victor Sjöström
VC PB

UNDER YOUR HAT (1940)
d Maurice Elvey
VC

UNEMPLOYMENT AND MONEY (1940)
d Michael Polanyi, Mary Field, John Jewkes,
Reginald Jeffryes
VC

UNITY IS STRENGTH (1945)
d Ralph Bond
VC

UNPUBLISHED STORY (1942)
d Harold French
VC PB

UNWANTED GUESTS (1943)
VC

UP COUNTRY WITH THE SETTLER (1930)
VC

UPSTREAM (1932)
d Arthur Elton
VC

UP THE POLL (1929)
d R E Jeffrey
VC

US AND US (1943)
VC

VAGABOND QUEEN, the (1929)
d Geza von Bolvary
VC SC

VANDERGILT DIAMOND MYSTERY, the
(1935)
d Randall Faye
PB

VARIETY HOUR (1937)
d Redd Davis
VC

VARIETY JUBILEE (1943)
d Maclean Rogers
VC

**VELVET AND SABLE; A NEW
PATHÉCOLOR MODE** (Eve's Film Review
series) (1929)
VC

VESSEL OF WRATH (1938)
d Erich Pommer
VC PB

VETERAN OF WATERLOO, the (1933)
d A V Bramble
PB

**VETERINARY TRAINING OF AFRICAN
NATIVES** (1936)
d L A Notcutt
VC

VICAR OF BRAY, the (1937)
d Henry Edwards
VC

VICTORIA THE GREAT (1937)
d Herbert Wilcox
VC PB

VICTORY! (1945)
VC

VICTORY WEDDING (1944)
d Jessie Matthews
VC

VILLAGE BAKERY, the (1935)
VC

VILLAGE SCHOOL (1940)
d John Eldridge
VC

VILLAGES OF LANKA, the (1934)
VC

VILLAGE SQUIRE, the (1935)
d Reginald Denham
PB

VILLAGE THAT FOUND ITSELF, the (1939)
d John E Lewis
VC

VILLAGE WEDDING, a (1930)
VC

VINQUISH IN HILL SHEEP (1941)
d George Dunlop
VC

VINTAGE WINE (1935)
d Henry Edwards
PB

VIOLIN VIRTUOSOS (1937)
VC

VISIT TO SUNNY SURREY, a (1935)
VC

**VISIT TO THE WORKS OF ICI METALS
LIMITED, a** (1931)
VC

VITAMINS (1937)
d Geoffrey Innes
VC

VOICE OF THE PEOPLE, the (1939)
d Frank Sainsbury
VC

VOLUNTEER, the (1943)
d Michael Powell, Emeric Pressburger
VC

V-1 (1944)
d Fletcher Markle
VC

VOYAGE OF DISCOVERY, a (1937)
VC

VOYAGE OF THE ASHANTI, the (1939)
VC

WAKE UP AND FEED (Secrets of Life series) (1936)
d J B Holmes
VC

WALES (1945)
VC

WALLPAPER FOR YOUR HOME (1934)
VC

WALSALL CORONATION CELEBRATIONS, 12 MAY 1937 (1937)
VC

WALTZES FROM VIENNA (1933)
d Alfred Hitchcock
VC SC

WANDERING JEW, the (1933)
d Maurice Elvey
VC

WAR AND ORDER (1940)
d Charles Hasse
VC

WARBLERS, the (1934)
d Mary Field
VC

WAR CLOUDS OVER ABYSSINIA (1934)
VC

WAR COMES TO LONDON (1940)
VC

WARE CASE, the (1929)
d Manning Haynes
VC

WARE CASE, the (1938)
d Robert Stevenson
VC SC

WAR IN THE PACIFIC (1943)
d Grahame Tharp, Geoffrey Bell
VC

WAR LIBRARY ITEMS 1, 2 AND 3 (1939)
VC

WARM CORNER, a (1930)
d Victor Saville
SC

WARNING, the (1939)
VC

WARN THAT MAN (1943)
d Lawrence Huntington
PB

WAR ON FIRE (1935)
VC

WARREN CASE, the (1934)
d Walter Summers
VC

WARTIME FACTORY (1940)
d Edgar Anstey
VC

WAR WITHOUT END (1936)
d Francis Searle
PB

WAS EVE SO SLOW THIRTY YEARS AGO? (Eve's Film Review series) (1930)
VC

WATCH AND WARD IN THE AIR (1937)
d Ralph Keene, Alexander Shaw
VC

WATCH BEVERLY (1932)
d Arthur Maude
PB

WATER (1942)
d Mary Field
VC

WATERCRESS (1942)
VC

WATER CYCLE, the (1943)
VC

WATER GIPSIES, the (1932)
d Maurice Elvey
VC

WATERLOO ROAD (1944)
d Sidney Gilliat
VC SC

WATER SERVICE (1945)
VC

WAVELL'S 30,000 (1942)
d John Monck
VC

WAY AHEAD, the (1944)
d Carol Reed
VC SC

WAY OF THE WILD, the (1935)
d F W Ratcliffe Holmes
PB

WAY OF YOUTH, the (1934)
d Norman Walker
PB

WAY TO THE SEA, the (1936)
d J B Holmes
VC

WAY TO THE STARS, the (1945)
d Anthony Asquith
VC SC

WEALTH OF A NATION (1938)
d Donald Alexander
VC

WE ARE THE ENGLISH (1936)
VC

WEATHER FORECAST (1934)
d Evelyn Spice
VC

WEAVING (1935)
VC

WEDDING EVE (1935)
d Charles Barnett
PB

WEDDING REHEARSAL (1932)
d Alexander Korda
VC PB

WEDDINGS ARE WONDERFUL (1938)
d Maclean Rogers
PB

WE DIVE AT DAWN (1943)
d Anthony Asquith
VC PB

WEDNESDAY'S LUCK (1936)
d George Pearson
PB

WEE BLUE BLOSSOM, the (1944)
d John Alderson
VC

WELCOME TO BRITAIN, a (1943)
d Anthony Asquith, Burgess Meredith
VC

WELDING HELPS THE FARMER (1943)
d Andrew Buchanan
VC

WELFARE OF THE WORKERS (1940)
d Humphrey Jennings
VC

WE LIVE IN TWO WORLDS (1937)
d Alberto Cavalcanti
VC

WELL DONE HENRY (1937)
d Wilfred Noy
PB

WE'LL MEET AGAIN (1942)
d Phil Brandon
VC PB

WELLS IN PORTUGAL (1936)
VC

WE'LL SMILE AGAIN (1942)
d John Baxter
PB

WENT THE DAY WELL? (1942)
d Alberto Cavalcanti
VC SC

WE OF THE WEST RIDING (1945)
d Ken Annakin
VC

WESTERN APPROACHES (1944)
d Pat Jackson
VC PB

WESTERN HIGHLANDS (Our Island series) (1934)
d Duncan Robbins
VC

WESTERN WATERWAY (1941)
VC

WEST INDIES CALLING (1944)
d John Page
VC

WESTLAND GLIMPSES (1930)
VC

WESTWARD HO! (1940)
d Thorold Dickinson
VC

WE TAKE OFF OUR HATS (1930)
d Harry Hughes
VC

WE'VE GOT TO GET RID OF THE RATS (1940)
d James Carr
VC

WHAT HAPPENED THEN? (1934)
d Walter Summers
VC SC

WHAT-HO-SHE-BUMPS (1937)
d George Pál
VC SC

WHAT'S IN A WISH? (1943)
VC

WHAT'S ON TODAY (1938)
d Richard Q McNaughton
VC

WHAT THE PARROT SAW (1935)
d Widgey R Newman
PB

WHAT WOULD YOU DO CHUMS? (1939)
d John Baxter
VC

WHAT WOULD YOU DO IF – (1931)
VC

WHEELWRIGHT, the (The Craftsman series) (1935)
d Peter Baylis
VC

WHEN KNIGHTS WERE BOLD (1936)
d Jack Raymond
VC

WHEN THE PIE WAS OPENED (1941)
d Len Lye
VC

WHEN THE SOLDER SETS (1934)
VC

WHEN WE ARE MARRIED (1943)
d Lance Comfort
VC PB

WHEN WE BUILD AGAIN (1943)
d Ralph Bond
VC

WHERE'S THAT FIRE? (1939)
d Marcel Varnel
PB

WHERE THERE'S A WILL (1936)
d William Beaudine
VC

WHERE THERE'S LIFE THERE'S SOAP (1936)
d D M Connan, H W Bush
VC

WHILE PARENTS SLEEP (1935)
d Adrian Brunel
VC

WHITE BATTLE FRONT (1940)
d Hans M Nieter
VC

WHITE CARGO (1929)
d Arthur W Barnes, J B Williams
VC

WHITE EAGLE, the (1941)
d Eugene Cekalski
VC

WHITE LINE, the (1935)
VC

WHO GOES NEXT? (1938)
d Maurice Elvey
VC

WHO'LL BUY A WARSHIP? (1942)
d Richard Massingham
VC

WHOM THE GODS LOVE (1936)
d Basil Dean
VC PB

WHOOPEE! (1932)
VC

WHO'S YOUR LADY FRIEND? (1937)
d Carol Reed
SC

WHY SAILORS LEAVE HOME (1930)
d Monty Banks
VC

WICKED LADY, the (1945)
d Leslie Arliss
VC PB

WIFE OF GENERAL LING (1937)
d Ladislao Vajda
PB

WILD BOY (1934)
d Albert de Courville
VC PB

WILL CIVILISATION CRASH? (1934)
VC

WILLIAM CAREY (1938)
VC

WILSON, KEPPEL AND BETTY (1943)
VC

WILSON, KEPPEL AND BETTY – EGYPTIAN DANCE (1943)
VC

WINDBAG THE SAILOR (1936)
d William Beaudine
VC

WINDFALL (1935)
d George King
VC

WINDJAMMER (1930)
d John Orton
VC

WINDMILL IN BARBADOS (1933)
d Basil Wright
VC

WINDOW IN LONDON, a (1939)
d Herbert Mason
VC

WINGED INVADERS (1942)
VC

WINGS FOR VICTORY WEEK – BEVERLEY AND DISTRICT 1943 (1943)
VC

WINGS OF THE MORNING (1936)
d Harold Schuster
VC PB

WINGS OVER AFRICA (1933)
d F Roy Tuckett
VC

WINGS OVER AFRICA (1936)
d Ladislao Vajda
VC

WINGS OVER EMPIRE (1939)
d Stuart Legg
VC

WINGS OVER EVEREST (1934)
d Ivor Montagu, Geoffrey Barkas
VC

WINTER (1936)
VC

WINTER ON THE FARM (1943)
d Ralph Keene
VC

WIRE ROPE MAKING (1936)
VC

WISDOM OF THE WILD (1940)
d Mary Field
VC

WITHIN THE WHITE LINE (1938)
VC

WIZARD IN THE WALL, the (1934)
VC

WOLVES (1930)
d Albert de Courville
PB

WOMAN ALONE, a (1936)
d Eugene Frenke
VC SC

WOMAN BETWEEN, the (1930)
d Miles Mander
VC SC

WOMAN FROM CHINA, the (1930)
d Edward Dryhurst
VC

WOMAN TO WOMAN (1929)
d Victor Saville
VC

WOMEN AREN'T ANGELS (1942)
d Lawrence Huntington
SC

WOMEN WHO PLAY (1932)
d Arthur Rosson
PB

WORDS AND ACTIONS (1943)
d Max Anderson
VC

WORDS FOR BATTLE (1941)
d Humphrey Jennings
VC

WORKER AND WARFRONT NO.1 (1942)
d Duncan Ross
VC

WORKER AND WARFRONT NO.2 (1942)
d Duncan Ross
VC

WORKER AND WARFRONT NO.3 (1942)
d Duncan Ross
VC

WORKER AND WARFRONT NO.4 (1943)
d Duncan Ross
VC

WORKER AND WARFRONT NO.5 (1943)
d Duncan Ross
VC

WORKER AND WARFRONT NO.6 (1943)
d Duncan Ross
VC

WORKER AND WARFRONT NO.7 (1943)
d Duncan Ross
VC

WORKER AND WARFRONT NO.8 (1943)
d Duncan Ross
VC

WORKER AND WARFRONT NO.9 (1943)
d Duncan Ross
VC

WORKER AND WARFRONT NO.10 (1944)
d Duncan Ross
VC

WORKER AND WARFRONT NO.11 (1944)
d Duncan Ross
VC

WORKER AND WARFRONT NO.12 (1944)
d Duncan Ross
VC

WORKER AND WARFRONT NO.13 (1944)
d Duncan Ross
VC

WORKER AND WARFRONT NO.14 (1945)
d Duncan Ross
VC

WORKER AND WARFRONT NO.15 (1945)
 d Duncan Ross
 VC

WORKER AND WARFRONT NO.16 (1945)
 d Duncan Ross
 VC

WORKER AND WARFRONT NO.17 (1945)
 d Duncan Ross
 VC

WORKER AND WARFRONT NO.18 (1945)
 d Duncan Ross
 VC

WORKERS AND JOBS (1935)
 d Arthur Elton
 VC

WORKERS' NEWSREEL NO.1 (1934)
 VC

WORKERS' NEWSREEL NO.2 (1934)
 VC

WORKERS' WEEKEND (1943)
 d Ralph Elton
 VC

WORK IN A STORE (1939)
 d John C Elder
 VC

WORKSHOP OF THE WORLD: BIRMINGHAM, the (Pathétone Weekly series) (1930)
 VC

WORLD GARDEN (1941)
 d Robin Carruthers
 VC

WORLD IN A WINEGLASS, a (Secrets of Nature series) (1931)
 d Mary Field
 VC

WORLD IN REVOLT (1937)
 VC

WORLD OF PLENTY (1943)
 d Paul Rotha
 VC

WORLD ON WHEELS, the (1929)
 VC

WORLD OWES ME A LIVING, the (1945)
 d Vernon Sewell
 PB

WORLD'S DIFFERENCE (1945)
 VC

WORLD THE FLESH AND THE DEVIL, the (1932)
 d George A Cooper
 PB

WORLD WINDOW series
 see
 GREEN GIRDLE, the (1941)

WOULD YOU BELIEVE IT? (1929)
 d Walter Forde
 VC

W PLAN, the (1930)
 d Victor Saville
 VC

W STAB, the (1935)
 VC

YANK AT OXFORD, a (1937)
 d Jack Conway
 VC PB

YELLOW CAESAR (1940)
 d Alberto Cavalcanti
 VC

YELLOW CANARY, the (1943)
 d Herbert Wilcox
 VC PB

YELLOW SANDS (1938)
 d Herbert Brenon
 VC

YELLOW STOCKINGS (1930)
 d Theodor Komisarjevsky
 PB

YES, MADAM? (1938)
 d Norman Lee
 VC SC

YESTERDAY IS OVER YOUR SHOULDER (1940)
 d Thorold Dickinson
 VC

YORK (1945)
 VC

YORKSHIRE WOOLLEN WORKERS DISCUSS SAFEGUARDING (Britain under National Government series) (1931)
 VC

YOU'D BE SURPRISED (1930)
 d Walter Forde
 VC

YOU MADE ME LOVE YOU (1933)
 d Monty Banks
 VC PB

YOUNG AND HEALTHY (1943)
 d Richard Massingham, Alex Strasser
 VC

YOUNG AND INNOCENT (1937)
 d Alfred Hitchcock
 VC PB

YOUNGERS' SHOPPERS GAZETTE (1930)
 VC

YOUNG MAN'S FANCY (1939)
 d Robert Stevenson
 VC SC

YOUNG MR PITT, the (1942)
 d Carol Reed
 VC PB

YOUNG THINGS (1934)
 d H E Turner
 VC

YOUNG VETERAN (1940)
 VC

YOUNG WOODLEY (1930)
 d Thomas Bentley
 VC

YOUR CHILDREN series
 see
 YOUR CHILDREN'S EARS (1945)
 YOUR CHILDREN'S EYES (1945)
 YOUR CHILDREN'S TEETH (1945)

YOUR CHILDREN'S EARS (Your Children series) (1945)
 d Albert Pearl
 VC

YOUR CHILDREN'S EYES (Your Children series) (1945)
 d Alex Strasser
 VC

YOUR CHILDREN'S TEETH (Your Children series) (1945)
 d Jane Massy
 VC

YOU'RE TELLING ME (1939)
 d A G Jackson, Anson Dyer
 VC

YOU'RE TELLING ME (1941)
 d Bladon Peake
 VC

YOUTH PEACE PILGRIMAGE FEBRUARY 1939 (1939)
 VC

YOUTH WILL BE SERVED (1933)
 d Anthony Asquith
 VC

YOU WILL REMEMBER (1940)
 d Jack Raymond
 PB

ZETLAND BIRDS (1939)
 VC

ABC XMAS AND NEW YEAR GREETINGS
(1946)
VC

ABERDEEN ANGUS (Scottish Livestock
series) (1947)
VC

A-B MECO MOORE CUTTER LOADER
(1953)
d John Shaw-Jones
VC

ABOMINABLE SNOWMAN, the (1957)
d Val Guest
PB

ABOVE US THE WAVES (1955)
d Ralph Thomas
VC SC

ACCOUNT RENDERED (1957)
d Peter Graham Scott
PB

ACHIEVEMENT IN HONG KONG (1958)
VC

ACROSS THE BRIDGE (1957)
d Ken Annakin
SC PB

ACT OF MURDER (1964)
d Alan Bridges
VC PB

ADAM AND EVELYNE (1949)
d Harold French
VC PB

ADMIRABLE CRICHTON, the (1957)
d Lewis Gilbert
VC SC

ADVENTURE IN THE HOPFIELDS (1954)
d John Guillermin
SC

ADVENTURERS, the (1950)
d David Macdonald
SC PB

ADVENTURES OF HAL 5, the (1958)
d Don Sharp
SC

ADVENTURES OF JANE, the (1949)
d Edward G Whiting
PB

ADVENTURES OF PC 49, the (1949)
d Godfrey Grayson
VC

**ADVENTURES OF QUENTIN DURWARD,
the** (1955)
d Richard Thorpe
PB

ADVENTURES OF REX, the (1959)
d Leonard Reeve
SC

ADVENTURES OF SOUPY series, the
see
JUMP TO IT (1950)

AFRICA; A RHODESIAN VILLAGE (1950)
VC

AFRICA HIGHWAY (1959)
VC

**AFRICAN AMBASSADOR; MEMOIRS OF
LADY ARABELLA APE** (1949)

AFRICAN BUILDS A CANOE, an (1950)
VC

AFRICAN HERITAGE (1956)
VC

AFRICAN QUEEN, the (1951)
d John Huston
PB

AFRICAN VISTA (1952)
d Jean Haines, Ronald Haines
SC

AFTER THE BALL (1957)
d Compton Bennett
VC

AGAINST THE WIND (1947)
d Charles Crichton
VC SC PB

AGRICULTURAL HOLIDAY CAMPS (1947)
d Richard Massingham
VC

AIRCRAFT TODAY AND TOMORROW
(1946)
d Sarah Erulkar
VC

AIR CROSSROADS (1958)
d John Arnold
VC

AIR OF MAGIC, an (The World of Life; a
Journal of the Outdoors series) (1961)
VC

AIR PARADE (1951)
d Bill Mason
VC

**A JYMPSON HARMAN ... AND ... 'GREAT
EXPECTATIONS' ...** (Critic and Film series)
(1949)
VC

ALBERT RN (1953)
d Lewis Gilbert
PB

ALI AND THE CAMEL (1960)
d Henry Geddes
SC

ALIAS JOHN PRESTON (1955)
d David Macdonald
PB

ALIEN ORDERS (1951)
VC

ALIVE AND KICKING (1958)
d Cyril Frankel
PB

ALL HALLOWE'EN (1953)
d Michael S Gordon
SC

ALL NIGHT LONG (1961)
d Michael Relph, Basil Dearden
VC PB

ALL OVER THE TOWN (1948)
d Derek Twist
VC SC

ALL THAT MIGHTY HEART (1963)
d R K Neilson Baxter
VC

ALWAYS A BRIDE (1953)
d Ralph Smart
SC

AMAZON, the (1959)
VC

AMELIA AND THE ANGEL (1958)
d Ken Russell
VC

AMOROUS PRAWN, the (1962)
d Anthony Kimmins
SC PB

ANAESTHESIA IN THE DENTAL CHAIR
(The Technique of Anaesthesia series) (1949)
VC

**ANAESTHESIA IN THE DENTAL CHAIR
FOR CHILDREN** (The Technique of
Anaesthesia series) (1949)
VC

ANASTASIA (1956)
d Anatole Litvak
PB

ANCESTRY OF SCIENCE series, the
see
TIME IS (1964)

ANDERTON SHEARER-LOADER, the
(1955)
d John Reid
VC

AND GLADLY WOULD HE LEARN (1964)
d Rodney Giesler
VC

ANGELS ONE FIVE (1952)
d George More O'Ferrall
VC SC

ANGEL WITH THE TRUMPET, the (1949)
d Anthony Bushell
VC SC

ANGRY HILLS, the (1959)
d Robert Aldrich
PB

ANGRY SILENCE, the (1960)
d Guy Green
VC SC

ANIMAL AFTERNOON (1958)
d Brian Salt
SC

ANIMALAND series
see
GINGER NUTT'S BEE BOTHER (1949)
GINGER NUTT'S CHRISTMAS CIRCUS
(1949)
GINGER NUTT'S FOREST DRAGON
(1949)
HOUSE CAT, the (1948)

ANIMAL FARM (1954)
d John Halas, Joy Batchelor
VC SC

ANIMAL HEALTH series
see
COCCIDIOSIS IN POULTRY (1952)

ANNA KARENINA (1947)
d Julien Duvivier
VC PB

ANOTHER CASE OF POISONING (1949)
d John Waterhouse
VC

ANOTHER SKY (1955)
d Gavin Lambert
VC

ANOTHER TIME, ANOTHER PLACE (1958)
d Lewis Allen
SC PB

ANTARCTIC CROSSING (1958)
VC

ANTARCTIC WHALE HUNT (This Modern
Age series) (1947)
VC

APPLE TREES, the (1951)
VC

APPOINTMENT WITH CRIME (1946)
d John Harlow
VC PB

APPOINTMENT WITH SUCCESS (1952)
VC

APPOINTMENT WITH VENUS (1951)
d Ralph Thomas
SC

APPROACHING THE SPEED OF SOUND
(High Speed Flight series) (1956)
d Peter de Normanville
VC

ARCTIC HARVEST (1946)
d Lewis Gilbert
SC

ARMAND AND MICHAELA DENIS AMONG THE HEADHUNTERS (1955)
d Armand Denis
PB

ARMAND AND MICHAELA DENIS ON THE BARRIER REEF (1955)
d Armand Denis
PB

ARMAND AND MICHAELA DENIS UNDER THE SOUTHERN CROSS (1954)
d Armand Denis
PB

ARTHUR ASKEY ON GOING TO THE DENTIST NO.1: THE APPOINTMENT (1947)
d Richard Massingham
VC

ARTHUR ASKEY ON GOING TO THE DENTIST NO.3: THE WAITING ROOM (1947)
d Richard Massingham
VC

ARTIST LOOKS AT CHURCHES, an (1960)
d John Taylor
VC

AS LONG AS THEY'RE HAPPY (1955)
d J Lee Thompson
SC PB

AS OLD AS THE HILLS (1950)
d Allan Crick
VC PB

ASPHYXIA AND ARTIFICIAL RESPIRATION (1958)
d Budge Cooper
VC

ASSASSIN FOR HIRE (1951)
d Michael McCarthy
VC

ASSIGNMENT REDHEAD (1956)
d Maclean Rogers
PB

ASTONISHED HEART, the (1950)
d Terence Fisher, Antony Darnborough
VC SC

ATLANTIC ISLES (1950)
VC

ATOMIC PHYSICS, PART 4: ATOM SMASHING – THE DISCOVERY OF THE NEUTRON (1947)
d Derek Mayne
VC

ATOMISATION (1948)
d Bill Mason
VC

ATOMS AT WORK (1952)
d Diana Pine
VC

AT THE PIRATE'S HEAD (1951)
d Alfred Goulding
SC

AUNT CLARA (1954)
d Anthony Kimmins
SC

AUTOMANIA 2000 (1963)
d John Halas
VC

AVE MARIA (1950)
VC

AWAKENING HOUR, the (1957)
d Donovan Winter
VC

AXE AND THE LAMP, the (1963)
d John Halas
VC

BABY AND THE BATTLESHIP, the (1956)
d Jay Lewis
PB

BACHELOR OF HEARTS (1958)
d Wolf Rilla
SC PB

BACKGROUND (1953)
d Daniel Birt
VC SC

BACK-ROOM OF THE SKY (Look at Life series) (1963)
VC

BADGER'S GREEN (1949)
d John Irwin
VC

BAD LORD BYRON, the (1948)
d David Macdonald
VC SC

BALANCE, the (1947)
VC

BALLAD IN BLUE (1964)
d Paul Henreid
PB

BALLET OF THE MERMAIDS (1953)
PB

BANDIT OF ZHOBE, the (1959)
d John Gilling
SC

BAND OF THIEVES (1962)
d Peter Bezencenet
VC

BANK HOLIDAY LUCK (1947)
d Baynham Honri
VC

BANK OF ENGLAND (1960)
d Ian Dalrymple
VC

BANK RAIDERS (1958)
d Maxwell Munden
PB

BARGEE, the (1964)
d Duncan Wood
SC PB

BARNACLE BILL (1957)
d Charles Frend
PB

BARRETTS OF WIMPOLE STREET, the (1956)
d Sidney A Franklin
PB

BASIC PRINCIPLES OF LUBRICATION, the (1952)
d Richard F Tambling
VC

BASUTO TROOPS ON ACTIVE SERVICE (1952)
VC

BATTLE OF THE RIVER PLATE, the (1956)
d Michael Powell, Emeric Pressburger
VC

BATTLE OF THE SEXES, the (1959)
d Charles Crichton
SC PB

BATTLE OF THE V-1 (1958)
d Vernon Sewell
PB

BATTLE OF WANGAPORE, the (1955)
d John Daborn
VC

BAY OF SAINT MICHEL, the (1963)
d John Ainsworth
VC

BEACHCOMBER, the (1954)
d Muriel Box
VC PB

'BEAT' GIRL (1959)
d Edmond T Gréville
VC PB

BEAU BRUMMELL (1954)
d Curtis Bernhardt
PB

BEAUTIFUL STRANGER (1954)
d David Miller
SC PB

BEAUTY ADVICE BY ANNE CRAWFORD (1949)
VC

BEAUTY AND THE BEAST (Look at Life series) (1960)
VC

BEAUTY JUNGLE, the (1964)
d Val Guest
VC PB

BECKET (1964)
d Peter Glenville
PB

BEDELIA (1946)
d Lance Comfort
VC PB

BEE WISE! (1946)
d Anson Dyer
VC

BEGGAR'S OPERA, the (1953)
d Peter Brook
VC PB

BEGINNING OF HISTORY (1946)
d Graham Wallace
VC SC

BEHEMOTH THE SEA MONSTER (1958)
d Douglas Hickox, Eugène Lourié
PB

BEHIND THE HEADLINES (1956)
d Charles Saunders
PB

BEHIND THE SCENES NO.3 (1953)
VC

BEHIND THE TON-UP BOYS (Look at Life series) (1964)
VC

BEHOLD THE MAN (1951)
d Walter Rilla
PB

BELADUNA NO.4 (1954)
VC

BELADUNA NO.8 (1954)
VC

BELADUNA NO.10 (1955)
VC

BELGIAN GRAND PRIX (1955)
d Geoffrey Hughes
VC

BELLES OF ST TRINIAN'S, the (1954)
d Frank Launder
VC PB

BERLIN AIRLIFT (1949)
VC

BERMUDA AFFAIR (1956)
d A Edward Sutherland
PB

BERNARD MILES ON GUN DOGS (1948)
d Basil Wright
VC

BERNARD SHAW (1957)
VC

BERNARD SHAW'S VILLAGE (1951)
d J S Frieze
VC

BERTH 24 (1950)
d J B Holmes
VC

BETRAYED (1954)
d Gottfried Reinhardt
PB

BETTER SAVE THAN SORRY (1946)
VC

BETTER WAYS series
see
INTRODUCING WORK STUDY (1955)
ONE MAN AND HIS JOB (1956)

BETWEEN TWO WORLDS (1955)
d W Hugh Baddeley
VC

BEVERCOTES NEW MINE (1958)
VC

BEWARE OF PITY (1946)
d Maurice Elvey
VC PB

BEWARE OF THE DOG (1963)
d Philip Ford
SC

BEYOND MOMBASA (1956)
d George Marshall
SC

BEYOND THE CURTAIN (1960)
d Compton Bennett
PB

BEYOND THE SPEED OF SOUND (High Speed Flight series) (1959)
d Denis Segaller
VC

BEYOND THIS PLACE (1959)
d Jack Cardiff
VC PB

BIG CHANCE, the (1957)
d Peter Graham Scott
PB

BIG DAY, the (1960)
d Peter Graham Scott
VC

BIG FOUR, the (1946)
d W M Larkins
VC

BIG MEETING, the (1963)
VC

BIG MONEY, the (1956)
d John Paddy Carstairs
PB

BILLY BUDD (1962)
d Peter Ustinov
VC SC

BILLY LIAR (1963)
d John Schlesinger
VC PB

BIRDS OF THE VILLAGE (1946)
d Eric Hosking
VC

BIRTHDAY PRESENT, the (1957)
d Pat Jackson
SC PB

BITTER HARVEST (1963)
d Peter Graham Scott
PB

BITTER SPRINGS (1950)
d Ralph Smart
VC PB

BLACKHILL CAMPAIGN (1963)
d Jack Parsons
SC

BLACK ICE, the (1957)
d Godfrey Grayson
SC

BLACK IN THE FACE (1954)
d John Irwin
SC

BLACKMAILED (1950)
d Marc Allégret
PB

BLACK MEMORY (1947)
d Oswald Mitchell
VC

BLACK NARCISSUS (1947)
d Michael Powell, Emeric Pressburger
VC PB

BLACK RIDER, the (1954)
d Wolf Rilla
PB

BLACK SWAN, the (1952)
d Leonard Reeve
VC

BLACK TENT, the (1956)
d Brian Desmond Hurst
SC

BLACK TORMENT, the (1964)
d Robert Hartford-Davis
PB

BLACK WINTER (1947)
VC

BLANCHE FURY (1947)
d Marc Allégret
VC SC

BLIND DATE (1959)
d Joseph Losey
VC PB

BLIND GODDESS, the (1948)
d Harold French
VC SC

BLITZ ON BRITAIN (1960)
d Harry Booth
VC PB

BLOOD AND FIRE (Look at Life series) (1964)
VC

BLOOD OF THE VAMPIRE (1958)
d Henry Cass
PB

BLOOD ORANGE (1953)
d Terence Fisher
VC

BLOOD TRANSFUSION (1955)
VC

BLOW YOUR OWN TRUMPET (1958)
d Cecil Musk
SC

BLUEBEARD'S TEN HONEYMOONS (1960)
d W Lee Wilder
SC

BLUE LAGOON, the (1948)
d Frank Launder
VC PB

BLUE LAMP, the (1949)
d Basil Dearden
VC PB

BLUE MURDER AT ST TRINIAN'S (1957)
d Frank Launder
SC PB

BLUE SCAR (1949)
d Jill Craigie
VC

BODY SAID NO!, the (1950)
d Val Guest
VC

BOLSHOI BALLET, the (1957)
d Paul Czinner
PB

BOMB IN THE HIGH STREET (1963)
d Terry Bishop, Peter Bezencenet
VC

BOND STREET (1948)
d Gordon Parry
PB

BONJOUR TRISTESSE (1957)
d Otto Preminger
VC PB

BONNIE PRINCE CHARLIE (1948)
d Anthony Kimmins
SC PB

BOOKIES AT THE CROSSROADS (Look at Life series) (1964)
VC

BORN TO BOATS (1958)
VC

BOTHERED BY A BEARD (1946)
d E V H Emmett
VC

BOTTOMS UP (1959)
d Mario Zampi
PB

BOUNCER BREAKS UP (1953)
d Don Chaffey
SC

BOUND FOR THE RIO GRANDE (Let's Sing Together series) (1948)
d David Hand
SC

BOY, A GIRL AND A BIKE, a (1949)
d Ralph Smart
VC SC

BOY AND THE BRIDGE, the (1959)
d Kevin McClory
SC

BOYS, the (1962)
d Sidney J Furie
VC PB

BOYS IN BROWN (1949)
d Montgomery Tully
VC SC

BOY WHO STOLE A MILLION, the (1960)
d Charles Crichton
PB

BRAIN MACHINE, the (1954)
d Ken Hughes
VC PB

BRANDY FOR THE PARSON (1951)
d John Eldridge
VC SC

BRASS MONKEY, the (1948)
d Thornton Freeland
PB

BRAVE DON'T CRY, the (1952)
d Philip Leacock
VC SC

BREAK, the (1962)
d Lance Comfort
PB

BREAKAWAY (1956)
d Henry Cass
PB

BREAKING POINT, the (1961)
d Lance Comfort
PB

BREAK IN THE CIRCLE (1955)
d Val Guest
PB

BREEDING BEHAVIOUR OF THE BLACK-HEADED GULL, the (1960)
d Nikolas Tinbergen
VC

BREEDING COLONY OF THE BLACK-HEADED GULL, a (1953)
d Nikolas Tinbergen
VC

BREEDING FOR MILK (1947)
d Jack Gowers
VC

BRIDAL PATH, the (1959)
d Frank Launder
PB

BRIDES OF DRACULA, the (1960)
d Terence Fisher
SC PB

BRIDGE, the (1946)
d J D Chambers
VC

BRIDGE OF TIME (1950)
d Geoffrey Boothby, David Eady
VC

BRIDGE ON THE RIVER KWAI, the (1957)
d David Lean
VC SC

BRIEF CITY (1952)
d Jacques Brunius, Maurice Harvey
VC

BRIGHTON ROCK (1947)
d John Boulting
VC SC

BRIGHTON STORY (1955)
d Pamela Bower
VC

BRITAIN CAN MAKE IT NO.1 (1946)
d Francis Gysin
VC

BRITAIN CAN MAKE IT NO.3 (1946)
VC

BRITAIN CAN MAKE IT NO.11 (1946)
VC

BRITAIN CAN MAKE IT NO.12 (1946)
VC

BRITAIN'S COMET (1952)
d James Hill
VC

BRITAIN'S FIRST JET PLANES (1949)
VC

BRITAIN'S NEW AIRCRAFT (1950)
VC

BRITAIN'S WEALTH FROM COAL (1959)
VC

BRITANNIA MEWS (1948)
d Jean Negulesco
PB

BRITISH AIRCRAFT REVIEW 1948 (1948)
d Geoffrey Hughes
VC

BRITISH AIRCRAFT REVIEW 1949 (1949)
d Bill Mason
VC

BRITISH – ARE THEY ARTISTIC?, the (This Modern Age series) (1947)
VC SC

BRITISH INDUSTRIES FAIR 1948 (1948)
d Charles de Lautour
VC

BRITISH POLICEMAN, the (1959)
d David Cobham
VC

BRITISH SPORTING PERSONALITIES series
see
PETER MAY (1962)

BRITISH TRADE UNION, a (1955)
VC

BROKEN HORSESHOE (1953)
d Martyn C Webster
PB

BROKEN JOURNEY (1947)
d Ken Annakin
VC SC

BROTHERS, the (1947)
d David Macdonald
VC PB

BROTHERS IN LAW (1956)
d Roy Boulting
PB

BROWNING VERSION, the (1951)
d Anthony Asquith
VC PB

BUILDERS, the (1948)
VC

BULLDOG BREED, the (1960)
d Robert Asher
SC PB

BULLFIGHTER (Look at Life series) (1960)
VC

BURIED FILM, the (1959)
d Alistair Sawrey-Cookson
VC

BURNT EVIDENCE (1954)
d Daniel Birt
PB

BUSH CHRISTMAS (1947)
d Ralph Smart
VC

BUT NOT IN VAIN (1948)
d Edmond T Gréville
PB

CAGE OF GOLD (1950)
d Basil Dearden
VC SC PB

CAIRO (1963)
d Wolf Rilla
PB

CALCULATED RISK (1963)
d Norman Harrison
VC

CALENDAR, the (1948)
d Arthur Crabtree
SC PB

CALLER HERRIN' (1948)
d Alan Harper
VC

CALLING ALL SPORTSMEN series
see
IT'S A GREAT GAME (1948)

CALLING BULLDOG DRUMMOND (1951)
d Victor Saville
PB

CALLING THE TUNE (Look at Life series) (1964)
VC

CALL ME BWANA (1963)
d Gordon Douglas
PB

CAMPBELL'S KINGDOM (1957)
d Ralph Thomas
PB

CAMP ON BLOOD ISLAND, the (1957)
d Val Guest
VC SC

CANDY'S CALENDAR (1946)
d Horace Shepherd
VC

CANTERBURY ROAD (Musical Paintbox series) (1949)
d Brian O'Hanlon
VC

CAN WE BE RICH? (Focus on the Future series) (1946)
d Cecil Musk
VC

CAPITAL CITIES OF THE NORTH (1956)
VC

CAPTAIN BOYCOTT (1947)
d Frank Launder
VC PB

CAPTAIN HORATIO HORNBLOWER RN
(1950)
d Raoul Walsh
VC PB

CAPTAIN'S PARADISE, the (1953)
d Anthony Kimmins
VC SC

CAPTAIN'S TABLE, the (1958)
d Jack Lee
PB

CAPTIVE HEART, the (1946)
d Basil Dearden
VC PB

CARAVAN (1946)
d Arthur Crabtree
VC

CARD, the (1952)
d Ronald Neame
VC SC

CARDBOARD CAVALIER (1948)
d Walter Forde
VC PB

CARE OF SAWS (1942)
VC

CARETAKER, the (1963)
d Clive Donner
VC SC

CARIBBEAN (1951)
d Graham Wallace
VC

CARING FOR CHILDREN (Is This the Job for Me? series) (1949)
VC

CARLTON-BROWNE OF THE FO (1958)
d Jeffrey Dell, Roy Boulting
VC

CARNIVAL (1946)
d Stanley Haynes
SC PB

CARRINGFORD SCHOOL MYSTERY, the (1958)
d William C Hammond
SC

CARRY ON CABBY (1963)
d Gerald Thomas
VC PB

CARRY ON CLEO (1964)
d Gerald Thomas
VC PB

CARRY ON, CONSTABLE (1960)
d Gerald Thomas
VC PB

CARRY ON CRUISING (1962)
d Gerald Thomas
VC PB

CARRY ON JACK (1964)
d Gerald Thomas
VC PB

CARRY ON NURSE (1958)
d Gerald Thomas
VC PB

CARRY ON REGARDLESS (1961)
d Gerald Thomas
VC SC

CARRY ON SERGEANT (1958)
d Gerald Thomas
VC PB

CARRY ON SPYING (1964)
d Gerald Thomas
VC PB

CARRY ON TEACHER (1959)
d Gerald Thomas
VC PB

CARVE HER NAME WITH PRIDE (1958)
d Lewis Gilbert
SC

CASE OF CHARLES PEACE, the (1949)
d Norman Lee
VC PB

CASE OF THE MUKKINESE BATTLEHORN, the (1955)
d Joseph Sterling
VC

CASE OF THE OLD ROPE MAN (1952)
d Darrel Catling
SC

CASH ON DEMAND (1961)
d Quentin Lawrence
SC PB

CAST A DARK SHADOW (1955)
d Lewis Gilbert
VC

CASTLE SINISTER (1947)
d Oscar Burn
VC

CAT GANG, the (1958)
d Darrel Catling
SC

CAT GIRL (1957)
d Alfred Shaughnessy
PB

CAUGHT IN THE NET (1960)
d John Haggarty
SC

CEILINGS WITH SIRAPITE FINISH (1949)
VC

CENTRE, the (1948)
d J B Holmes
VC

CENTURY OF ENGINEERING TOOL DEVELOPMENT, a (1956)
VC

CEYLON – THE NEW DOMINION (This Modern Age series) (1947)
VC

CHAIN OF EVENTS (1957)
d Gerald Thomas
SC PB

CHALK GARDEN, the (1964)
d Ronald Neame
VC PB

CHALLENGE, the (1959)
d John Gilling
SC PB

CHALLENGE IN NIGERIA (This Modern Age series) (1948)
VC

CHAMPIONS ON PARADE (1947)
d Joseph G Frankel, Michael H Goodman
VC

CHANCE OF A LIFETIME (1950)
d Bernard Miles
VC

CHAPTERS OF LLANDUDNO NO.5: MR CHURCHILL ON THE CHALLENGE OF SOVIET POLICY (1948)
VC

CHAPTERS OF LLANDUDNO NO.6: MR CHURCHILL ON CONSERVATIVE DUTY (1948)
VC

CHARLEY series
see
CHARLEY'S MARCH OF TIME (1948)
FARMER CHARLEY (1949)
ROBINSON CHARLEY (1948)

CHARLEY'S MARCH OF TIME (Charley series) (1948)
d John Halas, Joy Batchelor
VC

CHASE A CROOKED SHADOW (1957)
d Michael Anderson
PB

CHASING THE BLUES (1950)
d J D Chambers, Jack Ellitt
VC

CHECKPOINT (1956)
d Ralph Thomas
SC PB

CHICKENS IN THE MILL (Look at Life series) (1962)
VC

CHILD AND THE KILLER, the (1959)
d Max Varnel
PB

CHILDBIRTH WITHOUT FEAR (1956)
d Grantly Dick-Read
VC

CHILDREN GALORE (1954)
d Terence Fisher
PB

CHILDREN GROWING UP WITH OTHER PEOPLE (1947)
d Margaret Thomson
VC

CHILDREN LEARNING BY EXPERIENCE (1947)
d Margaret Thomson
VC

CHILDREN OF THE DAMNED (1963)
d Anton M Leader
PB

CHILDREN ON TRIAL (1946)
d Jack Lee
VC PB

CHILTERN HUNDREDS, the (1949)
d John Paddy Carstairs
VC PB

CHISOKO THE AFRICAN (1949)
d Donald Swanson
VC

CHRISTMAS PLAY, the (1959)
d Hazel Swift
VC

CHRISTOPHER COLUMBUS (1949)
d David Macdonald
VC SC

CHURCHILL RECEIVES FREEDOM OF PERTH (1948)
VC

CHURCHILL'S DECLARATION (1949)
VC

CINE-GAZETTE series
see
ELEPHANT WILL NEVER FORGET, the (1953)

CIRCLE OF DANGER (1950)
d Jacques Tourneur
VC

CIRCLE OF DECEPTION (1960)
d Jack Lee
SC PB

CIRCUS BOY (1947)
d Cecil Musk
PB

CIRCUS COMES TO TOWN (1946)
VC

CIRCUS FRIENDS (1956)
d Gerald Thomas
SC

CIRCUS OF HORRORS (1960)
d Sidney Hayers
SC PB

CIRCUS STORY (1946)
d Sammy Lee
VC

CITY AFTER DARK (1955)
d Ian K Barnes
VC

CITY OF CRISIS (Look at Life series) (1961)
VC

CITY OF THE DEAD (1960)
d John Moxey
PB

CITY SIDELIGHTS NO.1 (1951)
VC

CITY SIDELIGHTS NO.2 (1950)
VC

CITY SIDELIGHTS NO.3 (1950)
VC

CITY SIDELIGHTS NO.4 (1950)
VC

CITY SPEAKS, a (1947)
d Francis Gysin
VC

CLASH BY NIGHT (1963)
d Montgomery Tully
PB

CLOAK WITHOUT DAGGER (1955)
d Joseph Sterling
PB

CLOSE-UPS OF THE STARS – ANNE ZIEGLER (1946)
VC

CLOUDBURST (1951)
d Francis Searle
PB

CLOUDED YELLOW, the (1950)
d Ralph Thomas
VC SC

CLUE OF THE MISSING APE, the (1953)
d James Hill
SC

COACHING IN THE GAME (1948)
VC

COAL CRISIS (This Modern Age series) (1947)
VC

COALMINING AS A CRAFT series
see
ORIGIN OF COAL, the (1953)

COAL MINING TODAY (Post-War Jobs series) (1946)
VC

COAL PREPARATION (1956)
d Brian Salt
VC

COASTAL NAVIGATION AND PILOTAGE (1953)
d Louis Dahl
VC

COASTS OF CLYDE (1959)
d James Ritchie
VC

COCCIDIOSIS IN POULTRY (Animal Health series) (1952)
VC

COCKELL V LA STARZA, HEAVYWEIGHT CONTEST, EARLS COURT, LONDON (1954)
VC

COCKLESHELL HEROES, the (1955)
d José Ferrer
VC SC

COCOA HARVEST (1948)
d A R Taylor
VC

COLDITZ STORY, the (1954)
d Guy Hamilton
VC

COLONEL BOGEY (1948)
d Terence Fisher
VC

COLONEL CROMPTON, PIONEER AND PROPHET (1947)
d Terry Bishop
VC

COLORADO BEETLE; AN EXAMPLE OF INTERNATIONAL CO-OPERATION (1946)
VC

COLOUR (1947)
VC

COME DANCE WITH ME (1950)
d Mario Zampi
VC

COMEDY MAN, the (1963)
d Alvin Rakoff
SC

COME FLY WITH ME (1962)
d Henry Levin
PB

COME SATURDAY (1949)
d Leonard Reeve, Jim Davies
VC

COMIN' THRO' THE RYE (1947)
d Walter C Mycroft
VC

COMMANDO – THE STORY OF THE GREEN BERET (1952)
d Frank Cadman
PB

COMMONWEALTH JOURNEY (1959)
d Alan Masters
VC

COMMUNITY SINGING IN HYDE PARK (1948)
VC

COMPREHENSIVE SCHOOL (Looking at Britain series) (1962)
VC

CONE OF SILENCE (1960)
d Charles Frend
SC

CONFLICT OF WINGS (1954)
d John Eldridge
VC

CONFRONTATION IN BORNEO (1963)
VC

CONGO HARVEST (Wealth of the World series) (1951)
VC PB

CONJOINED TWINS OF KANO, the (1954)
VC

CONQUEST OF EVEREST, the (1953)
VC PB

CONSCIENCE BAY (1960)
d Norman Thaddeus Vane
SC

CONSPIRACY OF HEARTS (1960)
d Ralph Thomas
SC

CONSPIRATOR (1949)
d Victor Saville
PB

CONTRABAND – SPAIN (1955)
d Lawrence Huntington
PB

CONTROLLED HEAT (1955)
d Douglas Clarke, J D Chambers
VC

CONTROLS (How an Aeroplane Flies series) (1947)
d Bill Mason
VC

COPENHAGEN (1956)
d Michael Carreras
VC

COPY BOOK PLEASE (1948)
VC

CORNISH ENGINE, the (1948)
d Philip Armitage, Bill Mason
VC

CORNWALL (Musical Paintbox series) (1949)
d Pat Griffin
VC

CORONATION CEREMONY (1953)
VC

CORRECT STAMPING (1949)
VC

CORRIDOR OF MIRRORS (1948)
d Terence Young
VC PB

CORRIDORS OF BLOOD (1958)
d Robert Day
VC PB

COTTON COMEBACK (Post-War Jobs series) (1946)
VC

COUNTERBLAST (1948)
d Paul L Stein
VC PB

COUNTERFEIT PLAN, the (1956)
d Montgomery Tully
VC

COUNTERSPY (1953)
d Vernon Sewell
PB

COUNTRY HOMES (1947)
d Paul Dickson
VC

COUNTRY MANSIONS (1952)
VC

COUPE DES ALPES; THE STORY OF THE 1958 ALPINE RALLY (1958)
d John Armstrong
SC PB

COURTESY (1964)
d Richard Kilburn
VC

COURT MARTIAL OF MAJOR KELLER, the (1964)
d Ernest Morris
PB

COURTNEYS OF CURZON STREET, the (1947)
d Herbert Wilcox
VC PB

COVENTRY CATHEDRAL (1958)
d Dudley Shaw Ashton
VC

CRACKSMAN, the (1963)
d Peter Graham Scott
PB

CRAGSMEN, the (1948)
d J Blake Dalrymple
VC

CRAZY DAY WITH MAX WALL, a (1950)
d Horace Shepherd
VC

CRESCENT WING, the (1954)
VC

CRICKET (1950)
VC

CRIMINAL, the (1960)
d Joseph Losey
VC PB

CRIMSON PIRATE, the (1952)
d Robert Siodmak
PB

CRITICALITY (1957)
VC

CRITIC AND FILM series
see
A JYMPSON HARMAN ... AND ...
  'GREAT EXPECTATIONS' ... (1949)
DILYS POWELL ... AND 'THE
  OVERLANDERS' ... (1949)
E ARNOT ROBERTSON ... DISCUSSES
  '12 ANGRY MEN' ... (1959)

CROOKS ANONYMOUS (1962)
d Ken Annakin
PB

CROOKS IN CLOISTERS (1964)
d Jeremy Summers
PB

CROSS CHANNEL (1955)
d R G Springsteen
SC

CROWN DERBY (1949)
PB

CRUEL SEA, the (1952)
d Charles Frend
VC PB

CRY FROM THE STREETS, a (1958)
d Lewis Gilbert
PB

CRY, THE BELOVED COUNTRY (1951)
d Zoltan Korda
VC SC

CUMBERLAND STORY, the (1947)
d Humphrey Jennings
VC

CURE, the (1950)
d Richard Massingham, Michael Law
VC

CURE FOR LOVE, the (1949)
d Robert Donat
VC SC

CURE OF PINING DISEASE IN SHEEP (1952)
VC

CURSE OF SIMBA, the (1964)
d Lindsay Shonteff
VC

CURSE OF THE MUMMY'S TOMB, the (1964)
d Michael Carreras
VC SC

CURSE OF THE WEREWOLF, the (1961)
d Terence Fisher
PB

CURSE OF THE WRAYDONS, the (1946)
d Victor M Gover
VC

CURTAIN UP (1952)
d Ralph Smart
PB

CYPRUS IS AN ISLAND (1946)
d Ralph Keene
VC

CYRIL STAPLETON AND THE SHOW BAND (1955)
d Michael Carreras
PB

DAILY BREAD (1948)
d Ralph McCormick
VC

DAM BUSTERS, the (1955)
d Michael Anderson
VC PB

DAMNED, the (1961)
d Joseph Losey
VC PB

DANCE HALL (1950)
d Charles Crichton
VC PB

DANCE LITTLE LADY (1954)
d Val Guest
PB

DANCING FLEECE, the (1950)
d Frederick Wilson
VC

DANCING TIME (1957)
d Robert Henryson
VC

DANCING WITH CRIME (1947)
d John Paddy Carstairs
VC PB

DANCING YEARS, the (1949)
d Harold French
SC PB

DANGEROUS CARGO (1954)
d John Harlow
PB

DANGEROUS EXILE (1957)
d Brian Desmond Hurst
SC

DANGEROUS VOYAGE (1954)
d Vernon Sewell
SC PB

DARK MAN, the (1950)
d Jeffrey Dell
SC

DARK SECRET (1949)
d Maclean Rogers
PB

DATE WITH A DREAM, a (1948)
d Dicky Leeman
VC

DATE WITH IRIS (1956)
d Douglas Clarke
PB

DAUGHTER OF DARKNESS (1947)
d Lance Comfort
VC

DAVID (1951)
d Paul Dickson
VC

DAVY (1957)
d Michael Relph
VC SC

DAWN KILLER, the (1959)
d Donald Taylor
SC

DAY, the (1960)
d Peter Finch
PB

DAYBREAK (1948)
d Compton Bennett
VC PB

DAYBREAK IN UDI (1949)
d Terry Bishop
VC

DAYLIGHT ROBBERY (1964)
d Michael Truman
SC

DAY OF THE TRIFFIDS, the (1962)
d Steve Sekely
PB

DAY THE EARTH CAUGHT FIRE, the (1961)
d Val Guest
VC SC

DAY THEY ROBBED THE BANK OF ENGLAND, the (1959)
d John Guillermin
VC PB

DAY WITH 'BRUMAS' SUPPORTED BY 'IVY', a (1950)
VC

DEADLINE (1951)
VC

DEADLY LAMPSHADE (1948)
d Philip Leacock
VC

DEAD MAN'S EVIDENCE (1962)
d Francis Searle
SC

DEAR MR PROHACK (1949)
d Thornton Freeland
VC PB

DEAR MURDERER (1946)
d Arthur Crabtree
VC

DEATH DRUMS ALONG THE RIVER (1963)
d Lawrence Huntington
VC

DECONTAMINATION (1958)
VC

DEEP BLUE SEA, the (1955)
d Anatole Litvak
SC PB

DEFEATED PEOPLE, a (1946)
d Humphrey Jennings
VC

DEFENCE AGAINST POLIOMYELITIS (1956)
VC

DE HAVILLAND DIARY; A RANDOM MISCELLANY OF POST-WAR OCCASIONS, a (1951)
VC

DELAYED ACTION (1954)
d John Harlow
PB

DELAYED FLIGHT (1964)
d Anthony Young
SC

DENIS COMPTON (Players of Merit series) (1949)
VC

DENIS COMPTON (Sportshort series) (1954)
d Douglas Rankin
VC

DENTIST IN THE CHAIR (1960)
d Don Chaffey
VC PB

DENTIST ON THE JOB (1961)
d C M Pennington-Richards
VC PB

DEPTH CHARGE (1960)
d Jeremy Summers
SC

DERBY DAY (1952)
d Herbert Wilcox
PB

DESERT MICE (1959)
d Michael Relph
VC PB

DESERT ROAD (1954)
VC

DESPERATE MOMENT (1953)
d Compton Bennett
VC SC

DEVELOPMENT AREAS (This Modern Age series) (1947)
VC SC

DEVIL DOLL (1963)
d Lindsay Shonteff
VC

DEVIL NEVER SLEEPS, the (1962)
d Leo McCarey
PB

DEVIL'S BAIT (1959)
d Peter Graham Scott
VC

DEVIL'S DISCIPLE, the (1959)
d Guy Hamilton
PB

DEVIL-SHIP PIRATES, the (1963)
d Don Sharp
SC PB

DEVILS OF DARKNESS (1964)
d Lance Comfort
PB

DEVON WHEY (Musical Paintbox series) (1949)
d G Henry Stringer
VC

DIAL 999 (1955)
d Montgomery Tully
PB

DIAMOND, the (1954)
d Montgomery Tully
PB

DIAMOND CITY (1949)
d David Macdonald
VC SC

DIARY FOR TIMOTHY, a (1946)
d Humphrey Jennings
VC

DICK BARTON STRIKES BACK (1949)
d Godfrey Grayson
VC

DIESEL ON RAIL, the (1956)
SC

DIESEL ON THE FARM (1950)
d A H Luff
VC

DIESEL TRAIN DRIVER PART 2 (1959)
VC

DIGESTION (1949)
d Beryl Denman Lacey
VC

DIGGING UP THE PAST (Look at Life series) (1963)
VC

DILEMMA (1962)
d Peter Maxwell
SC

DILYS POWELL ... AND 'THE OVERLANDERS' ... (Critic and Film series) (1949)
VC

DIM LITTLE ISLAND, the (1948)
d Humphrey Jennings
VC

DISTANT NEIGHBOURS (1956)
d John Durst, Humphrey Swingler, Roland Stafford
VC

DISTANT TRUMPET (1952)
d Terence Fisher
SC

DIVIDED CITY, the (Look at Life series) (1959)
VC

DIVIDED HEART, the (1954)
d Charles Crichton
VC SC

DOCK BRIEF, the (1962)
d James Hill
PB

DOCTOR AT LARGE (1957)
d Ralph Thomas
SC

DOCTOR AT SEA (1955)
d Ralph Thomas
PB

DR CRIPPEN (1962)
d Robert Lynn
PB

DOCTOR IN DISTRESS (1963)
d Ralph Thomas
VC SC

DOCTOR IN LOVE (1960)
d Ralph Thomas
SC PB

DOCTOR IN THE HOUSE (1954)
d Ralph Thomas
VC

DR NO (1962)
d Terence Young
PB

DOCTOR'S DILEMMA (1948)
VC

DOCTOR'S DILEMMA, the (1958)
d Anthony Asquith
VC PB

DR STRANGELOVE; or, How I learned to stop worrying and love the bomb (1963)
d Stanley Kubrick
VC PB

DR SYN ALIAS THE SCARECROW (1963)
d James Neilson
SC PB

DO IT YOURSELF CARTOON KIT (1959)
d Bob Godfrey, Vera Linnecar, Nancy Hanna, Keith Learner
VC

DOLLARS AND SENSE (1949)
d Diana Pine
VC

DOMESTIC HELP (1952)
VC

DON GIOVANNI (1954)
d Paul Czinner
PB

DON'T BOTHER TO KNOCK (1961)
d Cyril Frankel
SC PB

DON'T EVER LEAVE ME (1949)
d Arthur Crabtree
VC PB

DON'T PANIC CHAPS (1959)
d George Pollock
SC

DON'T TALK TO STRANGE MEN (1962)
d Pat Jackson
SC PB

DOOLITTLE MAKES GOOD (1948)
VC

DOOR IN THE WALL, the (1956)
d Glenn H Alvey Jr
VC PB

DOUBLE CONFESSION (1950)
d Ken Annakin
SC PB

DOUBLECROSS (1955)
d Anthony Squire
VC

DOVER, SPRING 1947 (1947)
d Mary Beales
VC

DOWN LONDON RIVER (Look at Life series) (1959)
VC

DO YOU REMEMBER? 1903–1953 (1953)
VC

DRACULA (1958)
d Terence Fisher
PB

DRAG (How an Aeroplane Flies series) (1947)
d John Shearman
VC

DRAGON OF PENDRAGON CASTLE, the (1950)
d John Baxter
VC

DRAWINGS OF LEONARDO DA VINCI, the (1953)
d Adrian de Potier
PB

DRUMS FOR A HOLIDAY (1950)
d A R Taylor
VC

DRY HANDS (1964)
d Ian Clark
VC

d-TUBOCURARINE (1947)
VC

DUAL ALIBI (1947)
d Alfred Travers
PB

DUBLIN NIGHTMARE (1958)
d John Pomeroy
PB

DUEL IN THE JUNGLE (1954)
d George Marshall
SC PB

DUKE WORE JEANS, the (1958)
d Gerald Thomas
SC PB

DUNKIRK (1958)
d Leslie Norman
PB

DURING ONE NIGHT (1961)
d Sidney J Furie
VC PB

DUSTY BATES (1947)
d Darrell Catling
VC SC

EACH FOR ALL (1946)
d Montgomery Tully
VC

EAGLES OF THE FLEET (1950)
d Cyril Frankel
VC

EARLY STARTERS (Look at Life series) (1964)
VC

E ARNOT ROBERTSON ... DISCUSSES '12 ANGRY MEN' ... (Critic and Film series) (1959)
d Hazel Wilkinson
VC

EAST AFRICAN COLLEGE (1950)
d Robert Kingston Davies
VC

EAST IN THE WEST (1954)
d Margaret Thomson
VC

EAST OF SUDAN (1964)
d Nathan Juran
SC

EASY MONEY (1948)
d Bernard Knowles
VC PB

EDGE JOINTING (1947)
VC

EDINBURGH (1952)
d David Eady
SC

EDUCATION FOR LIVING (This Modern Age series) (1949)
VC SC

EDUCATION OF THE DEAF (1946)
d Jack Ellitt
VC

EDWARDIAN NEWSREEL (1948)
VC

EDWARDIANS AT SHELSLEY WALSH, the (1946)
VC

EDWARD, MY SON (1948)
d George Cukor
VC

80,000 SUSPECTS (1963)
d Val Guest
SC PB

EL DORADO (1951)
d John Alderson
VC

ELEPHANT WILL NEVER FORGET, the (Cine-Gazette series) (1953)
d John Krish
VC

ELSTREE STORY (1952)
d Gilbert Gunn
VC

ELUSIVE PIMPERNEL, the (1950)
d Michael Powell, Emeric Pressburger
SC PB

ELUSIVE VICTORY (1951)
VC

EMBEZZLER, the (1954)
d John Gilling
PB

EMERIC PRESSBURGER HOME MOVIES (1950)
VC

ENCORE (1951)
d Pat Jackson, Anthony Pélissier, Harold French
VC PB

ENDLESS ROPE HAULAGE (1955)
VC

END OF THE AFFAIR, the (1954)
d Edward Dmytryk
VC

END OF THE RIVER, the (1947)
d Derek Twist
VC PB

END OF THE ROAD, the (1954)
d Wolf Rilla
SC

ENGINEERS IN STEEL (1953)
VC

ENGLAND'S WEALTH FROM WOOL (1948)
d J B Napier-Bell
VC

ENGLISH CRIMINAL JUSTICE (1946)
d Ken Annakin
VC

ENGLISHMAN'S HOLIDAY, an (1946)
d A H Kingham
VC

ENGLISHMAN'S HOME, an (1946)
d Richard Massingham
VC

ENGLISH OILFIELD, an (1946)
d Francis Searle
VC

ENTERTAINER, the (1960)
d Tony Richardson
VC PB

ESCAPE (1948)
d Joseph L Mankiewicz
VC PB

ESCAPE DANGEROUS (1949)
d Digby Smith
VC

ESCAPE IN THE SUN (1955)
d George Breakston
PB

ESCAPEMENT (1957)
d Montgomery Tully
PB

ESCORT FOR HIRE (1960)
d Godfrey Grayson
PB

ESTHER WATERS (1948)
d Ian Dalrymple, Peter Proud
VC PB

EUREKA STOCKADE (1949)
d Harry Watt
VC SC

EUROPE GROWS TOGETHER (Look at Life series) (1963)
VC

EUROPE'S FISHERIES IN DANGER (This Modern Age series) (1949)
VC

EVERY DAY EXCEPT CHRISTMAS (1957)
d Lindsay Anderson
VC

EVERY DAY'S A HOLIDAY (1964)
d James Hill
VC

EVERY VALLEY (1957)
d Michael Clarke
VC

EVIL OF FRANKENSTEIN, the (1964)
d Freddie Francis
PB

EXERCISE MERMAID (1957)
VC

EXPRESSO BONGO (1959)
d Val Guest
VC PB

EXTENSIONS TO LONDON TRANSPORT (1946)
VC

EXTERIOR WALL WITH TYROLEAN FINISH (1951)
VC

EXTRA DAY, the (1956)
d William Fairchild
SC

EXTRAVAGANZA (1959)
d Robert Henryson
VC

EYES THAT KILL (1947)
d Richard Grey
VC

EYEWITNESS (1956)
d Muriel Box
SC PB

FABRICS OF THE FUTURE (This Modern
Age series) (1946)
VC SC

FACE OF A STRANGER (1965)
d John Moxey
SC PB

FACE THE MUSIC (1954)
d Terence Fisher
VC

FACTS AND FANCIES (1951)
d Michael Law
VC

FAIR RENT (1946)
d Mary Beales
VC

FALLEN IDOL, the (1948)
d Carol Reed
VC SC

FALL GUYS (1952)
d Ian K Barnes
VC

FALL OF THE HOUSE OF USHER, the
(1950)
d Ivan Barnett
PB

FAME IS THE SPUR (1947)
d Roy Boulting
VC PB

FAMILY AFFAIR, a (1950)
d Margaret Thomson
VC

FAMILY ALBUM (1953)
d Richard Massingham, Jacques Brunius
VC

FAMILY DOCTOR, the (1946)
d Richard Massingham
VC

FAMILY DOCTOR (1958)
d Derek Twist
PB

FAMILY PORTRAIT, a (1950)
d Humphrey Jennings
VC

FANTASY ON IRELAND, a (Musical Paintbox
series) (1949)
d G Henry Stringer
VC

FAR CRY, a (1958)
d Stephen Peet
SC

FARMER CHARLEY (Charley series) (1949)
d John Halas, Joy Batchelor
VC

FARMER MOVING SOUTH (1952)
d John Taylor
VC

FARMERS' MACHINERY SYNDICATES
(Looking at Britain) (1961)
VC

FARMYARD RISING, the (1947)
d Anson Dyer
VC

FASHION FANTASY (1946)
d Michel
VC

FAST AND LOOSE (1954)
d Gordon Parry
SC PB

FAST LADY, the (1962)
d Ken Annakin
SC PB

FAST PLOUGH, the (1954)
VC

FATE OF AN EMPIRE (This Modern Age
series) (1948)
VC

FATE TAKES A HAND (1961)
d Max Varnel
PB

FATHER BROWN (1954)
d Robert Hamer
VC SC

FATHER CAME TOO! (1963)
d Peter Graham Scott
SC PB

FATHER FORGOT, a (1954)
VC

FATHER'S DOING FINE (1952)
d Henry Cass
PB

FAWLEY ACHIEVEMENT (1954)
d Geoffrey Gurrin
VC

FEATHERED WHEEL, the (Films of the Sea
series) (1956)
d Alistair Sawrey-Cookson
VC

FELL LOCOMOTIVE, the (1952)
d Peter de Normanville, Roy Harris
VC

FERRY CROSS THE MERSEY (1964)
d Jeremy Summers
PB

FERRY TO HONG KONG (1959)
d Lewis Gilbert
VC SC

FESTIVAL IN EDINBURGH (1955)
d Douglas Clarke
VC

FESTIVAL IN LONDON (1951)
d Philip Leacock
VC

**FESTIVAL OF BRITAIN CELEBRATIONS,
LEYLAND, LANCS** (1951)
VC

FIEND WITHOUT A FACE (1957)
d Arthur Crabtree
PB

FIFTY YEARS OF BRITISH BOXING (1950)
d Bill MacDonnell
VC

FIGHT AGAINST DISEASE, the (1947)
VC

FIGHT FOR A FULLER LIFE (This Modern
Age series) (1949)
VC SC

FIGHT FOR THE ASHES, the (1962)
d E V H Emmett
VC

FIGHT IN MALAYA, the (This Modern Age
series) (1950)
VC SC

FIGURES IN A LANDSCAPE (1953)
d Dudley Shaw Ashton
VC

FILMAGAZINE NO.1 (1947)
d Henry Cooper
VC

FILMS AND THEIR STORY (1953)
VC

FILMS OF THE SEA series
see
FEATHERED WHEEL, the (1956)

FINAL APPOINTMENT (1954)
d Terence Fisher
PB

FINAL TEST, the (1953)
d Anthony Asquith
VC PB

FIND THE LADY (1956)
d Charles Saunders
PB

FINEST HOURS, the (1964)
d Peter Baylis
VC SC

**FIRE RISKS WITH UNDERGROUND
CONVEYORS** (1952)
d Grahame Tharp
VC

FIRE'S THE ENEMY (1951)
VC

FIRE UNDERGROUND (1955)
d Alun Falconer
VC

FIRST GENTLEMAN, the (1948)
d Alberto Cavalcanti
VC SC

FIRST MAN INTO SPACE (1958)
d Robert Day
SC PB

FIRST MEN IN THE MOON (1964)
d Nathan Juran
VC SC

FIRST ON THE ROAD (1960)
d Joseph Losey
VC

FIRST REPORT ON MODERNISATION
(1959)
VC

FIVE CLUES TO FORTUNE (1956)
d Joe Mendoza
SC

FIVE DAYS (1954)
d Montgomery Tully
PB

FIVE GOLDEN HOURS (1961)
d Mario Zampi
SC PB

FIVE HAVE A MYSTERY TO SOLVE (1964)
d Ernest Morris
SC

FIVE O'CLOCK FINISH (1954)
d John Irwin
SC

FIVE ON A TREASURE ISLAND (1957)
d Gerald Landau
SC

FIVE TO ONE (1963)
d Gordon Flemyng
PB

FIVE TOWNS (1947)
d Terry Bishop
VC

FLAME IN THE STREETS (1961)
d Roy Ward Baker
VC SC

FLAMINGO AFFAIR, the (1948)
d Horace Shepherd
VC

FLANAGAN BOY, the (1953)
d Reginald Le Borg
PB

FLAW, the (1955)
d Terence Fisher
VC

FLESH AND BLOOD (1951)
d Anthony Kimmins
VC SC

FLESH AND THE FIENDS, the (1959)
d John Gilling
PB

FLESH IS WEAK, the (1957)
d Don Chaffey
VC

FLIGHT FOR TOMORROW (1947)
d Sarah Erulkar
VC

FLOATING DUTCHMAN, the (1953)
d Vernon Sewell
PB

FLOATING FORTRESS (1959)
d Harold Baim
PB

FLOOD, the (1963)
d Frederic Goode
SC

FLOODS OF FEAR (1958)
d Charles Crichton
VC SC

FLOODTIDE (1949)
d Frederick Wilson
VC SC

FLYING EYE, the (1955)
d William C Hammond
SC

FLYING WITH PRUDENCE (1946)
SC

FOCUS ON ETHIOPIA (1952)
VC

FOCUS ON FLYING BOATS (1954)
VC

FOCUS ON KUWAIT (1953)
d A S Graham
VC

FOCUS ON THE DROVER (1953)
VC

FOCUS ON THE FUTURE series
see
CAN WE BE RICH? (1946)

FOCUS ON THE NILE (1952)
VC

FOLLOW A STAR (1959)
d Robert Asher
SC PB

FOLLOW THAT HORSE! (1960)
d Alan Bromly
PB

FOLLOW THAT MAN (1961)
d Jerry Epstein
VC

FOLLY TO BE WISE (1952)
d Frank Launder
VC

FOOD FLASHES (1946)
VC

FOOL AND THE PRINCESS, the (1948)
d William C Hammond
SC

FOOTSTEPS IN THE FOG (1955)
d Arthur Lubin
SC

FOR BETTER, FOR WORSE (1954)
d J Lee Thompson
SC PB

FORBIDDEN CARGO (1954)
d Harold French
SC

FORCES IN BALANCE (How an Aeroplane Flies series) (1947)
d John Shearman
VC

FORCES' SWEETHEART (1953)
d Maclean Rogers
PB

FORMING OF METALS (1957)
d Peter de Normanville
VC SC

FOR THEM THAT TRESPASS (1948)
d Alberto Cavalcanti
VC SC

FORWARD A CENTURY (1951)
d J B Napier-Bell
VC

FOUNDRY PRACTICE (1952)
d George H Sewell
VC

FOUR DAYS (1951)
d John Guillermin
VC

FOUR MEN IN PRISON (1950)
d Max Anderson
VC

XIVTH OLYMPIAD – THE GLORY OF SPORT (1948)
d Castleton Knight
VC

FOUR WINDS ISLAND (1961)
d David Villiers
SC

FOX AND THE CROW, the (1950)
VC

FOXHOLE IN CAIRO (1960)
d John Moxey
PB

FOXHUNTER; CHAMPION JUMPER (1953)
d Victor Wark
VC SC

FRANCHISE AFFAIR, the (1950)
d Lawrence Huntington
PB

FRENCH DRESSING (1963)
d Ken Russell
VC PB

FRENCH MISTRESS, a (1960)
d Roy Boulting
PB

FRIEDA (1947)
d Basil Dearden
VC PB

FRIENDLY INN, the (1958)
d Clare Ash
VC

FRIENDS AND NEIGHBOURS (1959)
d Gordon Parry
PB

FRIGHTENED CITY, the (1961)
d John Lemont
VC PB

FRIGHTENED MAN, the (1952)
d John Gilling
PB

FROM D-DAY TO PARIS (1946)
VC

FROM FEAR TO FAITH (1946)
d James Swackhammer
VC

FROM PARIS TO THE RHINE (1946)
VC

FROM RUSSIA WITH LOVE (1963)
d Terence Young
PB

FROM THE GROUND UP (1950)
VC

FROM THE RHINE TO VICTORY (1946)
VC

FROZEN IMAGES (1961)
d Gordon Rowley
VC

FULL TREATMENT, the (1960)
d Val Guest
VC SC

FUN AT ST FANNY'S (1955)
d Maurice Elvey
VC

FURNIVAL AND SON (1948)
d Denis Segaller
VC SC

FURTHER UP THE CREEK (1958)
d Val Guest
SC

FUTURE OF ONE MILLION AFRICANS, the (This Modern Age series) (1950)
VC SC

FUTURE OF SCOTLAND, the (This Modern Age series) (1947)
VC SC

GAIETY GEORGE (1946)
d George King
PB

GALA DAY (1963)
d John Irvin
VC

GALASHIELS AND BRAW LADS' GATHERING 1951 (1951)
VC

GALLOPING MAJOR, the (1951)
d Henry Cornelius
PB

GAMBLING (This Modern Age series) (1949)
VC SC

GAOLBREAK (1962)
d Francis Searle
PB

GAS IN BATTLEDRESS (1946)
VC

GAS TURBINE, the (1954)
d Peter de Normanville
VC SC

GAS TURBINE GOES TO SEA, the (1951)
d Philip Armitage
VC SC

GATEWAY TO HAPPINESS (1952)
VC

GAUMONT-KALEE SOUND-RECORDING SYSTEM, the (1949)
VC

GAY DOG, the (1954)
d Maurice Elvey
PB

GELIGNITE GANG, the (1956)
d Francis Searle
VC

GENERAL ELECTION (1946)
d Ronald H Riley
VC

GENEVIEVE (1953)
d Henry Cornelius
SC

GENTLE GUNMAN, the (1952)
d Michael Relph, Basil Dearden
SC PB

GENTLEMEN – THE QUEEN (1953)
d Castleton Knight
VC

GENTLE TRAP, the (1960)
d Charles Saunders
PB

GEORDIE (1955)
d Frank Launder
SC

GEORGE IN CIVVY STREET (1946)
d Marcel Varnel
VC

GHOST FOR SALE, a (1952)
d Victor M Gover
VC

GHOSTS OF BERKELEY SQUARE, the (1947)
d Vernon Sewell
VC PB

GIDEON'S DAY (1958)
d John Ford
VC

GIFT HORSE, the (1952)
d Compton Bennett
PB

GILBERT HARDING SPEAKING OF MURDER (1953)
d Paul Dickson
PB

GINGER NUTT'S BEE BOTHER (Animaland series) (1949)
d Bert Felstead
VC

GINGER NUTT'S CHRISTMAS CIRCUS (Animaland series) (1949)
d Bert Felstead
VC

GINGER NUTT'S FOREST DRAGON (Animaland series) (1949)
d Bert Felstead
VC

GIPSY AIRS (1950)
VC

GIRL IN THE HEADLINES (1963)
d Michael Truman
SC PB

GIRL ON APPROVAL (1961)
d Charles Frend
VC SC

GIRL ON THE BOAT, the (1962)
d Henry Kaplan
VC

GIRLS AT SEA (1958)
d Gilbert Gunn
PB

GIRLS OF LATIN QUARTER (1960)
d Alfred Travers
PB

GIRL WHO COULDN'T QUITE, the (1949)
d Norman Lee
VC PB

GIRL WITH GREEN EYES (1963)
d Desmond Davis
PB

GISELLE (1952)
d Henry Caldwell
VC

GIVE US THIS DAY (1949)
d Edward Dmytryk
VC PB

GLASGOW CIVICS series
see
GLASGOW OUR CITY (1947)
OUR HOMES (1947)
OUR POLICE (1947)
OUR PUBLIC PARKS (1947)
OUR SCHOOLS (1947)
OUR WATER SUPPLY (1947)

GLASGOW OUR CITY (Glasgow Civics series) (1947)
VC

GLASGOW'S YESTERDAYS; FIRST WORLD WAR PERIOD (1950)
VC

GLASSHOUSE SOILS (1949)
d Michael Orrom
VC

GLASS MOUNTAIN, the (1948)
d Henry Cass
VC SC

GODFREY EVANS (Players of Merit series) (1952)
VC

GOD WITHIN, the (1961)
d June Goodfield
PB

GOING AHEAD THE RIGHT WAY (1956)
VC

GOING SHOPPING WITH ELIZABETH ALLAN (1955)
VC

GO-KART GO (1963)
d Jan Darnley-Smith
SC

GOLDEN AGE, the (A History of Motor Racing series) (1961)
d Bill Mason
VC

GOLDEN AGE IN A SMALL WORLD, the (1950)
d Brian Smith
VC

GOLDEN DISC, the (1958)
d Don Sharp
PB

GOLDEN ELIXIR, the (1950)
VC

GOLDEN LINK, the (1954)
d Charles Saunders
PB

GOLDEN MADONNA, the (1949)
d Ladislao Vajda
PB

GOLDEN SALAMANDER (1949)
d Ronald Neame
VC SC

GOLDFINGER (1964)
d Guy Hamilton
PB

GONE TO EARTH (1950)
d Michael Powell, Emeric Pressburger
VC SC

GOODBYE TO ROSLIN (1955)
VC

GOOD COMPANIONS, the (1956)
d J Lee Thompson
PB

GOOD COMPANY series
see
HEMEL HOMESTEAD (1957)

GOOD NEIGHBOURS (1946)
d Humphrey Swingler
VC

GOOD PULL-UP, a (1953)
d Don Chaffey
SC

GOOD-TIME GIRL (1947)
d David Macdonald
VC SC

GOODWOOD (MacHARG) (1950)
VC

GORBALS STORY, the (1949)
d David MacKane
VC

GORGO (1960)
d Eugene Lourie
VC PB

GORGON, the (1964)
d Terence Fisher
VC SC

GO TO BLAZES (1962)
d Michael Truman
PB

GPO TRAINING FILM series
see
OVERHEAD LINE CONSTRUCTION – ERECTING HEAVY POLE BY DERRICK (1950)
OVERHEAD LINE CONSTRUCTION – ERECTION OF AN AERIAL CABLE SUSPENSION WIRE (1950)
OVERHEAD LINE CONSTRUCTION – ERECTION OF AERIAL CABLES (1950)
SAFETY BELTS (1949)

GRAND ESCAPADE, the (1946)
d John Baxter
PB

GRAND PRIX (1949)
d Bill Mason
VC

GRANTCHESTER (1958)
d J R F Stewart
VC

GRASS IS GREENER, the (1960)
d Stanley Donen
PB

GREAT EXPECTATIONS (1946)
d David Lean
VC SC

GREAT FAILURE, the (1946)
d Harold Purcell, James E Rogers
VC

GREAT GAME, the (1953)
d Maurice Elvey
PB

GREAT VAN ROBBERY, the (1959)
d Max Varnel
PB

GREED OF WILLIAM HART, the (1948)
d Oswald Mitchell
VC

GREEN BUDDHA, the (1954)
d John Lemont
PB

GREEN FOR DANGER (1946)
d Sidney Gilliat
VC PB

GREENGAGE SUMMER, the (1961)
d Lewis Gilbert
VC SC

GREEN GROW THE RUSHES (1951)
d Derek Twist
PB

GREEN HELMET, the (1961)
d Michael Forlong
PB

GREENHOUSE WHITE FLY (Plant Pests and Diseases series) (1950)
d J V Durden
VC

GREENSLEEVES (Melodies of England series) (1946)
d Michael Law
VC

GREEN YEARS, the (1946)
d Victor Saville
VC PB

GREYFRIARS BOBBY (1961)
d Don Chaffey
PB

GREY METROPOLIS, the (1953)
d Nigel McIsaac
PB

GRIP OF THE STRANGLER (1958)
d Robert Day
SC

GROWING GIRLS (1951)
VC

GROWING OLD (1959)
d Phillip Sattin
VC

GUILT IS MY SHADOW (1950)
d Roy Kellino
VC SC

GUILTY CHIMNEYS (1954)
VC

GUINEA PIG, the (1948)
d John Boulting
VC PB

GUNS AT BATASI (1964)
d John Guillermin
VC PB

GUNS OF DARKNESS (1962)
d Anthony Asquith
PB

GUNS OF NAVARONE, the (1961)
d J Lee Thompson
VC SC

GYPSY AND THE GENTLEMAN, the (1957)
d Joseph Losey
VC SC

GYPSY HOLIDAY (Look at Life series) (1963)
VC

HADRIAN'S WALL (1951)
d Derek Williams
SC

HAMLET (1948)
d Laurence Olivier
VC SC

HAND, the (1960)
d Henry Cass
PB

HAND HAULAGE (1953)
d Alun Falconer
VC

HAND IN HAND (1960)
d Philip Leacock
VC SC

HANDKERCHIEF DRILL (1949)
d Richard Massingham
VC

HANDS ACROSS THE OCEAN (1946)
d Harry Gordon
VC

HANGMAN WAITS, the (1947)
d A Barr-Smith
PB

HA'PENNY BREEZE (1950)
d Frank Worth
PB

HAPPIEST DAYS OF YOUR LIFE, the (1950)
d Frank Launder
VC PB

HAPPY EVER AFTER (1954)
d Mario Zampi
PB

HAPPY FAMILY, the (1952)
d Muriel Box
VC SC

HAPPY GO LOVELY (1951)
d H Bruce Humberstone
SC PB

HAPPY IS THE BRIDE (1957)
d Roy Boulting
PB

HARD DAY'S NIGHT, a (1964)
d Richard Lester
VC PB

HARNESSING THE HILLS (1949)
VC

HARVEST CAMP (1947)
d Richard Massingham
VC

HARVEST FROM THE WILDERNESS (This Modern Age series) (1948)
VC

HASLINGDEN GALA (1950)
VC

HASTY HEART, the (1949)
d Vincent Sherman
VC SC

HAUNTING, the (1963)
d Robert Wise
VC

HEART OF A CHILD (1958)
d Clive Donner
SC

HEART OF A MAN, the (1959)
d Herbert Wilcox
SC

HEART OF THE MATTER, the (1953)
d George More O'Ferrall
VC

HEART WITHIN, the (1957)
d David Eady
PB

HEATING RESEARCH FOR HOUSES (1949)
d Richard Warren
VC

HEIGHTS OF DANGER (1953)
d Peter Bradford
SC

HEIR TO THE THRONE (1947)
VC

HELL DRIVERS (1957)
d Cy Endfield
SC

HELLIONS, the (1961)
d Ken Annakin
SC PB

HELL IS A CITY (1959)
d Val Guest
VC PB

HELL IS SOLD OUT (1951)
d Michael Anderson
VC PB

HELLO LONDON (1958)
d Sidney Smith
PB

HELP YOURSELF (1950)
d John Waterhouse
VC

HELTER SKELTER (1949)
d Ralph Thomas
VC SC

HEMEL HOMESTEAD (Good Company series) (1957)
VC

HERE COME THE HUGGETTS (1948)
d Ken Annakin
VC SC

HERE IS THE GOLD COAST (1947)
d John Page
VC

HERE'S HEALTH (1948)
VC

HER FAVOURITE HUSBAND (1950)
d Mario Soldati
VC PB

HERITAGE (1949)
d John Oliver
VC

HEROIC DAYS, the (A History of Motor Racing series) (1960)
d Bill Mason
VC

HIDDEN HOMICIDE (1958)
d Tony Young
PB

HIDEOUT (1956)
d Peter Graham Scott
PB

HIGH FLIGHT (1957)
d John Gilling
PB

HIGH HELL (1958)
d Burt Balaban
PB

HIGHLIGHTS OF FARNBOROUGH 1951
(1951)
d Peter de Normanville, Bill Mason
VC

HIGHLY DANGEROUS (1950)
d Roy Ward Baker
VC SC

HIGH SPEED FLIGHT series
see
APPROACHING THE SPEED OF SOUND
(1956)
BEYOND THE SPEED OF SOUND (1959)
TRANSONIC FLIGHT (1957)

**HIGH SPEED SINKING AT PARKSIDE
COLLIERY** (1957)
VC

HIGH TIDE AT NOON (1957)
d Philip Leacock
SC

HIGH TREASON (1951)
d Roy Boulting
VC SC

HIGH, WIDE AND FASTER (Look at Life
series) (1963)
VC

HILL IN KOREA, a (1956)
d Julian Amyes
VC SC

HILLS OF DONEGAL, the (1947)
d John Argyle
PB

HINDLE WAKES (1952)
d Arthur Crabtree
PB

HIS AND HERS (1960)
d Brian Desmond Hurst
SC

HIS EXCELLENCY (1951)
d Robert Hamer
VC SC

HIS FIGHTING CHANCE (1949)
d Geoffrey Innes
VC

HIS GREATEST RIVAL (1952)
VC

HISTORY OF MR POLLY, the (1948)
d Anthony Pélissier
SC PB

HISTORY OF MODERN SCIENCE series
see
MIRROR IN THE SKY (1957)

HISTORY OF MOTOR RACING series, a
see
GOLDEN AGE, the (1961)
HEROIC DAYS, the (1960)
TITANS 1930–1934, the (1962)
TITANS 1935–1939, the (1962)

HISTORY OF THE HELICOPTER, the (1951)
d Sarah Erulkar
VC

HMS DEFIANT (1962)
d Lewis Gilbert
VC SC

HOBSON'S CHOICE (1953)
d David Lean
VC PB

HOLIDAY (1957)
d John Taylor
VC

HOLIDAY CAMP (1947)
d Ken Annakin
VC

HOLLY AND THE IVY, the (1952)
d George More O'Ferrall
SC PB

HOME AND BEAUTY (This Modern Age
series) (1947)
VC SC

HOME AT SEVEN (1952)
d Ralph Richardson
SC

HOME OF THE SEA BIRDS (1946)
VC

HOME OF YOUR OWN, a (1964)
d Jay Lewis
VC PB

HOME SERVICE (1957)
d John Alderson
VC

HOMES FOR ALL (This Modern Age series)
(1946)
VC SC

HOME TO DANGER (1951)
d Terence Fisher
VC

HONEYMOON DEFERRED (1951)
d Mario Camerini
SC

HORNET'S NEST, the (1955)
d Charles Saunders
PB

HORRORS OF THE BLACK MUSEUM, the
(1959)
d Arthur Crabtree
PB

HORSEMASTERS, the (1961)
d William Fairchild
PB

HORSE'S MOUTH, the (1958)
d Ronald Neame
PB

HOTEL SAHARA (1951)
d Ken Annakin
VC PB

HOT ENOUGH FOR JUNE (1964)
d Ralph Thomas
SC PB

HOUND OF THE BASKERVILLES, the
(1959)
d Terence Fisher
PB

HOUR OF 13, the (1952)
d Harold French
PB

HOUSE CAT, the (Animaland series) (1948)
d Bert Felstead
VC

HOUSE IN MARSH ROAD, the (1960)
d Montgomery Tully
PB

HOUSE OF BLACKMAIL (1953)
d Maurice Elvey
PB

HOUSE OF MYSTERY (1961)
d Vernon Sewell
VC

HOUSE OF SECRETS (1956)
d Guy Green
SC PB

HOUSE OF THE SEVEN HAWKS, the (1959)
d Richard Thorpe
PB

HOUSES IN HISTORY (1946)
VC

HOUSES IN THE TOWN (1951)
VC

HOUSING MAKES HISTORY (1953)
VC

HOUSING THE PEOPLE (1954)
VC

HOW A HOUSE IS BUILT (1960)
VC

HOW AN AEROPLANE FLIES series
see
CONTROLS (1947)
DRAG (1947)
FORCES IN BALANCE (1947)
LIFT (1947)
STABILITY (1947)
THRUST (1947)

HOW TELEVISION WORKS (1953)
d Colin Bell
VC

**HOW TO BECOME A DENTIST LESSON 1:
HOW TO PULL** (1947)
VC

**HOW TO BECOME A DENTIST LESSON 2:
HOW TO GIVE GAS** (1947)
VC

HOW TO MURDER A RICH UNCLE (1957)
d Nigel Patrick
VC SC

HOW TO PLAY CRICKET (1950)
VC

HOW TO USE THE TELEPHONE (1948)
d Michael Law
VC

HOW WHAT AND WHY NO.1 (1948)
VC

HOW WHAT AND WHY NO.2 (1948)
VC

HUE AND CRY (1946)
d Charles Crichton
VC PB

HUGGETTS ABROAD, the (1949)
d Ken Annakin
VC SC

**HUMORAL TRANSMISSION OF
SYMPATHETIC IMPULSES** (1947)
VC

HUMPTY DUMPTY (1951)
VC

HUNDRED YEARS UNDERGROUND, a
(1963)
d John Rowdon
VC

HUNGARIAN DANCE NO.5 (1950)
VC

HUNGRY HILL (1947)
d Brian Desmond Hurst
VC

HUNTED (1952)
d Charles Crichton
VC

HUNTED IN HOLLAND (1961)
d Derek Williams
SC

HYDE PARK CORNER (Look at Life series)
(1961)
VC

HYPNOTIST, the (1957)
d Montgomery Tully
PB

I BELIEVE IN YOU (1951)
d Michael Relph, Basil Dearden
VC

ICE COLD IN ALEX (1958)
d J Lee Thompson
PB

I COULD GO ON SINGING (1963)
d Ronald Neame
SC PB

IDEAL HUSBAND, an (1947)
d Alexander Korda
VC PB

IDLE ON PARADE (1958)
d John Gilling
SC

IDOL OF PARIS (1948)
d Leslie Arliss
VC PB

I HAD A DREAM LAST NIGHT (1951)
VC

I'LL TURN TO YOU (1946)
d Geoffrey Faithfull
PB

I'M ALL RIGHT JACK (1959)
d John Boulting
VC PB

IMPERSONATOR, the (1961)
d Alfred Shaughnessy
SC

IMPORTANCE OF BEING EARNEST, the
(1952)
d Anthony Asquith
VC PB

IMPULSE (1954)
d Charles de Lautour
VC

IN ALL WEATHERS (1949)
d John Rhodes
VC

INDIA AND PAKISTAN (This Modern Age
series) (1949)
VC

INDIA STRIKES (1946)
d Bishu Sen
VC

INDISCREET (1958)
d Stanley Donen
VC SC

INDUSTRIAL DERMATITIS (1950)
VC

INFLUENZA (1946)
d Richard Massingham
VC

INFORMERS, the (1963)
d Ken Annakin
VC SC

INLAND WATERWAYS (1950)
d R K Neilson Baxter
VC

INN FOR TROUBLE (1959)
d C M Pennington-Richards
SC

INNOCENTS, the (1961)
d Jack Clayton
VC SC

INNOCENT SINNERS (1958)
d Philip Leacock
VC SC

INNOCENTS IN PARIS (1953)
d Gordon Parry
PB

INN OF THE SIXTH HAPPINESS, the (1958)
d Mark Robson
VC

IN SEARCH OF THE CASTAWAYS (1962)
d Robert Stevenson
PB

INSIGHT – ANTHONY ASQUITH (1960)
d Peter Lee
VC

INSPECTOR, the (1962)
d Philip Dunne
PB

INSTRUMENTS OF THE ORCHESTRA
(1946)
d Muir Mathieson
VC

INSULIN (1949)
d Florence Anthony
VC

INTERNATIONAL REVIEW NO.12 (1951)
VC

INTERNATIONAL REVIEW NO.22 (1951)
VC

INTERNATIONAL REVIEW NO.46 (1951)
VC

INTERRUPTED JOURNEY, the (1949)
d Daniel Birt
VC PB

IN THE DOGHOUSE (1961)
d Darcy Conyers
VC SC

IN THE EVENT (1962)
VC

IN THE NICK (1959)
d Ken Hughes
SC PB

INTIMATE STRANGER, the (1956)
d Joseph Losey
VC PB

INTO THE BLUE (1950)
d Herbert Wilcox
VC SC

INTRODUCING WORK STUDY (Better Ways
series) (1955)
d Clifford Parris
VC

INTRODUCTION TO THE FROG (1950)
VC

INTRODUCTION TO TRACKWORK (1961)
VC

INTRUDER, the (1953)
d Guy Hamilton
SC PB

INVITATION TO THE DANCE (1954)
d Gene Kelly
SC

I ONLY ARSKED! (1958)
d Montgomery Tully
SC

IRISH INTERLUDE (1948)
d David Villiers
VC

IRON MAIDEN, the (1963)
d Gerald Thomas
PB

IRON PETTICOAT, the (1956)
d Ralph Thomas
PB

I SEE A DARK STRANGER (1946)
d Frank Launder
VC PB

ISLAND, the (1952)
d Peter Pickering, John Ingram
VC

ISLAND OF COAL (1963)
VC

ISLAND OF STEEL (1956)
d Geoffrey Hughes
VC

ISLE OF BAYS (1955)
SC

ISLE OF MAN TT 1950 (1950)
d Geoffrey Hughes
VC

ISN'T LIFE WONDERFUL! (1952)
d Harold French
PB

IS THIS THE JOB FOR ME? series
see
CARING FOR CHILDREN (1949)

IT ALWAYS RAINS ON SUNDAY (1947)
d Robert Hamer
VC PB

IT BEGAN ON THE CLYDE (1946)
d Ken Annakin
VC

I THANK A FOOL (1962)
d Robert Stevens
PB

IT HAPPENED HERE (1963)
d Kevin Brownlow, Andrew Mollo
VC PB

IT MIGHT BE YOU (1946)
d Michael S Gordon
VC

IT'S A GRAND LIFE (1953)
d John E Blakeley
PB

IT'S A GREAT DAY (1955)
d John Warrington
PB

IT'S A GREAT GAME (Calling All Sportsmen
series) (1948)
d Victor M Gover
VC

IT'S ALL HAPPENING (1963)
d Don Sharp
SC

IT'S ALL OVER TOWN (1963)
d Douglas Hickox
PB

IT'S A WONDERFUL WORLD (1956)
d Val Guest
PB

IT'S GREAT TO BE YOUNG! (1956)
d Cyril Frankel
VC PB

IT'S HARD TO BE GOOD (1948)
d Jeffrey Dell
VC

IT'S NOT CRICKET (1949)
d Alfred Roome, Roy Rich
SC PB

IT STARTED IN PARADISE (1952)
d Compton Bennett
SC

IT'S TRAD, DAD! (1962)
d Richard Lester
VC SC

IVANHOE (1951)
d Richard Thorpe
VC PB

IVEL TRACTOR, the (1952)
VC

I WANT TO GO TO SCHOOL (1959)
d John Krish
VC

I WAS MONTY'S DOUBLE (1958)
d John Guillermin
VC SC

I WENT TO BRITAIN (1955)
d Douglas Clarke, John Durst
VC

JACKPOT (1960)
d Montgomery Tully
PB

JACQUELINE (1956)
d Roy Ward Baker
SC PB

JAGUAR AT LE MANS 1955 (1955)
VC

JAMAICA PROBLEM (This Modern Age series) (1947)
SC

JAMAICA – THIRD TEST (1960)
d Edric Connor
VC

JASON AND THE ARGONAUTS (1963)
d Don Chaffey
VC PB

JASSY (1947)
d Bernard Knowles
VC SC

JAZZ ALL THE WAY (Look at Life series) (1963)
VC

JAZZBOAT (1959)
d Ken Hughes
SC PB

JET LIFT (1956)
VC

JET-PROPELLED GERMS (1948)
d John Krish
VC

JET STORM (1959)
d Cy Endfield
PB

JIGSAW (1962)
d Val Guest
VC

JOHN AND JULIE (1955)
d William Fairchild
VC SC

JOHN GILPIN (Poet and Painter series) (1951)
d John Halas
VC

JOHN MUIR DONALDSON, MC, EMINENT IN THE SUPPLY OF ELECTRICAL POWER (1949)
VC

JOHNNY ON THE RUN (1953)
d Lewis Gilbert
SC

JOHN OF THE FAIR (1952)
d Michael McCarthy
SC

JOIN THE ARMY (1946)
d W M Larkins
VC

JOLLY BAD FELLOW, a (1963)
d Don Chaffey
SC PB

JOURNEY INTO HISTORY (1952)
d Alexander Shaw, John Taylor
VC

JOURNEY INTO NOWHERE (1963)
d Denis Scully
VC

JOURNEY INTO SPRING (1957)
d Ralph Keene
VC

JOURNEY TO ADVENTURE; A FILM CHRONICLE OF CHERRY KEARTON (1947)
d Cherry Kearton
VC

JOURNEY TO THE SEA (1952)
d Terry Bishop
VC

JUDGMENT DEFERRED (1951)
d John Baxter
SC

JUMPING FOR JOY (1950)
VC

JUMPING FOR JOY (1955)
d John Paddy Carstairs
SC

JUMP TO IT (The Adventures of Soupy series) (1950)
d Anson Dyer
VC

JUNGLE STREET (1961)
d Charles Saunders
VC PB

JUNO HELPS OUT (1953)
d William C Hammond
SC

JUST AN IDEA (1957)
d Guy Blanchard
VC

JUST FOR FUN! (1963)
d Gordon Flemyng
SC PB

JUST MY LUCK (1957)
d John Paddy Carstairs
SC

JUST WILLIAM'S LUCK (1947)
d Val Guest
VC PB

KASHMIR CONFLICT (1951)
d Lawrence Mitchell, Peter Lennox
VC

KEEP IT CLEAN (1955)
d David Paltenghi
PB

KENSAL HOUSE (1946)
d Frank Sainsbury
VC

KEY, the (1958)
d Carol Reed
VC SC

KEY MAN, the (1957)
d Montgomery Tully
PB

KID FOR TWO FARTHINGS, a (1954)
d Carol Reed
PB

KID FROM CANADA, the (1957)
d Kay Mander
SC

KIDNAPPED (1960)
d Robert Stevenson
PB

KIDNAPPERS, the (1953)
d Philip Leacock
VC SC

KILLERS OF KILIMANJARO (1959)
d Richard Thorpe
SC PB

KILL HER GENTLY (1957)
d Charles Saunders
SC

KILL ME TOMORROW (1957)
d Terence Fisher
PB

KILL OR CURE (1962)
d George Pollock
PB

KILTIES ARE COMING, the (1951)
d Robert Jordan Hill
VC

KIND HEARTS AND CORONETS (1949)
d Robert Hamer
VC SC

KIND OF LOVING, a (1962)
d John Schlesinger
VC PB

KING & COUNTRY (1964)
d Joseph Losey
VC SC

KING GEORGE VI MEMORIAL FUND (1952)
VC

KING IN NEW YORK, a (1957)
d Charles Chaplin
PB

KING'S BREAKFAST, the (1963)
d Wendy Toye
VC

KISS OF THE VAMPIRE (1962)
d Don Sharp
PB

KITCHEN, the (1961)
d James Hill
VC SC

KNAVE OF HEARTS (1954)
d René Clément
VC PB

KNIGHTS OF THE AIR! (1946)
VC

KNIGHTS OF THE ROUND TABLE, the
(1953)
d Richard Thorpe
PB

KONGA (1960)
d John Lemont
PB

KRO GERMANY, 1947 (1948)
d Graham Wallace
VC

LADIES WHO DO (1963)
d C M Pennington-Richards
PB

LADY GODIVA RIDES AGAIN (1951)
d Frank Launder
VC SC

LADY IS A SQUARE, the (1958)
d Herbert Wilcox
PB

LADYKILLERS, the (1955)
d Alexander Mackendrick
PB

LADY MISLAID, a (1958)
d David Macdonald
PB

LADY TWEEDSMUIR MP IN A BRIEF TALK ABOUT POLITICS (1949)
VC

LADY WITH THE LAMP, the (1951)
d Herbert Wilcox
VC SC

LAMP IN ASSASSIN MEWS, the (1962)
d Godfrey Grayson
PB

LANCASHIRE'S TIME FOR ADVENTURE
(This Modern Age series) (1948)
VC

LANCELOT AND GUINEVERE (1962)
d Cornel Wilde
PB

LANDFALL (1949)
d Ken Annakin
SC PB

LAND OF PROMISE (1946)
d Paul Rotha
VC

LAND OF THE MAPLE LEAF (1946)
VC

LAND OF THE SAINTS (1946)
d A Stanley Williamson
SC

LAND SHORT OF PEOPLE (This Modern Age series) (1947)
VC SC

LAST DAYS OF DOLWYN, the (1949)
d Emlyn Williams
VC SC

LAST HOLIDAY (1950)
d Henry Cass
VC PB

LAST LOAD, the (1948)
d John Baxter
VC

LAST PAGE, the (1952)
d Terence Fisher
PB

LAST RHINO, the (1961)
d Henry Geddes
SC

LATE EDWINA BLACK, the (1951)
d Maurice Elvey
SC

LATITUDE AND LONGITUDE (1947)
d Margaret Simpson, Ken Hardy
VC

LAUGHING ANNE (1953)
d Herbert Wilcox
PB

LAUGHING LADY, the (1946)
d Paul L Stein
PB

LAUGHTER IN PARADISE (1951)
d Mario Zampi
VC SC

LAUNCH OF THE PUNTA MEDANOS AT WALLSEND, 1950, the (1950)
VC

LAVENDER HILL MOB, the (1951)
d Charles Crichton
VC PB

LAWRENCE OF ARABIA (1962)
d David Lean
VC SC

LAYOUT AND HANDLING IN FACTORIES
(1951)
VC

LEAGUE OF GENTLEMEN, the (1959)
d Basil Dearden
SC PB

LEARNING FOR LIVING (1955)
VC

LEASE OF LIFE (1954)
d Charles Frend
SC PB

LEATHER BOYS, the (1963)
d Sidney J Furie
VC SC

LE MANS 1952 (1952)
d Bill Mason
VC

LE MANS 1954 (1954)
VC

LE MANS 1956 (1956)
VC

LE MANS 1958 (1958)
VC

LEN HUTTON (Players of Merit series) (1946)
VC

LET'S BE HAPPY (1956)
d Henry Levin
PB

LET'S HAVE A MURDER (1950)
d John E Blakeley
PB

LET'S KEEP OUR TEETH (1952)
d Louise Witting
VC

LET'S SING TOGETHER series
see
BOUND FOR THE RIO GRANDE (1948)

LETTER FROM AYRSHIRE, a (1954)
d J E Ewins
SC

LETTER FROM EAST ANGLIA, a (1953)
d Cynthia Whitby
SC

LETTER FROM THE ISLE OF WIGHT, a
(1953)
d Brian Salt
SC

LETTER FROM WALES, a (1953)
d George Lloyd
SC

LIBEL (1959)
d Anthony Asquith
PB

LIFE CYCLE OF A MOSS, the (1946)
VC

LIFE FOR RUTH (1962)
d Basil Dearden
VC SC

LIFE IN DANGER (1959)
d Terry Bishop
PB

LIFE IN EMERGENCY WARD 10 (1958)
d Robert Day
PB

LIFE IN HER HANDS (1951)
d Philip Leacock
VC

LIFE IN THE ORKNEYS (1957)
d Alan J Harper
VC

LIFE IS A CIRCUS (1958)
d Val Guest
SC PB

LIFE OF THE THREE-SPINED STICKLEBACK, the (1949)
d Thora James
VC

LIFE WITH THE LYONS (1953)
d Val Guest
VC PB

LIFT (How an Aeroplane Flies series) (1947)
d J B Napier-Bell
VC

LIFTING YOUR POTATOES (1947)
VC

LIGHT FINGERS (1957)
d Terry Bishop
PB

LIGHTHOUSE, the (1948)
VC

LIGHT UP THE SKY (1960)
d Lewis Gilbert
VC SC

LIKE UNTO YOU (1961)
d Geoffrey Collyer
PB

LILACS IN THE SPRING (1954)
d Herbert Wilcox
SC PB

Tropical Breezes
(H Brian White,
Sidney G Griffiths,
A Goodman, 1930)

Fruitlands of Kent
(Mary Field, 1934)

Walter Forde, c. 1929
[588–589]

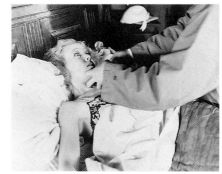

The Ghost Camera
(Bernard Vorhaus,
1933)

90° South (Herbert G
Ponting, 1933)

Astoria Cinema,
Purley. Programme.
LIS ephemera

Come Out of the Pantry
(Jack Raymond, 1935)
Press-book. LIS [458]

The Clairvoyant
(Maurice Elvey, 1935)

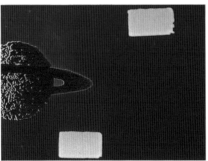

Above and below:
Trade Tattoo (Len
Lye, 1937), an NFTVA
restoration

Right: ***Things to Come***
(William Cameron
Menzies, 1936)

EXHIBITORS' CAMPAIGN BOOK

Alexander Korda presents
THE THIEF
OF BAGDAD
in Magic Technicolor!
CONRAD VEIDT · SABU · JUNE DUPREZ · JOHN JUSTIN · REX INGRAM · MARY MORRIS
Distributed by

Romance! Spectacle!
Adventure! Thrills!

The Thief of Bagdad
(Ludwig Berger,
Michael Powell,
Tim Whelan, 1940)
Press-book. LIS
[765–761, 939–945]

This Happy Breed
(David Lean, 1944),
an NFTVA restoration

Pimpernel Smith
(Leslie Howard, 1941)

**Caesar and
Cleopatra** (Gabriel
Pascal, 1945), an
NFTVA restoration

Far right: **Blithe Spirit**
(David Lean, 1944)
Press-book. LIS
[510–516]

NOEL COWARD'S
Super-Naturally Spicy Screen Entertainment
"Blithe
Spirit"
in Blushing
TECHNICOLOR

with
REX HARRISON · CONSTANCE CUMMINGS · KAY HAMMOND
and Margaret Rutherford ★ A TWO CITIES FILM · A NOEL COWARD·CINEGUILD PRODUCTION
RELEASED THRU UNITED ARTISTS

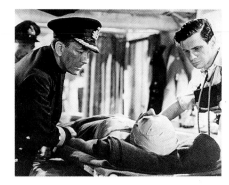

Far left: *Oh, Mr Porter!* (Marcel Varnel, 1937) [688–689]

Left: *In Which We Serve* (Noël Coward, David Lean, 1942)

They Drive by Night (Arthur Woods, 1939)

The Wicked Lady (Leslie Arliss, 1945)

A Diary for Timothy (Humphrey Jennings, 1944)

LIMESTONE IN NATURE (1946)
d Ronald Gardner
VC

LINCOLNSHIRE POACHER, the (1947)
d W M Larkins
VC

LION, the (1962)
d Jack Cardiff
SC

LISBON STORY (1946)
d Paul L Stein
VC SC

LITTLE BALLERINA, the (1947)
d Lewis Gilbert
VC PB

LITTLE BIG SHOT (1952)
d Jack Raymond
SC

LITTLE RED MONKEY (1954)
d Ken Hughes
PB

LIVE NOW, PAY LATER (1962)
d Jay Lewis
SC

LIVING SOIL, the (1960)
d Atma Ram
VC

LIVING WITH CARS (Look at Life series)
(1964)
VC

LOLITA (1961)
d Stanley Kubrick
VC PB

LONDON AIRPORT (1949)
VC

LONDON BELONGS TO ME (1948)
d Sidney Gilliat
VC PB

LONDON BUILDS AGAIN (1947)
VC

LONDON CONFERENCE HIGHLIGHTS
(1949)
VC

LONDON IN THE RAW (1964)
d Arnold Louis Miller
PB

LONDON TOWN (1946)
d Wesley Ruggles
VC PB

**LONDON TRANSPORT CINE REVIEW
NO.1** (1949)
VC

**LONDON TUBE EXTENSION TO
HAINAULT** (1948)
VC

**LONELINESS OF THE LONG DISTANCE
RUNNER, the** (1962)
d Tony Richardson
PB

**LONG AND THE SHORT AND THE TALL,
the** (1960)
d Leslie Norman
SC PB

LONG ARM, the (1956)
d Charles Frend
VC SC

LONG DARK HALL, the (1951)
d Anthony Bushell, Reginald Beck
VC

LONG, LONG TRAIL (1946)
d Richard Massingham
VC

LONG MEMORY, the (1952)
d Robert Hamer
VC SC

LONG NIGHT HAUL (1957)
d James Ritchie
VC

LOOK AT LIFE series
see
BACK-ROOM OF THE SKY (1963)
BEAUTY AND THE BEAST (1960)
BEHIND THE TON-UP BOYS (1964)
BLOOD AND FIRE (1964)
BOOKIES AT THE CROSSROADS (1964)
BULLFIGHTER (1960)
CALLING THE TUNE (1964)
CHICKENS IN THE MILL (1962)
CITY OF CRISIS (1961)
DIGGING UP THE PAST (1963)
DIVIDED CITY, the (1959)
DOWN LONDON RIVER (1959)
EARLY STARTERS (1964)
EUROPE GROWS TOGETHER (1963)
GYPSY HOLIDAY (1963)
HIGH, WIDE AND FASTER (1963)
HYDE PARK CORNER (1961)
JAZZ ALL THE WAY (1963)
LIVING WITH CARS (1964)
MARRAKESH (1959)
NEW UNIVERSITIES (1963)
OLD SCHOOL TIE, the (1964)
OVER MY SHOULDER (1963)
PINCH OF SALT, a (1963)
POWER NEEDS NO PASSPORT (1964)
PRICE OF VALOUR, the (1964)
RULERS OF RACING (1964)
TIDE ON THE TURN (1964)
TRADE WINDS BLOW, the (1963)
UNDER ONE UMBRELLA (1964)
WEALTH UNDER THE SEA? (1964)
WINNING THE HARD WAY (1964)

LOOK AT YOUR WORLD, 5TH ISSUE
(1957)
VC

LOOK BACK IN ANGER (1959)
d Tony Richardson
VC SC

LOOK BEFORE YOU LOVE (1948)
d Harold Huth
PB

LOOKING AT BRITAIN series
see
COMPREHENSIVE SCHOOL (1962)
FARMERS' MACHINERY SYNDICATES
(1961)
MARKET DAY IN BUCKINGHAM (1961)

LORD JIM (1964)
d Richard Brooks
VC

LORD OF THE FLIES (1963)
d Peter Brook
VC PB

LORD SIVA DANCED (1948)
d Sarah Erulkar
VC

LOSER TAKES ALL (1956)
d Ken Annakin
SC PB

LOST (1955)
d Guy Green
SC PB

LOST PEOPLE, the (1949)
d Bernard Knowles
VC SC

LOVE-BIRDS (1949)
VC

LOVE LOTTERY, the (1953)
d Charles Crichton
PB

LOVE ME, LOVE ME, LOVE ME (1962)
d Richard Williams
VC

LOVE'S A LUXURY (1952)
d Francis Searle
PB

LOVES OF JOANNA GODDEN, the (1947)
d Charles Frend
VC SC

LOWLANDS OF SCOTLAND (Travelling
Around series) (1947)
VC

L-SHAPED ROOM, the (1962)
d Bryan Forbes
VC SC

**LUBRICANTS FOR NUCLEAR POWER
STATIONS** (1958)
d Peter de Normanville
VC

LUCKY JIM (1957)
d John Boulting
SC PB

LYONS IN PARIS, the (1954)
d Val Guest
VC PB

MACBETH (1960)
d George Schaefer
SC PB

MAD ABOUT MEN (1954)
d Ralph Thomas
SC PB

MADAME LOUISE (1951)
d Maclean Rogers
VC

MADE IN HEAVEN (1952)
d John Paddy Carstairs
SC

MADELEINE (1949)
d David Lean
VC SC

MADNESS OF THE HEART (1949)
d Charles Bennett
VC PB

MAGGIE, the (1953)
d Alexander Mackendrick
VC PB

MAGIC BOW, the (1946)
d Bernard Knowles
VC PB

MAGIC BOX, the (1951)
d John Boulting
VC SC

MAGIC ELECTRONS series
see
TERRA INCOGNITA (1948)

MAGIC GLOBE series, the
see
POLAND (1947)

MAGIC THREAD, the (1951)
VC

MAGIC TOUCH, the (1950)
VC

MAGNET, the (1950)
d Charles Frend
VC SC

MAIN ATTRACTION, the (1962)
d Daniel Petrie
PB

MAIN STREET – MERSEY (1955)
d Christopher A Radley
VC

MAKE MINE A MILLION (1959)
d Lance Comfort
SC

MAKE MINE MINK (1960)
d Robert Asher
SC PB

MAKING A CHILD'S DRINKING VESSEL
(1951)
VC

MALAGA (1954)
d Richard Sale
SC PB

MALTA STORY (1953)
d Brian Desmond Hurst
PB

MAN ABOUT THE HOUSE, a (1947)
d Leslie Arliss
PB

MAN AT THE CARLTON TOWER (1961)
d Robert Tronson
VC

MAN BETWEEN, the (1953)
d Carol Reed
VC

MAN DETAINED (1961)
d Robert Tronson
VC

MANDY (1952)
d Alexander Mackendrick
VC SC

MAN FROM TANGIER (1957)
d Lance Comfort
PB

MANIAC (1963)
d Michael Carreras
SC PB

MAN IN THE MOON (1960)
d Basil Dearden
VC PB

MAN IN THE SHADOW (1957)
d Montgomery Tully
PB

MAN IN THE SKY, the (1956)
d Charles Crichton
VC SC

MAN IN THE WHITE SUIT, the (1951)
d Alexander Mackendrick
VC SC

MAN OF AFRICA (1953)
d Cyril Frankel
VC

MAN OF THE MOMENT (1955)
d John Paddy Carstairs
SC PB

MAN ONE FAMILY (1946)
d Ivor Montagu
VC

MAN ON THE BEACH, a (1955)
d Joseph Losey
VC

MAN ON THE RUN (1949)
d Lawrence Huntington
PB

MANUELA (1957)
d Guy Hamilton
SC PB

**MANUFACTURE OF POLISHED PLATE
GLASS, the** (1947)
d Alan T Dinsdale
VC

MAN UPSTAIRS, the (1958)
d Don Chaffey
VC

MAN WHO COULD CHEAT DEATH, the
(1959)
d Terence Fisher
PB

MAN WHO COULDN'T WALK, the (1960)
d Henry Cass
PB

MAN WHO FINALLY DIED, the (1962)
d Quentin Lawrence
SC PB

MAN WHO 'INVENTED' ST PATRICK, the
(1957)
VC

MAN WHO WATCHED TRAINS GO BY, the
(1952)
d Harold French
VC

MAN WHO WOULDN'T TALK, the (1957)
d Herbert Wilcox
SC PB

MAN WITHIN, the (1947)
d Bernard Knowles
PB

MARALINGA 1956 (1956)
VC

MARBLE RETURNS, the (1951)
d Darrel Catling
SC

**MARCH FROM ALDERMASTON TO
LONDON** (1959)
VC

MARCH HARE, the (1956)
d George More O'Ferrall
PB

MARCH TO ALDERMASTON (1959)
VC

MARDI AND THE MONKEY (1953)
d Kay Mander
VC SC

MARGAM MARSHALLING YARD (1961)
d G B M Dean
VC

MARINO V MONAGHAN FIGHT (1947)
VC

MARKET DAY IN BUCKINGHAM (Looking
at Britain series) (1961)
VC

MARK OF CAIN, the (1948)
d Brian Desmond Hurst
VC

MARK OF THE PHOENIX (1957)
d Maclean Rogers
PB

MARRAKESH (Look at Life series) (1959)
VC

MARRIAGE OF CONVENIENCE, a (1962)
d Ernest Morris
VC

MARY HAD A LITTLE... (1961)
d Edward Buzzell
PB

MARY'S BIRTHDAY (1950)
d Lotte Reiniger
VC

MASK OF DUST (1954)
d Terence Fisher
PB

MASQUE OF THE RED DEATH, the (1964)
d Roger Corman
PB

MASTER CONTROL CARBURETTOR
(1951)
VC

MASTER OF BANKDAM (1947)
d Walter Forde
VC PB

MASTERS OF VENUS (1962)
d Ernest Morris
SC

MASTER SPY (1963)
d Montgomery Tully
VC

MATTER OF LIFE AND DEATH, a (1946)
d Michael Powell, Emeric Pressburger
VC SC

MAYTIME IN MAYFAIR (1949)
d Herbert Wilcox
VC

MEASURING CRAFTSMANSHIP (1952)
d J A D Cartwright
VC

**MECHANICAL EFFECTS AT MONTE
BELLO** (1952)
VC

**MECHANISED PIT BOTTOM (SHILBOTTLE
COLLIERY)** (1952)
d Francis Gysin
VC

MEETING, the (1964)
d Mamoun Hassan
VC

MEET ME AT DAWN (1947)
d Thornton Freeland
VC

MEET ME TONIGHT (1952)
d Anthony Pélissier
SC

MEET MR LUCIFER (1953)
d Anthony Pélissier
SC PB

MELBA (1953)
d Lewis Milestone
PB

MELODY IN THE DARK (1948)
d Robert Jordan Hill
VC

MEN AGAINST THE SUN (1953)
d Brendan J Stafford
VC

MEN OF IRON (1947)
VC

MEN OF SHERWOOD FOREST, the (1954)
d Val Guest
PB

MEN OF TWO WORLDS (1946)
d Thorold Dickinson
VC PB

MIDDLE COURSE, the (1961)
d Montgomery Tully
PB

MIDLAND JOURNEY (Travelling Around series) (1947)
VC

MILESTONES IN ROAD TRANSPORT HISTORY 1896–1946 (1946)
VC

MILK FROM GRANGE HILL FARM, the (1946)
d J B Napier-Bell
VC

MILLIGAN AT LARGE series
    see
    SPIKE MILLIGAN MEETS JOE BROWN
    (1961)
    SPIKE MILLIGAN ON TREASURE
    ISLAND WC2 (1961)

MILLIONAIRESS, the (1960)
d Anthony Asquith
PB

MILLION AND ONE, a (1947)
VC

MILLION POUND NOTE, the (1953)
d Ronald Neame
SC

MIND BENDERS, the (1963)
d Basil Dearden
SC PB

MINE OWN EXECUTIONER (1947)
d Anthony Kimmins
VC SC

MINER, the (1950)
VC

MINING REVIEW 1ST YEAR NO.5 (1948)
VC

MINING REVIEW 1ST YEAR NO.7 (1948)
VC

MINING REVIEW 1ST YEAR NO.9 (1948)
VC

MINING REVIEW 1ST YEAR NO.11 (1948)
VC

MINING REVIEW 1ST YEAR NO.12 (1948)
VC

MINING REVIEW 2ND YEAR NO.1 (1948)
VC

MINING REVIEW 2ND YEAR NO.3 (1948)
VC

MINING REVIEW 2ND YEAR NO.4 (1948)
VC

MINING REVIEW 2ND YEAR NO.5 (1949)
VC

MINING REVIEW 2ND YEAR NO.11 (1949)
VC

MINING REVIEW 3RD YEAR NO.2 (1949)
VC

MINING REVIEW 3RD YEAR NO.6 (1950)
VC

MINING REVIEW 3RD YEAR NO.7 (1950)
VC

MINING REVIEW 3RD YEAR NO.12 (1950)
VC

MINING REVIEW 4TH YEAR NO.3 (1950)
VC

MINING REVIEW 4TH YEAR NO.4 (1950)
VC

MINING REVIEW 4TH YEAR NO.6 (1951)
VC

MINING REVIEW 4TH YEAR NO.11 (1951)
VC

MINING REVIEW 5TH YEAR NO.2 (1951)
VC

MINIVER STORY, the (1950)
d H C Potter
PB

MINX TO MOSCOW (1957)
VC

MIRACLE IN SOHO (1957)
d Julian Amyes
VC SC

MIRANDA (1948)
d Ken Annakin
VC SC

MIRROR CAN LIE, the (1946)
d Richard Massingham
VC

MIRROR IN THE SKY (History of Modern Science series) (1957)
d Alex Strasser
VC

MISSING NOTE, the (1961)
d Michael Brandt
SC

MISS ROBIN HOOD (1952)
d John Guillermin
PB

MR CHURCHILL ON THE AGRICULTURAL CHARTER (1949)
VC

MR DENNING DRIVES NORTH (1951)
d Anthony Kimmins
SC

MR DRAKE'S DUCK (1950)
d Val Guest
VC SC

MR PERRIN AND MR TRAILL (1948)
d Lawrence Huntington
VC SC

MR TOPAZE (1961)
d Peter Sellers
VC

MRS FITZHERBERT (1947)
d Montgomery Tully
PB

MRS GIBBONS' BOYS (1962)
d Max Varnel
PB

MIX ME A PERSON (1962)
d Leslie Norman
SC

MOBY DICK (1956)
d John Huston
PB

MODEL FLIGHT, the (1951)
d Alan Pride
VC

MODEL FOR MURDER (1959)
d Terry Bishop
SC

MODERN GUIDE TO HEALTH, a (1946)
d John Halas, Joy Batchelor
VC

MODERN IRELAND (1952)
d Eric Lindeman
VC

MODS AND ROCKERS (1964)
d Kenneth Hume
PB

MOMENT OF DANGER (1960)
d Laslo Benedek
PB

MOMENT OF INDISCRETION (1958)
d Max Varnel
PB

MOMMA DON'T ALLOW (1955)
d Karel Reisz, Tony Richardson
VC

MONKEY'S PAW, the (1948)
d Norman Lee
PB

MONSTER OF HIGHGATE PONDS, the (1960)
d Alberto Cavalcanti
VC SC

MONTE BELLO OCTOBER 1952 (1952)
VC

MOONRAKER, the (1957)
d David Macdonald
PB

MORE POWER FROM THE ATOM (1958)
VC

MORNING DEPARTURE (1950)
d Roy Ward Baker
VC PB

MORTISE AND TENON JOINT (1947)
VC

MOULIN ROUGE (1952)
d John Huston
PB

MOUNT KINABALU, NORTH BORNEO (1961)
VC

MOUSE ON THE MOON, the (1963)
d Richard Lester
PB

MOUSE THAT ROARED, the (1959)
d Jack Arnold
SC PB

MOVING HOUSE (1949)
d Richard Massingham
VC

MOVING MILLIONS (1947)
d Noel Arthur
VC

MUDLARK, the (1950)
d Jean Negulesco
VC

MURDER AHOY (1964)
d George Pollock
PB

MURDER AT THE GALLOP (1963)
d George Pollock
SC PB

MURDER AT THE WINDMILL (1949)
d Val Guest
PB

MURDER BY PROXY (1955)
d Terence Fisher
VC PB

MURDER IN THE CATHEDRAL (1951)
d George Hoellering
PB

MURDER MOST FOUL (1964)
d George Pollock
PB

MURDER SHE SAID (1961)
d George Pollock
PB

MURDER WITHOUT CRIME (1950)
d J Lee Thompson
PB

MUSICAL PAINTBOX series
see
CORNWALL (1949)
DEVON WHEY (1949)
FANTASY ON IRELAND, a (1949)
SOMERSET (1949)

MY BROTHER JONATHAN (1948)
d Harold French
VC SC

MY BROTHER'S KEEPER (1948)
d Alfred Roome
VC PB

MY DAUGHTER JOY (1950)
d Gregory Ratoff
VC SC

MY HANDS ARE CLAY (1948)
d Lionel Tomlinson
PB

MYRTLE'S MILLIONS (1949)
VC

MY SIGNATURE TUNE (1947)
VC

MY SISTER AND I (1948)
d Harold Huth
PB

MYSTERIOUS ISLAND (1961)
d Cy Endfield
SC

MYSTERIOUS POACHER, the (1950)
d Don Chaffey
VC

MYSTERY IN THE MINE (1959)
d James Hill
SC

**MYSTERY OF THE WHITE
HANDKERCHIEF, the** (1946)
VC

MYSTERY ON BIRD ISLAND (1954)
d John Haggarty
SC

MYSTERY SUBMARINE (1962)
d C M Pennington-Richards
PB

MY TEENAGE DAUGHTER (1956)
d Herbert Wilcox
PB

MY WIFE'S FAMILY (1956)
d Gilbert Gunn
PB

NAAMAN THE LEPER (Sermon Film series)
(1949)
d J B Sloan
VC

NAKED AS NATURE INTENDED (1961)
d Harrison Marks
PB

NAKED EDGE, the (1961)
d Michael Anderson
PB

NAKED FURY (1959)
d Charles Saunders
SC

NAKED HEART, the (1950)
d Marc Allégret
VC SC

NAKED TRUTH, the (1957)
d Mario Zampi
SC PB

NALORPHINE (1953)
d Florence Anthony
VC

NARROWING CIRCLE, the (1956)
d Charles Saunders
PB

**NATURAL HISTORY OF THE LARGE
SOUTH AMERICAN POUCHED TREE
FROG, GASTROTHECA MARSUPIATA,
the** (1954)
VC

NAVY LARK, the (1959)
d Gordon Parry
VC PB

NEAR HOME (1946)
d Kay Mander
VC

NEIGHBOURHOOD 15 (1948)
d Stanley Reed
VC

NET, the (1953)
d Anthony Asquith
VC SC

NETWORK (1962)
d Joe Mendoza
VC

NEVER BACK LOSERS (1961)
d Robert Tronson
VC

NEVER LET GO (1960)
d John Guillermin
VC SC

NEVER LET ME GO (1953)
d Delmer Daves
PB

NEVER LOOK BACK (1952)
d Francis Searle
PB

NEVER TAKE NO FOR AN ANSWER (1951)
d Maurice Cloche, Ralph Smart
VC

**NEVER TAKE SWEETS FROM A
STRANGER** (1960)
d Cyril Frankel
SC

**NEW DEVELOPMENTS IN COAL
PREPARATION** (1958)
VC

NEW ESSO REFINERY (1951)
d Darrel Catling
VC

NEW LEASE OF LIFE (1958)
d Guy Blanchard
VC

NEW LIFE IN NIGERIA (1961)
VC

NEW POWER IN THEIR HANDS (1959)
VC

**NEWS CHRONICLE 1846–1946
CENTENARY DINNER** (1946)
VC

NEW TENANT, the (1963)
d George Brandt
SC

NEW TOWN (1948)
d John Halas, Joy Batchelor
VC

NEW UNIVERSITIES (Look at Life series)
(1963)
VC

**NEW WING OF CHAHABAD TB
SANATORIUM, the** (1950)
VC

NEW ZEALAND, A WORLD POWER (This
Modern Age series) (1950)
VC

NEXT TO NO TIME! (1958)
d Henry Cornelius
PB

NICE TIME (1957)
d Claude Goretta, Alain Tanner
VC

NICHOLAS NICKLEBY (1947)
d Alberto Cavalcanti
VC

NIGERIAN COCOA FARMER (1949)
VC

NIGHT AND THE CITY (1950)
d Jules Dassin
VC

NIGHT BEAT (1948)
d Harold Huth
PB

NIGHT BOAT TO DUBLIN (1946)
d Lawrence Huntington
VC SC

NIGHT CARGOES (1962)
d Ernest Morris
SC

NIGHTMARE (1963)
d Freddie Francis
PB

NIGHT MUST FALL (1964)
d Karel Reisz
VC

NIGHT MY NUMBER CAME UP, the (1955)
d Leslie Norman
PB

NIGHT OF THE DEMON (1957)
d Jacques Tourneur
VC SC

NIGHT OF THE EAGLE (1962)
d Sidney Hayers
VC SC

NIGHT OF THE PROWLER (1962)
d Francis Searle
PB

NIGHT RIVER (1955)
d Cyril Coke
VC

NIGHT TO REMEMBER, a (1958)
d Roy Ward Baker
VC PB

NIGHT TRAIN FOR INVERNESS (1959)
d Ernest Morris
VC

NIGHT WAS OUR FRIEND (1951)
d Michael Anderson
SC PB

NIGHT WE DROPPED A CLANGER, the (1959)
d Darcy Conyers
PB

NIGHT WE GOT THE BIRD, the (1960)
d Darcy Conyers
SC

NIGHT WITHOUT STARS (1951)
d Anthony Pélissier
SC

NINE CENTURIES OF COAL (1958)
d J B Napier-Bell
VC

NINE, DALMUIR WEST (1962)
VC

NINES WAS STANDING (1949)
VC

1984 (1955)
d Michael Anderson
VC

NOBEL BEGAN IT (1948)
VC

NO HIGHWAY (1951)
d Henry Koster
VC PB

NOISY-LE-SEC (1947)
VC

NO KIDDING (1960)
d Gerald Thomas
SC PB

NO LOVE FOR JOHNNIE (1961)
d Ralph Thomas
VC SC

NO, MY DARLING DAUGHTER (1961)
d Ralph Thomas
SC PB

NONE BUT THE LONELY HEART (1950)
VC

NONE BUT THE TORTOISE (1963)
VC

NON-VITAL ROOT CANAL THERAPY
(1960)
VC

NO ORCHIDS FOR MISS BLANDISH (1948)
d St John Legh Clowes
VC SC

NOOSE (1948)
d Edmond T Gréville
VC PB

NOOSE FOR A LADY (1952)
d Wolf Rilla
PB

NO PLACE FOR JENNIFER (1949)
d Henry Cass
VC

NO RESTING PLACE (1951)
d Paul Rotha
VC SC

NO ROAD BACK (1956)
d Montgomery Tully
VC

NO ROOM AT THE INN (1948)
d Daniel Birt
VC PB

NORTH AND SOUTH OF THE NIGER (1947)
d John Page
VC

NOR THE MOON BY NIGHT (1958)
d Ken Annakin
VC SC

NORTH WEST FRONTIER (1959)
d J Lee Thompson
SC

NO SAFETY AHEAD (1958)
d Max Varnel
PB

NOT A HOPE IN HELL (1960)
d Maclean Rogers
PB

NOTHING BARRED (1961)
d Darcy Conyers
SC PB

NOTHING BUT THE BEST (1964)
d Clive Donner
VC PB

NO TIME FOR TEARS (1957)
d Cyril Frankel
SC

NO TIME TO DIE (1958)
d Terence Young
PB

NO TRACE (1950)
d John Gilling
VC

NO TREES IN THE STREET (1958)
d J Lee Thompson
PB

NOT WANTED ON VOYAGE (1957)
d Maclean Rogers
VC PB

NOW AND FOREVER (1955)
d Mario Zampi
SC PB

NO WAY BACK (1949)
d Stefan Osiecki
VC PB

NOW BARABBAS WAS A ROBBER...
(1949)
d Gordon Parry
VC SC

NOWHERE TO GO (1958)
d Seth Holt
VC SC

NOW IS THE TIME (1951)
d Norman Mclaren
VC

NUDIST PARADISE (1958)
d Charles Saunders
PB

NURSE ON WHEELS (1963)
d Gerald Thomas
PB

OBSESSION (1949)
d Edward Dmytryk
VC SC

OCEAN WEATHER SHIP (1949)
d Frank Chilton
VC

ODD MAN OUT (1947)
d Carol Reed
VC SC

ODETTE (1950)
d Herbert Wilcox
VC PB

O DREAMLAND (1953)
d Lindsay Anderson
VC

OFFBEAT (1960)
d Cliff Owen
VC

OH... ROSALINDA!! (1955)
d Michael Powell, Emeric Pressburger
PB

OIL (Wealth of the World series) (1950)
d Grahame Tharp
VC

OIL FROM KHUZISTAN (1949)
VC

OIL HELPS OUT (1947)
d Frank Sherwin Green
VC

OIL IN KUWAIT (1948)
VC

OIL REVIEW NO.1 (1950)
VC

OIL REVIEW NO.5 (1951)
VC

OIL REVIEW NO.6 (1951)
VC

OIL REVIEW NO.7 (1951)
VC

OIL REVIEW NO.8 (1951)
VC

OIL REVIEW NO.10 (1951)
VC

OIL REVIEW NO.11 (1951)
VC

OIL REVIEW NO.12 (1951)
VC

OLD MOTHER RILEY HEADMISTRESS
(1950)
d John Harlow
VC

**OLD MOTHER RILEY'S JUNGLE
TREASURE** (1951)
d Maclean Rogers
VC PB

OLD MOTHER RILEY'S NEW VENTURE
(1949)
d John Harlow
VC PB

OLD SCHOOL TIE, the (Look at Life series)
(1964)
VC

OLD SHERRY (1960)
d Patrick Young
VC

OLD WIVES' TALES (1946)
d John Halas, Joy Batchelor
VC

OLIVE GROWING IN THE MIDDLE EAST
(1951)
VC

OLIVER TWIST (1948)
d David Lean
VC PB

OLYMPIC PREVIEW (1948)
d Herbert Marshall
VC

ONCE AGAIN AT WIMBLEDON (1949)
VC

ONCE A JOLLY SWAGMAN (1948)
d Jack Lee
VC SC PB

ONCE A SINNER (1950)
d Lewis Gilbert
SC PB

ONCE UPON A DREAM (1949)
d Ralph Thomas
VC SC

ONCE UPON A LINE (1947)
VC

ONE GOOD TURN (1954)
d John Paddy Carstairs
VC SC

ONE JUMP AHEAD (1955)
d Charles Saunders
PB

ONE MAN AND HIS JOB (Better Ways series)
(1956)
d Denis Ward
VC

ONE MAN'S STORY (1948)
d Dennis Shand, Maxwell Munden
VC

ONE MORE RIVER (1961)
d John Brason
VC

ONE NIGHT WITH YOU (1948)
d Terence Young
VC

ONE POTATO, TWO POTATO (1957)
d Leslie Daiken
VC PB

ONE THAT GOT AWAY, the (1957)
d Roy Ward Baker
SC

**1000 MILES IN 14 HOURS – THE
SUNBEAM RAPIER STORY OF THE
MILLE MIGLIA** (1957)
VC

ONE WAY OUT (1955)
d Francis Searle
PB

ONE WAY PENDULUM (1964)
d Peter Yates
PB

ONE WILD OAT (1951)
d Charles Saunders
VC PB

ONE WISH TOO MANY (1956)
d John Durst
SC

ONLY TWO CAN PLAY (1961)
d Sidney Gilliat
SC PB

ON SUCH A NIGHT (1955)
d Anthony Asquith
VC

ON THE BEAT (1962)
d Robert Asher
VC SC

ON THE FIDDLE (1961)
d Cyril Frankel
PB

ON THE RECORD (1955)
d Michael Brandt
VC

ON WINNING RACES (1952)
VC

ON WITH THE DANCE (1954)
VC

**OPENING OF CECIL CINEMA KINGSTON-
UPON-HULL, 28TH NOVEMBER 1955**
(1955)
VC

**OPENING OF THE NEW BUILDING FOR
THE BFI AT 81 DEAN STREET** (1960)
d Hazel Wilkinson
VC

OPEN WINDOW, the (1952)
d Henri Storck
PB

OPERATION AMSTERDAM (1958)
d Michael McCarthy
VC SC

OPERATION BULLSHINE (1959)
d Gilbert Gunn
SC PB

OPERATION CROSSBOW (1964)
d Michael Anderson
VC

OPERATION DIPLOMAT (1953)
d John Guillermin
PB

**OPERATION GRAPPLE EXPLOSIONS
RECORD** (1957)
VC

OPERATION MALAYA (1953)
d David Macdonald
VC

OPERATION SNATCH (1962)
d Robert Day
SC PB

OPUS 65 (1952)
d John Taylor
VC

ORACLE, the (1953)
d C M Pennington-Richards
PB

ORDERS ARE ORDERS (1954)
d David Paltenghi
VC PB

ORDERS TO KILL (1958)
d Anthony Asquith
VC PB

ORIGIN OF COAL, the (Coalmining as a Craft
series) (1953)
d J B Napier-Bell
VC

**OROFACIAL MUSCLES; ASPECTS OF
THEIR BEHAVIOUR** (1955)
VC

OSCAR WILDE (1960)
d Gregory Ratoff
VC PB

OUR CLUB MAGAZINE NO.8 (1946)
VC

OUR CLUB MAGAZINE NO.9 (1946)
VC

OUR CLUB MAGAZINE NO.10 (1946)
VC

OUR CLUB MAGAZINE NO.12 (1946)
VC

OUR CLUB MAGAZINE NO.14 (1946)
VC

OUR CLUB MAGAZINE NO.15 (1946)
VC

OUR CLUB MAGAZINE NO.16 (1946)
VC

OUR CLUB MAGAZINE NO.17 (1946)
VC

OUR CLUB MAGAZINE NO.18 (1946)
VC

OUR CLUB MAGAZINE NO.20 (1946)
VC

OUR CLUB MAGAZINE NO.23 (1947)
VC

OUR CLUB MAGAZINE NO.24 (1947)
VC

OUR CLUB MAGAZINE NO.25 (1947)
VC

OUR CLUB MAGAZINE NO.26 (1947)
VC

OUR CLUB MAGAZINE NO.28 (1947)
VC

OUR CLUB MAGAZINE NO.30 (1948)
VC

OUR CLUB MAGAZINE NO.31 (1948)
VC

OUR CLUB MAGAZINE NO.34 (1948)
VC

OUR CLUB MAGAZINE NO.38 (1948)
VC

OUR CLUB MAGAZINE NO.39 (1948)
VC

OUR CLUB MAGAZINE NO.40 (1949)
VC

OUR CLUB MAGAZINE NO.41 (1948)
VC

OUR CLUB MAGAZINE NO.47 (1949)
VC

OUR CLUB MAGAZINE NO.58 (1949)
VC

OUR GIRL FRIDAY (1953)
d Noel Langley
VC PB

OUR HOMES (Glasgow Civics series) (1947)
VC

OUR KING AND QUEEN (1948)
VC

OUR MAGAZINE NO.1 (1952)
d J E Ewins
SC

OUR MAGAZINE NO.2 (1952)
d J E Ewins
SC

OUR MAGAZINE NO.3 (1952)
d J E Ewins
SC

OUR MAGAZINE NO.4 (1952)
d J E Ewins
SC

OUR MAGAZINE NO.5 (1953)
d J E Ewins
SC

OUR MAGAZINE NO.6 (1954)
d J E Ewins
SC

OUR MAGAZINE NO.7 (1954)
d J E Ewins
SC

OUR MAGAZINE NO.8 (1954)
d J E Ewins
SC

OUR MAGAZINE NO.9 (1954)
d J E Ewins
SC

OUR MAGAZINE NO.10 (1954)
d J E Ewins
SC

OUR MAGAZINE NO.11 (1955)
d J E Ewins
SC

OUR MAGAZINE NO.12 (1955)
d J E Ewins
SC

OUR MAGAZINE NO.13 (1955)
d J E Ewins
SC

OUR MAGAZINE NO.14 (1955)
d J E Ewins
SC

OUR MAGAZINE NO.15 (1955)
d J E Ewins
SC

OUR MAGAZINE NO.16 (1956)
d J E Ewins
SC

OUR MAN IN HAVANA (1959)
d Carol Reed
VC PB

OUR POLICE (Glasgow Civics series) (1947)
VC

OUR PUBLIC PARKS (Glasgow Civics series) (1947)
VC

OUR SCHOOLS (Glasgow Civics series) (1947)
VC

OUR WATER SUPPLY (Glasgow Civics series) (1947)
VC

OUTCAST OF THE ISLANDS (1951)
d Carol Reed
VC SC

OUTING FOR CHRISTOPHER, an (1949)
VC

OUT OF THE CLOUDS (1955)
d Basil Dearden
PB

OUT OF THE DARK (1951)
d John Durst
VC

OUT OF THE FOG (1962)
d Montgomery Tully
PB

OUT OF TRUE (1951)
d Philip Leacock
VC

OVERHEAD LINE CONSTRUCTION – ERECTING HEAVY POLE BY DERRICK (GPO Training Film series) (1950)
VC

OVERHEAD LINE CONSTRUCTION – ERECTION OF AERIAL CABLES (GPO Training Film series) (1950)
VC

OVERHEAD LINE CONSTRUCTION – ERECTION OF AN AERIAL CABLE SUSPENSION WIRE (GPO Training Film series) (1950)
VC

OVERLANDERS, the (1946)
d Harry Watt
VC PB

OVER MY SHOULDER (Look at Life series) (1963)
VC

OVER THE GARDEN WALL (1950)
d John E Blakeley
VC PB

OXFORD (1958)
VC

PACIFIC DESTINY (1956)
d Wolf Rilla
VC SC

PADDY'S MILESTONE (1947)
d J Blake Dalrymple
VC

PAINTING WITH FLOWERS (1957)
SC

PAIR OF BRIEFS, a (1961)
d Ralph Thomas
SC PB

PALESTINE (This Modern Age series) (1947)
VC

PANDORA AND THE FLYING DUTCHMAN (1950)
d Albert Lewin
SC PB

PAPER AND STRING (1948)
VC

PARANOIAC (1962)
d Freddie Francis
SC PB

PARTNERS IN CRIME (1961)
d Peter Duffell
PB

PART-TIME WIFE (1961)
d Max Varnel
SC

PARTY'S OVER, the (1963)
d Guy Hamilton
PB

PASSAGE HOME (1955)
d Roy Ward Baker
SC

PASSING STRANGER, the (1954)
d John Arnold
PB

PASSIONATE FRIENDS, the (1948)
d David Lean
VC

PASSIONATE STRANGER, the (1956)
d Muriel Box
PB

PASSIONATE SUMMER (1958)
d Rudolph Cartier
PB

PASSPORT TO PIMLICO (1949)
d Henry Cornelius
VC SC

PASSPORT TO SHAME (1958)
d Alvin Rakoff
VC PB

PATHÉ PICTORIAL NO.370 (1951)
VC

PATHÉ PICTORIAL NO.434 (1963)
VC

PATHS OF PROGRESS (1958)
d J R F Stewart
VC

PATHWAYS TO THE SKY (1952)
VC

PAUL TEMPLE RETURNS (1952)
d Maclean Rogers
PB

PAUL TEMPLE'S TRIUMPH (1950)
d Maclean Rogers
PB

PAYROLL (1961)
d Sidney Hayers
PB

PEACEDAY CELEBRATIONS, KINGSTON-UPON-HULL (1946)
VC

PEACEFUL REVOLUTION, the (1961)
d Atma Ram
VC

PEACEFUL YEARS, the (1948)
d Peter Baylis
VC

PEACHES, the (1964)
d Michael Gill
VC

PEDESTRIAN CROSSING (1948)
d Michael Law
VC

PEEP BEHIND THE SCENES (1947)
VC

PEEPING TOM (1959)
d Michael Powell
VC

PENNY AND THE POWNALL CASE (1948)
d Slim Hand
VC

PEN PICTURES FROM DENMARK; LETTER 1 (1949)
d Isabel Elder, John C Elder
VC

PEN PICTURES FROM DENMARK; LETTER 3 (1949)
d Isabel Elder, John C Elder
VC

PEN PICTURES FROM DENMARK; LETTER 4 (1949)
d Isabel Elder, John C Elder
VC

PEN PICTURES FROM RHODESIA; LETTER 1 (1948)
VC

PEN PICTURES FROM RHODESIA; LETTER 3 (1948)
VC

PEN PICTURES FROM RHODESIA; LETTER 5 (1948)
VC

PEOPLE AT NO.19, the (1949)
d J B Holmes
VC

PEOPLE OF MALAYA (1949)
VC

PERFECT HUSBAND, the (1952)
VC

PERFECT WOMAN, the (1949)
d Bernard Knowles
VC PB

PERIL FOR THE GUY (1956)
d James Hill
SC

PERSONAL AFFAIR (1953)
d Anthony Pélissier
PB

PETER MAY (British Sporting Personalities series) (1962)
VC

PETTICOAT PIRATES (1961)
d David Macdonald
PB

PHAGOCYTOSIS; MACROPHAGES IN TISSUE CULTURES OF EMBRYONIC CHICK LUNG (1946)
d A F W Hughes
VC

PHANTOM OF THE OPERA, the (1962)
d Terence Fisher
SC PB

PHASE-CONTRAST MICROSCOPE, the (1954)
VC

PHENYLKETONURIA (1962)
d F P Hudson
VC

PHYSIOLOGY OF THE KIDNEY (1947)
VC

PICCADILLY INCIDENT (1946)
d Herbert Wilcox
VC PB

PICCADILLY THIRD STOP (1960)
d Wolf Rilla
PB

PICKWICK PAPERS, the (1952)
d Noel Langley
VC PB

PICTURE PAPER (1946)
d Erik Cripps
VC

PIECE OF CAKE, a (1948)
d John Irwin
VC

PIGS ON EVERY FARM (1949)
d Richard Warren
VC

PINCH OF SALT, a (Look at Life series) (1963)
VC

PINNING MOSQUITOES (1954)
VC

PIPER'S TUNE, the (1961)
d Muriel Box
SC

PIPING HOT (1959)
d John Halas, Joy Batchelor
VC

PIT OF DARKNESS (1961)
d Lance Comfort
PB

PLACE TO GO, a (1963)
d Basil Dearden
SC PB

PLANE SAILING (1957)
VC

PLAN FOR COAL (1953)
VC

PLANTER'S WIFE, the (1952)
d Ken Annakin
VC SC

PLAN TO WORK ON, a (1948)
d Kay Mander
VC

PLANT PESTS AND DISEASES series
see
GREENHOUSE WHITE FLY (1950)
WINTER MOTH (1950)

PLAYBOY OF THE WESTERN WORLD, the (1962)
d Brian Desmond Hurst
SC

PLAYERS OF MERIT series
see
DENIS COMPTON (1949)
GODFREY EVANS (1952)
LEN HUTTON (1946)
STANLEY MATTHEWS (1946)

PLAYGROUND EXPRESS (1955)
d John Irwin
SC

PLAYING FIELDS (1951)
VC

PLAY IT COOL (1962)
d Michael Winner
PB

PLAYS FOR THE PEOPLE (1947)
d L Gordon Begg
VC

PLEASE TURN OVER (1960)
d Gerald Thomas
PB

POET AND PAINTER series
see
JOHN GILPIN (1951)

POET'S PUB (1949)
d Frederick Wilson
VC SC

POLAND (The Magic Globe series) (1947)
d Herbert Marshall
VC

POLICE FORCE, the (1947)
d Malcolm Stewart
VC

POLICEMAN, the (1947)
d Malcolm Stewart
VC

POLIO; DIAGNOSIS AND MANAGEMENT (1948)
d Geoffrey Innes
VC

POOL OF CONTENTMENT (1946)
d Richard Massingham
VC

POOL OF LONDON (1950)
d Basil Dearden
VC SC

PORT OF HULL, the (1963)
d John Taylor
VC

PORTRAIT FROM LIFE (1948)
d Terence Fisher
VC SC

PORTRAIT OF ALISON (1955)
d Guy Green
PB

PORTRAIT OF A MATADOR (1958)
d Theodore Zichy
VC

PORTRAIT OF CLARE (1950)
d Lance Comfort
SC

PORTRAIT OF QUEENIE (1964)
d Michael Orrom
SC

POSTMAN'S KNOCK (1961)
d Robert Lynn
PB

POSTMAN'S NIGHTMARE (1948)
VC

POSTSCRIPT TO EMPIRE (1962)
d Michael Alexander
VC

POST-WAR JOBS series
see
COAL MINING TODAY (1946)
COTTON COMEBACK (1946)

POTATO GROWING (1946)
d Andrew Buchanan
VC

POT CARRIERS, the (1962)
d Peter Graham Scott
PB

POTTERY IN THE GOLD COAST (1946)
VC

POULTRY ON THE GENERAL FARM (1949)
VC

POWERED FLIGHT; THE STORY OF THE CENTURY (1953)
VC

POWERED SUPPORTS (1960)
d Peter Pickering
VC

POWER NEEDS NO PASSPORT (Look at Life series) (1964)
VC

POWER ON THE FARM (1946)
d Henry Cooper
VC

PRECISE MEASUREMENT FOR ENGINEERS (1948)
d J D Chambers
VC

PRELUDE TO FAME (1950)
d Fergus McDonell
VC SC

PRELUDE TO PROGRESS (1951)
VC

PRELUDE TO PROSPERITY (1947)
d James E Rogers
VC

PREVENTION OF CROSS INFECTION; GASTRO-ENTERITIS IN INFANCY (1951)
VC

PREVENTION OF CROSS INFECTION; RESPIRATORY TRACT INFECTION IN CHILDREN'S WARDS (1953)
VC

PRICE OF SILENCE, the (1960)
d Montgomery Tully
PB

PRICE OF VALOUR, the (Look at Life series) (1964)
VC

PRIMITIVES, the (1962)
 d Alfred Travers
 PB

PRINCE AND THE SHOWGIRL, the (1957)
 d Laurence Olivier
 VC PB

PRINCESS'S WEDDING DAY (1947)
 VC

PRIVATE ANGELO (1949)
 d Peter Ustinov
 VC

PRIVATE POTTER (1962)
 d Casper Wrede
 VC PB

PRIVATE'S PROGRESS (1956)
 d John Boulting
 VC SC

PROBATION OFFICER (1949)
 d Donald Alexander
 VC

**PRODUCTION PLANNING IN CENTRAL
WORKSHOPS** (1960)
 VC

PROFESSIONALS, the (1960)
 d Don Sharp
 VC

PROGRESS REPORT NO.2 (1948)
 VC

**PROJECT MARK X; THE DEVELOPMENT
OF A NEW JAGUAR** (1962)
 VC

PROUD CANVAS (1949)
 d Aubrey Singer
 VC

PROUD CITY (1946)
 d Ralph Keene
 VC

PSYCHE 59 (1964)
 d Alexander Singer
 SC

PUMPKIN EATER, the (1964)
 d Jack Clayton
 VC PB

PUNCH AND JUDY (1948)
 d F W Ratcliffe Holmes
 SC

PUNCH AND JUDY MAN, the (1962)
 d Jeremy Summers
 VC SC

PURE HELL OF ST TRINIAN'S, the (1960)
 d Frank Launder
 PB

PURPLE PLAIN, the (1954)
 d Robert Parrish
 SC

QUARE FELLOW, the (1962)
 d Arthur Dreifuss
 SC

QUARTET (1948)
 d Arthur Crabtree, Harold French, Ralph
   Smart, Ken Annakin
 VC PB

QUATERMASS EXPERIMENT, the (1955)
 d Val Guest
 PB

QUEEN AT ELSTREE STUDIOS, the (1951)
 VC

QUEEN IS CROWNED, a (1953)
 VC

QUEEN OF SPADES, the (1948)
 d Thorold Dickinson
 VC SC PB

QUEEN OF THE FUTURE (1947)
 VC

QUEEN'S GUARDS, the (1961)
 d Michael Powell
 VC

QUESTIONING CITY, the (1959)
 d Eric Fullilove
 VC

QUESTION OF ADULTERY, a (1958)
 d Don Chaffey
 VC

QUESTION OF VALUES, a (Religion and Life
series) (1949)
 d J B Sloan
 VC

QUIET WEEKEND (1946)
 d Harold French
 VC SC

RAG DOLL (1960)
 d Lance Comfort
 PB

RAIDERS OF THE RIVER (1955)
 d John Haggerty
 SC

RAILWAYMEN, the (1946)
 d Richard Q McNaughton
 VC

RAINBOW JACKET, the (1954)
 d Basil Dearden
 VC SC

RAISING THE WIND (1961)
 d Gerald Thomas
 VC PB

RAMSBOTTOM RIDES AGAIN (1956)
 d John Baxter
 SC PB

RANDLE AND ALL THAT (1946)
 VC

RAPE OF THE EARTH, the (This Modern
Age series) (1947)
 VC

RATTLE OF A SIMPLE MAN (1964)
 d Muriel Box
 VC SC

RAWDON REBORN (1954)
 VC

RAY OF SUNSHINE, a (1950)
 d Horace Shepherd
 VC

REACH FOR THE SKY (1956)
 d Lewis Gilbert
 VC SC

READ ANY GOOD METERS LATELY?
(1947)
 d John Waterhouse
 VC

REBEL, the (1960)
 d Robert Day
 VC SC

RECLINING FIGURE, the (1959)
 d Dudley Shaw Ashton
 VC

RED BERET, the (1953)
 d Terence Young
 VC

RED SHOES, the (1948)
 d Michael Powell, Emeric Pressburger
 VC SC

RED SHOES SKETCHES, the (1948)
 VC

REFUGE ENGLAND (1959)
 d Robert Vas
 VC

RELIGION AND LIFE series
 see
 QUESTION OF VALUES, a (1949)

RELUCTANT HEROES (1951)
 d Jack Raymond
 SC

RELUCTANT WIDOW, the (1950)
 d Bernard Knowles
 VC

REPORT ON COAL (1947)
 VC

REPORT ON 60s (1961)
 d Philip Owtram
 VC

REPORT ON STEEL (1948)
 d Michael Orrom
 VC

**REPRODUCTIVE BEHAVIOUR OF THE
KITTIWAKE, the** (1955)
 d Nikolas Tinbergen
 VC

**REPRODUCTIVE BEHAVIOUR OF THE
STICKLEBACK, the** (1948)
 d Nikolas Tinbergen
 VC

RESCUE SQUAD, the (1963)
 d Colin Bell
 SC

RESEARCH AND MODERN HOUSING
(1951)
 d Richard F Tambling
 VC

RESHAPING BRITISH RAILWAYS (1963)
 VC

RETURN TO ACTION (1947)
 d Gilbert Gunn
 VC

REVENGE OF FRANKENSTEIN, the (1958)
 d Terence Fisher
 VC

RICHARD III (1955)
 d Laurence Olivier
 VC PB

**RIGHT HONOURABLE SIR ANDREW RAE
DUNCAN, the** (1948)
 VC

RIG 20 (1952)
 d Ronald H Riley, David Villiers
 PB

RING OF SPIES (1963)
 d Robert Tronson
 SC PB

RISE AND FALL OF EMILY SPROD, the
(1964)
 d Bob Godfrey
 VC

RIVAL WORLD, the (1955)
 d Bert Haanstra
 VC PB

RIVER BEAT (1953)
d Guy Green
PB

RIVER TO CROSS (1950)
d John Shearman
VC

ROAD TO HONG KONG, the (1961)
d Norman Panama
PB

ROBBERY UNDER ARMS (1957)
d Jack Lee
PB

ROBINSON CHARLEY (Charley series) (1948)
d John Halas, Joy Batchelor
VC

ROB ROY THE HIGHLAND ROGUE (1953)
d Harold French
SC PB

ROCKETS GALORE (1958)
d Michael Relph
PB

ROCKETS IN THE DUNES (1960)
d William C Hammond
SC

ROCKING HORSE, the (1962)
d James Scott
VC

ROCKING HORSE WINNER, the (1949)
d Anthony Pélissier
VC

RODE SAFELY (1955)
d Edwin Lambert
VC

ROLLO THE SQUIRREL (1949)
d Anson Dyer
VC

ROMAN SPRING OF MRS STONE, the (1961)
d José Quintero
PB

ROMANTIC AGE, the (1949)
d Edmond T Gréville
VC SC

ROMANTIC INDIA (1946)
SC

ROMEO AND JULIET (1954)
d Renato Castellani
SC

ROOF BOLTING IN GREAT BRITAIN (1958)
d Geoffrey Bell
VC

ROOM AT THE TOP (1958)
d Jack Clayton
VC PB

ROOM IN THE HOUSE (1955)
d Maurice Elvey
PB

ROONEY (1958)
d George Pollock
VC SC

ROOT OF ALL EVIL, the (1947)
d Brock Williams
VC SC

'ROSE MARIE' ON ICE (1952)
d John de Vere Loder
VC

ROUGH AND THE SMOOTH, the (1959)
d Robert Siodmak
VC SC

ROUGH SHOOT (1953)
d Robert Parrish
VC

ROVER AND ME (1949)
d Frank Chisnell
VC

ROVER MAKES GOOD (1952)
d John Dooley
SC

ROYAL BALLET, the (1959)
d Paul Czinner
PB

ROYAL BURGH OF DUMFRIES GUID NYCHBURRIS FESTIVAL (1950)
VC

ROYAL RIVER, the (1960)
d Kenneth Fairbairn
VC

ROYAL TOUR OF SOUTH AFRICA (1947)
VC

RULERS OF RACING (Look at Life series) (1964)
VC

RUN FOR YOUR MONEY, a (1949)
d Charles Frend
VC PB

RUNNING JUMPING & STANDING STILL FILM, the (1960)
d Richard Lester
VC

RUNNING MAN, the (1963)
d Carol Reed
PB

RUTH (1948)
d Donald Taylor
VC

SACRIFICE WE OFFER, the (1949)
PB

SADLER'S WELLS AND BRITISH BALLET (1956)
d John de Vere Loder
VC

SAFECRACKER, the (1957)
d Ray Milland
PB

SAFETY BELTS (GPO Training Film series) (1949)
VC

SAILOR'S RETURN, the (1947)
VC

SAINT JOAN (1957)
d Otto Preminger
PB

SAINTS AND SINNERS (1949)
d Leslie Arliss
VC

SALMON FISHING INDUSTRY OF BRITISH COLUMBIA (1947)
VC

SALT (1947)
d Max Anderson
VC

SALUTE THE TOFF (1952)
d Maclean Rogers
PB

SALVAGE GANG, the (1958)
d John Krish
SC

SAMMY GOING SOUTH (1963)
d Alexander Mackendrick
VC PB

SAPPHIRE (1959)
d Basil Dearden
VC PB

SARABAND FOR DEAD LOVERS (1948)
d Basil Dearden
VC PB

SATURDAY ISLAND (1952)
d Stuart Heisler
PB

SATURDAY MEN, the (1963)
d John Fletcher
VC

SATURDAY NIGHT AND SUNDAY MORNING (1960)
d Karel Reisz
VC PB

SATURDAY NIGHT OUT (1964)
d Robert Hartford-Davis
VC

SCAMP, the (1957)
d Wolf Rilla
PB

SCAPEGOAT, the (1958)
d Robert Hamer
PB

SCARLET BLADE, the (1963)
d John Gilling
VC

SCARLET SPEAR, the (1953)
d George Breakston, C Ray Stahl
PB

SCHERZO TARANTELLE (1950)
VC

SCHOOL FOR DANGER (1947)
d Edward Baird
SC

SCHOOL FOR SCOUNDRELS; or, How to win without actually cheating (1959)
d Robert Hamer
VC

SCHOOL FOR SECRETS (1946)
d Peter Ustinov
VC PB

SCHOOL IN COLOGNE (1948)
VC

SCHOOLMASTER, the (1953)
d Leonard Reeve
VC

SCIENCE IN THE ORCHESTRA (1950)
d Alex Strasser
VC

SCOTLAND YARD (This Modern Age series) (1946)
SC

SCOTTISH EXPRESS (1946)
d Paul Barralet
VC

SCOTTISH LIVESTOCK series
see
ABERDEEN ANGUS (1947)

SCOTT OF THE ANTARCTIC (1948)
d Charles Frend
VC PB

SCRAPBOOK FOR 1922 (1947)
d Peter Baylis, Leslie Baily
PB

SCRAPBOOK FOR 1933 (1949)
VC

SCROOGE (1951)
d Brian Desmond Hurst
VC SC

SEA DEVILS (1952)
d Raoul Walsh
PB

SEAGULLS OVER SORRENTO (1954)
d John Boulting, Roy Boulting
PB

SEANCE ON A WET AFTERNOON (1964)
d Bryan Forbes
VC SC

SEARCHLIGHT ON JAPAN (1949)
VC

SEARCHLIGHT ON STEEL (1949)
VC

SEA SHALL NOT HAVE THEM, the (1954)
d Lewis Gilbert
SC PB

SECOND FIDDLE (1957)
d Maurice Elvey
PB

SECOND MATE, the (1950)
d John Baxter
PB

SECOND MRS TANQUERAY, the (1952)
d Dallas Bower
VC

SECRET, the (1955)
d Cy Endfield
PB

SECRET CAVE, the (1953)
d John Durst
SC

SECRET MAN, the (1958)
d Ronald Kinnoch
PB

SECRET OF BLOOD ISLAND, the (1964)
d Quentin Lawrence
PB

SECRET OF THE FOREST, the (1955)
d Darcy Conyers
SC

SECRET PARTNER, the (1961)
d Basil Dearden
PB

SECRET PEOPLE (1951)
d Thorold Dickinson
VC PB

SECRET PLACE, the (1957)
d Clive Donner
VC

SECRET TENT, the (1956)
d Don Chaffey
PB

SECRET TUNNEL, the (1947)
d William C Hammond
VC

SECRET VENTURE (1955)
d R G Springsteen
SC

SEED OF PROSPERITY (1946)
d Alan J Harper
VC

SEEKERS, the (1954)
d Ken Annakin
PB

SEND FOR PAUL TEMPLE (1946)
d John Argyle
PB

SENSITIVITY TO ANTIBIOTIC INJECTIONS; IMPROVED INJECTION TECHNIQUE (1954)
VC

SERENA (1962)
d Peter Maxwell
PB

SERMON FILM series
see
NAAMAN THE LEPER (1949)

SERVANT, the (1963)
d Joseph Losey
VC PB

SERVANT OF THE PEOPLE (1947)
d John O Douglas
VC

SEVEN DAYS TO NOON (1950)
d John Boulting, Roy Boulting
VC PB

SEVEN PILLARS OF WISDOM – ARTISTS TEST: ALBERT FINNEY (1960)
d David Lean
VC

7TH DAWN, the (1964)
d Lewis Gilbert
SC PB

SEVEN YEARS IN TIBET (1956)
d Hans M Nieter
VC

SEWAGE DISPOSAL (1947)
d Malcolm Stewart
VC

SEWERMAN (1947)
d Malcolm Stewart
VC

SHADOW OF THE RUHR (This Modern Age series) (1948)
VC SC

SHAFT SURVEY (1957)
d Ralph Elton
VC

SHAKEDOWN, the (1959)
d John Lemont
VC

SHARE THY BREAD (1963)
d Leonard Cheshire
VC

SHE ALWAYS GETS THEIR MAN (1962)
d Godfrey Grayson
VC PB

SHE DIDN'T SAY NO (1958)
d Cyril Frankel
SC

SHE KNOWS Y'KNOW (1962)
d Montgomery Tully
PB

SHELL CINEMAGAZINE NO.9 (1947)
VC

SHELL CINEMAGAZINE NO.13 (1949)
VC

SHELL CINEMAGAZINE NO.14 (1949)
VC

SHELL CINEMAGAZINE NO.19 (1951)
VC

SHE'LL HAVE TO GO (1961)
d Robert Asher
VC PB

SHERIFF OF FRACTURED JAW, the (1958)
d Raoul Walsh
VC PB

SHIP COMES IN FROM TEXAS, a (1949)
VC

SHIPSHAPE (1963)
d Philip Dennis
VC

SHIP THAT DIED OF SHAME, the (1955)
d Michael Relph, Basil Dearden
SC

SHOP AT SLY CORNER, the (1946)
d George King
VC

SHORT VISION, a (1956)
d Peter Foldes, Joan Foldes
VC

SHOT IN THE DARK, a (1964)
d Blake Edwards
PB

SHOVEL, the (1953)
d Alun Falconer
VC

SHOWGROUND OF THE NORTH (1948)
d Tom Blakeley
PB

SHOWN BY REQUEST (1947)
d Colin Dean
VC

SIEGE OF PINCHGUT, the (1959)
d Harry Watt
VC

SIEGE OF SIDNEY STREET, the (1960)
d Robert S Baker, Monty Berman
PB

SILENT PLAYGROUND, the (1963)
d Stanley Goulder
PB

SILKEN AFFAIR, the (1956)
d Roy Kellino
SC

SILVER DARLINGS, the (1946)
d Clarence Elder
VC

SILVER LINING (1947)
VC

SIMBA (1955)
d Brian Desmond Hurst
SC

SIMON AND LAURA (1955)
d Muriel Box
VC

SINGAPORE; A STUDY OF A PORT (1951)
d Brian Salt
VC

SINGAPORE AND BACK (1960)
VC

SINGER NOT THE SONG, the (1960)
d Roy Ward Baker
VC PB

SINGING STREET, the (1952)
d Nigel McIsaac
PB

SINGLE POINT FUEL INJECTOR, a (1946)
d John Shearman
VC

SINK THE BISMARCK! (1960)
d Lewis Gilbert
VC

SIR BASIL SPENCE (1964)
VC

SIR CLIFFORD COPLAND PATERSON (1947)
VC

6.5 SPECIAL (1958)
d Alfred Shaughnessy
VC SC

SIX MEN, the (1951)
d Michael Law
VC

SIX-SIDED TRIANGLE, the (1963)
d Christopher Miles
VC

633 SQUADRON (1963)
d Walter Grauman
PB

SKID KIDS (1953)
d Don Chaffey
SC

SKIFFY GOES TO SEA (1947)
d Harry May
VC

SKY IS OURS, the (1956)
d Terry Ashwood
VC

SLEEPING CAR TO TRIESTE (1948)
d John Paddy Carstairs
PB

SLEEPING TIGER, the (1954)
d Joseph Losey
VC PB

SMALL BACK ROOM, the (1948)
d Michael Powell, Emeric Pressburger
VC

SMALL BAND JAZZ (1961)
d Robert Henryson
VC

SMALLEST SHOW ON EARTH, the (1957)
d Basil Dearden
VC PB

SMALL HOTEL (1957)
d David Macdonald
PB

SMALL WORLD OF SAMMY LEE, the (1962)
d Ken Hughes
PB

SMILEY (1956)
d Anthony Kimmins
PB

SMOKE SIGNALS (1950)
d Derek Stewart
PB

SMOKING AND YOU (1963)
d Derrick Knight
VC

SNAP IT IN COLOUR (1950)
VC

SNOWBOUND (1947)
d David Macdonald
VC

SNOWDRIFT AT BLEATH GILL (1955)
d Kenneth Fairbairn
VC

SOAPBOX DERBY (1957)
d Darcy Conyers
SC PB

SOCIETY OF BRITISH AIRCRAFT CONSTRUCTORS FLYING DISPLAY AT FARNBOROUGH, 1956 (1956)
VC

SO EVIL MY LOVE (1948)
d Lewis Allen
VC

SO EVIL SO YOUNG (1961)
d Godfrey Grayson
PB

SOLID EXPLANATION, a (1951)
d Peter Bradford
VC

SOLITARY CHILD, the (1958)
d Gerald Thomas
PB

SO LONG AT THE FAIR (1950)
d Terence Fisher, Antony Darnborough
VC PB

SOLUTION BY PHONE (1953)
d Alfred Travers
PB

SOME ASPECTS OF ACCESSIBLE CANCERS (1951)
VC

SOME OBSERVATIONS ON SOFT TISSUE BEHAVIOUR IN MALOCCLUSIONS (1950)
VC

SOMERSET (Musical Paintbox series) (1949)
d Pat Griffin
VC

SOMETHING IN THE CITY (1950)
d Maclean Rogers
PB

SOMETHING MONEY CAN'T BUY (1952)
d Pat Jackson
VC

SOMEWHERE IN POLITICS (1948)
d John E Blakeley
PB

SONG FOR TOMORROW (1948)
d Terence Fisher
PB

SONG OF PARIS (1952)
d John Guillermin
PB

SONG OF THE CLOUDS (1957)
d John Armstrong
PB

SON IS BORN, a (1946)
d Eric Porter
SC

SONS AND LOVERS (1960)
d Jack Cardiff
VC PB

SONS OF SINBAD (1946)
d Alan Villiers
VC

SOS PACIFIC (1959)
d Guy Green
PB

SOUND BARRIER, the (1952)
d David Lean
VC PB

SOURING OF MILK (1947)
d J B Napier-Bell
VC

SOUTHAMPTON DOCKS (1964)
d John Taylor
VC

SOUTHERN RHODESIA: IS THIS YOUR COUNTRY? (1947)
VC

SOUTH FROM CHILOÉ (1960)

SO WELL REMEMBERED (1947)
d Edward Dmytryk
VC PB

SPACEWAYS (1953)
d Terence Fisher
VC

SPANIARD'S CURSE, the (1957)
d Ralph Kemplen
PB

SPANISH GARDENER, the (1956)
d Philip Leacock
PB

SPANISH SWORD, the (1962)
d Ernest Morris
VC PB

SPARE THE ROD (1961)
d Leslie Norman
VC PB

SPARROWS CAN'T SING (1962)
d Joan Littlewood
VC PB

SPEEDBIRD TO SUNRISE (1953)
VC

SPEEDWAY (1947)
d Sammy Lee
VC

SPIDER AND THE FLY, the (1949)
d Robert Hamer
VC

SPIDER'S WEB, the (1960)
d Godfrey Grayson
VC PB

SPIKE MILLIGAN MEETS JOE BROWN (Milligan at Large series) (1961)
d Gerard Bryant
SC

SPIKE MILLIGAN ON TREASURE ISLAND WC2 (Milligan at Large series) (1961)
d Gerard Bryant
SC

SPIRIT OF LAMBETH, the (1962)
VC

SPORTSHORT series
see
DENIS COMPTON (1954)

SPOTLIGHT ON THE BEST SELLERS (1951)
d Anthony Gilkison
VC

SPOTLIGHT ON THE COLONIES (1950)
d Diana Pine
VC

SPOTLIGHT ON THE POOLS (1949)
VC

SPOTLIGHT ON THE SPOOKS (1951)
VC

SPRING IN PARK LANE (1948)
d Herbert Wilcox
VC

SPRING SONG (1946)
d Montgomery Tully
PB

SPRINGTIME IN BIRDLAND (1947)
d F W Ratcliffe Holmes
PB

SQUARE PEG, the (1958)
d John Paddy Carstairs
PB

SQUARE RING, the (1953)
d Michael Relph, Basil Dearden
VC PB

STABILITY (How an Aeroplane Flies series)
(1947)
d Bill Mason
VC

STABLE RIVALS (1952)
d Leonard Reeve
SC

STAGE FRIGHT (1949)
d Alfred Hitchcock
VC SC

STANLEY MATTHEWS (Players of Merit
series) (1946)
VC

STAR OF BETHLEHEM, the (1956)
d Vivian Milroy
PB

STAR OF MY NIGHT (1954)
d Paul Dickson
PB

STATION SIX SAHARA (1962)
d Seth Holt
PB

STEAM TURBINE (1946)
d Aubrey Singer, Lionel Pierce
VC

STEEL KEY, the (1953)
d Robert S Baker
PB

**STEPHANE GRAPPELLY AND HIS
QUINTET** (1946)
d Horace Shepherd
VC

STEPS OF THE BALLET (1948)
d Muir Mathieson
VC SC

STICKLEBACKS (1948)
VC

STITCH IN TIME, a (1963)
d Robert Asher
VC PB

STOCK CAR (1955)
d Wolf Rilla
PB

STOLEN AIRLINER, the (1955)
d Don Sharp
SC

STOLEN FACE (1952)
d Terence Fisher
VC

STOLEN HOURS (1963)
d Daniel Petrie
PB

STOLEN PLANS, the (1952)
d James Hill
SC

STOLEN TIME (1955)
d Charles Deane
PB

STOP-OVER FOREVER (1964)
d Frederic Goode
PB

STOP PRESS GIRL (1949)
d Michael Barry
VC PB

STORM OVER THE NILE (1955)
d Terence Young, Zoltan Korda
PB

STORY OF A STEEL-WIRE ROPE, the
(1946)
d Stanley Russell
VC

STORY OF DAVID, a (1960)
d Bob McNaught
SC

STORY OF GILBERT AND SULLIVAN, the
(1953)
d Sidney Gilliat
VC SC

STORY OF OMOLO, the (1946)
d Basil Wright
VC

STORY OF PAPER MAKING, the (1948)
d Peter Bradford
VC

STORY OF PENICILLIN, the (1947)
d Oliver Cheatle
VC

STORY OF PRINTING, the (1948)
d Peter Bradford
VC

**STORY OF ROBIN HOOD AND HIS
MERRIE MEN, the** (1952)
d Ken Annakin
SC PB

STORY OF SHIRLEY YORKE, the (1948)
d Maclean Rogers
PB

STORY OF THE BRISTOL BRABAZON, the
(1951)
VC

STRANGER CAME HOME, the (1954)
d Terence Fisher
PB

STRANGER LEFT NO CARD, the (1952)
d Wendy Toye
VC

STRANGERS' MEETING (1957)
d Robert Day
PB

STRANGE WORLD OF PLANET X, the
(1958)
d Gilbert Gunn
PB

STRANGLERS OF BOMBAY, the (1959)
d Terence Fisher
PB

STRAW MAN, the (1953)
d Donald Taylor
VC

STREET CORNER (1953)
d Muriel Box
VC

STRING OF BEADS, a (1947)
d Ralph Keene
SC

STRONGHOLD OF THE WILD (1952)
PB

STRONGROOM (1962)
d Vernon Sewell
PB

STRUGGLE FOR OIL (This Modern Age
series) (1948)
VC

STUDY IN MOVEMENT, a (1948)
VC

STUDY RESULTS (1957)
d Robert Kingsbury
VC

SUBWAY IN THE SKY (1958)
d Muriel Box
PB

SUCKLING (1950)
VC

SUDAN DISPUTE (This Modern Age series)
(1947)
VC

SUDDENLY, LAST SUMMER (1959)
d Joseph L Mankiewicz
VC SC

SUMMER HOLIDAY (1962)
d Peter Yates
VC SC

SUNDAY BY THE SEA (1953)
d Anthony Simmons
VC

SUNDOWNERS, the (1960)
d Fred Zinnemann
VC SC

SUNSHINE IN SOHO (1956)
d Burt Hyams
VC

SUNSHINE MINERS (1952)
d J D Chambers
VC

SUNSWEPT (1961)
d Michael Keatering
PB

SUPERSONIC SAUCER (1956)
d S G Ferguson
SC

SUPPLY LINE (1960)
VC

SURF BOATS OF ACCRA, the (1958)
d Sydney Latter
VC

SURPRISE ATTACK (1951)
VC

SURPRISE PACKAGE (1960)
d Stanley Donen
SC

SUSPECT (1960)
d John Boulting, Roy Boulting
VC PB

SUSPENDED ALIBI (1956)
d Alfred Shaughnessy
PB

SVENGALI (1954)
d Noel Langley
VC SC

SWIFT WATER (1952)
d Tony Thompson
SC

SWISS FAMILY ROBINSON (1960)
d Ken Annakin
PB

SWORD AND THE ROSE, the (1953)
d Ken Annakin
PB

SWORD OF SHERWOOD FOREST (1960)
d Terence Fisher
SC

SYSTEM, the (1964)
d Michael Winner
VC

TAHITI (1962)
d Philip Hudsmith
VC

TAKE MY LIFE (1947)
d Ronald Neame
VC PB

TALE OF FIVE CITIES, a (1951)
d Montgomery Tully, Romolo Marcellini,
Wolfgang Staudte, Emile-Edwin Reinert,
Geza von Cziffra
SC

TALE OF TEETH, a (1949)
VC

TALE OF TWO CITIES, a (1958)
d Ralph Thomas
VC

TALES OF HOFFMANN, the (1951)
d Michael Powell, Emeric Pressburger
VC PB

TALK OF A MILLION (1951)
d John Paddy Carstairs
SC

TAMAHINE (1962)
d Philip Leacock
VC PB

TARNISHED HEROES (1961)
d Ernest Morris
PB

TARZAN AND THE LOST SAFARI (1956)
d H Bruce Humberstone
SC PB

TARZAN GOES TO INDIA (1962)
d John Guillermin
PB

TARZAN'S GREATEST ADVENTURE (1959)
d John Guillermin
PB

TARZAN THE MAGNIFICENT (1960)
d Robert Day
PB

TASTE OF FEAR (1961)
d Seth Holt
SC PB

TASTE OF HONEY, a (1961)
d Tony Richardson
VC PB

TASTE OF MONEY, a (1960)
d Max Varnel
PB

TEA GROWING IN ASSAM (1950)
d G J Cons
VC

TECHNIQUE OF ANAESTHESIA series, the
see
ANAESTHESIA IN THE DENTAL CHAIR
(1949)
ANAESTHESIA IN THE DENTAL CHAIR
FOR CHILDREN (1949)

TECHNIQUES IN PLASTIC SURGERY
(1949)
d Alastair Scobie
VC

TEDDY BEARS (1946)
VC

TED HEATH AND HIS MUSIC (1961)
d Robert Henryson
VC

TEHERAN (1946)
d Frank Hurley
VC

TEHERAN (1947)
d William Freshman, Giacomo Gentilomo
VC

TELEPHONE CABLE PLUMBING (1948)
VC

TELEVISION IS HERE AGAIN (1946)
d Philip Dorté
VC

TELL-TALE HEART, the (1960)
d Ernest Morris
VC PB

TEMPTATION HARBOUR (1947)
d Lance Comfort
VC

TEMPTRESS, the (1949)
d Oswald Mitchell
PB

TEN BOB IN WINTER (1963)
d Lloyd Reckord
VC

TERMINUS (1961)
d John Schlesinger
VC

TERM OF TRIAL (1962)
d Peter Glenville
VC

TERRA INCOGNITA (Magic Electrons series)
(1948)
VC

TERRIBLE BEAUTY, a (1960)
d Tay Garnett
PB

TERROR OF THE TONGS, the (1960)
d Anthony Bushell
SC PB

THAT DANGEROUS AGE (1949)
d Gregory Ratoff
SC

THAT KIND OF GIRL (1963)
d Gerry O'Hara
VC PB

THAT'S AN ORDER (1955)
d John Irwin
SC

THAT'S ODD (1960)
d Horace Shepherd
VC

THAT WOMAN OPPOSITE (1957)
d Compton Bennett
PB

THEIRS IS THE GLORY (1946)
d Brian Desmond Hurst
VC

THEM NICE AMERICANS (1958)
d Anthony Young
PB

THERE GO THE BOATS (1951)
d R K Neilson Baxter
VC

THERE WAS A CROOKED MAN (1960)
d Stuart Burge
VC PB

THERE WAS A YOUNG LADY (1952)
d Lawrence Huntington
PB

THESE DANGEROUS YEARS (1957)
d Herbert Wilcox
VC

THEY MADE ME A FUGITIVE (1947)
d Alberto Cavalcanti
VC

THEY PLANTED A STONE (1953)
d Robin Carruthers
VC

THEY THINK I'M RICH (1964)
d Terrick Fitzhugh
VC

THEY WERE NOT DIVIDED (1950)
d Terence Young
VC

THEY WHO DARE (1953)
d Lewis Milestone
PB

THIRD ALIBI, the (1961)
d Montgomery Tully
VC PB

THIRD MAN, the (1949)
d Carol Reed
VC

THIRD MAN ON THE MOUNTAIN (1959)
d Ken Annakin
SC

THIRD PARTY RISK (1955)
d Daniel Birt
VC PB

THIRD REPORT ON MODERNISATION
(1961)
VC

THIRD RIVER, the (1952)
d Michael Clarke
PB

THIRD TIME LUCKY (1949)
d Gordon Parry
VC SC

THIRD VISITOR, the (1951)
d Maurice Elvey
PB

THIRTEEN CANTOS OF HELL (1955)
d Peter King
VC

13 EAST STREET (1952)
d Robert S Baker
VC PB

THIRTY MILES AN HOUR (1949)
d Michael Law
VC

39 STEPS, the (1958)
d Ralph Thomas
SC PB

THIRTY-SIX HOURS (1954)
d Montgomery Tully
PB

THIS FILM IS DANGEROUS (1948)
d Ronald Haines
VC

THIS IS BRITAIN NO.2 (1946)
VC

THIS IS BRITAIN NO.4 (1946)
VC

THIS IS BRITAIN NO.11 (1947)
VC

THIS IS BRITAIN NO.19 (1946)
VC

THIS IS BRITAIN NO.25 (1947)
VC

THIS IS BRITAIN NO.35 (1949)
VC

THIS IS CHINA (1946)
VC

THIS IS HONG KONG (1961)
d D S Lawrence
VC

THIS IS SALT (1949)
VC

THIS IS THE FILM OF PHILIP VASSAR HUNTER (1951)
VC

THIS IS THE LIFE (1950)
d Sidney A Coronel
VC

THIS IS YORK (1953)
d J B Holmes
VC

THIS LITTLE SHIP (1952)
VC

THIS MAN IS MINE (1946)
d Marcel Varnel
VC

THIS MODERN AGE series
see
ANTARCTIC WHALE HUNT (1947)
BRITISH – ARE THEY ARTISTIC?, the (1947)
CEYLON – THE NEW DOMINION (1947)
CHALLENGE IN NIGERIA (1948)
COAL CRISIS (1947)
DEVELOPMENT AREAS (1947)
EDUCATION FOR LIVING (1949)
EUROPE'S FISHERIES IN DANGER (1949)
FABRICS OF THE FUTURE (1946)
FATE OF AN EMPIRE (1949)
FIGHT FOR A FULLER LIFE (1949)
FIGHT IN MALAYA, the (1950)
FUTURE OF ONE MILLION AFRICANS, the (1950)
FUTURE OF SCOTLAND, the (1947)
GAMBLING (1949)
HARVEST FROM THE WILDERNESS (1948)
HOME AND BEAUTY (1947)
HOMES FOR ALL (1946)
INDIA AND PAKISTAN (1949)
JAMAICA PROBLEM (1947)
LANCASHIRE'S TIME FOR ADVENTURE (1948)
LAND SHORT OF PEOPLE (1947)
NEW ZEALAND, A WORLD POWER (1950)
PALESTINE (1947)
RAPE OF THE EARTH, the (1947)
SCOTLAND YARD (1946)
SHADOW OF THE RUHR (1948)
STRUGGLE FOR OIL (1948)
SUDAN DISPUTE (1947)
THOROUGHBREDS FOR THE WORLD (1947)
TOMORROW BY AIR (1946)
TRIESTE, PROBLEM CITY (1949)

TRUE FACE OF JAPAN, the (1950)
TURKEY, KEY TO THE MIDDLE EAST (1950)
WHEN YOU WENT AWAY (1949)
WHERE BRITAIN STANDS (1950)
WILL BRITAIN GO HUNGRY? (1947)
WILL EUROPE UNITE? (1949)
WOMEN IN OUR TIME (1948)

THIS SPORTING LIFE (1963)
d Lindsay Anderson
SC

THIS WAS A WOMAN (1948)
d Tim Whelan
VC

THOROUGHBREDS FOR THE WORLD
(This Modern Age series) (1947)
VC SC

THOSE WERE THE DAYS (1946)
d James M Anderson
PB

THREE As, the (1947)
VC

THREE CORNERED FATE (1955)
d David Macdonald
PB

THREE CROOKED MEN (1958)
d Ernest Morris
PB

THREE DAWNS TO SYDNEY (1948)
d John Eldridge
VC

THREE SPARE WIVES (1962)
d Ernest Morris
PB

THREE STEPS IN THE DARK (1953)
d Daniel Birt
PB

3 STEPS TO THE GALLOWS (1953)
d John Gilling
PB

THREE WEIRD SISTERS, the (1948)
d Daniel Birt
VC

THROUGH TEN REIGNS (1952)
PB

THRUST (How an Aeroplane Flies series) (1947)
d Lionel Cole
VC

TIARA TAHITI (1962)
d Ted Kotcheff
PB

TIDE ON THE TURN (Look at Life series) (1964)
VC

TIGER BAY (1959)
d J Lee Thompson
VC SC

TIGER IN THE SMOKE (1956)
d Roy Ward Baker
PB

TIM DRISCOLL'S DONKEY (1954)
d Terry Bishop
SC

TIME BOMB (1952)
d Ted Tetzlaff
PB

TIME GENTLEMEN PLEASE! (1952)
d Lewis Gilbert
VC SC

TIME IS (The Ancestry of Science series) (1964)
d Don Levy
VC

TIME LOCK (1957)
d Gerald Thomas
SC

TIMESLIP (1955)
d Ken Hughes
PB

TIME WITHOUT PITY (1957)
d Joseph Losey
VC PB

TINNED JAM (1946)
VC

TITANS 1930–1934, the (A History of Motor Racing series) (1962)
d Bill Mason
VC

TITANS 1935–1939, the (A History of Motor Racing series) (1962)
d Bill Mason
VC

TITFIELD THUNDERBOLT, the (1953)
d Charles Crichton
VC PB

TOBACCO SUPPLY OF THE WORLD (1949)
VC

TO BE A WOMAN (1951)
d Jill Craigie
VC

TODMORDEN AGRICULTURAL SHOW, the (1949)
VC

TO DOROTHY A SON (1954)
d Muriel Box
VC SC

TO END WITH A CURTSY (1959)
d Derrick Knight
PB

TOGETHER (1955)
d Lorenza Mazzetti, Denis Horne
VC

TOMB OF LIGEIA, the (1964)
d Roger Corman
PB

TOM BROWN'S SCHOOLDAYS (1950)
d Gordon Parry
VC

TOM JONES (1963)
d Tony Richardson
VC PB

TOMMY STEELE STORY, the (1957)
d Gerard Bryant
VC

TOMMY THE TOREADOR (1959)
d John Paddy Carstairs
VC PB

TOMORROW AT TEN (1962)
d Lance Comfort
VC

TOMORROW BY AIR (This Modern Age series) (1946)
VC SC

TOMORROW'S TODAY (1958)
d Henry Lewis, John Morley
VC

TOM THUMB (1958)
d George Pál
VC PB

TOM TOM TOPIA (1946)
d Frank Chisnell
SC

TONIGHT IN BRITAIN (1954)
d Gerard Bryant
PB

TONY DRAWS A HORSE (1950)
d John Paddy Carstairs
SC PB

TONY KINSEY QUARTET, the (1961)
d Robert Henryson
VC

TOO YOUNG TO LOVE (1959)
d Muriel Box
PB

TOP FLOOR GIRL (1959)
d Max Varnel
PB

TOP OF THE FORM (1953)
d John Paddy Carstairs
VC SC

TOP SECRET (1952)
d Mario Zampi
PB

TO THE PUBLIC DANGER (1948)
d Terence Fisher
VC

TO THE RESCUE (1952)
d Jacques Brunius
VC SC

TOTO AND THE POACHERS (1956)
d Brian Salt
SC

TOUCH OF DEATH (1962)
d Lance Comfort
VC

TOUCH OF LARCENY, a (1959)
d Guy Hamilton
PB

TOWER, the (1953)
d Peter Pickering, John Ingram
VC

TOWERS OPEN FIRE (1963)
d Antony Balch
VC

TOWN LIKE ALICE, a (1956)
d Jack Lee
VC

TRACING THE SPREAD OF INFECTION
(1949)
d Michael Clark
VC

TRACK BUCKLING AND ITS PREVENTION
(1952)
d Kenneth Fairbairn
VC

TRADERS IN LEATHER (1957)
d Sydney Latter
VC

TRADE WINDS BLOW, the (Look at Life
series) (1963)
VC

**TRADITIONAL DANCES OF
SUKUMALAND** (1947)
VC

TRAIN TIME (1952)
d John Shearman
VC

TRAITORS, the (1962)
d Robert Tronson
SC

TRANSATLANTIC (1960)
d Ernest Morris
PB

TRANSFERENCE OF HEAT (1947)
VC

TRANSMISSION OF ELECTRICITY (1947)
d Graham Murray, Neil Brown
VC

TRANSONIC FLIGHT (High Speed Flight
series) (1957)
d Denis Segaller
VC

TRANSPORT (1948)
d Peter Bradford
PB

TRAVELLERS, the (Two Thousand Years Ago
series) (1946)
d Mary Field
VC

TRAVELLER'S JOY (1949)
d Ralph Thomas
VC

TRAVELLING AROUND series
see
LOWLANDS OF SCOTLAND (1947)
MIDLAND JOURNEY (1947)
ULSTER STORY (1947)

TREASURE AT THE MILL (1957)
d Max Anderson
SC

TREASURE HUNT (1952)
d John Paddy Carstairs
SC

TREASURE IN MALTA (1963)
d Derek Williams
SC

TREASURE OF SAN TERESA (1959)
d Alvin Rakoff
PB

TRENT'S LAST CASE (1952)
d Herbert Wilcox
VC

TREPANNER, the (1956)
d Peter Pickering
VC

TRIAL BY WEATHER (1948)
d Mary Francis
VC

TRIALS OF OSCAR WILDE, the (1960)
d Ken Hughes
VC PB

TRIESTE, PROBLEM CITY (This Modern
Age series) (1949)
VC

TRIO (1950)
d Ken Annakin, Harold French
VC

TROLLENBERG TERROR, the (1958)
d Quentin Lawrence
VC

TROPICAL HARVEST (1949)
VC

TROTTIE TRUE (1948)
d Brian Desmond Hurst
VC

TROUBLED MIND, the (1954)
d Margaret Thomson
VC

TROUBLE IN THE GLEN (1954)
d Herbert Wilcox
PB

TROUBLE WITH EVE (1959)
d Francis Searle
PB

TRUE AS A TURTLE (1957)
d Wendy Toye
PB

TRUE FACE OF JAPAN, the (This Modern
Age series) (1950)
VC SC

TSETSE (1950)
d Frank Cadman
VC

TUNES OF GLORY (1960)
d Ronald Neame
PB

TURF CELEBRITIES NO.1 (1956)
VC

TURKEY, KEY TO THE MIDDLE EAST (This
Modern Age series) (1950)
VC SC

TURNING POINT (1951)
VC

TURNING POINT, the (1951)
VC

TURN THE KEY SOFTLY (1953)
d Jack Lee
VC

'TWAS ON A MONDAY MORNING (1946)
d Louise Birt
VC

25 YEARS OF BRITISH FILMS (1948)
VC

TWENTY-FOUR SQUARE MILES (1946)
d Kay Mander
VC

**TWENTY QUESTIONS MURDER
MYSTERY, the** (1949)
d Paul L Stein
PB

TWILIGHT FOREST, the (1957)
d Sydney Latter
VC

TWO AND TWO MAKE SIX (1962)
d Freddie Francis
SC PB

TWO FACES OF DR JEKYLL, the (1960)
d Terence Fisher
PB

TWO-SPEED SUPERCHARGER (1951)
VC

TWO THOUSAND YEARS AGO series
see
TRAVELLERS, the (1946)

TWO WAY STRETCH (1960)
d Robert Day
PB

TWO-YEAR-OLD GOES TO HOSPITAL, a
(1951)
d James Robertson
PB

UGLY DUCKLING, the (1959)
d Lance Comfort
PB

ULSTER COVENANT, the (1962)
d Richard F Tambling
VC

ULSTER STORY (Travelling Around series)
(1947)
VC

UNCLE SILAS (1947)
d Charles Frank
VC

UNDEFEATED, the (1950)
d Paul Dickson
VC

UNDER CAPRICORN (1949)
d Alfred Hitchcock
VC PB

UNDER NEW MANAGEMENT (1946)
d John E Blakeley
PB

UNDER NIGHT STREETS (1958)
d Ralph Keene
VC

UNDER ONE ROOF (1949)
d Lewis Gilbert
VC

UNDER ONE UMBRELLA (Look at Life
series) (1964)
VC

UNDER THE SUN (1957)
d Peter Hopkinson
VC

UNDER THE SURFACE (1952)
d Derek Mayne
VC

UNEARTHLY STRANGER (1963)
d John Krish
PB

UNILEVER MAGAZINE NO.1 (1951)
VC

UNILEVER MAGAZINE NO.8 (1956)
VC

UNITED IN PEACE (1948)
VC

UNSEEN ENEMIES (1959)
d Michael Clarke
PB

UNTITLED FILM, an (1964)
d David Gladwell
VC

UP FOR THE CUP (1950)
d Jack Raymond
SC

UP IN THE WORLD (1956)
d John Paddy Carstairs
VC PB

UPSTAIRS AND DOWNSTAIRS (1959)
d Ralph Thomas
PB

UP THE CREEK (1958)
d Val Guest
VC PB

UP THE POTATO (1946)
VC

UPTURNED GLASS, the (1947)
d Lawrence Huntington
VC SC

USES OF LIMESTONE (1950)
d Jane Massy
VC

VALIANT, the (1961)
d Roy Ward Baker
PB

VALLEY OF EAGLES (1951)
d Terence Young
VC

VALLEY OF SONG (1953)
d Gilbert Gunn
VC SC

VALLEY OF THE KINGS (1964)
d Frederic Goode
SC

VALUE FOR MONEY (1955)
d Ken Annakin
VC

VANISHING STREET, the (1962)
d Robert Vas
VC

VENEPUNCTURE (1953)
d Cyril Jenkins
VC

VENGEANCE (1962)
d Freddie Francis
PB

VENGEANCE IS MINE (1948)
d Alan J Cullimore
VC

VERY EDGE, the (1962)
d Cyril Frankel
PB

VERY IMPORTANT PERSON (1961)
d Ken Annakin
PB

VIA LONDON (1948)
VC

VICE VERSA (1947)
d Peter Ustinov
VC

VICTIM (1961)
d Basil Dearden
VC SC

VICTIM FIVE (1964)
d Robert Lynn
SC

VICTORS, the (1963)
d Carl Foreman
VC SC

VICTORY PARADE (1946)
VC

VICTORY PARADE, the (1946)
VC

VICTORY TRIAL 1952 (1952)
SC

VILLAGE OF THE DAMNED (1960)
d Wolf Rilla
VC PB

VINTAGE '28 (1953)
d Robert M Angell
VC

VIPs, the (1963)
d Anthony Asquith
VC

VIRGIN ISLAND (1958)
d Pat Jackson
PB

VISA TO CANTON (1960)
d Michael Carreras
PB

VISION OF WILLIAM BLAKE, the (1958)
d Guy Brenton
VC

VISIT, the (1959)
d Jack Gold
VC

VITAL FLAME, the (1952)
d J R F Stewart
VC

VOICES OF MALAYA (1948)
d Ralph Elton
VC

VOTE FOR HUGGETT (1948)
d Ken Annakin
VC

WAKEFIELD EXPRESS (1953)
d Lindsay Anderson
VC

WALK IN THE FOREST (1958)
d James Hill
VC

WALTZ OF THE TOREADORS (1962)
d John Guillermin
PB

WARDROBE, the (1958)
d George Dunning
VC

WATCH FROM FRANCE, a (1957)
d Theodore Zichy
VC

WATCH IT SAILOR! (1961)
d Wolf Rilla
PB

WATCH OUT! (1953)
d Don Chaffey
SC

WATCH YOUR STERN (1960)
d Gerald Thomas
PB

WATERFRONT (1950)
d Michael Anderson
VC

WATERS OF TIME (1951)
d Basil Wright, Bill Launder
VC

WATER SPOUT (1948)
VC

WAVERLEY STEPS (1948)
d John Eldridge
VC

WAY AHEAD, the (1963)
VC

WAY OF A SHIP, the (1954)
d Terry Ashwood
PB

WAY OF THE WORLD, the (1947)
d James Komisarjewsky
PB

WAY TO THE WEST, the (1947)
VC

WAY WE LIVE, the (1946)
d Jill Craigie
VC

WEAK AND THE WICKED, the (1953)
d J Lee Thompson
PB

WEAKER SEX, the (1948)
d Roy Ward Baker
VC

WEALTH OF THE WORLD series
see
CONGO HARVEST (1951)
OIL (1950)

WEALTH UNDER THE SEA? (Look at Life series) (1964)
VC

WE ARE THE LAMBETH BOYS (1959)
d Karel Reisz
VC PB

WEAVING IN A GOLD COAST VILLAGE (1948)
VC

WEAVING IN TOGOLAND (1948)
VC

WEB OF SUSPICION (1959)
d Max Varnel
PB

WEBSTER BOY, the (1962)
d Don Chaffey
SC

WEDDING OF LILLI MARLENE, the (1953)
d Arthur Crabtree
SC

WEEKEND WITH LULU, a (1961)
d John Paddy Carstairs
PB

WELCOME TO THE QUEEN (1956)
d Sydney Boyle
VC

WELDED STRUCTURES (1950)
VC

WEST COUNTRY GAZETTE NO.2 (1948)
d W H Quintrell
VC

WEST COUNTRY GAZETTE NO.15 (1948)
d W H Quintrell
VC

WEST COUNTRY JOURNEY (1953)
VC

WEST 11 (1963)
d Michael Winner
VC PB

WEST OF ENGLAND (1951)
d Humphrey Swingler
VC

WEST OF ZANZIBAR (1954)
d Harry Watt
PB

WHAT A CARRY ON! (1949)
d John E Blakeley
PB

WHAT A CARVE UP! (1961)
d Pat Jackson
PB

WHAT A CRAZY WORLD (1963)
d Michael Carreras
SC

WHAT A LIFE! (1948)
d Michael Law
VC

WHAT A WHOPPER! (1961)
d Gilbert Gunn
PB

WHAT EVERY WOMAN WANTS (1954)
d Maurice Elvey
PB

WHAT EVERY WOMAN WANTS (1962)
d Ernest Morris
PB

WHEN THE BOUGH BREAKS (1947)
d Lawrence Huntington
VC

WHEN YOU COME HOME (1947)
d John Baxter
PB

WHEN YOU WENT AWAY (This Modern Age series) (1949)
VC

WHERE BRITAIN STANDS (This Modern Age series) (1950)
SC

WHERE NO VULTURES FLY (1951)
d Harry Watt
VC PB

WHILE GERMANY WAITS (1946)
VC SC

WHILE I LIVE (1947)
d John Harlow
VC

WHILE THE SUN SHINES (1947)
d Anthony Asquith
VC

WHIRLPOOL (1959)
d Lewis Allen
VC

WHISKY GALORE! (1949)
d Alexander Mackendrick
VC PB

WHISTLE DOWN THE WIND (1961)
d Bryan Forbes
VC SC

WHITE CORRIDORS (1951)
d Pat Jackson
VC PB

WHITE CRADLE INN (1947)
d Harold French
VC

WHITE UNICORN, the (1947)
d Bernard Knowles
VC PB

WHO DONE IT? (1956)
d Basil Dearden
PB

WHO VOTED FOR THIS? (1948)
VC

WHY GLASSHOUSE SOILS ARE STERILIZED (1950)
VC

WHY NOT YOU? (1948)
VC

WHY WE HAVE BANKS (1949)
d Aubrey Singer
VC

WIDDICOMBE FAIR (1947)
d W M Larkins
VC

WILD AFFAIR, the (1963)
d John Krish
PB

WILD AND THE WILLING, the (1962)
d Ralph Thomas
PB

WILL ANY GENTLEMAN? (1953)
d Michael Anderson
PB

WILL BRITAIN GO HUNGRY? (This Modern Age series) (1947)
VC SC

WILL EUROPE UNITE? (This Modern Age series) (1949)
VC SC

WILLIAM COMES TO TOWN (1948)
d Val Guest
VC

WILLIAM HARVEY AND THE CIRCULATION OF BLOOD (1957)
VC

WILLIE DOES HIS STUFF (1948)
d Julius Pinschewer
VC

WILLOW TREE, the (1947)
d Claude Hudson, Thora James
VC

WIND CANNOT READ, the (1958)
d Ralph Thomas
PB

WINDOM'S WAY (1957)
d Ronald Neame
VC PB

WINDOW TO THE SKY (1959)
d Alex Strasser
VC

WINGS FOR PAULINE (1949)
VC

WINGS OF MYSTERY (1963)
d Gilbert Gunn
SC

WING TO WING (1951)
VC

WINNING THE HARD WAY (Look at Life series) (1964)
VC

WINSLOW BOY, the (1948)
d Anthony Asquith
VC

WINTER IN QUEBEC (1949)
d Jean Haines, Ronald Haines
VC

WINTER MOTH (Plant Pests and Diseases series) (1950)
d J V Durden
VC

WINTER TOUR (1949)
d J S Frieze
VC

WITCHCRAFT (1964)
d Don Sharp
PB

WITNESS IN THE DARK (1959)
d Wolf Rilla
VC

WOMAN IN A DRESSING GOWN (1957)
d J Lee Thompson
VC

WOMAN IN QUESTION, the (1950)
d Anthony Asquith
VC SC

WOMAN IN THE HALL, the (1947)
d Jack Lee
VC

WOMAN POSSESSED, a (1958)
d Max Varnel
PB

WOMAN WITH NO NAME, the (1950)
d Ladislao Vajda
SC

WOMEN AND SPORT (1946)
d Denis Kavanagh
PB

WOMEN IN OUR TIME (This Modern Age series) (1948)
VC SC

WOMEN OF TWILIGHT (1952)
d Gordon Parry
VC

WONDERFUL LIFE (1964)
d Sidney J Furie
SC

WONDERFUL THINGS (1957)
d Herbert Wilcox
SC

WONDER JET, the (1950)
VC

WOODCOCK V RALPH (1949)
VC

WOODEN HORSE, the (1950)
d Jack Lee
VC

WORLD IS RICH, the (1947)
d Paul Rotha
VC

WORLD OF LIFE; A JOURNAL OF THE OUTDOORS series, the
see
AIR OF MAGIC, an (1961)

WORLD OF SEMI-CONDUCTORS, the (1962)
d Michael Orrom
VC

WORLD OF SUZIE WONG, the (1960)
d Richard Quine
PB

WORLD TEN TIMES OVER, the (1963)
d Wolf Rilla
VC

WORM'S EYE VIEW (1951)
d Jack Raymond
PB

WORTH THE RISK? (1948)
VC

WRONG ARM OF THE LAW, the (1962)
d Cliff Owen
VC SC

X – THE UNKNOWN (1956)
d Leslie Norman
VC

YANGTSE INCIDENT (1956)
d Michael Anderson
PB

YEARS BETWEEN, the (1946)
d Compton Bennett
VC PB

YEARS OF ACHIEVEMENT (1952)
VC

YELLOW BALLOON, the (1952)
d J Lee Thompson
PB

YELLOW ROLLS-ROYCE, the (1964)
d Anthony Asquith
VC PB

YELLOW TEDDYBEARS, the (1963)
d Robert Hartford-Davis
VC

YESTERDAY'S ENEMY (1959)
d Val Guest
VC PB

YIELD TO THE NIGHT (1956)
d J Lee Thompson
VC

YOU AND YOUR MONEY (1951)
VC

YOU CAN'T ESCAPE (1955)
d Wilfred Eades
SC

YOUNG AND THE GUILTY, the (1958)
d Peter Cotes
SC PB

YOUNG CASSIDY (1964)
d Jack Cardiff
VC PB

YOUNG DETECTIVES, the (1963)
d Gilbert Gunn
SC

YOUNG JACOBITES, the (1959)
d John Reeve
SC

YOUNG LOVERS, the (1954)
d Anthony Asquith
VC

YOUNG ONES, the (1961)
d Sidney J Furie
SC PB

YOUNG WIVES' TALE (1951)
d Henry Cass
VC

YOU PAY YOUR MONEY (1957)
d Maclean Rogers
PB

YOUR CHILDREN series
see
YOUR CHILDREN AND YOU (1946)
YOUR CHILDREN'S MEALS (1947)
YOUR CHILDREN'S PLAY (1951)
YOUR CHILDREN'S SLEEP (1948)
YOUR CHILDREN WALKING (1951)

YOUR CHILDREN AND YOU (Your Children series) (1946)
d Brian Smith
VC

YOUR CHILDREN'S MEALS (Your Children series) (1947)
d Alex Strasser
VC

YOUR CHILDREN'S PLAY (Your Children series) (1951)
d Brian Smith
VC

YOUR CHILDREN'S SLEEP (Your Children series) (1948)
VC

YOUR CHILDREN WALKING (Your Children series) (1951)
d Alex Strasser
VC

YOUR LOCAL COUNCIL (1949)
d Gordon Lipman
VC

YOUR MONEY OR YOUR WIFE (1960)
d Anthony Simmons
PB

ZULU (1963)
d Cy Endfield
SC PB

ABDICATION, the (1974)
d Anthony Harvey
PB

**ABEL GANCE – THE CHARM OF
DYNAMITE** (1968)
d Kevin Brownlow
SC

ABOMINABLE DR PHIBES, the (1971)
d Robert Fuest
VC PB

ABOVE US THE EARTH (1977)
d Karl Francis
VC

ABSOLUTION (1978)
d Anthony Page
SC

ACCEPTABLE LEVELS (1983)
d John Davies
VC

ACCIDENT (1967)
d Joseph Losey
VC PB

ACES HIGH (1976)
d Jack Gold
SC PB

ACTING IN THE CINEMA (1985)
d Mark Nash, James Swinson
VC

ADAGIO (1990)
d Giancarlo Gemin
VC

ADERYN PAPUR (And Pigs Might Fly) (1984)
d Stephen Bayly
VC

**ADOLF HITLER – MY PART IN HIS
DOWNFALL** (1972)
d Norman Cohen
PB

**ADVENTURES OF A BROWN MAN IN
SEARCH OF CIVILISATION** (1971)
d James Ivory
PB

ADVENTURES OF A PRIVATE EYE (1977)
d Stanley Long
PB

ADVENTURES OF A TAXI DRIVER (1975)
d Stanley Long
PB

**ADVENTURES OF BARON
MUNCHAUSEN, the** (1988)
d Terry Gilliam
SC

ADVENTURES OF X, the (1967)
d Michael Newman, Andrew Fisher
VC PB

AFRICA – TEXAS STYLE (1967)
d Andrew Marton
PB

AFTER THE BALL (1984)
d Richard Anthony
VC

AFTER THE CORONATION (1991)
d Vipon Kumar
VC

AIRBORNE (Chimpmates second series) (1976)
d Harold Orton
SC

A IS FOR AUTISM (1992)
d Tim Webb
VC

ALF GARNETT SAGA, the (1972)
d Bob Kellett
PB

ALFIE (1965)
d Lewis Gilbert
PB

ALFIE DARLING (1975)
d Ken Hughes
SC PB

ALFRED THE GREAT (1969)
d Clive Donner
SC PB

ALICE AT SCHOOL (Chimpmates third series)
(1978)
d Harold Orton
SC

ALICE AT SEA (Chimpmates third series)
(1978)
d Harold Orton
SC

ALICE GOES MAGIC (Chimpmates third
series) (1978)
d Harold Orton
SC

ALICE GOES POP (Chimpmates second
series) (1976)
d Harold Orton
SC

ALICE'S ADVENTURES IN WONDERLAND
(1972)
d William Sterling
PB

ALL COPPERS ARE (1971)
d Sidney Hayers
SC PB

ALL CREATURES GREAT AND SMALL
(1974)
d Claude Whatham
VC PB

ALL IN A GOOD CAUSE (The Chiffy Kids
second series) (1978)
d David Bracknell
SC

ALL NEAT IN BLACK STOCKINGS (1969)
d Christopher Morahan
SC PB

ALL THE WAY UP (1970)
d James MacTaggart
VC SC

ALPHA BETA (1972)
d Anthony Page
PB

ALPHABET MURDERS, the (1965)
d Frank Tashlin
PB

AMARAVATI WEEKEND (1991)
VC

AMAZING MR BLUNDEN, the (1972)
d Lionel Jeffries
PB

AMBUSH AT DEVIL'S GAP (1966)
d David Eastman
SC

AMERICAN WEREWOLF IN LONDON, an
(1981)
d John Landis
SC PB

AM I A BUTTERFLY? (1973)
d Jini Rawlings
VC

**AMOROUS ADVENTURES OF MOLL
FLANDERS, the** (1965)
d Terence Young
PB

AMOROUS MILKMAN, the (1974)
d Derren Nesbitt
SC

AMSTERDAM AFFAIR (1968)
d Gerry O'Hara
PB

AMY! (1980)
d Laura Mulvey, Peter Wollen
VC

AND PIGS MIGHT FLY
see
ADERYN PAPUR

AND SOON THE DARKNESS (1970)
d Robert Fuest
SC PB

ANGEL IN THE HOUSE (1979)
d Jane Jackson
VC

ANGRY EARTH (1989)
d Karl Francis
VC

ANIMALS FILM, the (1981)
d Victor Schonfeld, Myriam Alaux
VC

ANIMATION FOR LIVE ACTION (1978)
d Vera Neubauer
VC

ANNEE 71, l' (1975)
d Giovanni Gnecchi-Ruscone
VC

ANNE OF THE THOUSAND DAYS (1969)
d Charles Jarrott
PB

ANNIVERSARY, the (1967)
d Roy Ward Baker
VC PB

ANOOP AND THE ELEPHANT (1972)
d David Eady
SC

ANOTHER TIME, ANOTHER PLACE (1983)
d Michael Radford
VC

ANTIQUES AT AUCTION (1970)
d Ronald Spencer
VC

ANYWHERE BUT HERE (1968)
d Richard Need
PB

ARABESQUE (1966)
d Stanley Donen
PB

ARCADE (1970)
d Tony Sinden
VC

ARENA OF CONFLICT (Faces of Industry
series) (1980)
d Peter Allen
VC

ARE YOU BEING SERVED? (1977)
d Bob Kellett
SC

ARGYLL FIELD – OIL AT 13:35 (1976)
d David Rees
VC

ARRIVALS (1983)
d Mari Peacock
PB

ARROW, the (1969)
d Mel Calman
VC

ARS MORIENDI (1983)
d Tom Pollock
PB

ART, INDUSTRY AND WEALTH (1980)
d Catherine Denford
VC

ASCENDANCY (1982)
d Edward Bennett
VC PB

ASPHYX, the (1972)
d Peter Newbrook
PB

ASSAM GARDEN, the (1985)
d Mary McMurray
VC

ASSASSINATION BUREAU, the (1968)
d Basil Dearden
PB

ASSAULT (1970)
d Sidney Hayers
VC SC

ASSIGNMENT K (1967)
d Val Guest
SC

ATTACK ON THE IRON COAST (1967)
d Paul Wendkos
PB

AT THE EARTH'S CORE (1976)
d Kevin Connor
VC

AT THE FOUNTAINHEAD (OF GERMAN STRENGTH) (1980)
d Anthea Kennedy, Nick Burton
VC

AU PAIR GIRLS (1972)
d Val Guest
PB

AUTOBIOGRAPHY OF A PRINCESS (1975)
d James Ivory
VC

AVALANCHE (1975)
d Frederic Goode
SC

BABYLON (1980)
d Franco Rosso
SC

BABYLON (Sweet Disaster series) (1986)
d David Sproxton, Peter Lord
VC

BABY LOVE (1967)
d Alastair Reid
PB

BABY SITTERS (Chimpmates first series) (1976)
d Harold Orton
SC

BAD TIMING (1980)
d Nicolas Roeg
SC PB

BAREFOOTIN' (1987)
d Richard Goleszowski
VC

BARRY LYNDON (1975)
d Stanley Kubrick
SC PB

BARTLEBY (1970)
d Anthony Friedmann
PB

BASE – WHO NEEDS IT?, the (1989)
d Stephen Connolly
VC

BASIL BUNTING (1982)
d Peter Bell
VC

BATTLE BENEATH THE EARTH (1967)
d Montgomery Tully
PB

BATTLE OF BILLY'S POND, the (1976)
d Harley Cokliss
SC

BATTLE OF BRITAIN (1969)
d Guy Hamilton
PB

BAWDY ADVENTURES OF TOM JONES, the (1975)
d Cliff Owen
PB

BAXTER! (1972)
d Lionel Jeffries
SC PB

BEACH, the (1967)
d Malcolm Graedeck
SC

BEARSKIN – AN URBAN FAIRYTALE (1989)
d Ann Guedes, Eduardo Guedes
VC

BEASTLY TREATMENT (1979)
d Bill Foulk
PB

BEAUBOURG (1980)
d Dennis Postle
VC

BEDAZZLED (1967)
d Stanley Donen
VC SC

BEDFORD INCIDENT, the (1965)
d James B Harris
SC PB

BED SITTING ROOM, the (1969)
d Richard Lester
PB

BEER AND SKITTLES series
see
BITTER SWEET DREAMS (1985)
GAMES PEOPLE PLAY (1985)
PUBLIC INCONVENIENCE (1985)
ROLL OUT THE BARREL (1985)
WIN SOME, LOSE SOME (1985)

BEFORE HINDSIGHT (1977)
d Jonathan Lewis
VC

BELLMAN AND TRUE (1987)
d Richard Loncraine
VC SC

BELLY OF AN ARCHITECT, the (1987)
d Peter Greenaway
VC PB

BELSTONE FOX, the (1973)
d James Hill
PB

BEQUEST TO THE NATION (1973)
d James Cellan Jones
PB

BERTHA (1969)
d Michael Sclater
VC

BEST HOUSE IN LONDON, the (1968)
d Philip Saville
PB

BEST KEPT SECRET, the (1985)
d Clive Donner
VC

BEST OF BENNY HILL, the (1974)
d John Robins
PB

BEST PAIR OF LEGS IN THE BUSINESS, the (1972)
d Christopher Hodson
SC PB

BETRAYAL (1983)
d David Jones
PB

BETTER LATE THAN NEVER (1983)
d Bryan Forbes
SC

BEYOND IMAGE (1969)
d Mark Boyle
VC

BICYCLETTES DE BELSIZE, les (1968)
d Douglas Hickox
VC

BIDDY (1983)
d Christine Edzard
SC PB

BIGGER SPLASH, a (1974)
d Jack Hazan
VC

BIGGEST BANK ROBBERY, the (1980)
d Ralph Thomas
SC

BIGGLES (1986)
d John Hough
SC

BIG JOB, the (1965)
d Gerald Thomas
PB

BIG KICK, the (Chimpmates first series) (1976)
d Harold Orton
SC

BIG SLEEP, the (1978)
d Michael Winner
PB

BIG ZAPPER (1973)
d Lindsay Shonteff
PB

BILLION DOLLAR BRAIN (1967)
d Ken Russell
PB

BILLY THE KID (Magnificent Six and ½ first series) (1968)
d Harry Booth
SC

BILLY THE KID AND THE GREEN BAIZE VAMPIRE (1985)
d Alan Clarke
VC

BINKY AND BOO (1987)
d Derek Hayes, Phil Austin
VC

BIRTH (1976)
d Julian Aston
VC

BIRTH RITES (1977)
d Robina Rose
VC

BITTER SWEET DREAMS (Beer and Skittles series) (1985)
d Andy Walker
VC

BLACK AND SILVER (1981)
d William Raban, Marilyn Raban
VC

BLACK BEAUTY (1971)
d James Hill
PB

BLACKBOARD JUNGLE (The Trouble with 2b series) (1972)
d Peter K Smith
SC

BLACK BOOK, the (1965)
d Michael Truman
VC

BLACK DOG (1987)
d Alison De Vere
VC

BLACK JOY (1977)
d Anthony Simmons
PB

BLACK WINDMILL, the (1974)
d Don Siegel
PB

BLESS THIS HOUSE (1972)
d Gerald Thomas
VC SC

BLIND JUSTICE series
see
MURDERS MOST FOUL (1987)
SOME PROTECTION (1987)

BLINKER'S SPY-SPOTTER (1971)
d Jack Stephens
SC

BLISS OF MRS BLOSSOM, the (1968)
d Joe McGrath
PB

BLOOD FROM THE MUMMY'S TOMB (1971)
d Seth Holt
SC

BLOOMFIELD (1969)
d Richard Harris
PB

BLOWUP (1966)
d Michelangelo Antonioni
VC SC

BLUE (1993)
d Derek Jarman
VC

BLUEBEARD'S LAST WIFE (1966)
d John Stoddart
VC

BLUE BLOOD (1973)
d Andrew Sinclair
PB

BLUE MAX, the (1966)
d John Guillermin
PB

BOB A JOB (The Magnificent Six and ½ first series) (1968)
d Harry Booth
SC

BOBO, the (1967)
d Robert Parrish
VC PB

BODY, the (1970)
d Roy Battersby
PB

BODY STEALERS, the (1969)
d Gerry Levy
PB

BOFORS GUN, the (1968)
d Jack Gold
SC PB

BOOLEAN PROCEDURE (1980)
d Nichola Bruce, Michael Coulson
VC

BOOM (1968)
d Joseph Losey
SC

BORN FREE (1965)
d James Hill
VC SC

BORN OF FIRE (1987)
d Jamil Dehlavi
VC

BORN TO BOOGIE (1972)
d Ringo Starr
PB

BOULE, la (1986)
d Simon Shore
VC

BOWES LINE, the (1975)
d Murray Martin
VC

BOY FRIEND, the (1971)
d Ken Russell
PB

BOYS IN BLUE, the (1983)
d Val Guest
SC

BOY WHO NEVER WAS, the (1979)
d Frank Godwin
SC

BOY WHO TURNED YELLOW, the (1972)
d Michael Powell
SC

BRAZIL (1985)
d Terry Gilliam
SC

BREAKING OF BUMBO, the (1970)
d Andrew Sinclair
SC PB

BREATH OF LIFE, a (1991)
d Navin Thapar
VC

BRED AND BORN (1984)
d Joanna Davis, Mary Pat Leece
VC SC

BRIDES OF FU MANCHU, the (1966)
d Don Sharp
PB

BRIDGE TOO FAR, a (1977)
d Richard Attenborough
VC PB

BRIDGET RILEY (1979)
d David Thompson
VC

BRIGAND OF KANDAHAR, the (1965)
d John Gilling
PB

BRIMSTONE & TREACLE (1982)
d Richard Loncraine
SC

BRITANNIA HOSPITAL (1982)
d Lindsay Anderson
VC

BRONCO BULLFROG (1969)
d Barney Platts-Mills
VC PB

BROTHERS AND SISTERS (1980)
d Richard Woolley
VC PB

BROWN ALE WITH GERTIE (1974)
d Alan Brown
VC

BUGSY MALONE (1976)
d Alan Parker
VC SC

BULLSHOT (1983)
d Dick Clement
VC

BUNNY LAKE IS MISSING (1965)
d Otto Preminger
VC PB

BURNING, the (1967)
d Stephen Frears
VC

BURNING AN ILLUSION (1981)
d Menelik Shabazz
VC

BUSINESS AS USUAL (1987)
d Lezli-An Barrett
VC

BUSINESS WITH FRIENDS (Continental Drift series) (1992)
d Uwe Jansen
VC

BUTTERCUP CHAIN, the (1970)
d Robert Ellis Miller
SC

CAFÉ BAR (1975)
d Alison De Vere
VC

CALAMITY THE COW (1967)
d David Eastman
SC

CALENDAR NO.119 (1965)
VC

CALENDAR NO.251 (1968)
VC

CAN HEIRONYMUS MERKIN EVER FORGET MERCY HUMPPE AND FIND TRUE HAPPINESS? (1969)
d Anthony Newley
PB

CAN HORSES SING? (1971)
d Elizabeth Sussex
VC

CAN'T STOP ME DREAMING (Continental Drift series) (1992)
d Bernard Rudden
VC

CAPTAIN NEMO AND THE UNDERWATER CITY (1969)
d James Hill
PB

CARAVAGGIO (1986)
d Derek Jarman
VC SC

CARNIVAL (1985)
d Susan Young
VC

CARRERA (1992)
d Martin Wallace
VC

CARRY ON ABROAD (1972)
d Gerald Thomas
VC PB

CARRY ON AGAIN DOCTOR (1969)
d Gerald Thomas
PB

CARRY ON AT YOUR CONVENIENCE
(1971)
d Gerald Thomas
VC PB

CARRY ON BEHIND (1975)
d Gerald Thomas
VC

CARRY ON CAMPING (1969)
d Gerald Thomas
VC PB

CARRY ON COWBOY (1965)
d Gerald Thomas
VC PB

CARRY ON DICK (1974)
d Gerald Thomas
VC

CARRY ON DOCTOR (1967)
d Gerald Thomas
PB

CARRY ON EMMANUELLE (1978)
d Gerald Thomas
VC

CARRY ON ENGLAND (1976)
d Gerald Thomas
VC SC

CARRY ON GIRLS (1973)
d Gerald Thomas
VC PB

CARRY ON HENRY (1971)
d Gerald Thomas
VC PB

CARRY ON LOVING (1970)
d Gerald Thomas
VC PB

CARRY ON MATRON (1972)
d Gerald Thomas
VC

CARRY ON SCREAMING (1966)
d Gerald Thomas
VC SC

CARRY ON UP THE JUNGLE (1970)
d Gerald Thomas
VC PB

CASINO ROYALE (1967)
d John Huston, Ken Hughes, Val Guest,
   Robert Parrish, Joe McGrath
PB

CASTAWAY (1986)
d Nicolas Roeg
VC

CATCH US IF YOU CAN (1965)
d John Boorman
VC SC

CATHEDRAL IN A VILLAGE (1968)
d Robin Carruthers
VC

CATLOW (1971)
d Sam Wanamaker
VC SC

CHALLENGE FOR ROBIN HOOD, a (1967)
d C M Pennington-Richards
SC PB

CHANCE, HISTORY, ART... (1979)
d James Scott
VC

CHANGE IN THE WEATHER, a (1984)
d Catherine Denford
VC

CHAPLIN (1992)
d Richard Attenborough
VC

CHARGE OF THE LIGHT BRIGADE, the
(1968)
d Tony Richardson
VC SC PB

CHARIOTS OF FIRE (1981)
d Hugh Hudson
VC

CHARLIE BUBBLES (1967)
d Albert Finney
PB

CHICAGO JOE AND THE SHOWGIRL
(1989)
d Bernard Rose
PB

CHIFFY KIDS first series, the
   see
   DECORATORS LIMITED (1976)
   GREAT SNAIL RACE, the (1976)
   MAGPIE LAYS AN EGG (1976)
   POT LUCK (1976)
   ROOM TO LET (1976)
   SHOVE TUESDAY (1976)

CHIFFY KIDS second series, the
   see
   ALL IN A GOOD CAUSE (1978)
   IT PAYS TO ADVERTISE (1978)
   JAM SESSION (1978)
   MAGPIE'S TALKING DUCK (1978)
   SLIMDERELLA (1978)
   WATERBIKES (1978)

CHILDREN (1977)
d Terence Davies
VC

CHILDREN, the (1990)
d Tony Palmer
VC

CHILDREN ON OUR CONSCIENCE (1965)
d Hans Casparius
VC

**CHILD'S GUIDE TO BLOWING UP A
MOTOR CAR, a** (1965)
d Ronald Spencer
VC

CHIMP CHAMP (Chimpmates third series)
(1978)
d Harold Orton
SC

CHIMPMATES first series
   see
   BABY SITTERS (1976)
   BIG KICK, the (1976)
   DOUBLE TROUBLE (1976)
   MONKEY TRICKS (1976)
   ON THE TILES (1976)
   WEDDING BELLS (1976)

CHIMPMATES second series
   see
   AIRBORNE (1976)
   ALICE GOES POP (1976)
   GO-KARTERS, the (1976)
   HOLIDAY SPIRIT (1976)
   TREASURE HUNT (1976)
   WAXWORKS (1976)
   ZOO TIME (1976)

CHIMPMATES third series
   see
   ALICE AT SCHOOL (1978)
   ALICE AT SEA (1978)
   ALICE GOES MAGIC (1978)
   CHIMP CHAMP (1978)
   GRAN'S MOVING DAY (1978)
   TIT FOR TAT (1978)

CHITTY CHITTY BANG BANG (1968)
d Ken Hughes
PB

CHRISTMAS FOR SALE (1984)
d Iain McCall
VC

CHRISTMAS TREE, the (1966)
d Jim Clark
SC

CHURCHILL – A NATION'S HOMAGE
(1965)
VC

CIRCLE OF GOLD (1988)
d Uday Bhattacharya
VC

CIRCUMSTANTIAL EVIDENCE (1984)
d Kez Cary, Penny Dedman, Terry Flaxton
VC

CIRCUS OF FEAR (1966)
d John Moxey
PB

CITY PORT (1971)
d Roger Dunton
SC PB

CITY UNDER THE SEA, the (1965)
d Jacques Tourneur
VC PB

CLASH OF THE TITANS (1981)
d Desmond Davis
SC PB

CLING FILM (1992)
d Anna Thew
VC

CLIP (1983)
d Nichola Bruce, Michael Coulson
VC

CLOCKTIME (1972)
d Stuart Pound
VC

CLOCKWISE (1986)
d Christopher Morahan
SC

CLOCKWORK ORANGE, a (1971)
d Stanley Kubrick
PB

CLOSE MY EYES (1991)
d Stephen Poliakoff
VC

COLLIERY LAYOUT UNDERGROUND
(1969)
VC

COLOUR – THE OUTSIDE STORY (1973)
VC

COMB, the (1990)
d Quay Brothers
VC

COMFORT AND JOY (1984)
d Bill Forsyth
SC

COMING UP ROSES
see RHOSYN A RHITH (1986)

COMMITMENTS, the (1991)
d Alan Parker
SC PB

COMMITTEE, the (1968)
d Peter Sykes
PB

COMPANY OF WOLVES, the (1984)
d Neil Jordan
VC SC

COMPELLANCE (1987)
d Bob Last
VC

COMPETITORS, the (1969)
d Joe Mendoza
SC

COMRADES (1986)
d Bill Douglas
VC SC

CONDUCT UNBECOMING (1975)
d Michael Anderson
SC

CONFESSIONS OF A POP PERFORMER
(1975)
d Norman Cohen
PB

CONFESSIONS OF A SEX MANIAC (1974)
d Alan Birkinshaw
PB

CONFESSIONS OF A WINDOW CLEANER
(1974)
d Val Guest
VC SC

CONNECTING ROOMS (1969)
d Franklin Gollings
PB

CONQUEST OF THE SOUTH POLE (1989)
d Gillies MacKinnon
VC

CONTINENTAL DRIFT series
see
BUSINESS WITH FRIENDS (1992)
CAN'T STOP ME DREAMING (1992)
SPRINGING LENIN (1992)

CONVERSATION PIECES series
see
EARLY BIRD (1983)
LATE EDITION (1983)
ON PROBATION (1983)
PALMY DAYS (1983)
SALES PITCH (1983)

**CONVERSATIONS BY A CALIFORNIAN
SWIMMING POOL** (Sweet Disaster series)
(1986)
d Andrew Franks
VC

**CONVERSION OF HECTOR THE
CHECKER, the** (1967)
d Bob Privett
VC

**COOK, THE THIEF, HIS WIFE AND HER
LOVER, the** (1989)
d Peter Greenaway
SC

COOLER, the (1982)
d Kevin Godley, Lol Creme
PB

COOL IT CAROL! (1970)
d Pete Walker
VC

COPING WITH CUPID (1991)
d Viviane Albertine
VC

CORNELIUS CARDEW (1986)
d Philippe Regniez
VC

**CORRECTION PLEASE; or, How we got
into pictures** (1979)
d Noël Burch
VC

CORRUPTION (1967)
d Robert Hartford-Davis
VC PB

COST, PROFIT AND BREAK-EVEN (1980)
d Peter Robinson
SC

COUNTESS DRACULA (1970)
d Peter Sasdy
VC

COUNTESS FROM HONG KONG, a (1966)
d Charles Chaplin
PB

COUNTRY GIRLS, the (1983)
d Desmond Davis
VC SC

COURTESANS OF BOMBAY (1982)
d Ismail Merchant
VC PB

COURT IN THE CAR, a (1993)
d Antonia Leslie
VC

COWBOYS series
see
OUTRAGE (1991)
SLIM'S PICKIN'S (1991)

**CRAFTY PREDATORS AND CRYPTIC
PREY** (1966)
d Nikolas Tinbergen
VC

CREATURE COMFORTS (Lip Synch series)
(1989)
d Nick Park
VC

CREATURES THE WORLD FORGOT (1970)
d Don Chaffey
PB

CRESCENDO (1969)
d Alan Gibson
PB

CROCODILE SAFARI (1967)
d Malcolm J Fancey
PB

CROMWELL (1970)
d Ken Hughes
VC PB

CROSS AND PASSION (1981)
d Kim Longinotto, Claire Pollak
VC

CROSS OF IRON (1977)
d Sam Peckinpah
VC PB

CRUCIBLE OF TERROR (1971)
d Ted Hooker
PB

CRY FREEDOM (1987)
d Richard Attenborough
VC SC

CRYING GAME, the (1992)
d Neil Jordan
VC

CRYSTAL GAZING (1983)
d Laura Mulvey, Peter Wollen
VC

CUL-DE-SAC (1966)
d Roman Polanski
PB

CUP FEVER (1965)
d David Bracknell
SC

CURSE OF THE CRIMSON ALTAR (1968)
d Vernon Sewell
PB

CURSE OF THE FLY (1965)
d Don Sharp
VC

CURTAIN CHANGES, the (Look at Life
series) (1966)
VC

**DADDY'S LITTLE BIT OF DRESDEN
CHINA** (1988)
d Karen Watson
VC

DAD'S ARMY (1971)
d Norman Cohen
VC SC

DAMON THE MOWER (1972)
d George Dunning
VC

DANCE OF THE VAMPIRES (1967)
d Roman Polanski
PB

DANCE WITH A STRANGER (1985)
d Mike Newell
VC

DANCING SILHOUETTES (1983)
d Felicity Field
VC

DANGER ON DARTMOOR (1980)
d David Eady
SC

DANGER POINT! (1971)
d John Davis
SC

DANGER ROUTE (1967)
d Seth Holt
SC PB

DANNY JONES (1971)
d Jules Bricken
PB

DANNY THE DRAGON (1966)
d C M Pennington-Richards
SC

DARK CRYSTAL, the (1982)
d Jim Henson, Frank Oz
VC SC

DARK WATER (1980)
d Andrew Bogle
SC

DARLING (1965)
d John Schlesinger
PB

DAVEY JONES' LOCKER (1966)
d Frederic Goode
VC SC

DAVID COPPERFIELD (1970)
d Delbert Mann
VC PB

DAVID LEACH (1977)
d John Anderson, Robert Fournier
VC

DAY IN THE DEATH OF JOE EGG, a (1970)
d Peter Medak
SC

DAY OF THE JACKAL, the (1973)
d Fred Zinnemann
VC PB

DEAD END CREEK (1965)
d Pat Jackson
SC

DEADFALL (1968)
d Bryan Forbes
SC PB

DEADLIER THAN THE MALE (1966)
d Ralph Thomas
SC

DEADLY AFFAIR, the (1966)
d Sidney Lumet
VC PB

DEADSY (1989)
d David Anderson
VC

DEAR ROSIE (1990)
d Peter Cattaneo
VC

DEATH AND TRANSFIGURATION (1983)
d Terence Davies
SC

DEATH OF A SPEECHWRITER (Sweet Disaster series) (1986)
d David Hopkins
VC

DEATH ON THE NILE (1978)
d John Guillermin
VC SC PB

DECEIVERS, the (1988)
d Nicholas Meyer
VC SC

DECISION, the (1981)
d Vera Neubauer
VC PB

DECORATORS LIMITED (The Chiffy Kids first series) (1976)
d David Bracknell
SC

DEFENDING A WAY OF LIFE (Home from Home series) (1980)
d Simon Heaven
VC

DEMONS OF THE MIND (1971)
d Peter Sykes
PB

DEUDA INTERNA, la (1987)
d Miguel Pereira
PB

DEVIL RIDES OUT, the (1967)
d Terence Fisher
SC

DEVILS, the (1971)
d Ken Russell
PB

DIALOGUE (1974)
d Chris Majka
VC

DIAMONDS ARE FOREVER (1971)
d Guy Hamilton
PB

DIAMONDS ON WHEELS (1972)
d Jerome Courtland
PB

DIGBY THE BIGGEST DOG IN THE WORLD (1973)
d Joe McGrath
VC

DIRTY DOZEN, the (1967)
d Robert Aldrich
VC SC

DISAPPEARANCE, the (1977)
d Stuart Cooper
SC PB

DISCIPLE OF DEATH (1972)
d Tom Parkinson
PB

DISTANT VOICES STILL LIVES (1988)
d Terence Davies
VC SC

DISTILLATION (1966)
d Rodney Giesler
VC

DOCTOR FAUSTUS (1967)
d Richard Burton, Nevill Coghill
VC

DOCTOR IN CLOVER (1966)
d Ralph Thomas
VC SC

DOCTOR IN TROUBLE (1970)
d Ralph Thomas
VC SC

DR JEKYLL & SISTER HYDE (1971)
d Roy Ward Baker
VC SC

DR PHIBES RISES AGAIN (1972)
d Robert Fuest
PB

DR WHO AND THE DALEKS (1965)
d Gordon Flemyng
SC PB

DOCTOR ZHIVAGO (1965)
d David Lean
PB

DOGS OF WAR, the (1980)
d John Irvin
SC

DO I DETECT A CHANGE IN YOUR ATTITUDE? (1980)
d Vera Linnecar
VC

DO IT ON THE WHISTLE (1965)
d Ludovic Kennedy
VC

DOLLAR BOTTOM, the (1981)
d Roger Christian
PB

DOLL'S EYE (1982)
d Jan Worth
SC

DOLL'S HOUSE, a (1973)
d Patrick Garland
PB

DOLLY MIXTURES (1983)
d Simon West
VC

DON'T JUST LIE THERE, SAY SOMETHING! (1973)
d Bob Kellett
VC SC

DON'T LOSE YOUR HEAD (1966)
d Gerald Thomas
SC PB

DOOR (1990)
d David Anderson
VC

DOPPELGÄNGER (1969)
d Robert Parrish
SC PB

DOUBLE TROUBLE (Chimpmates first series) (1976)
d Harold Orton
SC

DOWNSIDE UP (1985)
d Tony Hill
VC

DRACULA AD 1972 (1972)
d Alan Gibson
PB

DRACULA HAS RISEN FROM THE GRAVE (1968)
d Freddie Francis
VC

DRACULA – PRINCE OF DARKNESS (1965)
d Terence Fisher
VC PB

DREAMCHILD (1985)
d Gavin Millar
SC

DREAM DEMON, the (1988)
d Harley Cokliss
VC

DREAMING RIVERS (1988)
d Martina Attile
VC

DREAMLAND EXPRESS (1982)
d David Anderson
VC

DREAMLESS SLEEP (Sweet Disaster series) (1986)
d David Anderson
VC

DRESS, the (1984)
d Eva Sereny
VC

DRESSMAKER, the (1988)
d Jim O'Brien
VC

DROP DEAD DARLING (1966)
d Ken Hughes
PB

DROWNING BY NUMBERS (1988)
d Peter Greenaway
VC SC

DRUM BEAT (1991)
d Lol Gellor
VC

DUB AND VISUAL PERCEPTION (1983)
d Kelvin Richard
VC

DUELLISTS, the (1977)
d Ridley Scott
PB

DUFFY (1968)
d Robert Parrish
VC PB

DULCIMA (1971)
d Frank Nesbitt
SC PB

DUST SAMPLING IN ROADWAYS (1971)
d Ferdinand Fairfax
VC

DUTCHMAN (1966)
d Anthony Harvey
VC PB

EAGLE HAS LANDED, the (1976)
d John Sturges
SC

EAGLE'S WING (1978)
d Anthony Harvey
VC SC

EARLY BIRD, the (1965)
d Robert Asher
VC SC

EARLY BIRD (Conversation Pieces series) (1983)
d Peter Lord, David Sproxton
VC

EAST OF ELEPHANT ROCK (1976)
d Don Boyd
SC PB

EAST SIDE, WEST SIDE (1973)
d Arnold Louis Miller
VC

EAT THE RICH (1987)
d Peter Richardson
VC

EDUCATING RITA (1983)
d Lewis Gilbert
VC PB

EDWARD (1982)
d Marcus Thompson
PB

EDWARD HOPPER (1981)
d Ron Peck
VC

EDWARD II (1991)
d Derek Jarman
VC

EGGHEAD'S ROBOT (1970)
d Milo Lewis
SC

EGOLI (1989)
d Karen Kelly
VC

8MM FILM NOTES ON 16MM FILM (1971)
d Peter Gidal
VC

EIGHT OR NINE IN THE MORNING (One Man's China series) (1972)
d Felix Greene
SC

EISENSTEIN; A PROGRAMME OF ATTRACTIONS (1980)
d Terry Flaxton, Penny Dedman, Tony Cooper
VC

EK BAAR PHIR (1979)
d Vinod Pande
PB

ELECTRIC DREAMS (1984)
d Steve Barron
SC

ELECTRICITY AND THE ENVIRONMENT (1971)
d Marc Broadway
PB

ELENYA (1992)
d Steve Gough
VC

ELEPHANT CALLED SLOWLY, an (1969)
d James Hill
PB

ELIZABETH MACONCHY (1985)
d Margaret Williams
VC

EMBASSY (1972)
d Gordon Hessler
PB

EMERALD FOREST, the (1985)
d John Boorman
SC

EMILY (1976)
d Henry Herbert
PB

EMPIRE STATE (1987)
d Ron Peck
VC

ENEMY (1976)
d Tony Bagley
VC

ENERGY CONVERSION (1969)
VC

ENGLAND MADE ME (1972)
d Peter Duffell
SC

ENOUGH CUTS FOR A MURDER (1978)
d Chris Monger
PB

ENTERTAINING MR SLOANE (1969)
d Douglas Hickox
VC PB

ENVEROUNEN (1973)
d Simon Mallin, William Diver
VC

ENVIRONMENTAL DILEMMA, the (Faces of Industry series) (1980)
d Peter Allen
VC

EQUUS (1977)
d Sidney Lumet
PB

ERIK THE VIKING (1989)
d Terry Jones
SC

ESCAPE FROM THE SEA (1968)
d Peter Seabourne
SC

ESCAPE TO ATHENA (1979)
d George Pan Cosmatos
SC

ESKIMO NELL (1974)
d Martin Campbell
PB

EUREKA (1983)
d Nicolas Roeg
SC

EUROPE AFTER THE RAIN (1978)
d Mick Gold
VC SC

EUROPEANS, the (1979)
d James Ivory
PB

EVERYDAY (1969)
d Hans Richter
VC

EVERY HOME SHOULD HAVE ONE (1969)
d Jim Clark
VC PB

EVIL UNDER THE SUN (1981)
d Guy Hamilton
VC SC

EXECUTIONER, the (1970)
d Sam Wanamaker
PB

EXILES (1991)
d Jill Daniels
VC

EXPLORING NOVELTY (1967)
d Corinne Hutt
VC

EXPORT BY TRAIN (1965)
d James Ritchie
VC

EXTREMES (1971)
d Anthony Klinger, Michael Lytton
PB

EYE FOR QUALITY, an (1984)
d John McAdam
VC

EYE OF THE DEVIL (1966)
d J Lee Thompson
PB

EYEWITNESS (1970)
d John Hough
PB

FACE OF FU MANCHU, the (1965)
d Don Sharp
PB

FACES IN A CROWD (1971)
d Roger Dunton
PB

FACES OF INDUSTRY series
see
ARENA OF CONFLICT (1980)
ENVIRONMENTAL DILEMMA, the (1980)
MAN VERSUS MACHINES? (1980)
PATHWAY TO ETERNAL BOREDOM? (1980)
WHO TAKES THE MONEY? (1980)

FAHRENHEIT 451 (1966)
d François Truffaut
SC PB

FALL OUT (1985)
d El Glinoer
VC

FALLS, the (1980)
d Peter Greenaway
VC PB

FAMILY ALBUM (1991)
d Ellie O'Sullivan
VC

FAMILY LIFE (1971)
d Ken Loach
SC PB

FAMILY WAY, the (1966)
d Roy Boulting
PB

FANATIC (1965)
d Silvio Narizzano
VC

FAR FROM THE MADDING CROWD (1967)
d John Schlesinger
VC PB

FAST KILL, the (1972)
d Lindsay Shonteff
SC

FATHER DEAR FATHER (1972)
d William G Stewart
PB

FATHERLAND (1986)
d Ken Loach
VC PB

FATHERSPACE (1992)
d Kira Zurawska
VC

FEAR IN THE NIGHT (1972)
d Jimmy Sangster
SC

FEAR IS THE KEY (1972)
d Michael Tuchner
SC PB

FEET OF SONG (1988)
d Erica Russell
VC

FELLOW TRAVELLER (1989)
d Philip Saville
VC SC

FEVER HOUSE (1984)
d Howard Walmsley
VC

FFESTINIOG HOLIDAY (1985)
d Ronald Walker
VC

FIELD, the (1990)
d Jim Sheridan
VC

FIFTH REPORT ON MODERNISATION
(1965)
d John Taylor
VC

53°N 10°E (1975)
d Arnold Louis Miller
VC

FIGURES IN A LANDSCAPE (1970)
d Joseph Losey
SC PB

FILE OF THE GOLDEN GOOSE, the (1969)
d Sam Wanamaker
PB

FILM (1979)
d David Rayner Clark
VC PB

FILM PRINT (1974)
d Peter Gidal
VC

FILM WITHOUT (1976)
d Stuart Pound
VC

FINAL PROGRAMME, the (1973)
d Robert Fuest
PB

**FINNEGAN'S CHIN – TEMPORAL
ECONOMY** (1981)
d Malcolm Le Grice
PB

FIREFIGHTERS, the (1974)
d Jonathan Ingrams
SC

FIREPOWER (1979)
d Michael Winner
PB

FIRST GREAT TRAIN ROBBERY, the (1978)
d Michael Crichton
SC

FIRST YEARS OF THE SOVIET UNION, the
(1971)
d Lutz Becker
VC

FISH CALLED WANDA, a (1988)
d Charles Crichton
SC

FIT TO FLY (1976)
d Norman James
VC

FIVE DAYS ONE SUMMER (1982)
d Fred Zinnemann
VC SC

FIVE GOLDEN DRAGONS (1967)
d Jeremy Summers
PB

FIVE SURVIVE (The Magnificent Six and ½
third series) (1971)
d Peter Graham Scott
SC

FLASH GORDON (1980)
d Mike Hodges
VC PB

FLESH AND BLOOD SHOW, the (1972)
d Pete Walker
PB

FLYING MAN, the (1972)
d Colin Gregg
VC

FOCUS ON KODAK '84 (1984)
d Chris Pettit
VC

FOOTSTEPS (1974)
d Alan Parker
VC

FORBIDDEN (1986)
d Anthony Page
PB

FORCE 10 FROM NAVARONE (1978)
d Guy Hamilton
SC PB

FOREIGN BODY (1986)
d Ronald Neame
SC

FOR GOOD (1979)
d Christine Booth
VC

FOR QUEEN AND COUNTRY (1988)
d Martin Stellman
VC

FORTY YEARS ON (1978)
VC

FOUR DIMENSIONS OF GRETA, the (1972)
d Pete Walker
PB

FOUR IN THE MORNING (1965)
d Anthony Simmons
VC PB

14, the (1973)
d David Hemmings
VC PB

1492: CONQUEST OF PARADISE (1992)
d Ridley Scott
VC

FOURTH PROTOCOL, the (1987)
d John Mackenzie
SC

FRAGMENT OF FEAR (1970)
d Richard C Sarafian
PB

**FRAMED YOUTH – REVENGE OF THE
TEENAGE PERVERTS** (1983)
d Constantine Giannaris, Trill Burton, Jeff
Cole
VC

**FRANKENSTEIN AND THE MONSTER
FROM HELL** (1973)
d Terence Fisher
PB

FRANKENSTEIN CREATED WOMAN (1966)
d Terence Fisher
VC PB

FREEDOM RAILWAY (1975)
d Felix Greene
PB

FREE FALL (Look at Life series) (1967)
VC

FRENCH LIEUTENANT'S WOMAN, the
(1981)
d Karel Reisz
SC

FRENZY (1972)
d Alfred Hitchcock
SC PB

FRIENDS (1971)
d Lewis Gilbert
PB

**FRIENDSHIP FIRST, COMPETITION
SECOND** (One Man's China series) (1972)
d Felix Greene
SC

FRIENDSHIP'S DEATH (1987)
d Peter Wollen
SC

FRIGHT (1971)
d Peter Collinson
PB

FRONTIER series
see
HELP FOR THE HANDICAPPED
CHILDREN (1969)

FROZEN DEAD, the (1966)
d Herbert J Leder
VC

FRUIT MACHINE (1988)
d Philip Saville
VC

FULL CIRCLE (1971)
d Tim Wood
VC

FULL CIRCLE (1976)
d Richard Loncraine
SC

FULL METAL JACKET (1987)
d Stanley Kubrick
SC

FUN AND GAMES (1971)
d Ray Austin
PB

FUNERAL IN BERLIN (1966)
d Guy Hamilton
PB

GALILEO (1974)
d Joseph Losey
SC

GAMES, the (1969)
d Michael Winner
VC PB

GAMES PEOPLE PLAY (Beer and Skittles series) (1985)
d Andy Walker
VC

GANDHI (1982)
d Richard Attenborough
SC

GARDEN, the (1990)
d Derek Jarman
VC PB

GENERATION GAP (1973)
d Peter Hickling, Bob Godfrey
VC

GENESIS – A BAND IN CONCERT (1976)
d Tony Maylam
PB

GEORGE AND MILDRED (1980)
d Peter Frazer-Jones
VC

GEORGY GIRL (1966)
d Silvio Narizzano
VC PB

GERMFREE BABY (1968)
d Esmond Wilson, Guy Fergusson
VC

GET CARTER (1971)
d Mike Hodges
SC PB

GHOST OF A CHANCE (1967)
d Jan Darnley-Smith
SC

GHOSTS AND GHOULS (The Magnificent Six and ½ first series) (1968)
d Harry Booth
SC

GHOST STORY (1974)
d Stephen Weeks
SC

GHOUL, the (1975)
d Freddie Francis
SC

GIACOMETTI (1967)
d Michael Gill
VC

GIRL ON A MOTORCYCLE, the (1968)
d Jack Cardiff
VC

GIRLS' NIGHT OUT (1987)
d Joanna Quinn
VC

GIRO CITY (1982)
d Karl Francis
VC SC

GIVE US A SMILE (1983)
d Leeds Animation Workshop
SC

GLORY OF THE GARDEN, the (1982)
d Jan Kaplan
VC

GOAD, the (1965)
d Paul Joyce
SC

GOAL! WORLD CUP 1966 (1966)
d Abidine Dino, Ross Devenish
VC

GO-BETWEEN, the (1971)
d Joseph Losey
VC SC

GO FOR A TAKE (1972)
d Harry Booth
VC PB

GOING EQUIPPED (Lip Synch series) (1989)
d Peter Lord
VC

GOING LOCAL (1982)
d Kez Cary, Terry Flaxton
VC

GO-KARTERS, the (Chimpmates second series) (1976)
d Harold Orton
SC

GOLD (1974)
d Peter Hunt
SC

GOLD DIGGERS, the (1983)
d Sally Potter
VC PB

GOLDEN VOYAGE OF SINBAD, the (1973)
d Gordon Hessler
PB

GOLEM, the (1988)
d Möle Hill
VC

GOLFERS IN A SCOTTISH LANDSCAPE (1971)
d Norman Prouting
VC

GONKS GO BEAT (1965)
d Robert Hartford-Davis
PB

GOODBYE GEMINI (1970)
d Alan Gibson
SC PB

GOODBYE, MR CHIPS (1969)
d Herbert Ross
PB

GOOD FATHER, the (1986)
d Mike Newell
VC

GOOD RIDING GETS THERE (1969)
d John Tippey
VC

GRAN'S MOVING DAY (Chimpmates third series) (1978)
d Harold Orton
SC

GRASS IS SINGING, the (1981)
d Michael Raeburn
SC PB

GREAT CATHERINE (1967)
d Gordon Flemyng
PB

GREATEST HITS OF SCRATCH VIDEO, the (1985)
d George Barber, Duvet Brothers, Tim Morrison
VC

GREATEST HITS OF SCRATCH VIDEO VOLUME 2, the (1986)
d George Barber, Duvet Brothers, Tim Morrison
VC

GREAT McGONAGALL, the (1974)
d Joe McGrath
PB

GREAT PONY RAID, the (1968)
d Frederic Goode
SC

GREAT ROCK 'N' ROLL SWINDLE, the (1979)
d Julien Temple
PB

GREAT ST TRINIAN'S TRAIN ROBBERY, the (1966)
d Frank Launder, Sidney Gilliat
SC PB

GREAT SNAIL RACE, the (The Chiffy Kids second series) (1976)
d David Bracknell
SC

GREAT TREASURE HOUSE, a (One Man's China series) (1972)
d Felix Greene
SC

GREECE OF CHRISTIAN GREEKS (1971)
d Kostas Chronopoulos, Simon Louvish, Jorge Tsougarossa
SC

GREYSTOKE; THE LEGEND OF TARZAN, LORD OF THE APES (1984)
d Hugh Hudson
VC SC PB

GROUPIE GIRL (1970)
d Derek Ford
PB

GROVE MUSIC (1981)
d Henry Martin, Steve Shaw
VC

GUMSHOE (1971)
d Stephen Frears
VC SC

GUNDOWN (1973)
d Philip King
VC

GUNS IN THE HEATHER (1968)
d Robert Butler
PB

HAIR SET, the (Look at Life series) (1966)
VC

HALF A SIXPENCE (1967)
d George Sidney
PB

HAMLET (1969)
d Tony Richardson
VC PB

HAMLET (1976)
d Celestino Coronado
VC

HAMMERHEAD (1968)
d David Miller
VC PB

HANDFUL OF DUST, a (1987)
d Charles Sturridge
PB

HAND OF NIGHT, the (1966)
d Frederic Goode
PB

HANDS OF THE RIPPER (1971)
d Peter Sasdy
PB

HANDSWORTH SONGS (1986)
d John Akomfrah
VC

HANNIBAL BROOKS (1968)
d Michael Winner
PB

HANNIE CAULDER (1971)
d Burt Kennedy
PB

HANOVER STREET (1979)
d Peter Hyams
VC

HAPPY DAYS (The Trouble with 2b series)
(1972)
d Peter K Smith
SC

HAVING A LOVELY TIME (1970)
d Robert Bentley
VC

HAWKS (1988)
d Robert Ellis Miller
SC

HEADING FOR GLORY (1975)
d Michael Samuelson
SC

HEADLINE HUNTERS (1968)
d Jonathan Ingrams
SC

HEAR MY SONG (1991)
d Peter Chelsom
VC

HEARTS OF GOLD (1988)
d Jane Caldwell, Kate Cameron
VC

HEAT AND DUST (1982)
d James Ivory
VC SC

HEAVENLY PURSUITS (1986)
d Charles Gormley
VC PB

HELEN, QUEEN OF THE NAUTCH GIRLS
(1972)
d Anthony Korner
VC

HELL BOATS (1969)
d Paul Wendkos
PB

HELP! (1965)
d Richard Lester
PB

**HELP FOR THE HANDICAPPED
CHILDREN** (Frontier series) (1969)
VC

HELPING YOURSELF IN CYSTITIS (1974)
d S C Nicholas, Angela Kilmartin
VC

HENNESSY (1975)
d Don Sharp
PB

HENRI GAUDIER-BRZESKA (1968)
d Arthur Cantrill

**HERE WE GO ROUND THE MULBERRY
BUSH** (1967)
d Clive Donner
SC PB

HEROES OF TELEMARK, the (1965)
d Anthony Mann
VC PB

HEROSTRATUS (1967)
d Don Levy
VC PB

HER PRIVATE HELL (1967)
d Norman J Warren
PB

HETTY KING: PERFORMER (1970)
d David Robinson
VC

HE WHO RIDES A TIGER (1965)
d Charles Crichton
SC PB

HIDDEN CITY (1987)
d Stephen Poliakoff
VC

HIDE AND SEEK (1972)
d David Eady
SC

HIGH BRIGHT SUN, the (1965)
d Ralph Thomas
VC SC

HIGH HOPES (1988)
d Mike Leigh
VC

HIGHLANDER (1986)
d Russell Mulcahy
SC

HIGH RISE DONKEY (1980)
d Michael Forlong
SC

HIGH SEASON (1987)
d Clare Peploe
VC

HIGH SPIRITS (1988)
d Neil Jordan
SC PB

HIGH WIND IN JAMAICA, a (1965)
d Alexander Mackendrick
VC

HILDA WAS A GOODLOOKER (1985)
d Anna Thew
SC

HILL, the (1965)
d Sidney Lumet
VC SC

HIRELING, the (1973)
d Alan Bridges
VC PB

H IS FOR HOUSE (1976)
d Peter Greenaway
SC

HIT, the (1984)
d Stephen Frears
VC SC

HITCH IN TIME, a (1978)
d Jan Darnley-Smith
SC

HOFFMAN (1969)
d Alvin Rakoff
PB

HOGARTH (1977)
d Edward Bennett
VC

HOKUSAI (1978)
d Tony White
VC

HOLCROFT COVENANT, the (1985)
d John Frankenheimer
SC

HOLD ON TO YOUR STRUCTURE (1985)
d James Ewart
VC

HOLIDAY ON THE BUSES (1973)
d Bryan Izzard
PB

HOLIDAY SPIRIT (Chimpmates second series)
(1976)
d Harold Orton
SC

HOME (1977)
d Conny Templeman, Baudhuin Simon
VC

HOME AND DRY (1986)
d Jeff Dowson
VC

HOME FROM HOME series
see
DEFENDING A WAY OF LIFE (1980)
SAFE PLACE TO BE, a (1980)
WORKING TO A PATTERN (1980)

HOMEGROUND (1983)
d Anthony Harrild
VC

HONORARY CONSUL, the (1983)
d John Mackenzie
SC

HOPE AND GLORY (1987)
d John Boorman
VC

HORNSEY FILM, the (1970)
d Patricia Holland
VC

HORROR HOSPITAL (1973)
d Antony Balch
VC

HORROR OF FRANKENSTEIN, the (1970)
d Jimmy Sangster
PB

HORSE CALLED JESTER, a (1979)
d Kenneth Fairbairn
SC

HOSTAGES, the (1975)
d David Eady
SC

HOSTILE WITNESS (1968)
d Ray Milland
PB

HOTEL DU PARADIS (1986)
d Jana Bokova
VC PB

HOT MILLIONS (1968)
d Eric Till
VC PB

HOUSE IN NIGHTMARE PARK, the (1973)
d Peter Sykes
PB

HOUSE OF THE LONG SHADOWS (1982)
d Pete Walker
SC

HOUSE THAT DRIPPED BLOOD, the (1970)
d Peter Duffell
PB

HOUSING SOLUTIONS (1984)
d Derek Banham
VC

HOVERBUG (1971)
d Jan Darnley-Smith
SC

HOWARDS END (1992)
d James Ivory
VC

HOW CAN I IGNORE THE GIRL NEXT DOOR? (1987)
VC

HOW I WON THE WAR (1967)
d Richard Lester
PB

HOW STEAM IS PRODUCED (1971)
d Frank Goulding
PB

HULL NOW (1967)
d Bob Privett
VC

'HUMAN' FACTOR, the (1975)
d Edward Dmytryk
SC

HUNCH, the (1967)
d Sarah Erulkar
SC

HUNTED (1971)
d Peter Crane
PB

HUNTING PARTY, the (1971)
d Don Medford
SC PB

HUSH-A-BYE BABY (1989)
d Margo Harkin
VC

HYDROLOGICAL SIMULATION BY COMPUTER (1980)
d Gordon Thomson
VC

I CAN LICK ANY GIRL IN THE HOUSE! (1976)
d Eric Wallace
PB

IDENT (Lip Synch series) (1989)
d Richard Goleszowski
VC

IF.... (1968)
d Lindsay Anderson
VC SC

IMAGES OF NURSES (1987)
d Emma Whitlock
VC

IMMEDIATE SUBJECT, the (1986)
d Benita Raphan
VC

IMPERSONATION, the (1984)
d Noël Burch, Christopher Mason
VC

IMPOSSIBLE DECADE, the (1985)
d Juliet Miller
VC

IMPRESSIONS OF EXILE (1985)
d Ana Florin, Christine Wilkinson, Jane Harris
VC

IMPROMPTU (1991)
d James Lapine
SC

INADMISSIBLE EVIDENCE (1968)
d Anthony Page
PB

IN FADING LIGHT (1989)
d Murray Martin
VC

IN FLAGRANTE (1981)
d Neil Thomson
VC

IN MY MOTHER'S EYES (1988)
d Sarah Strickett
VC

INNER CITY (1987)
d Giles Herdman, Anne Riddlesdell
VC

INNOCENT BYSTANDERS (1972)
d Peter Collinson
PB

INSIGNIFICANCE (1985)
d Nicolas Roeg
VC PB

INSPECTOR CLOUSEAU (1968)
d Bud Yorkin
PB

INTELLIGENCE MEN, the (1965)
d Robert Asher
VC SC

INTERLUDE (1968)
d Kevin Billington
VC PB

INTERNATIONAL VELVET (1978)
d Bryan Forbes
SC PB

INTERNECINE PROJECT, the (1974)
d Ken Hughes
SC PB

INTERVIEW, the (1978)
d Michael Dudok De Wit
VC

IN THE FOREST (1978)
d Phil Mulloy
VC PB

INTIMATE GAMES (1976)
d Tudor Gates
SC PB

INTO THE WEST (1992)
d Mike Newell
VC

IN TOUCH (1966)
d George Brandt
VC

INVITATION TO THE WEDDING (1984)
d Joseph Brooks
SC

INVOCATION – MAYA DEREN (1987)
d JoAnn Kaplan
VC

IPCRESS FILE, the (1965)
d Sidney J Furie
PB

IRELAND – BEHIND THE WIRE (1974)
VC

IRON TREE WILL BLOSSOM AND THE DUMB WILL SPEAK, the (One Man's China series) (1972)
d Felix Greene
SC

ISAAC BUTTON – COUNTRY POTTER (1965)
d John Anderson, Robert Fournier
VC

ISADORA (1968)
d Karel Reisz
PB

ISLAND AWAKES, an (Look at Life series) (1966)
VC

ISLAND OF TERROR (1966)
d Terence Fisher
VC PB

I START COUNTING (1969)
d David Greene
PB

IT (1966)
d Herbert J Leder
VC

ITALIAN JOB, the (1969)
d Peter Collinson
SC PB

IT ALL DEPENDS ON YOU (1973)
VC

IT PAYS TO ADVERTISE (The Chiffy Kids second series) (1978)
d David Bracknell
SC

IT'S HAIR-EDITARY! (1991)
d Lynette Morris
VC

IT SHOULDN'T HAPPEN TO A VET (1976)
d Eric Till
SC PB

IT'S NOT ALL PAINTING AND DRAWING, YOU KNOW (1971)
d Ian Jones
VC

I'VE GOTTA HORSE (1965)
d Kenneth Hume
PB

I WANT TO BE HAPPY (1972)
d Patrick Lichfield
SC

I WANT WHAT I WANT (1971)
d John Dexter
PB

I WAS HAPPY HERE (1965)
d Desmond Davis
VC PB

JABBERWOCKY (1977)
d Terry Gilliam
VC SC

JAM SESSION (The Chiffy Kids second series) (1978)
d David Bracknell
SC

JANE AUSTEN IN MANHATTAN (1980)
d James Ivory
VC

JANET AND JOHN – GROW UP! (1974)
d Euan Duff
VC

JIGSAW (1980)
d Robina Rose
VC

JIGSAW MAN, the (1984)
d Terence Young
SC

JOANNA (1968)
d Mike Sarne
VC

JOBS FOR THE GIRLS (1978)
d Jenny Woodley
VC

JOE BROWN AT CLAPHAM (1965)
d Norman Prouting
VC

JOEY BOY (1965)
d Frank Launder
SC

JOHNSTOWN MONSTER, the (1971)
d Olaf Pooley
SC

JOKERS, the (1966)
d Michael Winner
SC PB

JORIS IVENS INTERVIEW (1979)
VC

JOSEPH ANDREWS (1976)
d Tony Richardson
SC

JULES VERNE'S ROCKET TO THE MOON
(1967)
d Don Sharp
PB

JULIUS CAESAR (1970)
d Stuart Burge
PB

JUNKET 89 (1970)
d Peter Plummer
SC

JUST A SECRETARY (1983)
d Sue Sudbury
VC

JUVENILE LIAISON (1975)
d Nicholas Broomfield, Joan Churchill
VC

KADOYNG (1972)
d Ian Shand
SC

KALEIDOSCOPE (1966)
d Jack Smight
PB

KEEP IT UP, JACK! (1973)
d Derek Ford
PB

KEEP OFF THE GRASS (1984)
d Paul Weiland
VC

KES (1969)
d Ken Loach
PB

KEY (1968)
d Peter Gidal
VC

KHARTOUM (1966)
d Basil Dearden
SC PB

KILLING TIME (1984)
d Christopher O'Reilly
VC

KING ALFRED'S COLLEGE, WINCHESTER
(1989)
VC

KING GEORGE V (1970)
d Paul Barnes
VC

KING'S STORY, a (1965)
d Harry Booth
VC

KISS (1991)
d Christopher Newby
VC

KITCHEN TOTO, the (1987)
d Harry Hook
VC

KNACK ...AND HOW TO GET IT, the (1965)
d Richard Lester
VC PB

KNOTS (1975)
d David Munro
PB

KONTIKI KIDS (The Magnificent Six and ½ first
series) (1968)
d Harry Booth
SC

KRAYS, the (1990)
d Peter Medak
SC

KRULL (1983)
d Peter Yates
SC

LABYRINTH (1986)
d Jim Henson
SC

LADDER OF SWORDS (1989)
d Norman Hull
VC

LADY CAROLINE LAMB (1972)
d Robert Bolt
SC PB

LADY JANE (1986)
d Trevor Nunn
PB

LADY VANISHES, the (1979)
d Anthony Page
VC SC

LAMB (1986)
d Colin Gregg
VC

LAND THAT TIME FORGOT, the (1974)
d Kevin Connor
PB

LAST GRAVE AT DIMBAZA (1974)
d Nana Mahomo
SC

LAST OF ENGLAND, the (1987)
d Derek Jarman
VC PB

LAST SAFARI, the (1967)
d Henry Hathaway
VC

LAST VALLEY, the (1970)
d James Clavell
PB

LATE EDITION (Conversation Pieces series)
(1983)
d Peter Lord, David Sproxton
VC

LATE SHOW, the (1969)
d Michael Wakely
VC

LAUGHTERHOUSE (1984)
d Richard Eyre
VC

LAUGHTER IN THE DARK (1969)
d Tony Richardson
SC PB

LAUTREC (1974)
d Geoff Dunbar
VC

LEARNING BY DISCOVERY (1968)
d Marc Broadway
PB

LEARNING TO READ (1967)
d Darrel Catling
SC

LEGEND OF HELL HOUSE, the (1973)
d John Hough
SC

**LEGEND OF THE 7 GOLDEN VAMPIRES,
the** (1974)
d Roy Ward Baker
VC

LEGEND OF THE WEREWOLF (1974)
d Freddie Francis
SC

LEGEND OF THE WITCHES (1970)
d Malcolm Leigh
PB

LEGEND OF YOUNG DICK TURPIN, the
(1965)
d James Neilson
SC PB

LEILA AND THE WOLVES (1984)
d Heiny Srour
VC

LEONARDO'S LAST SUPPER (1977)
d Peter Barnes
VC

LEOPARD IN THE SNOW (1977)
d Gerry O'Hara
SC

LEO THE LAST (1969)
d John Boorman
PB

LET IT BE (1970)
d Michael Lindsay-Hogg
PB

LET'S DO DAMNATION (1991)
d Alan Short
VC

LET'S GET LAID! (1977)
d James Kenelm Clarke
VC SC

LETTER TO BREZHNEV (1985)
d Chris Bernard
VC

LICENSED TO KILL (1965)
d Lindsay Shonteff
PB

LICENSED TO LOVE AND KILL (1979)
d Lindsay Shonteff
SC PB

LIFE AT THE TOP (1965)
d Ted Kotcheff
VC PB

LIFE IS SWEET (1990)
d Mike Leigh
VC

LIFE'S NORTH (1992)
d Karen Dunphie
VC

LIFE STORY OF BAAL, the (1978)
d Edward Bennett
PB

LIFETAKER, the (1975)
d Michael Papas
PB

LIKELY LADS, the (1976)
d Michael Tuchner
SC PB

LIMBO LINE, the (1968)
d Samuel Gallu
PB

LIMEHOUSE LINK (1991)
VC

LINESMAN, the (1965)
d Peter Griffiths
VC

LION IN WINTER, the (1968)
d Anthony Harvey
VC PB

LIP SYNCH series
see
CREATURE COMFORTS (1989)
GOING EQUIPPED (1989)
IDENT (1989)
NEXT (1989)
WAR STORY (1989)

LIQUIDATOR, the (1965)
d Jack Cardiff
VC PB

LISTENERS, the (1979)
d Keith Greig
VC

LISZTOMANIA (1975)
d Ken Russell
VC SC

LITTLE DORRIT (1987)
d Christine Edzard
SC

LITTLE ONES, the (1965)
d Jim O'Connolly
VC

LIVES OF ARTISTS NOT WIVES OF ARTISTS; WOMEN'S ART PRACTICE SINCE 1970 (1984)
d Sue Aron, Monika Morawietz, Rowena Rowling
VC

LIVING FREE (1972)
d Jack Couffer
PB

LLOYD COLE AND THE COMMOTIONS (1984)
d Mike Mansfield
VC

LOCK UP YOUR DAUGHTERS! (1969)
d Peter Coe
SC

LONDON STORY, the (1986)
d Sally Potter
VC

LONELY PLACES, the (1965)
d Peter Saunders
PB

LONG DAY CLOSES, the (1992)
d Terence Davies
SC

LONG DAY'S DYING, the (1968)
d Peter Collinson
SC PB

LONG DUEL, the (1967)
d Ken Annakin
VC SC

LONG GOOD FRIDAY, the (1979)
d John Mackenzie
VC

LOOK AT LIFE series
see
CURTAIN CHANGES, the (1966)
FREE FALL (1967)
HAIR SET, the (1966)
ISLAND AWAKES, an (1966)
MEMBERS ONLY (1965)
ROLL OUT THE BARREL (1966)
SUGARING THE PILL (1965)

LOOK AT THAT CLOUD (1981)
d Kim Flitcroft
VC

LOOKING GLASS WAR, the (1969)
d Frank R Pierson
VC

LOOKS AND SMILES (1981)
d Ken Loach
PB

LOOSE CONNECTIONS (1983)
d Richard Eyre
VC

LOOT (1970)
d Silvio Narizzano
VC PB

LORD HINTON OF BANKSIDE (1972)
VC

LOST CONTINENT (1968)
d Michael Carreras
VC

LOVE AND MARRIAGE (1970)
d Terry Gould
PB

LOVE CHILD, the (1987)
d Robert Smith
VC

LOVELY CRICKET (1967)
d Bill Latto
VC

LOVERS!, the (1972)
d Herbert Wise
VC PB

LOVES ME... LOVES ME NOT (1992)
d Jeffrey Newitt
VC

LOVE THY NEIGHBOUR (1973)
d John Robins
PB

LOVING MEMORY (1970)
d Anthony Scott
VC

LUST FOR A VAMPIRE (1970)
d Jimmy Sangster
PB

MACBETH (1971)
d Roman Polanski
SC

MACKINTOSH MAN, the (1973)
d John Huston
VC PB

MADAME SOUSATZKA (1988)
d John Schlesinger
VC PB

MADE (1972)
d John Mackenzie
SC PB

MADONNA AND CHILD (1980)
d Terence Davies
SC

MADWOMAN OF CHAILLOT, the (1969)
d Bryan Forbes
VC PB

MAGGOT, the (1973)
d George Dunning
VC

MAGNIFICENT SEVEN DEADLY SINS, the (1971)
d Graham Stark
PB

MAGNIFICENT SIX AND $\frac{1}{2}$ first series, the
see
BILLY THE KID (1968)
BOB A JOB (1968)
GHOSTS AND GHOULS (1968)
KONTIKI KIDS (1968)
PEEWEE'S PIANOLA (1968)
WHEN KNIGHTS WERE BOLD (1968)

MAGNIFICENT SIX AND $\frac{1}{2}$ third series, the
see
FIVE SURVIVE (1971)
SKI-WHEELERS (1971)
THAT'S ALL WE NEED (1971)
TIME FLIES (1971)
UP FOR THE CUP (1971)
UP THE CREEK (1971)

MAGNIFICENT TWO, the (1967)
d Cliff Owen
SC PB

MAGPIE LAYS AN EGG (The Chiffy Kids first series) (1976)
d David Bracknell
SC

MAGPIE'S TALKING DUCK (The Chiffy Kids second series) (1978)
d David Bracknell
SC

MAGRITTE; THE FALSE MIRROR (1970)
d David Sylvester
VC

MAHLER (1974)
d Ken Russell
SC PB

MAIDS, the (1974)
d Christopher Miles
VC

MAIDS AND MADAMS (1985)
d Mira Hamermesh
VC

MAJDHAR (1984)
d Ahmed A Jamal
VC

MAKE SURE (1972)
d Vivian Collins
VC

MAKE YOURSELF SAFE (1981)
d Mike Morgan
VC

MALEVITCH SUPREMATISM (1971)
d Lutz Becker
VC

MAN ABOUT THE HOUSE (1974)
d John Robins
VC SC

MANAGEMENT BY OBJECTIVES (1969)
d Frederic Goode
SC

MANAGING CHANGE – CHANGING THE MANAGERS (1988)
d Gavin Nettleton
VC

The Queen of Spades (Thorold Dickinson, 1948), Press-book. LIS [540–541, 558–560]

Saraband for Dead Lovers (Basil Dearden, 1948)

XIVth Olympiad – The Glory of Sport (Castleton Knight, 1948), an NFTVA restoration

Top: *Oliver Twist* (David Lean, 1948) Press-book. LIS [247]

Scott of the Antarctic (Charles Frend, 1948), an NFTVA restoration

The House Cat (Bert Felstead, 1949), an NFTVA restoration

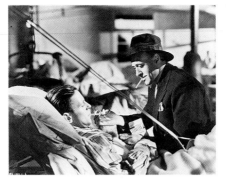

Above left: *A Modern Guide to Health* (John Halas, Joy Batchelor, 1946)

Above centre: *Green for Danger* (Sidney Gilliat, 1946)

Above right: *The Fallen Idol* (Carol Reed, 1948) [102–104]

British Aircraft Review 1948 (Geoffrey Hughes, 1948)

No Room at the Inn (Daniel Birt, 1948)

Caravan (Arthur Crabtree, 1946)

Above left: *The Card* (Ronald Neame, 1952)

Above centre: *The Dam Busters* (Michael Anderson, 1955)

Above right: *Thirteen Cantos of Hell* (Peter King, 1955)

No Resting Place (Paul Rotha, 1951)

Anthony Asquith on the set of *The Demi-Paradise*, 1943 [405–408]

Noose (Edmond T Gréville, 1948)

Cage of Gold (Basil Dearden, 1950), Press-book. LIS

The Servant (Joseph Losey, 1963) [293–294]

Nothing but the Best (Clive Donner, 1964) Press-book. LIS

Far left: *A Hard Day's Night* (Richard Lester, 1964), Press-book. LIS [130]

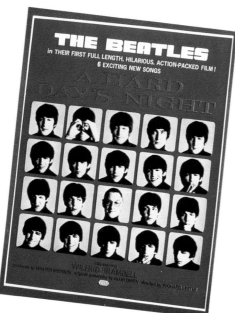

Carry on Cleo (Gerald Thomas, 1964) [1603]

MAN AT THE TOP (1973)
d Mike Vardy
SC PB

MAN FOR ALL SEASONS, a (1966)
d Fred Zinnemann
VC PB

MAN FRIDAY (1975)
d Jack Gold
SC

MAN IN THE CLOUDS (1967)
d Reg Spragg
VC

MANRIDING AT EPPLETON (1967)
d John Reid
VC

MAN VERSUS MACHINES? (Faces of Industry series) (1980)
d Peter Allen
VC

MAN WHO FELL TO EARTH, the (1976)
d Nicolas Roeg
VC PB

MAN WHO HAD POWER OVER WOMEN, the (1970)
d John Krish
PB

MAN WHO HAUNTED HIMSELF, the (1970)
d Basil Dearden
PB

MARC CHAGALL; THE COLOURS OF PASSION (1977)
d Charles Harris
VC

MAROC 7 (1966)
d Gerry O'Hara
SC

MARTIN'S DAY (1985)
d Alan Gibson
SC

MARY, QUEEN OF SCOTS (1971)
d Charles Jarrott
PB

MASKS AND FACES (1969)
VC

MASQUERADE (1965)
d Basil Dearden
PB

MASS (1976)
d Åsa Sjöström
VC

MATHEMATICIAN, the (1976)
d Stan Hayward
VC

MAURICE (1987)
d James Ivory
VC

MAURO THE GYPSY (1972)
d Laurence Henson
SC

MEANWHILE GARDENS (1983)
d Steve Shaw
VC

MELANCHOLIA (1989)
d Andi Engel
VC SC

MEMBERS ONLY (Look at Life series) (1965)
VC

MEMOIRS OF A SURVIVOR (1981)
d David Gladwell
VC

MEN AND THE BUOYS, the (1971)
d John Warrington
SC

MERCENARIES, the (1967)
d Jack Cardiff
SC PB

MERRY CHRISTMAS MR LAWRENCE (1982)
d Nagisa Oshima
SC

MESSAGE FROM THE WARDEN, a (1982)
d Anna Liebschner
VC

MIDNIGHT EXPRESS (1978)
d Alan Parker
SC

MIKADO, the (1966)
d Stuart Burge
PB

MILL, the (1992)
d Petra Freeman
VC

MILLENNIUM (1989)
d Michael Anderson
SC

MIND OF MR SOAMES, the (1969)
d Alan Cooke
VC PB

MINE AND THE MINOTAUR, the (1980)
d David Gowing
SC

MINIHOLIDAY (1968)
d Lawrence Moore
VC

MINI WEEKEND (1967)
d Georges Robin
PB

MIRACLE, the (1991)
d Neil Jordan
VC PB

MIROCLE, the (1976)
d Jack Daniel
VC

MIRROR (1970)
d Jon Schorstein
VC

MIRROR CRACK'D, the (1980)
d Guy Hamilton
VC

MIRROR, MIRROR (1980)
d Yugesh Walia
VC

MIRROR PHASE (1978)
d Carola Klein
VC

MISSIONARY, the (1982)
d Richard Loncraine
VC SC

MISS JULIE (1972)
d Robin Phillips, John Glenister
PB

MR FORBUSH AND THE PENGUINS (1971)
d Al Viola
SC PB

MR HORATIO KNIBBLES (1971)
d Robert Hird
SC

MISTER QUILP (1974)
d Michael Tuchner
VC

MISTER TEN PER CENT (1967)
d Peter Graham Scott
SC

MISTRESS PAMELA (1973)
d Jim O'Connolly
PB

MODEL MAKERS, the (This Week in Britain series) (1975)
VC

MODESTY BLAISE (1966)
d Joseph Losey
VC PB

MOMENT (1970)
d Stephen Dwoskin
VC

MONA LISA (1986)
d Neil Jordan
VC

MONKEY TRICKS (Chimpmates first series) (1976)
d Harold Orton
SC

MONSTER CLUB, the (1981)
d Roy Ward Baker
SC

MONSTER OF TERROR (1965)
d Daniel Haller
PB

MONTY PYTHON AND THE HOLY GRAIL (1974)
d Terry Jones
SC PB

MONTY PYTHON LIVE AT THE HOLLYWOOD BOWL (1982)
d Terry Hughes, Ian MacNaughton
VC

MONTY PYTHON'S LIFE OF BRIAN (1979)
d Terry Jones
VC

MOODS OF LOVE, the (1972)
d David Wickes
SC

MOON AND THE SLEDGEHAMMER, the (1971)
d Philip Trevelyan
VC PB

MOONLIGHTING (1983)
d Jerzy Skolimowski
VC

MOON OVER THE ALLEY, the (1975)
d Joseph Despins
VC

MORGAN; A SUITABLE CASE FOR TREATMENT (1966)
d Karel Reisz
PB

MORGAN'S WALL (1978)
d Caroline Goldie, Ron Orders, Geoff Richman, Marie Richman
PB

MOSQUITO SQUADRON (1968)
d Boris Sagal
PB

MOST DANGEROUS MAN IN THE WORLD, the (1969)
d J Lee Thompson
SC PB

MOTHER IRELAND (1988)
d Anne Crilly
VC

MOTOR WITH MORGAN (This Week in Britain series) (1974)
VC

MOVING THE GOALPOSTS (1990)
VC

MUMSY, NANNY, SONNY AND GIRLY (1969)
d Freddie Francis
PB

MURDER ON THE ORIENT EXPRESS (1974)
d Sidney Lumet
VC SC

MURDERS MOST FOUL (Blind Justice series) (1987)
d Gillian Lacey
VC

MURPHY'S WAR (1971)
d Peter Yates
PB

MUSIC! (1968)
d Michael Tuchner
SC

MUSIC LOVERS, the (1970)
d Ken Russell
PB

MUTINY ON THE BUSES (1972)
d Harry Booth
PB

MUYBRIDGE REVISITED (1986)
d George Snow
VC

MY AIN FOLK (1973)
d Bill Douglas
VC

MY BEAUTIFUL LAUNDRETTE (1985)
d Stephen Frears
VC SC

MY CHILDHOOD (1972)
d Bill Douglas
VC

MY WAY HOME (1978)
d Bill Douglas
VC

NAKED (1991)
d Yasmine Ramli
VC

NAKED EVIL (1966)
d Stanley Goulder
VC

NAKED WORLD OF HARRISON MARKS, the (1965)
d Harrison Marks
PB

NAKED YOGA (1975)
d Paul Cordsen, John Adams
SC

NANNY, the (1965)
d Seth Holt
VC PB

NANOU (1986)
d Conny Templeman
VC

NASTY HABITS (1976)
d Michael Lindsay-Hogg
PB

NATURE OF THE BEAST, the (1988)
d Franco Rosso
VC

NEAREST AND DEAREST (1972)
d John Robins
SC PB

NED KELLY (1970)
d Tony Richardson
PB

NEITHER THE SEA NOR THE SAND (1972)
d Fred Burnley
PB

NELLY'S VERSION (1983)
d Maurice Hatton
VC

NEVER MIND THE QUALITY FEEL THE WIDTH (1972)
d Ronnie Baxter
PB

NEXT (Lip Synch series) (1989)
d Barry Purves
VC

NIGHT AFTER NIGHT AFTER NIGHT (1969)
d Lindsay Shonteff
VC PB

NIGHT DIGGER, the (1971)
d Alastair Reid
PB

NIGHTHAWKS (1978)
d Ron Peck, Paul Hallam
VC

NIGHT OF THE BIG HEAT (1967)
d Terence Fisher
VC PB

NIGHT OF THE GENERALS, the (1966)
d Anatole Litvak
VC SC

NIGHT WATCH (1973)
d Brian G Hutton
SC PB

NINETEEN NINETEEN (1985)
d Hugh Brody
VC SC

1917 (1968)
d Stephen Weeks
SC

NINTH REPORT ON MODERNISATION (1969)
VC

NOBODY RUNS FOREVER (1968)
d Ralph Thomas
SC PB

NOCTURNA ARTIFICIALIA (1979)
d Quay Brothers
VC

NO MONEY, NO HONEY (1982)
d Jimmy Matthews
VC

NORTH (1986)
d Maxim Ford
VC

NORTHERN NEWSREEL NO.12 (1989)
VC

NORTHERN NEWSREEL NO.13 (1989)
VC

NORTHERN NEWSREEL NO.14 (1989)
VC

NORTHERN NEWSREEL NO.15 (1990)
VC

NORTHERN NEWSREEL NO.16 (1990)
VC

NORTHERN NEWSREEL NO.17 (1990)
VC

NORTHERN NEWSREEL NO.18 (1991)
VC

NO SEX PLEASE – WE'RE BRITISH (1973)
d Cliff Owen
VC PB

NO SURRENDER (1985)
d Peter K Smith
VC

NOT GUILTY (1988)
d Brenda Horsman
VC

NOTHING BUT THE NIGHT (1972)
d Peter Sasdy
SC

NOT NOW, COMRADE (1976)
d Harold Snoad, Ray Cooney
SC

NOT NOW, DARLING (1972)
d Ray Cooney, David Croft
SC PB

NUCLEAR FAMILY (1989)
d Kayla Parker
VC

NUCLEAR POWER '65 (1965)
d John S Green
VC

OBLONG BOX, the (1969)
d Gordon Hessler
PB

OCCUPY! (1976)
d Gael Dohany
VC

OFFENCE, the (1972)
d Sidney Lumet
SC PB

OH! WHAT A LOVELY WAR (1969)
d Richard Attenborough
PB

OLIVER! (1968)
d Carol Reed
PB

O LUCKY MAN! (1973)
d Lindsay Anderson
VC SC

ON APPROVAL (1967)
d Robin Carruthers
VC

ONE BRIEF SUMMER (1969)
d John Mackenzie
PB

ONE MAN'S CHINA series
see
EIGHT OR NINE IN THE MORNING (1972)
FRIENDSHIP FIRST, COMPETITION SECOND (1972)
GREAT TREASURE HOUSE, a (1972)
IRON TREE WILL BLOSSOM AND THE DUMB WILL SPEAK, the (1972)
ONE NATION, MANY PEOPLES (1972)
PEOPLE'S ARMY, the (1972)
PEOPLE'S COMMUNES, the (1972)
SELF RELIANCE (1972)

ONE MILLION YEARS BC (1966)
d Don Chaffey
PB

ONE MORE TIME (1969)
d Jerry Lewis
PB

ONE NATION, MANY PEOPLES (One Man's China series) (1972)
d Felix Greene
SC

ONE OF THE MISSING (1969)
d Anthony Scott
VC

ON HER MAJESTY'S SECRET SERVICE (1969)
d Peter Hunt
PB

ONLY WHEN I LARF (1968)
d Basil Dearden
PB

ON PROBATION (Conversation Pieces series) (1983)
d Peter Lord, David Sproxton
VC

ON THE AIR (The Trouble with 2b series) (1972)
d Peter K Smith
SC

ON THE BLACK HILL (1987)
d Andrew Grieve
SC

ON THE BUSES (1971)
d Harry Booth
SC PB

ON THE TILES (Chimpmates first series) (1976)
d Harold Orton
SC

OOH... YOU ARE AWFUL (1972)
d Cliff Owen
SC PB

OPEN FORUM (1966)
d Donovan Winter
VC

OPERATION THIRD FORM (1966)
d David Eady
SC

OPTIMISTS OF NINE ELMS, the (1973)
d Anthony Simmons
VC PB

OPUS (1967)
d Don Levy
PB

ORCHARD END MURDER, the (1981)
d Christian Marnham
SC

ORGANISING A SCHOOL TRIP (1991)
VC

ORIENTAL NIGHTFISH (1978)
d Ian Emes
PB

ORLANDO (1992)
d Sally Potter
SC PB

ORPHEUS AND EURYDICE (1984)
d Lesley H Keen, Michael Alexander
VC

OTHELLO (1965)
d Stuart Burge
VC PB

OTLEY (1968)
d Dick Clement
VC SC

OUCH! (1967)
d Gerard Bryant
VC

OUR CISSY (1974)
d Alan Parker
SC

OUR MAN IN MARRAKESH (1966)
d Don Sharp
PB

OUR MISS FRED (1972)
d Bob Kellett
SC PB

OUR MOTHER'S HOUSE (1967)
d Jack Clayton
VC PB

OUT OF ORDER (1988)
d Jonnie Turpie
VC SC

OUT OF SEASON (1975)
d Alan Bridges
SC PB

OUTRAGE (Cowboys series) (1991)
d Phil Mulloy
VC

OUTWARD BOUND (1973)
d Michael Birkett
SC

OVER HERE; IRISH DANCE AND MUSIC IN ENGLAND (1980)
d Carlo Gébler
VC

OVERTURE: 'ONE-TWO-FIVE' (1978)
d C David Lochner
VC

PAINTED FACES (1991)
d Tom Hooper
VC

PALACES OF A QUEEN (1966)
d Michael Ingrams
VC

PALMY DAYS (Conversation Pieces series) (1983)
d Peter Lord, David Sproxton
VC

PANTHER LZ, the (1979)
d Stuart Urban
VC

PAPAGENO (1991)
d Sarah Roper
VC

PAPER TIGER (1974)
d Ken Annakin
SC

PARADISE REGAINED (Sweet Disaster series) (1986)
d Andrew Franks
VC

PARAS (1983)
d Paul Grech-Ellul
VC

PARENTS' DAY (The Trouble with 2b series) (1972)
d Peter K Smith
SC

PARISH, PEOPLE AND PLACE (1992)
d Trevor Bailey, John Holman
VC

PARK, the (1967)
d Richard Saunders
VC

PASSAGE, the (1978)
d J Lee Thompson
SC

PASSAGE TO INDIA, a (1984)
d David Lean
SC PB

PASSION OF REMEMBRANCE, the (1986)
d Maureen Blackwood, Isaac Julien
VC

PATHWAY TO ETERNAL BOREDOM? (Faces of Industry series) (1980)
d Peter Allen
VC

PAUL RAYMOND'S EROTICA (1980)
d Brian Smedley-Aston
PB

PECKING ORDER (1989)
d Vicky Smith
VC

PEEWEE'S PIANOLA (The Magnificent Six and ½ first series) (1968)
d Harry Booth
SC

PENNY FOR YOUR THOUGHTS, a (1966)
d Donovan Winter
SC

PENNY GOLD (1973)
d Jack Cardiff
PB

PENTHOUSE, the (1967)
d Peter Collinson
PB

PEOPLE'S ARMY, the (One Man's China series) (1972)
d Felix Greene
SC

PEOPLE'S COMMUNES, the (One Man's China series) (1972)
d Felix Greene
SC

PERCY (1971)
d Ralph Thomas
SC

PERFECT FRIDAY (1970)
d Peter Hall
PB

PERFECT MURDER, the (1988)
d Zafar Hai
SC PB

PERFORMANCE (1970)
d Donald Cammell, Nicolas Roeg
VC SC

PERSECUTION AND ASSASSINATION OF JEAN-PAUL MARAT AS PERFORMED BY THE INMATES OF THE ASYLUM OF CHARENTON UNDER THE DIRECTION OF THE MARQUIS DE SADE, the (1966)
d Peter Brook
PB

PERSONAL SERVICES (1987)
d Terry Jones
SC

PHOELIX (1979)
d Anna Ambrose
PB

PHOENIX AND THE TURTLE, the (1972)
d Luigi V R Chiappini
VC

PHOTOGRAPHIC EXHIBITS (1984)
d Claire Barwell
VC

PICTURES AT AN EXHIBITION (1972)
d Nicholas Ferguson
PB

PICTURES ON PINK PAPER (1982)
d Lis Rhodes
VC

PILKIN'S PROGRESS (1976)
d Ronald Dunkley
SC

PING PONG (1986)
d Po-chih Leong
VC SC

PINK FLOYD – THE WALL (1982)
d Alan Parker
PB

PIONEERS OF THE BRITISH FILM (1968)
VC

PLACE OF MY OWN, a (1983)
d Andy Porter
VC

PLAGUE OF THE ZOMBIES, the (1966)
d John Gilling
PB

PLANK, the (1967)
d Eric Sykes
VC SC

PLANNING NEW MINES (1977)
d Euan Pearson
VC

PLAYBIRDS (1978)
d Willy Roe
PB

PLAY DIRTY (1968)
d André de Toth
PB

PLAYING AWAY (1986)
d Horace Ové
VC SC

PLAY ME SOMETHING (1989)
d Timothy Neat
SC

PLEASE SIR! (1971)
d Mark Stuart
PB

PLEASURE GIRLS, the (1965)
d Gerry O'Hara
VC PB

PLEASURE PRINCIPLE, the (1991)
d David Cohen
VC

PLOUGHMAN'S LUNCH, the (1983)
d Richard Eyre
VC

POETS AGAINST THE BOMB (1981)
d Francis Fuchs
VC

POND LIFE (1982)
VC

POPDOWN (1968)
d Fred Marshall
PB

POPE JOAN (1972)
d Michael Anderson
SC

PORRIDGE (1979)
d Dick Clement
VC SC

PORT OF GRIMSBY AND IMMINGHAM, the
(1967)
VC

PORTRAIT OF A CHALLENGE (1971)
d Robert Young
PB

PORTRAIT OF DAVID HOCKNEY (1972)
d David Pearce
VC

POSSESSION (1992)
d Phil Mulloy
VC

POT LUCK (The Chiffy Kids first series) (1976)
d David Bracknell
SC

**PRAISE MARX AND PASS THE
AMMUNITION** (1968)
d Maurice Hatton
VC PB

PRAYER BEFORE BIRTH, a (1991)
d Jacqui Duckworth
VC

PRAYER TO VIRACOCHA (1992)
d MarieCecille Pattisson
VC

PRESS FOR TIME (1966)
d Robert Asher
SC PB

PRESSURE (1975)
d Horace Ové
PB

PRETTY POLLY (1967)
d Guy Green
PB

PRICK UP YOUR EARS (1987)
d Stephen Frears
SC

PRIEST OF LOVE (1985)
d Christopher Miles
VC

**PRIMARY HEALTH CARE – A TEAM
APPROACH** (1983)
d Raymond Poole
VC

PRIME OF MISS JEAN BRODIE, the (1968)
d Ronald Neame
PB

PRINCE FOR WALES, a (1969)
d Martin D Harris
VC

PRIVATE ENTERPRISE, a (1974)
d Peter K Smith
VC

PRIVATE FUNCTION, a (1984)
d Malcolm Mowbray
VC PB

PRIVATE LIFE, a (1988)
d Francis Gerard
VC

PRIVATE RIGHT, the (1966)
d Michael Papas
PB

PRIVATE ROAD (1971)
d Barney Platts-Mills
PB

PRIVATES ON PARADE (1982)
d Michael Blakemore
VC

PRIVILEGE (1967)
d Peter Watkins
VC SC

PROGRAMMED LEARNING (1970)
d Richard Need
PB

PROJECT Z (1968)
d Ronald Spencer
SC

PROMENADE (1967)
d Donovan Winter
VC

PROSPERO'S BOOKS (1991)
d Peter Greenaway
VC PB

PRUDENCE AND THE PILL (1968)
d Fielder Cook
PB

PSYCHOMANIA (1972)
d Don Sharp
PB

PSYCHOPATH, the (1966)
d Freddie Francis
PB

PUBLIC INCONVENIENCE (Beer and Skittles
series) (1985)
d Andy Walker
VC

PULP (1972)
d Mike Hodges
SC

PUPPET ON A CHAIN (1970)
d Geoffrey Reeve
SC

QUADROPHENIA (1979)
d Franc Roddam
SC

QUARTET (1981)
d James Ivory
SC

QUATERMASS AND THE PIT (1967)
d Roy Ward Baker
VC

QUEEN OF HEARTS (1989)
d Jon Amiel
VC

QUEST FOR LOVE (1971)
d Ralph Thomas
SC

QUILLER MEMORANDUM, the (1966)
d Michael Anderson
VC PB

QUORN HUNT CRUELTY (1991)
VC

RACER, the (1975)
d Anthony Garner
VC

RADIO ON (1979)
d Christopher Petit
VC

RAGE IN HARLEM, a (1991)
d Bill Duke
VC PB

RAGMAN'S DAUGHTER, the (1971)
d Harold Becker
SC

RAILWAY CHILDREN, the (1970)
d Lionel Jeffries
VC SC

RAINDANCE (1991)
d Susan Hewitt
VC

RAISING THE ROOF (1971)
d Michael Forlong
SC

RAISING THE TITANIC (1984)
d Alan Ravenscroft
VC

RANGI'S CATCH (1972)
d Michael Forlong
SC

RANSOM (1974)
d Casper Wrede
PB

RASPUTIN THE MAD MONK (1965)
d Don Sharp
VC SC

RA; THE PATH OF THE SUN GOD (1990)
d Lesley H Keen
VC

RECKONING, the (1969)
d Jack Gold
VC

RED SKIRTS ON CLYDESIDE (1984)
d Jenny Woodley, Christine Bellamy
VC

REFLECTIONS (1984)
d Kevin Billington
VC PB

REFLEX ACTION (1986)
d Andrew Graham, David Kerr
VC

REGGAE (1970)
d Horace Ové
PB

REHEARSAL (1975)
d Robert Young
SC

RELAX (1991)
d Christopher Newby
VC

REMEMBRANCE (1982)
d Colin Gregg
VC

RENTADICK (1972)
d Jim Clark
SC PB

REPTILE, the (1966)
d John Gilling
PB

REQUIEM FOR A VILLAGE (1975)
d David Gladwell
VC

RESISTANCE (1976)
d Ken McMullen, Chris Rodrigues
PB

RESTLESS NATIVES (1985)
d Michael Hoffman
VC

RESURRECTED (1988)
d Paul Greengrass
VC

RETURN, the (1973)
d Sture Rydman
SC

RETURN FROM THE ASHES (1965)
d J Lee Thompson
PB

RETURN OF MR MOTO, the (1965)
d Ernest Morris
PB

RETURN OF THE SOLDIER (1982)
d Alan Bridges
PB

REVENGE (1971)
d Sidney Hayers
SC PB

REVENGE OF THE PINK PANTHER (1978)
d Blake Edwards
PB

RHOSYN A RHITH (Coming Up Roses) (1986)
d Stephen Bayly
VC PB

RICHARD'S THINGS (1980)
d Anthony Harvey
SC

RIDDLE OF THE SANDS, the (1978)
d Tony Maylam
PB

RIDDLES OF THE SPHINX (1977)
d Laura Mulvey, Peter Wollen
VC

RIDING HIGH (1980)
d Ross Cramer
SC

RIDING THE HURRICANE (1988)
VC

RIFF RAFF (1991)
d Ken Loach
VC

RING OF BRIGHT WATER (1969)
d Jack Couffer
PB

RITA, SUE AND BOB, TOO! (1987)
d Alan Clarke
VC

RITZ, the (1976)
d Richard Lester
PB

ROAD MOVIE (1984)
d Richard Philpott
VC

ROAD TO POPRICANI; THE CLEVELAND AID FOR ROMANIAN CHILDREN SPRING CONVOY 1991 (1992)
d Brian Shield
VC

ROBBERY (1967)
d Peter Yates
PB

ROCKALL PLATEAU – ROCK SAMPLING 1971 (1971)
VC

ROGER HOLMAN'S DACORUM FILM (1978)
VC

ROLL OUT THE BARREL (Look at Life series) (1966)
VC

ROLL OUT THE BARREL (Beer and Skittles series) (1985)
d Andy Walker
VC

ROMANTIC ENGLISHWOMAN, the (1975)
d Joseph Losey
SC PB

ROMANTIC ITALY (1975)
d Chris Garratt
VC

ROMEO AND JULIET (1966)
d Paul Czinner
VC PB

ROOM FILM 1973 (1973)
d Peter Gidal
VC

ROOM TO LET (The Chiffy Kids second series) (1976)
d David Bracknell
SC

ROOM WITH A VIEW, a (1987)
d James Ivory
VC

ROOTS ROCK REGGAE (1977)
d Jeremy Marre
VC

ROPE TRICK (1967)
d Bob Godfrey
VC

ROSEBUD (1992)
d Cheryl Farthing
VC

ROTTEN TO THE CORE (1965)
d John Boulting
SC PB

ROUGH CUT AND READY DUBBED (1981)
d Hasan Shah, Dom Shaw
VC

ROYAL HUNT OF THE SUN, the (1969)
d Irving Lerner
SC PB

RUDDIGORE (1967)
d Joy Batchelor
PB

RUDE BOY (1980)
d Jack Hazan, David Mingay
PB

RUE SAINT-SULPICE (1991)
d Ben Lewin
VC

RULING CLASS, the (1971)
d Peter Medak
PB

RUNAWAY RAILWAY (1965)
d Jan Darnley-Smith
SC

RUNNERS (1983)
d Charles Sturridge
VC

RUN WITH THE WIND (1966)
d Lindsay Shonteff
PB

RYAN'S DAUGHTER (1970)
d David Lean
SC PB

SAFE PLACE TO BE, a (Home from Home series) (1980)
d Simon Heaven
VC

SAILOR FROM GIBRALTAR, the (1967)
d Tony Richardson
PB

SAILOR'S RETURN, the (1978)
d Jack Gold
VC PB

SAILOR WHO FELL FROM GRACE WITH THE SEA, the (1976)
d Lewis John Carlino
SC

SALES PITCH (Conversation Pieces series) (1983)
d Peter Lord, David Sproxton
VC

SAMMY AND ROSIE GET LAID (1987)
d Stephen Frears
VC SC

SAMSON AND DELILAH (1984)
d Mark Peploe
VC

SANDBAGS AND TRENCHES (1979)
d Barry Bliss
VC

SANDS OF THE KALAHARI (1965)
d Cy Endfield
PB

SANDWICH MAN, the (1966)
d Robert Hartford-Davis
VC PB

SAN FRANCISCO (1968)
d Anthony Stern
VC

SANTA CLAUS (1985)
d Jeannot Szwarc
SC

SATURN 3 (1980)
d Stanley Donen
PB

SAVAGE MESSIAH (1972)
d Ken Russell
PB

SAY HELLO TO YESTERDAY (1970)
d Alvin Rakoff
PB

SCANDAL (1988)
d Michael Caton-Jones
PB

SCANDALOUS (1984)
d Rob Cohen
PB

SCARS OF DRACULA, the (1970)
d Roy Ward Baker
VC PB

SCHIZO (1976)
d Pete Walker
PB

SCRAMBLE (1970)
d David Eady
SC

SCREAM... AND DIE! (1973)
d Joseph Larraz
PB

SCROOGE (1970)
d Ronald Neame
PB

SCRUBBERS (1982)
d Mai Zetterling
VC

SCUM (1979)
d Alan Clarke
SC

SEA CHILDREN, the (1973)
d David Andrews
SC

SEA GULL, the (1968)
d Sidney Lumet
VC

SEASIDE WOMAN (1980)
d Oscar Grillo
PB

SEASPEED ACROSS THE CHANNEL (1969)
d R K Neilson Baxter
VC

SEAWEED CHILDREN, the (1973)
d Henry Herbert
PB

SEA WOLVES, the (1980)
d Andrew V McLaglen
SC

SEBASTIAN (1967)
d David Greene
SC PB

SECRET CEREMONY (1968)
d Joseph Losey
PB

SECRET FRIENDS (1992)
d Dennis Potter
VC

SECRET JOY (OF FALLING ANGELS) (1991)
d Simon Pummell
VC

SECRET OF MY SUCCESS, the (1965)
d Andrew L Stone
VC PB

SECRET PLACES (1984)
d Zelda Barron
PB

SECRET REEDS, the (1981)
d Michael W Richards
VC

SEEDS OF RESISTANCE (1985)
d Juliet Miller
VC

SELF RELIANCE (One Man's China series) (1972)
d Felix Greene
SC PB

SENDER, the (1982)
d Roger Christian
SC

SEVERED HEAD, a (1970)
d Dick Clement
VC SC

SEX AND THE OTHER WOMAN (1972)
d Stanley Long
PB

SEX WITH THE STARS (1980)
d Anwar Kawadri
PB

SHADEY (1985)
d Philip Saville
VC

SHALAKO (1968)
d Edward Dmytryk
PB

SHALLOW AND CROOKED (1990)
d Diane Scully, Martin Carter
VC

SHANGHAI SURPRISE (1986)
d Jim Goddard
VC

SHARPEVILLE SPIRIT (1986)
d Elaine Proctor
VC

SHE (1965)
d Robert Day
VC

SHE'LL BE WEARING PINK PYJAMAS (1985)
d John Goldschmidt
VC SC

SHELTERING SKY, the (1990)
d Bernardo Bertolucci
VC PB

SHINING, the (1980)
d Stanley Kubrick
SC

SHIP THAT NEVER RETURNED, the (1987)
d Nigel Atkinson, Nick Clark, Huw Davies
VC

SHOCK TREATMENT (1981)
d Jim Sharman
SC

SHOOTING PARTY, the (1984)
d Alan Bridges
SC

SHORELINE, the (1984)
d Peter Todd
VC

SHOUT, the (1978)
d Jerzy Skolimowski
SC PB

SHOVE TUESDAY (The Chiffy Kids first series) (1976)
d David Bracknell
SC

SHUTTERED ROOM, the (1966)
d David Greene
VC

SID AND NANCY (1986)
d Alex Cox
SC

SIDE BY SIDE (1975)
d Bruce Beresford
PB

SIDE EFFECTS (1980)
d Jacky Garstin, Delyse Hawkins
VC

SIDESHOW (1991)
d Christine Fotheringham
VC

SID'S FAMILY (1972)
d Nick Gifford
VC

SILENT PARTNER (1977)
d Peter Gidal
VC

SILENT SCREAM (1990)
d David Hayman
VC

SILENT WITNESS, the (1978)
d David W Rolfe
SC

SILVER DREAM RACER (1980)
d David Wickes
PB

SINBAD AND THE EYE OF THE TIGER (1977)
d Sam Wanamaker
PB

SINK OR SWIM (1977)
d John Michael Phillips
SC

64 DAY HERO; A BOXER'S TALE (1985)
d Franco Rosso
VC

SIZE M (1970)
d Tony Sinden
VC

SKI BUM (1969)
d Bruce Clark
SC

SKI-WHEELERS (The Magnificent Six and ½ third series) (1971)
d Peter Graham Scott
SC

SKULL, the (1965)
d Freddie Francis
SC

SKY BIKE, the (1967)
d Charles Frend
SC

SKY HIGH (1967)
d Arthur Boynton
VC

SKY WEST AND CROOKED (1965)
d John Mills
VC PB

SLAVE GIRLS (1966)
d Michael Carreras
PB

SLAYGROUND (1983)
d Terry Bedford
SC

SLIMDERELLA (The Chiffy Kids second series) (1978)
d David Bracknell
SC

SLIM'S PICKIN'S (Cowboys series) (1991)
d Phil Mulloy
VC

SLIPPER AND THE ROSE; THE STORY OF CINDERELLA, the (1976)
d Bryan Forbes
PB

SMACK AND THISTLE (1989)
d Tunde Ikoli
VC

SMASHING BIRD I USED TO KNOW, the (1969)
d Robert Hartford-Davis
PB

SMASHING TIME (1967)
d Desmond Davis
PB

SMOKEY JOE'S REVENGE (1974)
d Ronald Spencer
SC

SNOWMAN, the (1982)
d Diane Jackson
VC

SOFT WORDS; or, Life does not live (1984)
d Roger Noake
VC

SOHO SQUARE (1992)
d Mario Cavalli
VC

SOLO (1968)
d Misha Donat
VC

SOME KIND OF HERO (1972)
d Marvin Lichtner
SC

SOME MAY LIVE (1967)
d Vernon Sewell
PB

SOME PROTECTION (Blind Justice series) (1987)
d Marjut Rimminen
VC

SOMETHING TO HIDE (1971)
d Alastair Reid
PB

SON, ARE YOU DOWN THERE? (1984)
d Carl Johnson
VC

SONG OF THE SHIRT, the (1979)
d Sue Clayton, Jonathan Curling
PB

SONG REMAINS THE SAME, the (1976)
d Joe Massot, Peter Clifton
PB

SON OF THE SAHARA (1966)
d Frederic Goode
SC

SORCERERS, the (1967)
d Michael Reeves
PB

SOURSWEET (1988)
d Mike Newell
VC SC

SOUTH BANK (This Week in Britain series) (1973)
VC

SPACEFLIGHT IC-1 (1965)
d Bernard Knowles
VC

SPACE RIDERS (1984)
d Joe Massot
SC

SPICE OF WICKEDNESS, the (1983)
d Elka Tupiak
VC

SPLIT (1974)
d Roger Lambert
PB

SPRING AND PORT WINE (1969)
d Peter Hammond
PB

SPRINGFIELD (1986)
d Emma Calder
VC

SPRINGING LENIN (Continental Drift series) (1992)
d Andrei Nekrasov
VC

SPY WITH A COLD NOSE, the (1966)
d Daniel Petrie
PB

SREDNI VASHTAR (1983)
d Liz Spencer
VC

SS FRANCE (1970)
SC

STAIN, the (1991)
d Marjut Rimminen, Christine Roche
VC

STAND UP VIRGIN SOLDIERS (1977)
d Norman Cohen
PB

STANLEY SPENCER (1979)
d David Rowan
PB

STARDUST (1974)
d Michael Apted
VC

STEAMING (1985)
d Joseph Losey
VC SC

STEPTOE AND SON (1972)
d Cliff Owen
VC PB

STEPTOE & SON RIDE AGAIN (1973)
d Peter Sykes
PB

STILL WANTED (1967)
d Esmond Wilson
VC

STORIES FROM A FLYING TRUNK (1979)
d Christine Edzard
PB

STORMS OF AUGUST, the
see
STORMYDD AWST (1988)

STORMYDD AWST (The Storms of August) (1988)
d Endaf Emlyn
PB

STRANGER IN THE HOUSE (1967)
d Pierre Rouve
PB

STRANGER THAN FICTION (1985)
d Ian Potts
VC PB

STRAPLESS (1988)
d David Hare
VC SC

STRAW DOGS (1971)
d Sam Peckinpah
PB

STREET OF CROCODILES (1986)
d Quay Brothers
SC

STRIP POKER (1968)
d Pete Walker
SC

STUD, the (1978)
d Quentin Masters
PB

STUDENT POWER (1968)
d Daniel Schechter
VC

STUDY IN TERROR, a (1965)
d James Hill
PB

STUFFY OLD BANK (1972)
d Ronald Spencer
VC

SUBMARINE X-1 (1968)
d William A Graham
PB

SUCCESS IS THE BEST REVENGE (1984)
d Jerzy Skolimowski
VC PB

SUGARING THE PILL (Look at Life series) (1965)
VC

SUMMER HOLIDAY (1972)
d Philip Leacock
VC

SUMMER IS FOREVER (1972)
SC

SUMURU (1967)
d Lindsay Shonteff
PB

SUNDAY IN THE PARK (1970)
d Donovan Winter
VC

SUNFLOWERS (1968)
d Ian McMillan
VC

SUPERGIRL (1984)
d Jeannot Szwarc
SC PB

SUPERGRASS, the (1985)
d Peter Richardson
PB

SUPERMAN (1978)
d Richard Donner
SC

SUPERMAN II (1980)
d Richard Lester
PB

SUPER-SOFT, QUICK-MIX, AFTER-EIGHT WOMAN, the (1981)
d Norma Sullivan
VC

SURGICAL INSTRUMENTS (1968)
d Cedric Maggs
VC

SWALLOWS AND AMAZONS (1974)
d Claude Whatham
SC PB

SWEENEY! (1976)
d David Wickes
PB

SWEENEY 2 (1978)
d Tom Clegg
VC SC

SWEET AND SEXY (1970)
d Anthony Sloman
PB

SWEET DISASTER series
see
BABYLON (1986)
CONVERSATIONS BY A CALIFORNIAN
SWIMMING POOL (1986)
DEATH OF A SPEECHWRITER (1986)
DREAMLESS SLEEP (1986)
PARADISE REGAINED (1986)

SWEET WILLIAM (1979)
d Claude Whatham
SC

SWORD OF THE VALIANT – THE LEGEND OF GAWAIN AND THE GREEN KNIGHT (1983)
d Stephen Weeks
SC

SYMPTOMS (1974)
d Joseph Larraz
PB

TABLE, the (1973)
d Adrian Lyne
SC

TABOO OF DIRT (1987)
d Martyn Pick
VC

TAIWAN TODAY (1965)
VC

TAKE A GIRL LIKE YOU (1969)
d Jonathan Miller
PB

TAKE IT OR LEAVE IT (1981)
d David Robinson
SC

TAKE ME HIGH (1973)
d David Askey
PB

TAKES (1970)
d Peter Gidal
VC

TAKING A PART (1979)
d Jan Worth
VC

TALES FROM THE CRYPT (1972)
d Freddie Francis
PB

TALES OF BEATRIX POTTER (1971)
d Reginald Mills
VC PB

TALES OF THE NIGHT (1992)
d Michel Ocelot
VC

TALK ABOUT WORK (1971)
d Ken Loach
VC

TALL GUY, the (1989)
d Mel Smith
VC PB

TARKA THE OTTER (1978)
d David Cobham
VC

TAXI DRIVER 2 (THE RECLINE OF THE WEST) (1987)
d George Barber
VC

TELL ME LIES (1967)
d Peter Brook
VC

TELLY SAVALAS LOOKS AT PORTSMOUTH (1981)
VC

TENDER TOUCH OF LOVE, the (1966)
d Robin Cantelon
SC

TEN LITTLE INDIANS (1965)
d George Pollock
PB

10 RILLINGTON PLACE (1970)
d Richard Fleischer
VC PB

TERROR (1978)
d Norman J Warren
SC PB

TERRORNAUTS, the (1967)
d Montgomery Tully
VC

TESTAMENT (1988)
d John Akomfrah
PB

TESTIMONY (1987)
d Tony Palmer
SC PB

TG: PSYCHIC RALLY IN HEAVEN (1981)
d Derek Jarman
VC

THAT'LL BE THE DAY (1973)
d Claude Whatham
VC

THAT LUCKY TOUCH (1975)
d Christopher Miles
PB

THAT RIVIERA TOUCH (1966)
d Cliff Owen
SC PB

THAT'S ALL WE NEED (The Magnificent Six and ½ third series) (1971)
d Peter Graham Scott
SC

THAT SUMMER OF WHITE ROSES (1989)
d Rajko Grlic
VC PB

THAT'S YOUR FUNERAL (1972)
d John Robins
PB

THEATRE OF BLOOD (1973)
d Douglas Hickox
SC PB

THEATRE OF DEATH (1966)
d Samuel Gallu
PB

THERE GOES THE BRIDE (1979)
d Terry Marcel
SC

THERE'S A GIRL IN MY SOUP (1970)
d Roy Boulting
SC PB

THESE FOUR WALLS (1990)
VC

THEY CAME FROM BEYOND SPACE (1967)
d Freddie Francis
VC

THINGS – A LIFE OF THEIR OWN (1984)
d Roger Parsons
VC

THIRD WOMAN, the (1991)
d Mitra Tabrizian
VC

THIRTY NINE STEPS, the (1978)
d Don Sharp
SC PB

'36 TO '77 (1978)
d Marc Karlin, Jon Sanders, James Scott, H B Trevelyan
SC

THIRTY YEARS YOUNGER (The Trouble with 2b series) (1972)
d Peter K Smith
SC

THIS IS YOUR GUINNESS (1975)
d Arthur G Wooster
PB

THIS MADE NEWS (1971)
d Terry Ashwood
SC

THIS WEEK IN BRITAIN series
see
MODEL MAKERS, the (1975)
MOTOR WITH MORGAN (1974)
SOUTH BANK (1973)

THOSE BEAUTIFUL OLD CARS (1972)
d Derek Robbins
SC

THOSE MAGNIFICENT MEN IN THEIR FLYING MACHINES; or, How I flew from London to Paris in 25 hours and 11 minutes (1965)
d Ken Annakin
VC PB

THREE (1969)
d James Salter
PB

THREE HATS FOR LISA (1965)
d Sidney Hayers
PB

THREE INTO TWO WON'T GO (1968)
d Peter Hall
PB

THREE SISTERS (1970)
d Laurence Olivier
PB

THUNDERBALL (1965)
d Terence Young
PB

THUNDERBIRD 6 (1968)
d David Lane
SC PB

TIBET (1976)
d Felix Greene
SC PB

TIDE IS TURNING, the (1979)
d Paul Gane
VC

TIFFANY JONES (1973)
d Pete Walker
PB

TIGER LILY, the (1975)
d Paul Bernard
SC

TILL DEATH US DO PART (1969)
d Norman Cohen
VC SC

TIMBER MOVE (1965)
d Norman Prouting
VC

TIME BANDITS (1981)
d Terry Gilliam
VC

TIME FLIES (The Magnificent Six and ½ third series) (1971)
d Peter Graham Scott
SC

TIN BOX (1992)
d Steve Arnott
VC

TITANS OF TOMORROW (1968)
d Marc Broadway
PB

TIT FOR TAT (Chimpmates third series) (1978)
d Harold Orton
SC

TO KILL A CLOWN (1971)
d George Bloomfield
SC

TOMMY (1975)
d Ken Russell
SC PB

TOM PHILLIPS (1977)
d David Rowan
VC

TOOMORROW (1970)
d Val Guest
PB

TOPICAL BUDGET: THE GREAT BRITISH NEWS FILM (1992)
VC

TO SEE SUCH FUN (1977)
d Jon Scoffield
PB

TO SIR, WITH LOVE (1966)
d James Clavell
VC PB

TO THE DEVIL A DAUGHTER (1976)
d Peter Sykes
VC

TO THE WESTERN WORLD; THE TRAVELS OF J M SYNGE AND JACK YEATS IN CONNEMARA IN 1905 (1981)
d Margy Kinmonth
VC

TOUCH OF CLASS, a (1972)
d Melvin Frank
PB

TOUCH OF LOVE, a (1969)
d Waris Hussein
PB

TOWARDS INTUITION; AN AMERICAN LANDSCAPE (1980)
d Terry Flaxton, Penny Dedman, Tony Cooper
VC

TRACK 29 (1988)
d Nicolas Roeg
VC SC

TRAITOR'S GATE (1965)
d Freddie Francis
VC

TRAP, the (1966)
d Sidney Hayers
PB

TREASURE HUNT (Chimpmates second series) (1976)
d Harold Orton
SC

TREE OF HANDS (1988)
d Giles Foster
VC

TRIAL, the (1992)
d David Jones
SC

TRIAL BY COMBAT (1976)
d Kevin Connor
PB

TRIAL OF STRENGTH (The Trouble with 2b series) (1972)
d Peter K Smith
SC

TRIPLE ECHO, the (1972)
d Michael Apted
PB

TROUBLESOME DOUBLE, the (1971)
d Milo Lewis
SC

TROUBLE WITH 2B series, the
see
BLACKBOARD JUNGLE (1972)
HAPPY DAYS (1972)
ON THE AIR (1972)
PARENTS' DAY (1972)
THIRTY YEARS YOUNGER (1972)
TRIAL OF STRENGTH (1972)

TRUE ROMANCE ETC (1982)
VC

TRYGON FACTOR, the (1966)
d Cyril Frankel
PB

TSIAMELO – A PLACE OF GOODNESS (1984)
d Betty Wolpert, Ellen Kuzwayo, Blanche Tsimatsima
SC

TUNNYNG OF ELINOUR RUMMYNG, the (1976)
d Julien Temple
VC

TURNER (1966)
d David Thompson
PB

25 YEARS (1977)
d Peter Morley
PB

TWENTY-NINE (1969)
d Brian Cummins
VC

TWENTY-ONE (1991)
d Don Boyd
VC

TWISTED NERVE (1968)
d Roy Boulting
PB

TWIST OF SAND, a (1968)
d Don Chaffey
PB

TWO ARCHITECTS (1966)
d Ron Parks
VC

TWO FOR THE ROAD (1966)
d Stanley Donen
PB

200 MOTELS (1971)
d Frank Zappa, Tony Palmer
PB

TWO TRACK MIND (1984)
d Barrie Gavin
VC

UBU (1978)
d Geoff Dunbar
VC

UNBROKEN ARROW, the (1976)
d Matt McCarthy, John Black
SC

UNDERGROUND (1970)
d Arthur H Nadel
PB

UNDER MILK WOOD (1971)
d Andrew Sinclair
PB

UNDER SUSPICION (1991)
d Simon Moore
VC

UNDER THE DOCTOR (1976)
d Gerry Poulson
PB

UNIVERSAL SOLDIER (1971)
d Cy Endfield
PB

UNKNOWN WOMAN (1991)
d Kayla Parker
VC

UNSUITABLE JOB FOR A WOMAN, an (1982)
d Christopher Petit
VC SC

UP AND AWAY (1971)
d Arnold Louis Miller
SC

UP FOR THE CUP (The Magnificent Six and ½ third series) (1971)
d Peter Graham Scott
SC

UP JUMPED A SWAGMAN (1965)
d Christopher Miles
VC SC

UP POMPEII (1971)
d Bob Kellett
PB

UPS AND DOWNS OF A HANDYMAN
(1975)
d John Sealey
VC

UP THE CHASTITY BELT (1971)
d Bob Kellett
SC PB

UP THE CREEK (The Magnificent Six and ½
third series) (1971)
d Peter Graham Scott
VC SC

UP THE FRONT (1972)
d Bob Kellett
SC PB

UP THE JUNCTION (1967)
d Peter Collinson
PB

USER FRIENDLY (1991)
d Jack Grossman
VC

VALENTINO (1977)
d Ken Russell
SC

VALUE FOR MONEY (1970)
d Gale Tattersall, David Blest
VC

VAMPIRA (1974)
d Clive Donner
VC

VAMPIRE LOVERS, the (1970)
d Roy Ward Baker
VC

VANISHING POINT (1971)
d Richard C Sarafian
VC PB

VAULT OF HORROR, the (1973)
d Roy Ward Baker
VC

VENOM (1981)
d Piers Haggard
PB

VICTIM FIVE (1965)
d Robert Lynn
SC

VICTOR, the (1985)
d Derek Hayes, Phil Austin
VC

VICTOR/VICTORIA (1982)
d Blake Edwards
SC

VIEW FROM A PARKED CAR (1971)
d Robert Carter
VC

VIEW TO A KILL, a (1985)
d John Glen
PB

VIKING QUEEN, the (1966)
d Don Chaffey
VC

VILLAIN (1971)
d Michael Tuchner
SC PB

VIOLA (1967)
d Dunstan Pereira, Richard Davis
VC

VIOLENT ENEMY, the (1969)
d Don Sharp
PB

VIRGIN AND THE GYPSY, the (1970)
d Christopher Miles
SC PB

VIRGIN SOLDIERS, the (1969)
d John Dexter
VC

VIRTUES OF KNATURE (1987)
d Kaprice Kea
VC

VIRUS – HEPATITIS 'B'... THE RISKS
(1983)
d Neville Wortman
VC

VIRUS OF WAR (1977)
d Stuart Urban
PB

VOICES (1973)
d Kevin Billington
PB

VROOM (1988)
d Beeban Kidron
VC

WALK THROUGH H, a (1978)
d Peter Greenaway
PB

WALKING STICK, the (1970)
d Eric Till
PB

WALL OF LIGHT (1986)
d John Tchalenko
VC

WARLORDS OF ATLANTIS (1978)
d Kevin Connor
PB

WAR REQUIEM (1989)
d Derek Jarman
SC

WAR STORY (Lip Synch series) (1989)
d Peter Lord
VC

WAR TO THE LAST ITCH (1972)
d Alastair MacEwen
SC

WATCHERS, the (1969)
d Richard Foster
VC

WATER (1985)
d Dick Clement
VC PB

WATERBIKES (The Chiffy Kids second series)
(1978)
d David Bracknell
SC

WATERLAND (1992)
d Stephen Gyllenhaal
VC

WAXING BOOK, the (1989)
d Paul Rodgers
VC

WAXWORKS (Chimpmates second series)
(1976)
d Harold Orton
SC

WE ARE THE ELEPHANT (1987)
d Glenn Ujebe Masokoane
VC

WE CAME TO LEARN (1971)
SC

WEDDING BELLS (Chimpmates first series)
(1976)
d Harold Orton
SC

WELCOME TO THE SPIV ECONOMY (1986)
d Andy Metcalf
VC

WETHERBY (1985)
d David Hare
VC PB

WE THINK THE WORLD OF YOU (1988)
d Colin Gregg
VC

WHAT CAN I DO WITH A MALE NUDE?
(1985)
d Ron Peck
VC

WHAT'S UP SUPERDOC? (1978)
d Derek Ford
VC

WHAT THE BUTLER SAW! (1991)
d Ray Selfe
VC

WHEN DINOSAURS RULED THE EARTH
(1969)
d Val Guest
SC

WHEN EIGHT BELLS TOLL (1971)
d Etienne Périer
PB

WHEN KNIGHTS WERE BOLD (The
Magnificent Six and ½ first series) (1968)
d Harry Booth
SC

WHEN THE WIND BLOWS (1986)
d Jimmy T Murakami
PB

**WHEN WILL THEY REALISE WE'RE
LIVING IN THE TWENTIETH CENTURY?**
(1980)
d Peter Robinson
SC

WHERE ARE WE GOING? (1983)
VC

WHERE EAGLES DARE (1968)
d Brian G Hutton
SC

WHERE IS PARSIFAL? (1984)
d Henri Helman
PB

WHERE THE SPIES ARE (1965)
d Val Guest
VC PB

WHISPERERS, the (1966)
d Bryan Forbes
SC PB

WHISTLE BLOWER, the (1986)
d Simon Langton
SC

WHITE MISCHIEF (1987)
d Michael Radford
SC PB

WHITE ROCK (1976)
d Tony Maylam
PB

WHOEVER SLEW AUNTIE ROO? (1971)
d Curtis Harrington
PB

WHO KILLED THE CAT? (1966)
d Montgomery Tully
VC PB

WHOLLY COMMUNION (1965)
d Peter Whitehead
SC

WHO NEEDS A HEART (1991)
d John Akomfrah
VC

WHO TAKES THE MONEY? (Faces of Industry series) (1980)
d Peter Allen
VC

WHO TOOK THE CLOCK? (1987)
d Ann Latimer
VC

WICKER MAN, the (1973)
d Robin Hardy
VC PB

WIFE, the (1982)
d Brenda Horsman
VC

WIFE SWAPPERS, the (1970)
d Derek Ford
PB

WILBY CONSPIRACY, the (1974)
d Ralph Nelson
PB

WILD GEESE, the (1978)
d Andrew V McLaglen
SC PB

WILD GEESE II (1985)
d Peter Hunt
PB

WILT (1989)
d Michael Tuchner
SC

WINDVANE (1972)
d Chris Welsby
VC

WINGS OF DEATH (1985)
d Nichola Bruce, Michael Coulson
VC

WINNIE (1984)
d Peter Biddle
VC

WINNING IN COMPETITION (COMPULSORY COMPETITIVE TENDERING AT LEICESTER CITY COUNCIL) (1990)
VC

WIN SOME, LOSE SOME (Beer and Skittles series) (1985)
d Andy Walker
VC

WINSTANLEY (1975)
d Kevin Brownlow, Andrew Mollo
VC

WISH YOU WERE HERE (1987)
d David Leland
VC SC

WITCHES, the (1966)
d Cyril Frankel
VC

WITCHFINDER GENERAL (1968)
d Michael Reeves
PB

WITHNAIL & I (1987)
d Bruce Robinson
VC

WOMAN WHO MARRIED CLARK GABLE, the (1985)
d Thaddeus O'Sullivan
VC

WOMBLING FREE (1977)
d Lionel Jeffries
PB

WOMEN IN LOVE (1969)
d Ken Russell
PB

WOMEN IN TROPICAL PLACES (1990)
d Penny Woolcock
VC

WOMEN OF THE RHONDDA (1973)
d Mary Capps, Mary Kelly, Margaret Dickinson, Esther Ronay, Brigid Segrave, H B Trevelyan
VC

WOMEN OF THE T&G (1990)
VC

WONDER OF ICE CREAM, the (1966)
d David Grainger
VC

WONDERWALL (1968)
d Joe Massot
SC

WORK IS A FOUR LETTER WORD (1967)
d Peter Hall
VC PB

WORKERS FILMS OF THE THIRTIES (1981)
d Victoria Wegg-Prosser
VC

WORKING TO A PATTERN (Home from Home series) (1980)
d Simon Heaven
VC

WORLD APART, a (1987)
d Chris Menges
VC

WRECK RAISERS (1972)
d Harold Orton
SC

WRESTLING (1979)
d Gabrielle Bown
VC

WRONG BOX, the (1966)
d Bryan Forbes
SC PB

WUTHERING HEIGHTS (1970)
d Robert Fuest
PB

YANKS (1979)
d John Schlesinger
VC SC

YELLOW DOG (1973)
d Terence Donovan
PB

YELLOW SUBMARINE (1968)
d George Dunning
PB

YENTL (1983)
d Barbra Streisand
SC

YESTERDAY'S HERO (1979)
d Neil Leifer
PB

YOU BE MOTHER (1990)
d Sarah Pucill
VC

YOU MUST BE JOKING (1965)
d Michael Winner
SC PB

YOUNG AND OLD (1979)
d Neville Presho
VC

YOUNG SOUL REBELS (1991)
d Isaac Julien
PB

YOUNG WINSTON (1972)
d Richard Attenborough
VC SC

YOU ONLY LIVE TWICE (1967)
d Lewis Gilbert
PB

YOU'RE HUMAN LIKE THE REST OF THEM (1967)
d B S Johnson
VC

YOU WINNING? (1978)
d Barry Bliss
VC

ZARDOZ (1973)
d John Boorman
PB

ZED & TWO NOUGHTS, a (1985)
d Peter Greenaway
VC

ZEE & CO (1971)
d Brian G Hutton
PB

ZEPPELIN (1971)
d Etienne Périer
VC SC

ZINA (1985)
d Ken McMullen
VC

ZOO ROBBERY, the (1973)
d John Black
SC

ZOO TIME (Chimpmates second series) (1976)
d Harold Orton
SC

ZYGOSIS (1991)
d Gavin Hodge
SC

Part Two
BFI Library and Information Services
Books and Special Materials

FILM TITLES

A LA RECHERCHE DU TEMPS PERDU

1. The Proust Screenplay: A la Recherche du Temps Perdu by Harold Pinter.
    Methuen, 1978. 166p.
    Unrealised project.

ABSOLUTE BEGINNERS

2. The Beginners' Guide to Absolute Beginners edited by Vicky Hayward.
    Corgi Books, 1986. 112p. col.illus.
    Novelisation of the film.

3. Sandy Lieberson Special Collection.
    See item 818

ACCIDENT

4. Joseph Losey Special Collection.
    See item 828

    See also item 374

THE ADVENTURES OF BARON MUNCHAUSEN

5. The Adventures of Baron Munchausen by Charles McKeown & Terry Gilliam.
    Mandarin, 1989. 213p. illus.
    Novelisation based on the film.

6. The Adventures of Baron Munchausen: The Screenplay by Charles McKeown & Terry Gilliam.
    Applause, 1989. 175p. illus.

7. Losing the Light: Terry Gilliam and the Munchausen Saga by Andrew Yule.
    Applause, 1991. 247p. plates. appendix. index.

THE AFRICAN QUEEN

8. The African Queen by James Agee.
    Mcdowell Obolensky, 1960. 488p.
    In 'Agee on Film Volume Two: Five Film Scripts'.

9. The Making of The African Queen: Or How I Went to Africa with Bogart, Bacall and Huston and Almost Lost My Mind by Katharine Hepburn.
    Century, 1987. 133p. illus.

AGAINST THE WIND

10. Against the Wind by Arnold Meredith.
    World Film Publications, 1948. 88p. plates.
    Novelisation based on the screenplay by T.E.B. Clarke.

11. Aileen & Michael Balcon Special Collection.
    See item 417

AGATHA

12. David Puttnam Special Collection.
    See item 950

ALIEN

13. Alien by Dan O'Bannon & Richard Anobile.
    Futura Books, 1979. c100p. col.plates.

14. The Book of Alien by Paul Scanlon & Michael Gross.
    Star Books, 1979. Unpaged. illus.

15. Giger's Alien: Film Design by H.R. Giger.
    Big O Publications, 1979. 72p. plates. bibliog. filmog.

ALL FOR MARY

16. Adrian Pryce-Jones Special Collection.
    See item 949

ANGEL

17. Angel by Neil Jordan.
    Faber, 1989. 50p. illus.

ANIMAL FARM

18. The Animated Film with Pictures from the Film Animal Farm by Roger Manvell.
    Sylvan Press, 1954. 64p. illus. diagrs.

ARMS AND THE MAN

See item 366

THE ARSENAL STADIUM MYSTERY

19. Thorold Dickinson Special Collection.
    See item 540

THE BAD LORD BYRON

20. The Bad Lord Byron by Sydney Box & Vivian Cox.
    Convoy Press, 1949. 112p. illus.

THE BATTLE OF BRITAIN

21. The Battle of Britain: The Making of a Film by Leonard Mosley.
    Weidenfeld and Nicolson, 1969. 207p.

THE BATTLE OF THE RIVER PLATE

22. The Last Voyage of the Graf Spee by Michael Powell.
    White Lion, 1976. 192p.
    Novel inspired by the film.

BEDELIA

23. Bedelia: Film Edition by Vera Caspary & William R.T. Rodger.
    Cornfield Publications, 1947. 174p.
    Novel on which film is based.

BEHOLD A PALE HORSE

24. Behold a Pale Horse by Emeric Pressburger.
    Fontana Books, 1964. 192p.
    Novel on which the film is based.
    Originally published as *Killing a Mouse on Sunday*.

THE BELLES OF ST.TRINIANS

25. Adrian Pryce-Jones Special Collection.
    See item 949

THE BELLY OF AN ARCHITECT

26. The Belly of an Architect by Peter Greenaway.
    Faber, 1988. 182p. illus.

THE BEST MAN

See item 368

BHOWANI JUNCTION

See item 365

BILITIS

27. Hamilton's Movie Bilitis – Photographs by David Hamilton.
    Quill, 1982. 109p. illus.
    A photographic scrapbook of the film.

BILLION DOLLAR BRAIN

28. Billion Dollar Brain by Len Deighton.
    Penguin, 1966. 255p.
    Novel on which the film is based.

BLACK NARCISSUS

See item 365

BLANCHE FURY

29. Blanche Fury by Eric Britton.
    World Film Publications, 1948. 78p. illus. photos.
    Novelisation based on the screenplay by Audrey Lindop and Cecil McGivern.

THE BLIND GODDESS

30. The Blind Goddess by Patrick Hastings.
    W.H. Allen, 1948. 88p. illus.
    Novelisation based on the film.

BLOW-UP

31. Blow-up by Michelangelo Antonioni.
    Lorrimer Publishing, 1971. 119p. plates.

32. Focus on Blow-up edited by Roy Huss.
    Prentice-Hall, 1971. 171p. plates. index.

THE BLUE LAMP

33. The Blue Lamp: A Novel from the Film Script by Ted Willis.
    Convoy Publications, 1950. 173p. plates.

BOND STREET

34. Bond Street by Warwick Mannon.
    World Film Publications, 1948. 78p. plates.
    Novelisation based on the screenplay by Anatole de Grunwald.

BONJOUR TRISTESSE

35. Adrian Pryce-Jones Special Collection.
    See item 949

BOOM!

36. Joseph Losey Special Collection.
    See item 828

BORN FREE

37. Born Free: The Story of Elsa, the Lioness of Two Worlds by Joy Adamson.
    Fontana, 1962. 143p.
    Book on which the film is based.

A BRIDGE TOO FAR

38. The Arnhem Report: The Story Behind A Bridge Too Far by Iain Johnstone.
    Star Books, 1977. 173p.

39. William Goldman's Story of A Bridge Too Far by William Goldman.
    Coronet Books, 1977. Unpaged. illus.

BRIEF ENCOUNTER

40. Brief Encounter: A Screenplay by Noel Coward.
    Lorrimer, 1984. 80p. plates.

    See also items 372, 377

BRIMSTONE AND TREACLE

41. Brimstone and Treacle by Sarah Potter.
    Quartet Books, 1982. 112p. col.illus.
    Novelisation with stills from the film.

BRITAIN CAN TAKE IT

42. Britain Can Take It by Quentin Reynolds.
    John Murray, 1941. c40p. illus.
    Book based on the film.

BRITANNIA OF BILLINGSGATE

43. Britannia of Billingsgate: The Novel of the Gaumont-British Film by Christine Jope-Slade.
    Rich and Cowan, 1933. 255p.

BROKEN JOURNEY

44. Broken Journey by Warwick Mannon.
World Film Publications, 1948. 89p.
illus.
Novelisation based on the original
screenplay by Robert Westerby.

THE BROWNING VERSION

45. Teddy Baird Special Collection.
See item 414

BUGSY MALONE

46. Bugsy Malone by Alan Parker.
Armada, 1976. 126p. plates.
Novelisation of the film.

CAESAR AND CLEOPATRA

47. Meeting at the Sphinx: Gabriel Pascal's
Production of Bernard Shaw's Caesar and
Cleopatra by Marjorie Deans.
Macdonald, 1946. 146p. illus.

See also item 366

CAPTAIN BOYCOTT

48. Captain Boycott by Warwick Mannon.
World Film Publications, 1947. 89p.
illus.
Novelisation based on the screenplay by
Frank Launder and Wolfgang Wilhelm.

CARAVAGGIO

49. Derek Jarman Special Collection.
See item 737

50. Derek Jarman's Caravaggio: The
Complete Film Script and Commentaries
by Derek Jarman.
Thames and Hudson, 1986. 136p. plates.

CHARIOTS OF FIRE

51. David Puttnam Special Collection.
See item 950

THE CHASE

52. The Chase by Kit Porlock.
Hollywood Publications, 1947. 88p.
plates.
Novelisation of the film.

CITY OF JOY

53. City of Joy: The Illustrated Story of the
Film by Roland Joffé, Mark Medoff &
Jake Eberts.
Newmarket Press, 1992. 159p. illus.

CLASH OF THE TITANS

54. Clash of the Titans by Alan Dean Foster
& Beverley Cross.
Macdonald Futura, 1981. 223p.
col.plates.
Novelisation based on the screenplay by
Beverley Cross.

CLOCKWISE

55. Clockwise: A Screenplay by Michael
Frayn.
Methuen, 1986. 99p. plates.

A CLOCKWORK ORANGE

56. A Clockwork Orange by Anthony
Burgess.
Penguin, 1972. 144p.
Novel on which the film is based.

57. Stanley Kubrick's A Clockwork Orange
by Stanley Kubrick.
Lorrimer, 1972. 362p. illus.

THE COMFORT OF STRANGERS

See item 367

COMIN' THRO' THE RYE

58. Comin' Thro' the Rye by Helen Mathers.
Macmillan, 1898.
Novel on which the film is based.

COMPANY OF WOLVES

See item 373

COMRADES

59. Comrades by Bill Douglas.
Faber, 1987. 134p. illus.

THE COOK, THE THIEF, HIS WIFE
AND HER LOVER

60. The Cook, the Thief, His Wife and Her
Lover by Peter Greenaway.
Dis Voir, 1989. 96p. col.plates.

CORRECTION, PLEASE, OR HOW
WE GOT INTO PICTURES

61. Correction, Please, or How We Got into
Pictures by Noel Burch.
Arts Council of Great Britain, 1979.
23p. illus.
Book of the film.

CORRIDOR OF MIRRORS

62. Corridor of Mirrors by S. Evelyn Thomas
& Dennis Yates.
S. Evelyn Thomas, 1948. 103p. illus.
Novelisation based on the screenplay by
Rudolph Cartier and Edana Romney.

THE COURTNEYS OF CURZON
STREET

63. The Courtneys of Curzon Street by Kit
Porlock.
World Film Publications, 1947. 88p.
plates.
Novelisation adapted from the
screenplay by Nicholas Phipps, based on
a story by Florence Tranter.

THE CRIMINAL

64. Joseph Losey Special Collection.
See item 828

CRY FREEDOM

65. Cry Freedom: A Novel Based on His
Original Screenplay by John Briley.
Penguin Books, 1987. 272p. plates.

66. Filming with Attenborough: The Making
of Cry Freedom by Donald Woods.
Penguin, 1987. 163p. plates.

67. Richard Attenborough's Cry Freedom: A
Pictorial Record by Richard
Attenborough.
The Bodley Head, 1987. Unpaged. illus.
(chiefly col.).
Story of the film told mainly through
the use of pictures.

CUL-DE-SAC

See item 371

DAKOTA ROAD

68. Dakota Road by Nick Ward.
Faber, 1991. 65p. illus.

THE DAMNED (1961)

69. Joseph Losey Special Collection.
See item 828

THE DARK CRYSTAL

70. The Making of the Dark Crystal: Creating
a Unique Film by Christopher Finch.
Holt, Rinehart and Winston, 1983. 96p.
col.illus.

71. The World of The Dark Crystal by J.J.
Llewellyn.
Henson Organization Pubs/Mitchell
Beazley, 1983. 128p. col.illus.
Novelisation based on the story by Jim
Henson.

DARLING

72. Darling by Frederic Raphael.
Fontana, 1965. 157p.
Novelisation of the film.

See also item 368

DAVID COPPERFIELD

73. Copperfield '70: The Story of the Making
of the Omnibus/20th Century-Fox Film of
Charles Dickens' David Copperfield by
George Curry.
Pan Books, 1970. 194p. photos.

DAYBREAK

74. Daybreak by Arnold Meredith.
World Film Publications, 1948. 88p.
plates.
Novelisation based on the screenplay by
Muriel and Sydney Box.

THE DEAD

75. Joyce, Huston, and the Making of The
Dead by Clive Hart.
Colin Smythe, 1988. 38p.

THE DECEIVERS

76. Hullabaloo in Old Jeypore: The Making
of The Deceivers by Ismail Merchant.
Viking, 1988. 156p. col.plates.

THE DEEP BLUE SEA

77. Adrian Pryce-Jones Special Collection.
See item 949

THE DEVIL'S DISCIPLE

78. Adrian Pryce-Jones Special Collection.
See item 949

See also item 366

A DIARY FOR TIMOTHY

79. An Analysis of A Diary for Timothy, a
Film by Humphrey Jennings by Evan
Cameron.
The Experiment Press, 1967. 68p.

DIM LITTLE ISLAND

80. Humphrey Jennings Special Collection.
See item 742

THE DOCTOR AND THE DEVILS

81. The Doctor and the Devils by Dylan
Thomas.
J.M. Dent, 1953. 138p.
Formed the basis of the 1985 film
directed by Freddie Francis.

DOCTOR ZHIVAGO

82. Doctor Zhivago: The Screenplay by
Robert Bolt.
Collins and Harvill Press, 1966. 223p.

THE DRAUGHTSMAN'S CONTRACT

83. The Draughtsman's Contract Special
Collection.
20 items including production material.

84. Peter Greenaway: Plans and Conceits...'of doubtful authenticity'.
BFI, 1984. 32p. illus.

THE DRESSER

85. The Dresser: A Study Guide by Tony Fegan & Ian Wall.
Columbia Pictures, 1983. 29p. illus.

DROWNING BY NUMBERS

86. Drowning by Numbers by Peter Greenaway.
Faber, 1988. 118p. illus.

THE DUELLISTS

87. David Puttnam Special Collection.
See item 950

EASY MONEY

88. Easy Money by Arnold Meredith.
World Film Publications, 1948. 89p. plates.
Novelisation based on the original screenplay by Muriel and Sydney Box.

EDGE OF THE WORLD

89. Edge of the World by Michael Powell.
Faber, 1990. 334p. plates. maps. index.
Originally published in 1938 as 200,000 Feet on Foula.

EDWARD II

90. Queer Edward II by Derek Jarman.
British Film Institute, 1991. 169p. illus.

ELEPHANT BOY

91. Elephant Dance by Frances Hubbard Flaherty.
Faber, 1937. 138p. illus.

THE ELEPHANT MAN

92. The Elephant Man: The Book of the Film by Joy Kuhn.
Virgin Books, 1980. 90p. illus.

ELIZABETH OF LADYMEAD

93. Elizabeth of Ladymead by Warwick Mannon.
World Film Publications, 1949. 64p. illus.
Novelisation based on the screenplay by Frank Harvey.

THE EMERALD FOREST

94. Money into Light: The Emerald Forest, a Diary by John Boorman.
Faber, 1985. 241p. illus.

THE EMPIRE STRIKES BACK

95. The Art of The Empire Strikes Back by Vic Bulluck & Valerie Hoffman.
Ballantine Books, 1980. 176p. col.illus.

96. The Empire Strikes Back Notebook by Diana Attias & Lindsay Smith.
Ballantine Books, 1980. 127p. illus.
Contains the complete script by Lawrence Kasdan and Leigh Brackett, with selected storyboards.

97. Once Upon a Galaxy: A Journal of the Making of The Empire Strikes Back by Alan Arnold.
Sphere Books, 1980. 277p. plates.

98. Star Wars: The Empire Strikes Back Storybook by Shep Steneman.
Random House, 1980. Unpaged. col.illus.
Novelisation based on the screenplay by Leigh Brackett and Lawrence Kasdan.

ENCORE

99. Encore: Screen Adaptations of Stories by W. Somerset Maugham by T.E.B. Clarke, Arthur Macrae & Eric Ambler.
Heinemann, 1951. 165p. plates.
Original stories with screenplays.

ERIK THE VIKING

100. Erik the Viking: The Screenplay by Terry Jones.
Applause, 1990. 155p. illus.

FAHRENHEIT 451

101. Fahrenheit 451 by Ray Bradbury.
Corgi Books, 1957. 158p.
Novel on which the film is based.

THE FALLEN IDOL

102. Carol Reed Special Collection.
See item 963

103. Fiction and Film Adaptation: A Study of Narrative Structure and Style in Graham Greene's The Basement Room and Carol Reed's The Fallen Idol by Barbara Crowther.
M.Phil thesis, 1982. 283p. bibliog.

104. A Film Star in Belgrave Square by Robert Henrey.
Peter Davies, 1948. 186p. illus.

See also item 376

A FAMILY PORTRAIT

105. Humphrey Jennings Special Collection.
See item 742

THE FAMILY WAY

106. The Family Way by Roy Boulting & Jeffrey Dell.
Scholastic Book Services, 1974. 204p.
In 'Men and Women: Scripts of Splendor in the Grass, The Family Way and Nothing But a Man' edited by Richard A. Maynard.

FANNY HILL

107. Fanny Hill in Pictures: Memories of a Woman of Pleasure by John Cleland.
Mayflower-Dell, 1965. 96p. illus.
Story told mainly through the use of illustrative material.

FATHERLAND

108. Fatherland by Trevor Griffiths.
Faber, 1987. 77p. illus.

FIGURES IN A LANDSCAPE

109. Figures in a Landscape by Barry England.
Panther, 1970. 206p.
Novel on which the film is based.

110. Joseph Losey Special Collection.
See item 828

FIRES WERE STARTED

111. Humphrey Jennings Special Collection.
See item 742

A FISH CALLED WANDA

112. A Fish Called Wanda: A Screenplay by John Cleese & Charles Crichton.
Methuen, 1988. 102p. plates.

THE FRENCH LIEUTENANT'S WOMAN

113. The Screenplay of The French Lieutenant's Woman by Harold Pinter.
Cape/Eyre Methuen, 1981. 104p.

See also item 369

FULL METAL JACKET

114. Full Metal Jacket: The Screenplay by Stanley Kubrick, Michael Herr & Gustav Hasford.
Secker and Warburg, 1987. 129p. plates.

GANDHI

115. Gandhi: The Screenplay by John Briley.
Duckworth, 1982. 198p.

116. In Search of Gandhi by Richard Attenborough.
Bodley Head, 1982. 240p. illus. (many col.) index.

THE GHOST GOES WEST

117. Successful Film Writing: Illustrated by The Ghost Goes West by Seton Margrave.
Methuen, 1936. 216p. plates.

GIVE MY REGARDS TO BROAD STREET

118. Paul McCartney's Give My Regards to Broad Street by Andrew Harvey.
Pavilion, 1984. 128p. illus.

THE GO-BETWEEN

119. Joseph Losey Special Collection.
See item 828

See also item 374

GOODBYE, MR. CHIPS

120. Aileen & Michael Balcon Special Collection.
See item 417

121. Goodbye, Mr. Chips by R.C. Sheriff, Claudine West & Eric Maschwitz.
Gordon Press, 1975. 534p.
In 'The Best Pictures 1939–40' edited by Jerry Wald.

GREAT EXPECTATIONS

122. Great Expectations: The Book of the Film Based on the Novel by Charles Dickens.
World Film Publications, 1946. 89p. plates.
Adapted from the screenplay by David Lean, Ronald Neame and Anthony Havelock-Allan.

THE GREAT WHITE SILENCE

123. The Great White South, or with Scott in the Antarctic by Herbert C. Ponting.
Duckworth, 1923. 305p. illus.

GREGORY'S GIRL

124. Gregory's Girl: The Filmscript by Bill Forsyth.
Cambridge University Press, 1991. 112p.

THE GUINEA PIG

125. The Guinea Pig by Arnold Meredith.
World Film Publications, 1948. 96p. plates.
Novelisation based on the screenplay by Warren Chetham-Strode and Bernard Miles in association with Roy Boulting.

HAMLET

126. The Film Hamlet: A Record of Its Production edited by Brenda Cross.
Saturn Press, 1948. 76p. illus.

127. Hamlet: Presented by Laurence Olivier.
Scenes from the Film with Original Set Designs by Roger Furse.
Benjamin Pollock, 1948. c20p. illus.

128.	Hamlet: The Film and the Play edited by Alan Dent.
World Film Publications, 1948. 168p. illus.
Screen version of the play by William Shakespeare.

HANOVER STREET

129.	Hanover Street by Maureen Gregson. Corgi, 1979. 203p.
Novelisation based on the script by Peter Hyams.

A HARD DAY'S NIGHT

130.	The Beatles in Richard Lester's A Hard Day's Night: A Complete Pictorial Record of the Movie by J. Philip di Franco.
Chelsea House, 1977. 297p. illus.

See also item 368

HEADING HOME

See item 370

THE HEART OF THE MATTER

131.	Adrian Pryce-Jones Special Collection.
See item 949

HELP!

132.	The Beatles in Help! Novelisation by Al Hine.
Mayflower Books, 1965. 158p. plates.

HENRY V (1944)

133.	Film Scripts One edited by George P. Garrett.
Appleton–Century–Crofts, 1971. 544p. bibliog.
Includes Henry V.

134.	Filmguide to Henry V by Harry M. Geduld.
Indiana University Press, 1973. 82p. bibliog. filmog.

135.	Henry V: A Screenplay by Laurence Olivier, Alan Dent & Reginald Beck.
Lorrimer, 1984. 93p. illus.
Screen version of the play by William Shakespeare.

136.	The Making of Henry V by C. Clayton Hutton.
Author, 1945. 72p. illus.

HENRY V (1989)

137.	Henry V by William Shakespeare & Kenneth Branagh.
Chatto and Windus, 1989. 128p. illus.

HERE COME THE HUGGETTS

138.	Here Come the Huggetts by Warwick Mannon.
World Film Publications, 1948. 96p. illus.
Novelisation based on the screenplay by Mabel and Denis Constanduros and Peter Rogers.

HIDDEN CITY

See item 375

HIGH SPIRITS

139.	High Spirits by Neil Jordan.
Faber, 1989. 78p. illus.

HOBSON'S CHOICE

140.	Adrian Pryce-Jones Special Collection.
See item 949

HOPE AND GLORY

141.	Hope and Glory by John Boorman.
Faber, 1987. 149p. illus.

HUE AND CRY

142.	Aileen & Michael Balcon Special Collection.
See item 417

143.	Hue and Cry by Eric Britton.
World Film Publications, 1947. 89p. illus.
Novelisation based on the screenplay by T.E.B. Clarke.

HUSSY

144.	Hussy by Rosemary Kingsland.
Sphere Books, 1980. 190p.
Novel on which the film is based.

I KNOW WHERE I'M GOING!

145.	I Know Where I'm Going! by Eric Britton.
World Film Publications, 1946. 76p. plates.
Novelisation based on the script by Michael Powell and Emeric Pressburger.

IF....

146.	If.... by Lindsay Anderson & David Sherwin.
Lorrimer, 1969. 167p. plates.

147.	If: A Story by David Sherwin.
Sphere Books, 1969. 191p.
Novelisation of the film.

THE IMPORTANCE OF BEING EARNEST

148.	Teddy Baird Special Collection.
See item 414

INDIANA JONES AND THE LAST CRUSADE

149.	Indiana Jones and the Last Crusade by Rob MacGregor.
Sphere Books, 1989. 248p. col.plates.
Novelisation of the film based on the script by Jeffrey Boam.

INDIANA JONES AND THE TEMPLE OF DOOM

150.	Indiana Jones and the Temple of Doom: The Storybook Based on the Film by Michael French.
Fontana, 1984. Unpaged. col.illus.
Novelisation based on the screenplay by Willard Huyck and Gloria Katz.

151.	Indiana Jones and the Temple of Doom: The Illustrated Screenplay by Willard Huyck & Gloria Katz.
Ballantine Books, 1984. 122p. col.illus.

INSIGNIFICANCE

152.	Insignificance: The Book by Neil Norman & Jon Barraclough.
Sidgwick and Jackson, 1985. 128p. illus.

INTERNATIONAL VELVET

153.	International Velvet by Bryan Forbes.
Heinemann, 1978. 160p.
Novelisation of the film.

IT ALWAYS RAINS ON SUNDAY

154.	Aileen & Michael Balcon Special Collection.
See item 417

155.	A Film in the Making Featuring It Always Rains on Sunday by John W. Collier.
World Film Publications, 1947. 96p. illus.

156.	It Always Rains on Sunday by A.J. La Bern.
Nicholson and Watson, 1947. 256p. illus.
Novel on which the film is based.

IT HAPPENED HERE

157.	How It Happened Here by Kevin Brownlow.
Secker and Warburg, 1968. 184p. photos. filmog.

JESUS CHRIST SUPERSTAR

158.	Jesus Christ Superstar by David James.
Fountain Press, 1973. Unpaged. col.illus.
Largely illustrative material.

JEW SUSS

159.	Jew Suss by Arthur Richard Rawlinson, Dorothy Farnum & Ernest Betts.
Methuen, 1935. 174p.

THE JIGSAW MAN

160.	The Jigsaw Man by Dorothea Bennett.
Corgi Books, 1977. 204p.
Novel on which the film is based.

JUBILEE

161.	Derek Jarman Special Collection.
See item 737

KES

162.	A Kestrel for a Knave by Barry Hines.
Penguin, 1969. 160p.
Novel on which the film is based.

A KID FOR TWO FARTHINGS

163.	A Kid for Two Farthings: Information Folder by Bill Batchelor.
N.p., c1955. 75p.

THE KILLING FIELDS

164.	David Puttnam Special Collection.
See item 950

165.	The Killing Fields: The Facts Behind the Film by Sydney Schanberg & Dith Pran.
Weidenfeld and Nicolson, 1984. 128p. illus.

THE KILLING OF SISTER GEORGE

166.	The Killing of Sister George: A Comedy in Three Acts by Frank Marcus.
Hamish Hamilton, 1965. 88p.
Play on which the film is based.

KIND HEARTS AND CORONETS

167.	Aileen & Michael Balcon Special Collection.
See item 417

168.	Israel Rank by Roy Horniman.
Eyre and Spottiswoode, 1948. 312p.
Novel on which the film is based.

169.	Kind Hearts and Coronets by Robert Hamer & John Dighton.
Lorrimer, 1984. 88p. illus.

See also item 372

KING AND COUNTRY

170.	Joseph Losey Special Collection.
See item 828

KING SOLOMON'S MINES

171. King Solomon's Mines: Text from the MGM Technicolor Film Based on the Novel by H. Rider Haggard.
Ward Lock, n.d.. 96p. illus. col.plates.
Novelisation of the film.

THE KITCHEN TOTO

172. The Kitchen Toto by Harry Hook.
Faber, 1987. 63p. illus.

LABYRINTH

173. Goblins of the Labyrinth by Brian Froud & Terry Jones.
Pavilion/Michael Joseph, 1986. 137p. col.illus.

174. Labyrinth the Photo Album Based on the Jim Henson Film by Numerous Goblins & Rebecca Grand.
Virgin, 1986. 64p. illus.
Novelisation based on the Jim Henson film.

THE LADY VANISHES

175. The Lady Vanishes by Frank Launder & Sidney Gilliat.
Lorrimer, 1984. 101p. illus.

THE LAST DAYS OF DOLWYN

176. The First Days of Dolwyn by Emlyn Williams.
Transcript of BBC broadcast, 1949. 10p.

THE LAST OF ENGLAND

177. The Last of England by Derek Jarman.
Constable, 1987. 249p. illus.

THE LAST TYCOON

See item 369

THE LAVENDER HILL MOB

178. The Lavender Hill Mob Special Collection.
Material held in the Lavender Hill Mob Special Collection.

LAWRENCE OF ARABIA

179. Lawrence of Arabia by Sam Spiegel et al.
Journal of the Society of Film and Television Arts, 1962–3. 24p. illus.

180. Lawrence of Arabia: The 30th Anniversary Pictorial History by L. Robert Morris & Lawrence Raskin.
Doubleday, 1992. 237p. illus. bibliog.

181. Single Bed for Three: A Lawrence of Arabia Notebook by Howard Kent.
Hutchinson, 1963. 208p. illus.

THE LEAGUE OF GENTLEMEN

182. The League of Gentlemen by John Boland.
Pan Books, 1958. 160p.
Novel on which the film is based.

THE LEGEND OF THE WEREWOLF

183. The Legend of the Werewolf Special Collection.
Source material collected for the book by Ed Buscombe – 22 items.

184. Making Legend of the Werewolf by Edward Buscombe.
British Film Institute/Educational Advisory Service, 1976. 121p. illus.

LICENCE TO KILL

185. The Making of Licence to Kill by Sally Hibbin.
Hamlyn, 1989. 128p. illus. index.

THE LIFE AND DEATH OF COLONEL BLIMP

186. The Shame and Disgrace of Colonel Blimp by E.W. and M.M. Robson.
The Sidneyan Society, c1942. 31p.

THE LION HAS WINGS

187. The Lion Has Wings by John Ware.
Collins, 1940. 188p.
Novelisation based on the story by Ian Dalrymple.

THE LION IN WINTER

188. Best American Screenplays 2 edited by Sam Thomas.
Crown Publishers, 1990. 612p.
Includes The Lion in Winter.

LISTEN TO BRITAIN

189. Humphrey Jennings Special Collection.
See item 742

A LITTLE BIT OF FLUFF

190. A Little Bit of Fluff by Draycot M. Dell.
Readers Library, 1928. 252p. plates.
Novelisation of the film based on the play by Walter W. Ellis.

LITTLE DORRIT

191. Little Dorrit: A Story Told in Two Films Based on the Novel by Charles Dickens.
Sands Films Ltd, 1987. 47p. illus. (chiefly col.).
Novelisation based on the film script by Christine Edzard.

LIVE AND LET DIE

192. The James Bond Files: Live and Let Die by John Peel.
The Borgo Press, 1987. 51p. illus. filmog.

193. Roger Moore as James Bond: Roger Moore's Own Account of Filming Live and Let Die by Roger Moore.
Pan Books, 1973. 189p. col.plates.

LOCAL HERO

194. David Puttnam Special Collection.
See item 950

195. Local Hero by David Benedictus.
Penguin, 1983. 144p.
Novelisation based on the screenplay by Bill Forsyth.

196. Local Hero: The Making of the Film by Allan Hunter & Mark Astaire.
Polygon Books, 1983. 99p. illus. filmog.

LONDON KILLS ME

197. London Kills Me by Hanif Kureishi.
Faber, 1991. 95p.

THE LONELINESS OF THE LONG DISTANCE RUNNER

198. The Loneliness of the Long Distance Runner by Alan Sillitoe.
Scholastic Book Services, 1974. 192p.
In 'Identity: Scripts of That's Me, The Loneliness of the Long Distance Runner, Cool Hand Luke and Up the Down Staircase'.

THE LONG DARK HALL

199. Adrian Pryce-Jones Special Collection.
See item 949

THE LONG GOOD FRIDAY

200. The Long Good Friday by Russell Claughton.
Magnum, 1981. 176p.
Novelisation based on the original story and screenplay by Barrie Keefe.

201. The Long Good Friday by Barrie Keefe.
Methuen, 1984. 45p. illus.

LOOK BACK IN ANGER

202. Look Back in Anger: A Play in Three Acts by John Osborne.
Faber, 1957. 96p.
Stageplay on which the film is based.

LORD OF THE FLIES

203. Lord of the Flies: A Novel Illustrated with Stills from the Film by William Golding.
Faber, 1962. 248p.
Novel on which the film is based.

LOSER TAKES ALL

204. Adrian Pryce-Jones Special Collection.
See item 949

MACBETH

205. Macbeth: The Making of the Film by Clayton Hutton.
Max Parrish, 1960. 48p. illus.

THE MAHABHARATA

206. The Mahabharata: Peter Brook's Epic in the Making by Garry O'Connor.
Hodder and Stoughton, 1989. 159p. illus. col.plates. index.

MAJOR BARBARA

207. Major Barbara: A Screen Version by George Bernard Shaw.
Penguin, 1941. 160p.

See also item 366

THE MAN BETWEEN

208. Adrian Pryce-Jones Special Collection.
See item 949

MAN OF ARAN

209. Aileen & Michael Balcon Special Collection.
See item 417

210. Man of Aran by Pat Mullen.
Faber, 1934. 286p. illus.

THE MAN WHO COULD WORK MIRACLES

211. Man Who Could Work Miracles: A Film Story Based on the Material Contained in His Short Story 'Man Who Could Work Miracles' by H.G. Wells.
The Cresset Press, 1936. 96p.

See also item 378

THE MAN WHO KNEW TOO MUCH

212. The Man Who Knew Too Much by Ruth Alexander.
Arrowsmith, 1936. 264p.
Novelisation based on the script by Charles Bennett.

THE MAN WHO WATCHED TRAINS GO BY

213. Adrian Pryce-Jones Special Collection.
See item 949

A MATTER OF LIFE AND DEATH

214. A Matter of Life and Death by Michael Powell & Emeric Pressburger.
L'Avant Scène du Cinéma, Dec. 1980. 50p.
Language: French.

215. A Matter of Life and Death by Eric Warman.
World Film Publications, 1946. 124p. plates.
Novelisation based on the script by Emeric Pressburger and Michael Powell.

MEN OF TWO WORLDS

216. The Acceptable Face of British Colonialism: Men of Two Worlds by Chaim Litewski.
MA thesis, 1983. Various pages.

217. Men of Two Worlds by E. Fisher.
World Film Publications, 1946. 89p. plates.
Novelisation adapted from the screenplay by Herbert W. Victor and Thorold Dickinson, from a story by Joyce Cary.

218. Thorold Dickinson Special Collection.
See item 540

MIDNIGHT EXPRESS

219. David Puttnam Special Collection.
See item 950

MINE OWN EXECUTIONER

220. Mine Own Executioner by Nigel Balchin.
Collins, 1976. 256p.
Novel on which the film is based.

MIRANDA

221. Miranda by Warwick Mannon.
World Film Publications, 1948. 88p. plates.
Novelisation based on the screenplay by Peter Blackmore.

THE MISSION

222. David Puttnam Special Collection.
See item 950

223. The Mission: A Film Journal by Daniel Berrigan.
Harper and Row, 1986. 160p.

224. Sandy Lieberson Special Collection.
See item 818

THE MISSIONARY

225. The Missionary by Michael Palin.
Methuen, 1983. 127p. col.illus.

MODESTY BLAISE

226. Joseph Losey Special Collection.
See item 828

MONA LISA

227. Mona Lisa by Neil Jordan & David Leland.
Faber, 1986. 83p. illus.

MONTY PYTHON AND THE HOLY GRAIL

228. Monty Python and the Holy Grail: Monty Python's Second Film, a First Draft by Graham Chapman et al.
Eyre Methuen, 1977. Unpaged. illus. col.plates.

MONTY PYTHON'S LIFE OF BRIAN

229. Monty Python's The Life of Brian/ Monty Python's Scrapbook by Graham Chapman et al.
Eyre Methuen, 1979. 64p. illus.

MONTY PYTHON'S THE MEANING OF LIFE

230. Monty Python's The Meaning of Life by Graham Chapman et al.
Methuen. 126p. col.illus.

THE MUPPET MOVIE

231. The Muppet Movie by Steven Crist.
Fontana, 1979. 118p. illus.
Novelisation based on the film script by Jerry Juhl and Jack Burns.

MURDER IN THE CATHEDRAL

232. The Film of Murder in the Cathedral by T.S. Eliot & George Hoellering.
Faber, 1952. 126p. illus.

MY BEAUTIFUL LAUNDRETTE

233. My Beautiful Laundrette and The Rainbow Sign by Hanif Kureishi.
Faber, 1986. 111p.

MY BROTHER'S KEEPER

234. My Brother's Keeper by Eric Britton.
World Film Publications, 1948. 88p. plates.
Novelisation based on the screenplay by Frank Harvey.

MY LEFT FOOT

235. My Left Foot by Shane Connaughton & Jim Sheridan.
Faber, 1989. 67p. illus.

NELL GWYN

236. Nell Gwyn by Ladbroke Black.
Queensway Library, n.d. 316p. plates.
Novelisation based on the screenplay by Miles Malleson.

THE NEXT OF KIN

237. Thorold Dickinson Special Collection.
See item 540

NINETEEN EIGHTY-FOUR

238. Nineteen Eighty-Four by George Orwell.
Penguin, 1954. 268p.
Novel on which the film is based.

NINETEEN, NINETEEN

239. Nineteen, Nineteen by Hugh Brody & Michael Ignatieff.
Faber, 1985. 96p. illus.

NO ROOM AT THE INN

240. No Room at the Inn by Warwick Mannon.
World Film Publications, 1948. 96p. plates.
Novelisation adapted from the screenplay by Dylan Thomas and Ivan Foxwell, based on the play by Joan Temple.

NO SURRENDER

241. No Surrender: A Deadpan Farce by Alan Bleasdale.
Faber, 1986. 90p. illus.

O LUCKY MAN!

242. O Lucky Man! by Lindsay Anderson & David Sherwin.
Plexus, 1973. 192p. illus.

THE OCTOBER MAN

243. The October Man by Eric Britton.
World Film Publications, 1947. 88p. plates.
Novelisation based on the original screenplay by Eric Ambler.

ODD MAN OUT

244. Filmguide to Odd Man Out by James De Felice.
Indiana University Press, 1975. 85p. bibliog. filmog.

See also item 377

ODETTE

245. Odette by Jerrard Tickell.
Chapman and Hall, 1950. 87p. plates.
Novelisation of the film.

OLD BILL AND SON

246. Old Bill and Son by Bruce Bairnsfather & Ian Dalrymple.
Hutchinson, 1940. 191p. illus.
Novelisation of the film.

OLIVER TWIST

247. Charles Dickens' Oliver Twist by Russell Thorndike.
Raphael Tuck and Sons, c1948. 64p. plates.
Novelisation of the Cineguild film version of the Dickens book.

OTLEY

248. Otley by Martin Waddell.
Pan Books, 1966. 166p.
Novel on which the film is based.

THE OVERLANDERS

249. The Overlanders by Dora Birtles.
World Film Publications, 1946. 148p.
Novelisation based on the screenplay by Harry Watt.

PARIS BY NIGHT

250. Paris by Night by David Hare.
Faber, 1988. 83p. illus.

PERSONAL SERVICES

251. Personal Services by David Leland.
Pavilion Books, 1987. 159p. illus. col.plates.

PICCADILLY

252. Piccadilly: Story of the Film by Arnold Bennett.
The Readers Library Publishing Co, 1929. 187p. plates.
Novelisation of the film.

PICCADILLY INCIDENT

253. Piccadilly Incident by Eric Britton.
World Film Publications, 1947. 89p. illus.
Novelisation based on the screenplay by Nicholas Phipps.

PINK FLOYD – THE WALL

254. Pink Floyd – The Wall.
Avon Books, 1982. Unpaged. col.illus.
Story of the film told in pictures.

PLAYING AWAY

255. Playing Away by Caryl Phillips.
Faber, 1987. 79p. illus.

THE PLOUGHMAN'S LUNCH

256. The Ploughman's Lunch by Ian McEwan.
Methuen, 1985. 34p. illus.

PORRIDGE

257. Porridge: The Inside Story by Paul
Ableman.
Pan Books, 1979. 218p.
Novelisation based on the screenplay by
Dick Clement and Ian La Frenais.

PRICK UP YOUR EARS

258. Prick up Your Ears: The Screenplay by
Alan Bennett.
Faber, 1987. 75p. illus.

THE PRINCE AND THE SHOWGIRL

259. The Prince and the Showgirl: The Script
for the Film by Terence Rattigan.
New American Library, 1957. 127p.
plates.

PRIVATE ANGELO

260. Adrian Pryce-Jones Special Collection.
See item 949

A PRIVATE FUNCTION

261. A Private Function: A Screenplay by Alan
Bennett.
Faber/HandMade Films, 1984. 110p.
illus.

THE PRIVATE LIFE OF HENRY VIII

262. The Private Life of Henry VIII by Lajos
Biro, Arthur Wimperis & Ernest Betts.
Methuen, 1934. 107p.

PROSPERO'S BOOKS

263. Prospero's Books: A Film of
Shakespeare's The Tempest by Peter
Greenaway.
Chatto and Windus, 1991. 168p. illus.
Screenplay with material on the making
of the film.

PROVIDENCE

264. Providence: Un Film pour Alain Resnais
by David Mercer.
Gallimard, 1977. 107p.
Language: French.

THE PUMPKIN EATER

See item 374

PYGMALION

See item 366

THE QUILLER MEMORANDUM

See item 374

RAIDERS OF THE LOST ARK

265. The Making of Raiders of the Lost Ark by
Derek Taylor.
Ballantine Books, 1981. 182p. plates.

THE RAKE'S PROGRESS

266. The Rake's Progress by Warwick
Mannon.
World Film Publications, 1946. 90p.
plates.
Novelisation based on the screenplay by
Sidney Gilliat and Frank Launder.

THE RED SHOES

267. The Red Shoes Ballet: A Critical Study by
Monk Gibbon.
Saturn Press, 1948. 95p. illus.

REPULSION

See item 371

RETURN OF THE JEDI

268. The Art of Return of the Jedi Including
the Complete Script of the Film by
Lawrence Kasdan & George Lucas.
Ballantine Books, 1983. 153p.
col.illus.

269. The Making of Return of the Jedi by John
Phillip Peecher.
Del Rey/Ballantine Books, 1983. 292p.

270. Return of the Jedi by James Kahn.
Futura, 1983. 181p. col.plates.
Novelisation based on the screenplay by
Lawrence Kasdan and George Lucas.

271. Return of the Jedi Sketchbook by Joe
Johnstone & Nilo Rodis-Jamero.
Ballantine Books, 1983. 96p. illus.

REUNION

See item 367

REVOLUTION

272. Sandy Lieberson Special Collection.
See item 818

RHODES OF AFRICA

273. Thirty Thousand Miles for the Films: The
Story of the Filming of Soldiers Three
and Rhodes of Africa by Natalie Barkas.
Blackie, 1937. 197p. illus.

RICHARD III

274. King Richard III by Hugh M. Richmond.
Manchester University Press, 1989.
158p. illus. plates. appendix. bibliog.
index.

ROBIN HOOD PRINCE OF THIEVES

275. Robin Hood Prince of Thieves: The
Official Movie Book by Garth Pearce.
Hamlyn, 1991. 80p. illus.

ROSENCRANTZ AND
GUILDENSTERN ARE DEAD

276. Rosencrantz and Guildenstern Are Dead:
The Film by Tom Stoppard.
Faber, 1991. 64p. illus.

THE ROYAL BALLET

277. The Royal Ballet on Stage and Screen:
The Book of the Royal Ballet Film by
Maurice Moiseiwitsch & Eric Warman.
Heinemann, 1960. 56p. illus.

RUNNERS

278. Runners and Soft Targets by Stephen
Poliakoff.
Methuen, 1984. 117p. illus.

SAMMY AND ROSIE GET LAID

279. Sammy and Rosie Get Laid: The Script
and the Diary by Hanif Kureishi.
Faber, 1988. 127p.

SAN DEMETRIO LONDON

280. Aileen & Michael Balcon Special
Collection.
See item 417

281. The Saga of San Demetrio by F.
Tennyson Jesse.
HMSO, 1942. 64p. illus.
Novelisation of the film.

SARABAND FOR DEAD LOVERS

282. Aileen & Michael Balcon Special
Collection.
See item 417

283. Saraband for Dead Lovers: The Film and
Its Production at Ealing Studios by
Michael Balcon et al.
Convoy Publications, 1948. 103p. illus.

SATURDAY NIGHT AND SUNDAY
MORNING

See item 372

SCHOOL FOR SECRETS

284. School for Secrets by D.L. Ames.
World Film Publications, 1946. 89p.
plates.
Novelisation based on the film written
and directed by Peter Ustinov.

SCOTT OF THE ANTARCTIC

285. Aileen & Michael Balcon Special
Collection.
See item 417

286. Scott of the Antarctic: The Film and Its
Production by David James.
Convoy Publications, 1948. 151p.
photos. maps.

See also item 377

SEBASTIANE

287. Derek Jarman Special Collection.
See item 737

SECRET CEREMONY

288. Joseph Losey Special Collection.
See item 828

SECRET PEOPLE

289. Making a Film: The Story of Secret
People Together with the Shooting Script
of the Film by Thorold Dickinson and
Wolfgang Wilhelm edited by Lindsay
Anderson.
George Allen and Unwin, 1952. 223p.
illus.

290. Thorold Dickinson Special Collection.
See item 540

SECRETS OF NATURE

291. Secrets of Nature by Mary Field & Percy
Smith.
Faber, 1934. 248p. illus.

SERIOUS CHARGE

292. Adrian Pryce-Jones Special Collection.
See item 949

THE SERVANT

293. Joseph Losey Special Collection.
See item 828

294. The Servant: Film Issue edited by
Jonathan Gili.
Isis National, 1964. 38p. illus.

See also item 374

THE SEVENTH VEIL

295. The Seventh Veil by Kit Porlock.
World Film Publications, 1946. 89p.
plates.
Novelisation based on the original
screenplay by Muriel and Sydney Box.

SGT. PEPPER'S LONELY HEARTS CLUB BAND

296. The Official Sgt. Pepper's Lonely Hearts Club Band Scrapbook: The Making of a Hit Movie Musical by Robert Stigwood & Dee Anthony.
Pocket Books, 1978. 80p. illus. (many col.).

297. Sgt. Pepper's Lonely Hearts Club Band by Henry Edwards.
Pocket Books, 1978. 190p. illus.
Novelisation of the film.

THE SHADOW LINE

298. A Change of Tack: Making the Shadow Line by Boleslaw Sulik.
British Film Institute/Educational Advisory Service, 1976. 113p.

SHE'S BEEN AWAY

See item 375

SID & NANCY

299. Sid & Nancy by Alex Cox & Abbe Wool.
Faber, 1986. 143p. illus.

THE SILENT VILLAGE

300. Humphrey Jennings Special Collection.
See item 742

301. The Silent Village: A Story of Wales and Lidice Based on the Crown Film Unit Production by Noel Joseph.
The Pilot Press, 1943. 48p. illus.

THE SLIPPER AND THE ROSE

302. The Slipper and the Rose by Bryan Forbes.
Namara Publications/Quartet Books, 1976. 95p. illus.
Novelisation based on an original script by Bryan Forbes, Robert B. Sherman and Richard M. Sherman.

THE SMALL BACK ROOM

303. The Small Back Room by Nigel Balchin.
Oxford University Press, 1985. 192p.
Novel on which the film is based.

SOURSWEET

304. Soursweet: Screenplay by Ian McEwan.
Faber, 1988. 83p. illus.

SPRING IN PARK LANE

305. Spring in Park Lane by Warwick Mannon.
World Film Publications, 1948. 89p. plates.
Novelisation based on the screenplay by Nicholas Phipps, adapted from the novel by Alice Duer Miller.

STAR

306. Star by Bob Thomas.
Corgi Books, 1968. 150p. illus.
Novelisation based on the screenplay by William Fairchild.

STAR WARS

307. The Art of Star Wars Including the Complete Script of the Film by George Lucas edited by Carol Titelman.
Ballantine Books, 1979. 175p. col.illus.

308. A Guide to the Star Wars Universe: Illustrated Throughout by Raymond L. Velasco.
Ballantine Books, 1984. 215p. illus.

309. Star Wars: A Media Education Pack for Primary Schools by Fiona Wright.
British Film Institute/Education, 1990. 87p. illus. appendix.

310. Star Wars: From the Adventures of Luke Skywalker by George Lucas.
Del Rey/Ballantine Books, 1976. 183p.
Novelisation based on the script by George Lucas.

STEAMING

311. Joseph Losey Special Collection.
See item 828

STRAPLESS

312. Strapless by David Hare.
Faber, 1989. 87p. illus.

STRAW DOGS

313. The Siege of Trencher's Farm by Gordon M. Williams.
Mayflower Paperbacks, 1971. 159p.
Novel on which the film is based.

SUNDAY BLOODY SUNDAY

314. Sunday Bloody Sunday: The Original Screenplay of the John Schlesinger Film by Penelope Gilliatt.
Dodd, Mead and Company, 1986. 151p. illus.

SUPERMAN

315. The Making of Superman the Movie by David Michael Petrou.
W.H. Allen, 1978. 224p.

SUPERMAN III

316. The Great Superman Movie Book by Jovial Bob Stine & Chip Lovitt.
Scholastic Inc, 1981. 48p. illus.

THE TALES OF BEATRIX POTTER

317. The Tale of the Tales: The Beatrix Potter Ballet by Rumer Godden.
Frederick Warne, 1971. 208p. col.illus.

THE TALES OF HOFFMANN

318. The Tales of Hoffmann: A Study of the Film by Monk Gibbon.
Saturn Press, 1951. 96p. illus.

TARGET FOR TONIGHT

319. The Book of the Famous Film Target for Tonight: The Record in Text and Pictures of a Bombing Raid on Germany by Paul Holt.
Hutchinson, c1945. 31p. illus.
Adapted from the scenario by Harry Watt.

THE TECKMAN MYSTERY

320. Adrian Pryce-Jones Special Collection.
See item 949

THE TEMPEST (1979)

321. Derek Jarman Special Collection.
See item 737

THINGS TO COME

322. The Prophetic Soul: A Reading of H.G. Wells' Things to Come together with His Film Treatment Whither Mankind? and the Post Production Script by Leon Stover.
McFarland, 1987. 301p. plates. bibliog. index.
Script and a critical analysis.

323. Things to Come: A Film Story Based on the Material Contained in the History of the Future 'The Shape of Things to Come' by H.G. Wells.
Cresset Press, 1935. 142p.

See also item 378

THE THIRD MAN

324. Carol Reed Special Collection.
See item 963

325. The Third Man: A Film by Graham Greene & Carol Reed.
Lorrimer, 1984. 120p. illus.

See also item 376

THUNDERBALL

326. Thunderball by Ian Fleming.
Triad/Panther, 1978. 234p.
Novel on which the film is based, evolved from a screen treatment by Kevin McClory, J. Whittington and IF.

TIME BANDITS

327. Time Bandits: A Screenplay by Michael Palin & Terry Gilliam.
Hutchinson, 1981. 131p. illus. col. plates.

TIME WITHOUT PITY

328. Adrian Pryce-Jones Special Collection.
See item 949

TO THE DEVIL A DAUGHTER

329. The Facts about a Feature Film: Featuring Hammer Films by Marjorie Bilbow.
Whizzard Publications/André Deutsch, 1978. 53p. illus.
The book charts the production of To the Devil a Daughter.

TOM JONES

330. Tom Jones: A Film Script by John Osborne.
Faber, 1964. 142p.
Original shooting script.

331. Tom Jones: A Film Script by John Osborne.
Grove Press, 1964. 192p.
Script based on the released film.

TOMMY

332. The Story of Tommy by Richard Barnes & Pete Townshend.
Eel Pie Publishing, 1977. 128p. illus. (many col.).

THE TRUE STORY OF LILI MARLENE

333. Humphrey Jennings Special Collection.
See item 742

TURTLE DIARY

See item 367

TWENTY-FIVE YEARS A KING

334. Twenty-Five Years a King by Austen Chamberlain.
A. & C. Black, 1935. 96p. illus.
Book of the Pathé film.

TWO FOR THE ROAD

335. Two for the Road by Frederic Raphael.
Jonathan Cape, 1967. 142p.

TWO LIVING, ONE DEAD

336. Teddy Baird Special Collection.
See item 414

2001: A SPACE ODYSSEY

337.   2001: A Space Odyssey – A Novel by
        Arthur C. Clarke.
        Hutchinson, 1968. 224p.
        Novelisation based on the screenplay by
        Arthur C. Clarke and Stanley Kubrick.

338.   Filmguide to 2001: A Space Odyssey by
        Caroline Geduld.
        Indiana University Press, 1973. 87p.
        bibliog. filmog.

339.   The Lost Worlds of 2001 by Arthur C.
        Clarke.
        New American Library, 1972. 240p.

340.   The Making of Kubrick's 2001 edited by
        Jerome Agel.
        New American Library, 1970. 367p.
        plates.

2010

341.   The Odyssey File by Arthur C. Clarke &
        Peter Hyams.
        Panther, 1985. 133p. col.plates.

UNDER MILK WOOD

342.   Under Milk Wood by Dylan Thomas &
        Andrew Sinclair.
        Lorrimer, 1972. 95p. illus.

UP AGAINST IT

343.   Up Against It: A Screenplay for the
        Beatles by Joe Orton.
        Grove Press, 1979. 70p.
        Unrealised project.

THE UPTURNED GLASS

344.   The Upturned Glass by Kit Porlock.
        World Film Publications, 1947. 88p.
        plates.
        Novelisation based on the screenplay by
        Pamela Kellino and Jno P. Monaghan.

VALENTINO

345.   The Nureyev Valentino: Portrait of a Film
        by Alexander Bland.
        Studio Vista, 1977. 128p. illus.

VICE VERSA

346.   Vice Versa by Warwick Mannon.
        World Film Publications, 1947. 88p.
        illus.
        Novelisation based on the screenplay by
        Peter Ustinov.

THE WAR GAME

347.   The War Game by Peter Watkins.
        Sphere Books/André Deutsch, 1967.
        Unpaged. photos.
        Adaptation of the documentary film.

WAR REQUIEM

348.   War Requiem: The Film by Derek
        Jarman.
        Faber, 1989. 50p.

THE WAY TO THE STARS

349.   The Way to the Stars by Dilys Owen.
        World Film Publications, 1945. 93p.
        plates.
        Novelisation based on the screenplay by
        Terence Rattigan.

WENT THE DAY WELL?

350.   Went the Day Well? by Penelope
        Houston.
        British Film Institute, 1992. 61p.
        illus. bibliog.

WETHERBY

351.   Wetherby: A Film by David Hare.
        Faber, 1985. 92p. illus.

        See also item 370

WHEN THE BOUGH BREAKS

352.   Aileen & Michael Balcon Special
        Collection.
        See item 417

353.   When the Bough Breaks by Warwick
        Mannon.
        World Film Publications, 1947. 89p.
        illus.
        Novelisation adapted from a screenplay
        by Peter Rogers, based on a story by
        Moie Charles and Herbert Victor.

WHERE THE HEART IS

354.   Where the Heart Is by John Boorman &
        Telsche Boorman.
        Faber, 1990. 91p. illus.

WHO GOES THERE?

355.   Adrian Pryce-Jones Special Collection.
        See item 949

WINSTANLEY

356.   Comrade Jacob by David Caute.
        André Deutsch, 1961. 223p.
        Novel on which the film is based.

WISH YOU WERE HERE

357.   Wish You Were Here by David Leland.
        Faber, 1988. 75p. illus.

WORDS FOR BATTLE

358.   Humphrey Jennings Special Collection.
        See item 742

A WORLD APART

359.   A World Apart by Shawn Slovo.
        Faber, 1988. 111p. illus.
        Plus extract from Shawn Slovo's diary.

YOUNG SOUL REBELS

360.   Diary of A Young Soul Rebel by Isaac
        Julien & Colin MacCabe.
        British Film Institute, 1991. 217p.
        illus.
        Includes script by Isaac Julien,
        Derrick Saldaan McClintock and Paul
        Hallam.

YOUNG WINSTON

361.   The Screenplay of the Film Young
        Winston by Carl Foreman.
        Fontana/Collins, 1972. 157p. plates.

ZARDOZ

362.   Zardoz by John Boorman & Bill Stair.
        Pan Books, 1974. 130p.
        Novelisation based on the original
        screenplay by John Boorman.

A ZED & TWO NOUGHTS

363.   A Zed & Two Noughts by Peter
        Greenaway.
        Faber, 1986. 110p.

ZEE & CO.

364.   Zee & Co. by Edna O'Brien.
        Weidenfeld and Nicolson, 1971. 126p.

COLLECTED TITLES

365.   British Film and Independence in India: A
        Case Study of Black Narcissus and
        Bhowani Junction by Roy Stafford.
        MA thesis, 1985. 104p. bibliog.

366.   The Collected Screenplays of Bernard
        Shaw: Pygmalion, The Devil's Disciple,
        Major Barbara, Caesar and Cleopatra and
        Arms and the Man by George Bernard
        Shaw & Bernard F. Dukers.
        George Prior, 1980. 487p. plates.

367.   The Comfort of Strangers and Other
        Screenplays: The Comfort of Strangers,
        Reunion, Turtle Diary and Victory by
        Harold Pinter.
        Faber, 1990. 226p.

368.   Film Scripts Four: A Hard Day's Night,
        The Best Man and Darling edited by
        George P. Garrett.
        Appleton-Century-Crofts, 1972. 500p.
        bibliog.

369.   The French Lieutenant's Woman and
        Other Screenplays. Langrishe Go Down
        and The Last Tycoon by Harold Pinter.
        Faber, 1991. 277p.

370.   Heading Home, Wetherby and Dreams of
        Leaving by David Hare.
        Faber, 1991. 177p.

371.   Knife in the Water, Repulsion and Cul-
        de-Sac: Three Films by Roman Polanski.
        Lorrimer, 1975. 214p. plates.

372.   Masterworks of the British Cinema: Brief
        Encounter, The Third Man, Kind Hearts
        and Coronets. Saturday Night and Sunday
        Morning edited by John Russell Taylor.
        Lorrimer, 1974. 352p. plates.

373.   Reel Terror by Sebastian Wolfe.
        Carrol and Graf, 1992. 249p.
        A collection of original stories that
        inspired horror films including
        'Asylum' and 'Company of Wolves'.

374.   The Servant and Other Screenplays: The
        Servant, The Pumpkin Eater, The
        Quiller Memorandum, Accident and The
        Go-between by Harold Pinter.
        Faber, 1991. 367p.

375.   She's Been Away & Hidden City by
        Stephen Poliakoff.
        Methuen, 1989. 189p. illus.

376.   The Third Man and The Fallen Idol by
        Graham Greene.
        Heinemann, 1966. 195p.
        Stories on which the films are based.

377.   Three British Screen Plays: Brief
        Encounter, Odd Man Out and Scott of the
        Antarctic edited by Roger Manvell.
        Methuen, 1950. 299p. illus.

378.   Two Film Stories: Things to Come and
        The Man Who Could Work Miracles by
        H.G. Wells.
        Cresset Press, 1940. 238p.

PERSONALITIES

Joss ACKLAND

379.   I Must Be in There Somewhere by Joss
        Ackland.
        Hodder and Stoughton, 1989. 250p.
        plates. index.

Rodney ACKLAND

380.   The Celluloid Mistress: Or the Custard
        Pie of Dr. Caligari by Rodney Ackland &
        Elspeth Grant.
        Allan Wingate, 1954. 264p. plates.
        index.

Birt ACRES

381. Birt Acres by Hauke Lange-Fuchs.
Walter G. Mühlau, 1987. 128p. illus.
bibliog. filmog.
Language: German.

Brian AHERNE

382. Aileen & Michael Balcon Special
Collection.
See item 417

383. A Proper Job by Brian Aherne.
Houghton Mifflin Co, 1969. 355p.
plates. filmog.

William ALWYN

384. William Alwyn: A Catalogue of His Music
by Stewart Craggs & Alan Poulton.
Bravura, 1985. 129p. plates. bibliog.
discog.

Eric AMBLER

385. Aileen & Michael Balcon Special
Collection.
See item 417

386. Here Lies Eric Ambler: An
Autobiography by Eric Ambler.
Weidenfeld and Nicolson, 1985. 234p.
plates.

Lindsay ANDERSON

387. Growth and Enlightenment in the Major
Films of Lindsay Anderson by Margaret
Allison Graham.
University Microfilms International,
1979. 162p. bibliog.

388. Lindsay Anderson by Alberto Crespi.
La Nuova Italia, 1989. 111p. bibliog.
filmog. theatrog.
Language: Italian.

389. Lindsay Anderson by Allison Graham.
Twayne Publishers, 1981. 171p. illus.
bibliog. filmog. index.

390. Lindsay Anderson by Elizabeth Sussex.
Movie Paperbacks, 1969. 90p.

391. Lindsay Anderson: A Guide to
References and Resources by Charles
L.P. Silet.
G.K. Hall, 1979. 155p. bibliog. filmog.
index.

Michael ANDERSON

392. Michael Anderson by Terence Heelas.
N.p., 1967. 15p.
Typescript of interview.

Julie ANDREWS

393. Julie Andrews by John Cottrell.
Mayflower Books, 1969. 206p. plates.

394. Julie Andrews: A Bio-bibliography by Les
Spindle.
Greenwood Press, 1989. 153p. illus.
bibliog. filmog. teleog. theatrog.
index.

395. Julie Andrews: A Biography by Robert
Windeler.
Comet, 1984. 223p. illus. filmog.
teleog. theatrog. discog. index.

George ARLISS

396. Aileen & Michael Balcon Special
Collection.
See item 417

397. George Arliss, By Himself.
John Murray, 1940. 287p. illus.

398. My Ten Years in the Studios by George
Arliss.
Little, Brown and Co., 1940. 349p.
plates. index.

399. Up the Years from Bloomsbury: An
Autobiography by George Arliss.
Little, Brown and Co., 1942. 321p.
plates. index.

Richard ARNELL

400. Richard Arnell Special Collection.
Film scores.

Peggy ASHCROFT

401. Ashcroft by Robert Tanitch.
Hutchinson, 1987. 160p. illus. filmog.
teleog. theatrog. index.

402. Peggy Ashcroft by Michael Billington.
John Murray, 1988. 312p. plates. index.

403. Peggy Ashcroft: An Illustrated Study of
Her Work, with a List of Her
Appearances on Stage and Screen by Eric
Keown.
Rockliff, 1955. 102p. illus.

Arthur ASKEY

404. Before Your Very Eyes by Arthur Askey.
Woburn Press, 1975. 191p. plates.

Anthony ASQUITH

405. Anthony Asquith by Peter Noble.
British Film Institute, 1951. 44p.

406. Anthony Asquith Special Collection.
29 items, including diaries, notebooks,
letters and cuttings.

407. Anthony Asquith: A Tribute by George
Elvin et al.
British Film Institute, 1968. Unpaged.
illus.

408. Puffin Asquith: A Biography of the Hon.
Anthony Asquith, Aesthete, Aristocrat,
Prime Minister's Son and Film-maker by
R.J. Minney.
Leslie Frewin, 1973. 273p. plates.
filmog. index.

Richard ATTENBOROUGH

409. Aileen & Michael Balcon Special
Collection.
See item 417

410. Richard Attenborough by David
Robinson.
British Film Institute/National Film
Theatre, 1992. 120p. illus. biog.
filmog.

411. Richard Attenborough: A Pictorial Film
Biography by David Castell.
The Bodley Head, 1984. 128p. illus.
filmog. index.

David AYLOTT

412. From Flicker Alley to Wardour Street by
David Aylott.
Unpublished typescript, 1949. 205p.

Bert AYRES

413. Bert Ayres Special Collection.
26 items including diaries, notebooks,
letters and cuttings.

Teddy BAIRD

414. Teddy Baird Special Collection.
43 items including scripts, production
files, correspondence and personal
memorabilia.

Stanley BAKER

415. Joseph Losey Special Collection.
See item 828

416. Stanley Baker: Portrait of an Actor by
Anthony Storey.
W.H. Allen, 1977. 160p. plates. filmog.

Michael BALCON

417. Aileen & Michael Balcon Special
Collection.
Currently being catalogued, over 1,000
entries so far, dating from 1929.
Includes Gainsborough, Gaumont-British,
MGM and Ealing.

418. Michael Balcon Presents: A Lifetime of
Films by Michael Balcon.
Hutchinson, 1969. 239p.

419. Michael Balcon's 25 Years in Films edited
by Monja Danischewsky.
World Film Publications, 1947. 112p.
photos.

420. Michael Balcon: Producer edited by
Anthony Slide.
British Film Institute/National Film
Theatre, 1969. 14p.

421. Michael Balcon: The Pursuit of British
Cinema edited by Jane Fluegel.
Museum of Modern Art, 1984. 128p.
illus. bibliog. filmog. index.

422. Der Produzent: Michael Balcon und der
Englische Film edited by Geoff Brown.
Volker Spiess, 1981. 319p. illus.
bibliog. filmog. index.
Language: German. Compiled for the
Retrospektive Internationale
Filmfestspiele Berlin 1981.

Geoffrey BARKAS

423. Behind the Camera by Natalie Barkas.
Geoffrey Bles, 1934. 237p.

Joy BATCHELOR

424. Art and Animation: The Story of Halas
and Batchelor Animation Studio 1940–
1980 by Roger Manvell.
Tantivy Press, 1980. Unpaged. illus.
bibliog. filmog.

John BAXTER

425. The Common Touch: The Films of John
Baxter by Geoff Brown & Anthony
Aldgate.
British Film Institute/National Film
Theatre, 1989. 174p. illus. bibliog.
filmog. index.

426. John Baxter Special Collection.
Policy and programme of John Baxter
Productions Ltd.

Cecil BEATON

427. Cecil Beaton: Stage and Film Design by
Charles Spencer.
Academy Editions/St. Martin's Press,
1975. 115p. illus. col.plates. bibliog.

Ivor BEDDOES

428. Ivor Beddoes Special Collection.
16 items, including material on The
Empire Strikes Back, The Longest Day,
Superman, Superman II, The Turning
Point.

Mary Hayley BELL

429. What Shall We Do Tomorrow?: An
Autobiography by Mary Hayley Bell.
Cassell, 1968. 235p. plates.

Alan BENNETT

430. Beyond the Fringe...and Beyond: A
Critical Biography of Alan Bennett, Peter
Cook, Jonathan Miller and Dudley Moore
by Ronald Bergan.
Virgin, 1989. 311p. plates. filmog.
teleog. theatrog. discog. index.

Richard Rodney BENNETT

431. Richard Rodney Bennett: A Bio-bibliography by
Stewart R. Craggs.
Greenwood Press, 1990. 249p. bibliog.
discog.

Sidney BERNSTEIN

432. Sidney Bernstein: A Biography by
Caroline Moorehead.
Jonathan Cape, 1984. 329p. plates.
bibliog. index.

Richard BEST

433. Richard Best Special Collection.
Unpublished manuscript.

Lionel BLAIR

434. Stage-struck: An Autobiography by
Lionel Blair.
Weidenfeld and Nicolson, 1985. 161p.
plates. index.

Brian BLESSED

435. The Dynamite Kid by Brian Blessed.
Bloomsbury, 1992. 248p. plates.

Claire BLOOM

436. Limelight and After: The Education of an
Actress by Claire Bloom.
Weidenfeld and Nicolson, 1982. 187p.
plates.

Dirk BOGARDE

437. Backcloth by Dirk Bogarde.
Viking, 1986. 313p. illus. plates.
index.

438. Dirk Bogarde: Actor edited by Søren
Fischer.
British Film Institute/National Film
Theatre, 1970. 8p. filmog.

439. Dirk Bogarde: The Complete Career
Illustrated by Robert Tanitch.
Ebury Press, 1988. 192p. illus. filmog.
teleog. theatrog. index.

440. The Films of Dirk Bogarde by Margaret
Hinxman & Susan D'Arcy.
Literary Services and Production, 1974.
200p. illus. filmog.

441. Great Meadow by Dirk Bogarde.
Viking, 1992. 207p.

442. Joseph Losey Special Collection.
Material held in Joseph Losey Special
Collection.

443. An Orderly Man by Dirk Bogarde.
Chatto and Windus, 1983. 291p. plates.
index.

444. A Particular Friendship by Dirk Bogarde.
Viking, 1989. 200p. plates. index.
A selection of personal letters.

445. A Postillion Struck by Lightning by Dirk
Bogarde.
Chatto and Windus, 1977. 265p. illus.
plates. index.

446. Snakes and Ladders by Dirk Bogarde.
Chatto and Windus, 1978. 339p. plates.
index.

John BOORMAN

447. Bright Dreams, Hard Knocks: A Journal
for 1991 edited by John Boorman.
Faber, 1992. p.5–120.
In 'Projections: A Forum for
Filmmakers' edited by JB and Walter
Donoghue.

448. John Boorman by Michel Ciment.
Faber, 1986. 271p. illus. bibliog.
filmog. index.

449. John Boorman: Hope and glory =
Hoffnung und Ruhm: Das Portrait des
Kino-Magiers by Rolf Giesen.
Wilhelm Goldmann, 1987. 126p. illus.
bibliog.
Language: German.

John and Roy BOULTING

450. The Director's Approach to Film-making:
John and Roy Boulting by Catherine De
La Roche.
Transcript of BBC interview, 1947. 8p.

Muriel BOX

451. Odd Woman Out: An Autobiography by
Muriel Box.
Leslie Frewin, 1974. 272p. plates.
index.

Kenneth BRANAGH

452. Beginning by Kenneth Branagh.
Chatto and Windus, 1989. 244p. illus.

Clive BROOK

453. Clive Brook Special Collection.
88 items including theatrical material,
scrapbooks, correspondence, typescript
of unpublished autobiography.

Peter BROOK

454. Peter Brook: A Biography by J.C.
Trewin.
Macdonald, 1971. 216p. plates. bibliog.
theatrog. filmog. index.

Adrian BRUNEL

455. Aileen & Michael Balcon Special
Collection.
See item 417

456. Nice Work: The Story of Thirty Years in
British Film Production by Adrian
Brunel.
Forbes Robertson, 1949. 217p. photos.

Dora BRYAN

457. According to Dora by Dora Bryan & Kay
Hunter.
The Bodley Head, 1987. 199p. plates.

Jack BUCHANAN

458. Top Hat and Tails: The Story of Jack
Buchanan by Michael Marshall.
Elm Tree Books, 1978. 271p. illus.
bibliog. filmog. discog. index.

Richard BURTON

459. Burton by Hollis Alpert.
G.P. Putnam's Sons, 1986. 270p. plates.

460. Burton: The Man behind the Myth by
Penny Junor.
Sidgwick and Jackson, 1985. 210p.
plates. index.

461. Meeting Mrs. Jenkins by Richard Burton.
William Morrow, 1966. 25p. plates.

462. A Portrait of Richard Burton 1925–1984
by Paul Ferris.
Weidenfeld and Nicolson, 1984. 96p.
illus. filmog. theatrog.

463. Rich: The Life of Richard Burton by
Melvyn Bragg.
Hodder and Stoughton, 1988. 533p.
plates. filmog. teleog. theatrog.
discog. index.

464. Richard Burton by Fergus Cashin.
W.H. Allen, 1982. 191p. illus. index.

465. Richard Burton by Paul Ferris.
Weidenfeld and Nicolson, 1981. 212p.
plates. bibliog. index.

466. Richard Burton by Ruth Waterbury.
Mayflower Books, 1965. 172p. plates.

467. Richard Burton: A Biography by John
Cottrell & Fergus Cashin.
Arthur Barker, 1971. 376p. plates.

468. Richard Burton: My Brother by Graham
Jenkins & Barry Turner.
Michael Joseph, 1988. 248p. plates.

Max BYGRAVES

469. After Thoughts by Max Bygraves.
W.H. Allen, 1988. 206p. illus.

470. I Wanna Tell You a Story by Max
Bygraves.
W.H. Allen, 1976. 195p. plates. index.

Michael CAINE

471. Candidly Caine by Elaine Gallagher & Ian
Macdonald.
Robson Books/LWT, 1990. 318p. plates.
filmog. teleog. theatrog.
Incorporating original conversations
with Michael Caine and comments from
his friends and co-stars.

472. The Films of Michael Caine by Emma
Andrews.
Barnden Castell Williams Ltd., 1974.
47p. illus. filmog.

473. Michael Caine by Philip Judge.
Hippocrene/Spellmount Books, 1985. 96p.
illus. filmog.

474. Michael Caine: A Biography by Emma
Andrews.
LSP Books, 1982. 94p. illus. filmog.

475. My Name is Michael Caine: A Lifetime in
Films by Anne Billson.
Muller, 1991. 192p. illus. index.

476. Raising Caine: The Authorized Biography
by William Hall.
Sidgwick and Jackson, 1981. 260p.
plates. filmog. index.

477. What's It All About? by Michael Caine.
Century, 1992. 494p. plates. index.

Simon CALLOW

478. Being an Actor by Simon Callow.
Methuen, 1984. 190p. plates. index.

Geoffrey H. CARDER

479. The Man in the Box: Memoirs of a
Cinema Projectionist by Geoffrey H.
Carder.
United Writers, 1984. 96p.

Ian CARMICHAEL

480. Will the Real Ian Carmichael... by Ian
Carmichael.
Macmillan, 1979. 400p. illus. index.

John Paddy CARSTAIRS

481. Aileen & Michael Balcon Special
Collection.
See item 417

482. Hadn't We the Gaiety? by John Paddy
Carstairs.
Hurst and Blackett, 1940. 107p. illus.

483. Honest Injun! A Light-hearted
Autobiography by John Paddy Carstairs.
Hurst and Blackett, 1942. 168p. illus.

484. Kaleidoscope and a Jaundiced Eye: A
Further Experiment in Autobiography by
John Paddy Carstairs.
Hurst and Blackett, n.d.. 141p. plates.

Maurice CARTER

485. The Darker Side of the Screen by Maurice
Carter.
Unpublished typescript, 1981. 189p.

W. 'Bill' CARTLIDGE

486. Golden Hill to Golden Square by W. 'Bill' Cartlidge.
New Horizon, 1982. 505p.

Alberto CAVALCANTI

487. Alberto Cavalcanti by Lorenzo Pellizzari & Claudio M. Valentinetti.
Locarno Film Festival, 1988. 461p.
illus. filmog.
Language: Italian.

Ian CHARLESON

488. For Ian Charleson: A Tribute.
Constable, 1990. 130p. plates.

Julie CHRISTIE

489. Joseph Losey Special Collection.
See item 828

490. Julie Christie by Michael Feeney Callan.
W.H. Allen, 1984. 192p. illus.
col.plates. filmog. index.

Sarah CHURCHILL

491. Keep on Dancing: An Autobiography by Sarah Churchill.
Weidenfeld and Nicolson, 1981. 243p.
plates. index.

Petula CLARK

492. This Is My Song: A Biography of Petula Clark by Andrea Kon.
W.H. Allen, 1983. 256p. plates. index.

T.E.B. CLARKE

493. Aileen & Michael Balcon Special Collection.
See item 417

494. This Is Where I Came In by T.E.B. Clarke.
Michael Joseph, 1974. 207p. plates.

Jack CLAYTON

495. Jack Clayton: A Guide to References and Resources by Georg M.A. Gaston.
G.K. Hall, 1981. 133p. index.

John CLEESE

496. Cleese Encounters by Jonathan Margolis.
Chapmans, 1992. 286p. plates. filmog.
index.

Joan COLLINS

497. Past Imperfect by Joan Collins.
W.H. Allen, 1978. 252p. illus.

Sean CONNERY

498. The Films of Sean Connery by Robert Sellers.
Vision Press, 1990. 192p. plates.
bibliog. index.

499. The James Bond Man: The Films of Sean Connery by Andrew Rissik.
Elm Tree Books, 1983. 217p. plates.
filmog. index.

500. Sean Connery by Emma Andrews.
LSP Books, 1982. 92p. illus. filmog.

501. Sean Connery by Robert Tanitch.
Chapmans, 1992. 192p. illus. chron.
index.

502. Sean Connery: A Biography by Kenneth Passingham.
Sidgwick and Jackson, 1983. 160p.
plates. filmog. index.

503. Sean Connery: Gilt-edged Bond by Richard Gant.
Mayflower Books, 1967. 109p. plates.

504. Sean Connery: His Life and Films by Michael Feeney Callan.
W.H. Allen, 1983. 290p. plates. filmog.
index.

Peter COOK

505. Beyond the Fringe...and Beyond: A Critical Biography of Alan Bennett, Peter Cook, Jonathan Miller and Dudley Moore by Ronald Bergan.
Virgin, 1989. 311p. plates. filmog.
teleog. theatrog. discog. index.

Gladys COOPER

506. Gladys Cooper: A Biography by Sheridan Morley.
Heinemann, 1979. 314p. plates. bibliog.
filmog. index.

507. Without Veils: The Intimate Biography of Gladys Cooper by Sewell Stokes.
Davies, 1953. 243p. photos.

Cicely COURTNEIDGE

508. Aileen & Michael Balcon Special Collection.
See item 417

509. Cicely by Cicely Courtneidge.
Hutchinson, 1953. 224p. photos.

Noel COWARD

510. Coward and Company by Richard Briers.
Robson Books, 1987. 151p. illus.
plates.

511. Future Indefinite by Noel Coward.
Heinemann, 1954. 336p. plates.

512. The Life of Noel Coward by Cole Lesley.
Jonathan Cape, 1976. 499p. plates.
bibliog. index.

513. The Noel Coward Diaries edited by Graham Payn & Sheridan Morley.
Weidenfeld and Nicolson, 1982. 698p.
chron. index.

514. Noel Coward Special Collection.
Collection of press cuttings.

515. Present Indicative by Noel Coward.
Heinemann, 1951. 431p. plates.

516. A Talent to Amuse: A Biography of Noel Coward by Sheridan Morley.
Pavilion/Michael Joseph, 1986. 363p.
plates. bibliog. filmog. teleog.
theatrog. index.

Michael CRAWFORD

517. Phantom: Michael Crawford Unmasked by Anthony Hayward.
Weidenfeld and Nicolson, 1991. 196p.
plates. appendix. filmog. index.

The CRAZY GANG

518. The Crazy Gang: A Personal Reminiscence by Maureen Owen.
Weidenfeld and Nicolson, 1986. 150p.
plates. bibliog. index.

Roland CULVER

519. Not Quite a Gentleman by Roland Culver.
William Kimber, 1979. 192p. plates.

Peter CUSHING

520. Past Forgetting: Memoirs of the Hammer Years by Peter Cushing.
Weidenfeld and Nicolson, 1988. 112p.
illus. plates. filmog. teleog.
theatrog. index.

521. Peter Cushing: An Autobiography by Peter Cushing.
Weidenfeld and Nicolson, 1986. 157p.
plates. filmog. teleog. theatrog.
index.

522. Peter Cushing: The Gentle Man of Horror and His 91 Films by Deborah Del Vecchio & Tom Johnson.
McFarland, 1992. 465p. illus. index.
bibliog. filmog.

Claude DAMPIER

523. Claude Dampier Special Collection.
10 items, including scripts and programmes.

524. Claude Dampier, Mrs. Gibson and Me by Billie Carlyle.
Billie Carlyle, 1988. 116p. plates.
index.

Bebe DANIELS

525. Bebe and Ben by Jill Allgood.
Robert Hale, 1975. 192p. plates.
filmog.

526. Bebe Daniels Special Collection.
Scrapbooks.

527. Life with the Lyons: The Autobiography of Bebe Daniels and Ben Lyon by Bebe Daniels & Ben Lyon.
Odhams, 1953. 256p. plates. index.

Monja DANISCHEWSKY

528. White Russian, Red Face by Monja Danischewsky.
Gollancz, 1966. 192p. plates.

Albert DE COURVILLE

529. I Tell You by Albert De Courville.
Chapman and Hall, 1928. 253p. plates.
index.

Lee DE FOREST

530. A Conqueror of Space: An Authorised Biography of the Life and Work of Lee De Forest by Georgette Carneal.
Horace Liveright, 1930. 296p.

Catherine DE LA ROCHE

531. Performance by Catherine De La Roche.
The Dunmore Press, 1988. 243p. illus.
index.

Basil DEAN

532. Basil Dean Special Collection.
12 items including minutes, correspondence and budgets.

533. Mind's Eye: An Autobiography 1927–1972 by Basil Dean.
Hutchinson, 1973. 340p. plates. index.

534. Seven Ages: An Autobiography 1888–1927 by Basil Dean.
Hutchinson, 1970. 340p. index. illus.

Bernard DELFONT

535. East End, West End by Bernard Delfont & Barry Turner.
Macmillan, 1990. 250p. plates. filmog.
index.

Judi DENCH

536. Judi Dench, a Great Deal of Laughter: An Authorized Biography by Gerald Jacobs.
Weidenfeld and Nicolson, 1985. 167p.
plates. theatrog. index.

Michael DENISON

537. Double Act by Michael Denison.
Michael Joseph, 1985. 306p. plates.
index.

538. Overture and Beginners by Michael
Denison.
Gollancz, 1973. 255p. plates. index.

Florence DESMOND

539. Florence Desmond, by Herself by
Florence Desmond.
Harrap, 1953. 303p. photos.

Thorold DICKINSON

540. Thorold Dickinson Special Collection.
48 items including scripts, production
files for realised and unrealised
projects.

541. Thorold Dickinson: The Man and His
Films by Jeffrey Richards.
Croom Helm, 1986. 215p. plates.
bibliog. filmog. index.

Edward DMYTRYK

542. It's a Hell of a Life, But Not a Bad Living
by Edward Dmytryk.
New York Times Books, 1978. 310p.
illus. filmog. index.

Robert DONAT

543. Aileen & Michael Balcon Special
Collection.
See item 417

544. Mr. Chips: The Life of Robert Donat by
Kenneth Barrow.
Methuen, 1985. 208p. plates. filmog.
theatrog. index.

545. Robert Donat: A Biography by J.C.
Trewin.
Heinemann, 1968. 252p. plates. filmog.
index.

Diana DORS

546. Behind Closed Dors by Diana Dors.
W.H. Allen, 1979. 208p. illus.

547. Diana Dors: Only a Whisper Away by
Joan Flory & Damien Walne.
Lennard, 1987. 288p. plates. index.

548. Dors by Dors by Diana Dors.
Macdonald Futura, 1981. 317p. plates.

549. For Adults Only by Diana Dors.
W.H. Allen, 1978. 256p. illus.

550. Swingin' Dors by Diana Dors.
World Distributors, 1960. 187p. plates.

Charlie DRAKE

551. Drake's Progress by Charlie Drake.
Robson Books, 1986. 244p. plates.

Gerald DU MAURIER

552. Gerald du Maurier: The Last Actor-
Manager by James Harding.
Hodder and Stoughton, 1989. 198p.
plates. bibliog. index.

Charles DUNCAN

553. A Photographic Pilgrim's Progress: Being
the Adventures of an Itinerant
Photographer among Cameras, Cabbages
and Kings by Charles Duncan.
Focal Press, 1954. 155p.

Stephen DWOSKIN

554. Stephen Dwoskin by the Filmoteca
Nacional de España.
FNE, 1976. Unpaged. illus. biofilmog.
Language: Spanish.

Jimmy EDWARDS

555. Six of the Best by Jimmy Edwards.
Robson Books, 1984. 224p. plates.

Mary ELLIS

556. Those Dancing Years: An Autobiography
by Mary Ellis.
John Murray, 1982. 182p. plates. index.

Maurice ELVEY

557. The Commercial Imperative in the British
Film Industry: Maurice Elvey, a Case
Study by Linda Wood.
British Film Institute, 1987. 89p.
filmog.

Edith EVANS

558. Edith Evans: A Personal Memoir by Jean
Batters.
Hart-Davis MacGibbon, 1977. 159p.
illus. index.

559. Edith Evans: An Illustrated Study of
Dame Edith's Work, with a List of Her
Appearances on Stage and Screen by J.C.
Trewin.
Rockliff, 1954. 116p. photos.

560. Ned's Girl: An Authorised Biography of
Dame Edith Evans by Bryan Forbes.
Elm Tree Books, 1977. 297p. plates.
index.

Douglas FAIRBANKS JR.

561. Knight Errant: A Biography of Douglas
Fairbanks Jr. by Brian Connell.
Hodder and Stoughton, 1955. 288p.
photos.

562. The Salad Days by Douglas Fairbanks Jr..
Doubleday, 1988. 431p. illus. filmog.
index.

David FARRAR

563. Aileen & Michael Balcon Special
Collection.
See item 417

564. No Royal Road: Autobiography of David
Farrar.
Mortimer Publications, 1947. 171p.
plates.

Shirley Anne FIELD

565. A Time for Love: An Autobiography by
Shirley Anne Field.
Bantam, 1991. 255p. plates. index.

Sid FIELD

566. What a Performance: A Life of Sid Field
by John Fisher.
Seeley Service, 1975. 236p. plates.
index.

Gracie FIELDS

567. Aileen & Michael Balcon Special
Collection.
See item 417

568. Gracie Fields by Muriel Burgess &
Tommy Keen.
W.H. Allen, 1980. 125p. illus.

569. Gracie Fields: Her Life in Pictures by
Peter Hudson.
Robson Books, 1989. 120p. illus.

570. Our Gracie by Bert Aza.
Pitkins, 1951. 32p. photos.

571. Our Gracie: The Life of Dame Gracie
Fields by Joan Moules.
Robert Hale, 1983. 247p. plates.
discog. filmog. theatrog. index.

572. Sing as We Go: The Autobiography of
Gracie Fields.
Muller, 1960. 203p. illus.

Peter FINCH

573. Finch, Bloody Finch: A Biography of
Peter Finch by Elaine Dundy.
Michael Joseph, 1980. 320p. plates.
filmog. index.

574. Finchy: My Life with Peter Finch by
Yolande Finch.
Arrow Books, 1980. 216p. plates.

575. Peter Finch: A Biography by Trader
Faulkner.
Angus and Robertson, 1979. 312p.
plates. filmog. index.

Terence FISHER

576. The Charm of Evil: The Life and Films of
Terence Fisher by Wheeler Winston
Dixon.
Scarecrow Press, 1991. 574p. illus.
filmog. bibliog. index.

577. Terence Fisher by Stéphane Bourgoin.
Edilig, 1984. 127p. illus. bibliog.
filmog. index.
Language: French.

Robert FLAHERTY

578. Aileen & Michael Balcon Special
Collection.
See item 417

579. The Innocent Eye: The Life of Robert J.
Flaherty by Arthur Calder-Marshall,
Paul Rotha & Basil Wright.
W.H. Allen, 1963. 304p. illus. index.

580. The Odyssey of a Film-maker: Robert
Flaherty's Story by Frances Hubbard
Flaherty.
Beta Phi Mu, 1960. 45p. illus.

581. Robert Flaherty: A Guide to References
and Resources by William T. Murphy.
George Prior/G.K. Hall, 1978. 171p.
bibliog. filmog. index.

582. Robert J. Flaherty: A Biography by Paul
Rotha & Jay Ruby.
University of Pennsylvania Press, 1983.
359p. bibliog. filmog. index.

583. The Vision of Robert Flaherty: The Artist
as Myth and Filmmaker by Richard
Barsam.
Indiana University Press, 1988. 144p.
illus. index.

584. The World of Robert Flaherty by Richard
Griffith.
Gollancz, 1953. 165p. photos.

Bud FLANAGAN

585. My Crazy Life, the Autobiography of Bud
Flanagan.
Muller, 1961. 206p. plates.

Bryan FORBES

586. A Divided Life: Memoirs by Bryan
Forbes.
Heinemann, 1992. 376p. plates.
appendix. index.

587. Notes for a Life by Bryan Forbes.
Collins, 1974. 384p. plates. index.

Walter FORDE

588. Walter Forde edited by Geoff Brown.
British Film Institute, 1977. 51p.
filmog.

589. Walter Forde Special Collection.
79 items, mainly scripts and
pressbooks; some scrapbooks and
ephemera.

Denis FORMAN

590. Aileen & Michael Balcon Special
Collection.
See item 417

591. Son of Adam by Denis Forman.
André Deutsch, 1990. 201p. plates.

George FORMBY

592. Aileen & Michael Balcon Special
Collection.
See item 417

593. George Formby by John Fisher.
Woburn–Futura, 1975. 96p. illus.

594. George Formby: A Biography by Alan
Randall & Ray Seaton.
W.H. Allen, 1974. 192p. plates. filmog.
discog.

James FOX

595. Comeback: An Actor's Direction by
James Fox.
Hodder and Stoughton, 1983. 151p.
plates.

The FOX FAMILY

596. Completely Foxed by Angela Fox.
Collins, 1989. 189p. illus. index.

597. Slightly Foxed By My Theatrical Family
by Angela Fox.
Collins, 1986. 214p. plates. index.

William FOX TALBOT

598. Fox Talbot: Photographer by Robert
Lassam.
Compton Press/Dovecote Press, 1979.
90p. plates. bibliog.
Mainly illustrations.

Freddie FRANCIS

599. The Films of Freddie Francis by Wheeler
Winston Dixon.
Scarecrow Press, 1991. 304p. illus.
bibliog. filmog. index.

Harold FRENCH

600. I Swore I Never Would by Harold French.
Secker and Warburg, 1970. 206p.

William FRIESE-GREENE

601. Friese-Greene: Close up of an Inventor by
Ray Allister.
Marsland Publications, 1948. 192p.
photos.

602. William Friese-Greene and the Origins of
the Kinematography by Brian Coe.
19p. illus. diagrs.
Reprinted from March–April 1962 issues
of The Photographic Journal.

603. William Friese-Greene Special Collection.
Provisional specification for taking
photographs in rapid series.
Unidentified script.

Peter GIDAL

604. L' Avant-garde Cinématographique
Britannique 1960–1980: Examen des
Propositions des Cinéastes Peter Gidal et
Malcolm Le Grice. Contribution à une
Théorie Expérimental by Alain Alcide
Sudre.
Unpublished thesis, n.d.. 369p.
bibliog.
Language: French.

605. Peter Gidal by Paul Willemen.
British Film Institute/Film
Availability, 1979. 43p. filmog.

John GIELGUD

606. An Actor and His Time by John Gielgud,
John Miller & John Powell.
Sidgwick and Jackson, 1989. 300p.
illus. index.

607. The Ages of Gielgud: An Actor at Eighty
edited by Ronald Harwood.
Hodder and Stoughton, 1984. 182p.
plates. filmog. teleog. theatrog.
index.

608. Backward Glances. Part I: Times for
Reflection; Part II: Distinguished
Company by John Gielgud.
Hodder and Stoughton, 1989. 214p.
plates. index.

609. Early Stages by John Gielgud.
Falcon Press, 1953. 269p. photos.

610. Gielgud by Robert Tanitch.
Harrap, 1988. 192p. illus. filmog.
teleog. theatrog. index.

611. Gielgud Stories: Anecdotes, Sayings and
Impressions of Sir John Gielgud by
Clive Fisher.
Futura, 1988. 110p. bibliog.

612. John Gielgud: A Celebration by Giles
Brandreth.
Pavilion Books/Michael Joseph, 1984.
186p. illus. bibliog. filmog. teleog.
theatrog. index.

Sidney GILLIAT

613. Aileen & Michael Balcon Special
Collection.
See item 417

614. Launder and Gilliat by Geoff Brown.
British Film Institute, 1977. 159p.
filmog. index.

Lew GRADE

615. Last of a Kind: The Sinking of Lew Grade
by Quentin Falk & Dominic Prince.
Quartet Books, 1987. 183p. plates.
filmog. index.

616. Still Dancing: My Story by Lew Grade.
Collins, 1987. 314p. plates. index.

The GRADE FAMILY

617. The First Family of British Entertainment
by Hunter Davies.
Weidenfeld and Nicolson, 1981. 268p.
plates. index.

618. My Fabulous Brothers by Rita Grade
Freeman.
W.H. Allen, 1982. 203p. illus.

Roger GRAEF

619. Nothing But the Truth: Cinéma Vérité
and the Films of the Roger Graef Team
by John Wyver.
British Film Institute, 1982. 34p.
filmog.

Stewart GRANGER

620. Sparks Fly Upward by Stewart Granger.
Granada, 1981. 416p. plates. index.

Dulcie GRAY

621. Looking Forward, Looking Back: An
Autobiography by Dulcie Gray.
Hodder and Stoughton, 1991. 199p.
plates. filmog. index.

Hughie GREEN

622. Opportunity Knocked by Hughie Green.
Muller, 1965. 224p. plates.

Peter GREENAWAY

623. The Draughtsman's Contract Special
Collection.
Twenty items including production
material.

624. The Early Films of Peter Greenaway
edited by Liz Reddish.
British Film Institute, 1992. 12p.
illus.

625. The Films of Peter Greenaway by Laura
Denham.
MA thesis, 1992. 68p. bibliog.

626. Papers by Peter Greenaway.
Dis Voir, 1990. 125p. illus.
Language: English and French.

627. Peter Greenaway by Daniel Caux et al.
Dis Voir, 1987. 127p. illus. bibliog.
filmog.
Language: French.

628. Peter Greenaway by Michael Nyman et al.
Dis Voir, 1987. 127p. illus. filmog.
Language: French.

Graham GREENE

629. Graham Greene and Cinema by Judith
Adamson.
Pilgrim Books, 1984. 191p. illus.
filmog. bibliog. index.

630. Graham Greene: The Films of His Fiction
by Gene D. Phillips.
Teachers College Press, 1974. 203p.
illus. bibliog. filmog.

631. Joseph Losey Special Collection.
See item 828

632. The Other Man: Conversations with
Graham Greene by Marie-Françoise
Allain.
Bodley Head, 1983. 187p.

633. Travels in Greeneland: The Cinema of
Graham Greene by Quentin Falk.
Quartet Books, 1984. 229p. plates.
filmog. index.

John GREENWOOD

634. John Greenwood Special Collection.
Film scores.

Joyce GRENFELL

635. Darling Ma: Letters to Her Mother 1932–
1944 by Joyce Grenfell & James Roose-
Evans.
Hodder and Stoughton, 1988. 360p.
plates. index.

636. In Pleasant Places by Joyce Grenfell.
Macmillan, 1979. 304p. illus. index.

637. Joyce Grenfell Requests the Pleasure by
Joyce Grenfell.
Macmillan, 1976. 295p. illus. index.

638. Joyce Grenfell: The Time of My Life,
Entertaining the Troops, Her Wartime
Journals edited by Joyce Grenfell &
James Roose-Evans.
Hodder and Stoughton, 1989. 300p.
illus. plates. index.

639. Joyce, by Herself, and Her Friends edited
by Reggie Grenfell & Richard Garnett.
Macmillan, 1980. 200p. plates. index.

John GRIERSON

640. Aileen & Michael Balcon Special
Collection.
See item 417

641. The Colonized Eye: Rethinking the
Grierson Legend by Joyce Nelson.
Between the Lines, 1988. 197p. index.

642. Film and Reform: John Grierson and the
Documentary Film Movement by Ian
Aitken.
Routledge, 1990. 246p. illus. bibliog.
index.

643. Grierson on Documentary by John
Grierson & Forsyth Hardy.
Faber, 1979. 232p. index.

644. Grierson on the Movies by John Grierson & Forsyth Hardy.
Faber, 1981. 200p. index.

645. John Grierson: A Documentary Biography by Forsyth Hardy.
Faber, 1979. 298p. plates. index.

646. John Grierson: A Guide to References and Resources by Jack C. Ellis.
G.K. Hall, 1986. 262p. bibliog. filmog. index.

647. John Grierson: Film Master by James Beveridge.
Macmillan, 1978. 361p. illus. index.

648. John Grierson: The Man and the Memory by Denis Forman.
The John Grierson Archive/University of Stirling, 1978. 33p.

649. Researchers' Guide to John Grierson: Films, Reference Sources, Collections, Data edited by John Chittock.
Grierson Memorial Trust, 1990. 36p. illus. filmog. bibliog.

Alec GUINNESS

650. Aileen & Michael Balcon Special Collection.
See item 417

651. Alec Guinness by Kenneth Tynan.
Rockliff, 1953. 108p. photos.

652. Alec Guinness on Screen by Allan Hunter.
Polygon Books, 1982. 103p. illus. filmog. index.

653. Alec Guinness: A Celebration by John Russell Taylor.
Pavilion Books/Michael Joseph, 1984. 184p. illus. bibliog. teleog. theatrog.

654. Alec Guinness: The Films by Kenneth Von Gunden.
McFarland, 1987. 350p. illus. bibliog. filmog. index.

655. Blessings in Disguise by Alec Guinness.
Hamish Hamilton, 1985. 238p. plates. index.

656. Dear Alec: Guinness at 75 edited by Ronald Harwood.
Hodder and Stoughton, 1989. 140p. plates. index.

657. Guinness by Robert Tanitch.
Harrap, 1989. 168p. plates. filmog. teleog. theatrog. discog. index.

William HAGGAR

658. Biography of William Haggar: Actor, Showman and Pioneer of the Film Industry by Lily May Richards.
The Author, n.d. 36p.

John HALAS

659. Art and Animation: The Story of Halas and Batchelor Animation Studio 1940–1980 by Roger Manvell.
Tantivy Press, 1980. Unpaged. illus. bibliog. filmog.

Henry HALL

660. Here's to the Next Time by Henry Hall.
Odhams, 1955. 240p. photos.

Peter HALL

661. Peter Hall's Diaries: The Story of a Dramatic Battle edited by John Goodwin.
Hamish Hamilton, 1983. 507p. plates. index.

Leslie HALLIWELL

662. Seats in All Parts: Half a Lifetime at the Movies by Leslie Halliwell.
Granada, 1985. 202p. illus. index.

Robert HAMER

663. Aileen & Michael Balcon Special Collection.
See item 417

664. Robert Hamer 1911–1963 by Jacques Belmans.
L'Avant Scène du Cinéma, 1976. 39p. illus. filmog.
Language: French.

Sheila HANCOCK

665. Ramblings of an Actress by Sheila Hancock.
Hutchinson, 1987. 241p. plates. index.

Tony HANCOCK

666. Hancock by Freddy Hancock & David Nathan.
Ariel Books, 1986. 200p. plates.

667. Lady Don't Fall Backwards: A Memoir by Joan Le Mesurier.
Sidgwick and Jackson, 1988. 195p. plates.

668. Tony Hancock by Philip Oakes.
Woburn–Futura, 1975. 96p. illus.

669. Tony Hancock 'Artiste': A Tony Hancock Companion by Roger Wilmut.
Methuen, 1985. 271p. illus. bibliog. filmog. teleog. index.

Cedric HARDWICKE

670. A Victorian in Orbit: The Irreverent Memoirs of Sir Cedric Hardwicke by James Brough.
Methuen, 1961. 311p. illus.

David HARE

671. Writing Left-handed by David Hare.
Faber, 1991. 189p. filmog. appendix.

Robertson HARE

672. Yours Indubitably by Robertson Hare.
Robert Hale, 1956. 192p. illus.

Richard HARRIS

673. Richard Harris: An Actor by Accident by Gus Smith.
Robert Hale, 1990. 198p. plates. filmog. index.

Rex HARRISON

674. A Damned Serious Business by Rex Harrison.
Bantam Press, 1990. 290p. plates. bibliog. filmog. theatrog. index.

675. Fatal Charm: The Life of Rex Harrison by Alexander Walker.
Weidenfeld and Nicolson, 1992. 574p. plates. index.

676. Love, Honour and Dismay by Elizabeth Harrison.
Weidenfeld and Nicolson, 1976. 168p. plates. index.

677. Rex Harrison by Allen Eyles.
W.H. Allen, 1985. 240p. plates. bibliog. filmog. teleog. theatrog. index.

678. Rex Harrison: A Biography by Nicholas Wapshott.
Chatto and Windus, 1991. 341p. index.

679. Rex Harrison: The First Biography by Roy Moseley & Philip and Martin Masheter.
New English Library, 1987. 350p. plates. bibliog. filmog. theatrog. index.

680. Rex: An Autobiography by Rex Harrison.
Macmillan, 1974. 262p. plates. index.

Ray HARRYHAUSEN

681. Film Fantasy Scrapbook by Ray Harryhausen.
A.S. Barnes/Tantivy Press, 1981. 150p. illus. col.plates.

682. From the Land Beyond: The Films of Willis O'Brien and Ray Harryhausen by Jeff Rovin.
Berkley Windhover Books, 1977. 277p. illus. index.

683. Ray Harryhausen: Film Producer and Creator of Special Visual Effects by Richard Greene.
Southampton Film Theatre, 1974. 27p. illus. filmog.
Programme compiled for a discussion between Ray Harryhausen and Tony Dalton.

Laurence HARVEY

684. One Tear is Enough by Pauline Stone.
Michael Joseph, 1975. 176p. plates.

685. The Prince: Being the Public and Private Life of Larushka Mischa Skikne, a Jewish Lithuanian Vagabond, Otherwise Known as Laurence Harvey by Des Hickey & Gus Smith.
Leslie Frewin, 1975. 272p. plates. index.

Jack HAWKINS

686. Aileen & Michael Balcon Special Collection.
See item 417

687. Anything for a Quiet Life: The Autobiography of Jack Hawkins by Jack Hawkins.
Elm Tree Books/Hamish Hamilton, 1973. 180p. plates. index.

Will HAY

688. Good Morning Boys: Will Hay, Master of Comedy by Ray Seaton & Roy Martin.
Barrie and Jenkins, 1978. 174p. illus. filmog.

689. Will Hay Special Collection.
18 items including scrapbooks, notes for autobiography, letters and ephemera.

Patricia HAYES

690. A Funny Old Life by Patricia Hayes & Teresa Jennings.
Robson Books, 1990. 208p. illus.

Robert HELPMANN

691. Helpmann: The Authorised Biography of Sir Robert Helpmann, C.B.E. by Elizabeth Salter.
Angus and Robertson, 1978. 247p. illus. index.

Audrey HEPBURN

692. Audrey Hepburn by Ian Woodward.
W.H. Allen, 1984. 312p. plates. filmog. index.

693. Audrey: A Biography of Audrey Hepburn by Charles Higham.
New English Library, 1984. 184p. illus. index.

Cecil Milton HEPWORTH

694. Came the Dawn: Memories of a Film Pioneer by Cecil M. Hepworth.
Phoenix House, 1951. 207p. illus. photos.

Hubert von HERKOMER

695. Sir Hubert von Herkomer and His Film-making in Bushey 1912–1914 by Michael Pritchard.
Bushey Museum/Allm Books, 1987. 63p. plates.

Seymour HICKS

696. Night Lights: Two Men Talk of Life and Love and Ladies by Seymour Hicks.
Cassell, 1938. 244p. illus.

Thora HIRD

697. Scene and Hird by Thora Hird.
W.H. Allen, 1976. 238p. plates.

Alfred HITCHCOCK

698. Alfred Hitchcock and the British Cinema by Tom Ryall.
Croom Helm, 1986. 193p. plates. bibliog. filmog. index.

699. Alfred Hitchcock: A Guide to References and Resources edited by Jane E. Sloan.
G.K. Hall/Maxwell Macmillan, 1993. 602p. index.

700. The Art of Alfred Hitchcock: 50 Years of His Films by Donald Spoto.
Fourth Estate, 1992. 471p. illus. filmog. index.

701. The Films of Alfred Hitchcock by Robert A. Harris & Michael S. Lasky.
Citadel Press, 1976. 248p. illus.

702. Hitch: The Life and Work of Alfred Hitchcock by John Russell Taylor.
Faber, 1978. 320p. plates. index.

703. Hitchcock by François Truffaut & Helen G. Scott.
Grafton Books, 1986. 573p. illus. bibliog. filmog. index.

704. Hitchcock's British Films by Maurice Yacowar.
Archon Books, 1977. 314p. index.

705. Hitchcock's Films Revisited by Robin Wood.
Columbia University Press, 1989. 395p. plates. bibliog. index.

706. Hitchcock: The First Forty-four Films by Eric Rohmer, Claude Chabrol & Stanley Hochman.
Frederick Ungar, 1979. 178p. illus. filmog. index.

707. The Life of Alfred Hitchcock: The Dark Side of Genius by Donald Spoto.
Collins, 1983. 594p. illus. bibliog. filmog. index.

708. The Strange Case of Alfred Hitchcock; or, the Plain Man's Hitchcock by Raymond Durgnat.
Faber, 1974. 419p. plates. bibliog. filmog. index.

Stanley HOLLOWAY

709. Wiv a Little Bit o' Luck: The Life Story of Stanley Holloway by Dick Richards.
Leslie Frewin, 1967. 344p. plates.

Anthony HOPKINS

710. Anthony Hopkins: Too Good to Waste – a Biography by Quentin Falk.
Columbus Books, 1989. 210p. plates. filmog. theatrog. teleog. index.

Peter HOPKINSON

711. Split Focus: An Involvement in Two Decades by Peter Hopkinson.
Hart-Davis, 1969. 224p. illus. index.

Clifford HORNBY

712. Shooting Without Stars by Clifford Hornby.
Hutchinson, 1940. 252p. illus.

Bob HOSKINS

713. Bob Hoskins: An Unlikely Hero by Karen Moline.
Sidgwick and Jackson, 1988. 214p. plates.

Leslie HOWARD

714. Aileen & Michael Balcon Special Collection.
See item 417

715. Flight 777 by Ian Colvin.
Evans Brothers, 1957. 212p. illus.

716. In Search of My Father: A Portrait of Leslie Howard by Ronald Howard.
William Kimber, 1981. 255p. plates. filmog. index.

717. A Quite Remarkable Father by Leslie Ruth Howard.
Longmans, 1960. 280p. illus.

718. Trivial Fond Records by Leslie Howard & Ronald Howard.
William Kimber, 1982. 187p. plates. index.

Trevor HOWARD

719. Trevor Howard: A Gentleman and a Player by Vivienne Knight.
Muller, Blond and White, 1986. 280p. illus. filmog. teleog. theatrog. index.

720. Trevor Howard: The Man and His Films by Michael Munn.
Robson Books, 1989. 194p. plates. bibliog. filmog. teleog. theatrog. index.

Frankie HOWERD

721. On the Way I Lost It: An Autobiography by Frankie Howerd.
W.H. Allen, 1976. 288p. plates.

722. Titter Ye Not!: The Life of Frankie Howerd by William Hall.
Grafton Books, 1992. 186p. plates. filmog.

Jack HULBERT

723. Aileen & Michael Balcon Special Collection.
See item 417

724. The Little Woman's Always Right by Jack Hulbert.
W.H. Allen, 1975. 244p. plates. index.

Brian Desmond HURST

725. Brian Desmond Hurst: An Autobiography by Brian Desmond Hurst.
Unpublished, 1986. 212p.

John HURT

726. John Hurt: An Actor's Progress by David Nathan.
W.H. Allen, 1986. 223p. plates. filmog. teleog. theatrog. index.

James IVORY

727. The Films of Merchant Ivory by Robert Emmet Long.
Abrams, 1991. 208p. illus. bibliog. filmog. index.

728. James Ivory edited by Emanuela Martini.
Bergamo Film Meeting '85, 1985. 118p. illus.
Language: Italian.

729. Merchant/Ivory Productions by the Riverside Studios.
Riverside, 1979. 44p. illus. bibliog. Booklet to accompany season of films.

730. The Wandering Company: Twenty-One Years of Merchant Ivory Films by John Pym.
British Film Institute/Museum of Modern Art, 1983. 102p. illus.

Glenda JACKSON

731. Glenda Jackson by David Nathan.
Spellmount, 1984. 95p. illus. filmog. theatrog.

732. Glenda Jackson: A Study in Fire and Ice by Ian Woodward.
Weidenfeld and Nicolson, 1985. 225p. illus. plates. filmog. teleog. theatrog. index.

Derek JARMAN

733. At Your Own Risk: A Saint's Testament by Derek Jarman.
Hutchinson, 1992. 138p. plates.

734. The Complete Derek Jarman edited by Lindsey Merrison.
Arbeitsgemeinschaft Kommunales Kino, 1988. 38p. illus.
Language: German.

735. Dancing Ledge by Derek Jarman & Shaun Allen.
Quartet Books, 1984. 254p. illus.

736. Derek Jarman edited by Loredana Leconte.
L'Altra Comunicazione, 1990. 110p. illus. filmog. bibliog.
Language: Italian.

737. Derek Jarman Special Collection.
120 items including scripts and designs for Jubilee, Sebastiane, The Tempest and Caravaggio.

738. Modern Nature: The Journals of Derek Jarman by Derek Jarman.
Century, 1991. 314p. plates.

Humphrey JENNINGS

739. Heart of England by Robert Vas.
Unpaged.
Full transcripts of interviews used for the television documentary of that title on Humphrey Jennings.

740. Humphrey Jennings.
British Film Institute/Education Department, 1969. 33p. filmog. bibliog.

741. Humphrey Jennings – More Than a Maker of Films by Anthony W. Hodgkinson & Rodney E. Sheratsky.
University Press of New England, 1982. 205p. illus. bibliog. index.

742. Humphrey Jennings Special Collection.
21 items including production material for Fires Were Started, The Silent Village, etc.

743. Humphrey Jennings: Film-maker/Painter/Poet edited by Mary-Lou Jennings.
British Film Institute/Riverside Studios, 1982. 76p. illus. bibliog. filmog.

Celia JOHNSON

744. Celia Johnson: A Biography by Kate Fleming.
Weidenfeld and Nicolson, 1991. 244p. plates.

Cherry KEARTON

745. The Animals Came to Drink by Cherry Kearton.
Longmans, Green, 1932. 90p. illus.

746. In the Land of the Lion by Cherry Kearton.
Arrowsmith, 1946. 250p. illus.

747. Photographing Wild Life Across the World by Cherry Kearton.
Arrowsmith, c1913. 319p. plates.

748. The Shifting Sands of Algeria by Cherry Kearton.
Arrowsmith, 1924. 307p. illus.

Rachel KEMPSON

749. A Family and Its Fortunes by Rachel Kempson.
Duckworth, 1986. 242p. plates.

Henry KENDALL

750. I Remember Romano's: The Autobiography of Henry Kendall.
Macdonald, 1960. 224p. illus.

Deborah KERR

751. Deborah Kerr by Eric Braun.
W.H. Allen, 1977. 264p. plates. bibliog. filmog.

Hildegard KNEF

752. The Gift Horse by Hildegard Knef & D.A. Palastanga.
André Deutsch, 1971. 384p.

753. The Verdict by Hildegard Knef & D.A. Palastanga.
Weidenfeld and Nicolson, 1976. 377p.

Eric KNIGHT

754. Portrait of a Flying Yorkshireman, Letters from Eric Knight in the United States to Paul Rotha in England edited by Paul Rotha.
Chapman and Hall, 1952. 231p.

Esmond KNIGHT

755. Seeking the Bubble by Esmond Knight.
Hutchinson, 1943. 168p. plates.

Alexander KORDA

756. Aileen & Michael Balcon Special Collection.
See item 417

757. Alexander Korda by Paul Tabori.
Oldbourne, 1959. 324p. illus.

758. Alexander Korda: The Man Who Could Work Miracles by Karol Kulik.
W.H. Allen, 1975. 407p. plates. bibliog. filmog. index.

759. Charmed Lives: A Family Romance by Michael Korda.
Allen Lane, 1980. 498p. plates. index.

760. The Golden Years of Alexander Korda by Robert Vas.
N.p., 1968. 19p.
Photocopy of BBC post-production script.

761. The Korda Collection: Alexander Korda's Film Classics by Martin Stockham.
Boxtree, 1992. 128p. illus. bibliog. index.

Stanley KUBRICK

762. Cinéma Anglais: Autour de Kubrick et Losey by Freddy Buache.
Editions L'Age d'Homme, 1978. 327p. plates. index.
Language: French.

763. The Cinema of Stanley Kubrick by Norman Kagan.
Continuum, 1989. 249p. illus. filmog.

764. Kubrick by Michel Ciment.
Collins, 1983. 236p. illus. bibliog. filmog.

765. Kubrick: Inside a Film Artist's Maze by Thomas Allen Nelson.
Indiana University Press, 1982. 268p. illus. bibliog. filmog. index.

766. Stanley Kubrick A Film Odyssey by Gene D. Phillips.
Popular Library, 1975. 189p. illus.

767. Stanley Kubrick Directs by Alexander Walker.
Davis-Poynter, 1972. 272p. illus. filmog.

768. Stanley Kubrick: A Guide to References and Resources by Wallace Coyle.
G.K. Hall, 1980. 155p. bibliog. filmog. index.

Danny LA RUE

769. From Drags to Riches: My Autobiography by Danny La Rue & Howard Elson.
Viking, 1987. 254p. plates. index.

Elsa LANCHESTER

770. Elsa Lanchester Herself by Elsa Lanchester.
St. Martin's Press, 1983. 327p. plates. index.

Lupino LANE

771. Born to Star: The Lupino Lane Story by James Dillon White.
Heinemann, 1957. 304p. plates. index.

772. How to Become a Comedian by Lupino Lane.
Muller, 1945. unpaged.

Walter LASSALLY

773. Itinerant Cameraman by Walter Lassally.
John Murray, 1987. 258p. illus. bibliog. index.

Charles LAUGHTON

774. Charles Laughton by William Brown.
Falcon Press, 1970. 159p. illus. filmog.

775. Charles Laughton and I by Elsa Lanchester.
Faber, 1938. 271p. photos.

776. The Charles Laughton Story by Kurt Singer.
Robert Hale, 1954. 256p. photos.

777. Charles Laughton: A Difficult Actor by Simon Callow.
Methuen, 1987. 318p. plates. bibliog. filmog. theatrog. discog. index.

778. Charles Laughton: An Intimate Biography by Charles Higham.
W.H. Allen, 1976. 239p. plates. index.

779. Joseph Losey Special Collection.
See item 828

780. Pavilions by the Sea: The Memoirs of an Hotel-keeper by Tom Laughton.
Chatto and Windus, 1977. 216p. plates. index.

Frank LAUNDER

781. Launder and Gilliat by Geoff Brown.
British Film Institute, 1977. 159p. filmog. index.

Gertrude LAWRENCE

782. Gertrude Lawrence by Sheridan Morley.
Weidenfeld and Nicolson, 1981. 228p. plates. bibliog. filmog. theatrog. index.

783. Gertrude Lawrence as Mrs. A: An Intimate Biography of the Great Star by Her Husband by Richard Stoddard Aldrich.
Odhams, 1955. 351p. plates.

784. A Star Danced by Gertrude Lawrence.
W.H. Allen, 1945. 231p. plates.

Evelyn LAYE

785. Boo, to My Friends by Evelyn Laye.
Hurst and Blackett, 1957. 180p. illus.

Malcolm LE GRICE

786. L' Avant-garde Cinématographique Britannique 1960–1980: Examen des Propositions des Cinéastes Peter Gidal et Malcolm Le Grice. Contribution à une Théorie Expérimental by Alain Alcide Sudre.
Unpublished thesis, n.d.. 369p. bibliog.
Language: French.

John LE MESURIER

787. A Jobbing Actor by John Le Mesurier.
Elm Tree Books, 1984. 159p. plates. filmog.

David LEAN

788. The Cinema of David Lean by Gerald Pratley.
A.S. Barnes/Tantivy Press, 1974. 256p. illus. index.

789. David Lean by Michael A. Anderegg.
Twayne Publishers, 1984. 161p. illus. bibliog. filmog. index.

790. David Lean by Stephen M. Silverman.
Harry N. Abrams, 1989. 208p. plates. bibliog. filmog. index.

791. David Lean and His Films by Alain Silver & James Ursini.
Leslie Frewin, 1974. 255p. illus. bibliog. biofilmog. index.

792. David Lean: A Guide to References and Resources by Louis Phillip Castelli & Caryn Lynn Cleeland.
G.K. Hall, 1980. 134p. bibliog. filmog. index.

793. A Director's Approach to Film-making: David Lean by Catherine De La Roche.
Transcription of BBC interview, 1947. 7p.

794. Film Epic, a Generic Examination and an Application of Definitions to the Work of David Lean by Louis Phillip Castelli.
University Microfilms, 1978. 254p. bibliog. filmog.
Ph.D. dissertation.

Christopher LEE

795. Christopher Lee by G.R. Parfitt.
Author, 1971. 32p. filmog.

796. The Films of Christopher Lee by Robert W. Pohle Jr. & Douglas C. Hart.
Scarecrow Press, 1983. 227p. plates. bibliog. index.

797. Tall, Dark and Gruesome: An Autobiography by Christopher Lee.
W.H. Allen, 1977. 284p. plates. index.

Norman LEE

798. Log of a Film Director by Norman Lee.
Quality Press, 1949. 156p. photos.

Mike LEIGH

799. The Improvised Play: The Work of Mike Leigh by Paul Clements.
Methuen, 1983. 96p. teleog. theatrog.

Vivien LEIGH

800. Darlings of the Gods: One Year in the Lives of Laurence Olivier and Vivien Leigh by Garry O'Connor.
Hodder and Stoughton, 1984. 192p. plates. index.

801. Light of a Star by Gwen Robyns.
Leslie Frewin, 1968. 256p. plates. index.

802. Love Scene: The Story of Laurence Olivier and Vivien Leigh by Jesse Lasky Jr. & Pat Silver.
Angus and Robertson, 1978. 256p. illus. bibliog. index.

803. The Oliviers: A Biography by Felix Barker.
Hamish Hamilton, 1953. 313p. photos.

804. Vivien Leigh by John Russell Taylor.
Elm Tree Books, 1984. 128p. illus. filmog.

805. Vivien Leigh by Hugo Vickers.
Hamish Hamilton, 1988. 411p. plates. bibliog. filmog. theatrog. index.

806. Vivien Leigh: A Biography by Anne Edwards.
W.H. Allen, 1977. 318p. plates. filmog. index.

807. Vivien Leigh: A Bouquet by Alan Dent.
Hamilton, 1969. 219p.

808. Vivien: A Love Affair in Camera by Angus McBean & Adrian Woodhouse.
Phaidon Press, 1989. 112p. plates. bibliog. index.
Mainly photographs.

809. Vivien: The Life of Vivien Leigh by Alexander Walker.
Weidenfeld and Nicolson, 1987. 342p. plates. bibliog. index.

Caroline A. LEJEUNE

810. Aileen & Michael Balcon Special Collection.
See item 417

811. Thanks for Having Me by Caroline A. Lejeune.
Alexander Maclehose, 1964. 255p.

Mark LESTER

812. Mark Lester: The Boy, His Life and His Films by Paul Kidd.
Arthur H. Stockwell, 1975. 81p. plates.

Richard LESTER

813. The Films of Richard Lester by James Monaco.
The author, 1974. Various.

814. The Films of Richard Lester by Neil Sinyard.
Croom Helm, 1985. 174p. illus. filmog. index.

815. Richard Lester by Brenda Davies.
British Film Institute/National Film Theatre, 1968. 8p.

816. Richard Lester: A Guide to References and Resources by Diane Rosenfeldt.
G.K. Hall/George Prior, 1978. 152p. index.

Louis LEVY

817. Music for the Movies by Louis Levy.
Sampson Low, Marston, 1948. 182p. illus. index.

Sandy LIEBERSON

818. Sandy Lieberson Special Collection.
67 items, mainly scripts and production material, including Absolute Beginners, The Mission, Revolution etc.

Margaret LOCKWOOD

819. Lucky Star: The Autobiography of Margaret Lockwood.
Odhams, 1955. 191p. photos.

820. Once a Wicked Lady: A Biography of Margaret Lockwood by Hilton Tims.
Virgin Books, 1989. 237p. plates. bibliog. filmog. index.

John LODER

821. Hollywood Hussar by John Loder.
Howard Baker, 1977. 178p. plates. index.

Frederick LONSDALE

822. Freddy Lonsdale by Frances Donaldson.
Heinemann, 1957. 257p. plates. index.

Joseph LOSEY

823. Cinéma Anglais: Autour de Kubrick et Losey by Freddy Buache.
Editions L'Age d'Homme, 1978. 327p. plates. index.
Language: French.

824. The Cinema of Joseph Losey by James Leahy.
Zwemmer/A.S. Barnes, 1967. 175p. plates. bibliog. filmog.

825. Conversations with Losey by Michel Ciment.
Methuen, 1985. 436p. illus. biofilmog. index.

826. Joseph Losey by Foster Hirsch.
Twayne, 1980. 256p. illus. bibliog. filmog. index.

827. Joseph Losey by Edith de Rham.
André Deutsch, 1991. 316p. plates. bibliog. filmog. index.

828. Joseph Losey Special Collection.
Over 400 items covering entire career from 1930s to 1984, with detailed production files on all his major films, as well as unrealised projects. Extensive correspondence.

829. Losey on Losey edited by Tom Milne.
Secker and Warburg, 1967. 192p.

Bessie LOVE

830. From Hollywood with Love by Bessie Love.
Elm Tree, 1977. 160p. illus. filmog. index.

Joanna LUMLEY

831. Stare Back and Smile: Memoirs by Joanna Lumley.
Viking, 1989. 217p. plates.

Elisabeth LUTYENS

832. A Goldfish Bowl by Elisabeth Lutyens.
Cassell, 1972. 330p. plates. index.

Alexander MACKENDRICK

833. Aileen & Michael Balcon Special Collection.
See item 417

834. Lethal Innocence: The Cinema of Alexander Mackendrick by Philip Kemp.
Methuen, 1991. 298p. plates. bibliog. filmog. index.

William MACQUITTY

835. A Life to Remember by William MacQuitty.
Quartet, 1991. 390p. plates. index.

Geoffrey H. MALINS

836. How I Filmed the War: A Record of the Extraordinary Experiences of the Man Who Filmed the Great Somme Battles by Geoffrey H. Malins & Low Warren.
Jenkins, 1920. 307p. plates.

H.F. MALTBY

837. Ring Up the Curtain: Being the Stage and Film Memoirs of H.F. Maltby.
Hutchinson, 1950. 232p. plates. index.

Louis J. MANNIX

838. Memories of a Cinema Man by Louis J. Mannix.
Associated Tower Cinemas, 1988. 134p. illus.

James MASON

839. The Authorised Biography of James Mason by Jno P. Monaghan.
World Film Publications, 1947. 78p. plates.

840. Before I Forget: Autobiography and Drawings by James Mason.
Hamish Hamilton, 1981. 345p. plates. illus. index.

841. The Films of James Mason by Clive Hirschhorn & James Mason.
LSP Books, 1975. 256p. illus. filmog.

842. James Mason: A Personal Biography by Diana De Rosso.
Lennard Publishing, 1989. 193p. plates. index.

843. James Mason: Odd Man Out by Sheridan Morley.
Weidenfeld and Nicolson, 1989. 200p. plates. filmog. teleog. theatrog. radiog. index.

Raymond MASSEY

844. A Hundred Different Lives: An Autobiography by Raymond Massey.
Robson Books, 1979. 447p. illus. index.

845. When I Was Young by Raymond Massey.
Little, Brown and Co., 1976. 272p. plates.

Richard MASSINGHAM

846. Richard Massingham: A Tribute by His Friends and a Record of His Films by Jack Beddington et al.
Richard Massingham Memorial Fund, 1955. 24p.

A.E. MATTHEWS

847. Matty: An Autobiography by A.E. Matthews.
Hutchinson, 1952. 232p. photos.

Jessie MATTHEWS

848. Aileen & Michael Balcon Special Collection.
See item 417

849. Jessie Matthews: A Biography by Michael Thornton.
Hart-Davis MacGibbon, 1974. 359p. plates. bibliog. discog. filmog. index.

850. Over My Shoulder: An Autobiography by Jessie Matthews & Muriel Burgess.
W.H. Allen, 1974. 240p. plates. index.

Carl MAYER

851. Carl Mayer in England by Paul Rotha.
N.p., 1980. 18p.

Trial of Strength
(Peter K Smith, 1972)

***The Knack . . . and
How to Get It*** (Richard
Lester, 1965)

***Morgan – A Suitable
Case for Treatment***
(Karel Reisz, 1966)

Enverounen
(Simon Mallin,
William Diver, 1973)

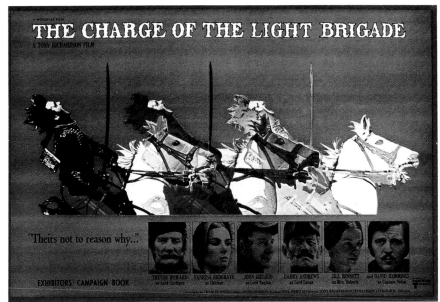

Billion Dollar Brain
(Ken Russell, 1967)
Press-book. LIS [28,
471–477, 992–1000]

Above right: *The Lion
in Winter* (Anthony
Harvey, 1968), Press-
book. LIS [188, 710,
902–904]

*The Charge of the
Light Brigade* (Tony
Richardson, 1968)
Press-book. LIS

Dulcima (Frank
Nesbitt, 1971), Press-
book. LIS [866–867,
1062]

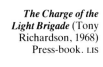

Left: *Akhenatan*
(Derek Jarman)
Sketch for an
unrealised project.
LIS [737]

Above and right:
Chariots of Fire (Hugh
Hudson, 1981)

Above: souvenir
programme. LIS
ephemera [51, 950–
951]

*Animation for Live
Action* (Vera
Neubauer, 1978)

Right: *Death on the
Nile* (John
Guillermin, 1978)
Press-book. LIS [1599]

Song of the Shirt (Sue
Clayton, Jonathan
Curling, 1979)

The Gold Diggers
(Sally Potter, 1983)

*Dub and Visual
Perception* (Kelvin
Richard, 1983)

Brazil
(Terry Gilliam, 1985)

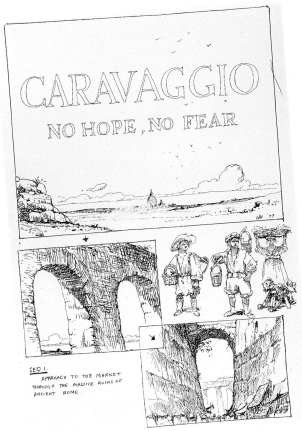

Caravaggio (Derek   Ink sketch. LIS
Jarman, 1986)   [49–50, 737]

Who Needs a Heart?
(John Akomfrah,
1991)

Rhosyn a Rhith
(Stephen Bayly, 1986)

Stewart McALLISTER

852. Portrait of an Invisible Man: The Working
Life of Stewart McAllister, Film Editor
by Dai Vaughan.
British Film Institute, 1983. 209p.
bibliog.

Alec McCOWEN

853. Double Bill by Alec McCowen.
Elm Tree Books, 1980. 198p. illus.

Ronald McINTYRE

854. Films Without Make-Up by Ronald
McIntyre.
R. Schindler, 1943. 338p.

Ian McKELLEN

855. Ian McKellen by Joy Leslie Gibson.
Weidenfeld and Nicolson, 1986. 190p.
plates. theatrog. index.

Ismail MERCHANT

856. The Films of Merchant Ivory by Robert
Emmet Long.
Abrams, 1991. 208p. illus. bibliog.
filmog. index.

857. Merchant/Ivory Productions by the
Riverside Studios.
Riverside, 1979. 44p. illus. bibliog.
Booklet to accompany season of films.

858. The Wandering Company: Twenty-One
Years of Merchant Ivory Films by John
Pym.
British Film Institute/Museum of Modern
Art, 1983. 102p. illus.

Oliver MESSEL

859. Oliver Messel: A Biography by Charles
Castle.
Thames and Hudson, 1986. 264p. illus.
col.plates. index.

Jonathan MILLER

860. Beyond the Fringe...and Beyond: A
Critical Biography of Alan Bennett, Peter
Cook, Jonathan Miller and Dudley Moore
by Ronald Bergan.
Virgin, 1989. 311p. plates. filmog.
teleog. theatrog. discog. index.

Max MILLER

861. For the Sake of Shadows by Max Miller.
E.P. Dutton, 1936. 200p.

862. Max Miller: The Cheeky Chappie by John
M. East.
W.H. Allen, 1977. 196p. plates. discog.
index.

Spike MILLIGAN

863. It Ends with Magic...: A Milligan Family
Story by Spike Milligan.
Michael Joseph, 1990. 243p. illus.

864. Milligan: The Life and Times of Spike
Milligan by Dominic Behan.
Methuen, 1988. 193p. plates. bibliog.
filmog. teleog. discog.

865. Spike Milligan: A Biography by Pauline
Scudamore.
Granada, 1985. 318p. plates. bibliog.
filmog. teleog. discog. index.

John MILLS

866. Aileen & Michael Balcon Special
Collection.
See item 417

867. Up in the Clouds, Gentlemen Please by
John Mills.
Weidenfeld and Nicolson, 1980. 290p.
plates. filmog. index.

Billy MILTON

868. Milton's Paradise Mislaid by Billy Milton.
Jupiter, 1976. 218p. illus. index.

Yvonne MITCHELL

869. Actress by Yvonne Mitchell.
Routledge and Kegan Paul, 1957. 111p.
illus.

Ivor MONTAGU

870. Ivor Montagu Special Collection.
463 items covering The Film Society,
early film career (Hitchcock,
Gainsborough, etc.), censorship, the
Russian connection (Eisenstein,
etc.), FIAF, ACTT.

871. The Youngest Son: Autobiographical
Sketches by Ivor Montagu.
Lawrence and Wishart, 1970. 384p.
plates. index.

Dudley MOORE

872. Beyond the Fringe...and Beyond: A
Critical Biography of Alan Bennett, Peter
Cook, Jonathan Miller and Dudley Moore
by Ronald Bergan.
Virgin, 1989. 311p. plates. filmog.
teleog. theatrog. discog. index.

Roger MOORE

873. The Films of Roger Moore by John
Williams.
Barnden Castell Williams, 1974. 47p.
illus. filmog.

874. Roger Moore by Paul Donovan.
W.H. Allen, 1983. 224p. illus.
col.plates. filmog. index.

875. Roger Moore: A Biography by Roy
Moseley & Philip and Martin Masheter.
New English Library, 1985. 249p.
plates. filmog. index.

Kenneth MORE

876. Happy Go Lucky: My Life by Kenneth
More.
Robert Hale, 1959. 192p. illus. index.

877. Kindly Leave the Stage by Kenneth More.
Michael Joseph, 1965. 128p. illus.

878. More or Less by Kenneth More.
Hodder and Stoughton, 1978. 249p.
plates. index.

879. Swings and Roundabouts: An
Autobiography by Angela Douglas.
Elm Tree Books, 1983. 255p. plates.

Robert MORLEY

880. Larger than Life: The Biography of
Robert Morley by Margaret Morley.
Robson Books, 1979. 206p. plates.
bibliog. filmog. playog.

881. The Pleasures of Age by Robert Morley.
Hodder and Stoughton, 1988. 159p.
illus.

882. Robert Morley: Responsible Gentleman
by Robert Morley & Sewell Stokes.
Heinemann, 1966. 222p. plates.

Stanley J. 'Percy' MUMFORD

883. Stanley J. 'Percy' Mumford Special
Collection.
Clippings and personal memorabilia.

Owen NARES

884. Myself and Some Others: Pure Egotism
by Owen Nares.
Duckworth, 1925. 204p.

Anna NEAGLE

885. Anna Neagle Special Collection.
Scrapbooks.

886. There's Always Tomorrow: An
Autobiography by Anna Neagle.
Futura, 1979. 224p. plates. filmog.
index.

Cathleen NESBITT

887. A Little Love and Good Company by
Cathleen Nesbitt.
Faber, 1975. 263p. plates. index.

David NIVEN

888. The Films of David Niven by Gerard
Garrett.
LSP Books, 1975. 256p. illus. filmog.

889. The Last Gentleman: A Tribute to David
Niven by Peter Haining.
W.H. Allen, 1984. 223p. illus. filmog.

890. The Moon's a Balloon: Reminiscences by
David Niven.
Hamish Hamilton, 1971. 312p. plates.
index.

891. The Other Side of the Moon: The Life of
David Niven by Sheridan Morley.
Weidenfeld and Nicolson, 1985. 300p.
plates. filmog. index.

Peter NOBLE

892. Reflected Glory: An Autobiographical
Sketch by Peter Noble.
Jarrolds, 1958. 235p. illus. index.

Ronald NOBLE

893. Shoot First! Assignments of a Newsreel
Cameraman by Ronnie Noble.
Harrap, 1955. 271p. photos.

Richard NORTON

894. Silver Spoon, Being Extracts from the
Random Reminiscences of Lord Grantley
by Richard Norton, Baron Grantley &
Mary and Alan Wood.
Hutchinson, 1954. 239p.

Ivor NOVELLO

895. Aileen & Michael Balcon Special
Collection.
See item 417

896. Ivor by Sandy Wilson.
Michael Joseph, 1975. 288p. illus.
bibliog. filmog. discog. index.

897. Ivor Novello by James Harding.
W.H. Allen, 1987. 258p. plates.
bibliog. theatrog. index.

898. Ivor Novello: Man of the Theatre by Peter
Noble.
Falcon Press, 1951. 306p. photos.

899. Ivor: The Story of an Achievement – A
Biography of Ivor Novello by W.
Macqueen-Pope.
W.H. Allen, 1952. 550p. photos.

900. The Life I Have Loved by Clara Novello
Davies.
Heinemann, 1940. 323p.

901. Perchance to Dream: The World of Ivor
Novello by Richard Rose.
Leslie Frewin, 1974. 199p. illus.

Peter O'TOOLE

902. Loitering with Intent: The Child by Peter
O'Toole.
Macmillan, 1992. 198p.

903. Peter O'Toole: A Biography by Michael
Freedland.
W.H. Allen, 1983. 237p. plates. index.

904. Peter O'Toole: A Biography by Nicholas Wapshott.
New English Library, 1983. 239p. plates. filmog. index.

Charles OAKLEY

905. Those Were the Years: The Autobiography of Charles Oakley.
Blackie, 1983. 166p. illus.

Merle OBERON

906. Merle: A Biography of Merle Oberon by Charles Higham & Roy Moseley.
New English Library, 1983. 227p. plates. filmog. index.

Laurence OLIVIER

907. The Complete Films of Laurence Olivier by Jerry Vermilye.
Carol, 1992. 287p. illus.

908. Confessions of an Actor by Laurence Olivier.
Weidenfeld and Nicolson, 1982. 305p. plates. index.

909. Cry God for Larry by Virginia Fairweather.
Calder and Boyars, 1969. 183p.

910. Darlings of the Gods: One Year in the Lives of Laurence Olivier and Vivien Leigh by Garry O'Connor.
Hodder and Stoughton, 1984. 192p. plates. index.

911. Laurence Olivier by Melvyn Bragg.
Hutchinson, 1984. 144p. illus. col.plates.

912. Laurence Olivier by John Cottrell.
Weidenfeld and Nicolson, 1975. 433p. plates. bibliog. index.

913. Laurence Olivier by W.A. Darlington.
Morgan Grampian Books, 1968. 92p. illus.

914. Laurence Olivier and the Art of Film Making by Dale Silviria.
Fairleigh Dickinson Univ. Press/ Associated Univ. Press, 1985. 309p. illus. bibliog. index.

915. Laurence Olivier Directs Shakespeare: A Study in Film Authorship by Susan Sugarman Singer.
Ph.D thesis, 1979. 233p. bibliog. filmog. gloss.

916. Laurence Olivier on Screen by Foster Hirsch.
Da Capo Press, 1984. 190p. illus. bibliog. filmog. index.

917. Laurence Olivier: A Biography by Donald Spoto.
HarperCollins, 1991. 387p. plates. bibliog. index.

918. Laurence Olivier: A Critical Study by Felix Barker.
Spellmount, 1984. 95p. illus. bibliog. filmog. theatrog.

919. Laurence Olivier: Theater and Cinema by Robert L. Daniels.
A.S. Barnes/Tantivy Press, 1980. 319p. illus. bibliog. index.

920. Love Scene: The Story of Laurence Olivier and Vivien Leigh by Jesse Lasky Jr. & Pat Silver.
Angus and Robertson, 1978. 256p. illus. bibliog. index.

921. My Father Laurence Olivier by Tarquin Olivier.
Headline, 1992. 271p. plates. index.

922. Olivier edited by Logan Gourlay.
Weidenfeld and Nicolson, 1973. 208p. plates.

923. Olivier by Anthony Holden.
Weidenfeld and Nicolson, 1988. 504p. plates. bibliog. index.

924. Olivier: The Complete Career by Robert Tanitch.
Thames and Hudson, 1985. 191p. illus. filmog. teleog. theatrog. index.

925. Olivier: The Films and Faces of Laurence Olivier edited by Margaret Morley.
LSP Books, 1978. 216p. illus. bibliog. filmog.

926. Olivier: The Life of Laurence Olivier by Thomas Kiernan.
Sidgwick and Jackson, 1981. 302p. illus. index.

927. The Oliviers: A Biography by Felix Barker.
Hamish Hamilton, 1953. 313p. photos.

John OSBORNE

928. Almost a Gentleman: An Autobiography – Volume 2 1955–1966 by John Osborne.
Faber, 1991. 283p. plates. index.

929. A Better Class of Person: An Autobiography – Volume 1 1929–1956 by John Osborne.
Faber, 1991. 285p. plates. index.

Lilli PALMER

930. Change Lobsters and Dance: An Autobiography by Lilli Palmer.
W.H. Allen, 1976. 310p. plates.

Gabriel PASCAL

931. The Disciple and His Devil by Valerie Pascal.
Michael Joseph, 1971. 319p. plates.

George PEARSON

932. Flashback: The Autobiography of a British Filmmaker by George Pearson.
George Allen and Unwin, 1957. 236p. illus. filmog. index.

933. George Pearson Special Collection.
40 items including autobiographical notes, diary, scripts and lectures.

Harold PINTER

934. Harold Pinter by William Baker & Stephen Ely Tabachnick.
Oliver and Boyd, 1973. 156p. bibliog.

935. Harold Pinter: You Never Heard Such Silence edited by Alan Bold.
Vision/Barnes and Noble, 1984. 184p. index.

936. Joseph Losey Special Collection.
See item 828

937. Making Pictures: The Pinter Screenplays by Joanne Klein.
Ohio State University, 1985. 215p. bibliog. index.

Herbert PONTING

938. Photographer of the World: The Biography of Herbert Ponting by H.J.P. Arnold.
Hutchinson, 1969. 175p. plates. index.

Michael POWELL

939. Arrows of Desire: The Films of Michael Powell and Emeric Pressburger by Ian Christie.
Waterstone, 1985. 127p. illus. col.plates. bibliog. filmog. index.

940. A Life in Movies: An Autobiography by Michael Powell.
Heinemann, 1986. 705p. filmog. index.

941. Michael Powell by Kevin Gough-Yates.
Brussels Filmmuseum, 1973. 48p. illus. filmog. index.

942. Million-Dollar Movie: The Second Volume of His Life in Movies by Michael Powell.
Heinemann, 1992. 612p. plates.

943. L' Oeuvre de Michael Powell, Cinéaste Britannique: Etude Biographique et Thématique by Claude Guiguet & Pierette Matalon.
Thesis, 1983. 588p.

944. Powell and Pressburger edited by Emanuela Martini.
Bergamo Film Meeting '86, 1986. 136p. illus.
Language: Italian.

945. Powell, Pressburger and Others edited by Ian Christie.
British Film Institute, 1978. 124p. filmog.

Emeric PRESSBURGER

946. Arrows of Desire: The Films of Michael Powell and Emeric Pressburger by Ian Christie.
Waterstone, 1985. 127p. illus. col.plates. bibliog. filmog. index.

947. Powell and Pressburger edited by Emanuela Martini.
Bergamo Film Meeting '86, 1986. 136p. illus.
Language: Italian.

948. Powell, Pressburger and Others edited by Ian Christie.
British Film Institute, 1978. 124p. filmog.

Adrian PRYCE-JONES

949. Adrian Pryce-Jones Special Collection.
72 items including production material for Hobson's Choice, Devil's Disciple, The Deep Blue Sea, etc.

David PUTTNAM

950. David Puttnam Special Collection.
Production files on Agatha, Chariots of Fire, The Duellists, The Killing Fields, Local Hero, Midnight Express, The Mission, etc.

951. Enigma: David Puttnam – The Story So Far by Andrew Yule.
Mainstream, 1988. 480p. illus. plates. index.

952. Out of Focus: Power, Pride and Prejudice – David Puttnam in Hollywood by Charles Kipps.
Silver Arrow Books/William Morrow, 1989. 336p. index.

Anthony QUAYLE

953. A Time to Speak by Anthony Quayle.
Barrie and Jenkins, 1990. 368p. plates. index.

Charlotte RAMPLING

954. Charlotte Rampling, with Compliments by Mareike Boom, Dirk Bogarde & Nagisa Oshima.
Quartet Books, 1987. 135p. plates. filmog.
Mainly illustrative material.

Frank RANDLE

955. King Twist: A Portrait of Frank Randle by Jeff Nuttall.
Routledge and Kegan Paul, 1978. 139p. plates.

J. Arthur RANK

956. The Influence of J. Arthur Rank on the History of the British Film by James L. Limbacher.
Temple University Seminar Paper, 1971. 56p. bibliog. filmog.

957. Mr. Rank: A Study of J. Arthur Rank and British Films by Alan Wood.
Hodder and Stoughton, 1952. 288p.

Terence RATTIGAN

958. Terence Rattigan: The Man and His Work by Michael Darlow & Gillian Hodson.
Quartet Books, 1979. 360p. plates. bibliog. playog. index.

Michael REDGRAVE

959. In My Mind's Eye: An Autobiography by Michael Redgrave.
Weidenfeld and Nicolson, 1983. 256p. plates. index.

960. Michael Redgrave – Actor by Richard Findlater.
Heinemann, 1956. 170p. photos.

Vanessa REDGRAVE

961. Vanessa Redgrave: An Autobiography by Vanessa Redgrave.
Hutchinson, 1991. 312p. plates. index.

Carol REED

962. Carol Reed edited by Brenda Davies.
British Film Institute, 1978. 33p. filmog.

963. Carol Reed Special Collection.
67 items including scrapbooks, production material, correspondence, scripts.

964. The Cinema of Carol Reed by Michael P.O. Voigt.
Unpublished typescript, 1970. 58p. bibliog. filmog.

965. The Films of Carol Reed by Robert F. Moss.
Macmillan, 1987. 312p. plates. bibliog. filmog. index.

966. The Man Between: A Biography of Carol Reed by Nicholas Wapshott.
Chatto and Windus, 1990. 376p. plates. bibliog. filmog. index.

Oliver REED

967. The Films of Oliver Reed by Susan d'Arcy.
Barnden Castell Williams, 1974. 47p. illus. filmog.

968. Reed All About Me: The Autobiography of Oliver Reed.
W.H. Allen, 1979. 261p. plates. index.

Beryl REID

969. So Much Love by Beryl Reid & Eric Braun.
Hutchinson, 1984. 295p. plates. filmog. teleog. theatrog.

Karel REISZ

970. Karel Reisz by Georg Gaston.
Twayne, 1980. 166p. illus. bibliog. filmog. index.

Ralph RICHARDSON

971. Ralph Richardson, an Illustrated Study of Sir Ralph's Work by Harold Hobson.
Rockliff, 1958. 98p. photos.

972. Ralph Richardson: A Tribute by Robert Tanitch.
Evans, 1982. 128p. illus. filmog. teleog. playog. index.

973. Ralph Richardson: An Actor's Life by Garry O'Connor.
Hodder and Stoughton, 1986. 281p. plates. bibliog. filmog. theatrog. index.

Jocelyn RICKARDS

974. The Painted Banquet: My Life and Loves by Jocelyn Rickards.
Weidenfeld and Nicolson, 1987. 172p. plates. index.

Rachel ROBERTS

975. No Bells on Sunday: The Journals of Rachel Roberts by Rachel Roberts & Alexander Walker.
Pavilion/Michael Joseph, 1984. 246p. plates.

Paul ROBESON

976. Paul Robeson by Edwin P. Hoyt.
Cassell, 1968. 228p.

977. Paul Robeson by Marie Seton.
Dennis Dobson, 1958. 254p. illus.

978. Paul Robeson: The Life and Times of a Free Black Man by Virginia Hamilton.
Harper and Row, 1974. 217p. plates. bibliog. index.

George ROBEY

979. George Robey by Peter Cotes.
Cassell, 1972. 212p. illus. index.

980. Looking Back on Life by George Robey.
Constable, 1933. 318p. photos.

Flora ROBSON

981. Flora Robson by Janet Dunbar.
Harrap, 1960. 276p. illus.

982. Flora: An Appreciation of the Life and Work of Dame Flora Robson by Kenneth Barrow.
Heinemann, 1981. 242p. plates. index.

Nicolas ROEG

983. The Films of Nicolas Roeg by Neil Sinyard.
Charles Letts, 1991. 167p. illus. filmog. bibliog. index.

984. The Films of Nicolas Roeg: Myth and Mind by John Izod.
Macmillan, 1992. 294p. plates. filmog. bibliog. gloss. index.

985. Fragile Geometry: The Films, Philosophy and Misadventures of Nicolas Roeg by Joseph Lanza.
PAJ Publications, 1989. 176p. illus. bibliog. filmog. index.

986. Nicolas Roeg by Neil Feineman.
Twayne, 1978. 153p. illus. bibliog. filmog. index.

Leonard ROSSITER

987. Leonard Rossiter by Robert Tanitch.
Robert Royce, 1985. 160p. illus. filmog. teleog. theatrog. index.

Paul ROTHA

988. Aileen & Michael Balcon Special Collection.
See item 417

989. Paul Rotha edited by Paul Marris.
British Film Institute, 1982. 113p. bibliog. filmog.

Harry ROWSON

990. Harry Rowson Special Collection.
26 items including notebooks, scripts, correspondence.

991. Ideals of Wardour Street by Harry Rowson.
Unpublished typescript, n.d.. 197p.

Ken RUSSELL

992. Altered States: The Autobiography of Ken Russell by Ken Russell.
Bantam Books, 1991. 337p. illus. index.

993. An Appalling Talent: Ken Russell by John Baxter.
Michael Joseph, 1973. 240p. illus. filmog. index.

994. A British Picture: An Autobiography by Ken Russell.
Heinemann, 1989. 293p.

995. Ken Russell edited by Thomas R. Atkins.
Monarch Press, 1976. 132p. illus. filmog.

996. Ken Russell by Gene D. Phillips.
Twayne, 1979. 200p. illus. bibliog. filmog. index.

997. Ken Russell's Films by Ken Hanke.
The Scarecrow Press, 1984. 460p. illus. filmog. index.

998. Ken Russell: A Director in Search of a Hero by Colin Wilson.
Intergroup, 1975. 71p. plates. filmog.

999. Ken Russell: A Guide to References and Resources by Diane Rosenfeldt.
G.K. Hall/George Prior, 1978. 140p. bibliog. filmog. index.

1000. Ken Russell: The Adaptor as Creator by Joseph A. Gomez.
Muller, 1976. 223p. plates. filmog. bibliog.

Margaret RUTHERFORD

1001. Margaret Rutherford by Eric Keown.
Rockliff, 1956. 94p. photos.

1002. Margaret Rutherford: A Blithe Spirit by Dawn Langley Simmons.
Arthur Barker, 1983. 196p. plates. bibliog. index.

1003. Margaret Rutherford: An Autobiography by Margaret Rutherford & Gwen Robyns.
W.H. Allen, 1972. 230p. plates. index.

SABU

1004. Sabu the Elephant Boy by Frances Hubbard Flaherty & Ursula Leacock.
J.M. Dent, 1937. 95p. photos.

George SANDERS

1005. A Dreadful Man: A Personal Intimate Book about George Sanders by Brian Aherne, George Sanders & Hume Benita.
Simon and Schuster, 1979. 224p. plates.

Victor SAVILLE

1006. Aileen & Michael Balcon Special Collection.
See item 417

1007. Victor Saville by the National Film Theatre.
British Film Institute, 1972. 24p. filmog.

John SCHLESINGER

1008. John Schlesinger by Gene D. Phillips.
Twayne Publishers, 1981. 199p. illus. bibliog. filmog. index.

1009. John Schlesinger: A Guide to References and Resources by Nancy J. Brooker.
G.K. Hall/George Prior, 1978. 132p. bibliog. filmog. index.

Jeanette SCOTT

1010. Act One by Jeanette Scott.
Thomas Nelson, 1953. 88p. photos.

Peter SELLERS

1011. P.S. I Love You: Peter Sellers 1925–1980 by Michael Sellers.
Collins, 1981. 238p. plates.

1012. Peter Sellers by Derek Sylvester.
Proteus, 1981. 128p. illus. filmog.

1013. Peter Sellers: A Film History by Michael Starr.
Robert Hale, 1992. 262p. illus. index.

1014. Peter Sellers: The Authorized Biography by Alexander Walker.
Weidenfeld and Nicolson, 1981. 240p. plates. filmog. index.

1015. Peter Sellers: The Mask behind the Mask by Peter Evans.
New English Library, 1980. 256p. plates. filmog. index.

1016. Remembering Peter Sellers by Graham Stark.
Robson Books, 1990. 210p. plates.

Omar SHARIF

1017. The Eternal Male by Omar Sharif, Marie-Thérèse Guinchard & Martin Sokolinsky.
W.H. Allen, 1977. 155p.

Alfred SHAUGHNESSY

1018. Both Ends of the Candle by Alfred Shaughnessy.
Peter Owen, 1978. 167p. plates. index.

Robert Cedric SHERIFF

1019. Aileen & Michael Balcon Special Collection.
See item 417

1020. No Leading Lady: An Autobiography by Robert Cedric Sheriff.
Gollancz, 1968. 352p.

Alastair SIM

1021. Dance and Skylark: Fifty Years with Alastair Sim by Naomi Sim.
Bloomsbury, 1987. 151p. plates.

Donald SINDEN

1022. Laughter in the Second Act by Donald Sinden.
Hodder and Stoughton, 1985. 228p. illus. plates. index.

1023. A Touch of the Memoirs by Donald Sinden.
Hodder and Stoughton, 1982. 256p. plates. index.

C. Aubrey SMITH

1024. Sir Aubrey: A Biography of C. Aubrey Smith by David Rayvern Allen.
Elm Tree Books, 1982. 172p. plates. bibliog. index.

Maggie SMITH

1025. Maggie Smith: A Bright Particular Star by Michael Coveney.
Gollancz, 1992. 286p. plates. bibliog. index.

Sam SPIEGEL

1026. Spiegel: The Man behind the Pictures by Andrew Sinclair.
Weidenfeld and Nicolson, 1987. 162p. plates. bibliog. index.

Terence STAMP

1027. Coming Attractions by Terence Stamp.
Bloomsbury, 1988. 216p. illus.

1028. Double Feature by Terence Stamp.
Bloomsbury, 1989. 336p. illus.

1029. Stamp Album by Terence Stamp.
Bloomsbury, 1987. 203p. illus.

Tommy STEELE

1030. Tommy Steele, the Facts about a Teenage Idol and an Inside Picture of Show Business by John Kennedy.
Souvenir Press, 1958. 166p. photos.

STING

1031. Sting: A Biography by Robert Sellers.
Omnibus Press, 1989. 123p. plates. filmog. teleog. discog.

Tom STOBART

1032. Adventurer's Eye: The Autobiography of Everest Film-man Tom Stobart.
Odhams, 1958. 256p. photos.

John STUART

1033. Caught in the Act by John Stuart.
The Silent Picture, 1971. 32p. illus. filmog.

Penrose TENNYSON

1034. Penrose Tennyson by C[harles] T[ennyson].
A.S. Atkinson, 1943. 164p. illus.

TERRY-THOMAS

1035. Filling the Gap by Terry-Thomas.
Max Parrish, 1959. 168p.

1036. Terry-Thomas Tells Tales: An Autobiography by Terry-Thomas & Terry Daum.
Robson Books, 1990. 213p. illus.

Sybil THORNDIKE

1037. Lewis and Sybil: A Memoir by John Casson.
Collins, 1972. 352p. plates. index.

1038. Sybil Thorndike Casson by Elizabeth Sprigge.
Gollancz, 1971. 348p. plates. index.

1039. Sybil Thorndike: A Life in the Theatre by Sheridan Morley.
Weidenfeld and Nicolson, 1977. 183p. illus. filmog. index.

1040. Sybil Thorndike: An Illustrated Study of Dame Sybil's Work, with a List of Her Appearances on Stage and Screen by J.C. Trewin.
Rockliff, 1955. 123p. illus.

Ann TODD

1041. The Eighth Veil by Ann Todd.
William Kimber, 1980. 173p. plates. index.

Richard TODD

1042. Caught in the Act: The Story of My Life by Richard Todd.
Hutchinson, 1986. 302p. plates. index.

1043. In Camera, an Autobiography Continued by Richard Todd.
Century Hutchinson, 1989. 386p. illus. index.

Harry Alan TOWERS

1044. Show Business: Stars of the World of Show Business by Harry Alan Towers.
Sampson Low, Marston, 1948. 110p. illus.

Ben TRAVERS

1045. A-Sitting on a Gate: Autobiography by Ben Travers.
W.H. Allen, 1978. 195p. plates. index.

TWIGGY

1046. Twiggy: An Autobiography by Twiggy.
Hart-Davis, MacGibbon, 1975. 156p. plates.

Peter USTINOV

1047. Dear Me by Peter Ustinov.
Heinemann, 1977. 280p. plates. index.

1048. The Universal Ustinov by Christopher Warwick.
Sidgwick and Jackson, 1990. 246p. plates. bibliog. filmog. teleog. theatrog. index.

1049. Ustinov in Focus by Tony Thomas.
Zwemmer/A.S. Barnes, 1971. 192p. illus.

Irene VANBRUGH

1050. To Tell My Story by Irene Vanbrugh.
Hutchinson, 1948. 217p. illus.

Conrad VEIDT

1051. Conrad Veidt Special Collection.
5 items including theatre contracts and British naturalisation certificate.

1052. Conrad Veidt: From Caligari to Casablanca by J.C. Allen.
Boxwood Press, 1987. 253p. illus. filmog. index.

Alexander WALKER

1053. 'It's Only a Movie Ingrid': Encounters On and Off Screen by Alexander Walker.
Headline, 1988. 312p. illus. index.

William WALTON

1054. William Walton: A Thematic Catalogue of His Musical Works by Stewart R. Craggs.
Oxford University Press, 1977. 273p. bibliog. index.

1055. William Walton: Behind the Facade by Susana Walton.
Oxford University Press, 1988. 255p. plates. index.

Jack WARNER

1056. Jack of All Trades: An Autobiography by Jack Warner.
W.H. Allen, 1975. 226p. plates.

Peter WATKINS

1057. Peter Watkins by Joseph A. Gomez.
Twayne, 1979. 214p. illus. bibliog. filmog. index.

1058. Peter Watkins: A Guide to References and Resources by James Michael Welsh.
G.K. Hall, 1986. 222p. bibliog. filmog. index.

Harry WATT

1059. Aileen & Michael Balcon Special Collection.
See item 417

1060. Don't Look at the Camera by Harry Watt.
Paul Elek, 1974. 198p. plates. filmog. index.

Alfred WEST

1061. Alfred J. West : An Autobiography by Alfred J. West.
Unpublished typescript, n.d. 212p.

Carol WHITE

1062. Carol Comes Home by Carol White & Clifford Thurlow.
New English Library, 1982. 284p. plates.

Herbert WILCOX

1063. Twenty-five Thousand Sunsets: The Autobiography of Herbert Wilcox. Bodley Head, 1967. 233p. plates.

Michael WILDING

1064. Apple Sauce: The Story of My Life by Michael Wilding & Pamela Wilcox. Allen and Unwin, 1982. 190p. plates. filmog. index.

Emlyn WILLIAMS

1065. Aileen & Michael Balcon Special Collection. See item 417

1066. Emlyn Williams by Richard Findlater. Rockliff, 1956. 112p. photos.

1067. Emlyn: An Early Autobiography 1927–35 by Emlyn Williams. Bodley Head, 1973. 424p. index.

Kenneth WILLIAMS

1068. Just Williams: An Autobiography by Kenneth Williams. J.M. Dent, 1985. 252p. index.

1069. Kenneth Williams: A Biography by Michael Freedland. Weidenfeld and Nicolson, 1990. 242p. illus. index.

Ted WILLIS

1070. Evening All: Fifty Years Over a Hot Typewriter by Ted Willis. Macmillan, 1991. 244p. plates. index.

1071. Whatever Happened to Tom Mix: The Story of One of My Lives by Ted Willis. Cassell, 1970. 197p.

Barbara WINDSOR

1072. Barbara: The Laughter and Tears of a Cockney Sparrow by Barbara Windsor & Joan Flory. Century, 1990. 195p. plates.

Julian WINTLE

1073. Julian Wintle: A Memoir by Anne Francis. Dukeswood, 1985. 138p. illus. filmog.

Norman WISDOM

1074. Don't Laugh at Me: An Autobiography by Norman Wisdom & William Hall. Century, 1992. 213p. plates.

1075. Trouble in Store: Norman Wisdom, a Career in Comedy by Richard Dacre. T.C. Farries, 1991. 183p. plates. filmog. bibliog. appendix. index.

Googie WITHERS

1076. Life with Googie by John McCallum. Heinemann, 1979. 275p. plates. index.

Patrick WYAND

1077. Patrick Wyand Special Collection. 13 items on newsreels and personal memorabilia.

Paul WYAND

1078. Useless if Delayed by Paul Wyand. Harrap, 1959. 256p. plates.

Michael YORK

1079. Travelling Player: An Autobiography by Michael York. Headline, 1991. 410p. plates. index.

Freddie YOUNG

1080. Freddie Young by the National Film Theatre. British Film Institute, 1972. 7p.

Fred ZINNEMANN

1081. Fred Zinnemann Special Collection. Mainly copies of correspondence.

1082. Fred Zinnemann: An Autobiography. Bloomsbury, 1992. 256p. illus.

1083. Zinnemann by Antje Goldau, Hans Helmut Prinzler & Neil Sinyard. Filmland Presse, 1986. 207p. illus. bibliog. filmog. index. Language: German.

COLLECTED PERSONALITIES

1084. Anger and After: A Guide to the New British Drama by John Russell Taylor. Methuen, 1969. 391p. plates. index.

1085. L' Attore nel Cinema Britannico by Mario Verdone. Bianco e Nero, 1960. 32p. Language: Italian.

1086. Behind the Scenes: Theatre and Film Interviews from the Transatlantic Review by Joseph F. McCrindle. Pitman, 1971. 341p.

1087. British Cinema: An Illustrated Guide by Denis Gifford. Zwemmer, 1968. 176p. plates. index.

1088. British Film Character Actors: Great Names and Memorable Moments by Terence Pettigrew. David and Charles, 1982. 208p. illus. index.

1089. British Film Stars at Home 1946–7 by Stephanie Lee. Findon Publications, 1947. c50p. illus.

1090. British Screen Stars edited by Peter Noble. British Yearbooks, 1947. 91p. illus. Also a 1946 edition.

1091. Close-up: The Contemporary Director by Jon Tuska. Scarecrow Press, 1981. 431p. illus. filmog. index.

1092. Comedy Greats: A Celebration of Comic Genius Past and Present by Barry Took. Equation/Thorsons Publishing, 1989. 240p. illus. bibliog. teleog. filmog. index.

1093. Directors and Directions: Cinema for the Seventies by John Russell Taylor. Eyre Methuen, 1975. 327p. bibliog. filmog.

1094. Do You Sleep in the Nude? by Rex Reed. New American Library, 1968. 276p.

1095. Documentary Explorations: 15 Interviews with Film-makers by G. Roy Levin. Doubleday, 1971. 420p. plates. bibliog. filmog. index.

1096. Dossiers du Cinéma: Cinéastes 2 by Jean-Louis Bory & Claude Michel Cluny. Tournai, Casterman, 1971. 51 fiches. Language: French.

1097. The Great Movie Stars 1: The Golden Years by David Shipman. Macdonald, 1989. 623p. illus.

1098. The Great Movie Stars 2: The International Years by David Shipman. Macdonald, 1989. 630p. illus.

1099. The Great Movie Stars 3: The Independent Years by David Shipman. Macdonald, 1991. 281p. illus.

1100. The Illustrated Who's Who in British Film by Denis Gifford. B.T. Batsford, 1978. 334p. illus. bibliog.

1101. New British Political Dramatists: Howard Brenton, David Hare, Trevor Griffiths and David Edgar by John Bull. Macmillan, 1984. 244p. plates. bibliog. index.

1102. A Paler Shade of Green by Des Hickey & Gus Smith. Leslie Frewin, 1972. 253p. plates.

1103. Playback by Ronald Hayman. Davis-Poynter, 1973. 166p.

1104. The Player by Lillian and Helen Ross. Simon and Schuster, 1962. 459p. illus.

1105. Screen Souvenir 1946–7 by Stephanie Lee. Findon Publications, 1947. c50p. illus.

1106. The Second Wave: British Drama for the Seventies by John Russell Taylor. Methuen, 1971. 236p. bibliog.

1107. Sixty Voices – Celebrities Recall the Golden Age of British Cinema by Brian McFarlane. British Film Institute, 1992. 260p. illus. index.

1108. Take Ten: Contemporary British Film Directors by Jonathan Hacker & David Price. Clarendon Press, 1991. 434p. illus. bibliog. filmog. index.

1109. Talking Films: The Best of The Guardian Film Lectures edited by Andrew Britton. Fourth Estate, 1991. 266p.

1110. Three Men and a Gimmick by Robert Hirst. The World's Work Ltd, 1957. 125p. On Peter Cushing, Arthur Askey and Terry-Thomas.

1111. A Who's Who of British Film Actors by Scott Palmer. Scarecrow Press, 1981. 561p. bibliog.

SUBJECTS

CINEMA HISTORY

1112. All Our Yesterdays: 90 Years of British Cinema edited by Charles Barr. British Film Institute, 1986. 446p. illus. bibliog. filmog. index.

1113. Best of British: Cinema and Society 1930–1970 by Jeffrey Richards & Anthony Aldgate. Basil Blackwell, 1983. 170p. illus. filmog. index.

1114. The Big Book of British Films by Robin Cross. Charles Herridge/Sidgwick and Jackson, 1984. 192p. illus. index.

1115. British Cinema History edited by James Curran & Vincent Porter. Weidenfeld and Nicolson, 1983. 445p. tables. bibliog.

1116. The British Cinema: The Unknown Cinema by Alan Lovell. British Film Institute/Education Department, 1969. 8p.

1117. The British Film Collection 1896–1984: A History of the British Cinema in Pictures by Patricia Warren. Elm Tree Books, 1984. 248p. illus. bibliog. index.

1118. The British Labour Movement and Film by Stephen G. Jones. Routledge and Kegan Paul, 1987. 248p. illus. bibliog. index.

1119. The Cinema Book edited by Pam Cook. British Film Institute, 1985. 377p. illus. bibliog. filmog. index.

1120. Cinema Great Britain: Seventy-five Years of British Films by Miriam Clore, David Robinson & Leon Clore.
Film Production Association, 1970. c125p. illus.
Language: English and French.

1121. Cinema in Britain: An Illustrated Survey by Ivan Butler.
A.S. Barnes/Tantivy Press, 1973. 307p. illus. index.

1122. Cinema Inglês (1933–1983) by the Cinemateca Portuguesa & the British Council.
Cinemateca Portuguesa, 1984. 296p. illus. biofilmog.
Language: Portuguese.

1123. Cinema Parade: Fifty Years of Film Shows by John H. Bird.
Cornish Brothers, 1947. 107p. illus. plates.

1124. A Critical History of the British Cinema by Roy Armes.
Secker and Warburg, 1978. 374p. illus. bibliog. index.

1125. The Film Business: A History of British Cinema 1896–1972 by Ernest Betts.
Allen and Unwin, 1973. 349p. illus. bibliog. index.

1126. The Film Game by Low Warren.
Werner Laurie, 1937. 256p. illus.

1127. From Limelight to Satellite: A Scottish Film Book edited by Eddie Dick.
Scottish Film Council/British Film Institute, 1990. 256p. illus. filmog. index.

1128. The Great British Picture Show by George Perry.
Hart-Davis, MacGibbon, 1974. 367p. plates. bibliog. index.

1129. The Miracle of the Movies by Leslie Wood.
Burke Publishing, 1947. 352p. illus.

1130. A Mirror for England: British Movies from Austerity to Affluence by Raymond Durgnat.
Faber, 1970. 336p. plates. bibliog. filmog. index.

1131. A Night at the Pictures: Ten Decades of British Film by Gilbert Adair & Nick Roddick.
Columbus Books/British Film Fair, 1985. 144p. illus.

1132. An Outline of British Film History 1896–1962 by David Grenfell.
British Film Institute, 1963. 25p. Unpublished typescript.

1133. Portraits of the British Cinema: 60 Glorious Years 1925–1985 by John Russell Taylor & John Kobal.
Arum, 1985. 160p. illus. index. Mainly illustrative.

1134. Retrospettiva del Film Inglese dal 1895 al 1948 by the Mostra Internazionale d'Arte Cinematografica di Venezia.
Mostra Internazionale d'Arte Cinematografica di Venezia, 1957. 57p. illus.
Language: Italian and English.

1135. Scotch Reels: Scotland in Cinema and Television edited by Colin McArthur.
British Film Institute, 1982. 122p. illus. tables.

1136. Scotland in Film by Forsyth Hardy.
Edinburgh University Press, 1990. 250p. index. illus.

1137. Spotlight on Filmland: A Book about British Films by Peter Noble.
Ward and Hitchon, 1947. 103p. plates.

1138. Storia del Cinema Inglese 1930–1990 by Emanuela Martini.
Marsilio, 1991. 461p. plates. filmog. index.
Language: Italian.

1139. 30 Ans de Cinéma Britannique by Raymond Lefevre & Roland Lacourbe.
Editions Cinéma 76, 1976. 491p. illus. bibliog. filmog. index.
Language: French.

1140. Twenty Years of British Film 1925–1945 by Michael Balcon, Forsyth Hardy, Roger Manvell et al.
Falcon, 1947. 96p. illus.

1141. 21 Years of the Scottish Film Council 1934–1955 by the Scottish Film Council.
SFC, 1955. 52p.

1142. Where We Came In: Seventy Years of the British Film Industry by Charles Oakley.
Allen and Unwin, 1964. 245p. plates.

CINEMA HISTORY – THE SILENT ERA

1143. Army Life; or, How Soldiers Are Made. Illustrated from a Series of Animatograph Pictures by R.W. Paul.
R.W. Paul, 1900. 24p.

1144. Before 1910: Kinematograph Experiences by R.W. Paul, Cecil Hepworth & W.G. Barker.
British Kinematograph Society, 1936. 16p.
BKS Proceedings No.38.

1145. The Beginnings of the Cinema in England by John Barnes.
David and Charles, 1976. 240p. illus. filmog. index.

1146. The Biograph in Battle, Its Story in the South African War Related with Personal Experiences by W.K.L. Dickson.
T. Fisher Unwin, 1901. 296p. illus.

1147. Cinema 1900–1906: An Analytical Study by the National Film Archive and the International Federation of Film Archives edited by Roger Holman.
Fédération Internationale des Archives du Film, 1982. 558p.
Language: English and French.

1148. Conference Papers of 34th Annual Conference by the Fédération Internationale des Archives du Film.
N.p., 1978. Various.
Programme, programme notes and complete set of papers.

1149. The Dream that Kicks: The Prehistory and Early Years of Cinema in Britain by Michael Chanan.
Routledge and Kegan Paul, 1980. 353p. bibliog. index.

1150. Early Film Makers of the South Coast by the Chichester District Museum.
Chichester District Museum, 1981. 16p. illus.
Exhibition catalogue.

1151. Filming the Boer War. The Beginnings of the Cinema in England 1894–1901 – Volume 4 by John Barnes.
Bishopsgate Press, 1992. 340p. illus. filmog. index.

1152. The History of the British Film 1896–1906 by Rachael Low & Roger Manvell.
Allen and Unwin, 1948. 136p. plates. index.
Based on research by the History Committee of the British Film Institute.

1153. The History of the British Film 1906–1914 by Rachael Low.
Allen and Unwin, 1949. 309p. plates. tables. bibliog. filmog. index.
Based on research of the History Committee of the British Film Institute, Chairman Cecil Hepworth.

1154. The History of the British Film 1914–1918 by Rachael Low.
Allen and Unwin, 1950. 332p. plates. tables. filmog. index.
Published under the auspices of the British Film Institute and the British Film Academy.

1155. The History of the British Film 1918–1929 by Rachael Low.
Allen and Unwin, 1971. 544p. plates. filmog. index.

1156. Our Lady Cinema; How and Why I went into the Photo-play World and What I Found There by Harry Furniss.
J.W. Arrowsmith/Simpkin, Marshall, 1914. 208p. illus.

1157. Pioneers of the British Film. The Beginnings of the Cinema in England 1894–1901, Volume 3: 1898 The Rise of the Photoplay by John Barnes.
Bishopsgate Press, 1983. 256p. illus. index.

1158. Provincial Cinematograph Theatres Ltd Special Collection.
Material held in Provincial Cinematograph Theatres Ltd Special Collection.

1159. Reminiscences of the British Film Trade by A.C. Bromhead.
British Kinematograph Society, 1933. 26p.

1160. The Rise of the Cinema in Great Britain. The Beginnings of the Cinema in England 1894–1901 – Volume 2: Jubilee Year 1897 by John Barnes.
Bishopsgate Press, 1983. 272p. illus. index.

CINEMA HISTORY – THE THIRTIES

1161. The Age of the Dream Palace: Cinema and Society 1930–1939 by Jeffrey Richards.
Routledge and Kegan Paul, 1984. 374p. plates. bibliog. index.

1162. British Films 1927–1939 by Linda Wood.
British Film Institute/Library Services, 1986. 143p. stats. bibliog.

1163. Deadly Parallels: Film and the Left in Britain 1929–1939 by Bert Hogenkamp.
Lawrence and Wishart, 1986. 240p. illus. bibliog. filmog. index.

1164. Enter the Dream House: The British Film Industry and the Working Classes in Depression England 1929–1939 by Stephen Craig Shafer.
University Microfilms International, 1982. 414p. tables. bibliog. filmog. discog.

1165. The History of the British Film 1929–1939: Film Making in 1930s Britain by Rachael Low.
Allen and Unwin/British Film Institute, 1985. 452p. illus. bibliog. filmog. index.

1166. Theatre and Film in Exile: German Artists in Britain 1933–1945 by Gunter Berghaus.
Berg Publishers, 1989. 275p. illus. bibliog. index.

CINEMA HISTORY – THE FORTIES

1167. Blackout: Reinventing Women for Wartime British Cinema by Antonia Lant.
Princeton University, 1991. 262p. illus. appendix. filmog. bibliog. index.

1168. Britain and the Cinema in the Second World War by Philip M. Taylor.
Macmillan, 1988. 210p. index.

1169. Britain Can Take It: The British Cinema in the Second World War by Anthony Aldgate & Jeffrey Richards.
Basil Blackwell, 1986. 312p. illus. filmog. index.

1170. Films 1945–1950 by Denis Forman.
Longmans Green for the British Council, 1952. 64p.

1171. Films and the Second World War by Roger Manvell.
A.S. Barnes/J.M. Dent, 1974. 388p. illus. bibliog. index.

1172. Films since 1939 by Dilys Powell.
Longmans Green for the British Council, 1948. 40p. illus.

1173. National Fictions: World War Two in British Films and Television edited by Geoff Hurd.
British Film Institute, 1984. 77p. illus. filmog. teleog.

1174. Progress of British Films 1946–47.
McKenzie, Vincent and Co, 1947. 72p. illus. biog.

1175. Progress of British Films: Part I and Part II.
McKenzie, Vincent and Co, 1946. 160p. illus.

1176. Realism and Tinsel: Cinema and Society in Britain 1939–1948 by Robert Murphy.
Routledge and Kegan Paul, 1989. 278p. illus. bibliog. index.

1177. The Representation of Women in British Films 1943–1953 by Sue Aspinall.
MA thesis, 1981. 43p.

1178. Vaudeville Patterns by A. Crooks Ripley & Peter Noble.
Brownlee, 1946. 124p. illus.

CINEMA HISTORY – THE FIFTIES

1179. The Film: United Kingdom by Stanley Reed.
British Film Institute, 1955. 15p.

1180. Sex, Class and Realism: British Cinema 1956–1963 by John Hill.
British Film Institute, 1986. 228p. illus. filmog.

CINEMA HISTORY – THE SIXTIES

1181. The Abortive Renaissance by Peter Graham.
Axle Publications, 1963. 12p.

1182. Breakthrough in Britain by Alan Lovell.
British Film Institute/Education Department, 1967. 19p.

1183. British Films – A Kind of Progress by David Childs & Vincent Porter.
Extract from 'Socialist Commentary', 1964. 4p.

1184. Free Cinema: Furisii Filmului Britanic by Adina Darian.
Meridane, 1970. 64p. plates. bibliog. filmog.
Language: Romanian.

1185. Hollywood, England: The British Film Industry in the Sixties by Alexander Walker.
Michael Joseph, 1974. 493p. plates. index.

1186. Jeune Cinéma Anglais by Jacques Belmans.
SERDOC, 1967. 126p. plates. bibliog.
Language: French.

1187. New Cinema in Britain by Roger Manvell.
Studio Vista/Dutton Picturebacks, 1969. 160p. illus. index.

1188. Sixties British Cinema by Robert Murphy.
British Film Institute, 1992. 353p. illus. appendix. notes. bibliog. index.

1189. Société et Cinéma: Les Années 1960 en Grande-Bretagne – Essai d'Interprétation by Alain Malassinet.
Lettres Modernes/Minard, 1979. 223p. bibliog. filmog.
Language: French.

1190. What's Happening to British Films by the Unit.
Unit, 1967. 20p.

CINEMA HISTORY – THE SEVENTIES

1191. National Heroes: British Cinema in the Seventies and Eighties by Alexander Walker.
Harrap, 1985. 296p. plates. index.

1192. The Once and Future Film: British Cinema in the Seventies and Eighties by John Walker.
Methuen, 1985. 184p. biofilmog. index.

CINEMA HISTORY – THE EIGHTIES

1193. British Cinema Now edited by Martin Auty & Nick Roddick.
British Film Institute, 1985. 168p. illus. index.

1194. British Cinema: The Lights that Failed by James Park.
B.T. Batsford, 1990. 192p. illus. bibliog. index.

1195. British Film-makers of the 80s by Clyde Jeavons.
British Council, 1990. 14p. illus. biofilmog.

1196. Fires Were Started: British Cinema and Thatcherism edited by Lester Friedman.
University of Minneapolis Press, 1993. 320p. illus. index.

1197. Learning to Dream: The New British Cinema by James Park.
Faber, 1984. 138p. illus.

1198. Local Heroes: Registi e Scrittori nel Cinema Britannico degli Anni Ottanta edited by Filippo D'Angelo et al.
La Casa Usher, 1986. 157p. illus. biofilmog.
Language: Italian.

1199. Le Nouveau Cinéma Britannique 1979–1988 by Philippe Pilard.
5 Continents/Hatier, 1989. 221p. illus. bibliog. filmog. index.
Language: French.

CINEMA HISTORY – THE COMPANIES

1200. Best of British: A Celebration of Rank Film Classics by Maurice Sellar et al.
Sphere, 1987. 154p. illus.

1201. Bungalow Town: Theatre and Film Colony by N.E.B. Wolters.
The Author, 1985. 62p. illus.

1202. Catalogue of the Film Studio Equipment at Film Studios, Shepperton, Middlesex for Sale by Auction by Fuller, Horsey, Sons and Cassell. 168p.

1203. Ealing Studios by Charles Barr.
Cameron and Tayleur/David and Charles, 1977. 198p. illus. filmog. index.

1204. Ealing Studios edited by Emanuela Martini.
Bergamo Film Meeting '88, 1988. 143p. illus. bibliog. filmog.
Language: Italian.

1205. The Elstree Story: Twenty-one Years of Film-making by Leslie Banks et al.
Clerke and Cockeran, 1949. 95p. illus.

1206. Elstree: The British Hollywood by Patricia Warren.
Elm Tree Books, 1983. 184p. illus. bibliog. filmog. index.

1207. Film Studio: A Bygone Age by Julien Caunter.
N.p., n.d.. 350p. filmog. index.
A history of Beaconsfield Studios.

1208. Forever Ealing: A Celebration of the Great British Film Studio by George Perry.
Pavilion/Michael Joseph, 1981. 200p. illus. bibliog. filmog. index.

1209. The Formation and Early History of Pinewood Studios by Gregg Glaser.
The Author, 1975. 44p. bibliog.

1210. Gainsborough Melodrama edited by Sue Aspinall & Robert Murphy.
British Film Institute, 1983. 93p. filmog.

1211. Gainsborough Pictures: A Popular Commercial Studio by Robert Murphy.
MA thesis, 1981. 29p. bibliog. filmog.

1212. The Golden Gong: Fifty Years of the Rank Organisation, Its Films and Its Stars by Quentin Falk.
Columbus Books, 1987. 208p. illus. bibliog. index.

1213. Hammer e Dintorni edited by Emanuela Martini.
Bergamo Film Meeting '90, 1990. 159p. illus. bibliog. filmog. teleog.
Language: Italian.

1214. Hammer: A Cinema Case Study by David Pirie.
British Film Institute, 1980. 64p. illus.

1215. The History of the British Mutoscope and Biograph Company and an Account of the Biograph Film Studios by Richard Brown.
The Author, 1992. 64p. tables.

1216. Hollywood a Go-go: An Account of the Cannon Phenomenon by Andrew Yule.
Sphere, 1987. 233p. tables.

1217. The House of Horror: The Story of Hammer Films edited by Allen Eyles & Nicholas Fry.
Lorrimer, 1981. 144p. illus. filmog.

1218. The House of Jury by Jury's Imperial Pictures.
Jury's, 1909. 15p. illus.
Publicity brochure.

1219. If it Moves – Film it: A History of Film-making in Walton-on-Thames, 1900–1939, Commemorating the Work of Cecil Hepworth and Clifford Spain by the Weybridge Museum.
Weybridge Museum, 1973. 13p. plates.

1220. Movies from the Mansion: A History of Pinewood Studios by George Perry.
Elm Tree Books, 1982. 191p. illus.

1221. My Indecision is Final by Jake Eberts & Terry Ilott.
Faber, 1990. 678p. plates. tables. index.

1222. Nettlefold Studios Special Collection.
20 items including agreements.

1223. Plan for Film Studios: A Plea for Reform by Helmut Junge.
Focal Press, 1945. 64p. plans. diagrs.

1224. Projecting Britain: Ealing Studios Film Posters edited by David Wilson.
British Film Institute, 1982. 67p. col.illus. index.

1225. The Rank Financial Disaster of 1949 by Pascale-Philippe Volle.
MSc thesis, 1987. 91p. illus. tables. bibliog. filmog.

1226. The Rank Organisation Ltd by The Cinema Press.
The Cinema Press, 1956. 108p. illus.

1227. Sam Shawcroft Special Collection.
Material relating to Elstree Studios.

1228. Stars by Day: A Tour in Words and Pictures of the British Film Studios by Robert Stannage.
Film Book Club, c1947. 103p. plates.

1229. Vampires: Hammer Style by Robert Marrero.
RGM Publications, 1982. 98p. illus. biofilmog. filmog.

THE FILM INDUSTRY

1230. A.I.P. Report: Recommendations to the Government Following the Prime Minister's Working Party Report on The Future of the British Film Industry and the Interim Action Committee's Report on the Setting Up of a British Film Authority by the Association of Independent Producers.
AIP, 1978. 31p.

1231. Action!: Fifty Years in the Life of a Union by the Association of Cinematograph, TV & Allied Technicians.
ACTT, 1983. 176p. illus. index.

1232. The Activities of the British Film Industry, Presented to the Delegates of the Monetary and Economic Conference of the Federation of British Industries by the Gaumont British Picture Corporation.
FBI, 1933. 20p.

1233. Britain: World Film Centre 1976 edited by Michael Relph.
Film Production Association of Great Britain, 1976. 96p. illus.

1234. The British Film Industry by John Davis.
Chartered Institute of Secretaries, 1958. 16p.
Paper given at the Annual Conference of CIS at Llandudno, May 1958.

1235. British Film Industry by Linda Wood.
British Film Institute/Library Services, 1980. Various pagings. stats.

1236. The British Film Industry: A Report on Its History and Present Organisation with Special Reference to the Economic Problems of British Feature Film Production by the Political and Economic Planning.
PEP, 1952. 307p. tables.
Supplement published in 1958.

1237. British Film Production Data by Stephen Romer.
N.p., 1990. 126p. illus. tables.

1238. British Film Production in the EEC: Background Papers by Vincent Porter.
Polytechnic of Central London, 1972. 77p.

1239. British Films by Paul Rotha.
World Review, n.d. pp. 47–51 illus.

1240. British Films: Fact, Forecast and Opinion by the Rank Organisation.
Rank, 1948. 33p.

1241. Business Monitor: M2 – Cinemas.
HMSO.
Published annually from 1968 to 1984.

1242. Business Start-up edited by Shelly Bancroft.
Association of Independent Producers, 1987. 63p.

1243. The Cinema Industries in the EEC and the United Kingdom by Jack Kershaw.
N.p., 1972. 168p. tables.

1244. The Cinema Industry 1950–1970 and Its Customers by P. Braithwaite.
CNAA thesis, 1970. 87p.

1245. A Competitive Cinema by Terence Kelly, Graham Norton & George Perry.
Institute of Economic Affairs, 1966. 204p. tables. diagrs. bibliog.

1246. Creativity and Constraint in the British Film Industry by Duncan Petrie.
Macmillan, 1991. 249p. plates. appendix. bibliog. index.

1247. The Crisis of British Films by the Film Industry Employees Council.
FIEC, 1951. 12p. tables.

1248. The Decline of the Cinema: An Economist's Report by John Spraos.
Allen and Unwin, 1962. 168p. tables.

1249. Developing the Independent Film and Video Sector by the Boyden Southwood Associates/Comedia.
Greater London Arts, 1989. 166p. tables. bibliog.

1250. Distribution and Exhibition edited by Shelly Bancroft.
Association of Independent Producers, 1987. 119p.

1251. Facts about Films by Donald Alexander.
London Bureau of Current Affairs, 1946. 20p. illus.

1252. The Fate of British Films by John Grierson.
Reprinted from 'The Fortnightly', 1937. 15p.

1253. Feature Film Development in the UK by Sarah Burton et al.
National Film and Television School, 1989. 57p. diagrs.

1254. Film and Cinema Statistics: A Preliminary Report on Methodology with Tables Giving Current Statistics by UNESCO.
UNESCO, 1956. 111p. tables.

1255. Film and Television: West Germany and Great Britain by the Polytechnic of Central London & the Goethe Institute.
PCL, 1976. 78p. tables. bibliog.
Papers from a two-day conference held in London in December 1976.

1256. Film Business is Big Business: An Investigation into Film Production Finance by the Association of Cine-Technicians.
ACT, 1940. 29p.

1257. The Film in Britain by the Central Office of Information Reference Division.
COI, 1963. 22p.

1258. Film in Europe: Proceedings of a Conference Held at the Polytechnic of Central London edited by Vincent Porter.
PCL, 1974. c150p.

1259. The Film Industry by Davidson Boughey.
Pitman, 1921. 110p. illus. diagrs.

1260. The Film Industry in Great Britain: Some Facts and Figures edited by John Gillett.
British Film Academy with Fredk. W. Kahn, 1950. 41p. appendix. tables.

1261. The Film Industry in Six European Countries by the Film Centre.
UNESCO, 1950. 156p. tables.

1262. The Film Industry: A Memorandum by the Communist Party.
Communist Party, 1947.

1263. Film Production Association of Great Britain, the EEC and the Film Industry by the Film Production Association.
N.p., 1971. 22p.
Transcript of a conference convened by the FPA at the National Film Theatre.

1264. Film, Video and Television: Market Forces, Fragmentation and Technological Advance by Graham Wade.
Comedia, 1985. 77p. tables.

1265. Films – An Alternative to Rank: An Analysis of Power and Policy in the British Film Industry by Frederic Mullally.
Socialist Book Centre, 1946. 32p.

1266. Films and Forecasts by L'Estrange Fawcett.
Geoffrey Bles, 1927. 277p. index.

1267. Films in Focus by Richard Auty.
Bureau of Current Affairs, 1949. 20p. illus.

1268. Films: A Financial Times Survey.
Financial Times, Sept. 1958. 32p.

1269. Financial Survey: Cinema, Television and Radio Producers by the ICC.
ICC. 1974/75 to date.

1270. The First Thirty Years: A Record of the National Association of Theatrical, Television and Kine Employees 1890 to 1920 by Syd Heath.
NATKE, 1973. 48p.

1271. The Focus Report: Recommendations to the Government Following the Prime Minister's Working Party Report Focus, 1978. Unpaged. diagrs. bibliog.

1272. From Downing Street to Centrepoint: A Review of Progress on the Downing Street Agenda by Wilf Stevenson.
British Film Institute, 20p.
Speech given to the BFI/CBI Conference on 5 March 1992.

1273. The Great Film Lock-out by the Group of Communist Film Workers.
Communist Party, 1949. 24p.

1274. A Guide to British Film Production by the British Film Producers Association.
BFPA, 1966. 27p.

1275. The Industry by Nicholas Garnham & Geoff Reeves.
Granta, Nov. 1960. pp. 36–42 illus.

1276. Inside Pictures, with Some Reflections from the Outside by Ernest Betts.
Cresset Press, 1960. 161p. illus.

1277. Intermission in the British Film Industry by John H. Davis.
National Provincial Bank Review, Aug. 1958. pp. 1–12.

1278. Labour Power in the British Film Industry by Michael Chanan.
British Film Institute, 1976. 57p. bibliog.

1279. A Level Playing Field? by Patricia Perilli.
British Film Institute, 1991. 48p. tables.

1280. The Malady of the British Film: Its Cause and Cure by Meyrick Milton.
Austin Leigh, 1925. 66p.

1281. A Memorandum on the Scarcity of the Film Supply together with a Scheme to Assist British Film Production by Sidney Bernstein.
Sidney Bernstein, 1939. 12p.

1282. Money behind the Screen: A Report Prepared on Behalf of the Film Council by F.D. Klingender & Stuart Legg.
Arno Press, 1978. 79p. illus. tables.
First published in 1937 by Lawrence and Wishart.

1283. Monopoly: The Future of British Film by Ralph Bond.
Association of Cine-Technicians, 1946. 32p.

1284. Nationalising the Film Industry: Report of the ACTT Nationalisation Forum, August 1973 by the Association of Cinematograph, TV & Allied Technicians.
ACTT, 1973. 59p. illus. tables.

1285. The Need for Tax Incentives by Michael Prescott.
British Film Institute, 1991. 33p. tables. appendix.

1286. New Questions of British Cinema edited by Duncan Petrie.
British Film Institute, 1992. 119p.

1287. A New Society of Leisure: Strategies for the Future of the British Film Industry by Anthony J.H. Burton.
Thesis, 1986. 56p. stats.

1288. Newsreel Agreement Between the Association of Cine-Technicians and the Newsreel Association.
Newsreel Association of Great Britain & Ireland, 1947. 23p.

1289. No Fine on Fun: The Comical History of the Entertainments Duty by A.P. Herbert.
Methuen, 1957. 200p.

1290. Patterns of Discrimination against Women in the Film and Television Industries by the Association of Cinematograph, TV and Allied Technicians.
ACTT, 1975. 62p. tables.

1291. Problems of the British Film Industry by Edouard Roditi.
N.p., c1937. 10p.

1292. Productive Relationship? by Nick Smedley & John Woodward.
British Film Institute, 1991. 30p. tables.

1293. Projection 2000: Cinemas by Projection 2000.
Projection 2000, 1989. 32p. tables.
Research report on spare-time.

1294. Promoting the Industry by Richard Lewis & Paul Marris.
British Film Institute, 1991. 44p.

1295. Proposals for Improvement in the British Film Industry: Report by the Labour Party Trade and Industry Group Films Sub-committee.
Labour Party, 1946. 5p.

1296. Quality not Cost is the Test of a Good British Film, by the Cinematograph Exhibitors' Association of Great Britain.
CEA, 1937. 8p.

1297. Raising Production Finance by Shelly Bancroft.
Association of Independent Producers, 1987. 134p.

1298. Recent Trends in British Films by John Alexander.
Extract from 'Soviet Literature', 1954. 3p.

1299. Report of the All-Industry Committee of the Film Industry by Robert Bolt.
Association of Independent Producers, 1977. 12p. appendix.

1300. Review of the UK Film Industry: Report to the British Screen Advisory Council by Richard Lewis.
N.p., 1990. 82p. diagrs. tables.

1301. Screen Digest Dossier: British Cinema and Film Statistics by Screen Digest.
Screen Digest, 1990. 17p. tables.

1302. Show Business and the Law by E.R. Hardy Ivamy.
Stevens, 1955. 188p. index.

1303. A Speech to the General Council of the Cinematograph Exhibitors' Association by J. Arthur Rank.
N.p., 1948. 4p.

1304. A Statistical Survey of the Cinema Industry in Great Britain in 1934 by Simon Rowson.
Reprinted from 'Journal of the Royal Statistical Society', 1936. 62p. tables.

1305. Statistics of the Film Industry in Europe by Michel Gyorgy & Gabrielle Glas.
European Centre for Research & Information on Film & Television, 1992. 280p. tables.

1306. Statistics on Film and Cinema 1955–1977 by the Division of Statistics on Culture and Communications.
UNESCO, 1981. 99p. tables.

1307. Submission to the Parliamentary Under-Secretary of State for Trade on 'The Future of the British Film Industry' by the Independent Filmmakers' Association.
IFA, 1978. 8p.

1308. Survival or Extinction? A Policy for British Films by the Association of Cinematograph, TV and Allied Technicians.
ACTT, 1964. 47p. tables.

1309. Talking of Films by R. J. Minney.
Home and Van Thal, 1947. 80p.

1310. U.K. Cinema Today 1980 by Euromonitor.
Euromonitor Publications, 1980. 114p.

1311. Whatever Happened to...The British Film...Or Could There Be Life after Death: An Enquiry, an Analysis, a Challenge, and Perhaps a Plan for Survival by John and Roy Boulting.
Charter Film Productions, 1980. 24p.

GOVERNMENT AND THE CINEMA

1312. AIP Report 1983: Recommendations to the Government on the Future of British Film Production by the Association of Independent Producers.
AIP, 1983. 16p.

1313. Cinema and State: The Film Industry and Government 1927–84 by Margaret Dickinson & Sarah Street.
British Film Institute, 1985. 280p. illus. stats. bibliog. index.

1314. Cinematograph (Amendment) Act, 1982.
HMSO, 1982. 14p.

1315. Cinematograph Act, 1952.
HMSO, 1952. 6p.

1316. Cinematograph Film Production (Special Loans) Acts, 1949–1954.
HMSO, 1949–54. Various pagings. Plus accounts.

1317. Cinematograph Films Act, 1909.
HMSO, 1909. 6p.

1318. Cinematograph Films Act, 1927.
HMSO, 1927. 23p.

1319. Cinematograph Films Act, 1938.
HMSO, 1938. 48p.
Plus Cinematograph Films Bill 1938, Standing Committee Proceedings and Debates in Parliament.

1320. Cinematograph Films Act, 1948.
HMSO, 1948. 38p.

1321. Cinematograph Films Act, 1957.
HMSO, 1957. 12p.

1322. Cinematograph Films Act, 1975.
HMSO, 1975. 2p.

1323. Concerning Legislation to Encourage Empire Films by Meyrick Milton.
Austin Leigh, 1927. 28p.

1324. Distribution and Exhibition of Cinematograph Films: Recommendations to the President of the Board of Trade on the Report of the Committee of Enquiry by the Cinematograph Films Council
Chair: Earl of Drogheda
HMSO, 1950. 16p.

1325. Distribution and Exhibition of Cinematograph Films: Report of the Committee of Enquiry Appointed by the President of the Board of Trade.
Chair: Sir Arnold Plant
HMSO, '949. 63p. tables.

1326. Eady Scheme by Anthony S. Gruner.
Daily Film Renter, 1952. 31p.

1327. Film Policy by the Department of Trade and Industry.
HMSO, 1984. 27p.

1328. Films Act, 1960.
HMSO, 1960. 66p.
Plus Films Bill.

1329. Films Act, 1970.
HMSO, 1970. 10p.

1330. Films Act, 1980.
HMSO, 1980. Various pagings.
Plus Films Bill, Standing Committees and Parliamentary Debates.

1331. Films Act, 1985.
HMSO, 1985. Various pagings.
Plus Films Bill, Amendments and Parliamentary Debates.

1332. Films: A Report on the Supply of Films for Exhibition in Cinemas by the Monopolies Commission.
HMSO, 1966. 113p. tables.
Chair: Ashton Roskill

1333. Films: A Report on the Supply of Films for Exhibition in Cinemas by the Monopolies and Mergers Commission.
HMSO, 1983. 123p. tables. index.
Chair: Sir Godfray Le Quesne

1334. Final Report of the Census of Production for 1948. Volume II–Trade G: Cinematograph Film Production by the Board of Trade.
HMSO, 1952. 20p.

1335. Future of the British Film Industry: Report of the Prime Minister's Working Party by John Terry.
HMSO, 1976. 34p.

1336. The Future of the Films Act by Simon Rowson.
The Author, 1935. 30p.
Expanded version of paper read at CEA Conference on 26 June 1935.

1337. Memorandum of Agreement between His Majesty's Government in the United Kingdom and the Motion Picture Industry of the United States of America by the Board of Trade.
HMSO, 1948.
2nd agreement for 1950.

1338. Memorandum on Cinematograph Films Bill with Detailed Notes on the Clauses by Simon Rowson.
N.p., Sept. 1927. 46p.

1339. Minutes of a Conference on the Subject of British Film Production, Held at the Offices of the Federation of British Industries by the Federation of British Industries.
N.p., 1925. Various pagings.
Conference took place May, November, December 1925.

1340. Minutes of Evidence Taken before the Departmental Committee on Cinematograph Films by the Board of Trade Committee on Cinematograph Films.
HMSO, 1936. 272p.
Chair: Lord Moyne.

1341. National Film Finance Corporation Act, 1981.
HMSO, 1981. 11p.

1342. Policy for British Films: Speech to the 15th Annual General Meeting of the Association of Cine-Technicians by Harold Wilson.
N.p., 1948. 11p.

1343. Proposals for Legislation on Cinematograph Films by the Board of Trade.
HMSO, 1937. 12p.

1344. Recommendations of the Cinematograph Films Council for New Legislation on Cinematograph Films by the Board of Trade/Cinematograph Films Committee.
HMSO, 1947. 12p.
Chair: Arnold Plant.

1345. Report of a Committee Appointed by the Board of Trade to Consider the Position of British Films by the Board of Trade Committee on Cinematograph Films.
HMSO, 1936. 41p.
Chair: Lord Moyne.

1346. Report of the Film Studio Committee by the Board of Trade Film Studio Committee.
HMSO, 1948. 18p.
Chair: Sir George Gater.

1347. Report of the Working Party on Film Production Costs by the Board of Trade.
HMSO, 1949. 32p. tables.
Chair: Sir George Gater.

1348. Report on Experimental Scheme to Test the Effectiveness of Recommendations in the Monopolies and Mergers Commission Report on the Supply of Films for Exhibition in Cinemas by the Office of Fair Trading.
N.p., 1987. c100p. tables.

1349. Reports of the Interim Action Committee. I: Proposals for the Setting Up of a British Film Authority; II: Financing the British Film Industry; III: Statistics, Technological Development and Cable Television; IV: Film and Television Co-operation; V: The Distribution of Films for Exhibition in Cinemas and by other means.
HMSO. Various pagings.
Series of reports published between 1978 and 1982.
Chair: Sir Harold Wilson.

1350. Review of Policy on Film Finance by the Department of Trade.
N.p., 1979. 28p. appendix.

1351. Sunday Entertainments Act, 1932.
HMSO, 1932. 9p.

1352. Tendencies to Monopoly in the Cinematograph Film Industry: Report of a Committee Appointed by the Cinematograph Films Council by the Board of Trade/Cinematograph Films Council.
HMSO, 1944. 41p. tables.
Chair: Albert Palache.

1353. The View from Downing Street by Jane Headland & Simon Relph.
British Film Institute, 1991. 34p. tables. appendix.

THE BRITISH FILM INSTITUTE

1354. Archive: A Study of the History, Work and Aims of Britain's National Film Archive by Neil Stephen Kendall.
BA thesis, 1979. 37p. illus.

1355. The British Film Institute and Regional Film Theatres: Developing a Profile of Subsidized Film Exhibition in Britain by Susan Feldman.
An Arts Administration Studies project, 1980. 103p. tables.

1356. British Film Institute Production Board edited by Alan Lovell.
British Film Institute, 1976. 68p.
Includes history of Experimental Film Fund.

1357. The Cinema and the Public: A Critical Analysis of the Origin, Constitution and Control of the British Film Institute by Walter Ashley.
Ivor Nicholson and Watson, 1934. 44p.

1358. Film in National Life: Being the Report of an Enquiry Conducted by the Commission on Educational and Cultural Films into the Service which the Cinematograph May Render to Education and Social Progress by the Commission on Educational and Cultural Films.
Allen and Unwin, 1932. 204p.
Report which led to the setting up of the BFI.

1359. The First Twenty-Five Years by the British Film Institute.
BFI, 1958. 39p. photos.

1360. Forty Years 1952–92: The World's Leading Cinematheque Celebrates Its Fortieth Anniversary by Deac Rossell.
British Film Institute/National Film Theatre, 1992. 30p. illus.

1361. Outside London: A Report to the Governors of the British Film Institute by James Quinn.
British Film Institute, 1965. 48p. illus.

1362. To Encourage the Art of the Film: The Story of the British Film Institute by Ivan Butler.
Robert Hale, 1971. 208p. plates. index.

1363. The Work of the British Film Institute by Denis Forman.
Quarterly of Film, Radio & Television, Winter 1954. pp. 147–58.

1364. The Work of the National Film Library by Ernest Lindgren.
British Kinematograph Society's Journal, March 1945. 12p.

FILM PRODUCTION

1365. Accent on Design: Four European Art Directors by Catherine A. Surowiec.
British Film Institute, 1992. 48p. illus. bibliog.
Entries on Vincent Korda, Hein Heckroth, Alfred Junge and Lazare Meerson.

1366. Acting in Film: An Actor's Take on Movie Making by Michael Caine.
Applause, 1990. 153p. illus. filmog.

1367. All about Cinema by Derek Bowskill.
W.H. Allen, 1976. 142p. illus. bibliog. index.

1368. Anatomy of the Film by H.H. Wollenberg.
Marsland Publications, 1947. 104p. illus.

1369. Animated Photograph: The A.B.C. of the Cinematograph, a Simple and Thorough Guide to the Projection of Living Photographs, with Notes on the Production of Cinematograph Negatives by Cecil Hepworth.
Hazell, Watson and Viney, 1897. 108p. illus.

1370. Art and Design in the British Film: A Pictorial Directory of British Art Directors and Their Work edited by Edward Carrick.
Dennis Dobson, 1948. 133p. illus.

1371. The Art of Film Production by Andrew Buchanan.
Pitman, 1936. 99p. illus.

1372. The Art of the Film by Ernest Lindgren.
Allen and Unwin, 1948. 258p. illus. glossary.

1373. Behind the Cinema Screen by Stuart Chesmore.
Thomas Nelson and Sons, c1933. 100p. illus.

1374. British Composers for the Film by Christopher Palmer.
Performing Right No.6, Nov. 1971. pp. 20–8, illus.

1375. British Creators of Film Technique. British Scenario Writers: The Creators of the Language of D.W. Griffith, G.A. Smith, Alfred Collins and Some Others by Georges Sadoul.
British Film Institute, 1948. 10p.

1376. British Film Music by John Huntley.
Skelton Robinson, 1947. 247p. illus.

1377. British Technicolor Films by John Huntley.
Skelton Robinson, 1949. 224p. plates. filmog.

1378. Continuity Girl by Martha Robinson.
Robert Hale, 1937. 253p. plates.

1379. Designing for Films by Edward Carrick.
Studio Publications, 1949. 128p. illus.

1380. Development by Shelly Bancroft & Sally Davies.
Association of Independent Producers, 1989. 82p.

1381. Directing Motion Pictures by Terence St. John Marner.
Tantivy Press/A.S. Barnes, 1972. 158p. illus. index.

1382. Film Credits: Art Department by the Association of Cinematograph and Allied Technicians.
ACTT. 1952: 34p.; 1953: 27p.

1383. Film Design by Terence St. John Marner & Michael Stringer.
Tantivy Press/A.S. Barnes, 1974. 165p. illus. index.

1384. A Film is Born: How 40 Film Fathers Bring a Modern Talking Film into Being by Norman Lee.
Jordan and Sons, 1945. 123p. illus.

1385. Film Production by Adrian Brunel.
Newnes, 1936. 184p.

1386. Film Publicity: A Handbook on the Production and Distribution of Propaganda Films by Sydney Box.
Lovat Dickson Ltd, 1937. 142p.

1387. Film Script: The Technique of Writing for the Screen by Adrian Brunel.
Burke Publishing Co., 1948. 192p. illus.

1388. Filmcraft: The Art of Picture Production by Adrian Brunel.
George Newnes, 1935. 238p. appendix.

1389. Footnotes to the Film edited by Charles Davy.
Lovat Dickson, 1937. 346p. illus.

1390. From Script to Screen edited by Bruce Woodhouse.
Winchester Publications, 1948. 192p. illus. index.

1391. How Films Are Made by Stanley Reed & John Huntley.
Educational Supply Association, 1955. 90p. illus.

1392. Ivor Beddoes Special Collection.
See item 428

1393. John Greenwood Special Collection.
See item 634

1394. Lectures Given to the British Film Institute's 1945 Summer School by Michael Balcon, Charles Frend, Bridget Boland et al.
British Film Institute, 1945. Various pagings.

1395. The Living Screen: Background to the Film and Television by Roger Manvell.
Harrap, 1961. 192p. index.

1396. Location – Cornwall by David Clarke.
Bossiney Books, 1990. 96p. illus.

1397. Made in Devon by Chips Barber, David Fitzgerald & Sally Barber.
Obelisk, 1988. 104p. illus.

1398. The Making of Feature Films: A Guide by Ivan Butler.
Penguin, 1971. 191p. plates. filmog. index.

1399. The March of the Movies by Harry Alan Towers & Leslie Mitchell.
Sampson Low Marston, 1947. 88p. photos.

1400. Money for Film Stories by Norman Lee.
Pitman, 1937. 206p. index.

1401. Moving Pictures: How They Are Made and Worked by Frederick A. Talbot.
Heinemann, 1912. 340p. illus. plates.
Copy amended by Birt Acres.

1402. My Studio Sketchbook by Emil Weiss.
Marsland/Falcon Press, 1948. 36p.
illus.
Mainly illustrative material.

1403. New Independents on Four by Channel
Four.
Channel Four, N.d.. 23p. illus.

1404. On Acting by Laurence Olivier.
Weidenfeld and Nicolson, 1986. 270p.
illus. index.

1405. Richard Arnell Special Collection.
See item 400

1406. Richard Best Special Collection.
See item 433

1407. Stage and Film Decor by R. Myerscough-
Walker.
Pitman, 1940. 192p. illus.

1408. The Technique of Film Editing by Karel
Reisz & Gavin Millar.
Focal Press, 1968. 411p. illus. index.

1409. The Technique of Film Music by Roger
Manvell & John Huntley.
Focal Press, 1957. 299p. illus.
British Film Academy Advisory
Committee.
Included William Alwyn, Ken Cameron,
Muir Mathieson and Basil Wright.

1410. The Use of Music edited by Shelly
Bancroft.
Association of Independent Producers,
1987. 43p.

1411. The Work of the Motion Picture
Cameraman by Freddie Young & Paul
Petzold.
Focal Press, 1972. 246p. illus.

1412. Working for the Films edited by Oswell
Blakeston.
Focal Press, 1947. 207p. diagrs.

SOCIAL ASPECTS OF THE CINEMA

1413. Black and Third Cinema: Film and TV
Bibliography by Chris Vieler-Porter.
British Film Institute, 1991. 247p.

1414. Black Film British Cinema edited by
Kobena Mercer.
Institute of Contemporary Arts, 1988.
62p. illus.

1415. Brickbats and Bouquets: Black Woman's
Critique, Literature, Theatre, Film by
Akua Rugg.
Race Today Publications, 1984. 96p.

1416. Britain's Self-portraiture in Feature Films
by Roger Manvell.
Geographical Magazine, Aug. 1953. pp.
222–34, illus.

1417. The British Board of Film Censors: Film
Censorship in Britain 1896–1950 by
James C. Robertson.
Croom Helm, 1985. 213p. plates.
bibliog. index.

1418. British Board of Film Classification
Special Collection.
Scenarios 1930–39, 1941–47 & Verbatim
Reports 1930–31, 1932–35.

1419. British Films by An Englishman.
Author/E.D. Paine, 1938. 54p.

1420. British Films for Liberated Europe by the
Ministry of Information.
N.p., 1944. 6p.
Lists British features and shorts shown
in France and Italy.

1421. British Influence through the Films by
Simon Rowson.
Royal Empire Society, 1933. 17p.

1422. The Censor's Reply by John Trevelyan.
Encounter, Sept. 1960. pp. 61–5.
A response to 'The Habit of Censorship'
by Derek Hill (Item 1449). Includes item
by Tony Richardson.

1423. The Censor, the Drama and the Film
1900–1934 by Dorothy Knowles.
Allen and Unwin, 1934. 294p.

1424. Censorship in Britain by Paul O'Higgins.
Nelson, 1972. 232p. bibliog. index.
appendix.

1425. Censorship in the 70s Special Collection.
Collection of press cuttings.

1426. Children and Films: A Study of Boys and
Girls in the Cinema. A Report to the
Carnegie United Kingdom Trustees on an
Enquiry into Children's Response to Films
by Mary Field.
Carnegie United Kingdom Trust, 1954.
56p. tables.

1427. Children and the Cinema: An Inquiry
Made by the Social Survey in October
1948 for a Departmental Committee by
Joy C. Ward.
Central Office of Information, 1949.
100p. tables.

1428. Children in the Cinema by Richard Ford.
Allen and Unwin, 1939. 232p. index.

1429. Children Out of School: An Inquiry into
the Leisure Interests and Activities of
Children Out of School Hours, Carried
out for the Central Advisory Council for
Education by Joy C. Ward.
Central Office of Information, 1948.
76p. tables.

1430. The Cinema and the Child: A Report of
Investigations June–October 1931 by the
Birkenhead Vigilance Committee.
P.W. Shone, 1931. 24p. tables.

1431. Cinema, Censorship and Sexuality 1909–
1925 by Annette Kuhn.
Routledge and Kegan Paul, 1988. 160p.
illus. bibliog. filmog. index.

1432. The Cinematograph in Science, Education
and Matters of State by Charles Urban.
Urban Trading Company, 1906. 56p.

1433. A Culture for Democracy: Mass
Communication and the Cultivated Mind
in Britain Between the Wars by D.L.
LeMahieu.
Clarendon Press, 1988. 396p. index.

1434. The Edinburgh Cinema Enquiry: Being an
Investigation Conducted into the
Influence of the Film on School Children
and Adolescents in the City by
John MacKie.
Edinburgh Cinema Enquiry Committee,
1933. 64p. tables.

1435. English Life and Leisure: A Social Study
by B. Seebohm Rowntree & G.R. Lavers.
Longmans Green and Co., 1951. 482p.
index.

1436. Eyes of Democracy by John Grierson &
Ian Lockerbie.
John Grierson Archive/University of
Stirling, 1990. 152p.

1437. Feature Films as History by K.R.M.
Short.
Croom Helm, 1981. 192p. index.

1438. Film and the Future by Andrew
Buchanan.
Allen and Unwin, 1945. 104p. photos.

1439. Film and the Working Class: The Feature
Film in British and American Society by
Peter Stead.
Routledge and Kegan Paul, 1989. 283p.
illus. index.

1440. Film Censors and the Law by Neville
March Hunnings.
Allen and Unwin, 1967. 474p. plates.
bibliog. filmog.

1441. Film Censorship by Guy Phelps.
Gollancz, 1975. 319p. index.

1442. Film Censorship: Exploratory Study by
Roger Jowell et al.
Social and Community Planning
Research,
1974. 40p. appendix.

1443. Film Censorship: The Cinema and the
Williams Committee by R.S. Camplin.
Cinematograph Exhibitors' Association,
1978. 22p.

1444. Film Propaganda and the War by Helen
Forman.
Paper read at Imperial War Museum
Conference, 1973. 15p.

1445. Films and the Labour Party: An Address
Delivered at a Special Labour Party
Conference on Film Propaganda by Paul
Rotha.
N.p., 1936. 15p.
Held at Edinburgh in 1936.

1446. The First Fifty Years: A History of the
Finchley Cine Society 1930–1980 by Pat
Brown.
John Morin for Finchley Cine Society,
1980. 53p. illus.

1447. Good Company: The Story of the
Children's Entertainment Film Movement
in Great Britain 1943–1950 by Mary Field.
Longmans Green and Co, 1952. 192p.
plates.

1448. A Good Reputation for British Films by
Stafford Cripps.
N.p., 1947.
A speech.

1449. The Habit of Censorship by Derek Hill.
Encounter, July 1960. pp. 52–62.
See item 1422 for response.

1450. The Hidden Cinema: British Film
Censorship in Action 1913–1972 by James
C. Robertson.
Routledge and Kegan Paul, 1989. 190p.
illus. bibliog. index.

1451. The Historian and Film edited by Paul
Smith.
Cambridge University Press, 1976. 208p.
bibliog. index.

1452. The Hollywood Feature Film in Postwar
Britain by Paul Swann.
Croom Helm, 1987. 168p. plates.
bibliog. index.

1453. I Don't Mind the Sex, It's the Violence:
Film Censorship Explored by Enid
Wistrich.
Marion Boyars, 1978. 160p. bibliog.
filmog. index.

1454. Ivor Montagu Special Collection.
See item 870.

1455. Keeping It Dark; or the Censor's
Handbook by Bernard Causton & G.
Gordon Young.
Mandrake Press, c1920. 83p. illus.

1456. The Leisure Activities of Schoolchildren:
A Report Based upon an Enquiry into the
Leisure Activities of Ilford
Schoolchildren, Conducted by Adult
Students edited by Mary Stewart.
Workers' Educational Association, 1946.
26p. tables.

1457. Ministry of Morale: Home Front Morale
and the Ministry of Information in World
War II by Ian McLaine.
Allen and Unwin, 1979. 325p. plates.
bibliog. index.

1458. Obscenity: An Account of Censorship
Laws and Their Enforcement in England
and Wales by Geoffrey Robertson.
Weidenfeld and Nicolson, 1979. 364p.
index.

1459. Official British Film Propaganda during
the First World War by Nicholas Reeves.
Croom Helm, 1986. 288p. plates.
bibliog. filmog. index.

1460. The Political Censorship of Films by Ivor Montagu.
Gollancz, 1929. 44p.

1461. Pornography and Politics: A Look Back to the Williams Committee by A.W.B. Simpson.
Waterlow Publishers, 1983. 143p. bibliog. index.

1462. Progress of British Films: parts I, II and 1946–7 volume.
McKenzie Vincent, 1945–6. Various paginations. illus.

1463. The Projection of England by Stephen Tallents.
Olen Press for Film Centre, 1955. 46p.
First published by Faber in 1932.

1464. Propaganda in War 1939–1945: Organisations, Policies and Publics in Britain and Germany by Michael Balfour.
Routledge and Kegan Paul, 1979. 520p. bibliog. index.

1465. Propaganda, Politics and Film 1918–45 by Nicholas Pronay & D.W. Spring.
Macmillan, 1982. 302p. index.

1466. Report of a Discussion Held at Dartmouth House on March 11th, 1937 on the Subject of 'The Film as an Agency of British–American Understanding' by the English Speaking Union.
ESU, 1937. 18p.

1467. Report of Investigations April 1930 – May 1931 by the Birmingham Cinema Enquiry Committee.
BCEC, 1931. c70p.
Plus notes of meeting held on 7 November 1930.

1468. Report of the Committee on Obscenity and Film Censorship by Bernard Williams.
HMSO, 1979. 270p. tables. bibliog. appendix.

1469. Report of the Departmental Committee on Children and the Cinema by the Home Office.
HMSO, 1950. 109p.

1470. Research for the Children's Film Foundation: The Children's Matinee by Group Marketing.
Group Marketing, 1965. 24p.

1471. Saturday Morning Cinema: 25 Years of Films for Children with a Full Catalogue of Children's Film Foundation Films.
CFF, 1969. 52p. illus.
There is a 1972 edition entitled Young Cinema but the CFF catalogue section is missing.

1472. Screen Violence and Film Censorship: A Review of Research by Stephen Brody.
HMSO, 1977. 179p. bibliog. index.

1473. Visions of Yesterday by Jeffrey Richards.
Routledge and Kegan Paul, 1973. 391p. illus. bibliog. filmog. index.

1474. What the Censor Saw by John Trevelyan.
Michael Joseph, 1973. 276p. plates. index.

1475. Young, British and Black: A Monograph on the Work of Sankofa Film/Video Collective and Black Audio Film Collective by Coco Fusco.
Hallwalls/Contemporary Arts Centre, 1988. 65p.

CINEMAS – THEIR HISTORY AND AUDIENCE

1476. 1980 Cinema Audience Research. Study Two: Review of Findings by Carrick James Market Research & the Advertising Association, 1980. 29p. tables. stats.

1477. 50 Years of the ABC Regal, Wakefield by Kate Taylor.
Wakefield Historical Publications, 1985. 12p. illus.

1478. ABC Mile End: The First 150 Years by David Jones & Kevin Wheelan.
Mercia Cinema Society. 16p. illus.

1479. The Amber Valley Gazeteer of Greater London's Suburban Cinemas 1946–86 by Malcolm Webb et al.
Amber Valley Typesetting Services, 1986. 96p. illus. bibliog.

1480. Amber/Side Catalogue and History of Work since 1968.
Amber/Side, 1987. Unpaged. illus.

1481. The Answer in the Q: An Enquiry (in the London Area) into What Sent People to See Brothers in Law by Theo Richmond.
Boulting Brothers, c1957. 41p.

1482. The Archaeology of the Cinema by C.W. Ceram.
Thames and Hudson, 1965. 264p. plates. bibliog.

1483. At the Mighty Organ by Geoffrey Wyatt.
Oxford Illustrated Press, 1974. 98p. illus.

1484. Bagatelle by Tony Moss.
Keytone Publications, 1993. c150p. illus.
Concentrates on Florence de Jong and Ena Baga, but looks at the history of the cinema organ generally.

1485. Bedfordshire Cinemas by G.C. Peck.
Bedfordshire County Council, 1981. Unpaged. illus.

1486. The Bernstein Film Questionnaire Reports by Sidney Bernstein.
Granada Group. 1934: 20p.; 1937: 29p.; 1946–7: 24p. tables.
A survey of Granada cinemas' audiences.

1487. Bijou Kinema: A History of Early Cinema in Yorkshire by Robert Benfield.
Sheffield City Polytechnic, 1976. 62p. plates.

1488. Birmingham Cinemas, Their Films and Stars 1900–1960: A Nostalgic Journey by Victor J. Price.
K.A.F Brewin Books, 1986. 104p. illus. index.

1489. British Cinemas and Their Audiences by J.P. Mayer.
Dobson, 1948. 279p. index.

1490. Cathedrals of the Movies: A History of British Cinemas and Their Audiences by David Atwell.
The Architectural Press, 1980. 194p. illus. bibliog. index.

1491. A Change of Scene: Nostalgic Appreciation of Barrow's Theatres and Cinemas by William M. Gibbon.
The Author, 1986. 88p. illus.

1492. The Cinema and its Customers: A Pilot Study by the McAlley Associates for the Barclay Committee.
McAlley Associates, 1968. 53p. tables. appendix.

1493. The Cinema and the Public: An Inquiry into Cinema Going Habits and Expenditure Made in 1946 by Kathleen Box.
Central Office of Information, 1947. 17p. tables.

1494. Cinema and Video Industry Audience Research
Caviar. Various pagings.
Study 4 (1986); Study 5 (1987); Study 6 (1988); Study 7 (1989).

1495. The Cinema Audience: A National Survey by the Screen Advertising Association.
SAA, 1961. 64p. tables.

1496. The Cinema Audience: An Inquiry Made by the Wartime Social Survey by Louis Moss & Kathleen Box.
Ministry of Information, 1943. 24p. tables.

1497. Cinema Going in Greater London: A Study of Attitudes and Behaviour by Marketing Trends.
British Federation of Film Makers, 1963. c200p. tables.

1498. The Cinema in Bournemouth, Poole and Christchurch by Eric A. George.
Bournemouth Local Studies Publications, 1980. 11p.

1499. Cinema on the Roman Wall by Peter Douglas.
Mercia Cinema Society, 1984. 12p. illus.

1500. The Cinema Organ by Reginald Foort.
The Vestal Press, 1970. 199p. illus.

1501. The Cinema Theatres of Salisbury by Alan A. Richardson.
The Author, 1981. 13p. illus.

1502. The Cinema-going Habits of the British: BIPO Survey 174 by Gallup.
Gallup Poll, 1948. 6 leaves.

1503. Cinemagoing by Karsten Grummitt.
Dadona Reasearch, 1989. 81p. tables. appendix.

1504. Cinemagoing 2: A Survey of UK Exhibition by Karsten Grummitt.
Dadona Research, 1991. 43p. tables.

1505. Cinemas and Cinema-going in Great Britain by H.E. Browning & A.A. Sorrell.
Journal of the Royal Statistical Society, Vol. 117, 1954. 67p. tables.

1506. Cinemas and Theatres: An Industry Sector Overview by Key Note.
Key Note Publications.
1979 to date.

1507. Cinemas in Portsmouth 1910–1950 by the Hampshire County Library.
Portsmouth Library Reference & Information Centre, 1975. 19p.

1508. The Cinemas of Aldridge and Brownhills by Ned Williams.
Mercia Cinema Society, 1984. 43p. illus.

1509. The Cinemas of Bradford by Geoff J. Mellor.
Robert E. Preedy, 1983. 64p. plates.

1510. The Cinemas of Croydon by Allen Eyles & Keith Skone.
Keystone Publications, 1989. 48p. illus. index.

1511. The Cinemas of Lincoln by George Clarke.
Mercia Cinema Society, 1991. 35p. illus.

1512. The Cinemas of Portsmouth by J. Barker, R. Brown & W. Greer.
Milestone Publications, 1981. 56p. illus.

1513. Cinemas of the Black Country by Ned Williams.
Uralia Press, 1982. 231p. illus. index.

1514. Cinemas: Picture Houses in the Borough of Bexley by Caroline Ellis.
Bexley Libraries and Museums Department, 1985. 5p. illus.

1515. A City and Its Cinemas by Charles Anderson.
Redcliffe Press, 1983. 104p. illus.

1516. City Cinemas 1903–1978: A Brief History of Cinema in Norwich by David Elgood.
Norfolk and Norwich Film Theatre, 1978. Unpaged. illus.

1517. The Complete Projectionist: A Textbook for All Who Handle Sound and Pictures in the Kinema by R. Howard Cricks.
Kinematograph Publications, 1943. 326p. illus.

1518. The Dream Palaces of Birmingham by Chris Clegg & Rosemary Clegg.
The Authors, 1983. 104p. illus.

1519. The Dream Palaces of Oxfordshire by Sean Currell.
Mercia Cinema Society, 1983. 44p. illus. index.

1520. The Dream Palaces of Richmond upon Thames by Fred T.P. Windsor.
Mercia Cinema Society, n.d.. 36p. illus.

1521. The Dream Palaces of Southend by Roy Dilley.
Mercia Cinema Society, n.d. 64p. illus.

1522. The Dream Palaces of Sunderland by Albert Anderson.
Mercia Cinema Society, 1982. 76p. illus. index.

1523. Early Oxford Picture Palaces by Paul J. Marriott.
The Author, 1978. 32p. illus.

1524. Enter the Dream-House: Memories of Cinemas in South London from the Twenties to the Sixties edited by Margaret O'Brien & Allen Eyles.
British Film Institute, 1993. 176p. illus.

1525. Fifty Years at the Pictures by the Scottish Film Council.
SFC, 1946. 16p. illus. plates.

1526. The Film Audience: An International Bibliography of Research with Annotations and an Essay by Bruce A. Austin.
Scarecrow Press, 1983. 177p. index.

1527. Films and the British Public by Hubert Griffith.
Constable, 1932. 11p.
Extract from 'The Nineteenth Century and After'.

1528. A Handbook on Rating of Cinemas by Alan D. Daly.
Bray House Press, 1940. 82p. illus. index.

1529. The Harwich Electric Palace by Chris Strachan.
The Author, 1979. 30p. illus.

1530. The History of Salford Cinemas by Tony Flynn.
Neil Richardson, 1987. 42p. illus.

1531. The History of the Cinema in Gainsborough by the Gainsborough Public Library.
Gainsborough Public Library, 1973. 8p.

1532. A History of the Theatres and Cinemas of Tameside by David Owen.
Neil Richardson, 1985. 30p. illus.

1533. The Home of Beautiful Pictures: The Story of the Playhouse Cinema, Beverley by Peter H. Robinson.
Hutton Press, 1985. 94p. illus.

1534. How to Reach the Cinema Audience by Rank Screen Advertising.
Rank, 1979. 22p. stats.

1535. How to Run a Picture Theatre by Kinematograph Weekly.
Kinematograph Weekly, 1912. 127p. illus.

1536. The Imperial Picturedome, Ryhill, Pontefract, Yorkshire by R. Benton.
The Author, 1977. 8p. illus.

1537. Independent Cinema and Regional Film Culture: Report of the 1980 British Film Institute Regional Conference.
University of London Institute of Education, 1981. 45p.

1538. The Influence of the Cinema on Contemporary Auditoria Design by Clifford Worthington.
Pitman and Sons, 1952. 123p. illus. index.

1539. Islington's Cinemas and Film Studios by Chris Draper.
London Borough of Islington, 1989. 120p. illus. bibliog. filmog.

1540. The Kinema at Kinver by Bill Parker & Ned Williams.
Uralia Press, 1986. 16p. illus.

1541. Last Complete Performance: In Memory of Hull's Cinemas by Robert Curry.
Hutton Press/Hull College of Further Education, 1992. 87p. illus.

1542. A Last Complete Performance: Watford's Cinema History in Focus by Ivor Buckingham.
The Author, 1989. 55p. illus. index.

1543. The Last Picture Show? Britain's Changing Film Audience by David Docherty, David Morrison & Michael Tracey.
British Film Institute, 1987. 152p. tables. bibliog. index.

1544. The Last Picture Shows Edinburgh: Ninety Years of Cinema Entertainment in Scotland's Capital City by Brendon Thomas.
Moorfoot Publishing, 1984. 79p. illus. index.

1545. Leeds Cinemas 2 by Robert E. Preedy.
The Author, 1982. 56p. illus. index.

1546. Leeds Cinemas Remembered by Robert E. Preedy.
Netherwood Dalton, 1980. 56p. illus.

1547. London's West End Cinemas by Allen Eyles & Keith Skone.
Premier Bioscope, 1984. 60p. illus.

1548. The Lost Empire: The Picture Houses of the Potteries and Newcastle-under-Lyme by Barry Blaize.
Brampton, 1990. 82p. illus.

1549. Mass-observation at the Movies by Jeffrey Richards & Dorothy Sheridan.
Routledge and Kegan Paul, 1987. 477p. index.

1550. Media and the Cinemagoer: A Study of the 100% Medium by the Screen Advertising Association.
SAA, 1964. 20p. tables.

1551. Memories of Buckinghamshire's Picture Palaces by Martin Tapsell.
Mercia Cinema Society, n.d.. 76p. illus.

1552. Memories of Kent Cinemas by Martin Tapsell.
Plateway Press, 1987. 104p. illus. map. index.

1553. The Mighty Screen: The Rise of the Cinema in Huddersfield by Stanley Chadwick.
Ventura Press, 1953. 128p. plates. tables.

1554. Modern Cinemas by Robert Cromie et al.
Architectural Press, 1936. 64p. illus.

1555. Modern Theatres and Cinemas: The Architecture of Pleasure by Morton P. Shand.
B.T. Batsford, 1930. 40p. illus.

1556. National Film Awards 1948: The Leading Films, Actors and Actresses in the ballot organised by the Daily Mail edited by Dennis Yates.
Dennis Yates Publications, 1948. 64p. illus.

1557. Odeon edited by Rosemary Clegg.
Mercia Cinema Society, 1985. 176p. illus. index.

1558. The Picture House in East Anglia by Stephen Peart.
Terence Dalton, 1980. 180p. illus. bibliog. index.

1559. The Picture House: A Photographic Album of Film and Cinema in Greater Manchester, Lancashire, Cheshire and Merseyside from the Collections of the North West Film Archive by Maryann Gomes.
The North West Film Archive, 1988. 91p. illus. index.

1560. The Picture Palace, and Other Buildings for the Movies by Dennis Sharp.
Hugh Evelyn, 1969. 224p. illus. diagrs. bibliog. index.

1561. Picture Palace: A Social History of the Cinema by Audrey Field.
Gentry Books, 1974. 160p. plates. index.

1562. Picture Pioneers: The Story of the Northern Cinema 1896–1971 by Geoff J. Mellor.
Frank Graham, 1971. 96p. plates. index.

1563. Pictures Past: Recollections of Scottish Cinemas and Cinema-Going by Janet McBain.
Moorfoot Publishing, 1985. 80p. illus. index.

1564. Price List of Everything Required for the Bioscope Business: From the Theatre to the Film by the Walturdaw Company.
Walturdaw, 1912. 360p. illus.

1565. Reading Theatres, Cinemas and Other Entertainments by Daphne Phillips.
Reading Libraries, 1978. 56p. illus.

1566. Red Roses Every Night: An Account of a London Cinema under Fire by Guy Morgan.
Quality Press, 1948. 127p. illus.

1567. Reels on Wheels: A Guide to Rural Community Film Shows edited by Ian Scott.
Dorset Community Council, 1978. 57p. illus. bibliog.

1568. A Refuge from Reality: The Cinemas of Brighton and Hove by D. Robert Elleray.
Olio Books, 1989. 64p. illus. bibliog. index.

1569. Remembering: Harrogate Cinemas and Theatres by Robert E. Preedy.
The Author, n.d. 24p. illus.

1570. Rugby Theatre: The First Forty Years – An Anniversary History by Roger Bentley-Carr.
Rugby Theatre Society, 1989. 74p. illus.

1571. Showtime in Walthamstow by Gregory Tonkin.
Walthamstow Antiquarian Society, 1983. 32p. plates.

1572. Silver Screen in the Silver City: A History of Cinemas in Aberdeen, 1896–1987 by Michael Thomas.
Aberdeen University Press, 1988. 352p. illus. index.

1573. Silver Screen Memories: A Look Back at the Cinemas of Telford, Newport, Much Wenlock and Broseley by Fred Brown.
Garnet Press, 1984. 34p. plates.

1574. Speak for Yourself: A Mass Observation Anthology 1937–49 by Angus Calder & Dorothy Sheridan.
Jonathan Cape, 1984. 259p. illus. plates. bibliog.

1575. Sunday Opening Special Collection.
Material held in Sunday Opening Special Collection.

1576. Theatre Organ World edited by Jack Courtnay.
Theatre Organ World Pubs, 1946. 216p. illus.

1577. Troxy: Where East is Best by David Jones.
Mercia Cinema Society. 32p. illus.

1578. Tuppenny Rush: The Arrival of Cinemas and Film-making in Swadlincote by Graham Nutt.
Trent Valley Publications, 1992. 45p. illus.

1579. Two Sixpennies Please: Lewisham's Early Cinemas by Ken George.
Lewisham Local History Society, 1987. 83p. illus.

1580. The West End Cinemagoer: A Detailed Study of an Audience at London Cinemas by Pearl & Dean.
Pearl and Dean, 1971. c100p. diagrs. tables. appendix.

1581. What We Have: An East Midlands Celebration by Tony Bloor & Sue Norman.
East Midlands Arts Association, 1980. 131p. illus.

1582. Wild Beasts and Living Pictures by the Orchard Theatre Company. [1983–4].
11p. illus. filmog.
Programme for an Orchard Theatre Company's production recreating the early touring Bioscope shows.

FILM CRITICISM AND THEORY

1583. Cinema by Roger Manvell.
Penguin, 1950–52. Various paginations. illus.
Annual.

1584. Experiment in the Film edited by Roger Manvell.
Grey Walls Press, 1949. 258p. illus.

1585. Film by Roger Manvell.
Penguin, 1950. 289p. illus. index.

1586. Film 1959 by Chris Slater.
Granta, 6 Nov. 1959. pp. 26–30 illus.

1587. The Film and the Public by Roger Manvell.
Penguin, 1955. 352p. illus.

1588. Film To-day: Screen and Audience edited by John E. Cross & Arnold Rattenbury.
Film To-day, 1947. 90p. illus.

1589. Film: Criticism and Caricatures 1943–53 by Richard Winnington & Paul Rotha.
Paul Elek, 1975. 196p. illus. index.

1590. Focus on Films by Jean-Philippe Le Harivel.
Thrift Books/C.A. Watts, 1952. 86p.

1591. Mass Communications and the Cultivated Mind in Britain between the Wars by D.L. LeMahieu.
Clarendon Press, 1988. 396p. index.

1592. Nobody Ordered Wolves by Jeffrey Dell.
Heinemann, 1939. 333p.
Novel about the film industry.

1593. On Cinema by Vincent Porter.
Pluto, 1985. 149p. bibliog. index.

1594. Penguin Film Review Nos. 1–9 by Roger Manvell.
Penguin, 1946–49. Various paginations. illus.
Succeeded by 'Cinema' (item 1583).

1595. Rotha on the Film: A Selection of Writings about the Cinema by Paul Rotha.
Faber, 1958. 338p. plates. index.

1596. A Seat at the Cinema by Roger Manvell.
Evans Brothers, 1951. 192p. illus.

1597. Shots in the Dark: A Collection of Reviewers' Opinions of Some of the Leading Films Released between January 1949 and February 1951 edited by Edgar Anstey & Roger Manvell.
International Federation of Film Critics/Allan Wingate, 1951. 268p. illus.

1598. A Study of Film and Television Courses and Uses in the United Kingdom 1979–1980 by Clyde Loft.
Caulfield Institute of Technology, 1980. 64p.

GENRES

1599. Agatha Christie: Murder in Four Acts by Peter Haining.
Virgin, 1990. 160p. illus.

1600. Avant Garde Film in England and Europe edited by Richard Cork.
Studio International, 1975. 75p. illus.

1601. Bond and Beyond: The Political Career of a Popular Hero by Tony Bennett & Janet Woollacott.
Macmillan Education, 1987. 315p. illus. index.

1602. British Genres: Cinema and Society 1930–1960 by Marcia Landy.
Princeton University Press, 1991. 553p. plates. filmog. bibliog. index.

1603. The Carry On Book by Kenneth Eastaugh.
David and Charles, 1978. 160p. illus. filmog.

1604. Cela s'Appelle l'Horror: Le Cinéma Fantastique Anglais 1955–1976 by Gérard Lenne.
Librarie Seguier, 1989. 383p. illus. filmog. bibliog. index.
Language: French.

1605. The Complete James Bond Movie Encyclopedia by Steven J. Rubin.
Contemporary Books, 1990. 467p. illus.

1606. Deerstalker!: Holmes and Watson on Screen by Ron Haydock.
Scarecrow Press, 1978. 313p. index.

1607. Doing Rude Things: The History of the British Sex Film 1957–1981 by David McGillivray.
Sun Tavern Fields, 1992. 141p. illus. index.

1608. English Avant-garde Cinema 1966–1974 by Peter de Kay Dusinberre III.
M.Phil thesis, 1977. 275p. bibliog.

1609. Film is... by Stephen Dwoskin.
Peter Owen, 1975. 268p. index. illus.

1610. The Films of Sherlock Holmes by Chris Steinbrunner & Norman Michaels.
Citadel Press, 1978. 252p. illus.

1611. Funny Way to Be a Hero by John Fisher.
Muller, 1973. 336p. illus. bibliog. index.

1612. Hammer Film Productions Special Collection.

1613. A Heritage of Horror: The English Gothic Cinema 1946–1972 by David Pirie.
Gordon Fraser, 1973. 192p. illus. filmog. index.

1614. The Incredible World of 007: An Authorised Celebration by Lee Pfeiffer & Philip Lisa.
Boxtree, 1992. 224p. illus.

1615. The James Bond Bedside Companion by Raymond Benson.
Dodd, Mead and Co., 1984. 257p. illus. index.

1616. The James Bond Dossier by Kingsley Amis.
Jonathan Cape, 1965. 159p.

1617. The James Bond Films: A Behind the Scenes History by Steven J. Rubin.
Talisman Books, 1981. 183p. illus. index.

1618. The James Bond Girls by Graham Rye.
Boxtree, 1989. 64p. col. illus.

1619. James Bond in the Cinema by James Brosnan.
A.S. Barnes/Tantivy Press, 1981. 309p. illus. filmog.

1620. James Bond: A Celebration by Peter Haining.
Planet Books, 1987. 200p. illus. col. plates. bibliog. filmog.

1621. James Bond: The Authorised Biography of 007 by John Pearson.
Granada, 1985. 314p.

1622. Life of Python by George Perry.
Pavilion/Michael Joseph, 1983. 192p. illus. filmog. teleog.

1623. Make 'em Laugh: Famous Comedians and Their Worlds by Eric Midwinter.
Allen and Unwin, 1979. 209p. illus. index.

1624. Materialist Film by Peter Gidal.
Routledge and Kegan Paul, 1989. 189p. illus. index.

1625. Monty Python: A Chronological Listing of the Troupe's Creative Output, and Articles and Reviews about Them 1969–1989 by Douglas L. McCall.
McFarland, 1991. 210p. appendix. index.

1626. The Official James Bond 007 Movie Book by Sally Hibbin.
Hamlyn, 1989. 128p. illus. (chiefly col.) filmog. index.

1627. Sherlock Holmes: A Centenary Celebration by Allen Eyles.
John Murray, 1986. 144p. illus.

1628. What a Carry On: The Official Story of the Carry On Film Series by Sally Hibbin & Nina Hibbin.
Hamlyn/Octopus, 1988. 127p. illus. (mostly col.) filmog. index.

FILM AND LITERATURE

1629. Cinema Arthuriana: Essays on Arthurian Film by Kevin J. Harty.
Garland, 1991. 255p. illus. bibliog. filmog. index.

1630. The English Novel and the Movies edited by Michael Klein & Gillian Parker.
Frederick Ungar, 1981. 383p. illus. bibliog. filmog. index.

1631. Filming Shakespeare's Plays: The Adaptations of Laurence Olivier, Orson Welles, Peter Brook and Akira Kurosawa by Anthony Davies.
Cambridge University Press, 1988. 219p. illus. bibliog. filmog. index.

1632. Focus on Shakespearean Film by Charles W. Eckert.
Prentice Hall, 1972. 184p. index.

1633. H.G. Wells in the Cinema by Alan Wykes.
Jupiter Books, 1977. 176p. illus. filmog.

1634. Screening the Novel: The Theory and Practice of Literary Dramatization by Robert Giddings, Keith Selby & Chris Wensley.
St. Martin's Press, 1990. 174p. plates. index.
Concentrates on Lean's 'Great Expectations'.

1635. The Serpent's Eye: Shaw and the Cinema by Donald P. Costello.
University of Notre Dame Press, 1965. 209p. illus. bibliog. filmog.

1636. Shakespeare and the Film by Roger Manvell.
J.M. Dent, 1971. 172p. plates. bibliog. index.

1637. Theater and Film: A Comparative Study of the Two Forms of Dramatic Art, and of the Problems of Adaptation of Stage Plays into Films by Roger Manvell.
Fairleigh Dickinson University Press/Associated University Presses, 1979. 303p. illus. bibliog. filmog. index.

ANIMATION

1638. Animation is Fun by Sheila Graber.
Tyneside Cinema Publications, 1984.
64p. illus.

1639. Animation: A Guide to Animated Film
Techniques by Roger Noke.
MacDonald Orbis, 1988. 160p. illus.
Includes a number of British examples.

1640. The Do-it-yourself Film Animation by
Bob Godfrey & Anna Jackson.
BBC Publications, 1974. 96p. illus.

1641. The Technique of Film Animation by
John Halas & Roger Manvell.
Focal Press, 1976. 351p. illus. plates.
bibliog. index.

NON-FICTION FILM

1642. L' Angleterre et Son Cinéma: Le Courant
Documentaire 1927–1965 by Olivier
Barrot et al.
Film Editions, 1977. 156p. illus.
bibliog.
Language: French.

1643. Bibliography: Free Cinema by David
Pester.
Unpubd., n.d. 13 leaves.
Compiled for Library Studies Diploma.

1644. The British Documentary Film Movement
1926–1946 by Paul Swann.
Cambridge University Press, 1989. 216p.
illus. bibliog. filmog. index.

1645. British Documentary Films 1929–1952.
Part I: Films Controlled by the Central
Office of Information by the British Film
Institute.
British Film Institute, 1952. 32p.
Chronological listing giving directors'
names.

1646. British Newsreels – Issue Sheets 1913–
1970: The Complete Collection Held by
the Slade Film History Register by the
Slade Film History Register.
Graphic Data Publishing, 1984. 275
microfiches.

1647. Cameramen at War by Ian Grant.
Patrick Stephens, 1980. 192p. illus.

1648. El Cine Realistista Británico by the
Filmoteca Nacional de España.
FNE, 1978. 70p. illus. bibliog.
biofilmog.
Language: Spanish.

1649. Cinema by Stephen Tallents.
35p.
Typescript of a chapter from his
unpublished autobiography, with related
correspondence and notes.

1650. Cinema and History: British Newsreels
and the Spanish Civil War by Anthony
Aldgate.
Scolar Press, 1979. 234p. plates.
bibliog. filmog. index.

1651. The Cinema Newsreels and Politics 1929–
1939 by T.J. Hollins.
Ph.D thesis, 1981. pp. 616–694.

1652. Coal Film Makers: An Appreciation by
Henry Donaldson.
National Coal Board, n.d. 72p.

1653. Documentaries on the Arts: Arts Council
Film Library Catalogue by the Arts
Council of Great Britain.
ACGB, 1984. 72p. illus.

1654. Documentary Diary: An Informal History
of the British Documentary Film 1928–
1939 by Paul Rotha.
Secker and Warburg, 1973. 305p. plates.
bibliog. index.

1655. Documentary Film in Great Britain: A
Selective Bibliography by Mary E.
Welch.
N.p., 1959. 37p.

1656. Documentary Film: The Use of the Film
Medium to Interpret Creatively and in
Social Terms the Life of the People as It
Exists in Reality by Paul Rotha.
Faber, 1952. 412p. plates. filmog.
index.

1657. Documentary is Neither Short Nor Long
by Paul Rotha.
13 leaves.
Typescript dated 9 August 1946.

1658. Die Englische Dokumentarfilmschule in
den Dreissiger Jahren: Zur
Begriffsbestimmung des
Dokumentarismus im Film by Rolf
Reemtsen.
PhD thesis, 1976. 233p. bibliog. filmog.
Language: German.

1659. The Factual Film: A Survey Sponsored by
the Dartington Hall Trustees by the Arts
Enquiry.
Political and Economic Planning/Oxford
University Press, 1947. 260p.

1660. The Film in Education by Andrew
Buchanan.
Phoenix House, 1951. 256p. plates.
bibliog. tables.

1661. Free Cinema: Programme Notes for the
Seasons of Free Cinema Held at the
National Film Theatre during 1956–59 by
the National Film Theatre.
British Film Institute/National Film
Theatre, 1956–59. 30 leaves.

1662. The History of the British Film 1929–
1939: Documentary and Educational
Films of the 1930s by Rachael Low.
Allen and Unwin, 1979. 244p. illus.
bibliog. filmog. index.

1663. The History of the British Film 1929–
1939: Films of Comment and Persuasion
of the 1930s by Rachael Low.
Allen and Unwin, 1979. 256p. illus.
bibliog. filmog. index.

1664. Hommage au G.P.O. Film Unit by the
Cinémathèque Française/Musée du
Cinéma.
Cinémathèque Française, 1966. 19p.
photos. filmog.
Language: French.

1665. Journey to a Legend and Back: The
British Realistic Film by Eva Orbanz.
Edition Volker Spiess, 1977. 213p.
illus. filmog.

1666. A Long Look at Short Films: An ACTT
Report on the Short Entertainment and
Factual Film by Derrick Knight & Vincent
Porter.
Pergamon Press, 1967. 185p. figs.
tables. index. (See 1670.)

1667. Meet '...the Common People...':
Photographs from the Documentary Films
Made between 1939 and 1942 by Edward
Carrick & Gerry Bradley.
Studio Publications, 1942. 94p. illus.

1668. New Directions in Documentary: Report
of the International Conference Held at
Edinburgh by John Grierson et al.
Edinburgh Film Festival, 1952. 41p.

1669. Newsreel Association of Great Britain
Special Collection.
Material held in Newsreel Association
of Great Britain Special Collection.

1670. No Case for Compulsion by the Rank
Organisation.
Rank, 1967. 20p. tables.
A reply to 'A Long Look at Short
Films'. (Item 1666.)

1671. Nonfiction Film: A Critical History by
Richard Meran Barsam.
E.P. Dutton, 1973. 332p. illus.
bibliog. filmog. index.

1672. Patrick Wyand Special Collection.
See item 1077.

1673. The Public's Progress edited by A.G.
Weidenfeld.
Contact Publications, 1947. 104p.
illus.
Two essays on factual film by Basil
Wright and Paul Rotha.

1674. Researcher's Guide to British Newsreels
edited by James Ballantyne.
British Universities Film and Video
Council, 1983. 119p. index.

1675. Researcher's Guide to British Newsreels
Volume II edited by James Ballantyne.
British Universities Film and Video
Council, 1988. 47p. illus. index.

1676. The Rise and Fall of British
Documentary: The Story of the Film
Movement Founded by John Grierson by
Elizabeth Sussex.
University of California Press, 1975.
219p. illus. index.

1677. The Slade Film History Register: Report
of the Working Party to Consider the
Future Development of the Slade Film
History Register by the British
Universities Film Council.
British Universities Film Council,
1977. 37p.

1678. Sound and the Documentary Film by Ken
Cameron.
Pitman, 1947. 157p. illus. index.

1679. Stanley J. 'Percy' Mumford Special
Collection.
Mumford Special Collection. (See item
883.)

1680. Studies in Documentary by Alan Lovell &
Jim Hillier.
Secker and Warburg, 1972. 176p. illus.
bibliog. filmog.

1681. Ten Years of British Short Films Abroad:
A Survey of Past Successes, Present
Problems and Future Action. A Guide to
100 Film Festivals with Lists of
Prizewinners edited by Robert Dunbar.
National Panel for Film
Festivals/British Council, 1976. 88p.

1682. Topical Budget: The Great British News
Film by Luke McKernan.
British Film Institute, 1992. 180p.
illus. appendix. index.

1683. Traditions of Independence: British
Cinema in the Thirties edited by Don
Macpherson & Paul Willemen.
British Film Institute, 1980. 226p.
bibliog. filmog.

1684. What is Cinéma Vérité? by M. Ali Issari
& Doris A. Paul.
Scarecrow Press, 1979. 208p. illus.
bibliog. filmog. index.

1685. Workers Newsreels in the 1920s and 1930s
by Bert Hogenkamp.
Communist Party History Group, 1980.
36p. illus.

REFERENCE BOOKS

1686. British Animated Films 1895–1985: A
Filmography by Denis Gifford.
McFarland, 1987. 345p. illus. index.

1687. East End on Screen: A Catalogue of East
London Film and Video edited by Hilary
Dunn.
T.H.A.P. Books, 1985. 24p. illus.

1688. Independent Cinema: One – Directory of
Independent British Cinema edited by
Jane Hopkins & David Hopkins.
Independent Cinema Magazine, 1978.
108p. illus. index.

1689. Independent Film Workshops in Britain
edited by Rod Stoneman.
Grael Communications, 1979. 64p.

1690. Reel Practices: A Directory of
Independent Film from the North-East by
York Film.
York Film, 1981. 68p. illus. index.

1691. Regional Film Directory: Films and Video Made with the Assistance of the English Regional Arts Associations by Frank Challenger.
West Midlands Arts, 1984. 104p. index.

1692. South West Film Directory edited by Rod Stoneman.
South West Arts, 1980. 136p. illus.

1693. Survey of Film in Greater London March 1972 by Tim Horrocks.
Greater London Arts Association's Film Panel, 1972. 65p. tables.

1694. Twenty Years On: A Review of the Independent Film and Video Sector in London by the Independent Film and Video Producers Association & the London Strategic Policy Unit.
IFVPA/LSPU, 1987.

1695. West Midlands Film and Video Handbook by the Birmingham Film and Video Workshop.
1985. 72p.

REFERENCE BOOKS – ANNUALS AND CATALOGUES

1696. 1951–76: British Film Institute Productions; a Catalogue of Films Made under the Auspices of the Experimental Film Fund 1951–1966 and the Production Board 1966–1976 by John Ellis.
British Film Institute, 1977. 135p. illus. index.

1697. Animated Photograph Films: Section A by R.W. Paul.
R.W.Paul, 1902. 72p. illus.
Issued 1902, re-issued 1906.

1698. Animated Photographs for the Cinematograph 1901–2 by Walker, Turner and Dawson.
WTD, c1902. Various pagings.
Collection of catalogues bound in one volume.

1699. Association of Cinematograph and Allied Technicians Year Book
ACT.
1947, 1948/9, 1950, 1951.

1700. Association of Cinematograph, TV and Allied Technicians Annual Report ACT/ACTT.
1940/41, 1944/45–1946/47, 1948/49–1990.

1701. Bioscope Annual and Trades Directory 1915.
Ganes, 613p.

1702. Blue Book of 'Warwick' and 'Star' Selected Film Subjects by the Warwick Trading Company.
Warwick, 1902. 143p. illus.

1703. The Boys' & Girls' Film Book edited by Mary Field & Maud Miller.
Burke Publishing, 1948. 192p. illus.

1704. The Boys' and Girls' Book of Films and Television edited by Mary Field, Maud Miller & Roger Manvell.
Burke, 1961. 143p. diagrs. illus.

1705. Boys' and Girls' Cinema Clubs Annual.
Juvenile Productions.
1949, 1950, 1953, 1954.

1706. British Academy of Film and Television Arts Report and Financial Statements.
BAFTA.
1981–86, 1988, 1989.

1707. British Board of Film Classification Report.
BBFC.
1928–33, 1935–7, 1985 to date. Formerly British Board of Film Censorship.

1708. British Film and Television Yearbook edited by Peter Noble.
1945, 1947/48, 1949/50, 1952, 1955/56–1975. Formerly British Film Yearbook (became Screen International Film & TV Yearbook).

1709. The British Film Annual (Daily Mail Film Award Annual) edited by Jeffrey Truby.
Winchester Publications.
1948, 1949.

1710. The British Film Catalogue 1895–1985: A Guide to Entertainment Films by Denis Gifford.
David and Charles, 1986. Unpaged. bibliog. index.

1711. British Film Fund Agency Annual Report.
HMSO.
1958–60, 1962–87.

1712. British Film Industry Yearbook by John Sullivan.
Film Press, 1948. 207p.
Gives cast and credits of British features produced during 1947.

1713. British Film Institute Annual Report.
BFI.
1934 to date – incorporated in BFI Yearbook 1983–87.

1714. British Film Institute Film and Television Handbook.
British Film Institute.
1983 to date.

1715. British Film Institute Production Board Catalogue by the British Film Institute.
1977–78, 1978–79, 1981–82, 1983–84, 1990 to date.

1716. British Film Institute Production Board edited by Alan Lovell.
British Film Institute, 1976. 67p. filmog.

1717. British Films by the British Film and Television Producers Association et al.
BFTPA.
1960–63, 1982/3–1985.

1718. British Films 1971–1981 edited by Linda Wood.
British Film Institute/Library Services, 1983. 154p.

1719. British Films Catalogue by the Cannes Action Committee.
1986, 1987, 1989 to date.

1720. British Lion Report and Accounts by British Lion.
BL.
1955/56–1972.

1721. British National Film and Video Catalogue.
British Film Institute.
Published annually from 1963 to 1991. Formerly British National Film Catalogue.

1722. British Official Films in the Second World War: A Descriptive Catalogue by Frances Thorpe, Nicholas Pronay & Clive Coultass.
Clio Press, 1980. 321p. illus. index.

1723. British Screen Finance Annual Report by British Screen Finance.
BSF.
1985 to date.

1724. British Sound Films: The Studio Years 1928–1959 by David Quinlan.
B.T. Batsford, 1984. 407p. illus. bibliog.

1725. Cardiff Media City: Database 1991/2 by Cardiff Media City, 1992. Unpaged.

1726. Catalogue and Price List by the Hepworth Manufacturing Company.
Hepworth, c1903. 56p. illus.

1727. Catalogue of Films in the East Anglian Film Archive Vol I–IV by David Cleveland et al.
East Anglian Film Archive, 1977. Unpaged.

1728. Catalogue of Paul's Animatographs and Films by R.W. Paul.
R.W. Paul. 1901: 104p. 1902: unpaged. illus.

1729. Catalogue of Selected Animated Photograph Films: Section B 1906–7 by R.W. Paul.
R.W. Paul, c1907. 88p. illus. index.

1730. Catalogue of the Book Library of the British Film Institute by the Library and Information Services/British Film Institute.
G.K. Hall, 1975. 5 volumes.
Supplement published in 1983.

1731. Catalogue of the Lions Head Brand Kinematograph Films by Cricks and Martin.
Cricks and Martin, 1908. 78p. illus.

1732. Catalogue of the Sheffield Photo Company Films and Cinematograph Apparatus by the Sheffield Photo Company.
Sheffield PC, 1906. 35p. illus.

1733. Catalogue: Scientific and Educational Subjects by the Urban Trading Company.
Urban, 1908. 252p.

1734. The Cinema edited by Roger Manvell & R.K. Neilson Baxter.
Penguin. 1950–53. Replaced The Penguin Film Review. (See 1787.)

1735. Cinema News and Property Gazette Yearbook and Diary.
Cinema News and Property Gazette, 1915. 330p.

1736. Cinematograph Exhibitors' Association of Great Britain Annual Report by the Cinematograph Exhibitors' Association of Great Britain.
CEA. 1920–21, 1923, 1926, 1932, 1935, 1936, 1950, 1953 to date.

1737. Cinematograph Exhibitors' Diary by Low Warren.
S. Pressbury. 1927, 1928.

1738. Cinematograph Films Council Annual Report by the Cinematograph Films Council.
CFC. 1939, 1946, 1950–53, 1951–61, 1963 to date.

1739. Collins Film Book for Young People edited by Eric Gillett.
Collins. 1948, 1949, 1950, 1951.

1740. Cricks and Sharp Catalogue by Cricks and Sharp.
C&S, 1906. 32p.

1741. Daily Express Film Book edited by Ernest Betts.
Daily Express Publications, 1935. 208p. illus. index.

1742. Directory of British Film and Television Producers by PACT.
1991 to date.

1743. Directory of Members. Directors Guild of Great Britain.
DGGB. 1984 to date.

1744. Directory of Women Working in Film, TV and Video by Alison Butler.
Women's Film, TV and Video Network, 1987. 159p.

1745. E.M.B. Film Catalogue by the Empire Marketing Board.
EMB, 1932. 32p.

1746. Early Rare British Film-makers' Catalogues 1896–1913.
World Microfilm Publications. 8 reels on microfilm.
The collection of Library and Information Services (BFI), with additional contributions by the Barnes Museum of Cinematography, the Science Museum, the Kodak Museum, David Francis, Charles Musser and David Robinson.

1747. East Anglia on Film by David Cleveland.
Poppyland Publishing, 1987. 76p. illus.
index.
Some of the films and film-makers that
have recorded the region's past,
through films in the East Anglian Film
Archive.

1748. Empire Cinematograph Catalogue,
Including The Cinematograph and How to
Operate It by Butcher and Sons.
Butcher, 1911. 160p. illus.

1749. Empire Cinematographs and Accessories
by Butcher and Sons.
Butchers, 1906. 64p.

1750. Empire Film Library Catalogue by the
Imperial Institute.
Imperial Institute, 1937. 47p.

1751. Fifty Classic British Films 1932–1982: A
Pictorial Record by Anthony Slide.
Dover Publications, 1985. 152p. illus.
bibliog.

1752. Film Bang: Scotland's Film and Video
Directory by the Film Bang Society.
1976 to date. Published irregularly.

1753. Film Review edited by F. Maurice Speed
et al.
Macdonald/W.H. Allen/Virgin.
1944 to date.

1754. Film User Year Book: A Manual of
Review and Reference for All Concerned
with the Screening of 16mm Film and
35mm Filmstrip – in Industry, Education
and Entertainment edited by Bernard
Dolman.
Current Affairs, 1949 & '50. c300p.
index.

1755. Films for Hire by the Magnet Film
Company.
Magnet, c1910. 16p.

1756. Films from Britain 1964–65 by the Central
Office of Information.
COI, 1964. 427p. illus. index.
Catalogue of films available from COI.

1757. Films of Britain by the British Council
Film Department.
British Council. c55p. illus. index.
Catalogue of British shorts [and]
documentaries: 1942/43, updated
1944/45.

1758. G.P.O. Film Library: Notes and Synopses
for the Use of Teachers and Lecturers by
the G.P.O. Film Library.
G.P.O., 1937. 31p.

1759. General Catalogue of Classified Subjects,
'Urban', 'Eclipse', 'Radios' Film
Subjects and 'Urbanora' Educational
Series by the Urban Trading Company.
Urban, 1909. 432p. illus.

1760. Goldcrest Films and Television Annual
Report and Accounts.
Goldcrest. 1984–87.

1761. The Great British Films by Jerry
Vermilye.
Citadel Press, 1978. 255p.

1762. Hepwix Films for the Cinematograph by
the Hepworth Manufacturing Company.
Hepworth, 1906. 141p. illus.

1763. Illustrated Catalogue of a New and
Original Series of Standard-sized
Animated Photograph Films. List No. 15,
August 1898 by R.W. Paul.
R.W. Paul, 1898. 32p. illus.

1764. Illustrated Catalogue of the Prestwich
Specialities for Animated Photography
by the Prestwich Manufacturing
Company.
Prestwich MC, 1905. 14p. illus.

1765. International Film Annual.
John Calder, 1957–59.

1766. International Film Guide edited by Peter
Cowie.
Various publishers 1964 to date.

1767. Jury's Imperial Bioscope: Animated
Photographs by Jury's Imperial Pictures.
Jury's, c1905. Various pagings.
Several catalogues bound in one volume.

1768. Kemp's International Film and Television
Year Book.
Kemp Publishing Group. 1956–59, 1961,
1963–66, 1968 to date. Formerly Kemp's
Short and Specialised Film and
Independent TV Directory.

1769. Kemps Production Diary/The AIP
Handbook.
1978 to date.

1770. Kinematograph Year Book.
Kinematograph Pubs/Odhams/Go
Magazine/Longacres Pubs.
1914–64, 1967–71. Also called
Kinematograph and Television Year
Book.

1771. List of Cinematograph Films: New
English Subjects on Clear Transparent
Celluloid of Even Thickness by the
Prestwich Manufacturing Company.
Prestwich MC, 1898. 8p.

1772. List of Films for Hire by Butcher and
Sons.
Butcher, 1907. 23p. illus.

1773. List of Urban Film Subjects, November
1903 by the Urban Trading Company.
Urban, 1903. 202p. illus.
Plus supplements 1902–8.

1774. Missing Believed Lost: The Great British
Film Search by Allen Eyles & David
Meeker.
British Film Institute, 1992. 107p.
illus. appendix.

1775. Mr. W.F. Jury's List of Select
Entertainments by Jury's Entertainment
Bureau.
Jury's Entertainment Bureau, n.d. 14p.
illus.
Publicity brochure.

1776. National Film Archive Catalogue of
Viewing Copies 1985 by the National Film
Archive.
British Film Institute, 1984. 216p.
index.

1777. National Film Archive Catalogue. Part I:
Silent News Films 1895–1933 by the
National Film Archive.
British Film Institute, 1965. 308p.
index.

1778. National Film Archive Catalogue. Part II:
Silent Non-Fiction Films 1895–1934 by
the National Film Archive.
British Film Institute, 1960. 195p.
illus.

1779. National Film Archive Catalogue. Part
III:
Silent Fiction Films 1895–1930 by the
National Film Archive.
British Film Institute, 1966. 326p.
plates.

1780. National Film Archive Catalogue. Volume
I: Non-fiction Films by the National Film
Archive.
British Film Institute, 1980. 808p.
plates. index.

1781. National Film Finance Corporation
Annual Report by the National Film
Finance Corporation.
HMSO. 1950 to Ap/Oct 1985.

1782. New 'Hepwix' Films, June 1904. Third
Supplement to the Revised and Abridged
Catalogue by the Hepworth
Manufacturing Company.
Hepworth, 1904. 39p.

1783. The New Social Function of Cinema:
Catalogue of British Film Institute
Productions 1979–80 edited by Rod
Stoneman & Hilary Thompson.
British Film Institute, 1981. 147p.
illus.

1784. North West Film Archive Film Catalogue
1985 by Marion Hewitt.
Manchester University Press, 1985.
127p. illus. index.

1785. Northern Lights by Helen Bingham &
John Bradshaw.
Northern Arts, 1990. 120p. illus.

1786. PACT Annual Report by PACT.
PACT. 1942 to date. Formerly British and
TV Producers Assoc./Film Producers
Assoc./Film Production Assoc. of Great
Britain.

1787. The Penguin Film Review edited by
Roger Manvell.
Penguin. No.1–9 (1947–49).

1788. Picture Show Annual.
Amalgamated Press.
1926–41, 1947–61.

1789. Picturegoer Film Annual.
Odhams. 1949–1961/62.

1790. Preview.
Various publishers. 1945–58, 1960–63.

1791. The Rank Organisation Annual Report by
the Rank Organisation.
Rank. 1946 to date.

1792. Register of Feature Film Credits 1944–46
by the Association of Cine-Technicians.
ACT, 1947. 120p. index.

1793. Researcher's Guide to British Film &
Television Collections.
British Universities Film and Video
Council, 1993. 250p. illus.

1794. Revised List of High-class Original
Copyrighted Bioscope Films, Urban
Films, Geo. Méliès' Star Films and the
Best Productions of Messrs. Lumière,
G.A. Smith, West's 'Our Navy',
Williamson, Nordon and Other Makers by
the Urban Trading Company.
Urban, 1905. 332p. illus.

1795. The Royal Bioscope: Animated
Photographs by Jury's Imperial Pictures.
Jury's. Various pagings.
Two editions: c1906–7 and c1909.

1796. Screen International Film and Television
Yearbook by Peter Noble.
1976/77 to date. Formerly British Film
and Television Yearbook.

1797. A Selected Catalogue of the Best and
Most Interesting 'Hepwix' Films by
Hepworth and Company.
Hepworth, 1903. 64p.

1798. Some Film Material Relating to Newcastle
upon Tyne and Surrounding Areas by
James Ballantyne & Kate Black.
British Universities Film Council,
1979. 27p.

1799. Thorn–EMI Annual Reports.
Thorn–EMI. 1955 to date. Formerly
Associated British Picture Corporation/
EMI.

1800. Walturdaw Catalogues 1904–11 by the
Walturdaw Company.
Various pagings.
Collection of catalogues bound in one
volume.

1801. Warwick Trading Company Catalogue.
Warwick, 1898. 63p. illus.

1802. Warwick Trading Company Catalogue.
Warwick, 1901. 224p. illus.
Plus supplement.

1803. Winchester's Screen Encyclopedia edited
by Maud Miller.
Winchester Publications, 1948. 386p.
illus.

1804. The Year's Work in the Film edited by
Roger Manvell.
Longmans Green for the British Council.
1949, 1950.

Index to Part One
(by Director)

ACKLAND, Rodney
LADY BE KIND (1941)
THURSDAY'S CHILD (1943)

ACRES, Birt
ROUGH SEA AT DOVER (1895)
TOM MERRY, LIGHTNING CARTOONIST, SKETCHING KAISER WILHELM II (1895)

ADAMS, John
NAKED YOGA (1975)

AINSWORTH, John
BAY OF SAINT MICHEL, the (1963)

AITKEN, William Maxwell
THEY FORGOT TO READ THE DIRECTIONS (1924)

AKOMFRAH, John
HANDSWORTH SONGS (1986)
TESTAMENT (1988)
WHO NEEDS A HEART (1991)

ALAUX, Myriam
ANIMALS FILM, the (1981)

ALBERTINE, Viviane
COPING WITH CUPID (1991)

ALDERSON, John
EL DORADO (1951)
HOME SERVICE (1957)
SILVER LINING (1935)
WEE BLUE BLOSSOM, the (1944)

ALDRICH, Robert
ANGRY HILLS, the (1959)
DIRTY DOZEN, the (1967)

ALEXANDER, Donald
ALL THOSE IN FAVOUR (1941)
EASTERN VALLEY (1937)
FIVE AND UNDER (1941)
JOB TO BE DONE, a (1940)
LIFE BEGINS AGAIN (1942)
OUR SCHOOL (1941)
PROBATION OFFICER (1949)
WEALTH OF A NATION (1938)

ALEXANDER, Michael
ORPHEUS AND EURYDICE (1984)

ALLÉGRET, Marc
BLACKMAILED (1950)
BLANCHE FURY (1947)
NAKED HEART, the (1950)

ALLEN, Lewis
ANOTHER TIME, ANOTHER PLACE (1958)
SO EVIL MY LOVE (1948)
WHIRLPOOL (1959)

ALLEN, Peter
ARENA OF CONFLICT (1980)
ENVIRONMENTAL DILEMMA, the (1980)
MAN VERSUS MACHINES? (1980)
PATHWAY TO ETERNAL BOREDOM? (1980)
WHO TAKES THE MONEY? (1980)

ALLEN, Stanley
OLD SUSSEX (1933)

ALLEN, T D
POLYCHROME FANTASY (1935)

ALVEY, Glenn H, Jr
DOOR IN THE WALL, the (1956)

AMBROSE, Anna
PHOELIX (1979)

AMIEL, Jon
QUEEN OF HEARTS (1989)

AMYES, Julian
HILL IN KOREA, a (1956)
MIRACLE IN SOHO (1957)

ANDERSON, David
DEADSY (1989)
DOOR (1990)
DREAMLAND EXPRESS (1982)
DREAMLESS SLEEP (1986)

ANDERSON, James M
THOSE WERE THE DAYS (1948)

ANDERSON, J S
SMOKE FROM GRAND-PA'S PIPE, the (1920)

ANDERSON, John
DAVID LEACH (1977)
ISAAC BUTTON – COUNTRY POTTER (1965)

ANDERSON, Lindsay
BRITANNIA HOSPITAL (1982)
EVERY DAY EXCEPT CHRISTMAS (1957)
IF.... (1968)
O DREAMLAND (1953)
O LUCKY MAN! (1973)
THIS SPORTING LIFE (1963)
WAKEFIELD EXPRESS (1953)

ANDERSON, Max
FOUR MEN IN PRISON (1950)
HARVEST SHALL COME, the (1942)
OUT OF THE NIGHT (1941)
SALT (1947)
TREASURE AT THE MILL (1957)
WORDS AND ACTIONS (1943)

ANDERSON, Michael
CHASE A CROOKED SHADOW (1957)
CONDUCT UNBECOMING (1975)
DAM BUSTERS, the (1955)
HELL IS SOLD OUT (1951)
MILLENNIUM (1989)
NAKED EDGE, the (1961)
NIGHT WAS OUR FRIEND (1951)
1984 (1955)
OPERATION CROSSBOW (1964)
POPE JOAN (1972)
QUILLER MEMORANDUM, the (1966)
WATERFRONT (1950)
WILL ANY GENTLEMAN? (1953)
YANGTSE INCIDENT (1956)

ANDREWS, David
SEA CHILDREN, the (1973)

ANGELL, Robert M
VINTAGE '28 (1953)

ANNAKIN, Ken
ACROSS THE BRIDGE (1957)
BROKEN JOURNEY (1947)
CROOKS ANONYMOUS (1962)
DOUBLE CONFESSION (1950)
ENGLISH CRIMINAL JUSTICE (1946)
FAST LADY, the (1962)
FENLANDS (1945)
FLYING START, (1944)
HELLIONS, the (1961)
HERE COME THE HUGGETTS (1948)
HOLIDAY CAMP (1947)
HOTEL SAHARA (1951)
HUGGETTS ABROAD, the (1949)
INFORMERS, the (1963)
IT BEGAN ON THE CLYDE (1946)
LANDFALL (1949)
LONDON 1942 (1942)
LONG DUEL, the (1967)
LOSER TAKES ALL (1956)
MIRANDA (1948)
NEW CROP, the (1944)
NOR THE MOON BY NIGHT (1958)
PAPER TIGER (1974)
PLANTER'S WIFE, the (1952)
QUARTET (1948)
RIDE WITH UNCLE JOE, a (1943)
SEEKERS, the (1954)
STORY OF ROBIN HOOD AND HIS MERRIE MEN, the (1952)
SWISS FAMILY ROBINSON (1960)
SWORD AND THE ROSE, the (1953)
THIRD MAN ON THE MOUNTAIN (1959)

THOSE MAGNIFICENT MEN IN THEIR FLYING MACHINES; or, How I flew from London to Paris in 25 hours and 11 minutes (1965)
TRIO (1950)
VALUE FOR MONEY (1955)
VERY IMPORTANT PERSON (1961)
VOTE FOR HUGGETT (1948)
WE OF THE WEST RIDING (1945)

ANSTEY, Edgar
DINNER HOUR (1935)
ENOUGH TO EAT (1936)
HOUSING PROBLEMS (1935)
MEN BEHIND THE METERS (1936)
ON THE WAY TO WORK (1936)
SIX-THIRTY COLLECTION (1934)
WARTIME FACTORY (1940)

ANTHONY, Florence
INSULIN (1949)
NALORPHINE (1953)

ANTHONY, Richard
AFTER THE BALL (1984)

ANTONIONI, Michelangelo
BLOWUP (1966)

APTED, Michael
STARDUST (1974)
TRIPLE ECHO, the (1972)

ARCH, Albert H
SCOTLAND, THE MAGIC NORTH (1934)
SUNSHINE, FUN AND LAUGHTER (1932)

ARGYLE, John
HILLS OF DONEGAL, the (1947)
SEND FOR PAUL TEMPLE (1946)

ARLISS, Leslie
FARMER'S WIFE, the (1941)
IDOL OF PARIS (1948)
LOVE STORY (1944)
MAN ABOUT THE HOUSE, a (1947)
MAN IN GREY, the (1943)
NIGHT HAS EYES, the (1942)
SAINTS AND SINNERS (1949)
WICKED LADY, the (1945)

ARMITAGE, Philip
CORNISH ENGINE, the (1948)
GAS TURBINE GOES TO SEA, the (1951)

ARMSTRONG, Charles
CLOWN AND HIS DONKEY, the (1910)

ARMSTRONG, John
COUPE DES ALPES; THE STORY OF THE 1958 ALPINE RALLY (1958)
SONG OF THE CLOUDS (1957)

ARNOLD, Jack
MOUSE THAT ROARED, the (1959)

ARNOLD, John
AIR CROSSROADS (1958)
PASSING STRANGER, the (1954)

ARNOTT, Steve
TIN BOX (1992)

ARON, Sue
LIVES OF ARTISTS NOT WIVES OF ARTISTS; WOMEN'S ART PRACTICE SINCE 1970 (1984)

ARTHUR, Noel
MOVING MILLIONS (1947)

ASH, Clare
FRIENDLY INN, the (1958)

ASHER, Robert
BULLDOG BREED, the (1960)
EARLY BIRD, the (1965)
FOLLOW A STAR (1959)
INTELLIGENCE MEN, the (1965)
MAKE MINE MINK (1960)
ON THE BEAT (1962)

BARRINGER, Michael
Q-SHIPS (1928)

BARRINGTON, A F C
LANGFORD REED'S LIMERICKS (1935)

BARRON, Steve
ELECTRIC DREAMS (1984)

BARRON, Zelda
SECRET PLACES (1984)

BARRY, Gerald
LAST WALTZ, the (1936)

BARRY, Michael
STOP PRESS GIRL (1949)

BARWELL, Claire
PHOTOGRAPHIC EXHIBITS (1985)

BATCHELOR, Joy
ABU AND THE POISONED WELL (1943)
ANIMAL FARM (1954)
CHARLEY'S MARCH OF TIME (1948)
DUSTBIN PARADE (1942)
FARMER CHARLEY (1949)
MODERN GUIDE TO HEALTH, a (1946)
NEW TOWN (1948)
OLD WIVES' TALES (1946)
PIPING HOT (1959)
ROBINSON CHARLEY (1948)
RUDDIGORE (1967)

BATLEY, Ethyle
BULLDOG GRIT (1915)
THERE'S GOOD IN THE WORST OF US
(1913)

BATTERSBY, Roy
BODY, the (1970)

BAXTER, John
COMMON TOUCH, the (1941)
CROOK'S TOUR (1940)
DOSS HOUSE (1933)
DRAGON OF PENDRAGON CASTLE, the
(1950)
DREAMING (1944)
ELLA SHIELDS (1936)
FLOOD TIDE (1934)
GRAND ESCAPADE, the (1946)
HEARTS OF HUMANITY (1936)
HERE COMES THE SUN (1945)
JUDGMENT DEFERRED (1951)
KENTUCKY MINSTRELS (1934)
LAST LOAD, the (1948)
LAUGH IT OFF (1940)
LEST WE FORGET (1934)
LET THE PEOPLE SING (1942)
LOVE ON THE DOLE (1941)
MEN OF YESTERDAY (1936)
OLD MOTHER RILEY IN BUSINESS
(1940)
OLD MOTHER RILEY IN SOCIETY (1940)
OLD MOTHER RILEY'S GHOSTS (1941)
RAMSBOTTOM RIDES AGAIN (1956)
REAL BLOKE, a (1935)
SAY IT WITH FLOWERS (1934)
SECOND MATE, the (1950)
SECRET JOURNEY (1939)
SHIPBUILDERS, the (1943)
SONG OF THE ROAD (1937)
TALKING FEET (1937)
THEATRE ROYAL (1943)
WE'LL SMILE AGAIN (1942)
WHAT WOULD YOU DO CHUMS? (1939)
WHEN YOU COME HOME (1947)

BAXTER, Ronnie
NEVER MIND THE QUALITY FEEL THE
WIDTH (1972)

BAYLIS, Peter
DISTILLATION (1940)
FINEST HOURS, the (1964)
PEACEFUL YEARS, the (1948)
SCRAPBOOK FOR 1922 (1947)
TURN OF THE FURROW (1941)
WHEELWRIGHT, the (1935)

BAYLY, Stephen
ADERYN PAPUR (1984)
RHOSYN A RHITH (1986)

BEALES, Mary
DOVER, SPRING 1947 (1947)
FAIR RENT (1946)

BEAUDINE, William
BOYS WILL BE BOYS (1935)
DANDY DICK (1935)
FEATHER YOUR NEST (1937)
IT'S IN THE BAG (1936)
SAID O'REILLY TO McNAB (1937)
SO YOU WON'T TALK! (1935)
WHERE THERE'S A WILL (1936)
WINDBAG THE SAILOR (1936)

BECK, Reginald
LONG DARK HALL, the (1951)

BECKER, Harold
RAGMAN'S DAUGHTER, the (1971)

BECKER, Lutz
FIRST YEARS OF THE SOVIET UNION
(1971)
MALEVITCH SUPREMATISM (1971)

BEDFORD, Terry
SLAYGROUND (1983)

BEE-MASON, J C
BEE HUNTER, the (1910)
BEES AND THEIR ENEMIES (1910)
BEE'S EVICTION, the (1909)
HORNET AND HER NEST, the (1911)

BEGG, L Gordon
PLAYS FOR THE PEOPLE (1947)

BEHR, John
PICTURE PEOPLE (1943)

BELL, Colin
HOW TELEVISION WORKS (1953)
RESCUE SQUAD, the (1963)

BELL, Geoffrey
CONTROL ROOM (1942)
ROOF BOLTING IN GREAT BRITAIN
(1958)
TRANSFER OF POWER; THE HISTORY
OF THE TOOTHED WHEEL (1939)
TRANSFER OF SKILL (1940)
WAR IN THE PACIFIC (1943)

BELL, Peter
BASIL BUNTING (1982)

BELLAMY, Christine
RED SKIRTS ON CLYDESIDE (1984)

BENEDEK, Laslo
MOMENT OF DANGER (1960)

BENNETT, Charles
MADNESS OF THE HEART (1949)

BENNETT, Compton
AFTER THE BALL (1957)
BEYOND THE CURTAIN (1960)
DAYBREAK (1948)
DESPERATE MOMENT (1953)
FIND, FIX AND STRIKE (1942)
GIFT HORSE, the (1952)
IT STARTED IN PARADISE (1952)
SEVENTH VEIL, the (1945)
THAT WOMAN OPPOSITE (1957)
YEARS BETWEEN, the (1946)

BENNETT, Edward
ASCENDANCY (1982)
HOGARTH (1977)
LIFE STORY OF BAAL, the (1978)

BENNETT, F S
SMALLEST CAR IN THE LARGEST CITY
IN THE WORLD, the (1913)

BENTLEY, Robert
HAVING A LOVELY TIME (1970)

BENTLEY, Thomas
AFTER OFFICE HOURS (1932)
AMERICAN PRISONER, the (1929)
ANTIDOTE, the (1927)
BEAU BROCADE (1916)
CAVALCADE OF VARIETY (1941)
COMPROMISING DAPHNE (1930)
DAVID COPPERFIELD (1913)
DEAD MAN'S SHOES (1939)
GENERAL POST (1920)
GREAT DEFENDER, the (1934)
HARMONY HEAVEN (1930)
KEEPERS OF YOUTH (1931)
LAST COUPON, the (1932)
LUCKY TO ME (1939)
MARIGOLD (1938)
ME AND MY PAL (1939)
MIDDLE WATCH, the (1939)
MUSIC HATH CHARMS (1935)
NIGHT ALONE (1938)
NOT QUITE A LADY (1928)
OLD BILL 'THROUGH THE AGES' (1924)
OLD CURIOSITY SHOP, the (1935)
OLD MOTHER RILEY'S CIRCUS (1941)
ROMANCE OF MAYFAIR, a (1925)
SILVER BLAZE (1937)
SILVER LINING, the (1927)
SLEEPLESS NIGHTS (1932)
THOSE WERE THE DAYS (1934)
THREE SILENT MEN (1940)
YOUNG WOODLEY (1930)

BERESFORD, Bruce
SIDE BY SIDE (1975)

BERGER, Ludwig
EARLY TO BED (1933)
THIEF OF BAGDAD, the (1940)

BERMAN, Monty
SIEGE OF SIDNEY STREET, the (1960)

BERNARD, Chris
LETTER TO BREZHNEV (1985)

BERNARD, Paul
TIGER LILY, the (1975)

BERNHARDT, Curtis
BEAU BRUMMELL (1954)

BERTOLUCCI, Bernardo
SHELTERING SKY, the (1990)

BEST, Joseph
MY SONG GOES FORTH (1937)
WHATSOEVER A MAN SOWETH (1917)

BETTS, John
OUR FIGHTING NAVY (1933)
RACING OUTLOOK NO.1 –
STEEPLECHASING (1924)
RACING OUTLOOK NO.2 –
STEEPLECHASING (1924)
RACING OUTLOOK NO.4 –
STEEPLECHASING (1924)
RACING OUTLOOK NO.5 –
STEEPLECHASING (1924)
RACING OUTLOOK NO.7 (1924)
RACING OUTLOOK NO.8 (1924)
RACING OUTLOOK NO.9 (1924)
RACING OUTLOOK NO.10 (1924)
RACING OUTLOOK NO.11 (1924)
RACING OUTLOOK NO.12 (1924)
RUNNING; A SPORT THAT CREATES
BOTH BODILY AND MENTAL
HEALTH PLUS ENDURANCE AND
COURAGE (1924)
SPORT AND INTEREST IN A FRESH
LIGHT (1926)
SWIMMING (1924)
TENNIS; THE MOST DEMOCRATIC OF
GAMES FOR BOTH SEXES (1924)

BEZENCENET, Peter
BAND OF THIEVES (1962)
BOMB IN THE HIGH STREET (1963)

BHATTACHARYA, Uday
CIRCLE OF GOLD (1988)

BRABIN, Charles J
DAUGHTER OF ROMANY, a (1914)

BRACKNELL, David
ALL IN A GOOD CAUSE (1978)
CUP FEVER (1965)
DECORATORS LIMITED (1976)
GREAT SNAIL RACE, the (1976)
IT PAYS TO ADVERTISE (1978)
JAM SESSION (1978)
MAGPIE LAYS AN EGG (1976)
MAGPIE'S TALKING DUCK (1978)
POT LUCK (1976)
ROOM TO LET (1976)
SHOVE TUESDAY (1976)
SLIMDERELLA (1978)
WATERBIKES (1978)

BRADFORD, Peter
HEIGHTS OF DANGER (1953)
SOLID EXPLANATION, a (1951)
STORY OF PAPER MAKING, the (1948)
STORY OF PRINTING, the (1948)
TRANSPORT (1948)

BRADSHAW, L
LITTLE ANNIE'S RAG BOOK (1942)

BRAHM, John
BROKEN BLOSSOMS (1936)

BRAMBLE, A V
LUCKY SWEEP, a (1931)
MAN WHO CHANGED HIS NAME, the (1928)
MRS DANE'S DEFENCE (1933)
SHOOTING STARS (1927)
VETERAN OF WATERLOO, the (1933)
ZEEBRUGGE (1924)

BRANDON, Phil
HAPPIDROME (1943)
WE'LL MEET AGAIN (1942)

BRANDT, George
IN TOUCH (1966)
NEW TENANT, the (1963)

BRANDT, Michael
MISSING NOTE, the (1961)
ON THE RECORD (1955)

BRASON, John
ONE MORE RIVER (1961)

BRAYNE, William
JUDGEMENT (1985)

BREAKSTON, George
ESCAPE IN THE SUN (1955)
SCARLET SPEAR, the (1953)

BRENON, Herbert
BLACK EYES (1939)
DOMINANT SEX, the (1937)
FLYING SQUAD, the (1940)
HOUSEMASTER (1938)
LIVING DANGEROUSLY (1936)
ROYAL CAVALCADE (1935)
SPRING HANDICAP (1937)
VICTORY AND PEACE (1918)
YELLOW SANDS (1938)

BRENTON, Guy
VISION OF WILLIAM BLAKE, the (1958)

BRICKEN, Jules
DANNY JONES (1971)

BRIDGES, Alan
ACT OF MURDER (1964)
HIRELING, the (1973)
OUT OF SEASON (1975)
RETURN OF THE SOLDIER (1982)
SHOOTING PARTY, the (1984)

BROADWAY, Marc
ELECTRICITY AND THE
ENVIRONMENT (1971)
LEARNING BY DISCOVERY (1968)
TITANS OF TOMORROW (1968)

BRODY, Hugh
NINETEEN NINETEEN (1985)

BROMLY, Alan
FOLLOW THAT HORSE! (1960)

BROOK, Clive
ON APPROVAL (1944)

BROOK, Peter
BEGGAR'S OPERA, the (1953)
LORD OF THE FLIES (1963)
PERSECUTION AND ASSASSINATION
OF JEAN-PAUL MARAT AS
PERFORMED BY THE INMATES OF
THE ASYLUM OF CHARENTON
UNDER THE DIRECTION OF THE
MARQUIS DE SADE, the (1966)
TELL ME LIES (1967)

BROOKS, Joseph
INVITATION TO THE WEDDING (1984)

BROOKS, Richard
LORD JIM (1964)

BROOMFIELD, Nicholas
JUVENILE LIAISON (1975)

BROWN, Alan
BROWN ALE WITH GERTIE (1974)

BROWN, Neil
TRANSMISSION OF ELECTRICITY (1947)

BROWNLOW, Kevin
ABEL GANCE – THE CHARM OF
DYNAMITE (1968)
IT HAPPENED HERE (1963)
WINSTANLEY (1975)

BRUCE, Neville
VERY UNSUCCESSFUL COMPETITOR
IN THE TOFFEE APPLE
COMPETITION, a (1920)

BRUCE, Nichola
BOOLEAN PROCEDURE (1980)
CLIP (1983)
WINGS OF DEATH (1985)

BRUNEL, Adrian
BADGER'S GREEN (1934)
BLIGHTY (1927)
BOOKWORMS (1920)
BUMP, the (1920)
CITY OF BEAUTIFUL NONSENSE (1935)
CROSS CURRENTS (1935)
CROSSING THE GREAT SAGRADA
(1924)
CUT IT OUT; A DAY IN THE LIFE OF A
CENSOR (1925)
ELSTREE CALLING (1930)
INVADER, the (1936)
LIGHT WOMAN, a (1928)
LION HAS WINGS, the (1939)
LOVE AT SEA (1936)
MAN WITHOUT DESIRE, the (1922)
SALVAGE WITH A SMILE (1940)
SHIMMY SHEIK (1923)
TYPICAL BUDGET; THE ONLY
UNRELIABLE FILM REVIEW (1925)
VORTEX, the (1927)
WHILE PARENTS SLEEP (1935)

BRUNIUS, Jacques
BRIEF CITY (1952)
FAMILY ALBUM (1953)
TO THE RESCUE (1952)

BRUUN, Einar J
CORNER MAN, the (1921)

BRYANT, Gerard
CHANNEL ISLANDS 1940–45, the (1945)
CHILDREN'S CHARTER (1945)
OUCH! (1967)
SPIKE MILLIGAN MEETS JOE BROWN
(1961)

SPIKE MILLIGAN ON TREASURE
ISLAND WC2 (1961)
TOMMY STEELE STORY, the (1957)
TONIGHT IN BRITAIN (1954)

BRYCE, Alex
AGAINST THE TIDE (1937)
ANSWER, the (1940)
ANYBODY'S BUGBEAR (1940)
BIG NOISE, the (1936)
LONDONDERRY AIR, the (1938)
MY IRISH MOLLY (1938)

BUCHAN, John
ENGLAND AWAKE (1932)

BUCHANAN, Andrew
BACKYARD FRONT, the (1940)
CEREAL SEED DISINFECTION (1943)
FINE FEATHERS, the (1941)
HOW TO COOK GREEN VEGETABLES
(1944)
LAND OF INVENTION (1941)
LEARNING A JOB (1944)
LONDON RIVER (1939)
OUTDOOR TOMATO GROWING (1945)
OUT OF THE SHADOW (1938)
POTATO GROWING (1946)
RELIGION AND THE PEOPLE (1940)
START A LAND CLUB (1942)
TRACTOR ENGINE OVERHAUL (1945)
TRAINING FOR MECHANISED MINING
(1945)
WELDING HELPS THE FARMER (1943)

BUCHANAN, Jack
SKY'S THE LIMIT, the (1937)
THAT'S A GOOD GIRL (1933)

BUCKLAND, Warwick
AT THE FOOT OF THE SCAFFOLD (1913)
CHURCH AND STAGE (1912)
CORPORAL'S KIDDIES, the (1914)
MIDNIGHT MAIL, the (1915)
MYSTERY OF MR MARKS, the (1914)
WOMAN'S WIT, a (1913)

BUCKSEY, Colin
BLUE MONEY (1984)

BUNDY, A Frank
CAMPANIONS (1938)
JAMAICAN HARVEST (1938)
NEW FIELDS FOR INDUSTRY (1939)

BURCH, Noël
CORRECTION PLEASE; or, How we got
into pictures (1979)
IMPERSONATION, the (1984)

BURGE, Stuart
JULIUS CAESAR (1970)
MIKADO, the (1966)
OTHELLO (1965)
THERE WAS A CROOKED MAN (1960)

BURGER, Germain
BORDER COLLIE (1939)
DEVIL'S ROCK (1938)
FAITHFUL FOR EVER (1941)
ROSE OF TRALEE, the (1942)
TWO GOOD FAIRIES (1944)

BURN, Oscar
CASTLE SINISTER (1947)

BURNLEY, Fred
NEITHER THE SEA NOR THE SAND
(1972)

BURTON, Nick
AT THE FOUNTAINHEAD (OF GERMAN
STRENGTH) (1980)

BURTON, Richard
DOCTOR FAUSTUS (1967)

BURTON, Trill
FRAMED YOUTH – REVENGE OF THE
TEENAGE PERVERTS (1983)

CAVALCANTI, Alberto
ALICE IN SWITZERLAND (1940)
CAUSE COMMUNE, la (1940)
CHAMPAGNE CHARLIE (1944)
COAL FACE (1935)
DEAD OF NIGHT (1945)
FILM AND REALITY (1942)
FIRST GENTLEMAN, the (1948)
FOR THEM THAT TRESPASS (1948)
FOUR BARRIERS, the (1937)
HAPPY IN THE MORNING (1938)
LINE TO THE TSCHIERVA HUT (1937)
MASTERY OF THE SEA (1940)
MEN OF THE ALPS (1937)
MESSAGE FROM GENEVA (1936)
MID-SUMMER DAY'S WORK (1939)
MONSTER OF HIGHGATE PONDS, the
   (1960)
NICHOLAS NICKLEBY (1947)
PETT AND POTT (1934)
SKY'S THE LIMIT, the (1945)
THEY MADE ME A FUGITIVE (1947)
WE LIVE IN TWO WORLDS (1937)
WENT THE DAY WELL? (1942)
YELLOW CAESAR (1940)

CAVALLI, Mario
SOHO SQUARE (1992)

CEDER, Ralph
CAPTAIN BILL (1935)

CEKALSKI, Eugene
DIARY OF A POLISH AIRMAN (1942)
LONDON SCRAPBOOK (1942)
SEAMAN FRANK GOES BACK TO SEA
   (1942)
WHITE EAGLE, the (1941)

CHAFFEY, Don
BOUNCER BREAKS UP (1953)
CREATURES THE WORLD FORGOT
   (1970)
DENTIST IN THE CHAIR (1960)
FLESH IS WEAK, the (1957)
GOOD PULL-UP, a (1953)
GREYFRIARS BOBBY (1961)
JASON AND THE ARGONAUTS (1963)
JOLLY BAD FELLOW, a (1963)
MAN UPSTAIRS, the (1958)
MYSTERIOUS POACHER, the (1950)
ONE MILLION YEARS BC (1966)
QUESTION OF ADULTERY, a (1958)
SECRET TENT, the (1956)
SKID KIDS (1953)
TWIST OF SAND, a (1968)
VIKING QUEEN, the (1966)
WATCH OUT! (1953)
WEBSTER BOY, the (1962)

CHAMBERS, J D
BATTLE OF THE BOOKS, the (1941)
BRIDGE, the (1946)
CHASING THE BLUES (1950)
CONTROLLED HEAT (1955)
HOW THE TELEPHONE WORKS (1938)
NIGHT SHIFT (1942)
POWER FOR THE HIGHLANDS (1943)
PRECISE MEASUREMENT FOR
   ENGINEERS (1948)
SUNSHINE MINERS (1952)

CHAPLIN, Charles
COUNTESS FROM HONG KONG, a (1966)
KING IN NEW YORK, a (1957)

CHEATLE, Oliver
STORY OF PENICILLIN, the (1947)

CHELSOM, Peter
HEAR MY SONG (1991)

CHESHIRE, Leonard
SHARE THY BREAD (1963)

CHIAPPINI, Luigi V R
PHOENIX AND THE TURTLE, the (1972)

CHILTON, Frank
OCEAN WEATHER SHIP (1949)

CHISNELL, Frank
ROVER AND ME (1949)
TOM TOM TOPIA (1946)

CHORLTON, Michael C
SALUTE THE SOLDIER (1944)

CHRISTIAN, Roger
DOLLAR BOTTOM, the (1981)
SENDER, the (1982)

CHRONOPOULOS, Kostas
GREECE OF CHRISTIAN GREEKS (1971)

CHURCHILL, Joan
JUVENILE LIAISON (1975)

CLAIR, René
BREAK THE NEWS (1938)
GHOST GOES WEST, the (1935)

CLANCEY, Vernon J
ENGLAND'S PLAYGROUND (1934)

CLARK, Bruce
SKI BUM (1969)

CLARK, David Rayner
FILM (1979)

CLARK, Geoffrey
AIR POST (1934)

CLARK, Ian
DRY HANDS (1964)

CLARK, Jim
CHRISTMAS TREE, the (1966)
EVERY HOME SHOULD HAVE ONE
   (1969)
RENTADICK (1972)

CLARK, Michael
TRACING THE SPREAD OF INFECTION
   (1949)

CLARK, Nick
SHIP THAT NEVER RETURNED, the
   (1987)

CLARKE, Alan
BILLY THE KID AND THE GREEN
   BAIZE VAMPIRE (1985)
RITA, SUE AND BOB, TOO! (1987)
SCUM (1979)

CLARKE, Douglas
CONTROLLED HEAT (1955)
DATE WITH IRIS (1956)
FESTIVAL IN EDINBURGH (1955)
I WENT TO BRITAIN (1955)

CLARKE, James Kenelm
LET'S GET LAID! (1977)

CLARKE, Michael
EVERY VALLEY (1957)
THIRD RIVER, the (1952)
UNSEEN ENEMIES (1959)

CLAVELL, James
LAST VALLEY, the (1970)
TO SIR, WITH LOVE (1966)

CLAVERING, Albert
SOUTHWARD ON THE QUEST (1922)

CLAYTON, Jack
INNOCENTS, the (1961)
MEMENTO MORI (1993)
OUR MOTHER'S HOUSE (1967)
PUMPKIN EATER, the (1964)
ROOM AT THE TOP (1958)

CLAYTON, Sue
SONG OF THE SHIRT, the (1979)

CLEGG, Tom
SWEENEY 2 (1978)

CLEMENT, Dick
BULLSHOT (1983)
OTLEY (1968)
PORRIDGE (1979)
SEVERED HEAD, a (1970)
WATER (1985)

CLÉMENT, René
KNAVE OF HEARTS (1954)

CLIFT, Denison
CITY OF PLAY, the (1929)
DIANA OF THE CROSSWAYS (1922)
HIGH SEAS (1929)
PARADISE (1928)

CLIFTON, Peter
SONG REMAINS THE SAME, the (1976)

CLOCHE, Maurice
NEVER TAKE NO FOR AN ANSWER
   (1951)

CLOWES, St John Legh
DORA (1933)
NO ORCHIDS FOR MISS BLANDISH
   (1948)

COBB, Norman
BINGO THE BATTLING BRUISER (1930)

COBHAM, David
BRITISH POLICEMAN, the (1959)
TARKA THE OTTER (1978)

COBHAM, John
BACK CHAT (1935)

COE, Peter
LOCK UP YOUR DAUGHTERS! (1969)

COGHILL, Nevill
DOCTOR FAUSTUS (1967)

COHEN, David
PLEASURE PRINCIPLE, the (1991)

COHEN, Norman
ADOLF HITLER – MY PART IN HIS
   DOWNFALL (1972)
CONFESSIONS OF A POP PERFORMER
   (1975)
DAD'S ARMY (1971)
STAND UP VIRGIN SOLDIERS (1977)
TILL DEATH US DO PART (1969)

COHEN, Rob
SCANDALOUS (1984)

COKE, Cyril
NIGHT RIVER (1955)

COKLISS, Harley
BATTLE OF BILLY'S POND, the (1976)
DREAM DEMON, the (1988)

COLDSTREAM, William
FAIRY OF THE PHONE, the (1936)
KING'S STAMP, the (1935)
ROADWAYS (1937)

COLE, Jeff
FRAMED YOUTH – REVENGE OF THE
   TEENAGE PERVERTS (1983)

COLE, Lionel
THRUST (1947)

COLE, Sidney
BEHIND THE SPANISH LINES (1938)
ROADS ACROSS BRITAIN (1939)
SPANISH ABC (1938)

COLE, Teresa
SHEEP, the (1986)

THEY WERE SISTERS (1945)
WEDDING OF LILLI MARLENE, the
(1953)

CRAIGIE, Jill
BLUE SCAR (1949)
OUT OF CHAOS (1944)
TO BE A WOMAN (1951)
WAY WE LIVE, the (1946)

CRAMER, Ross
RIDING HIGH (1980)

CRANE, Frank Hall
TONS OF MONEY (1924)

CRANE, Peter
HUNTED (1971)

CRAVENNE, Marcel
PRÉSENCE AU COMBAT (1945)

CREIGHTON, Walter
CASTLES AND FISHERFOLK (1933)
MESSAGE OF THE DRUM, the (1930)
NIGHTWATCHMAN'S STORY; A
ROMANCE OF INDUSTRY, the (1933)
ONE FAMILY (1930)
ROMANCE OF A RAILWAY (1935)

CREME, Lol
COOLER, the (1982)

CRICHTON, Charles
AGAINST THE WIND (1947)
BATTLE OF THE SEXES, the (1959)
BOY WHO STOLE A MILLION, the (1960)
DANCE HALL (1950)
DEAD OF NIGHT (1945)
DIVIDED HEART, the (1954)
FISH CALLED WANDA, a (1988)
FLOODS OF FEAR (1958)
FOR THOSE IN PERIL (1944)
HE WHO RIDES A TIGER (1965)
HUE AND CRY (1946)
HUNTED (1952)
LAVENDER HILL MOB, the (1951)
LOVE LOTTERY, the (1953)
MAN IN THE SKY, the (1956)
PAINTED BOATS (1945)
TITFIELD THUNDERBOLT, the (1953)

CRICHTON, Michael
FIRST GREAT TRAIN ROBBERY, the
(1978)

CRICK, Allan
AS OLD AS THE HILLS (1950)

CRILLY, Anne
MOTHER IRELAND (1988)

CRIPPS, Erik
PICTURE PAPER (1946)

CROFT, David
NOT NOW, DARLING (1972)

CROISE, Hugh
ALWAYS TELL YOUR WIFE (1923)
KENSINGTON MYSTERY, the (1924)

CROSSMAN, Joe
OUR CAVALCADE (1937)

CUKOR, George
EDWARD, MY SON (1948)

CULLIMORE, Alan J
VENGEANCE IS MINE (1948)

CUMMINS, Brian
TWENTY-NINE (1969)

CURLING, Jonathan
SONG OF THE SHIRT, the (1979)

CUTLER, Ralph
AT SCHOOL IN TANGANYIKA (1936)
DAY IN THE LIFE OF A MSUKUMA
CALLED KINGA MKONO BARA, a
(1937)

CUTTS, Graham
AREN'T MEN BEASTS! (1937)
AS GOOD AS NEW (1933)
BLACKGUARD, the (1925)
CAR OF DREAMS (1935)
COCAINE (1922)
JUST WILLIAM (1939)
LET'S MAKE A NIGHT OF IT (1937)
LOOKING ON THE BRIGHT SIDE (1932)
OH DADDY (1935)
OVER SHE GOES (1937)
PRUDE'S FALL, the (1924)
QUEEN WAS IN THE PARLOUR, the
(1927)
RAT, the (1925)
SEA URCHIN, the (1926)
SIGN OF FOUR, the (1932)
THREE MEN IN A BOAT (1933)
TRIUMPH OF THE RAT, the (1926)
WONDERFUL STORY, the (1922)

CYRAN, A
LOVE WAGER, the (1933)

CZIFFRA, Geza von
TALE OF FIVE CITIES, a (1951)

CZINNER, Paul
AS YOU LIKE IT (1936)
BOLSHOI BALLET, the (1957)
CATHERINE THE GREAT (1934)
DON GIOVANNI (1954)
DREAMING LIPS (1937)
ESCAPE ME NEVER (1935)
ROMEO AND JULIET (1966)
ROYAL BALLET, the (1959)
STOLEN LIFE (1939)
WOMAN HE SCORNED, the (1928)

DABORN, John
BATTLE OF WANGAPORE, the (1955)

DAHL, Louis
COASTAL NAVIGATION AND
PILOTAGE (1953)

DAIKEN, Leslie
ONE POTATO, TWO POTATO (1957)

DALRYMPLE, Ian
BANK OF ENGLAND (1960)
ESTHER WATERS (1948)
OLD BILL AND SON (1940)
SEA FORT (1940)
STORM IN A TEACUP (1937)

DALRYMPLE, J Blake
CRAGSMEN, the (1948)
PADDY'S MILESTONE (1947)

DANIEL, Jack
MIROCLE, the (1976)

DANIELS, Jill
EXILES (1991)

DARNBOROUGH, Antony
ASTONISHED HEART, the (1950)
SO LONG AT THE FAIR (1950)

DARNLEY-SMITH, Jan
GHOST OF A CHANCE (1967)
GO-KART GO (1963)
HITCH IN TIME, a (1978)
HOVERBUG (1971)
RUNAWAY RAILWAY (1965)

DASSIN, Jules
NIGHT AND THE CITY (1950)

DAUMERY, John
LETTER OF WARNING, a (1932)
MEET MY SISTER (1933)
OVER THE GARDEN WALL (1934)

DAVES, Delmer
NEVER LET ME GO (1953)

DAVIES, Huw
SHIP THAT NEVER RETURNED, the
(1987)

DAVIES, Jim
COME SATURDAY (1949)

DAVIES, John
ACCEPTABLE LEVELS (1983)

DAVIES, Robert Kingston
EAST AFRICAN COLLEGE (1950)

DAVIES, Roland
STEVE OF THE RIVER (1937)
STEVE STEPS OUT (1937)

DAVIES, Terence
CHILDREN (1977)
DEATH AND TRANSFIGURATION (1983)
DISTANT VOICES STILL LIVES (1988)
LONG DAY CLOSES, the (1992)
MADONNA AND CHILD (1980)

DAVIS, Barry
COUNTRY PARTY, the (1977)

DAVIS, Desmond
CLASH OF THE TITANS (1981)
COUNTRY GIRLS, the (1983)
GIRL WITH GREEN EYES (1963)
I WAS HAPPY HERE (1965)
SMASHING TIME (1967)

DAVIS, Joanna
BRED AND BORN (1984)

DAVIS, John
DANGER POINT! (1971)

DAVIS, Redd
ANYTHING TO DECLARE? (1938)
ASK BECCLES (1933)
DISCOVERIES (1939)
EASY MONEY (1934)
GIRL IN THE FLAT, the (1934)
HANDLE WITH CARE (1935)
KING OF THE CASTLE (1936)
SING AS YOU SWING (1937)
SPECIAL EDITION (1938)
UMBRELLA, the (1933)
VARIETY HOUR (1937)

DAVIS, Richard
VIOLA (1967)

DAY, Robert
CORRIDORS OF BLOOD (1958)
FIRST MAN INTO SPACE (1958)
GRIP OF THE STRANGLER (1958)
LIFE IN EMERGENCY WARD 10 (1958)
OPERATION SNATCH (1962)
REBEL, the (1960)
SHE (1965)
STRANGERS' MEETING (1957)
TARZAN THE MAGNIFICENT (1960)
TWO WAY STRETCH (1960)

DEAN, Basil
AUTUMN CROCUS (1934)
BIRDS OF PREY (1930)
CONSTANT NYMPH, the (1933)
ESCAPE (1930)
IMPASSIVE FOOTMAN, the (1932)
LOOKING ON THE BRIGHT SIDE (1932)
LOOK UP AND LAUGH (1935)
LORNA DOONE (1934)
LOYALTIES (1933)
SHOW GOES ON, the (1937)
21 DAYS (1937)
WHOM THE GODS LOVE (1936)

DEAN, Colin
SHOWN BY REQUEST (1947)

DEAN, G B M
MARGAM MARSHALLING YARD (1961)

DEANE, Charles
STOLEN TIME (1955)

DOUGLAS, John O
SERVANT OF THE PEOPLE (1947)

DOWSON, Jeff
HOME AND DRY (1986)

DOXAT-PRATT, B E
CIRCUS JIM (1921)
LAUGHTER AND TEARS (1921)

DREIFUSS, Arthur
QUARE FELLOW, the (1962)

DRYDEN, Wheeler
LITTLE BIT OF FLUFF, a (1928)

DRYHURST, Edward
DIZZY LIMIT, the (1930)
WOMAN FROM CHINA, the (1930)

DUCKWORTH, Jacqui
PRAYER BEFORE BIRTH, a (1991)

DUDOK DE WIT, Michael
INTERVIEW, the (1978)

DUFF, Euan
JANET AND JOHN – GROW UP! (1974)

DUFFELL, Peter
ENGLAND MADE ME (1972)
HOUSE THAT DRIPPED BLOOD, the (1970)
PARTNERS IN CRIME (1961)

DUKE, Bill
RAGE IN HARLEM, a (1991)

DUNBAR, Geoff
LAUTREC (1974)
UBU (1978)

DUNKLEY, Ronald
PILKIN'S PROGRESS (1976)

DUNLOP, George
VINQUISH IN HILL SHEEP (1941)

DUNNE, Philip
INSPECTOR, the (1962)

DUNNING, George
DAMON THE MOWER (1972)
MAGGOT, the (1973)
WARDROBE, the (1958)
YELLOW SUBMARINE (1968)

DUNPHIE, Karen
LIFE'S NORTH (1992)

DUNTON, Roger
CITY PORT (1971)
FACES IN A CROWD (1971)

DUPONT, E A
ATLANTIC (1929)
CAPE FORLORN (1930)
MOULIN ROUGE (1928)
PICCADILLY (1929)
TWO WORLDS (1930)

DURDEN, J V
AND NOW THEY REST (1939)
ARACHNIDA (1940)
ASTACUS (1940)
CLIMBING PLANTS (1938)
COELENTERATA (1937)
DEVELOPMENT OF THE TROUT, the (1938)
GREENHOUSE WHITE FLY (1950)
HEREDITY IN MAN (1937)
PARAMECIUM (1937)
WINTER MOTH (1950)

DURRANT, Fred W
HUSBAND HUNTER, the (1920)

DURST, John
DISTANT NEIGHBOURS (1956)
I WENT TO BRITAIN (1955)

ONE WISH TOO MANY (1956)
OUT OF THE DARK (1951)
SECRET CAVE, the (1953)

DUVET BROTHERS
GREATEST HITS OF SCRATCH VIDEO, the (1985)
GREATEST HITS OF SCRATCH VIDEO VOLUME 2, the (1986)

DUVIVIER, Julien
ANNA KARENINA (1947)

DWAN, Allan
HER FIRST AFFAIRE (1932)
I SPY (1933)

DWOSKIN, Stephen
MOMENT (1970)

DYALL, Franklin
DUKE'S SON (1920)

DYER, Anson
AGITATED ADVERTS (1918)
ALL THE FUN OF THE 'AIR (1937)
BEE WISE! (1946)
CARMEN (1936)
DAY IN LIVERPOOL, a (1929)
DICKY DEE CARTOONS NO.3 (1915)
FARMYARD RISING, the (1947)
JUMP TO IT (1950)
KING WITH A TERRIBLE TEMPER, the (1937)
KING WITH THE TERRIBLE HICCUPS, the (1937)
LITTLE RED RIDING HOOD (1922)
OTHELLO (1920)
PETER'S PICTURE POEMS (1918)
'PLANE TALE, a (1918)
ROBBIE FINDS A GUN (1945)
ROLLO THE SQUIRREL (1949)
SAM AND HIS MUSKET (1935)
THIS BUTTON BUSINESS (1938)
THREE LITTLE PIGS, the (1918)
YOU'RE TELLING ME (1939)

EADES, Wilfred
YOU CAN'T ESCAPE (1955)

EADY, David
ANOOP AND THE ELEPHANT (1972)
BRIDGE OF TIME (1950)
DANGER ON DARTMOOR (1980)
EDINBURGH (1952)
HEART WITHIN, the (1957)
HIDE AND SEEK (1972)
HOSTAGES, the (1975)
OPERATION THIRD FORM (1966)
SCRAMBLE (1970)

EASTMAN, David
AMBUSH AT DEVIL'S GAP (1966)
CALAMITY THE COW (1967)

EDWARDS, Blake
REVENGE OF THE PINK PANTHER (1978)
SHOT IN THE DARK, a (1964)
VICTOR/VICTORIA (1982)

EDWARDS, Henry
AGAINST THE GRAIN (1918)
ANNE ONE HUNDRED (1933)
ARE YOU A MASON? (1934)
BARGAIN, the (1921)
BARTON MYSTERY, the (1932)
BEAUTY AND THE BARGE (1937)
BROTHER ALFRED (1932)
DISCORD (1932)
EAST IS EAST (1916)
ELIZA COMES TO STAY (1936)
FAILURE, the (1917)
FLAG LIEUTENANT, the (1932)
GIRL OF LONDON, a (1925)

IN THE SOUP (1936)
JUGGERNAUT (1936)
KING OF THE CASTLE (1925)
LASH, the (1934)
LORD EDGWARE DIES (1934)
LORD OF THE MANOR (1933)
ONE COLOMBO NIGHT (1926)
ONE PRECIOUS YEAR (1933)
OWD BOB (1924)
POSSESSION (1919)
PRIVATE SECRETARY, the (1935)
PURSE STRINGS (1933)
ROCKS OF VALPRÉ, the (1935)
SCROOGE (1935)
SQUIBS (1935)
STRANGLEHOLD (1931)
VICAR OF BRAY, the (1937)
VINTAGE WINE (1935)
WHAT'S THE USE OF GRUMBLIN'? (1918)

EDWARDS, James
FEAR SHIP, the (1933)

EDZARD, Christine
BIDDY (1983)
LITTLE DORRIT (1987)
STORIES FROM A FLYING TRUNK (1979)

EICHBERG, Richard
LET'S LOVE AND LAUGH (1931)
FLAME OF LOVE, the (1930)

ELDER, Clarence
SILVER DARLINGS, the (1946)

ELDER, Isabel
PEN PICTURES FROM DENMARK; LETTER 1 (1949)
PEN PICTURES FROM DENMARK; LETTER 3 (1949)
PEN PICTURES FROM DENMARK; LETTER 4 (1949)

ELDER, John C
GRAIN HARVEST (1936)
INLAND VOYAGE; OBAN TO INVERNESS, the (1937)
PEN PICTURES FROM DENMARK; LETTER 1 (1949)
PEN PICTURES FROM DENMARK; LETTER 3 (1949)
PEN PICTURES FROM DENMARK; LETTER 4 (1949)
SOUTHERN UPLANDS (1937)
WORK IN A STORE (1939)

ELDRIDGE, John
ASHLEY GREEN GOES TO SCHOOL (1940)
BRANDY FOR THE PARSON (1951)
CITY REBORN, a (1945)
CONFLICT OF WINGS (1954)
CONQUEST OF A GERM (1944)
FUEL FOR BATTLE (1944)
NEW TOWNS FOR OLD (1942)
OUR COUNTRY (1944)
SOLDIER COMES HOME, a (1945)
SOS (1940)
THREE DAWNS TO SYDNEY (1948)
TIME AND TIDE (1945)
VILLAGE SCHOOL (1940)
WAVERLEY STEPS (1948)

ELLES, Fred
MRS PYM OF SCOTLAND YARD (1939)

ELLIOTT, William J
CAB, the (1926)

ELLITT, Jack
ABCD OF HEALTH (1942)
BRITAIN'S YOUTH (1940)
CHASING THE BLUES (1950)
EDUCATION OF THE DEAF (1946)
HOW TO DIG (1941)
SOWING AND PLANTING (1941)
THIS IS COLOUR (1942)

FERGUSSON, Guy
GERMFREE BABY (1968)

FERNO, John
LAST SHOT, the (1945)

FERRER, José
COCKLESHELL HEROES, the (1955)

FEYDER, Jacques
KNIGHT WITHOUT ARMOUR (1937)

FFENNELL, Hazel
DAYS OF CHIVALRY (1928)

FFENNELL, Raymond
DOOR IN THE WALL, the (1934)

FIELD, Felicity
DANCING SILHOUETTES (1983)

FIELD, Mary
ANIMAL MOVEMENT (1939)
APHIS, the (1930)
ATLANTIC (1940)
BABES IN THE WOOD (1940)
BABY ON THE ROCKS (1934)
BREWSTER'S MAGIC (1933)
CIVILIAN FRONT (1940)
DEFERRED PAYMENT (1929)
DEVELOPMENT OF THE ENGLISH
    TOWN (1942)
DOUBLE THREAD (1943)
FARM FACTORY, the (1935)
FARMING IN SPRING (1934)
FARMING IN SUMMER (1934)
FARMING IN WINTER (1934)
FILTER, the (1934)
4 AND 20 FIT GIRLS (1940)
FRIENDLY FLIES (1931)
FROTHBLOWER (1932)
FRUITLANDS OF KENT (1934)
LIFE CYCLE OF THE MAIZE, the (1942)
LIFE CYCLE OF THE NEWT, the (1942)
LIFE CYCLE OF THE PIN MOULD, the
    (1942)
LIFE HISTORY OF THE ONION, the
    (1944)
LONDON PIGEON, the (1940)
MAGIC MYXIES (1931)
MARKET TOWN (1942)
MERLIN, the (1930)
MYSTERY OF MARRIAGE, the (1931)
NEW GENERATION, the (1937)
PAWS AND CLAWS (1944)
ROGER THE RAVEN (1936)
SCARLET RUNNER & CO (1930)
STRICTLY BUSINESS (1932)
SUNDEW (1930)
SWAN SONG (1938)
THEY MADE THE LAND (1938)
TOUGH 'UN, the (1938)
TRAVELLERS, the (1946)
UNEMPLOYMENT AND MONEY (1940)
WARBLERS, the (1934)
WATER (1942)
WISDOM OF THE WILD (1940)
WORLD IN A WINEGLASS, a (1931)

FINCH, Peter
DAY, the (1960)

FINLAYSON, W H
POLYCHROME FANTASY (1935)

FINNEY, Albert
CHARLIE BUBBLES (1967)

FISHER, Andrew
ADVENTURES OF X, the (1967)

FISHER, Terence
ASTONISHED HEART, the (1950)
BLOOD ORANGE (1953)
BRIDES OF DRACULA, the (1960)
CHILDREN GALORE (1954)
COLONEL BOGEY (1948)
CURSE OF THE WEREWOLF, the (1961)
DEVIL RIDES OUT, the (1967)
DISTANT TRUMPET (1952)

DRACULA (1958)
DRACULA – PRINCE OF DARKNESS
    (1965)
FACE THE MUSIC (1954)
FINAL APPOINTMENT (1954)
FLAW, the (1955)
FRANKENSTEIN AND THE MONSTER
    FROM HELL (1973)
FRANKENSTEIN CREATED WOMAN
    (1966)
GORGON, the (1964)
HOME TO DANGER (1951)
HOUND OF THE BASKERVILLES, the
    (1959)
ISLAND OF TERROR (1966)
KILL ME TOMORROW (1957)
LAST PAGE, the (1952)
MAN WHO COULD CHEAT DEATH, the
    (1959)
MASK OF DUST (1954)
MURDER BY PROXY (1955)
NIGHT OF THE BIG HEAT (1967)
PHANTOM OF THE OPERA, the (1962)
PORTRAIT FROM LIFE (1948)
REVENGE OF FRANKENSTEIN, the
    (1958)
SO LONG AT THE FAIR (1950)
SONG FOR TOMORROW (1948)
SPACEWAYS (1953)
STOLEN FACE (1952)
STRANGER CAME HOME, the (1954)
STRANGLERS OF BOMBAY, the (1959)
SWORD OF SHERWOOD FOREST (1960)
TO THE PUBLIC DANGER (1948)
TWO FACES OF DR JEKYLL, the (1960)

FITZHAMON, Lewin
BLACK BEAUTY (1906)
BLIND MAN'S DOG, a (1912)
BUSY MAN, the (1907)
CATCHING A BURGLAR (1908)
CHEAP REMOVAL, a (1909)
DEATH OF NELSON, the (1905)
DOG OUTWITS THE KIDNAPPERS, the
    (1908)
DUMB SAGACITY (1907)
FALSELY ACCUSED (1905)
FATHER'S LESSON (1908)
GAMIN'S GRATITUDE, a (1909)
HAPPY EVENT IN THE POORLUCK
    FAMILY, a (1911)
HEART OF A FISHERGIRL, the (1910)
INTERRUPTED HONEYMOON, an (1905)
INVISIBILITY (1909)
JIM OF THE MOUNTED POLICE (1911)
JOHN GILPIN'S RIDE (1908)
JONAH MAN; or, The traveller bewitched,
    the (1904)
JUST IN TIME (1906)
MR POORLUCK BUYS SOME CHINA
    (1911)
MR POORLUCK'S LUCKY HORSESHOE
    (1910)
NEW HAT FOR NOTHING, a (1910)
OTHER SIDE OF THE HEDGE, the (1905)
POET AND HIS BABIES, a (1906)
POISON OR WHISKEY (1904)
POORLUCKS' FIRST TIFF, the (1910)
PREHISTORIC PEEPS (1905)
RACE FOR A KISS, a (1904)
RESCUED BY ROVER (1905)
SEASIDE GIRL, a (1907)
SEASIDE INTRODUCTION, a (1911)
SISTER MARY JANE'S TOP NOTE (1907)
SQUATTER'S DAUGHTER, the (1906)
STOLEN CLOTHES (1909)
STOLEN GUY, the (1905)
THAT FATAL SNEEZE (1907)
TILLY'S PARTY (1911)
TILLY THE TOMBOY VISITS THE POOR
    (1910)
TOMKINS BUYS A DONKEY (1908)
WHAT THE CURATE REALLY DID
    (1905)

FITZHUGH, Terrick
THEY THINK I'M RICH (1964)

FITZPATRICK, James A
LADY OF THE LAKE, the (1928)

FLAHERTY, Robert
ELEPHANT BOY (1937)
INDUSTRIAL BRITAIN (1931)
MAN OF ARAN (1934)

FLAXTON, Terry
CIRCUMSTANTIAL EVIDENCE (1984)
EISENSTEIN; A PROGRAMME OF
    ATTRACTIONS (1980)
GOING LOCAL (1982)
TOWARDS INTUITION; AN AMERICAN
    LANDSCAPE (1980)

FLEISCHER, Richard
10 RILLINGTON PLACE (1970)

FLEMYNG, Gordon
DR WHO AND THE DALEKS (1965)
FIVE TO ONE (1963)
GREAT CATHERINE (1967)
JUST FOR FUN! (1963)

FLETCHER, John
SATURDAY MEN, the (1963)

FLETCHER, Paul
IT COMES FROM COAL (1940)
STRICKEN PENINSULA (1945)

FLETCHER, Yvonne
CARBON DIOXIDE ABSORPTION
    TECHNIQUE, the (1944)
CHILDREN SEE IT THRU, the (1941)
INTRAVENOUS ANAESTHESIA (1944)
SPINAL ANAESTHESIA (1944)

FLITCROFT, Kim
LOOK AT THAT CLOUD (1981)

FLOOD, James
LONELY ROAD, the (1936)

FLORIN, Ana
IMPRESSIONS OF EXILE (1985)

FOGWELL, Reginald
MURDER AT THE CABARET (1936)
WARNING, the (1928)

FOLDES, Joan
SHORT VISION, a (1956)

FOLDES, Peter
SHORT VISION, a (1956)

FORBES, Bryan
BETTER LATE THAN NEVER (1983)
DEADFALL (1968)
INTERNATIONAL VELVET (1978)
L-SHAPED ROOM, the (1962)
MADWOMAN OF CHAILLOT, the (1969)
SEANCE ON A WET AFTERNOON (1964)
SLIPPER AND THE ROSE; THE STORY
    OF CINDERELLA, the (1976)
WHISPERERS, the (1966)
WHISTLE DOWN THE WIND (1961)
WRONG BOX, the (1966)

FORD, Aleksander
CHILDREN MUST LAUGH (1944)

FORD, Derek
GROUPIE GIRL (1970)
KEEP IT UP, JACK! (1973)
WHAT'S UP SUPERDOC? (1978)
WIFE SWAPPERS, the (1970)

FORD, John
GIDEON'S DAY (1958)

FORD, Maxim
NORTH (1986)

FORD, Philip
BEWARE OF THE DOG (1963)

FORDE, Eugene
INSPECTOR HORNLEIGH (1939)

FORDE, Walter
ATLANTIC FERRY (1941)
BED AND BREAKFAST (1930)
BULLDOG JACK (1935)
CARDBOARD CAVALIER (1948)
CHARLEY'S (BIG-HEARTED) AUNT
(1940)
CHEER, BOYS, CHEER (1939)
CHU-CHIN-CHOW (1934)
CONDEMNED TO DEATH (1932)
ECONOMIST, the (1921)
FLYING FORTRESS (1942)
FOREVER ENGLAND (1935)
FOUR JUST MEN, the (1939)
GAUNT STRANGER, the (1938)
GHOST TRAIN, the (1931)
GHOST TRAIN, the (1941)
INSPECTOR HORNLEIGH GOES TO IT
(1941)
INSPECTOR HORNLEIGH ON HOLIDAY
(1939)
IT'S THAT MAN AGAIN (1943)
JACK AHOY! (1934)
JACK'S THE BOY (1932)
KING OF THE DAMNED (1936)
LAND WITHOUT MUSIC (1936)
LET'S BE FAMOUS (1939)
MASTER OF BANKDAM (1947)
ONE EXCITING NIGHT (1944)
ORDERS IS ORDERS (1933)
PETERVILLE DIAMOND, the (1942)
RED PEARLS (1930)
RINGER, the (1931)
ROME EXPRESS (1932)
SAILORS THREE (1940)
SALOON BAR (1940)
SILENT HOUSE, the (1929)
SPLINTERS IN THE NAVY (1932)
TOMMY HANDLEY (1943)
WAIT AND SEE (1928)
WALTER MAKES A MOVIE (1922)
WALTER THE PRODIGAL (1926)
WOULD YOU BELIEVE IT? (1929)
YOU'D BE SURPRISED (1930)

FOREMAN, Carl
VICTORS, the (1963)

FORLONG, Michael
GREEN HELMET, the (1961)
HIGH RISE DONKEY (1980)
RAISING THE ROOF (1971)
RANGI'S CATCH (1972)

FORSYTH, Bill
COMFORT AND JOY (1984)

FOSS, Kenelm
HOUSE OF PERIL, the (1922)
ROMANCE OF OLD BAGDAD, a (1922)

FOSTER, Giles
TREE OF HANDS (1988)

FOSTER, Peter Le Neve
WITCH'S FIDDLE, the (1924)

FOSTER, Richard
WATCHERS, the (1969)

FOTHERINGHAM, Christine
SIDESHOW (1991)

FOULK, Bill
BEASTLY TREATMENT (1979)

FOURNIER, Robert
DAVID LEACH (1977)
ISAAC BUTTON – COUNTRY POTTER
(1965)

FRANCIS, Freddie
DRACULA HAS RISEN FROM THE
GRAVE (1968)
EVIL OF FRANKENSTEIN, the (1964)
GHOUL, the (1975)
LEGEND OF THE WEREWOLF (1974)
MUMSY, NANNY, SONNY AND GIRLY
(1969)

NIGHTMARE (1963)
PARANOIAC (1962)
PSYCHOPATH, the (1966)
SKULL, the (1965)
TALES FROM THE CRYPT (1972)
THEY CAME FROM BEYOND SPACE
(1967)
TRAITOR'S GATE (1965)
TWO AND TWO MAKE SIX (1962)
VENGEANCE (1962)

FRANCIS, Karl
ABOVE US THE EARTH (1977)
ANGRY EARTH (1989)
GIRO CITY (1982)

FRANCIS, Mary
TRIAL BY WEATHER (1948)

FRANK, Charles
UNCLE SILAS (1947)

FRANK, Melvin
TOUCH OF CLASS, a (1972)

FRANKEL, Cyril
ALIVE AND KICKING (1958)
DON'T BOTHER TO KNOCK (1961)
EAGLES OF THE FLEET (1950)
IT'S GREAT TO BE YOUNG! (1956)
MAN OF AFRICA (1953)
NEVER TAKE SWEETS FROM A
STRANGER (1960)
NO TIME FOR TEARS (1957)
ON THE FIDDLE (1961)
SHE DIDN'T SAY NO (1958)
TRYGON FACTOR, the (1966)
VERY EDGE, the (1962)
WITCHES, the (1966)

FRANKEL, Joseph G
CHAMPIONS ON PARADE (1947)

FRANKENHEIMER, John
HOLCROFT COVENANT, the (1985)

FRANKLIN, Sidney A
BARRETTS OF WIMPOLE STREET, the
(1956)

FRANKS, Andrew
CONVERSATIONS BY A CALIFORNIAN
SWIMMING POOL (1986)
PARADISE REGAINED (1986)

FRAZER-JONES, Peter
GEORGE AND MILDRED (1980)

FREARS, Stephen
BURNING, the (1967)
GUMSHOE (1971)
HIT, the (1984)
MY BEAUTIFUL LAUNDRETTE (1985)
PRICK UP YOUR EARS (1987)
SAMMY AND ROSIE GET LAID (1987)

FREELAND, Thornton
ACCUSED (1936)
AMATEUR GENTLEMAN, the (1936)
BRASS MONKEY, the (1948)
BREWSTER'S MILLIONS (1935)
DEAR MR PROHACK (1949)
GANG'S ALL HERE, the (1939)
HOLD MY HAND (1938)
JERICHO (1937)
MEET ME AT DAWN (1947)
OVER THE MOON (1937)
PARADISE FOR TWO (1937)

FREEMAN, Petra
MILL, the (1992)

FRENCH, Harold
ADAM AND EVELYNE (1949)
BLIND GODDESS, the (1948)
DANCING YEARS, the (1949)
DAY WILL DAWN, the (1942)
DEAD MEN ARE DANGEROUS (1939)
DEAR OCTOPUS (1943)

ENCORE (1951)
ENGLISH WITHOUT TEARS (1944)
FORBIDDEN CARGO (1954)
HOUR OF 13, the (1952)
HOUSE OF THE ARROW, the (1940)
ISN'T LIFE WONDERFUL! (1952)
JEANNIE (1941)
MAN WHO WATCHED TRAINS GO BY,
the (1952)
MR EMMANUEL (1944)
MY BROTHER JONATHAN (1948)
OUR FILM (1942)
QUARTET (1948)
QUIET WEEKEND (1946)
ROB ROY THE HIGHLAND ROGUE
(1953)
SECRET MISSION (1942)
TRIO (1950)
UNPUBLISHED STORY (1942)
WHITE CRADLE INN (1947)

FREND, Charles
BARNACLE BILL (1957)
BIG BLOCKADE (1942)
CONE OF SILENCE (1960)
CRUEL SEA, the (1952)
FOREMAN WENT TO FRANCE, the (1942)
GIRL ON APPROVAL (1961)
JOHNNY FRENCHMAN (1945)
LEASE OF LIFE (1954)
LONG ARM, the (1956)
LOVES OF JOANNA GODDEN, the (1947)
MAGNET, the (1950)
RETURN OF THE VIKINGS (1944)
RUN FOR YOUR MONEY, a (1949)
SAN DEMETRIO – LONDON (1943)
SCOTT OF THE ANTARCTIC (1948)
SKY BIKE, the (1967)

FRENGUELLI, Alfonse
CHRISTMAS EVE (1915)

FRENKE, Eugene
WOMAN ALONE, a (1936)

FRESHMAN, William
TEHERAN (1947)

FRIEDMANN, Anthony
BARTLEBY (1970)

FRIESE-GREENE, Claude
KINO THE GIRL OF COLOUR (1920)

FRIESE-GREENE, William
KINO THE GIRL OF COLOUR (1920)

FRIEZE, J S
BERNARD SHAW'S VILLAGE (1951)
WINTER TOUR (1949)

FRYER, J Bertram
FEATHER BED, the (1933)

FUCHS, Francis
POETS AGAINST THE BOMB (1981)

FUEST, Robert
ABOMINABLE DR PHIBES, the (1971)
AND SOON THE DARKNESS (1970)
DR PHIBES RISES AGAIN (1972)
FINAL PROGRAMME, the (1973)
WUTHERING HEIGHTS (1970)

FULLILOVE, Eric
QUESTIONING CITY, the (1959)

FURIE, Sidney J
BOYS, the (1962)
DURING ONE NIGHT (1961)
IPCRESS FILE, the (1965)
LEATHER BOYS, the (1963)
WONDERFUL LIFE (1964)
YOUNG ONES, the (1961)

GALLONE, Carmine
CITY OF SONG (1930)
FOR LOVE OF YOU (1933)
GOING GAY (1933)
MY HEART IS CALLING (1934)
TWO HEARTS IN WALTZ TIME (1934)

GALLU, Samuel
LIMBO LINE, the (1968)
THEATRE OF DEATH (1966)

GANE, Paul
TIDE IS TURNING, the (1979)

GARDNER, Cyril
PERFECT UNDERSTANDING (1933)

GARDNER, Ronald
LIMESTONE IN NATURE (1946)

GARLAND, Patrick
DOLL'S HOUSE, a (1973)

GARMES, Lee
DREAMING LIPS (1937)
SKY'S THE LIMIT, the (1937)

GARNER, Anthony
RACER, the (1975)

GARNETT, Tay
TERRIBLE BEAUTY, a (1960)

GARRATT, Chris
ROMANTIC ITALY (1975)

GARSTIN, Jacky
SIDE EFFECTS (1980)

GATES, Tudor
INTIMATE GAMES (1976)

GAUSDEN, Sidney
NOEL (1944)
PERMANENT WAY, the (1944)

GAVIN, Barrie
TWO TRACK MIND (1984)

GAYE, Howard
BONNIE SCOTLAND CALLS YOU (1938)

GÉBLER, Carlo
OVER HERE; IRISH DANCE AND
MUSIC IN ENGLAND (1980)

GEDDES, Henry
ALI AND THE CAMEL (1960)
LAST RHINO, the (1961)

GELLOR, Lol
DRUM BEAT (1991)

GEMIN, Giancarlo
ADAGIO (1990)

GENEEN, Sasha
INFATUATION (1930)

GENTILOMO, Giacomo
TEHERAN (1947)

GERARD, Francis
PRIVATE LIFE, a (1988)

GERRARD, Gene
IT'S IN THE BLOOD (1938)
LET ME EXPLAIN DEAR (1932)
OUT OF THE BLUE (1931)

GIANNARIS, Constantine
FRAMED YOUTH – REVENGE OF THE
TEENAGE PERVERTS (1983)

GIBBS, Gerald
COD – A MELLOW DRAMA (1928)

GIBSON, Alan
CRESCENDO (1969)
DRACULA AD 1972 (1972)
GOODBYE GEMINI (1970)
MARTIN'S DAY (1985)

GIDAL, Peter
8MM FILM NOTES ON 16MM FILM (1971)
FILM PRINT (1974)

KEY (1968)
ROOM FILM 1973 (1973)
SILENT PARTNER (1977)
TAKES (1970)

GIESLER, Rodney
AND GLADLY WOULD HE LEARN
(1964)
DISTILLATION (1966)

GIFFORD, John
TURNING HER ROUND (1934)

GIFFORD, Nick
SID'S FAMILY (1972)

GILBERT, Lewis
ADMIRABLE CRICHTON, the (1957)
ALBERT RN (1953)
ALFIE (1965)
ARCTIC HARVEST (1946)
CARVE HER NAME WITH PRIDE (1958)
CAST A DARK SHADOW (1955)
CRY FROM THE STREETS, a (1958)
EDUCATING RITA (1983)
FERRY TO HONG KONG (1959)
FRIENDS (1971)
GREENGAGE SUMMER, the (1961)
HMS DEFIANT (1962)
JOHNNY ON THE RUN (1953)
LIGHT UP THE SKY (1960)
LITTLE BALLERINA, the (1947)
ONCE A SINNER (1950)
REACH FOR THE SKY (1956)
SEA SHALL NOT HAVE THEM, the (1954)
7TH DAWN, the (1964)
SINK THE BISMARCK! (1960)
TEN YEAR PLAN, the (1945)
TIME GENTLEMEN PLEASE! (1952)
UNDER ONE ROOF (1949)
YOU ONLY LIVE TWICE (1967)

GILKISON, Anthony
SPOTLIGHT ON THE BEST SELLERS
(1951)

GILL, Michael
GIACOMETTI (1967)
PEACHES, the (1964)

GILLETT, Roland
FIND THE LADY (1936)

GILLIAM, Terry
ADVENTURES OF BARON
MUNCHAUSEN, the (1988)
BRAZIL (1985)
JABBERWOCKY (1977)
TIME BANDITS (1981)

GILLIAT, Sidney
GREAT ST TRINIAN'S TRAIN
ROBBERY, the (1966)
GREEN FOR DANGER (1946)
LONDON BELONGS TO ME (1948)
MILLIONS LIKE US (1943)
ONLY TWO CAN PLAY (1961)
PARTNERS IN CRIME (1942)
RAKE'S PROGRESS, the (1945)
STORY OF GILBERT AND SULLIVAN,
the (1953)
WATERLOO ROAD (1944)

GILLING, John
BANDIT OF ZHOBE, the (1959)
BRIGAND OF KANDAHAR, the (1965)
CHALLENGE, the (1959)
EMBEZZLER, the (1954)
FLESH AND THE FIENDS, the (1959)
FRIGHTENED MAN, the (1952)
HIGH FLIGHT (1957)
IDLE ON PARADE (1958)
NO TRACE (1950)
PLAGUE OF THE ZOMBIES, the (1966)
REPTILE, the (1966)
SCARLET BLADE, the (1963)
3 STEPS TO THE GALLOWS (1953)

GINEVER, Aveling
CROSS BEAMS (1940)
IN OUR TIME (1933)
THIS PROGRESS (1934)

GLADWELL, David
MEMOIRS OF A SURVIVOR (1981)
REQUIEM FOR A VILLAGE (1975)
UNTITLED FILM, an (1964)

GLEN, John
VIEW TO A KILL, a (1985)

GLENISTER, John
MISS JULIE (1972)

GLENVILLE, Peter
BECKET (1964)
TERM OF TRIAL (1962)

GLINOER, El
FALL OUT (1985)

GLYN, Elinor
KNOWING MEN (1930)

GNECCHI-RUSCONE, Giovanni
ANNÉE 71, l' (1975)

GOBBETT, T J
BAD DAY FOR LEVINSKY, a (1909)

GODDARD, Jim
SHANGHAI SURPRISE (1986)

GODFREY, Bob
DO IT YOURSELF CARTOON KIT (1959)
GENERATION GAP (1973)
RISE AND FALL OF EMILY SPROD, the
(1964)
ROPE TRICK (1967)

GODFREY, Peter
DOWN RIVER (1931)

GODLEY, Kevin
COOLER, the (1982)

GODWIN, Frank
BOY WHO NEVER WAS, the (1979)

GOLD, Jack
ACES HIGH (1976)
BOFORS GUN, the (1968)
MAN FRIDAY (1975)
RECKONING, the (1969)
SAILOR'S RETURN, the (1978)
VISIT, the (1959)

GOLD, Mick
EUROPE AFTER THE RAIN (1978)

GOLDIE, Caroline
MORGAN'S WALL (1978)

GOLDMAN, Bosworth
PLANE SAILING (1937)

GOLDSCHMIDT, John
SHE'LL BE WEARING PINK PYJAMAS
(1985)

GOLESZOWSKI, Richard
BAREFOOTIN' (1987)
IDENT (1989)

GOLLINGS, Franklin
CONNECTING ROOMS (1969)

GOODE, Frederic
AVALANCHE (1975)
DAVEY JONES' LOCKER (1966)
FLOOD, the (1963)
GREAT PONY RAID, the (1968)
HAND OF NIGHT, the (1966)
MANAGEMENT BY OBJECTIVES (1969)
SON OF THE SAHARA (1966)
STOP-OVER FOREVER (1964)
VALLEY OF THE KINGS (1964)

GOODFIELD, June
GOD WITHIN, the (1961)

GOODMAN, A
TROPICAL BREEZES (1930)

HELL IS A CITY (1959)
I'LL BE YOUR SWEETHEART (1945)
IT'S A WONDERFUL WORLD (1956)
JIGSAW (1962)
JUST WILLIAM'S LUCK (1947)
LIFE IS A CIRCUS (1958)
LIFE WITH THE LYONS (1953)
LYONS IN PARIS, the (1954)
MEN OF SHERWOOD FOREST, the (1954)
MR DRAKE'S DUCK (1950)
MURDER AT THE WINDMILL (1949)
NOSE HAS IT, the (1942)
QUATERMASS EXPERIMENT, the (1955)
TOOMORROW (1970)
UP THE CREEK (1958)
WHEN DINOSAURS RULED THE
    EARTH (1969)
WHERE THE SPIES ARE (1965)
WILLIAM COMES TO TOWN (1948)
YESTERDAY'S ENEMY (1959)

GUILLERMIN, John
ADVENTURE IN THE HOPFIELDS (1954)
BLUE MAX, the (1966)
DAY THEY ROBBED THE BANK OF
    ENGLAND, the (1959)
DEATH ON THE NILE (1978)
FOUR DAYS (1951)
GUNS AT BATASI (1964)
I WAS MONTY'S DOUBLE (1958)
MISS ROBIN HOOD (1952)
NEVER LET GO (1960)
OPERATION DIPLOMAT (1953)
SONG OF PARIS (1952)
TARZAN GOES TO INDIA (1962)
TARZAN'S GREATEST ADVENTURE
    (1959)
WALTZ OF THE TOREADORS (1962)

GUISSART, René
SWEET DEVIL (1938)

GULLIVER, Clifford
LOVE UP THE POLE (1936)
MUSEUM MYSTERY (1937)

GUNDREY, V Gareth
HOUND OF THE BASKERVILLES, the
    (1931)
STRONGER SEX, the (1930)
SYMPHONY IN TWO FLATS (1930)

GUNN, Gilbert
ELSTREE STORY (1952)
GIRLS AT SEA (1958)
HOUSING IN SCOTLAND (1945)
MY WIFE'S FAMILY (1956)
OPERATION BULLSHINE (1959)
ORDER OF LENIN (1943)
RETURN TO ACTION (1947)
STAR AND THE SAND, the (1945)
STRANGE WORLD OF PLANET X, the
    (1958)
VALLEY OF SONG (1953)
WHAT A WHOPPER! (1961)
WINGS OF MYSTERY (1963)
YOUNG DETECTIVES, the (1963)

GURRIN, Geoffrey
FAWLEY ACHIEVEMENT (1954)

GYLLENHAAL, Stephen
WATERLAND (1992)

GYSIN, Francis
BRITAIN CAN MAKE IT NO.1 (1946)
CITY SPEAKS, a (1947)
MECHANISED PIT BOTTOM
    (SHILBOTTLE COLLIERY) (1952)

HAANSTRA, Bert
RIVAL WORLD, the (1955)

HAGGAR, William
DESPERATE POACHING AFFRAY (1903)
LIFE OF CHARLES PEACE, the (1905)
MESSAGE FROM THE SEA, a (1905)

HAGGAR, William, Jr
LOVE STORY OF ANN THOMAS THE
    MAID OF CEFN YDFA, the (1914)

HAGGARD, Piers
VENOM (1981)

HAGGARTY, John
CAUGHT IN THE NET (1960)
MYSTERY ON BIRD ISLAND (1954)
RAIDERS OF THE RIVER (1955)

HAI, Zafar
PERFECT MURDER, the (1988)

HAINES, Jean
AFRICAN VISTA (1952)
WINTER IN QUEBEC (1949)

HAINES, Ronald
AFRICAN VISTA (1952)
ALL ABOUT CARROTS (1941)
SIMPLE SOUPS (1941)
THIS FILM IS DANGEROUS (1948)
WINTER IN QUEBEC (1949)

HALAS, John
ABU AND THE POISONED WELL (1943)
ANIMAL FARM (1954)
AUTOMANIA 2000 (1963)
AXE AND THE LAMP, the (1963)
CHARLEY'S MARCH OF TIME (1948)
DUSTBIN PARADE (1942)
FARMER CHARLEY (1949)
JOHN GILPIN (1951)
MODERN GUIDE TO HEALTH, (1946)
NEW TOWN (1948)
OLD WIVES' TALES (1946)
PIPING HOT (1959)
ROBINSON CHARLEY (1948)

HALDANE, Bert
BRIGADIER GERARD (1915)
BURGLAR FOR ONE NIGHT, a (1911)
EAST LYNNE (1913)
GERMAN SPY PERIL, the (1914)
HILDA'S LOVERS (1911)
JANE SHORE (1915)
LURE OF LONDON, the (1914)
ROAD TO RUIN, the (1913)

HALE, Sonnie
GANGWAY (1937)
HEAD OVER HEELS (1937)
SAILING ALONG (1938)

HALES, Gordon
MR ENGLISH AT HOME (1940)

HALL, George Edwardes
NOBODY'S CHILD (1919)

HALL, Peter
THREE INTO TWO WON'T GO (1968)
WORK IS A FOUR LETTER WORD (1967)

HALLAM, Paul
NIGHTHAWKS (1978)

HALLER, Daniel
MONSTER OF TERROR (1965)

HAMER, Robert
DEAD OF NIGHT (1945)
FATHER BROWN (1954)
HIS EXCELLENCY (1951)
IT ALWAYS RAINS ON SUNDAY (1947)
KIND HEARTS AND CORONETS (1949)
LONG MEMORY, the (1952)
PINK STRING AND SEALING WAX (1945)
SCAPEGOAT, the (1958)
SCHOOL FOR SCOUNDRELS; or, How to
    win without actually cheating (1959)
SPIDER AND THE FLY, the (1949)

HAMERMESH, Mira
MAIDS AND MADAMS (1985)

HAMILTON, Guy
BATTLE OF BRITAIN (1969)
COLDITZ STORY, the (1954)
DEVIL'S DISCIPLE, the (1959)
DIAMONDS ARE FOREVER (1971)
EVIL UNDER THE SUN (1981)
FORCE 10 FROM NAVARONE (1978)
FUNERAL IN BERLIN (1966)
GOLDFINGER (1964)
INTRUDER, the (1953)
MANUELA (1957)
MIRROR CRACK'D, the (1980)
PARTY'S OVER, the (1963)
TOUCH OF LARCENY, a (1959)

HAMMOND, Peter
SPRING AND PORT WINE (1969)

HAMMOND, William C
CARRINGFORD SCHOOL MYSTERY, the
    (1958)
FLYING EYE, the (1955)
FOOL AND THE PRINCESS, the (1948)
JUNO HELPS OUT (1953)
ROCKETS IN THE DUNES (1960)
SECRET TUNNEL, the (1947)

HANBURY, Victor
ADMIRALS ALL (1935)
BALL AT SAVOY (1936)
HOTEL RESERVE (1943)
NO FUNNY BUSINESS (1933)
THERE GOES SUSIE (1934)

HAND, David
BOUND FOR THE RIO GRANDE (1948)

HAND, Slim
PENNY AND THE POWNALL CASE
    (1948)

HANKINSON, Michael
CARRY ON CHILDREN (1940)
CHICK (1936)
DARTMOUTH; THE ROYAL NAVAL
    COLLEGE (1942)
DIG FOR VICTORY (1941)
HOUSE BROKEN (1936)
LIFT YOUR HEAD, COMRADE (1942)
NEURO-PSYCHIATRY (1943)
SUPPLIES TO THE SOVIETS (1945)
TICKET OF LEAVE (1935)

HANMER, Charles
BLACK DIAMONDS (1932)
TOUR OF A BRITISH COALMINE (1928)

HANNA, Nancy
DO IT YOURSELF CARTOON KIT (1959)

HARDY, Ken
LATITUDE AND LONGITUDE (1947)

HARDY, Robin
WICKER MAN, the (1973)

HARE, David
STRAPLESS (1988)
WETHERBY (1985)

HARKIN, Margo
HUSH-A-BYE BABY (1989)

HARLOW, John
APPOINTMENT WITH CRIME (1946)
BAGGED (1934)
CANDLES AT NINE (1944)
DANGEROUS CARGO (1954)
DARK TOWER, the (1943)
DELAYED ACTION (1954)
ECHO MURDERS, the (1945)
MEET SEXTON BLAKE (1944)
MY LUCKY STAR (1933)
OLD MOTHER RILEY HEADMISTRESS
    (1950)
OLD MOTHER RILEY'S NEW VENTURE
    (1949)
WHILE I LIVE (1947)

HILL, Sinclair
BOADICEA (1926)
BRITANNIA OF BILLINGSGATE (1933)
CHINESE BUNGALOW, the (1926)
COMMAND PERFORMANCE (1937)
DARK RED ROSES (1929)
DRUM, the (1924)
FIRST MRS FRASER, the (1932)
FOLLOW YOUR STAR (1938)
GENTLEMAN OF PARIS, a (1931)
GREEK STREET (1930)
GUNS OF LOOS, the (1928)
KING'S HIGHWAY, the (1927)
MAN FROM TORONTO, the (1933)
MIDNIGHT MENACE (1937)
MY OLD DUTCH (1934)
ONE ARABIAN NIGHT (1923)
OPEN COUNTRY (1922)
OTHER PEOPLE'S SINS (1930)
SECRET KINGDOM, the (1925)
SQUIRE OF LONG HADLEY, the (1925)
SUCH IS THE LAW (1930)
TAKE A CHANCE (1937)
TIDAL WAVE, the (1920)
WOMAN REDEEMED, a (1927)

HILL, Tony
DOWNSIDE UP (1985)

HIRD, Robert
MR HORATIO KNIBBLES (1971)

HISCOTT, Leslie
ANNIE, LEAVE THE ROOM! (1935)
CLEANING UP (1933)
FAME (1936)
FEATHER, the (1929)
FINE FEATHERS (1937)
FIRE HAS BEEN ARRANGED, a (1935)
GREAT STUFF (1933)
INTERRUPTED HONEYMOON, the (1936)
MAN I WANT, the (1934)
MAROONED (1933)
NIGHT IN MONTMARTRE, a (1931)
SEVENTH SURVIVOR, the (1941)
SHE SHALL HAVE MUSIC (1935)
THREE WITNESSES (1935)
TRIUMPH OF SHERLOCK HOLMES, the (1935)

HITCHCOCK, Alfred
ALWAYS TELL YOUR WIFE (1923)
AVENTURE MALGACHE (1944)
BLACKMAIL (1929)
BON VOYAGE (1944)
CHAMPAGNE (1928)
DOWNHILL (1927)
EASY VIRTUE (1927)
FARMER'S WIFE, the (1928)
FRENZY (1972)
JAMAICA INN (1939)
JUNO AND THE PAYCOCK (1930)
LADY VANISHES, the (1938)
LODGER; A STORY OF THE LONDON FOG, the (1926)
MAN WHO KNEW TOO MUCH, the (1934)
MANXMAN, the (1929)
MURDER (1930)
NUMBER SEVENTEEN (1932)
PLEASURE GARDEN, the (1925)
RICH AND STRANGE (1932)
RING, the (1927)
SABOTAGE (1936)
SECRET AGENT (1936)
SKIN GAME, the (1931)
STAGE FRIGHT (1949)
39 STEPS, the (1935)
UNDER CAPRICORN (1949)
WALTZES FROM VIENNA (1933)
YOUNG AND INNOCENT (1937)

HODGES, C E
LAND OF THE VIKINGS (1933)

HODGES, Mike
FLASH GORDON (1980)
GET CARTER (1971)
PULP (1972)

HODSON, Christopher
BEST PAIR OF LEGS IN THE BUSINESS, the (1972)

HOELLERING, George
MESSAGE FROM CANTERBURY (1944)
MURDER IN THE CATHEDRAL (1951)

HOFFMAN, Michael
RESTLESS NATIVES (1985)

HOLLAENDER, Friedrich
ONLY GIRL, the (1933)

HOLLAND, Patricia
HORNSEY FILM, the (1970)

HOLMES, J B
BERTH 24 (1950)
CENTRE, the (1948)
COASTAL COMMAND (1942)
DAISY BELL COMES TO TOWN (1937)
HOW TO COOK (1937)
MEDIAEVAL VILLAGE (1936)
MERCHANT SEAMEN (1941)
PEOPLE AT NO.19, the (1949)
POTS AND PLANS (1937)
THIS IS YORK (1953)
WAKE UP AND FEED (1936)
WAY TO THE SEA, the (1936)

HOLT, Seth
BLOOD FROM THE MUMMY'S TOMB (1971)
DANGER ROUTE (1967)
NANNY, the (1965)
NOWHERE TO GO (1958)
STATION SIX SAHARA (1962)
TASTE OF FEAR (1961)

HONRI, Baynham
BANK HOLIDAY LUCK (1947)

HOOK, Harry
KITCHEN TOTO, the (1987)

HOOKER, Ted
CRUCIBLE OF TERROR (1971)

HOOPER, Tom
PAINTED FACES (1991)

HOPKINS, Albert
FAUST (1936)

HOPKINS, David
DEATH OF A SPEECHWRITER (1986)

HOPKINSON, Peter
UNDER THE SUN (1957)

HOPPIN, Hector
FOX HUNT (1936)

HOPWOOD, R A
BOTTLE PARTY (1936)
DIGGING FOR GOLD (1936)
FULL STEAM (1935)

HORNE, Denis
TOGETHER (1955)

HORSMAN, Brenda
NOT GUILTY (1988)
WIFE, the (1982)

HOSKING, Eric
BIRDS OF THE VILLAGE (1946)

HOUGH, Harold
GREAT TEMPTATION, a (1906)

HOUGH, John
BIGGLES (1986)
EYEWITNESS (1970)
LEGEND OF HELL HOUSE, the (1973)

HOWARD, Leslie
FIRST OF THE FEW, the (1942)
GENTLE SEX, the (1943)
PIMPERNEL SMITH (1941)
PYGMALION (1938)

HOWARD, William K
FIRE OVER ENGLAND (1937)
SQUEAKER, the (1937)

HUDSMITH, Philip
TAHITI (1962)

HUDSON, Claude
WILLOW TREE, the (1947)

HUDSON, F P
PHENYLKETONURIA (1962)

HUDSON, Hugh
CHARIOTS OF FIRE (1981)
GREYSTOKE; THE LEGEND OF TARZAN, LORD OF THE APES (1984)

HUGHES, A F W
PHAGOCYTOSIS; MACROPHAGES IN TISSUE CULTURES OF EMBRYONIC CHICK LUNG (1946)

HUGHES, Geoffrey
BELGIAN GRAND PRIX (1955)
BRITISH AIRCRAFT REVIEW 1948 (1948)
ISLAND OF STEEL (1956)
ISLE OF MAN TT 1950 (1950)

HUGHES, Harry
BACHELOR'S BABY (1932)
BARNACLE BILL (1934)
FACING THE MUSIC (1933)
GABLES MYSTERY, the (1938)
IMPROPER DUCHESS, the (1936)
JOY RIDE (1935)
MAN AT SIX, the (1931)
SONG AT EVENTIDE (1934)
SOUTHERN MAID, a (1933)
THEIR NIGHT OUT (1933)
TROUBLESOME WIVES (1928)
WE TAKE OFF OUR HATS (1930)

HUGHES, Ken
ALFIE DARLING (1975)
BRAIN MACHINE, the (1954)
CASINO ROYALE (1967)
CHITTY CHITTY BANG BANG (1968)
CROMWELL (1970)
DROP DEAD DARLING (1966)
IN THE NICK (1959)
INTERNECINE PROJECT, the (1974)
JAZZBOAT (1959)
LITTLE RED MONKEY (1954)
SMALL WORLD OF SAMMY LEE, the (1962)
TIMESLIP (1955)
TRIALS OF OSCAR WILDE, the (1960)

HUGHES, Terry
MONTY PYTHON LIVE AT THE HOLLYWOOD BOWL (1982)

HULBERT, Jack
FALLING FOR YOU (1933)
JACK OF ALL TRADES (1936)

HULL, Norman
LADDER OF SWORDS (1989)

HUMBERSTONE, H Bruce
HAPPY GO LOVELY (1951)
TARZAN AND THE LOST SAFARI (1956)

HUME, Kenneth
I'VE GOTTA HORSE (1965)
MODS AND ROCKERS (1964)

HUMPHREY, William
TANGLED HEARTS (1920)

HUNT, John
OUR ISLAND NATION (1937)

HUNT, Peter
GOLD (1974)
ON HER MAJESTY'S SECRET SERVICE (1969)
WILD GEESE II (1985)

FAMILY PORTRAIT, a (1950)
FIRES WERE STARTED (1943)
FIRST DAYS, the (1939)
HEART OF BRITAIN, the (1941)
LISTEN TO BRITAIN (1942)
LOCOMOTIVES (1934)
LONDON CAN TAKE IT (1940)
MAKING FASHION (1938)
PENNY JOURNEY (1938)
POST HASTE (1934)
SILENT VILLAGE, the (1943)
SPARE TIME (1939)
SPEAKING FROM AMERICA (1938)
SPRING OFFENSIVE (1940)
SS IONIAN (1939)
STORY OF THE WHEEL (1935)
THIS IS ENGLAND (1941)
TRUE STORY OF LILI MARLENE, the
   (1944)
WELFARE OF THE WORKERS (1940)
WORDS FOR BATTLE (1941)

JEWKES, John
UNEMPLOYMENT AND MONEY (1940)

JOHNSON, B S
YOU'RE HUMAN LIKE THE REST OF
   THEM (1967)

JOHNSON, Carl
SON, ARE YOU DOWN THERE? (1984)

JONES, Andrew Miller
DEVELOPMENT OF THE ENGLISH
   RAILWAYS, the (1936)
EXPANSION OF GERMANY 1870–1914,
   the (1936)

JONES, David
BETRAYAL (1983)
TRIAL, the (1992)

JONES, Ian
IT'S NOT ALL PAINTING AND
   DRAWING, YOU KNOW (1971)

JONES, James Cellan
BEQUEST TO THE NATION (1973)

JONES, Terry
ERIK THE VIKING (1989)
MONTY PYTHON AND THE HOLY
   GRAIL (1974)
MONTY PYTHON'S LIFE OF BRIAN
   (1979)
PERSONAL SERVICES (1987)

JORDAN, Neil
COMPANY OF WOLVES, the (1984)
CRYING GAME, the (1992)
HIGH SPIRITS (1988)
MIRACLE, the (1991)
MONA LISA (1986)

JOYCE, Paul
GOAD, the (1965)

JULIEN, Isaac
PASSION OF REMEMBRANCE, the (1986)
YOUNG SOUL REBELS (1991)

JURAN, Nathan
EAST OF SUDAN (1964)
FIRST MEN IN THE MOON (1964)

KANTUREK, Otto
STUDENT'S ROMANCE, the (1935)

KAPLAN, Henry
GIRL ON THE BOAT, the (1962)

KAPLAN, Jan
GLORY OF THE GARDEN, the (1982)

KAPLAN, JoAnn
INVOCATION – MAYA DEREN (1987)

KARLIN, Marc
'36 TO '77 (1978)

KAVANAGH, Denis
STARLIGHT SERENADE (1943)
WOMEN AND SPORT (1946)

KAWADRI, Anwar
SEX WITH THE STARS (1980)

KEA, Kaprice
VIRTUES OF KNATURE (1987)

KEARTON, Ada
DASSAN; AN ADVENTURE IN SEARCH
   OF LAUGHTER FEATURING
   NATURE'S GREATEST LITTLE
   COMEDIANS (1930)

KEARTON, Cherry
BIG GAME OF LIFE, the (1935)
DASSAN; AN ADVENTURE IN SEARCH
   OF LAUGHTER FEATURING
   NATURE'S GREATEST LITTLE
   COMEDIANS (1930)
JOURNEY TO ADVENTURE; A FILM
   CHRONICLE OF CHERRY KEARTON
   (1947)
ON THE EQUATOR (1923)
TEMBI (1929)

KEATERING, Michael
SUNSWEPT (1961)

KEEN, Lesley H
ORPHEUS AND EURYDICE (1984)
RA; THE PATH OF THE SUN GOD (1990)

KEENE, Ralph
ADESTE FIDELES (1941)
AIR OUTPOST (1937)
CROWN OF THE YEAR, the (1943)
CYPRUS IS AN ISLAND (1946)
GRASSY SHIRES, the (1944)
GREEN GIRDLE, the (1941)
JOURNEY INTO SPRING (1957)
NEW BRITAIN, the (1940)
PROUD CITY (1946)
SPRING ON THE FARM (1943)
STRING OF BEADS, a (1947)
SUMMER ON THE FARM (1943)
ULSTER (1940)
UNDER NIGHT STREETS (1958)
WATCH AND WARD IN THE AIR (1937)
WINTER ON THE FARM (1943)

KELLETT, Bob
ALF GARNETT SAGA, the (1972)
ARE YOU BEING SERVED? (1977)
DON'T JUST LIE THERE, SAY
   SOMETHING! (1973)
OUR MISS FRED (1972)
UP POMPEII (1971)
UP THE CHASTITY BELT (1971)
UP THE FRONT (1972)

KELLINO, Roy
GUILT IS MY SHADOW (1950)
I MET A MURDERER (1939)
LAST ADVENTURERS, the (1937)
SILKEN AFFAIR, the (1956)

KELLINO, W P
ALF'S CARPET (1929)
ANGEL ESQUIRE (1919)
AROMA OF THE SOUTH SEAS (1931)
BULL RUSHES (1931)
DUMMY, the (1916)
MY OLD CHINA (1931)
NOBBY THE NEW WAITER (1913)
NOT FOR SALE (1924)
PAYBOX ADVENTURE (1936)
ROB ROY (1922)
ROYAL CAVALCADE (1935)
SOMETIMES GOOD (1934)
YOUNG LOCHINVAR (1923)

KELLY, Gene
INVITATION TO THE DANCE (1954)

KELLY, Karen
EGOLI (1989)

KELLY, Mary
WOMEN OF THE RHONDDA (1973)

KEMPLEN, Ralph
SPANIARD'S CURSE, the (1957)

KENNEDY, Anthea
AT THE FOUNTAINHEAD (OF GERMAN
   STRENGTH) (1980)

KENNEDY, Burt
HANNIE CAULDER (1971)

KENNEDY, Ludovic
DO IT ON THE WHISTLE (1965)

KERR, David
REFLEX ACTION (1986)

KEYNES, Geoffrey
CARCINOMA OF THE BREAST
   TREATED WITH RADIUM (1929)

KIDRON, Beeban
VROOM (1988)

KILBURN, Richard
COURTESY (1964)

KILMARTIN, Angela
HELPING YOURSELF IN CYSTITIS (1974)

KIMMINS, Anthony
AMOROUS PRAWN, the (1962)
AUNT CLARA (1954)
BONNIE PRINCE CHARLIE (1948)
CAPTAIN'S PARADISE, the (1953)
COME ON, GEORGE! (1939)
FLESH AND BLOOD (1951)
I SEE ICE! (1938)
IT'S IN THE AIR (1938)
KEEP FIT (1937)
MINE OWN EXECUTIONER (1947)
MR DENNING DRIVES NORTH (1951)
ONCE IN A NEW MOON (1935)
SMILEY (1956)
TROUBLE BREWING (1939)

KINDER, Stuart
FLYING DESPATCH, the (1912)

KING, George
ADVENTURE LIMITED (1934)
BLUE SQUADRON, the (1934)
CANDLELIGHT IN ALGERIA (1943)
CASE OF THE FRIGHTENED LADY, the
   (1940)
CHINESE BUNGALOW, the (1940)
CRIMES AT THE DARK HOUSE (1940)
CRIMES OF STEPHEN HAWKE, the (1936)
FACE AT THE WINDOW, the (1939)
GAIETY GEORGE (1946)
GAY OLD DOG, the (1935)
JOHN HALIFAX, GENTLEMAN (1938)
LITTLE STRANGER (1934)
MAN WITHOUT A FACE, the (1935)
MAYFAIR GIRL (1933)
MEN OF STEEL (1932)
NUMBER, PLEASE (1931)
OH NO DOCTOR! (1934)
SHOP AT SLY CORNER, the (1946)
SILVER TOP (1938)
SWEENEY TODD, THE DEMON
   BARBER OF FLEET STREET (1936)
TO BE A LADY (1934)
TOO MANY CROOKS (1930)
TWO WAY STREET (1931)
UNDER A CLOUD (1937)
WINDFALL (1935)

KING, Peter
THIRTEEN CANTOS OF HELL (1955)

KING, Philip
GUNDOWN (1973)

KINGHAM, A H
ENGLISHMAN'S HOLIDAY, an (1946)

KINGSBURY, Robert
STUDY RESULTS (1957)

LAWRENCE OF ARABIA (1962)
MADELEINE (1949)
OLIVER TWIST (1948)
PASSAGE TO INDIA, a (1984)
PASSIONATE FRIENDS, the (1948)
RYAN'S DAUGHTER (1970)
SEVEN PILLARS OF WISDOM – ARTISTS
    TEST: ALBERT FINNEY (1960)
SOUND BARRIER, the (1952)
THIS HAPPY BREED (1944)

LEARNER, Keith
DO IT YOURSELF CARTOON KIT (1959)

LE BORG, Reginald
FLANAGAN BOY, the (1953)

LEDER, Herbert J
FROZEN DEAD, the (1966)
IT (1966)

LEE, Jack
CAPTAIN'S TABLE, the (1958)
CHILDREN ON TRIAL (1946)
CIRCLE OF DECEPTION (1960)
ONCE A JOLLY SWAGMAN (1948)
PILOT IS SAFE, the (1941)
ROBBERY UNDER ARMS (1957)
TOWN LIKE ALICE, a (1956)
TURN THE KEY SOFTLY (1953)
WOMAN IN THE HALL, the (1947)
WOODEN HORSE, the (1950)

LEE, Norman
ALMOST A HONEYMOON (1938)
BULLDOG DRUMMOND AT BAY (1937)
CASE OF CHARLES PEACE, the (1949)
DANGEROUS FINGERS (1938)
DR JOSSER KC (1931)
DOCTOR'S ORDERS (1934)
DOOR WITH SEVEN LOCKS, the (1940)
FARMER'S WIFE, the (1941)
FORGOTTEN MEN; THE WAR AS IT
    WAS (1934)
FRENCH LEAVE (1937)
GIRL WHO COULDN'T QUITE, the (1949)
HAPPY DAYS ARE HERE AGAIN (1936)
HOW A BICYCLE IS MADE (1945)
JOSSER IN THE ARMY (1932)
JOSSER JOINS THE NAVY (1932)
JOSSER ON THE RIVER (1932)
KATHLEEN MAVOURNEEN (1937)
MR REEDER IN ROOM 13 (1938)
MONEY TALKS (1932)
MONKEY'S PAW, the (1948)
MURDER IN SOHO (1938)
NO ESCAPE (1936)
OUTCAST, the (1934)
PRIDE OF THE FORCE, the (1933)
ROYAL CAVALCADE (1935)
SATURDAY NIGHT REVUE (1937)
SAVE A LITTLE SUNSHINE (1938)
STRANGLER, the (1932)
STRIP! STRIP!! HOORAY!!! (1932)
YES, MADAM? (1938)

LEE, Peter
INSIGHT – ANTHONY ASQUITH (1960)

LEE, Rowland V
LOVE FROM A STRANGER (1937)
THAT NIGHT IN LONDON (1932)

LEE, Sammy
CIRCUS STORY (1946)
SPEEDWAY (1947)

LEECE, Mary Pat
BRED AND BORN (1984)

LEEDS ANIMATION WORKSHOP
GIVE US A SMILE (1983)

LEEMAN, Dicky
DATE WITH A DREAM, a (1948)

LEGG, Stuart
BBC THE VOICE OF BRITAIN (1935)
CABLE SHIP (1933)

CAMBRIDGE (1931)
COMING OF THE DIAL, the (1933)
NEW OPERATOR, the (1934)
ROADWAYS (1937)
TELEPHONE WORKERS (1933)
WINGS OVER EMPIRE (1939)

LE GRICE, Malcolm
FINNEGAN'S CHIN – TEMPORAL
    ECONOMY (1981)

LEIFER, Neil
YESTERDAY'S HERO (1979)

LEIGH, Malcolm
LEGEND OF THE WITCHES (1970)

LEIGH, Mike
HIGH HOPES (1988)
LIFE IS SWEET (1990)

LELAND, David
WISH YOU WERE HERE (1987)

LEMONT, John
FRIGHTENED CITY, the (1961)
GREEN BUDDHA, the (1954)
KONGA (1960)
SHAKEDOWN, the (1959)

LENNOX, Peter
KASHMIR CONFLICT (1951)

LEONG, Po-chih
PING PONG (1986)

LE PRESLE, Robert
LET'S SEE (1945)

LERNER, Irving
ROYAL HUNT OF THE SUN, the (1969)

LESLIE, Antonia
COURT IN THE CAR, a (1993)

LESTER, Richard
BED SITTING ROOM, the (1969)
HARD DAY'S NIGHT, a (1964)
HELP! (1965)
HOW I WON THE WAR (1967)
IT'S TRAD, DAD! (1962)
KNACK ...AND HOW TO GET IT, the
    (1965)
MOUSE ON THE MOON, the (1963)
RITZ, the (1976)
RUNNING JUMPING & STANDING STILL
    FILM, the (1960)
SUPERMAN II (1980)

LEVIN, Henry
COME FLY WITH ME (1962)
LET'S BE HAPPY (1956)

LEVY, Benn W
LORD CAMBER'S LADIES (1932)

LEVY, Don
HEROSTRATUS (1967)
OPUS (1967)
TIME IS (1964)

LEVY, Gerry
BODY STEALERS, the (1969)

LEWIN, Albert
PANDORA AND THE FLYING
    DUTCHMAN (1950)

LEWIN, Ben
RUE SAINT-SULPICE (1991)

LEWIS, Cecil
ARMS AND THE MAN (1932)
HOW HE LIED TO HER HUSBAND (1931)
INDISCRETIONS OF EVE (1932)

LEWIS, Henry
TOMORROW'S TODAY (1958)

LEWIS, Jay
BABY AND THE BATTLESHIP, the (1956)
HERRINGS (1940)
HOME OF YOUR OWN, a (1964)
LIVE NOW, PAY LATER (1962)
MOBILE CANTEEN (1941)
ROOTS OF VICTORY, the (1941)
STEAMING (1940)

LEWIS, Jerry
ONE MORE TIME (1969)

LEWIS, John E
BRINGING IT HOME (1940)
HOT EVIDENCE (1939)
STEEL GOES TO SEA (1941)
TALKING SHOP (1939)
VILLAGE THAT FOUND ITSELF, the
    (1939)

LEWIS, Jonathan
BEFORE HINDSIGHT (1977)

LEWIS, Milo
EGGHEAD'S ROBOT (1970)
TROUBLESOME DOUBLE, the (1971)

LIEBSCHNER, Anna
MESSAGE FROM THE WARDEN, a (1982)

LICHFIELD, Patrick
I WANT TO BE HAPPY (1972)

LICHTNER, Marvin
SOME KIND OF HERO (1972)

LINDEMAN, Eric
MODERN IRELAND (1952)

LINDSAY-HOGG, Michael
LET IT BE (1970)
NASTY HABITS (1976)

LINNECAR, Vera
DO I DETECT A CHANGE IN YOUR
    ATTITUDE? (1980)
DO IT YOURSELF CARTOON KIT (1959)

LIPMAN, Gordon
YOUR LOCAL COUNCIL (1949)

LIPSCOMB, W P
COLONEL BLOOD (1933)

LITTLEWOOD, Joan
SPARROWS CAN'T SING (1962)

LITVAK, Anatole
ANASTASIA (1956)
DEEP BLUE SEA, the (1955)
NIGHT OF THE GENERALS, the (1966)
SLEEPING CAR (1933)

LLOYD, George
LETTER FROM WALES, a (1953)

LLOYD, Major
IT MIGHT BE YOU...! (1938)

LOACH, Ken
FAMILY LIFE (1971)
FATHERLAND (1986)
KES (1969)
LOOKS AND SMILES (1981)
RIFF RAFF (1991)
TALK ABOUT WORK (1971)

LOCHNER, C David
OVERTURE: 'ONE-TWO-FIVE' (1978)

LOCKWOOD, Roy
AIRPORT (1934)
MUTINY OF THE ELSINORE, the (1937)

LODER, John de Vere
'ROSE MARIE' ON ICE (1952)
SADLER'S WELLS AND BRITISH
    BALLET (1956)

LOGAN, Jacqueline
STRICTLY BUSINESS (1932)

MARRE, Jeremy
ROOTS ROCK REGGAE (1977)

MARSHALL, Fred
POPDOWN (1968)

MARSHALL, George
BEYOND MOMBASA (1956)
DUEL IN THE JUNGLE (1954)

MARSHALL, Herbert
OLYMPIC PREVIEW (1948)
POLAND (1947)

MARTIN, Henry
GROVE MUSIC (1981)

MARTIN, J H
DANCER'S DREAM, the (1905)

MARTIN, Murray
BOWES LINE, the (1975)
IN FADING LIGHT (1989)

MARTIN, Paul
HAPPY EVER AFTER (1932)

MARTINEK, H O
ANTIQUE VASE, the (1913)
HER FATHER'S PHOTOGRAPH (1911)
PLUCKY LAD, a (1910)
PLUM PUDDING STAKES, the (1911)
TABLES TURNED, the (1910)

MARTON, Andrew
AFRICA – TEXAS STYLE (1967)
SCHOOL FOR HUSBANDS (1937)
SECRET OF STAMBOUL, the (1936)

MASHWARI, Rashid
PRICE OF BREAD, the (1992)

MASON, Bill
AIR PARADE (1951)
ATOMISATION (1948)
BRITISH AIRCRAFT REVIEW 1949 (1949)
CONTROLS (1947)
CORNISH ENGINE, the (1948)
GOLDEN AGE, the (1961)
GRAND PRIX (1949)
HEROIC DAYS, the (1960)
HIGHLIGHTS OF FARNBOROUGH 1951
   (1951)
LE MANS 1952 (1952)
STABILITY (1947)
TITANS 1930–1934, the (1962)
TITANS 1935–1939, the (1962)

MASON, Christopher
IMPERSONATION, the (1984)

MASOKOANE, Glenn Ujebe
WE ARE THE ELEPHANT (1987)

MASON, Herbert
BACK-ROOM BOY (1942)
BRIGGS FAMILY, the (1940)
EAST MEETS WEST (1936)
FIRST OFFENCE (1936)
HIS LORDSHIP (1936)
MR PROUDFOOT SHOWS A LIGHT
   (1941)
ONCE A CROOK (1941)
SILENT BATTLE, the (1939)
STRANGE BOARDERS (1938)
TAKE MY TIP (1937)
WINDOW IN LONDON, a (1939)

MASSINGHAM, Richard
AGRICULTURAL HOLIDAY CAMPS
   (1947)
ARTHUR ASKEY ON GOING TO THE
   DENTIST NO.1: THE APPOINTMENT
   (1947)
ARTHUR ASKEY ON GOING TO THE
   DENTIST NO.3: THE WAITING ROOM
   (1947)
AT THE THIRD STROKE (1939)
CAMBRIDGE (1944)
COME FOR A STROLL (1938)

COUGHS AND SNEEZES (1945)
CURE, the (1950)
DAILY ROUND (1937)
DANGERS IN THE DARK (1941)
DOWN AT THE LOCAL (1945)
ELOPEMENT IN FRANCE (1944)
ENGLISHMAN'S HOME, an (1946)
FAMILY ALBUM (1953)
FAMILY DOCTOR, the (1946)
FEAR AND PETER BROWN (1940)
FIRST AID IN ACTION (1944)
HANDKERCHIEF DRILL (1949)
HARVEST CAMP (1947)
INFLUENZA (1946)
IN WHICH WE LIVE (1943)
LONG, LONG TRAIL (1946)
MIRROR CAN LIE, the (1946)
MOVING HOUSE (1949)
POOL OF CONTENTMENT (1946)
SOME LIKE IT ROUGH (1944)
WHO'LL BUY A WARSHIP? (1942)
YOUNG AND HEALTHY (1943)

MASSOT, Joe
SONG REMAINS THE SAME, the (1976)
SPACE RIDERS (1984)
WONDERWALL (1968)

MASSY, Jane
USES OF LIMESTONE (1950)
YOUR CHILDREN'S TEETH (1945)

MASTERS, Alan
COMMONWEALTH JOURNEY (1959)

MASTERS, Quentin
STUD, the (1978)

MATHIAS, John
LOBSTERS (1936)

MATHIESON, Muir
INSTRUMENTS OF THE ORCHESTRA
   (1946)
STEPS OF THE BALLET (1948)

MATTHEWS, Jessie
VICTORY WEDDING (1944)

MATTHEWS, Jimmy
NO MONEY, NO HONEY (1982)

MAUDE, Arthur
LURE, the (1933)
LYONS MAIL, the (1931)
POPPIES OF FLANDERS (1927)
RINGER, the (1928)
TONI (1928)
WATCH BEVERLY (1932)

MAXWELL, Peter
DILEMMA (1962)
SERENA (1962)

MAY, Harry
SKIFFY GOES TO SEA (1947)

MAY, Joe
TWO HEARTS IN WALTZ TIME (1934)

MAYLAM, Tony
GENESIS – A BAND IN CONCERT (1976)
RIDDLE OF THE SANDS, the (1978)
WHITE ROCK (1976)

MAYNE, Derek
ATOMIC PHYSICS, PART 4: ATOM
   SMASHING – THE DISCOVERY OF
   THE NEUTRON (1947)
UNDER THE SURFACE (1952)

MAZZETTI, Lorenza
TOGETHER (1955)

McADAM, John
EYE FOR QUALITY, an (1984)

McALLISTER, Stewart
LISTEN TO BRITAIN (1942)

McCALL, Iain
CHRISTMAS FOR SALE (1984)

McCAREY, Leo
DEVIL NEVER SLEEPS, the (1962)

McCARTHY, Matt
UNBROKEN ARROW, the (1976)

McCARTHY, Michael
ASSASSIN FOR HIRE (1951)
JOHN OF THE FAIR (1952)
OPERATION AMSTERDAM (1958)

McCLORY, Kevin
BOY AND THE BRIDGE, the (1959)

McDONELL, Fergus
PRELUDE TO FAME (1950)

McDOUGALL, Roger
CONTRARIES (1943)
MAN ON THE BEAT, the (1944)

McDOWELL, J B
CHEEKIEST MAN ON EARTH, the (1908)

McGANN, William
LITTLE FELLA (1932)
MURDER ON THE SECOND FLOOR
   (1932)

McGRATH, Joe
BLISS OF MRS BLOSSOM, the (1968)
CASINO ROYALE (1967)
DIGBY THE BIGGEST DOG IN THE
   WORLD (1973)
GREAT McGONAGALL, the (1974)

McISAAC, Nigel
GREY METROPOLIS, the (1953)
SINGING STREET, the (1952)

McLAGLEN, Andrew V
SEA WOLVES, the (1980)
WILD GEESE, the (1978)

McLAREN, Norman
BOOK BARGAIN (1937)
CAMERA MAKES WHOOPEE (1935)
HELL UNLTD (1936)
LOVE ON THE WING (1939)
NOW IS THE TIME (1951)
OBEDIENT FLAME, the (1939)
POLYCHROME FANTASY (1935)

McMILLAN, Ian
SUNFLOWERS (1968)

McMULLEN, Ken
ZINA (1985)

McMURRAY, Mary
ASSAM GARDEN, the (1985)

McNAUGHT, Bob
STORY OF DAVID, a (1960)

McNAUGHTON, Richard Q
RAILWAYMEN, the (1946)
WHAT'S ON TODAY (1938)

MEDAK, Peter
DAY IN THE DEATH OF JOE EGG, a
   (1970)
KRAYS, the (1990)
RULING CLASS, the (1971)

MEDFORD, Don
HUNTING PARTY, the (1971)

MELBOURNE-COOPER, Arthur
DREAMS OF TOYLAND (1908)
MacNAB'S VISIT TO LONDON (1905)
MOTOR PIRATES (1906)
TALE OF THE ARK, the (1909)
WOODEN ATHLETES, the (1912)

MELFORD, Austin
CAR OF DREAMS (1935)
OH DADDY (1935)

194

MULLOY, Phil
IN THE FOREST (1978)
OUTRAGE (1991)
POSSESSION (1992)
SLIM'S PICKIN'S (1991)

MULVEY, Laura
AMY! (1980)
CRYSTAL GAZING (1983)
RIDDLES OF THE SPHINX (1977)

MUNDEN, Maxwell
BANK RAIDERS (1958)
OFF DUTY (1943)
ONE MAN'S STORY (1948)
SHUNTER BLACK'S NIGHT OFF (1941)

MUNRO, David
KNOTS (1975)

MURAKAMI, Jimmy T
WHEN THE WIND BLOWS (1986)

MURRAY, Graham
TRANSMISSION OF ELECTRICITY (1947)

MUSK, Cecil
BLOW YOUR OWN TRUMPET (1958)
CAN WE BE RICH? (1946)
CIRCUS BOY (1947)
LOOKING THROUGH GLASS (1943)

MYCROFT, Walter C
BANANA RIDGE (1941)
COMIN' THRO' THE RYE (1947)
MY WIFE'S FAMILY (1941)
SPRING MEETING (1941)

NADEL, Arthur H
UNDERGROUND (1970)

NAKHIMOFF, Edward
IMMORTAL SWAN, the (1935)

NAPIER-BELL, J B
ENGLAND'S WEALTH FROM WOOL
  (1948)
FORWARD A CENTURY (1951)
GREAT CIRCLE (1944)
LIFT (1947)
MILK FROM GRANGE HILL FARM, the
  (1946)
NEW FIRE BOMB, a (1942)
NINE CENTURIES OF COAL (1958)
ORIGIN OF COAL, the (1953)
SOURING OF MILK (1947)

NARIZZANO, Silvio
FANATIC (1965)
GEORGY GIRL (1966)
LOOT (1970)

NASH, Mark
ACTING IN THE CINEMA (1985)

NASH, Percy
CROXLEY MASTER, the (1921)
HOW KITCHENER WAS BETRAYED
  (1921)
MOTHERHOOD; A LIVING PICTURE OF
  LIFE TODAY (1917)
OXFORD UNIVERSITY PRESS AND THE
  MAKING OF A BOOK, the (1925)

NATHAN, Matthew
HOUSING PROGRESS (1937)

NEAME, Elwin
SLEEPING BEAUTY, the (1912)

NEAME, Ronald
CARD, the (1952)
CHALK GARDEN, the (1964)
FOREIGN BODY (1986)
GOLDEN SALAMANDER (1949)
HORSE'S MOUTH, the (1958)
I COULD GO ON SINGING (1963)
MILLION POUND NOTE, the (1953)

PRIME OF MISS JEAN BRODIE, the (1968)
SCROOGE (1970)
TAKE MY LIFE (1947)
TUNES OF GLORY (1960)
WINDOM'S WAY (1957)

NEAT, Timothy
PLAY ME SOMETHING (1989)

NEED, Richard
ANYWHERE BUT HERE (1968)
PROGRAMMED LEARNING (1970)

NEGULESCO, Jean
BRITANNIA MEWS (1948)
MUDLARK, the (1950)

NEILL, Roy William
DR SYN (1937)
GOOD OLD DAYS, the (1939)
GYPSY (1937)
HOOTS MON! (1939)
MANY TANKS MR ATKINS (1938)

NEILSON, James
DR SYN ALIAS THE SCARECROW (1963)
LEGEND OF YOUNG DICK TURPIN, the
  (1965)

NEILSON BAXTER, R K
ALL THAT MIGHTY HEART (1963)
HOUSE OF SILENCE, the (1937)
INLAND WATERWAYS (1950)
NEW ACRES (1941)
SEASPEED ACROSS THE CHANNEL
  (1969)
THERE GO THE BOATS (1951)

NEKRASOV, Andrei
SPRINGING LENIN (1992)

NELSON, Ralph
WILBY CONSPIRACY, the (1974)

NESBITT, Derren
AMOROUS MILKMAN, the (1974)

NESBITT, Frank
DULCIMA (1971)

NETTLEFOLD, Archibald
WHAT NEXT? (1928)

NETTLETON, Gavin
MANAGING CHANGE – CHANGING
  THE MANAGERS (1988)

NEUBAUER, Vera
ANIMATION FOR LIVE ACTION (1978)
DECISION, the (1981)

NEWALL, Guy
ADMIRAL'S SECRET, the (1934)
FOX FARM (1922)
MAID OF THE SILVER SEA, a (1922)
RODNEY STEPS IN (1931)
STARLIT GARDEN, the (1923)
TESTIMONY (1920)

NEWBROOK, Peter
ASPHYX, the (1972)

NEWBY, Christopher
KISS (1991)
RELAX (1991)

NEWELL, Mike
DANCE WITH A STRANGER (1985)
GOOD FATHER, the (1986)
INTO THE WEST (1992)
SOURSWEET (1988)

NEWITT, Jeffrey
LOVES ME... LOVES ME NOT (1992)

NEWLEY, Anthony
CAN HEIRONYMUS MERKIN EVER
  FORGET MERCY HUMPPE AND FIND
  TRUE HAPPINESS? (1969)

NEWMAN, Michael
ADVENTURES OF X, the (1967)

NEWMAN, Widgey R
BROADCASTING (1926)
HERITAGE OF THE SOIL, the (1937)
HOME CONSTRUCTION (1926)
HOT WATER AND VEGETABUEL (1928)
HOW I BEGAN (1926)
IMMORTAL GENTLEMAN, the (1935)
JOHN CITIZEN (1927)
LISTENING IN (1926)
LOUD SPEAKER, the (1926)
MEN WITHOUT HONOUR (1939)
OSCILLATION (1926)
ROAD TO YESTERDAY (1944)
WHAT THE PARROT SAW (1935)

NIBLO, Fred
DIAMOND CUT DIAMOND (1932)
TWO WHITE ARMS (1932)

NIETER, Hans M
BLOOD TRANSFUSION (1942)
GOOD VALUE (1942)
SEVEN YEARS IN TIBET (1956)
THUNDER IN THE AIR (1935)
UNCLE TIMOTHY'S TEA PARTY (1944)
WHITE BATTLE FRONT (1940)

NICHOLAS, S C
HELPING YOURSELF IN CYSTITIS (1974)

NOAKE, Roger
SOFT WORDS; or, Life Does Not Live
  (1984)

NOBLE, Joe
ELSTREE 'ERBS, the (1930)
MEET MR YORK! A SPEAKING
  LIKENESS (1929)
SECOND ADVENTURE OF 'ORACE THE
  'ARMONIOUS 'OUND, the (1929)

NOEL, J B L
CLIMBING MOUNT EVEREST (1922)
EPIC OF EVEREST (1924)

NOLBANDOV, Sergei
SHIPS WITH WINGS (1941)
UNDERCOVER (1943)

NORMAN, Leslie
DUNKIRK (1958)
LONG AND THE SHORT AND THE
  TALL, the (1960)
MIX ME A PERSON (1962)
NIGHT MY NUMBER CAME UP, the
  (1955)
SPARE THE ROD (1961)
X – THE UNKNOWN (1956)

NORTHCOTE, Sidney
TRAGEDY ON THE CORNISH COAST
  (1912)

NORTON, Charles Goodwin
BILL POSTER, the (1899)
COUNTRY CATTLE SHOW, a (1897)
FIRE BRIGADE TURN-OUT IN THE
  COUNTRY (1899)
POSTMAN AND THE NURSEMAID, the
  (1899)

NOTCUTT, L A
AFRICAN PEASANT FARMS – THE
  KINGOLWIRA EXPERIMENT (1937)
TROPICAL HOOKWORM (1936)
VETERINARY TRAINING OF AFRICAN
  NATIVES (1936)

NOXON, G F
CAMBRIDGE (1931)

NOY, Wilfred
BUSINESS IS BUSINESS (1912)
DADDY'S DID'UMS ON A HOLIDAY
  (1912)
DADDY'S LITTLE DID'UMS DID IT?
  (1910)
DR BRIAN PELLIE AND THE SECRET
  DESPATCH (1912)
FOILED BY A GIRL (1912)
PASSIONS OF MEN, the (1914)
WELL DONE HENRY (1937)

PATTISSON, MarieCecille
PRAYER TO VIRACOCHA (1992)

PAUL, Fred
BROKEN MELODY, the (1929)
GAME FOR TWO, a (1921)
HER GREATEST PERFORMANCE (1916)
IN A LOTUS GARDEN (1930)
JEST, the (1921)
LADY WINDERMERE'S FAN (1916)
LAST APPEAL, the (1921)
LUCK OF THE NAVY, the (1927)
MASKS AND FACES (1917)
OATH, the (1921)
TORTURE CAGE, the (1928)
WARWICK CASTLE IN FEUDAL DAYS
   (1926)

PAUL, R W
CHESS DISPUTE, a (1903)
CHILDREN IN THE NURSERY (1898)
COME ALONG, DO! (1898)
COMIC COSTUME RACE (1896)
COUNTRYMAN AND THE
   CINEMATOGRAPH, the (1901)
DEONZO BROTHERS, the (1901)
HIS BRAVE DEFENDER (1901)
RETURN OF TRH THE PRINCE AND
   PRINCESS OF WALES (1903)
ROBBERY (1897)
TETHERBALL, OR DO-DO (1898)
TOMMY ATKINS IN THE PARK (1898)
TWINS' TEA PARTY, the (1896)

PEACOCK, Mari
ARRIVALS (1983)

PEAKE, Bladon
DEFEAT DIPHTHERIA (1941)
YOU'RE TELLING ME (1941)

PEARCE, David
PORTRAIT OF DAVID HOCKNEY (1972)

PEARL, Albert
YOUR CHILDREN'S EARS (1945)

PEARSON, Euan
PLANNING NEW MINES (1977)

PEARSON, George
ACE OF SPADES, the (1935)
BRITISH MADE (1939)
CHECKMATE (1935)
CHRISTMAS DAY IN THE WORKHOUSE
   (1914)
EAST LYNNE ON THE WESTERN
   FRONT (1931)
FATAL HOUR, the (1937)
FOUR MASKED MEN (1934)
GENTLEMEN'S AGREEMENT (1935)
I LOVE A LASSIE (1931)
JUBILEE WINDOW (1935)
LITTLE PEOPLE, the (1926)
MIDNIGHT AT MADAME TUSSAUD'S
   (1936)
NOTHING ELSE MATTERS (1920)
ONCE A THIEF (1935)
OPEN ALL NIGHT (1934)
REVEILLE (1924)
RIVER WOLVES, the (1933)
ROAMIN' IN THE GLOAMIN' (1931)
SAFTEST O' THE FAMILY, the (1931)
SHOT IN THE DARK, a (1933)
SQUIBS (1921)
SQUIBS MP (1923)
SQUIBS WINS THE CALCUTTA SWEEP
   (1922)
THAT'S MY UNCLE (1935)
ULTUS AND THE THREE-BUTTON
   MYSTERY (1917)
WEDNESDAY'S LUCK (1936)

PECK, Ron
EDWARD HOPPER (1981)
EMPIRE STATE (1987)
NIGHTHAWKS (1978)
WHAT CAN I DO WITH A MALE NUDE?
   (1985)

PECKINPAH, Sam
CROSS OF IRON (1977)
STRAW DOGS (1971)

PEDELTY, Donovan
BEHIND YOUR BACK (1937)
EARLY BIRD, the (1936)
FALSE EVIDENCE (1937)
FIRST NIGHT (1937)
FLAME IN THE HEATHER (1935)
LANDSLIDE (1937)
LUCK OF THE IRISH, the (1935)
MURDER TOMORROW (1938)
SCHOOL FOR STARS (1935)

PEET, Stephen
FAR CRY, a (1958)

PÉLISSIER, Anthony
ENCORE (1951)
HISTORY OF MR POLLY, the (1948)
MEET ME TONIGHT (1952)
MEET MR LUCIFER (1953)
NIGHT WITHOUT STARS (1951)
PERSONAL AFFAIR (1953)
ROCKING HORSE WINNER, the (1949)

PENNINGTON-RICHARDS, C M
CHALLENGE FOR ROBIN HOOD, a
   (1967)
DANNY THE DRAGON (1966)
DENTIST ON THE JOB (1961)
INN FOR TROUBLE (1959)
LADIES WHO DO (1963)
MYSTERY SUBMARINE (1962)
ORACLE, the (1953)

PEPLOE, Clare
HIGH SEASON (1987)

PEPLOE, Mark
SAMSON AND DELILAH (1984)

PEREIRA, Dunstan
VIOLA (1967)

PEREIRA, Miguel
DEUDA INTERNA, la (1987)

PÉRIER, Etienne
WHEN EIGHT BELLS TOLL (1971)
ZEPPELIN (1971)

PETIT, Christopher
RADIO ON (1979)
UNSUITABLE JOB FOR A WOMAN, an
   (1982)

PETRIE, Daniel
MAIN ATTRACTION, the (1962)
SPY WITH A COLD NOSE, the (1966)
STOLEN HOURS (1963)

PETTIT, Chris
FOCUS ON KODAK '84 (1984)

PHILLIPS, Bertram
MEET MR YORK! – A SPEAKING
   LIKENESS (1929)
TOPSEY TURVEY (1926)

PHILLIPS, John Michael
SINK OR SWIM (1977)

PHILLIPS, Robin
MISS JULIE (1972)

PHILPOTT, Richard
ROAD MOVIE (1984)

PICK, Martyn
TABOO OF DIRT (1987)

PICKERING, Peter
ISLAND, the (1952)
POWERED SUPPORTS (1960)
SABOTAGE! (1942)
TOWER, the (1953)
TREPANNER, the (1956)

PIERCE, Lionel
STEAM TURBINE (1946)

PIERSON, Frank R
LOOKING GLASS WAR, the (1969)

PIKE, Oliver
FAMILY OF GREAT TITS, a (1934)
ST KILDA, ITS PEOPLE AND BIRDS
   (1908)

PINE, Diana
ATOMS AT WORK (1952)
DOLLARS AND SENSE (1949)
SPOTLIGHT ON THE COLONIES (1950)

PINSCHEWER, Julius
WILLIE DOES HIS STUFF (1948)

PLAISETTY, René
BROKEN ROAD, the (1921)

PLATTS-MILLS, Barney
BRONCO BULLFROG (1969)
PRIVATE ROAD (1971)

PLUMB, Hay
ALL'S FAIR (1913)
BLOOD & BOSH (1913)
COCK O' THE WALK (1915)
HAMLET (1913)
HAWKEYE, SHOWMAN (1913)
LIEUTENANT LILLY AND THE
   SPLODGE OF OPIUM (1913)
MAGIC GLASS, the (1914)
TOPPER TRIUMPHANT (1914)

PLUMMER, Peter
JUNKET 89 (1970)

POLANSKI, Roman
CUL-DE-SAC (1966)
DANCE OF THE VAMPIRES (1967)
MACBETH (1971)

POLANYI, Michael
UNEMPLOYMENT AND MONEY (1940)

POLIAKOFF, Stephen
CLOSE MY EYES (1991)
HIDDEN CITY (1987)

POLLAK, Claire
CROSS AND PASSION (1981)

POLLARD, William
DUCHY OF CORNWALL, the (1938)
OF ALL THE GAY PLACES; AN
   INTERLUDE IN BATH (1938)

POLLOCK, George
DON'T PANIC CHAPS (1959)
KILL OR CURE (1962)
MURDER AHOY (1964)
MURDER AT THE GALLOP (1963)
MURDER MOST FOUL (1964)
MURDER SHE SAID (1961)
ROONEY (1958)
TEN LITTLE INDIANS (1965)

POLLOCK, Tom
ARS MORIENDI (1983)

POMEROY, John
DUBLIN NIGHTMARE (1958)

POMMER, Erich
VESSEL OF WRATH (1938)

PONTING, Herbert G
90° SOUTH (1933)

POOLE, Raymond
PRIMARY HEALTH CARE – A TEAM
   APPROACH (1983)

POOLEY, Olaf
JOHNSTOWN MONSTER, the (1971)

PORTER, Andy
PLACE OF MY OWN, a (1983)

PORTER, Eric
SON IS BORN, a (1946)

NIGHT OF THE GARTER (1933)
NO PARKING (1938)
RELUCTANT HEROES (1951)
ROYAL DIVORCE, a (1938)
SORRELL AND SON (1933)
SPLINTERS (1929)
UP FOR THE CUP (1950)
WHEN KNIGHTS WERE BOLD (1936)
WORM'S EYE VIEW (1951)
YOU WILL REMEMBER (1940)

RECKORD, Lloyd
TEN BOB IN WINTER (1963)

REDFERN, Jasper
MONKEY AND THE ICE CREAM, the (1904)

REED, Carol
BANK HOLIDAY (1938)
CLIMBING HIGH (1938)
FALLEN IDOL, the (1948)
GIRL IN THE NEWS, the (1940)
GIRL MUST LIVE, a (1939)
IT HAPPENED IN PARIS (1935)
KEY, the (1958)
KID FOR TWO FARTHINGS, a (1954)
KIPPS (1941)
LABURNUM GROVE (1936)
LETTER FROM HOME (1941)
MAN BETWEEN, the (1953)
MIDSHIPMAN EASY (1935)
NIGHT TRAIN TO MUNICH (1940)
ODD MAN OUT (1947)
OLIVER! (1968)
OUR MAN IN HAVANA (1959)
OUTCAST OF THE ISLANDS (1951)
PENNY PARADISE (1938)
RUNNING MAN, the (1963)
STARS LOOK DOWN, the (1939)
TALK OF THE DEVIL (1936)
THIRD MAN, the (1949)
WAY AHEAD, the (1944)
WHO'S YOUR LADY FRIEND? (1937)
YOUNG MR PITT, the (1942)

REED, Stanley
NEIGHBOURHOOD 15 (1948)

REES, David
ARGYLL FIELD – OIL AT 13:35 (1976)

REEVE, Geoffrey
PUPPET ON A CHAIN (1970)

REEVE, John
YOUNG JACOBITES, the (1959)

REEVE, Leonard
ADVENTURES OF REX, the (1959)
BLACK SWAN, the (1952)
COME SATURDAY (1949)
SCHOOLMASTER, the (1953)
STABLE RIVALS (1952)

REEVES, Michael
SORCERERS, the (1967)
WITCHFINDER GENERAL (1968)

REGNIEZ, Philippe
CORNELIUS CARDEW (1986)

REID, Alastair
BABY LOVE (1967)
NIGHT DIGGER, the (1971)
SOMETHING TO HIDE (1971)

REID, John
ANDERTON SHEARER-LOADER, the (1955)
MANRIDING AT EPPLETON (1967)

REINERT, Emile-Edwin
TALE OF FIVE CITIES, a (1951)

REINHARDT, Gottfried
BETRAYED (1954)

REINIGER, Lotte
HPO, the (1938)
KING'S BREAKFAST, the (1937)
MARY'S BIRTHDAY (1950)
TOCHER; A FILM BALLET BY LOTTE REINIGER, the (1938)

REISCH, Walter
MEN ARE NOT GODS (1936)

REISZ, Karel
FRENCH LIEUTENANT'S WOMAN, the (1981)
ISADORA (1968)
MOMMA DON'T ALLOW (1955)
MORGAN; A SUITABLE CASE FOR TREATMENT (1966)
NIGHT MUST FALL (1964)
SATURDAY NIGHT AND SUNDAY MORNING (1960)
WE ARE THE LAMBETH BOYS (1959)

RELPH, Michael
ALL NIGHT LONG (1961)
DAVY (1957)
DESERT MICE (1959)
GENTLE GUNMAN, the (1952)
I BELIEVE IN YOU (1951)
ROCKETS GALORE (1958)
SHIP THAT DIED OF SHAME, the (1955)
SQUARE RING, the (1953)

RENOIR, Louis
TERROR ON TIPTOE (1936)

RHODES, John
IN ALL WEATHERS (1949)

RHODES, Lis
PICTURES ON PINK PAPER (1982)

RICH, Roy
IT'S NOT CRICKET (1949)

RICHARD, Kelvin
DUB AND VISUAL PERCEPTION (1983)

RICHARDS, Lloyd T
COD – A MELLOW DRAMA (1928)

RICHARDS, Michael W
SECRET REEDS, the (1981)

RICHARDSON, Peter
EAT THE RICH (1987)
SUPERGRASS, the (1985)

RICHARDSON, Ralph
HOME AT SEVEN (1952)

RICHARDSON, Tony
CHARGE OF THE LIGHT BRIGADE, the (1968)
ENTERTAINER, the (1960)
HAMLET (1969)
JOSEPH ANDREWS (1976)
LAUGHTER IN THE DARK (1969)
LONELINESS OF THE LONG DISTANCE RUNNER, the (1962)
LOOK BACK IN ANGER (1959)
MOMMA DON'T ALLOW (1955)
NED KELLY (1970)
SAILOR FROM GIBRALTAR, the (1967)
TASTE OF HONEY, a (1961)
TOM JONES (1963)

RICHMAN, Geoff
MORGAN'S WALL (1978)

RICHMAN, Marie
MORGAN'S WALL (1978)

RICHTER, Hans
EVERYDAY (1969)

RIDDLESDELL, Anne
INNER CITY (1987)

RIDGWELL, George
ABBEY GRANGE, the (1922)
BECKET (1923)
BRUCE PARTINGTON PLANS, the (1922)
CARDBOARD BOX, the (1923)
CROOKED MAN, the (1923)
DISAPPEARANCE OF LADY FRANCES CARFAX, the (1923)
FINAL PROBLEM, the (1923)
FOUR JUST MEN, the (1921)
GLORIA SCOTT, the (1923)
HIS LAST BOW (1923)
MISSING THREE QUARTER, the (1923)
MUSGRAVE RITUAL, the (1922)
MYSTERY OF THOR BRIDGE, the (1923)
RED CIRCLE, the (1922)
STOCKBROKER'S CLERK, the (1922)
STONE OF MAZARIN, the (1923)

RIDLEY, Arnold
ROYAL EAGLE (1936)

RIDLEY, Charles
DOWN ON THE FARM (1942)
GERMANY CALLING (1941)

RIESNER, Charles F
EVERYBODY DANCE (1936)

RILEY, Ronald H
GENERAL ELECTION (1946)
RIG 20 (1952)

RILLA, Walter
BEHOLD THE MAN (1951)

RILLA, Wolf
BACHELOR OF HEARTS (1958)
BLACK RIDER, the (1954)
CAIRO (1963)
END OF THE ROAD, the (1954)
NOOSE FOR A LADY (1952)
PACIFIC DESTINY (1956)
PICCADILLY THIRD STOP (1960)
SCAMP, the (1957)
STOCK CAR (1955)
VILLAGE OF THE DAMNED (1960)
WATCH IT SAILOR! (1961)
WITNESS IN THE DARK (1959)
WORLD TEN TIMES OVER, the (1963)

RIMMINEN, Marjut
SOME PROTECTION (1987)
STAIN, the (1991)

RITCHIE, James
COASTS OF CLYDE (1959)
EXPORT BY TRAIN (1965)
LONG NIGHT HAUL (1957)

ROBBINS, Derek
THOSE BEAUTIFUL OLD CARS (1972)

ROBBINS, Duncan
AROUND SNOWDONIA (1937)
WESTERN HIGHLANDS (1934)

ROBBINS, Jess
LITTLE BIT OF FLUFF, a (1928)

ROBERTS, Adam
MICKEY FINN (1991)

ROBERTSON, James
TWO-YEAR-OLD GOES TO HOSPITAL, a (1951)

ROBIN, Georges
MINI WEEKEND (1967)

ROBINS, John
BEST OF BENNY HILL, the (1974)
LOVE THY NEIGHBOUR (1973)
MAN ABOUT THE HOUSE (1974)
NEAREST AND DEAREST (1972)
THAT'S YOUR FUNERAL (1972)

ROBINSON, Bruce
WITHNAIL & I (1987)

SALT, Brian
AND NOW THEY REST (1939)
ANIMAL AFTERNOON (1958)
COAL PREPARATION (1956)
LETTER FROM THE ISLE OF WIGHT,
(1953)
ROAD TO HEALTH, the (1938)
SCOTLAND FOR FITNESS (1938)
SINGAPORE; A STUDY OF A PORT
(1951)
TOTO AND THE POACHERS (1956)

SALTER, James
THREE (1969)

SAMUELSON, Michael
HEADING FOR GLORY (1975)

SANDERS, Jon
'36 TO '77 (1978)

SANDERSON, Challis N
BROADCASTING (1926)
COCK O' THE NORTH (1935)
HOME CONSTRUCTION (1926)
HOW I BEGAN (1926)
LISTENING IN (1926)
LOUD SPEAKER, the (1926)
OSCILLATION (1926)
SCALLYWAG, the (1921)
SCRAGS (1930)
SIR RUPERT'S WIFE (1922)
STARS ON PARADE (1936)

SANDGROUND, Maurice
LAMBS OF DOVE COURT, the (1920)

SANGSTER, Jimmy
FEAR IN THE NIGHT (1972)
HORROR OF FRANKENSTEIN, the (1970)
LUST FOR A VAMPIRE (1970)

SARAFIAN, Richard C
FRAGMENT OF FEAR (1970)
VANISHING POINT (1971)

SARNE, Mike
JOANNA (1968)

SASDY, Peter
COUNTESS DRACULA (1970)
HANDS OF THE RIPPER (1971)
NOTHING BUT THE NIGHT (1972)

SATTIN, Phillip
GROWING OLD (1959)

SAUNDERS, Charles
BEHIND THE HEADLINES (1956)
FIND THE LADY (1956)
GENTLE TRAP, the (1960)
GOLDEN LINK, the (1954)
HORNET'S NEST, the (1955)
JUNGLE STREET (1961)
KILL HER GENTLY (1957)
NAKED FURY (1959)
NARROWING CIRCLE, the (1956)
NUDIST PARADISE (1958)
ONE JUMP AHEAD (1955)
ONE WILD OAT (1951)
TAWNY PIPIT (1944)

SAUNDERS, Peter
LONELY PLACES, the (1965)

SAUNDERS, Richard
PARK, the (1967)

SAVILLE, Philip
BEST HOUSE IN LONDON, the (1968)
FELLOW TRAVELLER (1989)
FRUIT MACHINE (1988)
SHADEY (1985)

SAVILLE, Victor
CALLING BULLDOG DRUMMOND
(1951)
CONSPIRATOR (1949)
DARK JOURNEY (1937)
DICTATOR, the (1935)
EVENSONG (1934)
EVERGREEN (1934)
FAITHFUL HEART, the (1932)
FIRST A GIRL (1935)
FRIDAY THE THIRTEENTH (1933)
GOOD COMPANIONS, the (1933)
GREEN YEARS, the (1946)
HINDLE WAKES (1931)
IRON DUKE, the (1935)
IT'S LOVE AGAIN (1936)
I WAS A SPY (1933)
KITTY (1929)
LIQUID SUNSHINE (1921)
LOVE ON WHEELS (1932)
ME AND MARLBOROUGH (1935)
MICHAEL AND MARY (1931)
SOUTH RIDING (1938)
STORM IN A TEACUP (1937)
STORY OF OIL, the (1921)
SUNSHINE SUSIE (1931)
WARM CORNER, a (1930)
WOMAN TO WOMAN (1929)
W PLAN, the (1930)

SAWREY-COOKSON, Alistair
BURIED FILM, the (1959)
FEATHERED WHEEL, the (1956)

SCHAEFER, George
MACBETH (1960)

SCHAUDER, Leon
FATHER AND SON (1945)
NONQUASSI (1939)
TWELVE OP (1940)

SCHECHTER, Daniel
STUDENT POWER (1968)

SCHERTZINGER, Victor
MIKADO, the (1938)

SCHLESINGER, John
BILLY LIAR (1963)
DARLING (1965)
FAR FROM THE MADDING CROWD
(1967)
KIND OF LOVING, a (1962)
MADAME SOUSATZKA (1988)
TERMINUS (1961)
YANKS (1979)

SCHONFELD, Victor
ANIMALS FILM, the (1981)

SCHORSTEIN, Jon
MIRROR (1970)

SCHUSTER, Harold
DINNER AT THE RITZ (1937)
QUEER CARGO (1938)
WINGS OF THE MORNING (1936)

SCHWARZ, Hanns
RETURN OF THE SCARLET
PIMPERNEL, the (1937)

SCLATER, Michael
BERTHA (1969)

SCOBIE, Alastair
TECHNIQUES IN PLASTIC SURGERY
(1949)

SCOFFIELD, Jon
TO SEE SUCH FUN (1977)

SCOTT, Anthony
LOVING MEMORY (1970)
ONE OF THE MISSING (1969)

SCOTT, James
CHANCE, HISTORY, ART... (1979)
ROCKING HORSE, the (1962)
'36 TO '77 (1978)

SCOTT, Peter Graham
ACCOUNT RENDERED (1957)
BIG CHANCE, the (1957)
BIG DAY, the (1960)
BITTER HARVEST (1963)
CRACKSMAN, the (1963)
DEVIL'S BAIT (1959)
FATHER CAME TOO! (1963)
FIVE SURVIVE (1971)
HIDEOUT (1956)
MISTER TEN PER CENT (1967)
POT CARRIERS, the (1962)
SKI-WHEELERS (1971)
THAT'S ALL WE NEED (1971)
TIME FLIES (1971)
UP FOR THE CUP (1971)
UP THE CREEK (1971)

SCOTT, Ridley
1492: CONQUEST OF PARADISE (1992)
DUELLISTS, the (1977)

SCULLY, Denis
JOURNEY INTO NOWHERE (1963)

SCULLY, Diane
SHALLOW AND CROOKED (1990)

SEABOURNE, Peter
ESCAPE FROM THE SEA (1968)

SEALEY, John
UPS AND DOWNS OF A HANDYMAN
(1975)

SEARLE, Francis
CITIZEN'S ADVICE BUREAU (1941)
CLOUDBURST (1951)
DEAD MAN'S EVIDENCE (1962)
ENGLISH OILFIELD, an (1946)
FARES FAIR (1936)
GAOLBREAK (1962)
GELIGNITE GANG, the (1956)
HOSPITAL NURSE (1941)
LOVE'S A LUXURY (1952)
NEVER LOOK BACK (1952)
NIGHT OF THE PROWLER (1962)
ONE WAY OUT (1955)
STUDENT NURSE (1945)
TROUBLE WITH EVE (1959)
WAR WITHOUT END (1936)

SEGAL, Alex
HEDDA GABLER (1962)

SEGALLER, Denis
BEYOND THE SPEED OF SOUND (1959)
FURNIVAL AND SON (1948)
TRANSONIC FLIGHT (1957)

SEGRAVE, Brigid
WOMEN OF THE RHONDDA (1973)

SEKELY, Steve
DAY OF THE TRIFFIDS, the (1962)

SELFE, Ray
WHAT THE BUTLER SAW! (1991)

SELLERS, Peter
MR TOPAZE (1961)

SEN, Bishu
INDIA STRIKES (1946)

SERENY, Eva
DRESS, the (1984)

SEWELL, George H
FOUNDRY PRACTICE (1952)

SEWELL, Vernon
BATTLE OF THE V-1 (1958)
COUNTERSPY (1953)
CURSE OF THE CRIMSON ALTAR (1968)
DANGEROUS VOYAGE (1954)
FLOATING DUTCHMAN, the (1953)
GHOSTS OF BERKELEY SQUARE, the
(1947)
HOUSE OF MYSTERY (1961)

SMITH, Herbert
ALL AT SEA (1939)
CALLING ALL STARS (1937)
HOME FROM HOME (1939)
IT'S A GRAND OLD WORLD (1937)
I'VE GOT A HORSE (1938)
ON THE AIR (1934)
SOFT LIGHTS AND SWEET MUSIC (1936)

SMITH, J W
THEY FORGOT TO READ THE
DIRECTIONS (1924)

SMITH, Jack
MIND YOUR OWN BUSINESS (1907)
ROBBERS AND THE JEW, the (1908)

SMITH, Mel
TALL GUY, the (1989)

SMITH, Percy
BERTIE'S CAVE (1925)
MAGIC MYXIES (1931)
PIT AND THE PLUM, the (1925)
TALE OF A TENDRIL, the (1925)

SMITH, Peter K
BLACKBOARD JUNGLE (1972)
HAPPY DAYS (1972)
NO SURRENDER (1985)
ON THE AIR (1972)
PARENTS' DAY (1972)
PRIVATE ENTERPRISE, a (1974)
THIRTY YEARS YOUNGER (1972)
TRIAL OF STRENGTH (1972)

SMITH, Robert
LOVE CHILD, the (1987)

SMITH, Sidney
HELLO LONDON (1958)

SMITH, Vicky
PECKING ORDER (1989)

SMYTHE, F S
KAMET CONQUERED; AN EPIC
ADVENTURE ON THE ROOF OF THE
WORLD (1932)

SNOAD, Harold
NOT NOW, COMRADE (1976)

SNOW, George
MUYBRIDGE REVISITED (1986)

SOLDATI, Mario
HER FAVOURITE HUSBAND (1950)

SPEAR, Eric
HIGHWAY (1933)

SPEED, Lancelot
BULLY BOY (1914)
GENERAL FRENCH'S CONTEMPTIBLE
LITTLE ARMY (1914)
SEA DREAMS (1914)
SLEEPLESS (1914)
WONDERFUL ADVENTURES OF PIP,
SQUEAK AND WILFRED, THE
FAMOUS 'DAILY MIRROR' PETS, the
(1921)

SPENCER, Liz
SREDNI VASHTAR (1983)

SPENCER, Ronald
ANTIQUES AT AUCTION (1970)
CHILD'S GUIDE TO BLOWING UP A
MOTOR CAR, a (1965)
PROJECT Z (1968)
SMOKEY JOE'S REVENGE (1974)
STUFFY OLD BANK (1972)

SPICE, Evelyn
AROUND THE VILLAGE GREEN (1937)
BEHIND THE SCENES (1938)
BIRTH OF THE YEAR (1938)
CALENDAR OF THE YEAR (1936)

JOB IN A MILLION, a (1937)
SHELTERED WATERS (1934)
SPRING ON THE FARM (1933)
WEATHER FORECAST (1934)

SPRAGG, Reg
MAN IN THE CLOUDS (1967)

SPRINGSTEEN, R G
CROSS CHANNEL (1955)
SECRET VENTURE (1955)

SPROXTON, David
BABYLON (1986)
EARLY BIRD (1983)
LATE EDITION (1983)
ON PROBATION (1983)
PALMY DAYS (1983)
SALES PITCH (1983)

SQUIRE, Anthony
DOUBLECROSS (1955)

SROUR, Heiny
LEILA AND THE WOLVES (1984)

STAFFORD, Brendan J
MEN AGAINST THE SUN (1953)

STAFFORD, John
NO FUNNY BUSINESS (1933)
THERE GOES SUSIE (1934)

STAFFORD, Roland
DISTANT NEIGHBOURS (1956)

STAHL, C Ray
SCARLET SPEAR, the (1953)

STARK, Graham
MAGNIFICENT SEVEN DEADLY SINS,
the (1971)

STARR, Ringo
BORN TO BOOGIE (1972)

STAUDTE, Wolfgang
TALE OF FIVE CITIES, a (1951)

STEIN, Paul L
BLACK LIMELIGHT (1938)
BLOSSOM TIME (1934)
CAFE COLETTE (1937)
COUNTERBLAST (1948)
HEART'S DESIRE (1935)
JANE STEPS OUT (1938)
JUST LIKE A WOMAN (1938)
LAUGHING LADY, the (1946)
LILY CHRISTINE (1932)
LISBON STORY (1946)
MIMI (1935)
OUTSIDER, the (1939)
POISON PEN (1939)
RED WAGON (1934)
SONG YOU GAVE ME, the (1933)
TALK ABOUT JACQUELINE (1942)
TWENTY QUESTIONS MURDER
MYSTERY, the (1949)

STEINHOFF, Hans
ALLEY CAT, the (1929)

STELLMAN, Martin
FOR QUEEN AND COUNTRY (1988)

STEPHENS, Jack
BLINKER'S SPY-SPOTTER (1971)

STERLING, Joseph
CASE OF THE MUKKINESE
BATTLEHORN, the (1955)
CLOAK WITHOUT DAGGER (1955)

STERLING, William
ALICE'S ADVENTURES IN
WONDERLAND (1972)

STERN, Anthony
SAN FRANCISCO (1968)

STEVENS, Robert
I THANK A FOOL (1962)

STEVENSON, Robert
FALLING FOR YOU (1933)
HAPPY EVER AFTER (1932)
IN SEARCH OF THE CASTAWAYS (1962)
JACK OF ALL TRADES (1936)
KIDNAPPED (1960)
KING SOLOMON'S MINES (1937)
MAN WHO CHANGED HIS MIND, the
(1936)
NON-STOP NEW YORK (1937)
OWD BOB (1938)
RETURN TO YESTERDAY (1940)
TUDOR ROSE (1936)
WARE CASE, the (1938)
YOUNG MAN'S FANCY (1939)

STEWART, Derek
SMOKE SIGNALS (1950)

STEWART, J R F
GRANTCHESTER (1958)
PATHS OF PROGRESS (1958)
VITAL FLAME, the (1952)

STEWART, Malcolm
POLICE FORCE, the (1947)
POLICEMAN, the (1947)
SEWAGE DISPOSAL (1947)
SEWERMAN (1947)

STEWART, William G
FATHER DEAR FATHER (1972)

STODDART, John
BLUEBEARD'S LAST WIFE (1966)

STONE, Andrew L
SECRET OF MY SUCCESS, the (1965)

STORCK, Henri
OPEN WINDOW, the (1952)

STOW, Percy
ALGY'S YACHTING PARTY (1908)
ALICE IN WONDERLAND (1903)
ALL'S FAIR IN LOVE (1912)
ANXIOUS DAY FOR MOTHER, an (1907)
BOBBY THE BOY SCOUT; or, The boy
detective (1909)
CONVICT AND THE CURATE, the (1904)
COSTER'S WEDDING, the (1913)
ELECTRIC TRANSFORMATION (1909)
FREE RIDE, a (1904)
FRUSTRATED ELOPEMENT, the (1902)
GLASS OF GOAT'S MILK, a (1909)
HOW TO STOP A MOTOR CAR (1902)
INVADERS, the (1909)
IT'S LOVE THAT MAKES THE WORLD
GO ROUND (1913)
JEALOUS DOLL; or, The frustrated
elopement, the (1910)
JUGGINS' MOTOR SKATES (1909)
LESSON ON ELECTRICITY, a (1909)
LIEUTENANT ROSE AND THE CHINESE
PIRATES (1910)
LIEUTENANT ROSE AND THE
GUNRUNNERS (1910)
LIEUTENANT ROSE AND THE HIDDEN
TREASURE (1912)
LIEUTENANT ROSE AND THE
ROBBERS OF FINGALL'S CREEK
(1910)
LIEUTENANT ROSE AND THE ROYAL
VISIT (1911)
LIEUTENANT ROSE AND THE SEALED
ORDERS (1914)
LIEUTENANT ROSE AND THE STOLEN
CODE (1911)
LIEUTENANT ROSE RN AND HIS
PATENT AEROPLANE (1912)
LIEUTENANT ROSE RN AND THE
STOLEN BATTLESHIP (1912)
LOVE AND THE VARSITY (1913)
MAUDIE'S ADVENTURE (1913)
MILLING THE MILITANTS; A COMICAL
ABSURDITY (1913)
MISS SIMPKINS' BOARDERS; THE
INCIDENT OF THE CURATE AND THE
GHOST (1910)
MISTLETOE BOUGH, the (1904)
NEVER LATE; or, The conscientious clerk
(1909)

CARRY ON REGARDLESS (1961)
CARRY ON SCREAMING (1966)
CARRY ON SERGEANT (1958)
CARRY ON SPYING (1964)
CARRY ON TEACHER (1959)
CARRY ON UP THE JUNGLE (1970)
CHAIN OF EVENTS (1957)
CIRCUS FRIENDS (1956)
DON'T LOSE YOUR HEAD (1966)
DUKE WORE JEANS, the (1958)
IRON MAIDEN, the (1963)
NO KIDDING (1960)
NURSE ON WHEELS (1963)
PLEASE TURN OVER (1960)
RAISING THE WIND (1961)
SOLITARY CHILD, the (1958)
TIME LOCK (1957)
WATCH YOUR STERN (1960)

THOMAS, Howard
BBC BRAINS TRUST NO.1, the (1943)

THOMAS, Ralph
ABOVE US THE WAVES (1955)
APPOINTMENT WITH VENUS (1951)
BIGGEST BANK ROBBERY, the (1980)
CAMPBELL'S KINGDOM (1957)
CHECKPOINT (1956)
CLOUDED YELLOW, the (1950)
CONSPIRACY OF HEARTS (1960)
DEADLIER THAN THE MALE (1966)
DOCTOR AT LARGE (1957)
DOCTOR AT SEA (1955)
DOCTOR IN CLOVER (1966)
DOCTOR IN DISTRESS (1963)
DOCTOR IN LOVE (1960)
DOCTOR IN THE HOUSE (1954)
DOCTOR IN TROUBLE (1970)
HELTER SKELTER (1949)
HIGH BRIGHT SUN, the (1965)
HOT ENOUGH FOR JUNE (1964)
IRON PETTICOAT, the (1956)
MAD ABOUT MEN (1954)
NOBODY RUNS FOREVER (1968)
NO LOVE FOR JOHNNIE (1961)
NO, MY DARLING DAUGHTER (1961)
ONCE UPON A DREAM (1949)
PAIR OF BRIEFS, a (1961)
PERCY (1971)
QUEST FOR LOVE (1971)
TALE OF TWO CITIES, a (1958)
39 STEPS, the (1958)
TRAVELLER'S JOY (1949)
UPSTAIRS AND DOWNSTAIRS (1959)
WILD AND THE WILLING, the (1962)
WIND CANNOT READ, the (1958)

THOMPSON, David
BRIDGET RILEY (1979)
TURNER (1966)

THOMPSON, J Lee
AS LONG AS THEY'RE HAPPY (1955)
EYE OF THE DEVIL (1966)
FOR BETTER, FOR WORSE (1954)
GOOD COMPANIONS, the (1956)
GUNS OF NAVARONE, the (1961)
ICE COLD IN ALEX (1958)
MOST DANGEROUS MAN IN THE
    WORLD, the (1969)
MURDER WITHOUT CRIME (1950)
NORTH WEST FRONTIER (1959)
NO TREES IN THE STREET (1958)
PASSAGE, the (1978)
RETURN FROM THE ASHES (1965)
TIGER BAY (1959)
WEAK AND THE WICKED, the (1953)
WOMAN IN A DRESSING GOWN (1957)
YELLOW BALLOON, the (1952)
YIELD TO THE NIGHT (1956)

THOMPSON, Marcus
EDWARD (1982)

THOMPSON, Roffe
MUSIC HATH CHARMS (1935)

THOMPSON, Tony
SWIFT WATER (1952)

THOMSON, Gordon
HYDROLOGICAL SIMULATION BY
    COMPUTER (1980)

THOMSON, Margaret
CHILDREN GROWING UP WITH OTHER
    PEOPLE (1947)
CHILDREN LEARNING BY
    EXPERIENCE (1947)
DITCHING (1942)
EAST IN THE WEST (1954)
ENDOTRACHEAL ANAESTHESIA (1944)
FAMILY AFFAIR, a (1950)
GARDEN TOOLS (1943)
HEATHLANDS (1938)
HEDGING (1942)
MAKING A COMPOST HEAP (1941)
MAKING GRASS SILAGE (1943)
NITROUS OXIDE-OXYGEN-ETHER
    ANAESTHESIA (1944)
OPEN DROP ETHER (1944)
RESEEDING FOR BETTER GRASS (1943)
SIGNS AND STAGES OF ANAESTHESIA,
    the (1945)
STORING VEGETABLES INDOORS
    (1942)
TROUBLED MIND, the (1954)

THOMSON, Neil
IN FLAGRANTE (1981)

THORNTON, F Martin
IF THOU WERT BLIND (1917)
JANE SHORE (1915)
MAN WHO FORGOT, the (1919)
MELODY OF DEATH (1922)
RIVER OF STARS, the (1921)
ROMANY LASS, a (1918)
TEMPTER, the (1913)
WARRIOR STRAIN, the (1919)

THORPE, Richard
ADVENTURES OF QUENTIN
    DURWARD, the (1955)
HOUSE OF THE SEVEN HAWKS, the
    (1959)
IVANHOE (1951)
KILLERS OF KILIMANJARO (1959)
KNIGHTS OF THE ROUND TABLE, the
    (1953)

THUMWOOD, T R
IT ALL DEPENDS ON YOU (1942)
PRODUCTION AND DISTRIBUTION OF
    MEDICAL GASES, the (1939)

TILL, Eric
HOT MILLIONS (1968)
IT SHOULDN'T HAPPEN TO A VET
    (1976)
WALKING STICK, the (1970)

TINBERGEN, Nikolas
BREEDING BEHAVIOUR OF THE
    BLACK-HEADED GULL, the (1960)
BREEDING COLONY OF THE BLACK-
    HEADED GULL, a (1953)
CRAFTY PREDATORS AND CRYPTIC
    PREY (1966)
REPRODUCTIVE BEHAVIOUR OF THE
    KITTIWAKE, the (1955)
REPRODUCTIVE BEHAVIOUR OF THE
    STICKLEBACK, the (1948)

TIPPEY, John
GOOD RIDING GETS THERE (1969)

TODD, Peter
SHORELINE, the (1984)

TOMLINSON, Lionel
MY HANDS ARE CLAY (1948)

TOURNEUR, Jacques
CIRCLE OF DANGER (1950)
CITY UNDER THE SEA, the (1965)
NIGHT OF THE DEMON (1957)

TOURNEUR, Maurice
KOENIGSMARK (1936)

TOYE, Wendy
KING'S BREAKFAST, the (1963)
STRANGER LEFT NO CARD, the (1952)
TRUE AS A TURTLE (1957)

TRACY, Bert
BOOTS! BOOTS! (1934)

TRAVERS, Alfred
DUAL ALIBI (1947)
GIRLS OF LATIN QUARTER (1960)
PRIMITIVES, the (1962)
SOLUTION BY PHONE (1953)

TRENKER, Luis
CHALLENGE, the (1938)

TREVELYAN, H B
'36 TO '77 (1978)
WOMEN OF THE RHONDDA (1973)

TREVELYAN, Philip
MOON AND THE SLEDGEHAMMER, the
    (1971)

TRONSON, Robert
MAN AT THE CARLTON TOWER (1961)
MAN DETAINED (1961)
NEVER BACK LOSERS (1961)
RING OF SPIES (1963)
TRAITORS, the (1962)

TRUFFAUT, François
FAHRENHEIT 451 (1966)

TRUMAN, Michael
BLACK BOOK, the (1965)
DAYLIGHT ROBBERY (1964)
GIRL IN THE HEADLINES (1963)
GO TO BLAZES (1962)

TSIMATSIMA, Blanche
TSIAMELO – A PLACE OF GOODNESS
    (1984)

TSOUGAROSSA, Jorge
GREECE OF CHRISTIAN GREEKS (1971)

TUCHNER, Michael
FEAR IS THE KEY (1972)
LIKELY LADS, the (1976)
MISTER QUILP (1974)
MUSIC! (1968)
VILLAIN (1971)
WILT (1989)

TUCKETT, F Roy
WINGS OVER AFRICA (1933)

TULLY, Montgomery
BATTLE BENEATH THE EARTH (1967)
BOYS IN BROWN (1949)
CLASH BY NIGHT (1963)
COUNTERFEIT PLAN, the (1956)
DAILY BREAD (1940)
DIAL 999 (1955)
DIAMOND, the (1954)
EACH FOR ALL (1946)
ESCAPEMENT (1957)
FIVE DAYS (1954)
FROM ACORN TO OAK (1938)
HOUSE IN MARSH ROAD, the (1960)
HYPNOTIST, the (1957)
I ONLY ARSKED! (1958)
JACKPOT (1960)
KEY MAN, the (1957)
MAN IN THE SHADOW (1957)
MASTER SPY (1963)
MIDDLE COURSE, the (1961)
MRS FITZHERBERT (1947)
MURDER IN REVERSE (1945)
NO ROAD BACK (1956)
OUT OF THE FOG (1962)
PRICE OF SILENCE, the (1960)
SHE KNOWS Y'KNOW (1962)
SPRING SONG (1946)
TALE OF FIVE CITIES, a (1951)
TERRORNAUTS, the (1967)
THIRD ALIBI, the (1961)
THIRTY-SIX HOURS (1954)
WHO KILLED THE CAT? (1966)

WATSON, Karen
DADDY'S LITTLE BIT OF DRESDEN
CHINA (1988)

WATT, Harry
BBC – DROITWICH (1935)
BIG MONEY (1938)
BRITAIN AT BAY (1940)
BRITAIN CAN TAKE IT (1940)
CHRISTMAS UNDER FIRE (1941)
EUREKA STOCKADE (1949)
FIDDLERS THREE (1944)
FIRST DAYS, the (1939)
FRONT LINE, the (1940)
LONDON CAN TAKE IT (1940)
NIGHT MAIL (1936)
NINE MEN (1942)
NORTH SEA (1938)
OVERLANDERS, the (1946)
SAVING OF BILL BLEWITT, the (1936)
SIEGE OF PINCHGUT, the (1959)
SIX-THIRTY COLLECTION (1934)
SQUADRON 992 (1940)
TARGET FOR TONIGHT (1941)
21 MILES (1942)
WEST OF ZANZIBAR (1954)
WHERE NO VULTURES FLY (1951)

WATTS, Fred
GREAT CRUSADE; THE STORY OF A
MILLION HOMES, the (1936)
PATHÉTONE PARADE OF 1940 (1940)

WATTS, Tom
TOILERS, the (1919)

WEBB, Millard
HAPPY ENDING (1931)

WEBB, Tim
A IS FOR AUTISM (1992)

WEBSTER, Martyn C
BROKEN HORSESHOE (1953)

WEEKS, Stephen
GHOST STORY (1974)
1917 (1968)
SWORD OF THE VALIANT – THE
LEGEND OF GAWAIN AND THE
GREEN KNIGHT (1983)

WEGG-PROSSER, Victoria
WORKERS FILMS OF THE THIRTIES
(1981)

WEILAND, Paul
KEEP OFF THE GRASS (1984)

WEISS, Fred
TA-RA-RA BOOM DE-AY (1945)

WEISS, Jiří
BEFORE THE RAID (1943)
ETERNAL PRAGUE (1942)
JOHN SMITH WAKES UP (1940)
NIGHT AND DAY (1945)
SECRET ALLIES (1939)

WELLESLEY, Gordon
SILVER FLEET, the (1943)

WELSBY, Chris
WINDVANE (1972)

WENDHAUSEN, Fritz
RUNAWAY PRINCESS, the (1929)

WENDKOS, Paul
ATTACK ON THE IRON COAST (1967)
HELL BOATS (1969)

WERKER, Alfred
LOVE IN EXILE (1936)

WEST, Simon
DOLLY MIXTURES (1983)

WEST, Walter
BED AND BREAKFAST (1938)
DAUGHTER OF LOVE, a (1925)
KNIGHT OF THE PIGSKIN, a (1926)
LADY OWNER, the (1923)
MYSTERY OF A LONDON FLAT, the
(1915)
SWEENEY TODD (1928)
WHEN GREEK MEETS GREEK (1922)

WESTON, Charles
VENGEANCE OF NANA, the (1915)

WETHERELL, M A
LIVINGSTONE (1925)
SOMME, the (1927)

WHATHAM, Claude
ALL CREATURES GREAT AND SMALL
(1974)
SWALLOWS AND AMAZONS (1974)
SWEET WILLIAM (1979)
THAT'LL BE THE DAY (1973)

WHELAN, Tim
ACTION FOR SLANDER (1937)
ADAM'S APPLE (1928)
AUNT SALLY (1933)
CAMELS ARE COMING, the (1934)
DIVORCE OF LADY X, the (1938)
FAREWELL AGAIN (1937)
IT'S A BOY! (1933)
Q PLANES (1939)
ST MARTIN'S LANE (1937)
THIEF OF BAGDAD, the (1940)
THIS WAS A WOMAN (1948)

WHITBY, Cynthia
LETTER FROM EAST ANGLIA, a (1953)

WHITE, E W
MOVIE MIXTURE (1945)

WHITE, H Brian
TROPICAL BREEZES (1930)

WHITE, Lance
ADOLF'S BUSY DAY (1940)

WHITE, Tony
HOKUSAI (1978)

WHITEHEAD, Peter
WHOLLY COMMUNION (1965)

WHITING, Edward G
ADVENTURES OF JANE, the (1949)

WHITLOCK, Emma
IMAGES OF NURSES (1987)

WHYBROW, George F
WHEN GEORGE WAS KING (1922)

WICKES, David
MOODS OF LOVE, the (1972)
SILVER DREAM RACER (1980)
SWEENEY! (1976)

WILCOX, Herbert
BITTER SWEET (1933)
COURTNEYS OF CURZON STREET, the
(1947)
DAWN (1928)
DECAMERON NIGHTS (1924)
DERBY DAY (1952)
GOODNIGHT VIENNA (1932)
HEART OF A MAN, the (1959)
I LIVE IN GROSVENOR SQUARE (1945)
INTO THE BLUE (1950)
KING'S CUP, the (1933)
LADY IS A SQUARE, the (1958)
LADY WITH THE LAMP, the (1951)
LAUGHING ANNE (1953)
LILACS IN THE SPRING (1954)
LIMELIGHT (1936)
LITTLE DAMOZEL, the (1932)
LOVES OF ROBERT BURNS, the (1930)
MADAME POMPADOUR (1927)

MAN WHO WOULDN'T TALK, the (1957)
MAYTIME IN MAYFAIR (1949)
MONEY MEANS NOTHING (1932)
MY TEENAGE DAUGHTER (1956)
NELL GWYN (1934)
ODETTE (1950)
ONLY WAY, the (1926)
PEG OF OLD DRURY (1935)
PICCADILLY INCIDENT (1946)
QUEEN'S AFFAIR (1934)
SIXTY GLORIOUS YEARS (1938)
SPRING IN PARK LANE (1948)
THESE DANGEROUS YEARS (1957)
THEY FLEW ALONE (1942)
THIS'LL MAKE YOU WHISTLE (1936)
TIPTOES (1927)
TRENT'S LAST CASE (1952)
TROUBLE IN THE GLEN (1954)
VICTORIA THE GREAT (1937)
WONDERFUL THINGS (1957)
YELLOW CANARY, the (1943)

WILDE, Cornel
LANCELOT AND GUINEVERE (1962)

WILDER, W Lee
BLUEBEARD'S TEN HONEYMOONS
(1960)

WILKINSON, Christine
IMPRESSIONS OF EXILE (1985)

WILKINSON, Hazel
E ARNOT ROBERTSON ... DISCUSSES
'12 ANGRY MEN' ... (1959)
OPENING OF THE NEW BUILDING FOR
THE BFI AT 81 DEAN STREET (1960)

WILLIAMS, Brock
ROOT OF ALL EVIL, the (1947)

WILLIAMS, Derek
HADRIAN'S WALL (1951)
HUNTED IN HOLLAND (1961)
TREASURE IN MALTA (1963)

WILLIAMS, Emlyn
LAST DAYS OF DOLWYN, the (1949)

WILLIAMS, J B
WHITE CARGO (1929)

WILLIAMS, Margaret
ELIZABETH MACONCHY (1985)

WILLIAMS, Richard
LOVE ME, LOVE ME, LOVE ME (1962)

WILLIAMSON, A Stanley
BOYS OF THE OLD BRIGADE (1945)
LAND OF THE SAINTS (1946)

WILLIAMSON, James
ARE YOU THERE? (1901)
ATTACK ON A CHINESE MISSION –
BLUEJACKETS TO THE RESCUE
(1900)
BIG SWALLOW, the (1901)
BROWN'S HALF HOLIDAY (1905)
DEAR BOYS HOME FOR THE
HOLIDAYS, the (1904)
FIRE! (1901)
FLYING THE FOAM AND SOME FANCY
DIVING (1906)
INTERESTING STORY, an (1905)
MAGIC EXTINGUISHER, the (1901)
OLD CHORISTER, the (1904)
£100 REWARD (1908)
OUR NEW ERRAND BOY (1905)
PUZZLED BATHER AND HIS
ANIMATED CLOTHES, the (1901)
RESERVIST, BEFORE THE WAR, AND
AFTER THE WAR, a (1902)
RIVAL BARBERS, the (1906)
RIVAL CYCLISTS, the (1908)
SOLDIER'S RETURN, the (1902)
STOP THIEF! (1901)
TWO LITTLE WAIFS (1905)
WASHING THE SWEEP (1898)
WHERE THERE'S A WILL THERE'S A
WAY (1906)

Index to Part Two
(by Book Author)

Index to Part Two (by Book Author)

University College of
Ripon & York St. John
YORK CAMPUS
REFERENCE ONLY
NOT TO BE TAKEN OUT
OF THE LIBRARY